SOWING THE WORD

Bible in the Modern World, 3

Series Editors
J. Cheryl Exum, Jorunn Økland and Stephen D. Moore

Editorial Board
Alison Jasper, Tat-siong Benny Liew, Hugh Pyper,
Yvonne Sherwood, Caroline Vander Stichele

SOWING THE WORD

The Cultural Impact of the British and Foreign Bible Society 1804–2004

edited by
Stephen Batalden, Kathleen Cann and John Dean

SHEFFIELD PHOENIX PRESS

2006

Copyright © 2004, 2006 Sheffield Phoenix Press

First published in hardback, 2004
Reprinted in paperback, 2006

Published by Sheffield Phoenix Press
Department of Biblical Studies, University of Sheffield
Sheffield S10 2TN

www.sheffieldphoenix.com

All rights reserved.
No part of this publication may be reproduced or transmitted
in any form or by any means, electronic or mechanical, including
photocopying, recording or any information storage or retrieval system,
without the publishers' permission in writing.

A CIP catalogue record for this book
is available from the British Library

Printed on acid-free paper by Lightning Source

ISBN 1-905048-65-3

TABLE OF CONTENTS

List of Illustrations   viii
Foreword
    Rowan Williams, Archbishop of Canterbury   x

Introduction
    The Editors   1

The Archives of the British and Foreign Bible Society
    Kathleen Cann   14

Part One: The BFBS at Home

The Bible Society and the Book Trade
    Leslie Howsam   24

Women and the Bible Society
    Roger Martin   38

Forgotten Labours: Women's Bible Work and the BFBS
    Sarah Lane   53

"Without Note or Comment":
Yesterday, Today, and Tomorrow
    Roger Steer   63

London Bible House in the 1950s:
An Illustrated Reminiscence
    John Dean   81

Part Two: The BFBS Abroad

West Africa
    John Hill and the Early Attempt to Study a West African Language
       Patricia Mirrlees   98

East Asia

Anonymous Bible Translators: Native Literati and the
Translation of the Bible into Chinese, 1807–1907
  Thor Strandenaes — 121

Problems in Translating the Bible into Manchu:
Observations on Louis Poirot's Old Testament
  Erling von Mende — 149

Russia

The BFBS Petersburg Agency and Russian Biblical Translation,
1856–1875
  Stephen Batalden — 169

Bishop Cassian's BFBS-Sponsored Russian Translation of the
New Testament
  Sergei Ovsiannikov — 197

Minority Language Biblical Translation Work in Russia:
Then and Now
  David Clark — 217

The Levant and Southeastern Europe

Enlightening "A Poor, Oppressed, and Darkened Nation":
Some Early Activities of the BFBS in the Levant
  Richard Clogg — 234

The Bible Society's South Slavic Bible in the
Balkan Maelstrom
  Peter Kuzmič — 251

Western Europe

Robert Pinkerton: Principal Agent of the BFBS in the
Kingdoms of Germany
  Wayne Detzler — 268

Obedience and Disobedience: George Borrow's Idiosyncratic
Relationship with the Bible Society
  Ann Ridler — 286

The Bible in Spain and Gibraltar
  Sue Jackson — 305

North America

The BFBS and Native Language Literature in Nineteenth-Century Canada
  Joyce Banks 316

At Sea

Sowing by Sea: Empowering Seafarers with the Gospel
  Roald Kverndal 327

Appendix: A Summary Catalogue of the BFBS Archives
  Kathleen Cann 344

List of Contributors 360

Index 363

LIST OF ILLUSTRATIONS

[1]	Bible House, 10 Earl Street, Blackfriars	15
[2]	Stanhope stereotype printing press, 1805	28
[3]	Women Workers at Watkins Bindery, 1905	32
[4]	Charles Stokes Dudley (1780–1862)	41
[5]	Ellen Ranyard (1810–1879)	56
[6]	Gospel of John in Mohawk and English	68
[7]	Bible House, 146 Queen Victoria Street	82
[8]	Bible House Main Staircase	83
[9]	Bible House Mezzanine Floor	85
[10]	Bible House General Office	85
[11]	Bible House Packing Room	86
[12]	Office of an BFBS General Secretary	88
[13]	Bible House Committee Room	89
[14]	Plan of Bible House First Floor, Early 1900s	90
[15]	Bible House Library	92
[16]	BFBS Staff on Bible House Roof	94
[17]	The Island of Gorée	104
[18]	Robert Morrison with Chinese Co-workers Chen Laoyi and Li Shigong	129

List of Illustrations ix

[19]	Walter Medhurst with Chinese Co-worker Ju Dilang	137
[20]	Job, Chap. 14, in Manchu, Copied by George Borrow	163
[21]	First Edition (1860) of the Synodal Russian Text of the Gospels	180
[22]	William Nicolson, BFBS Agent in St. Petersburg, 1869–1897	183
[23]	Bishop Cassian and Russian Translation Committee	202
[24]	Gospel of Mark in Kalmyk (1887)	219
[25]	Gospel of John and Epistles of John and James in Yakut (2000)	223
[26,27]	Imprimatur of Patriarch Kyrillos VI for the BFBS New Testament in Modern and Ancient Greek, with English Translation	238, 239
[28]	Vuk Karadžić about 1816	252
[29]	Serbian New Testament (1847)	264
[30]	Robert Pinkerton (1780–1859)	269
[31]	George Borrow (1803–1881)	287
[32]	Andrew Brandram, BFBS Secretary 1823–1850	291
[33]	Letter from George Borrow, Cadiz, 21 September 1839	301
[34]	Gibraltar from the North-West, 1845	305
[35]	Cree New Testament (1859) in Syllabic Script	322
[36]	Distributing Scriptures to Sailors	337

Foreword[1]

Rowan Williams, Archbishop of Canterbury

Of all the great world religions, it is Christianity that has the most obvious and pervasive investment in translation. We do not have a sacred language; from the very first, Christians have been convinced that every human language can become the bearer of scriptural revelation. The words in which revelation is first expressed are not solid, impenetrable containers of the mystery; they are living realities which spark recognition across even the deepest of gulfs between cultures, and generate new words native to diverse cultures which will in turn become alive and prompt fresh surprise and recognition. Biblical translation represents an enormous act of faith — the faith that what is given by God in one context is capable of being equally transfiguring and authoritative in all other human environments. Jesus speaks Greek and Aramaic; but the whole narrative of his words and work, his ministry and death and resurrection, is such that he can speak to call, to judge, to forgive and to bless in every human language that has been or will be.

Translating the Bible is thus a deeply theological action. It witnesses to what Christians believe about the humanity of Jesus as a human identity that can be recognized by every human person as speaking to them — and speaking for them. If he can be heard and understood in every human environment, all human beings can recognize that — stranger though he is — he shares their distinctive world, their history and experience. We all know how hard it is fully to trust anyone who doesn't speak our language, in the sense of speaking out of a world we recognize as ours. As St Augustine put it, Jesus is able to "play the part" of every created person, to speak from the depth of their humanity in all its darkness and confusion and turn their words Godwards. If scripture can be "re-created" in different languages, the humanity of the saviour who speaks in scripture must be an extraordinary humanity, a unique humanity.

What is more, the act of translating tells us something about humanity itself and its speech. Every language and culture has in it a sort of "homing

---

1. Dr. Williams' foreword was first presented at the "Service to Celebrate the Bicentenary of the British and Foreign Bible Society," St. Paul's Cathedral, 8 March 2004.

instinct" for God—deeply buried by the sin and corruption that affects all cultures, yet still there, a sleeping beauty to be revived by the word of Christ. Hence the recurrent pattern in the history of mission and biblical translation whereby cultures and languages seem to reach a new level of energy and individuality as the biblical story is uncovered in their own words. The West African theologian Lamin Sanneh, probably the most significant theologian of mission in the English-speaking world today, has noted that there are important differences between Christianized African societies in which native names for God have been retained and those in which it was thought necessary to import an alien word. The former show greater levels of Christian stability and of social vigour and engagement within the churches. But we could point equally to all those societies in the past in which the translation of scripture prompted unprecedented levels of sophistication in the study and analysis of a language, and helped to create utterly new possibilities for literature and thought. From the first translations into Georgian and Armenian in the early Christian era to the great labours of Tyndale and Bishop Morgan in the sixteenth century (Bishop Morgan whose Bible it was that Mary Jones set out to acquire for herself, helping to prompt the foundation of the Society), the re-creation of the Bible in a language has opened the wellsprings of creativity. And how many Native American, Polynesian, African languages owe their grammars and lexicons to the labours of translators?

Just as the kingdoms of this world, we are told, will become the kingdoms of our God and of his Christ, so the languages of this world will become dialects of heaven; the tongues of this world will become tongues of flame. When a language speaks of God in Christ it is a language of the Spirit, since it is the Spirit who witnesses to Christ's Lordship. We are celebrating not just a history of human skill today but an outpouring of the Spirit—in the apparently routine work of poring over dictionaries, seeking apt phrases, wrestling with the perennial challenge of making what is strange familiar—and what is familiar strange; always the task of the translator.

In recent years, though, the Bible Society has increasingly been asking not just about translation in the ordinary sense but about the larger question of how to bridge the gulf between two or more cultures sharing one and the same language. We may be familiar with the rhythms and shapes of the Bible in our tongue, we may know (or think we know) something of God's revelation. But however potent and weighted with meaning the Bible is to us as believers, its language as we have received it is not instantly recognizable to so many others who at one level speak the same language. How do we translate into the manifold cultures of Britain and other Western countries today? And what is being done with such imagination and energy by the Society is to go out to meet our culture in its own terms, through drama and art, through bold advertisement, by all sorts of means designed to find the sleeping beauty in our environment, the hidden pull towards Christ that we believe to be at work even where the style and words of a culture seem least in touch with God.

In this way, the history we celebrate today gives us grounds for hope. For two millennia we have been translating; for two centuries this Society has organized the work, sponsored the labours of translation and overseen the distribution of the results. Again and again in Christian history, the Bible has proved itself a living, transforming partner for the world's cultures. We feel ourselves now to be in the middle of a deeply unreceptive society, for whom the Bible's categories and assumptions and expectations are alien as never before; but what our history and our theology alike tell us is that no human style or speech is finally impermeable to Scripture, because the Word of God in his incarnation has made all human languages his own, has identified with the heart of all human experience and taken it upon him to speak for us to the Father, sharing our condition. We do well to approach our world, however forbidding, however apparently unreceptive, with confidence.

But with challenge also. The Society counted William Wilberforce among its founders, a reminder that the Word transfigures as well as affirming. Looking back again to the flowering of cultures that has so often accompanied the translation of scripture, we must say to our own environment, "You will not find the fulness and depth of your human nature in all its ruin and all its glory without this lifegiving partnership with the biblical revelation". We have a gift to share that will enlarge any and every culture — because without the scriptural vision of covenant and justice, mercy and fidelity and generosity, in personal relations and political structures alike, we shall find our cultures becoming less and less human, less and less simply sustainable, less liveable. This is the full implication of where we began, the vision of a gospel that always seeks to be at home in the human world, yet reshapes that world more radically than we could have imagined.

And so we give thanks not only for the Society and its history of faithful, creative ministry; not only even for Scripture itself as the vehicle of God's great promise to creation and its fulfilment in Jesus, but for that fulfilment itself, for the Word made flesh. May all tribes and tongues and nations learn to praise him in the pentecostal symphony stirred up by the Spirit from age to age.

INTRODUCTION: TWO HUNDRED YEARS OF THE BRITISH AND FOREIGN BIBLE SOCIETY

Marking its two-hundredth anniversary in 2004, the British and Foreign Bible Society (BFBS) has been one of the most dynamic and successful institutions spawned by the great evangelical awakening of the late eighteenth and early nineteenth centuries. In its creative commercial appeal to an expanded literate audience, the BFBS played a leading role in the transformation of modern religious culture. It did so by launching market-oriented mass publication and circulation of Holy Scripture. Extending that effort beyond the shores of the British Isles in sponsored projects of biblical translation and dissemination, the Society became a genuinely global institution, contributing both to the development and standardization of national and tribal languages and cultures.

While the second century of its existence has seen the Society's global outreach subsumed within larger international confederative bodies, notably the United Bible Societies, the historical records of the BFBS remain a hidden gold mine. BFBS records today document a virtually unlimited set of significant historical issues ranging from biblical text studies and the study of the book and printing, to the global extension of Christianity, and even issues of national identity and the national politics of modern religious culture.

With an eye toward illuminating the two-hundred-year history of the BFBS and documenting the importance of its rich archival repository now housed in Cambridge University Library, a group of colleagues who had conducted research in the BFBS library and archive over the past generation gathered at Goodenough College in London in March 2004 to share the results of their research and celebrate together the bicentenary of the Bible Society. The proceedings of that symposium, "Sowing the Word," augmented by other invited papers, constitute the basis for this volume. Before turning to some of the broader interpretive issues posed at the Goodenough College symposium, it may be helpful to review in broad outline the basic course of BFBS institutional history.

The British and Foreign Bible Society was founded in London on 7 March 1804, following a year of gestation when the matter came under discussion in the committee of the Religious Tract Society (RTS). The RTS committee was responding to a plea for Welsh Bibles from the Reverend Thomas Charles of Bala. Religious revival and the growth of literacy were fuelling a demand for Scripture that, in the eyes of its founders, could not be met by traditional publishers such as the Society for Promoting Christian Knowledge (SPCK). The RTS committee decided that a separate society was called for, and that its purpose should be to publish Bibles in Welsh and other languages. The problems posed by the French Revolution and the ensuing Napoleonic wars were much on the mind of the founders, and the pastor of the German Lutheran church in London, Karl Friedrich August Steinkopf, argued on behalf of the war-torn German lands. The secretary of the RTS, the Reverend Joseph Hughes, wrote a pamphlet setting out the aims of the proposed Society. It would be, like the RTS itself, non-denominational, and would confine itself to the publication of the Bible alone. Thus, it was hoped to "cut off the occasion of theological hostilities, and invite christians in general to associate for the more extensive propagation of their common faith."[1]

Neither non-denominational societies nor Bible societies were entirely new phenomena, for there had been a flurry of such institutional development—the Society for Promoting Religious Knowledge among the Poor (1750), the Naval and Military Bible Society (1779), the Sunday School Society (1785), the London Missionary Society (1795), and the Religious Tract Society (1799), among others—inspired by the evangelical revival of the eighteenth century.[2] The BFBS was therefore able to profit from the experiences of other comparable societies and frame its own constitution so as to maximize support and minimize cause for controversy. Its original committee of thirty-six were all laymen—fifteen Anglican, fifteen dissenting, and six foreign. Its three secretaries (ordained men) included one from each of those categories. From the RTS came Joseph Hughes (dissenting) and Karl Steinkopf (German). The third secretary was John Owen, Anglican chaplain to the bishop of London.

The Society was a publisher and distributor of Bibles. Translators were not on the permanent staff, and printing was done by commercial firms. Supporters of the Society paid an annual subscription and were entitled to buy copies of the Society's Bibles at preferential rates. From 1809, local "auxiliary" societies were formed throughout the United Kingdom, and their rapid increase over the next decade led to BFBS status as the

---

1. [J. Hughes], *The Excellence of the Holy Scriptures, an Argument for their more general dispersion at home and abroad* (London: Thomas Bensley, 1803). For the discussions in the RTS committee, see Henry Morris, *A Memorable Room: The Story of the Inception and Foundation of the British and Foreign Bible Society* (London: BFBS, 1898).

2. Roger H. Martin, *Evangelicals United: Ecumenical Stirrings in Pre-Victorian Britain, 1795–1830* (Metuchen, N.J., and London: Scarecrow Press, 1983), chap. 2.

wealthiest of the religious societies in London.[3] Members of auxiliaries were also the principal distributors of Bibles in their localities. The prominence of women in this enterprise has been featured in two of the articles in this collection—those by Sarah Lane and Roger Martin.

In accordance with its second law, the Society tried to "add its endeavours to those employed by other Societies for circulating the Scriptures."[4] Foreign Secretary Steinkopf had spent five years as secretary of the Deutsche Christentumsgesellschaft in Basel and had access to a network of people and local religious societies across Germany, Switzerland, and Scandinavia. Indeed, the first continental Bible society was formed in Nürnberg in 1804. BFBS committee member Josiah Roberts encouraged his associate Robert Ralston in Philadelphia to form the Philadelphia Bible Society in 1808, the first Bible society to be established in the United States. Colonial Bible societies were founded in Calcutta in 1811, in Halifax, Nova Scotia, in 1813, and in Sydney, New South Wales, in 1817. The Russian Bible Society was founded at the end of 1812. Following the defeat of Napoleon in 1814, as noted in the essay by Wayne Detzler, BFBS representatives such as Robert Pinkerton toured the Continent, helping to launch Bible societies throughout northern Europe.

The Society's publishing programme was also expanding. For the United Kingdom, there were, by 1815, Bibles or New Testaments available in English, Welsh, Scottish Gaelic, Irish, and Manx. For the rest of the world, modern Scriptures were available in a further 50 languages. Ten years later the Society had 142 languages to its credit. In 39 of the languages the BFBS had itself printed these Scriptures, the remaining 103 were published by other Bible societies, often with the financial assistance of the BFBS, as for example in the case of those published by the Russian Bible Society and by British missionaries in India. As noted in the contribution to this anthology by Joyce Banks, the BFBS financed missionary translations into native languages of Canada throughout the nineteenth century. The translations marked in several cases the only published literature in these languages.

Significant questions unforeseen by the founders quickly came to the fore in this process of cross-cultural translation and interpretation: Which base text should be followed? What should constitute the scriptural

---

3. "Receipts of the principal religious charities in London, for the year ending Lady Day 1821," *The Scotsman* (21 July 1821), in A. Aspinall and E. Anthony Smith, eds., *English Historical Documents, 1783–1832* (London: Eyre & Spottiswoode, 1969), p. 662. The BFBS received £89,154 that year; the next richest society was the SPCK, with £53,100.

4. Law 2 of the BFBS constitution, established in 1804 and published in the *First Report of the BFBS* (London, 1805) and in subsequent *Reports*.

canon? Should marginal notes be added? How should critical terminology such as "to baptize" be translated? Undoubtedly the Society's initial policy was to publish Protestant Bibles in Protestant form, but this soon came up against the fact that Lutheran, as well as Catholic and Orthodox, churches demanded the inclusion of the deutero-canonical books in their Bibles. In 1813 it was agreed that foreign Bible societies with funding from the BFBS could publish Scriptures in their own canonical form. By 1819 the BFBS had supplemented its Protestant French, Italian, Portuguese, and Spanish versions with authorized Catholic texts. In 1821, it went so far as to publish Bibles in these languages with the deutero-canonical books as part of the Old Testament.[5] Unfortunately, the Society had not carried its supporters with it in these developments, resulting in the explosion of the "Apocrypha controversy" that by 1825, when the facts were brought forcefully to their attention, rallied British evangelicals against any and all BFBS publication of deutero-canonical texts.[6] The weight of Protestant opinion among the Society's supporters, especially in Scotland, forced the Society to abandon its ecumenical experiment and restrict itself in 1826 to a Protestant canon without the deutero-canonical texts (a decision that was only reversed in 1966). The distrust generated by the controversy was such that the Scottish Bible societies withdrew their support and ultimately, in 1861, linked up to form the National Bible Society of Scotland. The Apocrypha controversy also meant the severing of links to several European Bible societies, which in turn found their operations affected by the loss of BFBS funding for their Bible publishing.

From the beginning, individual BFBS co-workers helped to found new societies and distribute Scriptures. In 1814 three such figures were taken on as salaried "agents," who were commissioned to travel and promote the interests of the Society.[7] Three more were added in 1820-1821.[8] Gradually a system of "territorial" agencies developed, with an agent resident in a particular area controlling translation, publication, and distribution in his territory. This system developed particularly in the second half of the nineteenth century, a time when some notable agents ruled large fiefdoms: Robert Pinkerton throughout the German principalities and central Europe (1830-1857), Edward Millard in the Austrian Empire (1864-1887),

---

5. T. H. Darlow and H. F. Moule, comps., *Historical Catalogue of the Printed Editions of Holy Scripture in the Library of the British and Foreign Bible Society*, 2 vols. in 4 (London: BFBS, 1903-1911), nos. 3860, 5621, 7496, and 8498.

6. See George Browne, *A History of the British and Foreign Bible Society, From Its Institution in 1804, to the Close of Its Jubilee in 1854*, 2 vols. (London: BFBS, 1859), vol. 1, chap. 7; and Martin, *Evangelicals United*, pp. 123-31.

7. John Paterson, Ebenezer Henderson, and Robert Pinkerton.

8. Jean Daniel Kieffer in Paris, Henry Leeves in Constantinople (later in Athens), and Benjamin Barker in Smyrna.

Alexander Thomson in the Turkish Empire (1860-1895), William Nicolson for European Russia and much of Eurasia (1869-1897), and a succession of agents for Spain from 1869, Italy from 1860, and China from 1863. It was the agent for France, Victor de Pressensé, who in 1837 persuaded the Society to experiment with hiring door-to-door salesmen (*colporteurs*, in French). Colportage eventually became one of the Society's most successful means of distribution, not least in publicity terms, as tales of the heroic exploits of colporteurs filled the Society's published annual *Report* and popular magazines, providing material also for children's books.[9]

Agents were not needed, nor were they suitable, for all countries. In the British dominions local auxiliary Bible societies continued to do the work of fundraising and distribution. The BFBS supplied them with Scriptures and sponsored translation work in local languages. In India, six auxiliary Bible societies divided the country between them, each with a full-time secretary and a staff of assistants and colporteurs. In Africa and East Asia, there were relatively few local societies, so the BFBS worked through missionaries, whose translations it published, and whom it encouraged to engage in local distribution.

Like the British Empire, the Bible Society in the early years of the twentieth century experienced its greatest extent and influence. At the time of the Society's centenary, the BFBS employed thirty foreign agents, all male, whose territories often covered several countries. These agents had sub-agents, depot-keepers, and colporteurs, all adding up to a total of approximately one thousand staff. In the British dominions there were about two thousand affiliated Bible societies, and there were five thousand auxiliaries in England and Wales. The annual expenditure of the Bible Society had reached £254,000 and its annual circulation five million books. It was a time of self-confident certainty in the righteousness and permanence of the cause, when the BFBS felt able to count on a "singular and special Providence, which has guided the Society's fortunes and shielded its agents, and blessed its efforts so abundantly in the waste places of the earth."[10]

Nevertheless, there were worries: circulation was increasing, but income was not keeping pace. The Society wondered whether doubts about the authority of the Bible were affecting its supporters, or whether

---

9. For examples of these children's books, see Edwin Smith, *Tales of God's Packmen* (London: BFBS, 1928); and Mary Carter, *Tales from India* (London: BFBS, 1950). There were also many publicity leaflets, such as *The Man with the Book* (1904), *Perils of Bible-selling* (1911), *Wayfaring Biblemen* (1921), *The Colporteurs at Work* (1937), *Round the World with the Colporteurs* (1940), and *The Men with the Book* (1956).

10. *After a Hundred Years: A Popular Illustrated Report of the BFBS for the Centenary Year 1903-4* (London, 1904), p. 5.

they were under the common misconception that the BFBS was very wealthy. It noted that the Reformed churches of Christendom were suffering from "the parching breath of secularity, which dries up the springs of spiritual life."[11] The Centenary Fund, which raised £281,141, gave the Society a temporary boost and allowed it to embark on the purchase of property overseas, but the hoped-for progress was soon shattered by the First World War. The Russian Revolution wiped out most of the Society's massive circulation in Eurasia, including a far-flung system of colportage overseen by an expanded set of agencies in Petersburg, Ekaterinburg, and Odessa. Similar changes, if more gradual, affected the attitudes and activities of Bible societies in other parts of the world.

Although they lacked the size and scope of BFBS operations, other Bible societies began to conduct significant international work. Hanna Hodacs has argued that British evangelicals occasionally stigmatized their cross-cultural Swedish counterparts until BFBS-led efforts to establish a Swedish Bible Society effectively drew Swedish evangelicals into a common pan-Protestant European view of global mission.[12] Yet, the overseas work of the Netherlands Bible Society in the Dutch East Indies was pioneering and did not rest upon BFBS leadership. Founded in 1814, the Netherlands society early on employed its own linguists to learn local languages and translate the Bible. The National Bible Society of Scotland also felt the need to support Scottish missions in the field, including its active centers in Africa and China. The largest of all these other Bible societies, second only to the BFBS itself, was the American Bible Society (ABS), founded in New York in 1816. Not only did the ABS tackle the enormous task of supplying the United States with Bibles, but from its origins it had a strong missionary interest. The ABS often followed in the path of American missionaries, as for example in the Ottoman Empire, where it sent its representative to Smyrna in 1837. The BFBS agent working in the same Ottoman territories, Benjamin Barker, thought this strange and unnecessary. Richard Clogg's essay in this collection sets the background to these Levantine issues. The ABS naturally regarded central and south America as its particular field of influence, something that the BFBS did not altogether concede, though it did hand over the work in Mexico to the ABS in 1876. In 1911, the ABS surrendered its Persian field to the BFBS, in exchange for Central America; and in 1918 it exchanged Korea for the Philippines.

---

11. *One Hundred and First Report of the BFBS* (London, 1905), p. 3.

12. See her published doctoral dissertation, *Converging World Views: The European Expansion and Early-Nineteenth-Century Anglo-Swedish Contacts*, Studia Historica Upsaliensia, no. 207 (Uppsala: Uppsala University, 2003).

In 1919, the American Bible Society farsightedly suggested the formation of an association of national Bible societies to promote coordination and prevent overlapping jurisdiction. This was indignantly rejected by the BFBS, which declared that it was *not* a national Bible society, but an international organization whose "world operations might be seriously hampered by any control of the nature suggested."[13]

The post-World War I ideology of national self-determination and emergent colonial self-rule movements no doubt contributed to a rethinking of the need for international collaboration. The retirements of antagonistic BFBS and ABS secretaries John Ritson and William Haven in 1931 also paved the way for a less competitive attitude. Their successors, Arthur Wilkinson and Eric North, not only got along well personally, but were both convinced that cooperation, not competition, was the way forward. In 1932 a system of "joint agencies" was set up, whereby administration of an area was left to one society alone, although two or more might provide financial support. In other parts of the world, nationalism and national movements raised questions about the BFBS as a colonial enterprise and London as the only international center for biblical work.

Political pressures, such as those felt during and after the Russian Revolution, had their effect too. This was perhaps most starkly illustrated in the case of China. From the 1860s, the BFBS, the ABS, and the National Bible Society of Scotland (NBSS) all had significant operations in China, each with its own separate staff, depots, and colporteurs. This led to much overlapping and competition.[14] The growth of nationalism was viewed with some suspicion, not least when a group of Chinese Christians wanted to form a South China Bible Society in 1927, intending eventually to replace societies of foreign origin. The civil unrest of the 1930s forced further changes. In 1937, the BFBS and ABS came together to form one organization, China Bible House (the NBSS joined in 1946). The China Bible House was handed over to Chinese leadership in 1950 as western missionaries were forced out by the new communist government.

The Second World War again reduced the operations of the BFBS, and the need for closer international cooperation became more obvious to most Bible society leaders. The United Bible Societies (UBS) was formed in 1946 as a forum for the exchange of ideas and mutual support. Starting with thirteen societies, the UBS grew steadily, and its fiftieth anniversary meeting in 1996 was attended by representatives of 135 societies. From

---

13. BFBS Minutes of Staff Subcommittee for Review, 14 April 1919, p. 2 (BSA/C30/5).

14. These Bible societies had, of course, been financing the Bible translations of missionaries for far longer. The BFBS made its first grant to the pioneer Chinese translator Robert Morrison in 1812.

1966 the UBS has managed a world service budget and employed experts to help societies with their financial, publishing, and translation programmes—work such as that of the "translation consultant" described in the essay by David Clark.

By the 1940s, the BFBS also faced new challenges at home. There was the need to consider more modern translations of the English Bible.[15] There was the notable decline in the vibrancy of the BFBS auxiliary system. There was even the need to rethink some of the BFBS first principles, such as the commitment to publish only Bibles "without note or comment" (see the essay of Roger Steer), in light of the possibility that occasional non-doctrinal "note and comment" might make the Bible more intelligible to modern readers. Similarly, the BFBS issued its first illustrated Bible in 1954. As the marketplace changed, BFBS publishing also adjusted to include magazine-format Gospels and modern advertising methods. The renewed post-World War II effort to involve women and young people is noted in John Dean's essay on the London Bible House.

Although the BFBS was not to hand over administrative responsibility for its overseas agencies for another twelve years, the Third Jubilee in 1954 was perhaps the last time the BFBS could present itself as an international organization. Even as the British Empire had collapsed in the wake of the Second World War, so also the BFBS ceased to be the sole international hub for modern biblical translation and publication. National Bible societies throughout the world were exercising their own independence. Their international cooperation took the form not of subordination to the BFBS, but rather of confederative national membership in the United Bible Societies. The result of this transformation was that the BFBS had at last to see itself as but one national Bible society alongside many others.

So the BFBS had to develop a new identity. While continuing to raise funds for and publicize Bible work overseas, its attention increasingly turned to England and Wales as a mission field. The problem was no longer the scarcity or dearness of the Bible, but the unwillingness of the general public to read it. One answer was new, easy-to-read versions, notably the Good News Bible of 1976—begun by the ABS with the New Testament in 1966 and culminating in the complete Bible with the deuterocanonical books in 1979—the first such English Bible to be published by the BFBS. Another answer was a greater emphasis on selections adapted to a particular audience and the provision of study aids. These were made possible by a change to the Society's charter in 1984, which redefined its

---

15. In 1901 the BFBS altered Law 1 of its constitution in order to publish the English Revised Version of 1885, as well as the Authorized (King James) Bible. In 1951 it removed these restrictions and allowed itself to publish any version approved by the Committee.

aim as being to "encourage the wider circulation *and use* of the Bible [emphasis added]," as noted in the accompanying essay by Roger Steer.

Despite the transformation of the BFBS in the last half of the twentieth century, and the resulting transferral of most of its international agenda to the United Bible Societies, the BFBS archive and library have continued to document the critical role that the organization played both from a global perspective and within the development of a modern religious culture closely attuned to the marketplace. As is appropriate on the occasion of this anniversary year, the essays that follow examine the historical significance of the British and Foreign Bible Society in the context of larger issues confronting modern society in the past two hundred years.

The first of these larger interpretive issues is clearly that of modernity itself, and the place of the British and Foreign Bible Society in fashioning a modern literate religious culture. Elsewhere in this volume, Stephen Batalden has sought to clarify the place of the BFBS within the conceptual framework of modernity, adopting in the process the language of the German critical theorist, Jürgen Habermas. According to this view, the BFBS was a part of the "architecture of modernity," adapting the prevailing religious culture to an emergent "public sphere," a discursive world separate and distinct from the authority of the state in which commercial, bourgeois agents became the harbingers of a new nineteenth-century British civil society. As Leslie Howsam has noted in her essay in this volume and in her separate monograph, *Cheap Bibles*, not only did the BFBS instinctively capitalize upon the greatest instrument of this new civil society—namely, the press and, specifically, stereotype printing—but BFBS leaders, many of them entrepreneurs in their own right, were also among the most effective spokesmen for the new civil society.[16] The Bible Society's early patron, William Wilberforce, saw no conflict between his devotion to the cause of the BFBS and his popular civil society leadership in the anti-slavery movement. Ultimately, by adapting itself to the needs of an expanding literate public and to state-of-the-art commercial developments in the marketplace, the BFBS became a catalyst in the transformation of traditional religious culture. The universalism and self-confidence of the Bible Society, expressed in John Dean's comment on his BFBS employment in the 1950s (see his essay on the London Bible House), reflected this engagement of the BFBS with modernity. For it was in the embrace of the "public sphere" that the BFBS became a crucial link between religious culture and modernity.

The modern, commercial side of BFBS operations was not without its built-in tensions. The most obvious of these tensions was the difference

---

16. Leslie Howsam, *Cheap Bibles: Nineteenth-Century Publishing and the British and Foreign Bible Society* (Cambridge: Cambridge University Press, 1991).

between the commercial goals of the BFBS—it was, after all, in the business of selling Bibles and it was meant to be run like a business—and the missionary impulse that spawned its creation. Officially appointed BFBS agents, Robert Pinkerton (see the essay by Wayne Detzler), William Nicolson (see the essay by Stephen Batalden), and even the independent-minded writer George Borrow (see the essay by Ann Ridler) all understood the priority that the Society placed upon good business practices. Alexander Thomson, agent for the Turkish Empire, was criticized by BFBS Secretary Samuel Bergne for being unbusinesslike, and maintaining depots where the expenses far outweighed the receipts from sales. Bergne commented, "Dr Thomson thinks that to place a man of christian character in a dark and corrupt place must exert a valuable influence.... It is possible that he may look at the thing too strongly in a missionary point of view and rather aside from the exclusive object which this society proposes to accomplish."[17]

Nevertheless, the appeal of the BFBS to its far-flung auxiliaries and local associations grew out of the philanthropic and missionary goals attributed to the BFBS. The spirit of those missionary goals is well captured in several of the essays in this volume—especially Sue Jackson's work on the BFBS and the Methodists in Spain and Gibraltar, and Roald Kverndal's essay on the BFBS and missions to seafarers. Leslie Howsam has argued that the commercial goals of the Society effectively defined the dominant operational culture within the BFBS. The fact that these commercial realities may often have trumped the missionary side of BFBS operations testifies not to the exclusion of one by the other, but rather to the built-in creative tension between marketplace and mission.

If the Bible Society's engagement with the marketplace suggests a need for redefining the BFBS as an institutional catalyst of modernity and modern religious culture, then it is the Society's complicated international posture that, at the end of its second century, most draws the BFBS into contemporary debate over globalization and empire. From its earliest years, the Bible Society viewed its task internationally. Not only was its first publication of Scripture an edition of the Gospel of John in Mohawk (see the essay by Joyce Banks), but it also reserved a prominent place on its committee and among its leading secretaries for international representatives. In this respect, the BFBS was continuing squarely in the tradition of wider missionary movements that had dominated the Scottish and English evangelical awakening at the end of the eighteenth century. As Leslie Howsam notes in her accompanying essay, one of the founding

---

17. S. B. Bergne, Report of European tour, 3 vols., 1872 (BSA/D2/8), vol. 2, pp. 161-65. The Scutari depot cost £40 over six months, while sales amounted to £1.12.6. The figures for Sarajevo were £50 and £5.

BFBS committeemen, the Quaker Luke Howard, had questioned whether the BFBS was a religious society, claiming instead that it was rather "a society for furnishing the means of religion."[18] But such a quibble did not hide the fact that the BFBS carefully cultivated the collaboration of missionary translators (as Thor Strandenaes has described in his essay on early Chinese translations) and considered its work to be an integral part of the wider, globalizing missionary enterprise.

While the BFBS greatly expanded the range of its translations into African and indigenous Native American languages in the last half of the nineteenth and early twentieth centuries, even its earliest translation efforts, symbolized by the Mohawk Gospel of John, were ambitious by international standards of the day.[19] As Patricia Mirrlees has noted in her essay, the Bible Society did not support John Hill's proposed translation of Scripture into Wolof, but its failure to do so may well have reflected BFBS concern over paying salary to an untried translator, rather than any lack of commitment to West African languages. By 1965, the last year for which BFBS statistics were given separately from those of other Bible societies, the number of languages encompassed in BFBS scriptural publications had expanded to 877, including many of the less commonly taught indigenous languages of Africa, Latin America, and Eurasia.[20]

At this bicentenary crossroads, during a period of broad public debate on globalization, empire, and post-colonialism—a debate that has intensified in the wake of the war in Iraq—how are we to interpret the deep involvement of the BFBS in international biblical translation and global Christian missions? Was the global mission of the BFBS part of a Eurocentric colonial or imperial enterprise that sought western hegemony in the name of a Christian God? The Comaroffs, in their ambitious two-volume study, *Of Revelation and Revolution*, argue that "Non-conformist

---

18. Quoted in William Canton, *A History of the British and Foreign Bible Society*, 5 vols. (London: John Murray, 1904–1910), vol. 2, p. 359. See how this passage is also used in Leslie Howsam's essay in this volume.

19. Although many of the translations were published by the Russian Bible Society and other affiliated societies and missionaries, the fact that the BFBS contributed to the translation and publication of the Scriptures in 142 languages by 1825 suggests that its international agenda extended well beyond the typical early nineteenth-century Eurocentric focus upon power languages. Eric Hobsbawm, in *Nations and Nationalism Since 1780: Programme, Myth, Reality* (Cambridge: Cambridge University Press, 1990), has coined the term "threshold principle" to describe this Eurocentric idea that "the nation" was by definition restricted to empires or nations having reached a sufficient "threshold" in size or world power. By contrast, the BFBS publishing programme broke with such a limited perspective, contributing early on to the preservation and study of less commonly taught non-European languages.

20. *One Hundred and Sixty-First Report of the BFBS, year ending December 31st 1965* (London, n.d.), p. 218.

Christian missionaries in South Africa became the footsoldiers of British colonialism."[21] Should the BFBS agents and their sub-agents, depot-keepers, colporteurs, and collaborating translators — a global army estimated above at approximately one thousand employees by the time of the Society's centennial in 1904 — be viewed simply as unwitting agents in some larger western colonialist agenda?

The essays in this collection point to a quite different, more nuanced, approach to issues of globalization and post-colonialism. In the first place, the overseas work of the British and Foreign Bible Society invariably became "self-transforming," broadening the world of those most deeply engaged in such cross-cultural communication. Thus, BFBS efforts were rarely unidirectional in imposing some westernizing impact, but rather involved a dynamic reciprocal process of cross-cultural exchange — one particularly well documented in the case study of the Manchu translation project addressed in Erling von Mende's essay. The Comaroffs have also recognized this reciprocal cultural exchange relationship in global interactions, which they rightly view as "incorrigibly plural."[22]

Furthermore, those who would see the Bible Society as narrowly colonialist in its agenda face an even more substantial counter-argument posed by Lamin Sanneh and others addressing the preservation of indigenous cultural identity in the face of globalization or westernization. Sanneh, an Africanist leader in the joint University of Edinburgh/Yale University project on the history of Christian missions, has demonstrated how biblical translation became critically important in the preservation and standardization of national and tribal languages. The "native informants" identified in the essays by Thor Strandenaes and David Clark have their counterparts wherever the BFBS became involved in early biblical translation and dissemination. As Lamin Sanneh has noted in the case of West Africa, "African languages were developed in order to translate the Scriptures and to provide an effective medium of instruction in the schools established by the missions."[23] His point, of course, is not only that this development of African languages contributed to modern education and learning, but that in helping to preserve local African languages the Bible Society also offered a foundation upon which indigenous people might

---

21. Jean Comaroff and John Comaroff, *Of Revelation and Revolution*, vol. 1, *Christianity, Colonialism, and Consciousness in South Africa* (Chicago and London: University of Chicago Press, 1991), p. xi. See also their companion study, *Of Revelation and Revolution*, vol. 2, *The Dialectics of Modernity on a South African Frontier* (Chicago and London: University of Chicago Press, 1997).

22. See their edited anthology, *Modernity and its Malcontents: Ritual and Power in Postcolonial Africa* (Chicago and London: University of Chicago Press, 1993), p. xi.

23. Lamin Sanneh, *West African Christianity: The Religious Impact* (London and New York: George Allen & Unwin, 1983), p. 106.

seek their own cultural and religious identity, oftentimes in movements that would take on a decidedly anti-colonial character.

The indigenization of Christianity ironically now poses a more subtle challenge for Bible societies, not only in Africa or Latin America, but also notably in Eurasia. In Russia, as Father Sergei Ovsiannikov and Stephen Batalden note in their essays on the politics of modern Russian biblical translation, despite the commitment to interconfessional biblical translation, there have occasionally been disconnects between the traditionally Protestant Bible Society movement and modern Orthodox religious culture. As Ovsiannikov observes in the conclusion to his essay on the émigré Russian translation project of Bishop Cassian, the United Bible Societies and its participating post-Soviet Bible Society in Russia at times have failed to address the real needs of a Russian Orthodox world. It is with respect to this issue — full indigenization of biblical translation and dissemination — that the legacy of the British and Foreign Bible Society presents the greatest challenge to its post-colonial United Bible Societies stepchild.

In addressing the larger interpretive issues of religious culture, modernity, and post-colonialism, these essays document the importance of the living legacy left by the BFBS in its library and archives now on permanent loan at Cambridge University Library. The history of that archive, written by its first archivist Kathleen Cann, opens this collection of essays. Appended to this volume is Kathleen Cann's important guide to the catalogue of the British and Foreign Bible Society archives. Readers will note that, in line with the new BFBS archival catalogue, all the essays in this collection employ the standardized notational format recommended for future users of the archives, a feature of the volume that is owing to the editorial labours of Kathleen Cann.

The editors are particularly pleased to acknowledge the support received in the preparation of this volume. Goodenough College generously offered its facilities in the heart of London for the bicentenary scholarly symposium, "Sowing the Word." The audience at the symposium contributed to animated discussion that has helped sharpen the issues posed within the papers. The scholars who joined in the conference and have added their essays to this volume, while they do not necessarily share the same views on the larger historical issues posed within the volume, nevertheless have all had the good fortune of exploring the archival treasures of the BFBS under the guiding hand of its longstanding archivist Kathleen Cann. To her we add a special note of gratitude. For permission to publish material from the Bible Society's archives we give grateful thanks to the Society (www.biblesociety.org.uk) and to the Syndics of Cambridge University Library. Finally, we wish to thank Archbishop of Canterbury Rowan Williams for contributing the foreword to this volume.

THE ARCHIVES OF THE BRITISH AND FOREIGN BIBLE SOCIETY

Kathleen Cann

History of the Archives

The British and Foreign Bible Society moved into its first official premises at 10 Earl Street, Blackfriars, in 1816, bringing together under one roof its stock of Bibles, its library, and the administrative documents that had hitherto been kept at the homes of its officials.

It must have taken a while to get everything in order, since a committee member complained in June 1817, "Our Library, & original letters etc., remain in confusion; the Catalogue is also unfinished, & we cannot find any documents when they are wanted for consultation!"[1] Over the next five years the Scripture library was put in order: it had grown from an initial donation of 39 books in 1804 to the 800 items that were described in the first catalogue published with the BFBS annual *Report* in 1822. Today, most of the 35,000 books in the Scripture library are catalogued online as part of Cambridge University Library holdings.[2]

In spite of the above complaint, the arrangement of the archives proper seems to have been fairly orderly, thanks to BFBS Assistant Secretary Joseph Tarn. He held that post from the beginning and explained to the Committee that the work at first provided "a pleasant occupation of leisure hours". By 1807 the work was taking two hours a day, and by 1809 it consumed more time than his job in the City.[3] In 1810 he took on the work of the BFBS accountant as well, and thus became the Society's first full-time paid employee, turning a room in his house into a Bible Society office. In 1811 he was authorized to purchase "a set of Drawers and letter holes" to contain the Society's papers and a "copying machine, or polygraph" for the Society's use.[4] In 1815 he was invited to move into the

---

1. William Blair to Joseph Tarn, 24 June 1817, BFBS Home Correspondence Inwards (BSA/D1/1/20).
2. This can be consulted at www.lib.cam.ac.uk.
3. J. Tarn to the Committee, 3 August 1810, BFBS Home Correspondence Inwards (BSA/D1/1/6).
4. BFBS Minutes of the Printing Subcommittee, 16 December 1811, vol. 2, p. 92 (BSA/C1/1/2).

Picture 1. *Bible House, 10 Earl Street, Blackfriars.* Reprinted from William Canton, *A History of the BFBS*, vol. 1 (London: John Murray, 1904), facing p. 102.

the new Bible House, and he was still in harness at his death in 1837, aged 71. Joseph Tarn laid down a filing system that persisted, more or less, until the 1930s. Minutes of the Committee and of subcommittees, as well as the principal financial records, were kept in numerous series of bound volumes. Letters were filed in four chronological series: incoming home, incoming foreign, outgoing home, and outgoing foreign. The incoming foreign letters were bound up in large volumes (to 1851), each with its index of correspondents. The home letters were endorsed by name of writer and filed alphabetically in the above-mentioned letter holes, later to be tied in bundles and boxed. They were not indexed. Copies of outgoing letters, presumably made by the polygraph, were bound up and indexed by addressee. Some BFBS departments were still doing this in 1938, when a major administrative reorganization was carried through by outside consultants, who commented, "It will be appreciated that the method of endorsing letters and filing them in pigeon holes has long since been dispensed with by business houses in favour of filing cabinets".[5]

The simplicity of the system is both a strength and a weakness: it makes it easy to follow a transaction in detail, from the arrival of a letter, through its presentation to the Committee, its referral to a subcommittee, and on to the copy of the reply sent back. The limitation lies in the fact that the material is neither arranged geographically, nor grouped by person or subject. Some attempt to overcome this problem was made by copying letters into several series of copybooks: one, for example, arranged geographically according to the Bible Society agency, and another organized on a subject basis, namely, letters on translation matters. But essentially any subject approach to Bible Society history has to start with the published sources, the histories, and the annual reports.

The archives are by no means complete. The first recorded loss occurred in 1850, when the door of the muniment room was left open to air it, and eleven volumes of committee minutes went missing. The police searched the whole of the Metropolitan District — so they said — but found nothing. Two years later, one volume was brought back by a friend of a grocer in Lambeth, who had bought three volumes as waste paper from a youth of about nineteen — no, he would not recognize him again — and had used two of them in the course of business.[6] The next disruption came in 1868, when the Earl Street premises were pulled down to make way for a new road, and the Society had to move into temporary accommodation for almost a year, until their new office on Queen Victoria Street was ready.

5. "Re-organisation of administration", report by Price, Waterhouse & Co., 9 December 1938, appendix 8, p. 5, in BFBS Finance Department records (BSA/E1/1/10/8).

6. BFBS Minutes of the Finance Subcommittee, 13 November and 11 December 1850, 13 and 15 April 1853, vol. 5, pp. 64, 66, 129, 131 (BSA/C4/5).

The archives were then stored in a brick-vaulted strong room, known as the crypt, where they remained until 1977.

The minutes of the House Subcommittee (1868–1937) provide occasional glimpses of the archives over the next sixty years. In 1897 it was reported that the crypt "greatly needed cleansing and re-arrangement", and Taylor & Son were paid £5 to do this.[7] Perhaps they were not very efficient, for only a year later it was urged that "early action should be taken for the cleaning out of the Crypt and the removal of lumber and useless records therefrom".[8] This led to a major inspection by several of the Society's officials in May 1898, who found "such a quantity of old newspapers, old Reports of various Societies, magazines etc., together with a considerable quantity of old woodwork—like church-pews, gas-chandeliers, old directories etc., that nearly all the time was consumed in moving them out of the crypt.... The dirt was something dreadful—in fact the place was something like the stables of Augeas, King of Elis, on a small scale". The "old and useless papers" were duly removed, and orders were given that "nothing should be put there but important records of the Society".[9]

The Society's ignorance of its archives at this period can be illustrated by the efforts of George Borrow's first biographer, William Knapp, to consult Borrow's letters. When Knapp wrote to the Society in 1887, he was told that the letters could not be found or were not accessible; the same information was repeated when he called in person in 1895, and he had to manage without them.[10] His biography of Borrow appeared in 1899—soon after the great clearance of the crypt—and on reading it the BFBS secretary went to investigate and found all the letters, in their proper places. The Society's embarrassment led eventually to its own publication of Borrow's letters in 1911.

The story continued through the first half of the twentieth century. In 1907 the House Subcommittee drew attention to the "necessity for thoroughly clearing out and re-arranging the Crypt". No one on the staff had time for this, so a young man was employed for several months at fifteen shillings a week to do the job. New shelves and cupboards were erected, and boxes to store letters were purchased for 4s.6d per dozen.[11] In 1927 it was reported that the crypt had become very congested, and a schedule

---

7. BFBS Minutes of the House Subcommittee, 4 January 1897, vol. 1 (unpaginated) (BSA/C9/1).
8. BFBS Minutes of the House Subcommittee, 24 January 1898, vol. 1 (BSA/C9/1).
9. BFBS Minutes of the House Subcommittee, 17 June 1898, vol. 2, pp. 6-9 (BSA/-C9/2).
10. Letter of John Murray in *The Times*, 26 April 1899.
11. BFBS Minutes of the House Subcommittee, 13 February, 22 March, 29 May 1907, vol. 4, pp. 33, 41, 46 (BSA/C9/4).

was drawn up of "what may be dispensed with safely".[12] During the 1938 administrative reorganization the crypt was "cleared of much of the material in store".[13] In 1941 some promising discussion took place on classifying documents for retention for periods of three years, seven years, or permanently, but wartime conditions seem to have prevented anything being done.[14]

At some point fifty years' worth of incoming correspondence was lost: the Foreign Correspondence Inwards (1857–1900) and the Home Correspondence Inwards for almost exactly the same years. There is no evidence as to when and why this correspondence disappeared, but the loss of the foreign letters is probably the most serious gap in the Society's records.

Cataloguing the Archives

In 1962 the Society asked the librarian of Lambeth Palace Library, E. G. W. Bill, to survey the archives. His report made a series of recommendations for a programme of conservation, cataloguing, and indexing.[15] He suggested that the archival material up to 1912 be catalogued by employing three archivists for a period of seven years. In the event, the Society employed one archivist for twenty-one years — which may or may not amount to the same thing. Be that as it may, the Society sent me to qualify as an archivist, and I took up the post officially in 1966.

I had as a starting point a brief list of the main archive series, compiled by previous library staff, and I was able to expand on this, making lists of the many series of minute books, correspondence books, and accounts, but naturally I took Dr. Bill's report as my principal guide. Stating that "the most urgent task is the preparation of comprehensive indexes of the correspondence", the report drew attention in particular to the unindexed Home Correspondence Inwards. So, I took down the bundle of letters for 1804, and started to construct a card index. This was my main task for the next two years, by which time I had reached 1836, a total of eighty-six boxes, and about thirty thousand letters. I then amalgamated onto cards the entries from the hundred-odd contemporary indexes to the Foreign Correspondence Inwards series, while several temporary assistants helped to do the same for the copybooks. Between us we built up a card index of some

---

12. BFBS Minutes of the House Subcommittee, 24 November 1927, vol. 5, p. 21 (BSA/C9/5).

13. "Re-organisation of administration", in BFBS Finance Department records (BSA/E1/1/10/8).

14. BFBS Minutes of the General Purposes Subcommittee, 11 March 1941, vol. 2, p. 32 (BSA/C3/1/2).

15. E. G. W. Bill, "Report on the archives of the BFBS", 1962, in BFBS Translations Department records, archives policy file (BSA/E3/6/1/2).

ten thousand nineteenth-century correspondents. Meanwhile, research enquiries began to increase. In 1966, there were 19 postal enquiries, four years later 70, and from the mid-1970s onward about 120 a year. Much of the correspondence remains unindexed, including the Home Inwards (1837–1856), and the Home and Foreign Inwards (1901–1905), a total of 177 boxes, each holding about 350 letters.

Reading the early letters was an education in the Society's activities and attitudes. There were a great many routine letters from clergy and others wanting Bibles for their parishioners, Sunday schools, workhouses, or the local poor in general. So I was intrigued by a request in 1817 from a Mr. Parish of Bath, on behalf of his son, Sir John Parish, who had recently purchased the Principality of Senftenberg in Bohemia (two market towns, twenty villages, and fifteen thousand inhabitants) and wanted Scriptures for the schools he was establishing. The Society duly obliged, and two months later 250 German Catholic New Testaments were received with thanks by Baron Parish of Senftenberg Castle.[16] One of the early personalities that came to life in the letters was the Anglican Secretary John Owen, who directed a constant stream of instructions to Mr. Tarn: please call a subcommittee meeting for Monday, send me the latest letters from India, copy and despatch the enclosed drafts, insert advertisements in the following papers, get two thousand publicity leaflets printed immediately. As a subsequent writer put it, "At that time the late highly-gifted John Owen dominated in Earl-Street as Clerical Secretary, and owing to his abilities and energy, was known as the 'Dictator'".[17] If Owen did stand on his dignity as a clergyman of the Established Church, it was for a reason: he had the worldly wisdom to know that the Society had to keep the Church of England on its side if it was to be successful, which was not at all certain in the early years. But Owen was also a man of vision, who saw the BFBS as "a Society, which studies to unite the Christian world, by distributing among them, according to their respective versions, the common standard of their faith and their practice".[18]

Further upheavals occurred during my time as archivist: not only was there building work going on in the 1960s, but in the late 1970s Bible House was radically remodelled, which meant moving the library and the archives temporarily to other parts of the building. Finally, during the

16. J. Parish, Bath, 18 April, 2 and 15 May 1817, Samuel Whitchurch, Bath, 4 April 1817, BFBS Home Correspondence Inwards (D1/1/21, 22); Baron Parish, Senftenberg Castle, 16 June 1817, BFBS Foreign Correspondence Books, no. 6, p. 311 (BSA/D1/6/6).

17. *The History of the Trinitarian Bible Society*, reprinted from *The Record* newspaper, 27 April 1881.

18. J. Owen, Strasburg, 11 September 1818, published in the *Fifteenth Report of the BFBS* (London, 1819), appendix, p. 8.

period 1984–1985, the Bible Society sold the building on Queen Victoria Street and moved to Swindon, Wiltshire. The library and archives were deposited in Cambridge University Library on permanent loan. The library van came down from Cambridge every week, and the London staff at Bible House packed up the boxes that were later unpacked by staff at Cambridge after the return trip. I spent two years in Cambridge getting the archives in order and continuing the cataloguing, and then I moved on, ultimately to a job in the Manuscripts Department of Cambridge University Library. I only resumed my connection with the archives twelve years later, when the then BFBS librarian took early retirement.

Missionary Archives Project

In today's world, missionary societies can rarely afford to employ archivists, and even large research libraries have tight budgetary constraints. New work, however, can sometimes be done by getting short-term funding from a granting agency. Thus, in 1999 Cambridge University Library was invited to participate in a three-year project funded by the Research Support Libraries Programme, whose aim was to improve and facilitate access to missionary collections in the United Kingdom. Eight institutions were given money to carry out a variety of cataloguing and conservation projects, under the leadership of the archivist of the School of Oriental and African Studies in London. The project culminated in the creation of a web-based guide to more than four hundred collections of missionary material.[19] Cambridge University Library's main contribution to this project was the creation of a web-based catalogue of the BFBS archives; it was my rash suggestion, so in due course I found myself supervising two very capable assistants in doing just that.

I had intended simply to revise my existing lists and get them marked up for mounting on the web, as had been done for a number of the university library collections. But discussions with colleagues persuaded me to take advantage of a database that had been recently developed by a group of Cambridge archivists for cataloguing purposes. It is a customized version of Microsoft's Access database, which enables descriptions of archives to be created in a consistent fashion and in a way that conforms to modern archival standards.[20] The information on the database can be exported as a Word document, to provide a hard copy of the catalogue, and it can also

---

19. The Mundus Gateway, maintained at the School of Oriental and African Studies. See www.mundus.ac.uk.

20. These standards are the International Standard Archival Description (General), the National Council on Archives rules for the construction of names, the UNESCO thesaurus, and the Getty geographical thesaurus.

be exported in Encoded Archival Description (EAD) format, which is a marked-up text that can be put onto the web. Thus, there is being built up at Cambridge a collection of catalogues of archives — those of some of the colleges, the university archives themselves, and other Cambridge institutions — which is mounted on a server in the university library, and is accessible via the library's website.[21] The site is named Janus after the Roman god of gateways, who looks in two directions, back to ancient archives, and forward to modern technology.

So here was a brave new world. My descriptions had to be analyzed and entered in the relevant boxes: title, originator, description, quantity, and covering dates. Each description had to relate to all the others in a hierarchical pattern as a "parent", "child", or "grandchild", or in archival terms, as a "collection", a "series", or an "item". The BFBS archives are on the whole hierarchical in their arrangement, so much of the task was straightforward. It gave me the opportunity to standardize descriptions as far as possible, shortening some and expanding others, and indeed making proper catalogue entries for material that had previously been noted only briefly.

What the database also required was a unique code for each description, which would relate one description to the others and print things out in the correct sequence. Finally I had to face up to a proper classification of the archives, something I had avoided up to then (to the horror of my fellow-archivists). This was mainly because I was afraid of devising a classification that might prove unworkable, and also because I found I could manage without one; it was sufficient to use the names of the series — Editorial Subcommittee, Home Correspondence Inwards, and so on. But now my chief assistant and I had to grasp the nettle and create something logical. We settled for an alphanumeric system that grouped the records into eight major categories, A-G, and subdivided each one by numbers. I should add that the codes followed the natural hierarchy of the archives, and did not involve any major rearrangement. Thus, the Foreign Correspondence Inwards is still the Foreign Correspondence Inwards, and can be cited as such, even though it has the code D1/2. The system seems to work satisfactorily and allows for expansion as later material is added.[22]

For me personally it is a satisfactory conclusion to twenty years' work. My old typed and handwritten lists of the archives are summed up in a consistent format and are available worldwide via the Internet. The archives themselves are not likely to be stolen from Cambridge University Library, and I trust the papers are in less confusion than they were in 1817 and can be found when they are wanted for consultation.

---

21. See http://www.lib.cam.ac.uk, or go directly to http://janus.lib.cam.ac.uk.
22. See the full summary catalogue appended at the end of this volume.

Part One

THE BFBS AT HOME

THE BIBLE SOCIETY AND THE BOOK TRADE

Leslie Howsam

One of the founders of the British and Foreign Bible Society articulated in all seriousness a principle that, two hundred years later, sounds absurd. Luke Howard, a chemist and meteorologist, and a Quaker, insisted that the BFBS was not a religious society. "It is a society for furnishing the means of religion", he explained, "but not a religious society".[1] He was right: it was a publisher. The Society's leaders, most of whom were lay businessmen and professionals, had undertaken to furnish the means of religion by an extensive program of translation, composition, printing, binding, and distribution of a single book. Because the Bible is not like other books, the nineteenth-century Bible Society was not exactly like other contemporary publishers. The secretaries and the Committee members who held power in the organization did not share with Longman's or Rivington's, for example, the problem of choosing among new manuscripts by aspiring or established authors. The divine authorship of the single book on the Society's list was not a matter for copyrights or payments on account; nor did the Society's products appear in Hatchard's or other retail booksellers' shops. Nevertheless, the nineteenth-century BFBS was an organization that devoted most of its inexhaustible energy and considerable wealth to the products of the book trade. To argue that the BFBS was *not* a publisher would be as difficult as trying to make the case that it was not an evangelical organization. This chapter concerns both elements of its activity, the times when the Society behaved like a publisher, and those when it went its own way irrespective of the customs of the book trade.

A contemporary entrepreneurial publisher like Longman or Rivington was headed by an individual businessman and driven by a combination of cultural and commercial impulses. Besides bringing out important, interesting, or beautiful works of literature, the businessman also sought

---

1. William Canton, *A History of the British and Foreign Bible Society*, 5 vols. (London: John Murray, 1904-1910), vol. 2, p. 359. This essay is drawn from the author's own work, *Cheap Bibles: Nineteenth-Century Publishing and the British and Foreign Bible Society* (Cambridge: Cambridge University Press, 1991).

to make a profit. The evangelical publisher BFBS was headed by a committee of businessmen, but the cultural impulses that drove it were not abstract: they had a human face, replicated many times over. The faces of middle-class Britons by the thousand were alight with evangelical religious enthusiasm, and these Britons were wracked by anxiety about the changing social conditions of their rapidly industrializing nation. They regarded the publishing activity of the Society as their business. They took a passionate interest in the new technologies of stereotype composition, they worried about the conditions of labour in the binderies, and they undertook personally the task of distribution. If publishing is conceptualized in terms of "making public", then the men and women who made up local auxiliaries and ladies' Bible associations were just as much the publishers of BFBS books as the powerful men at the Earl Street headquarters who placed the orders for paper and print.[2] These men and women were, after all, enjoined to spread the gospel. Theirs was not an oral culture where news was spread solely by word of mouth. Even in 1804, association members were "modern", receiving their news and opinion from newspapers and pamphlets, demonstrating thereby how evangelicalism and print culture developed simultaneously.

The Politics of Evangelicalism

The Bible Society's publishing activities were shaped by the politics, as well as the passions, of contemporary evangelicalism. The leadership of the organization was carefully balanced between Anglicans and Dissenters, who agreed to disagree about matters of doctrine.[3] Although controversy and criticism could not be avoided altogether, the "fundamental principle" of publishing the Scriptures "without note or comment" made the project possible. Bibles and New Testaments published by the Society in any language would not contain prefaces or explanatory notes interpreting or supplementing the text according to specific doctrines or customs — no Book of Common Prayer for England and Wales, no Metrical Psalms for Scotland, and no dogmatic interpretations authorized by the papacy

---

2. Leslie Howsam, "Book History Unbound: Transactions of the Written Word Made Public", *Canadian Journal of History* 38 (April 2003), pp. 69-81.

3. The Committee was made up of equal numbers (fifteen each) of Anglicans and Dissenters, as well as six members of foreign churches. The senior staff also included an Anglican, a Dissenter, and a representative of foreign churches in the triumvirate secretariat. Roger Martin has characterized this principle as "pan-evangelicalism" (see his *Evangelicals United: Ecumenical Stirrings in Pre-Victorian Britain, 1795-1830* [Metuchen, N.J., and London: Scarecrow Press, 1983]). The energy of religious enthusiasm in those days was sometimes exhibited in an impatience with denominational barriers between sincere Christians.

for Roman Catholic countries. So strictly was this principle adhered to that local auxiliaries and Bible associations were forbidden to open their meetings with prayer.

Equally fundamental was the resolution that "the translation of the Scripture established by Public Authority, be the only one in the English language to be accepted by the Society".[4] Because the text of cheap Bibles in English was required to conform to the Authorized Version, such books had to be printed by one of three presses entrusted by the state with the Bible "privilege", namely, the King's (or Queen's) printer in London, or one of the two ancient university presses at Cambridge and Oxford. Only Scriptures in foreign languages could be contracted out to the lowest bidder in the printing shops of London and the provinces. In all these places, printers already knew what Luke Howard and his Bible Society colleagues were about to learn, that the Bible is a difficult work to print. P. M. Handover in *Printing in London* explains:

> To many people in this country, the Bible is a sacred book, perhaps even the inspired word of God, and that fact is relevant; but to its publishers the Bible is a book with certain physical features that make it different from all other books. First: the Authorized Version contains 774,746 words. Compositors and pressmen will quickly work out what that means in terms of ens, in paper orders and machining time. Secondly: there exists a considerable and constant demand for the Bible. Thirdly: the Bible must be produced without a single misprint. And fourthly: the Bible is required in the whole range of sizes, from folio to the smallest.

As a result, Handover concludes, the printing of Bibles attracts "the most shrewd businessmen in the trade", people "with a talent for organization and a keen analytical mind".[5] Such people needed all their skill and intelligence when dealing with the exigencies of the British and Foreign Bible Society.

New Technologies

Behind the Society's commitment to the new technologies of the publishing industry lay a powerful demand. Joseph John Gurney wrote from Norwich in 1813 that "poor people who have paid their money are very anxious — I might say very importunate for bibles".[6] So were the wealthier people who were collecting that money, as well as paying out their own,

---

4. Martin, *Evangelicals United*, p. 84.
5. P. M. Handover, *Printing in London from 1476 to Modern Times* (London: George Allen and Unwin Ltd., 1960), pp. 74-75.
6. Gurney to Tarn, 3 July 1813, BFBS Home Correspondence Inwards (BSA/D1/1/11).

to support both the domestic and foreign work of the Society. It was vital that the demand be supplied, even if this meant obliging the book trades to adopt new technologies and labour practices.

Fortunately (or, as most members believed, providentially), the technologies of communication were changing as rapidly in 1804 as they are in 2004. The promise at that time of stereotype was similar to contemporary panegyrics to the Internet or to the optimism generated twenty years ago by early experiences with word processing. Conventional practice required compositors to work with a limited supply of moveable type, which meant that they set up each book afresh whenever new copies were required. A German printer had experimented with keeping the type for Bibles standing, in other words, not distributing it in order to make the sorts available for other work; his books became more, rather than less, accurate over time, because errors could be caught and corrected without new ones creeping in. The privileged presses in England were not interested in keeping type standing, but they were prepared to experiment with an innovative technology, the production of stereotype plates, which offered similar advantages. Andrew Wilson, not quite the inventor but an early promoter of the technology, called it "a new era in the history of Literary Science".[7]

Stereotype plates began with conventional typeset pages, grouped as usual into formes. Rather than printing from this type, the platemaker took a plaster-of-paris mould of the whole forme and then poured in molten lead that would harden to form a single plate with all the words, punctuation marks, and spaces intact. Not only would this process ensure accuracy, its promoters hoped that it would also drastically reduce the price of printing. These promoters emphatically included the secretaries and the Committee of the Bible Society, who were so keen that they waited until the Cambridge University Press was equipped for stereotyping before placing their first order, in November 1804, for 6,000 Bibles and 5,000 New Testaments in English, along with 20,000 Bibles and 5,000 New Testaments in Welsh. Before long the university press at Oxford, and the printing firm of Eyre and Strahan, which held the royal privilege in London, were also striving to fill the Society's massive orders.

Stereotype plates solved the problems of accurate composition, but they did nothing to speed up the human-powered iron printing press, which was entirely too slow for the urgent needs of the Society. The Society's printers were also urged to experiment with the untried technology of steam power, and Richard Mackenzie Bacon of Norwich (now almost forgotten as an also-ran to Friedrich Koenig, who patented the

---

7. Andrew Wilson to "The Chairman & Gentlemen of the Printing Committee", 23 December 1806, BFBS Home Correspondence Inwards (BSA/D1/1/2).

first successful printing machine) was offered a contract to print some French New Testaments on his newly invented contraption. The experiment was a failure, and the resulting sheets ended up rotten, not even fit for "remanufacture", or recycling. At both the composition and presswork stages, printers found themselves responding to evangelical urgency, mediated by the pragmatic and entrepreneurial standards of contemporary business. "Like modern printers' customers, they wanted the work done 'yesterday'. As well as hounding their suppliers about deadlines and quality control, [the Society was] fully prepared to exert the economic pressure of the large customer".[8]

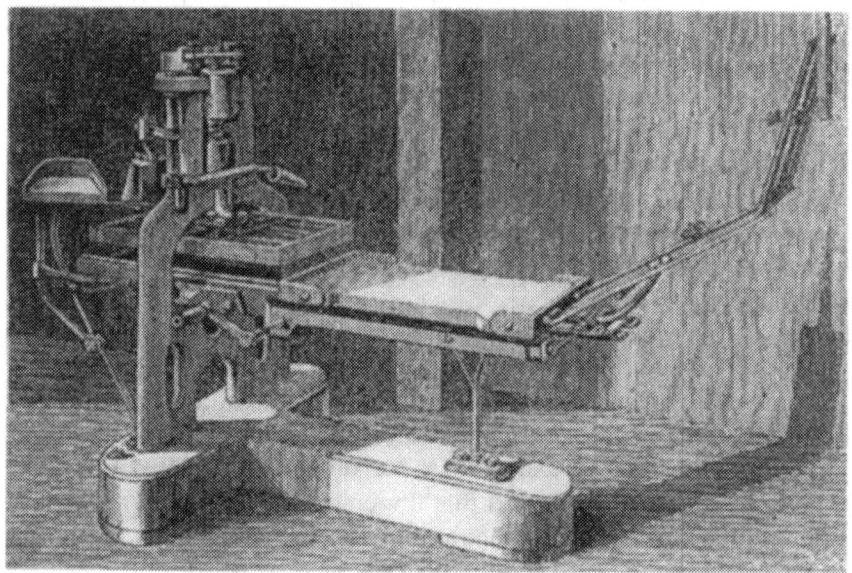

Picture 2. *A Stanhope stereotype printing press 1805, used by Cambridge University Press for printing Bibles.* Reproduced from Caleb Stower, *The Printer's Grammar; or, Introduction to the Art of Printing...* (London: Printed by the editor for B. Crosby and co., 1808). Courtesy Cary Graphic Arts Collection, RIT, Rochester, NY, USA.

Printers could not exercise their craft without paper, and here too the Society got involved at the level of both production and innovation. Long before the days of paper made from wood pulp, papermakers had to depend on the supply of white linen and cotton rags. When these were difficult to import because of wartime conditions, rags of poor quality had to be used, but the resulting paper was subject to weakness because of the use of bleach. Initially the privileged presses purchased their own paper, but the Society often provided paper to the commercial London

8. Howsam, *Cheap Bibles*, p. 94.

shops that had been made responsible for printing foreign-language Bibles. When complaints began to arise of English books having "come to pieces" in the hands of readers in the Kentish village of Maidstone, the Committee took matters into their own hands. An indication of how serious the problem was can be found in a Victorian history of papermaking: "Of a quantity of Bibles printed by the British and Foreign Bible Society, one was found two years later crumbling to dust, although it had not been used, owing to the process used in bleaching the paper at the mill".[9] Painstaking instructions were issued to the papermakers and to all the printers, even the privileged presses. Luke Howard's skill as a chemist and status as a Fellow of the Royal Society was put to use for an investigation of the effects of bleach upon paper-manufacturing processes. After all, most of the people who would be purchasing the end product were among "that description of persons, to whom durability enhances twofold the value of every gift or purchase".[10] As with their view of new technologies within the printing shop, the Bible Society's leaders were wide open to innovation, and unconcerned about offending the traditions of the papermaking trade.

To sum up the Society's attitude toward technology, it was complex, apparently contradictory, but in fact consistent. The Society admired stereotype openly, because of its dramatic promise to maintain the accuracy of the text. They were just as enthusiastic about machine printing and unbleached paper, but in these cases the members of local auxiliaries and Bible associations were not invited to share in the excitement lest it shock pre-industrial sensibilities. The Committee were "hard-headed businessmen of the industrial revolution, questioning the competence of traditional practitioners and seeking ways to cut costs and increase efficiency".[11] They used their *naiveté* about the printing process to their advantage, refusing to accept the authority of traditional practitioners. By 1845, Charles Stokes Dudley was talking about "Railway Speed in printing"![12] But five years later the Society was in trouble with its own members for equally aggressive approaches to new technologies and practices in the binding trades.

---

9. Joel Munsell, *Chronology of the Origin and Progress of Paper and Paper-Making*, 5th ed. (New York: Garland, 1980), p. 70. Originally published in 1876.

10. BFBS Minutes of Printing and General Purposes Subcommittee, 23 September 1818, vol. 4, pp. 47-54 (BSA/C1/1/4).

11. Howsam, *Cheap Bibles*, p. 119.

12. Letter from C. S. Dudley, 15 May 1845, BFBS Home Correspondence Inwards (BSA/D//1/114).

New Labour Practices

The fundamental principle ("without note or comment") made it essential that the Society sell its Bibles already bound. Contemporary practice was such that most books were sold in sheets with only temporary covers straight from the printer, ready for the purchaser to bind in leather that matched his or her own standards and tastes. Most bookbinders were geared for this custom work, or for producing batches of a dozen or two, at most, for booksellers or circulating libraries. These practices would not meet the needs of the Society, for it had to ensure that the pages of its Bibles not be jumbled together with tracts or prayers, thereby casting doubts upon its carefully preserved doctrinal neutrality.

The cliché that one cannot know a book by its cover might seem singularly inappropriate for sacred Scripture, but given that BFBS published cheap Bibles for the wealthy, as well as the poor, the range of bindings was an important part of the first impression created by a Society that was well on the way to becoming a Victorian institution. Well-to-do subscribers looking to fill the needs of their own families sought books bound in calf, and could have selected even higher-quality leathers, such as Persian basil and morocco, which were also available. But when these same subscribers purchased Bibles for their dependents, or to distribute among the poor in their communities, they expected to find the price moderated by covers that were made from sheepskin, not calf, or from an even cheaper alternative, canvas. "The materials and design of the packaging around the text clearly signaled the social assumptions of the BFBS members and leadership. The cheapest bibles were designated by a 'charity brand', a stamp indicating that distribution at this low price was limited 'to schools and the poor'".[13]

Thomas Burn, of Kirby Street in London, was one of the Society's first binders. A delegation of gentlemen from the Society asked him to tender for all their work. His descendants remember that Burn's "first impulse was to refuse; he thought it was an attempt to get work done at less than a fair price, or an inducement to try and undersell his neighbours; but his wife pointed out that all he was asked to do was to state the terms on which he could do the work". Burn's suspicions offer another indication of how startling the scale of the Society's undertaking was, both to contemporary printers and bookbinders and to the Society's own members and supporters. The risk that Mrs. Burn recommended worked out well, and the family business benefited from the Society's equally modern custom of settling its accounts on a regular, monthly, basis.[14] Like the printers,

---

13. Howsam, *Cheap Bibles*, p. 122.
14. Lionel S. Darley, *Bookbinding Then and Now: A Survey of the First Hundred and*

English bookbinders were prodded into new ways of doing their traditional crafts by the exigencies of the Bible Society's evangelical project. Since the Society's books were expected to be read much more intensively than a novel or a work of philosophy, the binding had to be durable, and above all, it had to be cheap.

In the early days of that first contract with Burn, nobody imagined that a Bible could be too cheap. But in the late eighteenth and early nineteenth centuries, employers — and contractors such as the BFBS — in bookbinding, among many other industries, often reduced the price of goods by undercutting the wages of workers. Trades unions were created to protect the interests of workers, and bookbinding became a trade in which union-management disputes proliferated.[15] The practice of strike action was risky in an industry where the number of workers exceeded the amount of work available; instead, unions often engaged in "controversies in print" to support their members and publicize their cause. When the master-bookbinder held a lucrative contract for Bible work, one such way was to accuse the contractor of hypocrisy.

T. J. Dunning, the secretary of the Journeymen Bookbinders' Union, used the Bible Society's fragile reputation, and the innocence of its members and subscribers about how business was practiced at the London headquarters, as a tool to further his cause. Dunning's gifts have been described as "the power of reasoning, the capacity for lucid expression, and a personal magnetism that caused him to be almost worshipped by his followers".[16] First in 1833, again a decade later, and once more in 1849-1850, Dunning put these talents to work to discredit the Bible Society. Rather than focus on the men in the binding industry, who belonged to his union, he appealed to middle-class sensibilities by targeting the plight of women workers who were not union members. Dunning respectfully submitted that "making it more difficult, and in some cases impossible, for females to earn an honest subsistence, by their labour, is in the same proportion to give potency to the seducers of female virtue".[17] Untangled from his early Victorian circumlocutions, what Dunning meant was that sweated women workers were driven into prostitution because the Society's tightfisted contract made it impossible for employers to pay them a living wage. In the 1842-1843 dispute, Dunning published pamphlets and

Seventy-Eight Years of James Burn & Company (London: Faber and Faber, 1959), pp. 15-16, quoted from the diary of Sarah Bain.

15. For contemporary labour practices see Ramsay MacDonald, *Women in the Printing Trades* (London: P. S. King and Son, 1904).

16. Ellic Howe and John Child, *The Society of London Bookbinders, 1780-1951* (London: Sylvan Press, 1952), p. 146.

17. Quoted in MacDonald, *Women*, p. 32.

wrote to the newspapers. Members of local auxiliaries and ladies' Bible associations responded with outrage. George Cartwright of Lyme Regis in Dorset, for example, observed that:

> Such low wages...appear very much like pandering to the vicious and selfish public, who in their morbid desire for cheapness, are reckless & indifferent to the misery & want of the Producers, who are thus forced (by a professing Religious Society) to work for the most inadequate wages, a sin condemn'd continually throughout the very Book we publish & take such pains to propagate.[18]

Cheap Bibles could indeed be too cheap.

Picture 3. *Women Workers at Watkins Bindery, 1905*. Reprinted from *The Bible in the World* (London: BFBS, March 1905), p. 90.

The secretaries and BFBS Committee were deeply troubled by these accusations and made some efforts to defend themselves, largely by distancing the Society from the practices of the workshop in question. Behind the scenes there were efforts at limiting the damage, but the efforts met with only partial success. The Society's reputation was injured for some time: its supporters, who regarded themselves as publishers of the gospel in an abstract sense, suddenly found themselves identified with the darker and dirtier side of the book trade and with the economic reality that their

---

18. George Cartwright to Brandram, 1 September 1849, BFBS Home Correspondence Inwards (BSA/D1/1/128, in bundle on Binders' Appeal).

policies implied "grinding the faces of the poor". These same supporters had gloried in policies that used the new technologies of stereotype and machine printing, without considering how compositors and handpress printers might be put out of work. The bookbinders' agitation put the emphasis upon workers, rather than the equipment that made them redundant.

Patterns of Distribution in Britain

The business of publishing involves three main activities. As described above, the BFBS addressed both printing and bookbinding in the same way that others in the trade did, indeed they were leaders in some crucial aspects. But when it came to distribution, the Bible Society went their own way. For the most part, Society Bibles did not appear in town bookshops or in the packs of hawkers who retailed books and pamphlets to the rural poor. Instead, initially, there was a subscription plan, whereby Society members could buy books at a discount for personal distribution; this plan was soon supplanted by an arrangement in which auxiliaries and associations collected penny-a-week subscriptions from their working-class neighbours. Only half of the funds from these subscriptions went directly to the purchaser's book; the other half was applied to the project of printing the Scriptures in foreign languages and distributing them abroad.

Later still, borrowing from successful practices in continental Europe, a system of "colportage" was developed whereby books were sold by a hawker, or a "Biblewoman", who specialized in selling one book only. The outrage over Dunning's accusations of hypocrisy is understandable in light of the popular appeal of Bible work. Rather to the surprise of the founders, who seem to have been focused on providing Bibles in Welsh and other languages, middle-class people in early nineteenth-century England undertook to supply their own humble neighbours with cheap Bibles in English, and to use the same books, somewhat more elegantly bound, for themselves. And these people also quickly formed auxiliaries, deaf to criticisms that such groups might endanger the position of the Established Church or sully the reputations of respectable ladies by exposing them to public discourse.

The momentum for this lay, particularly women's, movement was intensified by Charles Stokes Dudley, who set out guidelines in his 1821 *Analysis of the System of the Bible Society* and backed them up by personal appearances as the Society's domestic agent.[19] Dudley quickly grasped

---

19. Charles S. Dudley, *An Analysis of the System of the Bible Society throughout its Various Parts* (London: R. Watts, 1821).

and brilliantly articulated the principles of the Bible transaction, the intimate relationship between local activity and a national program for global action, which was secured by the equally powerful link between cheap Bibles designed for charitable distribution and other Bibles meant for the member's personal use. The economics of the transaction required that books be sold, not given away,[20] and stipulated that out of every shilling collected by an auxiliary, sixpence go for translation and publication of Bibles for distribution abroad. This "system" would even prevent the importation from abroad of revolutionary ideologies. Middle-class Britons joined BFBS auxiliaries, but they also sponsored the work of local Bible associations made up of working-class people. "The very principle of those Associations", an 1817 report stated, "is calculated to operate as a monitory and restraining influence on the members of them".[21] Far from being a tax on the poor, as some critics represented, "the institution of a Bible Society gives you the whole benefit of such a tax without its odiousness".[22]

The early decades of powerful evangelical enthusiasm fuelled by the novelty of the BFBS idea gave way by mid-century to a less intense involvement on the part of wealthy subscribers. Going door-to-door collecting weekly pence themselves was neither desirable nor successful in the new conditions of urban life, and those who could afford it turned instead to hiring agents. The system drew on the success of colportage in continental Europe, where pious peddlers had developed a method of distributing Protestant translations while circumventing both the authority of post-Napoleonic France and that of the Roman Catholic church.[23] Colporteurs were not volunteers, but neither were they mere employees: narratives of their exploits became part of the Bible Society's public relations rhetoric. Although George Borrow was hardly a typical colporteur, the popularity of *The Bible in Spain* (1843) reinforced popular interest in the work of the colporteurs. By the time of the Society's Jubilee in 1853–1854, colportage throughout Great Britain was the first fund-raising objective.

As the cost of producing books decreased, the Society found itself incurring increased expenses for distribution, by means of "the seasonable and kindly visit of the Bible Hawker".[24] It nevertheless remained essential

---

20. Leslie Howsam, "The Nineteenth-Century Bible Society and 'The Evil of Gratuitous Distribution'", in *Free Print and Non-commercial Publishing since 1700*, ed. James Raven (London: Ashgate Publishing, 2000), pp. 119-34.

21. *Thirteenth Report of the BFBS* (London, 1817), p. xciii.

22. Thomas Chalmers, *The Influence of Bible Societies on the Temporal Necessities of the Poor* (London, 1814).

23. Laurence Fontaine, *History of Pedlars in Europe* (Cambridge: Polity Press; Durham, N.C.: Duke University Press, 1996).

24. *Fifty-second Report of the BFBS* (London, 1856), p. ccxxxviii.

that Bible distribution be kept separate from secular bookselling. As BFBS Secretary Samuel Bergne argued in 1854:

> To sanction the disposal of our books with a miscellaneous collection... would give a latitude that would become very embarrassing.... By the large discount we allowed, we might furnish the means of disseminating works which we should be far from approving. The hawker would of course push his sales wherever he could and not confine them to the poor, and by this means many who are now willing and able to pay full price for copies purchased would be able to buy at a reduction.... The Committee cannot help thinking that the simplest and *safest* mode of carrying on the operation of colportage is to make that of this society distinct and complete in itself and quite free from any kind of admixture.[25]

And apart from the expense of maintaining a separate system, the introduction of colportage marked a change in the dynamics of evangelicalism. What it lacked "was the personal involvement, the gift of time and trouble, the link between rich and poor, upon which the Bible transaction had traditionally been based".[26]

Ellen Ranyard, a latter-day feminine incarnation of Charles Stokes Dudley, offered a solution. Her paid agents were called "Biblewomen", working under the direction of "lady superintendents". Unlike in colportage, Ranyard's solution had a strong volunteer element, and volunteerism had become an important evangelical activity for middle-class ladies, similar to the direct communication their mothers and grandmothers had enjoyed with working-class women. Ranyard spoke of a "missing link" between rich and poor, something that other men and women of her class were finding increasingly troubling. By this time the fear was not of revolution, but of "demoralization" or even "degeneration" on the part of a "casual residuum" living in slums at the bottom of prosperous Victorian society.[27] Paid Biblewomen would combat these trends, bringing salvation along with social work, and offering a recipe for soup guaranteed to "go far to prevent the craving for gin".[28]

The Bible transaction was burdened with so much ideological and cultural freight that the leadership had to be constantly vigilant about its image. In the first five or six decades, keeping Bibles as much as possible out of common bookshops was an important part of the strategy.

---

25. Copy of a letter from Samuel Bergne to John Angel James, 20 December 1854, Minutes of Birmingham Auxiliary Bible Society, vol. 1, pp. 288-90 (BSA/F1/Warks1/1).
26. Howsam, *Cheap Bibles*, p. 170.
27. Gareth Stedman Jones, *Outcast London: A Study in the Relationship between Classes in Victorian Society* (Oxford: Oxford University Press, 1971), chap. 16.
28. Ellen Ranyard, *The Missing Link* (London: James Nisbet and Co., 1859), p. 302.

Changes in the Book Trade, Changes in the BFBS

The members of the Bible Society's Committee, during its first sixty years of existence, were mostly men of business — merchants, lawyers, and bankers.[29] Only one of the founders, the law bookseller Joseph Butterworth, knew anything about the book trades, and his initial subscription was unusually generous in anticipation of the economic realities that his colleagues were about to discover. The Committee were also sincere Christians and fervid evangelicals, but they interpreted their religion in the vernacular of the time, that of political economy and free trade. They were unapologetic about keeping costs low and income high and remained remarkably unsentimental about the plight of people who might, in other circumstances, have received their charity.

After mid-century, the Society continued to be a publisher and, hence, to share the great changes experienced by others in the book trades. Before about 1840, books in general had been costly to produce, expensive to purchase, and relatively scarce, but by the 1860s, cheap literature was everywhere, printed by steam in massive quantities.[30] The problem of cheap Bibles had been solved, but other books were now accessible too. The BFBS had become a Victorian institution; it remained a publisher in material terms, but not in the cultural idiom of the time. Awash in novels and newspapers, supporters now took for granted the availability of print, paper, and binding, and focused almost entirely on the missionary work of colporteurs and Biblewomen at home and abroad. Echoing Luke Howard half a century earlier, J. P. Hewlett, who replaced Dudley as a district secretary in 1857, noted the changes: "The Society is increasingly *religious*", he observed. Moreover, it had "acquired the appearance and the reputation of being a *commercial* institution, and this, in some respects, greatly to its disadvantage. In earlier days the *charitable* nature of our operations was constantly kept before the public. There was an urgent necessity to be met, and it *was* met...in the way of handing over a plain, cheap Bible, with what has been called the 'charity brand' upon it, in return for the small

---

29. Howsam, *Cheap Bibles*, pp. 18-31.

30. There is an extensive literature on Victorian publishing, beginning with Richard Altick, *The English Common Reader* (Chicago: University of Chicago Press, 1957); for several useful articles see John O. Jordan and Robert L. Patten, *Literature in the Marketplace: Nineteenth-century British Publishing and Reading Practices* (Cambridge: Cambridge University Press, 1995). For an overview of the structure of the trade, see Simon Eliot, *Some Patterns and Trends in British Publishing, 1800–1919* (London: The Bibliographical Society, 1994).

cost received in weekly pence through the medium of our Ladies' Associations". Now times had changed, "Our depots and our elegant Bibles are everywhere".[31] Distribution had joined printing and bookbinding as elements of the publishing process that the Society shared with others in the secular book trades.

---

31. J. P. Hewlett, *A Paper Read at the Conference of the District Secretaries of the British and Foreign Bible Society, February 5th, 1867, and at Their Request Printed for Private Circulation* (London, [1867]).

Women and the Bible Society

Roger H. Martin

The important role that women played in the evangelical revival of the eighteenth and nineteenth centuries is a matter of record. Few persons in the annals of evangelical hagiography have received more attention than Susanna Wesley, the strong-willed and theologically astute woman who undeniably had a great influence over her celebrated son and through him over the revival itself. In a later decade, Selina, Countess of Huntingdon, about whom much has been written, actually created a denomination bearing her own name. Great female literary figures such as Hannah More and Sarah Trimmer were celebrities well known even to historians writing at the turn of the century, who had all but relegated women to inferior roles in the revival. Less well known or not known at all is a small army of middle-class women who played a significant role in the revival throughout its history. Women's participation was certainly evident during the initial eighteenth-century phase of the revival, when women openly served as itinerants and local preachers, particularly in the Wesleyan camp.[1] But women's involvement was also seen during the first two decades of the nineteenth century, even when the active participation of women in ministry was increasingly frowned upon by second-generation evangelicals.

An organization that actively sought the participation of middle-class women in its affairs was the British and Foreign Bible Society, which was founded in 1804 and grew to become one of the largest evangelical organizations in the United Kingdom. Yet like so many evangelical organizations of this period, one would not suspect from reading its many accounts that women played any role at all in the Society's long and illustrious history. Women were not voting members of the Bible Society until much later in its history, they were not officially permitted to attend the Society's general meetings until 1831, and it was only in the twentieth century that they could join the Society's General Committee.[2] But in fact women played a

---

1. See Earl Kent Brown, *Women of Mr. Wesley's Methodism* (New York: Edwin Mellen Press, 1983), pp. xv-xvii.
2. Frank K. Prochaska, *Women and Philanthropy in Nineteenth-Century England* (Oxford: Clarendon Press, 1980), pp. 26-27, 31 fn. 41.

very important though largely unchronicled role in the Bible Society's early history and may have done much to save the organization from financial difficulties not long after it was founded. This essay will examine the role of women in some detail and in doing so provide at least a glimpse of one aspect of women in ministry during the pre-Victorian period.[3]

The British and Foreign Bible Society was the largest of four interdenominational or pan-evangelical societies established in Britain at the end of the eighteenth and the beginning of the nineteenth century. The Bible Society and its sister organizations were precursors of the modern-day ecumenical movement, in which Baptists and Congregationalists, Anglicans and Presbyterians, and even Quakers and Roman Catholics joined together to engage in one simple and seemingly uncontroversial activity — the distribution of Bibles.[4] Indeed, the "fundamental principle" of the Bible Society was to distribute these Bibles "without note or comment" in order to protect the Society from charges of sectarianism or heresy. And because of this principle, the Bible Society was successful not only in distributing large quantities of Bibles, but also in avoiding the kind of internecine warfare that had disrupted and, in far too many cases, destroyed other ventures in pan-evangelical accord. With a couple of exceptions, the Bible Society avoided controversy and grew in size and importance. Today, the successor organizations of the Bible Society and its sister societies are the largest publishers and distributors of Bibles in the world. But the Bible Society was not always prosperous, especially in its early years, and it is the story of the Society's struggle to gain financial solvency, and the eventual use of women in this struggle, that will now be related.

From its inception, the Bible Society's parent Committee governed from its center in London, but the strength of the Society lay in the many auxiliary Bible societies that grew up around Britain, starting toward the end of the first decade of the nineteenth century. Officially, these auxiliaries had only two purposes: to distribute Bibles (and Bibles only!) and to raise funds. By 1814, the Bible Society had auxiliaries in every county in

---

3. Because primary and even secondary source material documenting the involvement of women in the affairs of the Bible Society is limited, data for this study is drawn from a variety of alternative sources. References to women in the Society's official minute books are limited in large part because they deal mostly with the routine of administration but also conceivably because the recorders, all men, filtered out material they thought to be irrelevant. Official histories of the Society, also written by men, simply fail to deal with the subject. References to women in anti-Bible Society tracts abound, but these are largely negative, written for propaganda purposes, and cannot always be trusted. Much of the material used, therefore, must be gleaned from casual references in Society correspondence and occasionally from the literature of the day.

4. See Roger H. Martin, *Evangelicals United: Ecumenical Stirrings in Pre-Victorian Britain, 1795-1830* (Metuchen, N. J., and London: Scarecrow Press, 1983).

Britain — 162 in England alone — and in the first few years of its life distributed well over 150,000 Testaments.[5] Three years later, however, the Bible Society experienced a 17 percent drop in total financial support after several years of steady increase.[6]

Though the Society had been established with a constitution that encouraged consensus, it was still an evangelical organization and as such was vigorously attacked by high church Anglicans, who claimed it was not only a threat to the older Society for Promoting Christian Knowledge (an all-Anglican group) but was also highly irregular in admitting into its deliberations Dissenters, the sworn enemies of the Established Church. The attacks from the Anglican camp between 1804 and the second decade of the century were vitriolic and effective. By 1817, Anglican patrons were deserting the Society in alarming numbers and morale was low.[7] This drop in membership was accompanied by a widespread fear that the loss of Anglican patronage might jeopardize the Society financially. C. S. Dudley, however, came to the fore with a small army of enthusiastic women, all ready to devote their considerable energies to the cause.

Charles Stokes Dudley, the principal proponent and organizer of the women's Bible auxiliaries, was born in 1780 in Prior Lane, near Clonmell, Ireland, the son of Mary Dudley, one of the greatest and most influential Quaker ministers of the eighteenth century. His mother's activities as an itinerant Quaker minister no doubt explain Dudley's openness to the participation of women in activities traditionally reserved for men.[8] After suffering the tragic loss of both his wife and baby, Dudley underwent a conversion experience in 1807 and soon thereafter commenced his work with the Bible Society. By 1812, he and his Quaker colleague Richard Phillips were helping to organize the Society's auxiliary system, then in its infancy. Seven years later Dudley was appointed the Society's domestic agent in charge of its home organization. In this position he traveled more than 4,500 miles on behalf of the Society, attending 107 committee meetings and 128 general meetings by 1818. His *Analysis of the System of the Bible Society*, published in 1821, was said to have been an inspiration behind the poor law system then being established in England.[9]

---

5. Ford Keeler Brown, *Fathers of the Victorians* (Cambridge: Cambridge University Press, 1961), p. 250.

6. See figures in William Canton, *A History of the British and Foreign Bible Society*, 5 vols. (London: John Murray, 1904-1910), vol. 1, pp. 50-53.

7. See BFBS Paterson Papers, vol. 2, item 12: J. Owen to J. Paterson, 10 May 1817; and vol. 2, item 31: J. Owen to J. Paterson, 16 December 1817 (BSA/F3/Paterson/2/2).

8. For Dudley's biography, see G. T. Edwards, "Charles Stokes Dudley," *The Bible Society Monthly Reporter*, September 1892, pp. 152-54; and October 1892, pp. 167-69.

9. Edwards, "Dudley," pp. 154, 167. Leslie Howsam, *Cheap Bibles* (Cambridge:

Picture 4. *Charles Stokes Dudley (1780–1862)*. Portrait courtesy of BFBS collections, Cambridge University Library.

Even before Dudley began recruiting women, his work at the Bible Society had become controversial. Like John Wesley, Dudley had a genius for organization and engaged himself in the task of helping to design and organize the nascent auxiliary and Bible association system with great zeal and effectiveness. The Southwark auxiliary, the first auxiliary to be

Cambridge University Press, 1991), pp. 41-42. See also Charles S. Dudley, *An Analysis of the System of the Bible Society throughout its Various Parts* (London: R. Watts, 1821).

founded in London itself, became under Dudley's supervision the model for similar auxiliaries in other parts of Britain. Here Dudley systematically subdivided the Southwark area of London into districts and subdistricts, each with a Bible association and a group of workers engaged in fundraising and Bible distribution activities. By 1814, the Southwark auxiliary had twelve Bible associations in union with it and employed 650 active agents. Dudley poetically likened the evolution of the auxiliary system to "a pebble cast into the untroubled ocean," which creates ripples "that extend in magnitude, until they are lost in the boundless expanse."[10] But the thoroughness of Dudley's work led paranoid critics of the Society to see in it a conspiracy against church and nation. Suggestions were made that Dudley had based his Southwark system on the Welsh Union and the Puritan Committee, two seditious organizations then in the news. It was feared that if the Southwark system spread to other parts of the country, Britain might be organized by foreign agents for political purposes.[11] The coordinated and centralized nature of the Bible Society with its intricate network of auxiliaries and associations that cut across the Anglicans' parochial system frightened Anglican clergymen, the more so since the Church of England was still decentralized, without synods or convocations. With the desertion from the Society of those Anglicans who were beginning to react to the unrelenting barrage of criticism from their high church colleagues, Dudley entered into the next and by far the most controversial phase of his activities at the Bible Society. Under orders to shore up the Society's financial base and expand its activities, Dudley introduced into the Bible Society a new and unique type of auxiliary, organized and managed exclusively by women, who would help save the Society from an uncertain future.

The involvement of women in the Bible Society was not new. Women's associations in one form or another had been in existence as early as 1811. But the dramatic growth of these new associations between 1812 and 1817 increased the Society's visibility and caused its opponents to fear even more than before that the Society might become a dangerous and largely

---

10. Quoted from an "Extract from the Second Report of the Southwark Auxiliary Bible Society," in *Reports of the British and Foreign Bible Society, with Extracts of Correspondence, &c. Volume the Third, for the years 1814 and 1815*. Reprinted from the Original Reports (London: BFBS, 1815), pp. 197-99.

11. Charles S. Dudley, *An Address to the Committee of the Bible Society in Horsham and its Neighborhood* (London, 1818), p. 28. Dudley's methods were compared to those of the Continental Illuminati. See H. H. Norris, *A Respectful Letter to the Earl of Liverpool* (London: F. C. and J. Rivington, 1822), p. 41; also H. H. Norris, *Practical Exposition of the Tendency and Proceedings of the British and Foreign Bible Society*, 2nd ed. (London: F. C. and J. Rivington, 1814), p. 483; and W. Dealtry, *A Review of Mr. Norris's Attack* (London: John Hatchard, 1815), p. 55.

unwanted force within the church. Using the Southwark auxiliary as a model, Dudley was able to open twenty-eight new women's associations in 1817, followed by seventy more in the following year![12]

Most of the women's auxiliaries followed very carefully the laws of the Society and restricted their activities to distributing the Bible and raising money. One example, drawn from literally hundreds in the Society's literature, illustrates how scrupulous most women were about this activity: the women of the ladies' Bible association in Hitchin worked in teams as they traveled through their assigned neighborhoods. On one occasion such a delegation came upon a poor, forlorn woman standing in a doorway and holding a baby. Without commenting on her state of affairs or in any other way imposing themselves on this poor woman, the delegation simply asked her whether she possessed a Bible. She said that as much as she would like to, her financial circumstances would not permit it. Much like the Fuller Brush salesperson, the delegation then told her how she could purchase a Bible on the Society's installment plan. As a matter of procedure, the Society rarely gave away free Bibles, even to the poor. On the following Monday the delegation was surprised to see the woman again. This time she had a sixpence and thus started paying for her Bible. Each Monday for a month she made a payment until the Bible was finally purchased. When later asked how she had managed to find the money she told the following story, itself a morality lesson the Bible Society loved to share with the public. After first meeting the Bible Society delegation, the poor woman had convinced her husband, a wayward man who spent his weekly salary in the local public house, to bring home his wages. She saved from this the sixpence needed to pay the weekly installments. Soon the Bible had been purchased and the family engaged in daily Bible readings. As a result, the husband reformed his ways, opened a savings account, and in time the family became prosperous. Here was a perfect example of what could be achieved by the Bible alone, without a tract or a sermon or for that matter anything else to accompany it. Because of the Bible, a family had been saved from perdition![13]

Not all women's auxiliaries, however, were as exemplary as the Hitchin society. Some bold spirits did much more than just distribute Bibles. They itinerated without invitation in the parishes of the very clergymen who opposed the Society, distributed their Bibles, and then gave a short sermon or made inquiry into the spiritual state of the recipients. Sometimes violations of the Society's laws were benign and therefore went unnoticed

.12 Dudley, *Analysis*, p. 55.

13. *Third Report of the Committee of the Ladies' Bible Association for Hitchin and its Vicinity* (Hitchin: T. Paternoster, 1821). For a discussion of women's Bible associations, especially in Liverpool, see Howsam, *Cheap Bibles*, pp. 52-60.

by the parent committee. The Covent Garden Bible Association, for example, encouraged its female agents to follow up Bible distribution activities with inquiries about the well-being of their recipients.[14] This was a technical violation of the fundamental principle, but not something that would draw a great deal of attention. The Southwark auxiliary went a bit further: it required agents to make a personal visit to every family within their field of labor, much as the parish priest did, and to determine the family's needs, spiritual and otherwise. If a Bible recipient was homeless or malnourished, the Bible Society agent was encouraged to take action, in the manner of a modern-day social worker.[15]

Other women's auxiliaries more blatantly violated the Society's fundamental principle. Such was the case of the women's auxiliary connected to the Hibernian Bible Society in Dublin, where according to an alarmed Bible Society patron:

> ...two or three [women] call from house to house to circulate addresses on the subject of the Society, to inquire into the want of Bibles and Testaments, to talk about the Bible, and thus wholly independent of the minister of the parish—in most cases in neglect of his counsels, and in defiance of his injunctions—issue forth under God's special guidance in order to establish a spiritual intercourse of weekly and daily visits with the parishioners.

The person who had observed these indiscretions expressed fear that "from the character and qualifications of the agents, the opinions so inculcated will be pernicious and enthusiastic."[16]

Society advocates tried to mitigate charges such as these by claiming that they were gross exaggerations. Thus, John Langley of Shrewsbury, an evangelical Anglican member of the Bible Society, reported after a tour of the women's auxiliaries: "I do not find that in any instance where I have attended [their meetings] the ladies violated the principle of distributing the Bible...without note or comment." However, he had to admit that "in some instances they do something so very like it *viva voce* that I am not prepared to say that it is not an *evasion* of the principle."[17] But evasions like these continued unabated, sometimes in embarrassing ways, as when William Conybeare, another clergyman, complained that a group

---

14. BFBS, Westminster Auxiliary Bible Society, Reports of the Bible Associations, 1815-1818: Covent Garden Bible Association, April 1815 (BSA/F1/London19/2).

15. "Extract from the Second Report of the Southwark Auxiliary Bible Society," in *Reports of the British and Foreign Bible Society*. Reprinted from the Original Reports (London: BFBS, 1815), p. 198.

16. J. E. Jackson, *Reasons for Withdrawing from the Hibernian Bible Society* (Dublin: Richard Milliken, 1822), pp. 154-55. See also, Norris, *A Respectful Letter*, p. 50.

17. J. Langley to J. Tarn, 20 April 1820, BFBS Home Correspondence Inwards (BSA/D1/1/30).

of Bible Society women had introduced themselves into the household of a "very religious clergyman—and one who was little likely to neglect making a due provision for the spiritual wants of his [household]."[18] A similar story is told by Richard Lloyd, vicar of St. Dunstan's in London, of a female parishioner visited by some Bible Society women who "inquired whether her servants had any Bibles. They also asked her, whether she heard them read, and instructed them." Although the parishioner apparently wondered about the propriety of the questions, "these perambulating ladies told [Lloyd's friend] that they felt it their duty to make enquiries."[19]

Women, of course, had few outlets for ministry, especially in the nineteenth century, and it should therefore not be surprising that the Bible Society quickly became an organization in which they could practice suppressed vocational aspirations. But the violations were unnerving to the parent Committee in London, because they once again opened the Society to new and potentially damning charges of irregularity and mismanagement, especially from high church Anglican critics looking for additional ammunition to use against the Bible Society. As one friend of the Society put it: "Bible Associations, like wheels employed in machinery, require considerable management to preserve them from retrograde motion."[20] Because London was having difficulty managing some outlying auxiliaries, these activities definitely seemed retrograde.

The complex issues surrounding the involvement of women in the Bible Society can perhaps best be seen in the "Henley controversy" of 1817. The Henley Women's Auxiliary Bible Society had been organized in March 1817 by Charles Dudley along the lines of the Southwark system, in part to shore up the flagging financial affairs of the local men's auxiliary.[21] Within a short period of time, the women's auxiliaries were working in six districts involving 158 women. By October, only eight short months after the auxiliaries were established, 3,349 Bibles had been distributed and £2,302 collected.[22]

18. Bodleian Library (Oxford) Manuscripts, Montagu, d. 12, vol. 2, Fols. 131, 132.
19. Richard Lloyd, *Strictures on a Recent Publication Entitled "The Church Her Own Enemy"* (London: F. C. and J. Rivington, 1818), p. 132.
20. BFBS, Westminster Auxiliary Bible Society, Reports of the Bible Associations, 1815-1818: Lincolns Inn Fields Bible Association, April 1815 (BSA/F1/London19/2).
21. The first auxiliary was established at Watlington, in part because this organization had a large deficit. See BFBS Henley Auxiliary Bible Society Minutes, 4 March 1817 (BSA/F1/Oxon1/1). Interestingly, because of later charges that the auxiliaries met in "suspect" places, the founding meeting of this ladies' auxiliary took place in a barn.
22. BFBS Henley Auxiliary Bible Society Minutes, 9 October 1817 (BSA/F1/Oxon1/1).

Normally this level of success would have evoked public praise. But Henley was located in ultra-conservative Oxfordshire, and the activities of the Henley women were especially visible to hostile Society critics. Not only did these women deliver sermons with their Bibles, but many also engaged in social work activities at a time when this type of involvement was the traditional responsibility of the local Anglican vicar.[23] Alarmed by the irregularity of these activities, R. B. Fisher, vicar of Basildon and secretary of the nearby Wallingford Auxiliary Bible Society, wrote a strong letter of protest to Joseph Hughes, one of the founders of the BFBS. This letter is of special interest because it defines the kind of activity the Henley women were involved in. Quoting from sections of the annual report of the Henley women's auxiliary, Fisher complained that this organization

> informs the minds and expands the affections of the people by its frequent public meetings. At the same time the Bible is given [the women] point out its value and importance. Nor does the care of the Society here cease. It is a moral cultivator that must be alert and attentive. [The Society] gives attention to the moral welfare of the district and not only encourages a serious perusal of the sacred volume but even provides Readers for the poor. Its agents are regularly [required] to examine the objects of its bounty [i.e., the recipients of the Bibles] as to their moral and by implication their spiritual state.[24]

A second letter from Fisher, written in April 1817 after the Henley women tried to infiltrate his own auxiliary, complained to Lord Teignmouth, the Bible Society's president, that the Henley meetings "are frequently held in Barns and assembled in opposition to the Clergymen of the Parish."[25] But the problem only continued and, by June, Fisher was again complaining that "Dudley's women" had now organized an "illegal" society in Benson in which "the public quarterly distribution of Bibles [is] accompanied by a variety of speeches."[26] Soon the bishop of Durham was requesting that his name be withdrawn as a patron of the White Church and Goring Bible Association, one of the offending groups, though in a moment of remorse he said that he would continue to pray for the success of the

---

23. George Eliot describes these women ca. 1799 in *Adam Bede*. For this citation, see Dale A. Johnson, *Women in English Religion* (New York: Edwin Mellen Press, 1983), pp. 80-87, 267-323.

24. R. B. Fisher to J. Hughes, 18 March 1817, BFBS Home Correspondence Inwards (BSA/D1/1/20).

25. R. B. Fisher to Lord Teignmouth, 22 April 1817, BFBS Home Correspondence Inwards (BSA/D1/1/20).

26. R. B. Fisher to Lord Teignmouth, 22 April 1817, BFBS Home Correspondence Inwards (BSA/D1/1/20).

Bible Society.[27] This probably brought J. W. Cunningham, vicar of Harrow and a very influential force in evangelical circles, to intervene with the directors in London, causing them to take direct action.[28]

On 31 May 1817, the BFBS Printing Subcommittee responded to Fisher's complaints by admonishing the Henley auxiliary that "the delivery of any public addresses...directed to such recipients of the Scripture...is in the judgment of the Committee not sanctioned by the regulations of this Society." Furthermore, "enquiries among the poor who have received Bibles with respect to their moral and religious improvement, and circumstances of their families" were also not authorized.[29] To reinforce these points with other auxiliaries, the parent Bible Society passed legislation in November prohibiting "devotional exercises at the opening and conclusion of their meetings for business, official inquiries into the use made of the Bibles by those who had received them, and specific addresses to the recipients of Bibles on occasions of public deliveries."[30]

Concerned about "the most proper mode of turning to advantageous account the zeal, so generally and laudably manifested in the female sex in favor of the Society's object," the parent Society next presented Henley with suggested changes to their by-laws in the hope that these suggestions would "be found serviceable in modelling that class of Associations, which, if regularly constituted and discreetly conducted, are likely to become instruments of extensive and permanent good."[31] At first the Henley auxiliary resisted these recommended changes, claiming that the ladies' auxiliaries were already in compliance. But after substantial pressure, Henley acquiesced and adopted London's recommendations.[32] By 1819 the Henley controversy had diminished to the point where at least one correspondent to the *Monthly Extracts* could express the opinion that "although, at the commencement, there were those who intimated an

---

27. BFBS Henley Auxiliary Bible Society Minutes, 4 April and 1 July 1817 (BSA/F1/Oxon1/1).

28. J. W. Cunningham to J. Owen, 24 October 1817, BFBS Home Correspondence Inwards (BSA/D1/1/20).

29. BFBS Subcommittee for Printing and General Purposes, 31 May 1817, vol. 3, p. 130 (BSA/C1/1/3); Henley Auxiliary Bible Society Minutes, 31 May 1817 (BSA/F1/Oxon1/1).

30. BFBS Minutes of the Committee, 17 November 1817, vol. 8, p. 364 (BSA/B1/8); J. Scholefield, *A Second Letter to the Right Hon. Earl of Liverpool* (London: L.B. Seeley, 1822), pp. 65-66.

31. BFBS Local Subcommittee Minutes, 17 November 1817, vol. 3, p. 205 (BSA/C1/1/3); Henley Auxiliary Bible Society Minutes, 2 December 1817 (BSA/F1/Oxon1/1).

32. BFBS Henley Auxiliary Bible Society Minutes, 3 March, 13 October, and 1 December 1818 (BSA/F1/Oxon1/1).

unfriendliness to [the Henley auxiliary's] proceedings, yet the expression of disapprobation has almost entirely subsided."[33]

Why did the women of Henley and women associated with other societies precipitate so much controversy? On the surface, at least three reasons can be given. In the first place, there was a great fear that the women's auxiliaries might be used for seditious purposes. Charles Dudley already had a reputation for organizing the Southwark auxiliary along potentially dangerous lines. There was, therefore, speculation that Dudley's women might clandestinely infiltrate neighborhoods and then report back to enemy agents everything they had seen. This fear was articulated by Fisher, when in his initial letter of protest about the activities of the Henley society, he expressed fear that alien and unwanted powers associated with the Society might do irreparable damage to church and nation. "What security can you give the friends of the Society," Fisher asked, "that it will not be the instrument of errors? What security can you give the government that it will not be perverted to political purposes?"[34] Others expressed similar concerns. For example, Henry Brooks of Wells, a friend of the Bible Society, feared that if the Henley women were not disciplined, the Society would be seen as a "popular [e.g., republican] organization, independent of the laws of the country."[35] Richard Lloyd needn't have reminded his readers that "the French and German Illuminati had their female adepts."[36]

The second reason the Henley women were so opposed was related to Anglican concern that their activities were inimical to the Established Church. Thus, Fisher wondered whether irregular meetings for worship held by the Henley women outside church was injurious to the Church of England, since Anglicans were involved, a sentiment shared by J. W. Cunningham and others. Referring to the extra-parochial services held by the women, most of whom were Dissenters, and echoing the frustration many evangelical Anglicans felt in choosing between their allegiance to the Church of England on the one hand and their spiritual affinity with evangelicals outside of the church on the other, Fisher wrote: "I am a firm

---

33. *Monthly Extracts from the Correspondence of the British and Foreign Bible Society*, no. 25, (London, August 1819), p. 31. This comment came from the Oxford Ladies Bible Association.

34. R. B. Fisher to J. Hughes, 18 March 1817, BFBS Home Correspondence Inwards (BSA/D1/1/20).

35. H. Brooks to J. Owen, 19 September 1817, BFBS Home Correspondence Inwards (BSA/D1/1/20).

36. Lloyd, *Strictures*, p. 119. See also Charles James Burton, *A Short Inquiry into the Directions and Designs of the British and Foreign Bible Society* (Canterbury: Rouse, Kirkby and Lawrence, n.d.).

friend to a full Toleration and feel a high regard for very many Dissenters, but I cannot, consistently with my principles or duty, sanction any plan which will injure the interests of the church to which I belong."[37]

Finally, Anglicans as well as Dissenters were alarmed by possible violations of the Society's sacred fundamental principle, especially during a time when the Society as a whole had been put under the magnifying glass of hostile critics. From the Society's inception in 1804, it had been mandated that Bibles were to be distributed by members of the Society without note or comment. But was it not a violation of that rule to accompany Bibles with religious instruction, as was the practice at Henley, or even to engage in social work activities, as was the case in some of the other women's auxiliaries?[38] J. W. Cunningham was therefore very concerned "that if some decisive measure is not adopted to confine these [women's] com[mittee]s to the prosecution of the great fundamental object of the Society we shall have a storm excited that we may find difficult to weather."[39]

There was much more to the controversy, however, than just these surface issues. Underlying the complaints leveled against the women at Henley and elsewhere was a general and largely suppressed fear that through organizations like the Bible Society, old and familiar societal patterns were breaking down as women began to compete with men. This fear was communicated through patronizing and often demeaning comments made by detractors — as well as supporters — of the Society. Thus, one critic of the Bible Society reported that some ladies associated with a women's auxiliary near Liverpool, when pressed to give up their activities, said that they would leave their husbands rather than leave their Bible auxiliary. This critic feared that "with the zeal and spirit, the forwardness and intrusive boldness of an active member of a Ladies' Bible Association, how is it possible to retain the softened diffidence and virgin modesty which form the greatest charm of the female bosom [sic]?"[40] Another critic asked:

> Is it delicate and proper that ladies should associate, as they do, in large assemblies, form committees, and collect in their own persons, subscriptions, donations, and even [pennies] from the lowest classes of the community?

---

37. R. B. Fisher to Lord Teignmouth, 22 April 1817, BFBS Home Correspondence Inwards (BSA/D/1/120).

38. R. B. Fisher to J. Hughes, 18 March 1817, BFBS Home Correspondence Inwards (BSA/D1/1/20).

39. J. W. Cunningham to J. Owen, 24 October 1817, BFBS Home Correspondence Inwards (BSA/D1/1/20).

40. *A Letter to the Church Members of the Auxiliary Society, Liverpool* (Liverpool: F. B. Wright, 1819), p. 18.

> Does it comport with their soft and more retiring manners, to occupy seats industriously prepared for them, and ostentatiously announced in the public prints, in order to hear speeches of a violent and party nature? ... Is it correct, particularly in females, to go from house to house, and sow seeds of discord between husbands and wives, parents and children, masters and servants? ... I appeal to husbands, parents, and masters of families, whether they can deliberately sanction such proceedings in their wives, daughters, and other female relatives and dependents.[41]

According to Dudley, the two most common objections raised against the participation of women in the Bible Society involved questions of social status and decorum. Not only would women be taken away from their domestic obligations, but they would be forced to witness "unpleasant scenes" that might violate their fragile constitutions.[42]

As women became even more active in the Bible Society, suppressed male chauvinism came out into the open. Some more prurient minds now saw perverted, surrogate sexuality behind the women's auxiliaries. A London newspaper, for instance, claimed that Olinthus Gregory, the Baptist mathematical master at the Royal Military Academy, once told the women's Bible association in Hertford that "God would be their lover" if they distributed Bibles for the Society.[43] But it was the issue of equality that disturbed these people the most. Thus, Henry Handley Norris, quoting from the Bath auxiliary report of 1812, wrote unapprovingly that female members of the Bible Society "were reminded of their 'gratitude to a Book which had emancipated them from the degradation of slavery and subserviency, and [here is the point Norris wanted to drive home] had made them the equal of men.'"[44]

Underlying these rather hostile comments was a very basic change taking place in nineteenth-century society, namely the demise of what Deborah Gorham has called the "cult of domesticity."[45] The evangelical revival, long the *bête noir* of high church Anglicans and of the status quo, was challenging, no doubt unwittingly, the long-held notion that identified men with the public sphere of the marketplace and women with the private sphere of the home. Early revival leaders like John Wesley were urging regenerate sinners, men and women alike, to holiness and perfection. But a manifestation of salvation was good works and charitable

---

41. Lloyd, *Strictures*, pp. 114-15.
42. Dudley, *Analysis*, pp. 347-48.
43. R. Everett to J. Tarn, 14 January 1823, BFBS Home Correspondence Inwards (BSA/D1/1/38); O. Gregory to J. R. Payne, 3 November 1824, BFBS Home Correspondence Inwards (BSA/D1/1/42).
44. H. H. Norris, *A Respectful Letter*, p. 33.
45. Deborah Gorham, *The Victorian Girl and the Feminine Ideal* (Bloomington, Ind.: Indiana University Press, 1982), pp. 4, 76.

deeds, mission and the active conversion of sinners.[46] This imperative to do good works — to be actively involved in the real world — placed evangelical women in a paradoxical situation. On the one hand, society had been teaching them self-abnegation and reinforcing their domestic roles. On the other, evangelical theology often stressed activity outside the domestic sphere. Thus women increasingly became involved in philanthropic and charitable concerns like the Bible Society that were outside the traditional work of a woman.[47] It is against the background of this social development that one can perhaps understand not only why women were increasingly prone to enter the male domain, but also why the upholders of the status quo, mostly non-evangelicals, were vigorously protesting what in their minds seemed to be the feminization of society. Commenting on the evangelical revival in general, one of these upholders of traditional society, Richard Lloyd, an Anglican critic of the Bible Society, expressed well what others had a difficult time articulating when he wrote that "the evangelical piety of the present times...generates a low, vulgar spirit of equality, without a due sense of subordination."[48] This sentiment could well have been applied to the Bible Society and the way it incorporated women into its activities.

Now, it is only left to comment briefly on the important contribution women made to the Bible Society and through it to society in general. Whether the charges were accurate that these women were destroying, by their irregular activities, the frail cocoon of consensus that enabled Dissenters to work with Anglicans, the fact remains that women helped to keep the Society together financially when it was facing difficulties. Of course, contemporaries of the Society, even supporters, would not admit this. R. B. Fisher said, for example, that the annual subscriptions of the Henley women's auxiliary in 1816 amounted to little more "than was sufficient to defray incidental expenses"[49] The evidence, however, suggests that the contribution was far more substantial. As Prochaska has shown, between 1805, a year after the Society was founded, and 1817, the period when its financial need was greatest, the percentage of women contributing to the Society almost doubled from 12 percent to 23 percent. By 1840, when the Society was prospering financially, 40 percent of the contributors were

---

46. See Roger H. Martin, "English Evangelicals and the Golden Age of Private Philanthropy," *The Princeton Seminary Bulletin*, vol. 4, no. 3 (1983), p. 189. The Calvinists somewhat modified Wesley's Arminianism by suggesting that good works were a sign of election.

47. Gorham, *The Victorian Girl and the Feminine Ideal*, p. 79. Prochaska, *Women and Philanthropy*, p. 119.

48. Lloyd, *Strictures*, p. 120.

49. R. B. Fisher to J. Hughes, 18 March 1817, BFBS Home Correspondence Inwards (BSA/D1/1/20).

women.[50] These figures reveal that not only did women give generously, but also that the women, who in turn raised most of this money, were effective workers and fundraisers, even though they may have caused some embarrassment to the Society when it came to obeying its fundamental principle.

Finally, these women were in a very real sense the pioneers of the modern-day women's movement. Women's emancipation, of course, was not part of the evangelical agenda, and evangelical women did not see themselves as feminists in the modern sense. Yet the women at Henley and in other Bible Society auxiliaries were, for the first time, playing more than just a supportive role to men. Indeed, they had their own ministry, whether or not recognized as such, and they were extremely effective in it. It is only fitting in this era of equal rights that the early contribution made by evangelical women in the Bible Society receive due recognition.[51]

---

50. Prochaska, *Women and Philanthropy*, pp. 27, 29, and 231.
51. For a discussion of women's involvement in the Bible Society during a later period, see Howsam, *Cheap Bibles*, pp. 170-78.

FORGOTTEN LABOURS: WOMEN'S BIBLE WORK AND THE BFBS

Sarah Lane

This paper provides a broad overview of women's Bible work within and beyond the structures of the British and Foreign Bible Society during the Society's first century. The work of women was crucial to the development of the Bible Society as a widespread movement. More broadly, the work of "Biblewomen" had an impact on other areas of social development, especially in the case of the involvement of working-class women. As is natural, the history of the Bible Society is often told through the stories of those most prominent within the organization and within society at large. The aim of this study is to reclaim the forgotten history of the labours of the many ordinary, as well as some of the extraordinary, women who devoted themselves to the distribution of Scriptures and actively involved themselves in the lives of the recipients.

Female Bible associations under the broad umbrella of the British and Foreign Bible Society seem to have arisen without any official prompting. As the structures became more defined and relationships between the different groupings were formalized, the ladies' associations were accountable to the (male) auxiliary societies, which in turn related to the BFBS parent or governing Committee. Charles Dudley, an early BFBS organizer of the auxiliary system, aimed to increase the effectiveness of female associations by encouraging them to follow the pattern of an efficient model. By 1821 he had completed his *Analysis of the System of the Bible Society*, which became the standard handbook for the organization of auxiliaries and associations, and was influential throughout the century.[1] The main key to the success of the ladies' associations, apart from the talents and energies of the ladies themselves, was the division of each area into smaller districts, enabling the collectors to acquire a more intimate knowledge of local needs.

To see the participation of women in the work of the Bible Society simply as the labours of the visitors and collectors is to disregard a key element that made the Society distinctive from other philanthropic organizations. The Bible Society was not a charity, and those who paid a weekly

---

1. Charles S. Dudley, *An Analysis of the System of the Bible Society throughout its Various Parts* (London: R. Watts, 1821).

subscription either toward a Bible or as a free contribution were seen as partners in the work. Anecdotal evidence, for example, found in the accounts of subscribers in various associations' minute books, suggests that the majority of subscribers amongst the poor were women. One of the effects of the ladies' associations' extensive schemes of visiting was to put women in touch with other women from different class backgrounds. Other factors such as the time of day when the collectors called to visit each week, usually during the daytime, and the public expectation that women were to be seen as more naturally religious, also came into play. Thus, even from the very beginning, working-class women participated in the work of the Bible Society, to the extent that many continued to subscribe their penny a week even when they had their own Bible.

By 1819, only fifteen years after the Society was founded, there were 350 female associations, and Charles Dudley estimated that ten thousand women were engaged in the work.[2] From these figures alone it is impossible to deny that the contribution of women to the work of the Society was significant and extensive, and it is all the more remarkable that their labours have since been forgotten. There is no suggestion that women could have funded and sustained the work of the British and Foreign Bible Society without the contribution made by men, but it is also worth examining the distinctive nature of women's work in this field.

The Origins of Women's Bible Work

It has already been noted that women began to participate in the work of the Bible Society at a very early stage of the organization's development. Many middle-class women were involved in philanthropic work, but it is important to examine why significant numbers of women were motivated to become involved in the work of Bible distribution, and how the Bible Society so quickly became established as a successful and influential organization at a time when other opportunities for women's work were emerging.

The nineteenth-century woman, particularly among the middle and upper classes, was seen as a religious role model. At a time when evangelical influences had a very real effect on the nature of society, women were seen as providing the moral tone of the family and as being more "naturally" religious than men. William Wilberforce, a leading evangelical of the Clapham sect, argued that women were particularly disposed to religion, as their education was limited and they had not been exposed to the "moral dangers of the classics".

---

2. Dudley, *Analysis*, p. 501.

> We would make them [women] as it were the medium of our intercourse with the heavenly world, the faithful repositories of the religious principle, for the benefit both of the present and the rising generation.[3]

By the period of the 1830s and the 1840s, the view of woman as domestic being was well established, and this led to the view of the home as the ideal model of society. Within the home, the mother could combat sin and promote an orderly environment based on sound biblical principles. When women's work extended beyond the home, the basic model still applied, and women, especially ladies, were seen as fit agents to bring about in society at large the same order and moral framework as existed in the home. Women used the Bible to make sense of their own lives. They read Scripture in a distinctive way, looking for a means of identifying with biblical women. Prochaska points out that "women sought in Scripture what could explain or give meaning to their more mundane existence".[4]

It is possible to demonstrate that these factors did actually motivate women involved in Bible work. Ellen Henrietta Ranyard (1810–1879), founder in 1858 of a female Bible mission in central London and the originator of the "Biblewomen", refers to the women of the Bible as examples who should inspire others to make known God's word.[5] She sees women's work as participating in the act of redemption, saying, "It would seem that as a woman brought sin into the world, so God would overthrow the designs of Satan by the instrumentality of women; that 'where sin abounded, grace might much more abound'".[6] In becoming involved in the work of the Bible Society, women identified an outlet for their talents and enthusiasm, and they identified absolutely with the Society's goals. In fact, it might be argued that in their participation they redefined the Society's goals. There are suggestions that early proposals put forward by the Religious Tract Society identified Bible distribution and translation overseas as a primary aim, yet the work of women in the Society emphasized the urgent domestic needs for the Bible amongst the poor. This ensured that the Society had a firm basis in its home mission and enabled it to gain support as a movement, ultimately ensuring the effectiveness of its work abroad in terms of financial support.

---

3. William Wilberforce, internally quoted in Catherine Hall, "The Early Formation of Victorian Domestic Ideology," in Sandra Burman, ed., *Fit Work for Women* (New York: St. Martin's Press and London: Croom Helm, for Oxford University Women's Studies Committee, 1979), p. 26.

4. Frank K. Prochaska, *Women and Philanthropy in Nineteenth-Century England* (Oxford: Oxford University Press, 1980), p. 14.

5. L. N. R. [Ellen H. Ranyard], *The Book and its Missions*, vol. 6 (London, 1861), pp. 69-73. For biographical information on Ranyard, see her entry in the *Dictionary of National Biography*.

6. Ranyard, *The Book and its Missions*, vol. 6, p. 69.

Picture 5. *Ellen Ranyard (1810–1879)*. Reprinted from William Canton, *A History of the BFBS*, vol. 3 (London: John Murray, 1910), facing p. 248.

Opposition and Support

The initial involvement of women in the Society was not without tension. This was to be expected inasmuch as the Society, in its fundamental principles, stated that Bible distribution was to be viewed as a business transaction, not a charitable or philanthropic exercise. The public involvement of ladies in business would not have been looked upon favourably. As a result, the ladies came to ignore these restrictions in practice and rather reinterpreted the principles in order to carve out their own distinctive role in the organization. It even seems that they deliberately understated their involvement and the nature of their work in order to be able to continue it unimpeded. Otherwise, how could the ladies of the Hackney, Clapton and Homerton Bible Association remark in their annual report of 1827:

> The [members] are sensible that so limited a sphere of action is destitute of materials for fascinating narrative or interesting detail, and were they persuaded their report would be read to a meeting convened in the expectation of being excited by surprising facts and remarkable adventures, their inducement to prepare it would be feeble indeed.[7]

Women's work was tolerated by the Bible Society, but it was never really valued in the same way as the work of men. Canton, in his account, records a tribute to one of the Society's secretaries: "To eminence in learning he conjoined a masculine mind, an uncompromising spirit, active habits, strong affections and devoted piety".[8] It is highly unlikely that the possession of a feminine mind would ever have been seen as a valuable asset, or used for purposes of a tribute.

Charles Dudley, probably the most outspoken supporter of women's work within the British and Foreign Bible Society, showed his practical commitment to women in his role as the Society's agent, travelling around the country and helping to set up and organize ladies' Bible associations. Dudley could not see that Bible work could be wrong for women as he compared it with other forms of charitable work.

> If it is deemed consistent with the highest attributes of the Female character, to administer to the temporal necessities of the poor and destitute, but inconsistent to supply them with spiritual food, we admit a paradox which reason and Scripture alike reject...that the evil is dependent on the value of the blessing conferred.[9]

Dudley's most powerful and pragmatic argument in favour of the work of women for the British and Foreign Bible Society was the sheer effectiveness of that work. In his correspondence and in his *Analysis* he cited numerous examples of the superior practical results of the work of the ladies' associations over those of the gentlemen's. Even with such strong support from those sharing Dudley's views, individual women and individual associations still faced opposition. Maria Hope of Liverpool, writing in 1819, remarked,

---

7. The annual report is appended to the Minutes of the Hackney, Clapton and Homerton Ladies' Bible Association, 2 May 1827 (BSA/F1/London6/1).

8. William Canton, *A History of the British and Foreign Bible Society*, 5 vols. (London: John Murray, 1904–1910), vol. 2, pp. 166-67.

9. Dudley, *Analysis*, p. 344.

> I have faced so many difficulties that had I been engaged in any other service I should long ago have given it up—but the opposition of the Clergyman has been overruled of God to accomplish the object it appeared designed to breach.[10]

Such comments surely dispel the notion that women only took part in this type of activity in order to fill their otherwise empty days. Women were obviously very determined to carve out a role for themselves within the Bible Society's work and were not deterred by the obstacles they faced. In agreeing to conduct their work within a structure that hid them from public view, women were able to secure for themselves the freedom they required to carry out their labours in the most effective way. Despite the Society's principle of Scripture distribution without note or comment, there was no way that the interaction between individuals could be regulated, and women who were not allowed to preach from the pulpit may have realized their vocation by less formal preaching to the poor, from whom they collected subscriptions for Bibles. By the time the most perceptive critics raised their voices, women were already indispensable, and the BFBS governing Committee was astute enough to realize that the survival of the Society was at stake if the work of the ladies' associations was regulated too strictly.

The Relationship between Spiritual and Temporal Relief

Critics of the Bible Society suggested that the ladies were trying to provide spiritual relief to the detriment of the temporal needs of the poor, but this was fiercely denied. Although the scope of the Society's work was limited to the distribution of the Bible, the nature of women's work in the associations meant that it actually extended far beyond this. Charles Dudley viewed the work of the Bible associations as complementary to the work of those agencies providing temporal relief, but argued that the Society's focus was crucial to the salvation of the whole person. The district system of the associations' organization led to collectors having an extensive knowledge of their areas and of the people who lived in their district. They would know who was working and who was unemployed, how many children there were, the state of the house, the health of the inhabitants, and many other details that could only be gained by systematic and regular visiting. The auxiliary society in Boston commented that

> furnishing the poor with the sacred Scriptures has not been the only advantage arising from the Ladies' Bible Association. It has produced its collateral advantages also. By weekly visits to such poor families as are subscribing

---

10. Maria Hope to Joseph Tarn, 3 September 1819, BFBS Home Correspondence Inwards (BSA/D1/1/26).

for Bibles, the collectors have obtained a correct acquaintance not only with their moral, but also with their temporal domestic wants. These wants have kindly been supplied; the sick have been furnished with medicine; the hungry have been fed, and the naked have been clothed.[11]

In the early years of the Society's existence this additional work continued, but little was disclosed publicly. As the century wore on, the increase of visiting societies meant that Bible Society collectors were more likely to alert agents of other societies to the particular needs of individuals, than to feel they should provide the means for meeting temporal needs themselves. At no time, however, was the Bible Society completely removed from a knowledge and appreciation that spiritual needs could not be met in isolation from physical or material needs. This realization was actually strengthened later in the century when Ellen Ranyard's Biblewomen, and later, Bible nurses, set out to deal with both the physical and spiritual needs of the poor, while maintaining a very strong connection with the British and Foreign Bible Society.

Although reading of the Bible was regarded by evangelicals as sufficient in itself for attaining knowledge of salvation, the early literature of the Society emphasizes certain collateral benefits arising from Bible distribution, particularly connected with the visiting work of the ladies' associations. The advantages gained from subscribing for a Bible were those changes in the individual's or family's life that brought them more into line with the values and behaviour of middle- and upper-class evangelicals. The collector aimed to consolidate family values. Dudley provided an illuminating insight into the way that the changes were perceived.

> The poor, taught by the visits of the collectors how they may acquire a Bible at a sacrifice that is rarely felt even by the most indigent, gladly embrace the opportunity. Gratified by the regular weekly calls of their superiors, they endeavour to render their humble abodes more cleanly and attractive: the effort is noticed with approbation, and comparative comfort and order are enjoyed. The husband and father no longer spends his evening from his family; he begins to taste the pleasures of home; and to consider whether his weekly earnings may not be more profitably expended than in sensual and degrading pursuits.[12]

This was all supposed to have happened before the Bibles were even delivered, reflecting thereby the influence of the lady collector and the values that she embodied. Considering that she was only supposed to have been concerned with encouraging the poor to subscribe for Bibles, the influence of the collector seems to have been remarkably far-reaching.

11. From the "Fifth Report of the Auxiliary Bible Society," Boston, Lincolnshire, 28 May 1819, in *Monthly Extracts from the Correspondence of the British and Foreign Bible Society* (London: BFBS, July 1819), p. 17.
12. Dudley, *Analysis*, pp. 208-209

It was as if all that was needed was a little prompting for the poor to recognize the error of their former ways, and the collector would be ready to teach them, as she would her own children, how to change their circumstances. The benefits increased once the Bible was delivered, as the family realized that the penny subscription had been easily afforded and they could continue to give it every week, in the form of a free subscription, for the benefit of others. This, of course, would bring with it the advantage that the collector would continue to call each week and would be able to provide further encouragement and instruction.

The evangelical condemnation of alcohol influenced the way in which many collectors viewed their work. In asking for a penny each week to be spent on a subscription for a Bible, the ladies realized that that penny would not then be available for the purchase of alcohol, in particular gin. The consumption of alcohol was viewed by many evangelicals as the beginning of a process that would eventually ruin a family materially and morally. It follows, therefore, that women connected with Bible work tended to be involved in temperance societies, many of which had a similar, evangelical emphasis. The concern about alcohol was not limited to the ladies. Ellen Ranyard's Biblewomen were eager to divert people's money and interest away from drink, and "Marian B's" theory was that people drank gin to "stupefy their misery".[13] If these people were offered an alternative in the form of a Bible, they would take it. Nowhere did there seem to be any recognition that the father might continue to drink, while the mother sacrificed other things the family needed in order to set aside the penny for the Bible subscription.

Frequently a lady collector would spend time reading the Bible with the subscribers, for there were many of the poor who were illiterate. On receiving their own Bible, these people then often wanted to learn to read themselves. Ample evidence supports the claim that increased literacy was one of the benefits of the ladies' work. Some of the teaching took place in Sunday schools, but there were other organizations that also taught the poor to read. The Hackney, Clapton and Homerton Ladies' Association noted this very point:

> It may also be reckoned among the incidental benefits of the visits that several Adult persons unable to read have been stirred up by the prospect of obtaining the Scriptures, to a desire of reading them, and have attended the schools…in the District for that benevolent purpose.[14]

---

13. Ranyard, *The Book and its Missions*, vol. 3 (1858), p. 117. "Marian B." was Marian Bower, Ranyard's first Biblewoman.

14. Hackney, Clapton and Homerton Ladies' Bible Association Minute Book, 16 March 1819 (BSA/F1/London6/1). The minutes were from a special meeting held to prepare the annual report for the auxiliary society.

Dudley notes the desire for literacy as the most prominent additional benefit of Bible distribution, saying that "of the collateral advantages which have been remarked in our own country, none are more prominent than the desire manifest by children and adults to learn to read".[15]

The regular setting aside of a penny for a Bible subscription also introduced the poor to the habit of regular saving, for the subscription was often continued after the receipt of a Bible. Such a habit was encouraged by collectors, who recommended the use of a savings bank. This scheme, extended over the years until being formalized in the work of the Biblewomen, was expressed in the principle stated by Ellen Ranyard, "the easy purchase of a Bible first shows them [the poor] what else may be done in the same way towards the provision of their own family comforts".[16]

"Women" and "Ladies"

It is easy to see that a common bond was felt between women of similar social backgrounds. The main strength of Ellen Ranyard's system of Biblewomen lay in the way that working-class women were trained and paid to reach others of similar backgrounds. Ranyard, sensing intuitively that ladies could not reach those women who were the poorest of the poor, realized that "the 'woman' goes where the 'lady' might not enter". Ranyard explained this attitude by saying that "those who would be ashamed to be seen by a Clergyman, a City missionary, or a Lady Visitor, have no objection to be a little cleared and set straight in their afflictions by one like themselves".[17]

Many of those who lived in the poorest conditions were victims of industrialization and urbanization. They had moved from closely knit, rural communities to the anonymity of crowded urban areas. Ellen Ranyard's scheme aimed to recover the tradition of self-help amongst the poor by encouraging poor Christian women to devote themselves to the task of relieving suffering and distributing Bibles within their local area. Biblewomen already had the advantage of knowing the area and comprehending the lives of those who lived there, and this enabled them to have a deeper understanding of the nature of local needs than was possible for the ladies of the Bible associations.

Biblewomen spent time and energy in developing effective networks of women who could support each other, whilst the women were in turn

---

15. Dudley, *Analysis*, p. 103.
16. Ranyard, *The Book and its Missions*, vol. 3 (1858), p. 95.
17. L. N. R. [Ellen H. Ranyard], *The Missing Link* (London: James Nisbet and Co., 1859), cited internally in Anne Summers, "A Home from Home", in Burman, *Fit Work for Women*, p. 45.

being supported by the professional Biblewoman who lived in their midst. It was inevitable that the Biblewomen, whose origins lay in the experiences of middle-class women, should be part of the process of perpetuating the middle-class value structure that was an intrinsic part of evangelical religion, but there is ample evidence that they did reach those who might otherwise have been condemned by being labelled the "undeserving poor".

Conclusion: Women's Bible Work in Historical Perspective.

It is not possible to do justice to the hundreds and thousands of forgotten women who laboured throughout the nineteenth century on behalf of the British and Foreign Bible Society. These women shaped the development of the Society, and it is unlikely that without their influence and hard work the organization could have achieved its rapid growth both in Britain and throughout the world.

The Bible was an important influence on women's lives and it was no accident that many women were drawn to this work. Evangelical women valued the Bible and felt impelled to share it with those to whom it was often inaccessible. Although the motives of these women were genuine, it is often difficult for the twenty-first-century mind to see beyond what may appear to be patronizing or arrogant attitudes. Some of the benefits of distributing the Bible that were perceived by nineteenth-century women may now appear as forms of social control. The work must, however, be evaluated in reference to its own context, and it must be remembered that many of the women involved in Bible work were interested only in practical responses to practical problems, rather than intellectual analysis of issues. These women also stressed the importance of the individual, rather than a concern with structures.

A few of the women involved in Bible work have secured wider recognition in recent years, as in the case of Mildred Cable, the early twentieth-century missionary of the China Inland Mission, whose Bible distribution work included notable travels through the Gobi desert. Too often, however, the insight into the Society's past provided by these women and their labours has been forgotten. Although the names of some of the many individual women involved in Bible Society work cannot be recovered, and much of the written examples of their work has been destroyed, there is still ample evidence for the important contributions women made to Bible work. It would have been impossible for the British and Foreign Bible Society to achieve such widespread success without the labours of these often forgotten women.

"WITHOUT NOTE OR COMMENT":
YESTERDAY, TODAY, AND TOMORROW[1]

Roger Steer

In 1835 the British and Foreign Bible Society's colourful and eccentric agent George Borrow visited Colhares, a village picturesquely situated between Sintra and the Portuguese coast. When Borrow asked to see the village school, he was taken to a small upstairs room, where he found a master with about a dozen pupils standing in a row. After embracing Borrow, the master offered him the only chair in the room. Borrow asked the schoolteacher whether he had a copy of the New Testament. The master showed him an edition of the Epistles translated in the previous century by a Roman Catholic priest, with extensive note and comment.

> I asked him whether he considered that there was harm in reading the Scriptures without notes: he replied that there was certainly no harm in it, but that simple people, without the help of notes, could derive but little benefit from Scripture, as the greatest part would be unintelligible to them; whereupon I shook hands with him, and on departing said that there was no part of Scripture so difficult to understand as those very notes which were intended to elucidate it, and that it would never have been written if not calculated of itself to illume [sic] the minds of all classes of mankind.[2]

Here one sees George Borrow at his most patronizing, but the incident also reveals something else: that at the beginning of the fourth decade of the Society's history its agents had already been thoroughly briefed on the "without note or comment" principle and were apparently convinced of its rightness. What was the background to the Society's decision to adopt the principle?

Tyndale's Marginal Notes

William Tyndale, who completed a translation of the New Testament into English in 1525 and was still working on the complete Bible at the time of

---

1. See also the author's recent bicentenary volume, *Good News for the World, 200 Years of Making the Bible Heard: The Story of Bible Society* (Oxford, UK, and Grand Rapids, Michigan: Monarch Books, 2004).
2. George Borrow, *The Bible in Spain* (London: John Murray, 1899), chap. 1.

his death in 1536, included extensive marginal notes, many of them polemical in nature, which defended both his translation and the Protestant position against attack. For example, where Jesus replies to Peter's confession at Caesarea Philippi with the words, "Thou art Peter..." (Matt. 16.17-19), Tyndale was well aware that Roman Catholics used these verses to defend their belief that Peter was the first pope. Therefore, in his note on this verse, Tyndale wrote, "Whosoever then this wise confesseth of Christ, the same is called Peter. Now is this confession come to all that are true Christian. Then is every Christian man and woman Peter".[3] There are many examples like this in Tyndale's marginal notes.

By no means are all of Tyndale's notes like this, however: many of them were simply designed to make the text easier to understand by providing what would now be called "cultural context". For example, alongside the words, "Do not the publicans even so"? (Matt. 5.46), Tyndale noted helpfully, "Publicans gathered rents, toll, customs and tribute for the Romans, and were commonly heathen men thereunto appointed of the Romans".[4] Some of Tyndale's marginal notes in his Pentateuch of 1530 make amusing reading today (and he perhaps had a pained smile on his face when he wrote them). Accompanying Exodus 32.35, where one reads of the plague that broke out among the Israelites after their worship of the golden calf, he comments, "The Pope's bull slayeth more than Aaron's calf". To Exodus 36.5-7, where the people are asked not to bring any more offerings for the building of the tabernacle, because they have already contributed more than enough, he writes, "When will the Pope say 'Hoo! [Hold!]' and forbid an offering for the building of St Peter's church? And when will our spirituality say 'Hoo!' and forbid to give them more land? Never until they have all".[5]

When Tyndale revised later editions of his work, he restrained himself, removed the more polemical notes reflecting particular points of view, and was content mainly with supplying notes that explained, summarized, or applied the text in a generally helpful and uncontroversial style. In the Gospels he gave marginal references to parallel passages.

Geneva and Bishops' Bibles

In 1560, the translators of the Geneva Bible, commenting on "the beast that cometh out of the bottomless pit" (Rev. 11.7), wrote in their notes that this is "the Pope, which hath his power out of hell and cometh thence".[6] There

---

3. Internally quoted, with modernized spelling, from F. F. Bruce, *The English Bible, a History of Translations* (London: Lutterworth Press, 1961), p. 34.
4. Quoted in Bruce, *The English Bible*, p. 35.
5. Quoted in Bruce, *The English Bible*, p. 42.
6. Quoted in Bruce, *The English Bible*, p. 90.

were many comments in a similar vein in the Geneva Bible, thus making it popular with Puritans and other Dissenters. On the other hand, the committee that prepared the 1568 Bishops' Bible tried to avoid the polemics of the Geneva Bible by agreeing to add no bitter or controversial annotations to the text.

Catholic Douai-Rheims Bible

Just as Protestant Bible translators found it difficult to resist the temptation to use marginal notes to attack their opponents, so the Catholics were equally guilty. In the Catholic Douai-Rheims Bible (1582–1610), the translators wrote the following note to the words "Come, Lord Jesus" in Rev. 22.20 (the penultimate verse of the Bible):

> And now, O Lord Jesus Christ, most just and merciful, we thy poor creatures that are so afflicted for confession and defence of the holy Catholic and Apostolic truth, contained in this thy sacred book, and in the infallible doctrine of thy dearest spouse our mother the Church, we cry unto thy Majesty with tenderness of our hearts unspeakable: COME LORD JESUS QUICKLY, and judge betwixt us and our adversaries, and in the mean time give patience, comfort, and constancy to all that suffer for thy name, and trust in thee. O Lord God, our only helper and protector, tarry not long. Amen.[7]

The translators' notes in the Douai-Rheims Bible included other anti-Protestant comments.

The Authorized Version

When at the Hampton Court Conference in January 1604, John Reynolds of Corpus Christi College, Oxford, suggested that a new translation of the Bible be made, King James seized eagerly on the proposal. He is reported to have said:

> I profess I could never yet see a Bible well translated in English; but I think that, of all, that of Geneva is the worst. I wish some special pains were taken for an uniform translation, which should be done by the best-learned men in both Universities, then reviewed by the Bishops, presented to the Privy Council, lastly ratified by Royal authority, to be read in the whole Church, and none other.

Richard Bancroft, bishop of London (soon to be archbishop of Canterbury), was not as keen on the idea as the king and complained that "if every man's humour were followed there would be no end of translating. *But if there were to be a new translation, it should be without notes* [italics added]." The king heartily agreed on the matter of the notes:

---

7. Quoted in Bruce, *The English Bible*, pp. 123-24.

> I have seen among the notes annexed to the Geneva Bible some that are very partial, untrue, seditious, and savouring too much of dangerous and traitorous conceits.

Thus, the resolution at the end of the Hampton Court Conference read:

> That a translation be made of the whole Bible, as consonant as can be to the original Hebrew and Greek; and this to be set out and printed, *without any marginal notes*, and only to be used in all Churches of England in time of divine service [italics added].[8]

Though a Protestant, James I favoured lenient treatment of Roman Catholics, made peace with Catholic Spain, and persuaded the Assembly of the Church of Scotland to agree to the introduction of bishops. He probably objected to the unashamedly Calvinist tone of the notes in the Geneva Bible.

The stipulation that the King James Bible should have no such notes was surely wise. No one could reasonably object, however, to notes intended to make the sense plainer. In fact, the conference issued guidelines to the translators that said that while no notes were to be placed in the margins, parallel passages could be noted, and where a Hebrew or Greek word allowed two similar meanings, one was to be expressed in the text, the other in the margin. Marginal notes were also allowed to clarify places where ancient manuscripts had variant readings, and where difficult Hebrew and Greek expressions required explanation.

When it was finally published in 1611, the new translation did include a surprising total of 17,000 translators' textual, linguistic, and explanatory notes and cross-references. While there were a number of anti-Catholic asides in the preface to the King James Bible and some notes that went a little beyond explanations of a textual, linguistic, or cultural/historical nature, these were exceptions rather than the rule. Notes reflecting confessional points of view in theology or church practice could only limit the usefulness of a Bible intended for all English people. If the Bible was to commend itself to all schools of thought, it must not include features that would unnecessarily offend any one group of readers.

Foundation of the British and Foreign Bible Society

What was new and distinctive about the British and Foreign Bible Society was its interdenominational nature and the enthusiasm and single-mindedness of its founders, who decided to print the Scriptures without note or comment and distribute them in Britain and throughout the world. Similar bodies had confined themselves to taking the Bible to particular

---

8. This exchange and the Hampton Court Conference resolution have been adapted from internal quotes in Bruce, *The English Bible*, pp. 96-97.

classes and groups of people. But, as Joseph Hughes (secretary of the Religious Tract Society and one of the founders of the BFBS) put it, this was to be an institution that originated in one nation for the good of all.

The phrase in the first paragraph of the Society's laws and regulations, which stated that the sole object of the Society was "to encourage a wider circulation of the Holy Scriptures without note or comment", reflected the non-sectarian, non-denominational approach of the Society. Since the Society wanted to serve the Bible cause generally and to enlist the help of Christians from across the church spectrum, the founders of the Bible Society were wise to adopt the policy of excluding note and comment. Each of the founders held cherished theological positions and interpretations of the Bible on such matters as baptism, the bread and wine at communion, the second coming, church order, the primacy of the papacy, and even (as the Society's history sadly demonstrated) the deity of Christ. But by restraining themselves and the translators they used from adopting and advertising argumentative positions on any issues, and by being ready to work cooperatively in a spirit of tolerance — agreeing to differ — they guaranteed the maximum support for their new Society and ensured its rapid growth.

Mohawk-English Gospel of John

The first use of Bible Society funds to produce a non-English version of the Scriptures under BFBS direction was made with a grant for publication of two thousand copies of a Mohawk-English Gospel of John. This translation provided an early test of the General Committee's commitment to the "without note or comment" principle. The Mohawks were one of the six Indian tribes, or nations, making up the Iroquois Confederacy. They lived mainly in what is now the state of New York (USA). During the American War of Independence, the Mohawks, who were pro-British, followed their leader Joseph Brant to Canada.

The Mohawk-English Gospel was translated by Tyonenhokarawen, a chief of the Mohawks, whose father, a Cherokee, had served in the British army. The chief himself had been a captain in the army and usually assumed the English name of John Norton. Captain Norton did most of the translation work while staying as a guest of the Teignmouths in Clapham. Lord Teignmouth, a former governor-general of India, was the Bible Society's first president. As Lord Teignmouth's memoirs describe it, Norton "sometimes appeared at his host's table in his native dress and performed the war-dance, tomahawk in hand, to the astonishment of his guests."[9]

---

9. Charles J. Shore, *Memoir of the Life and Correspondence of John Lord Teignmouth*, 2 vols. (London: Hatchard and Son, 1843), vol. 2, pp. 80-82.

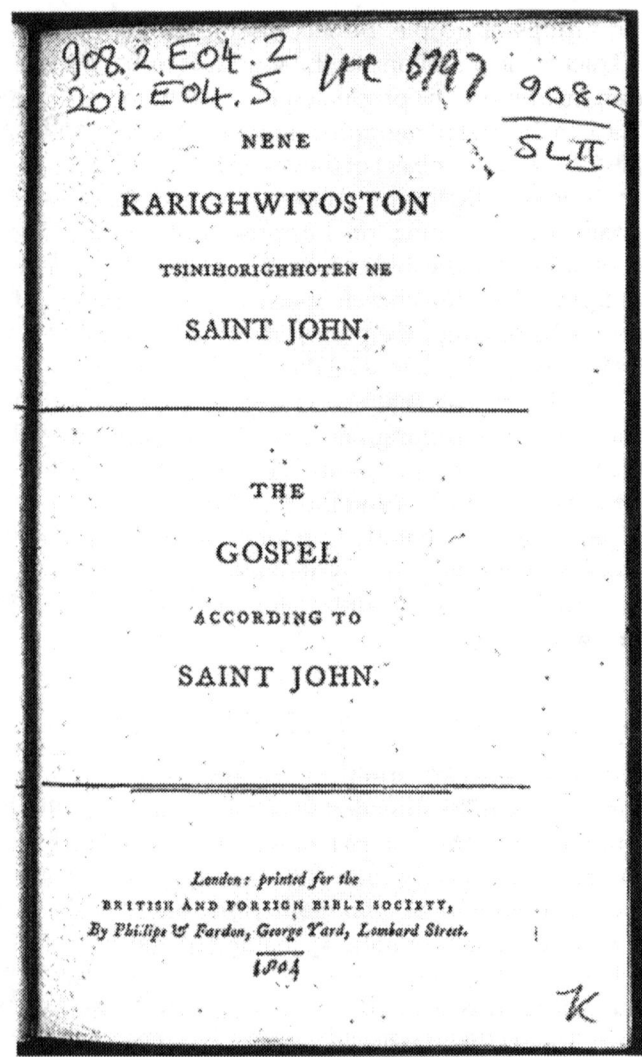

Picture 6. *Gospel of John in Mohawk and English.* Specimen courtesy of BFBS collections, Cambridge University Library

The principle of "without note or comment" was first and firmly put into practice when Captain Norton wrote a lively introduction to the gospel in the form of a spirited *Address to the Six Nations*. As soon as the Committee discovered this, they ordered it to be withdrawn as incompatible with a fundamental rule of the Society.[10]

10. John Owen, *The History of the Origin and First Ten Years of the British and Foreign Bible Society*, 2 vols. (London: Tilling and Hughes, 1816), vol. 1, pp. 126-35.

Launch of the Society's Staffordshire Auxiliary

When the Staffordshire Auxiliary was launched in 1811, the Reverend Thomas Gisborne was the keynote speaker. Gisborne was one of the best scholars of his year at Cambridge in 1780. A lifetime friend of William Wilberforce, he had written the book, *Principles of Moral Philosophy* (1789), as well as other works on the slave trade and the duties of women. In addition, he had published collections of hymns, poems, and sermons, and served locally as a curate in Staffordshire before being appointed prebendary of Durham.

At the launch of the Staffordshire auxiliary, Gisborne rose to the occasion and delivered a witty address. Warming to his task, he turned to the subject of "without note and comment", which had already become a controversial talking point:

> The charges advanced against the British and Foreign Bible Society at different periods of its progress, were they not likely to be occasionally mischievous, might furnish considerable entertainment. At one time it was clamorously alleged, "Notes and comments and interpretations will be inserted into your Bibles; you will undermine the Church of England by the expositions which you will interweave into the sacred volume". "It is impossible", replied the Society, "it is a fundamental law of our constitution that neither note nor comment shall ever be added". Then succeeds an accusation from the opposite corner of the sky, "Why do you send forth the Scriptures without an interpretation? The Established Church will be ruined by your dispersion of the Bible without note or comment!" I leave these two classes of objectors to settle accounts each with the other. For the overthrow of the Bible Society both are equally anxious.[11]

The Staffordshire audience smiled and felt better for Gisborne's spirited defence of the cause it supported.

Foundation of the American Bible Society

At the end of the six days of talks that led to the foundation of the American Bible Society in 1816, one of the founders, Peter Jay, spoke at a meeting in the New York City Hall. Peter was the eldest son of John Jay, first chief justice of the Supreme Court of the United States.

> Our object is to distribute the Holy Scriptures without note or comment. At this, no politician can be alarmed, no Sectary can be reasonably jealous. We shall distribute no other book, we shall teach no disputed doctrine. Laying aside for this purpose the banners of our respective corps, we assemble

---

11. Gisborne, internally quoted in William Canton, *A History of the British and Foreign Bible Society*, 5 vols. (London: John Murray, 1904–1910), vol. 1, p. 69.

under the sole standard of the great captain of our salvation. We endeavor to extend his reign, and in his name alone we contend.[12]

Thus, the American Bible Society (ABS) from its inception followed the lead of the BFBS in upholding the "without note or comment" guidelines in its operations.

After 1825, the BFBS never supplied anyone with Bibles *in sheets*: every Bible was sold bound in order to prevent the so-called apocryphal books from being inserted within the covers of a Society edition, and to avoid a preface, note, or comment being added. However, as early as 1816, the BFBS published its first Authorized Version Bible with the translators' references and alternate readings (edited since 1611) in the margin, and the ABS followed suit in 1833. Thus, despite the stance taken on "without note or comment", it seems that from the early years the two English language Bible societies saw no conflict with the insertion of marginal references and alternate readings. Such features were not seen as doctrinally divisive or contentious.

Borrow in Spain

In the summer of 1836, BFBS agent George Borrow visited the interior ministry in Madrid and was shown into the office of the Duke of Rivas, who headed the ministry. Rivas, an Andalucian, received Borrow affably and listened politely to his request to publish and circulate the Bible Society's New Testament in Spanish. The following exchange was then recorded by Borrow in his work, *The Bible in Spain*:

> "Go to my secretary; go to my secretary - *El hará por usted el gusto* [he will gratify your fancy]". So I went to the secretary, whose name was Oliban, an Aragonese, and whose manners were neither elegant nor affable. "You want permission to print the New Testament?" "I do," I said. "And you have come to his Excellency about it?" continued Oliban. "Very true," I replied. "I suppose you intend to print it without notes?" "Yes." "Then his Excellency cannot give you permission," said the Aragonese Secretary. "It was determined by the Council of Trent that no part of the Scripture should be printed in any Christian country without the notes of the church." "How many years was that ago?" I demanded. "I do not know how many years ago it was," said Oliban, "but such was the decree of the Council of Trent." "Is Spain at present governed according to the decrees of the Council of Trent?" I inquired. "In some points she is," answered the Aragonese, "and this is one. But tell me, who are you? Are you known to the British minister?" "Oh yes, and he takes a great interest in the matter." "Does he?" said

---

12. Peter A Jay, "Address to the Founders," in *Proceedings of a Meeting of the Citizens of New York and Others*, convened in the City Hall on 13 May 1816 at the request of the Board of Managers, American Bible Society (New York: ABS, 1816).

Oliban; "that indeed alters the case: if you can show me that his Excellency takes an interest in this business, I certainly shall not oppose myself to it."

Borrow paid a visit to the British embassy. Ambassador George Villiers, who later became British foreign secretary, performed marvellously on behalf of Borrow and the Bible Society. He visited the duke of Rivas and spoke to him at length on the matter. The duke was all smiles and courtesy. Villiers followed this up with a private letter to the duke, which he gave to Borrow and asked him to present to the duke on his next visit. He wrote a letter addressed to Borrow in which he said that nothing would give him greater pleasure than to hear that he had obtained the permission he sought.

When Borrow returned to the interior ministry to see the duke and deliver the letter, Rivas read the letter, smiled sweetly, and extended his arms in a theatrical gesture: "*Al secretario, el hará por usted el gusto*". Borrow, with a strong sense of déjà vu, hurried to see the secretary, who received him coldly, and again referred to the decrees of the Council of Trent.

Some weeks later, when friends had smoothed the way for him to make a further visit to the interior ministry, Borrow had a third interview with Oliban. This time the official was more expansive. He took out a box of cigars, lit one, and offered Borrow one. The English agent of the Bible Society declined. Oliban put his feet on the table and began to speak to Borrow in French.

> It is with great pleasure that I see you in this capital, and, I may say, upon this business. I consider it a disgrace to Spain that there is no edition of the Gospel in circulation, at least such a one as would be within the reach of all classes of society, the highest or poorest; one unencumbered with notes and commentaries, human devices, swelling it to an unwieldy bulk. I have no doubt that such an edition as you propose to print would have a most beneficial influence on the minds of the people, who, between ourselves, know nothing of pure religion; how should they? Seeing that the Gospel has always been sedulously kept from them, just as if civilization could exist where the light of the Gospel beameth not. The moral regeneration of Spain depends on the free circulation of the Scriptures; to which alone England, your own happy country, is indebted for its high state of civilization and the unmatched prosperity which it at present enjoys. All this I admit, in fact, reason compels me to do so, but—"Now for it," thought I. "But—" And then he began to talk once more of the wearisome Council of Trent.[13]

Borrow retained his cool and slipped away dejected.

While Mendizábal was prime minister of Spain, government officials constantly frustrated Borrow's plans to print the New Testament in

---

13. For the foregoing quotes and related description, see Borrow, *The Bible in Spain*, chap. 13.

Spanish by referring to the decree of the Council of Trent that Bibles should only be published with the notes of the Catholic church. However, Mendizábal's successor Istúriz personally gave Borrow not written but oral permission to go ahead with his publishing plans. Encouraged by Ambassador Villiers, Borrow therefore arranged publication of five thousand copies of a Spanish edition of the New Testament, which he took with him on a donkey and sold in many Spanish villages as well as from an elaborately furnished shop in Madrid and in depots in many towns.

Changes to the "Without Note or Comment" Principle

It is not unusual to read statements in the Society's publications in the first half of the twentieth century to the effect that the work of the Society was not finished when the Bible was delivered to its destination. But the first major signs of a twentieth-century reassessment and limited relaxation in the "without note and comment" rule came when the Netherlands Bible Society (NBS) celebrated its 125th anniversary in July 1939. It invited representatives from nine Bible societies to attend a conference in Woudschoten, Zeist. Three were unable to accept, but representatives from the BFBS, ABS, NBSS (National Bible Society of Scotland), the Norwegian Bible Society, and Bible Work in France joined the Netherlands society.

Professor Hendrick Kraemer, a layman who had been to Indonesia as a translation expert on behalf of the NBS and was one of the principal figures in the emerging ecumenical movement, made the opening speech and issued a powerful challenge to Bible societies to cooperate with the churches to encourage the *use* of the Bible. His opening address included two points directly bearing on the issue of "without note or comment". First, Professor Kraemer acknowledged the important work of the Bible societies in translating, printing, and distributing the Bible, but called for a systematic and well-planned movement for teaching those who bought a Bible how to read and *use* it for private and family worship. Second, he noted that, while most Bible societies issued the Bible only, some published additional material as well. He suggested that more was needed: "All Bible Societies ought to include in their activities the preparation, printing, and distribution of books with collections of tales from the Bible".[14]

These two proposals sparked lively discussion. Undeterred, Kraemer went on to criticize the quality of translations, questioning the instructions given by Bible societies to their translators. For example, he didn't like the requirement that "the translation of the Scriptures, if possible

---

14. Kraemer, as quoted in Edwin H. Robertson, *Taking the Word to the World: 50 Years of the United Bible Societies* (Nashville: Thomas Nelson, 1996), pp. 9-10.

without loss of idiom, dignity and beauty of phrase, should be made in a language that average people can understand without explanation". The logic of what he was saying seemed to be leading to the proposal that Bibles should be issued with explanations. This cut across the basic Bible Society principle that Bibles should be published without note or comment. Some delegates thought that Kraemer was asking Bible societies to take on the task of the churches.[15]

In preparation for the Woudschoten conference, the BFBS drew up a report stating that the object of the Society "will be fully carried out provided that the Holy Scriptures circulated by the Society neither contain nor have bound with them any matter of any description which either in any way interprets, or attempts to interpret, the inspired word, or can in any way be regarded as having a doctrinal bias".[16]

The Woudschoten meeting represented a key turning point in the history of the Bible society movement in that it recognized the need for a more nuanced understanding of the traditional "without note or comment" stance and foreshadowed the revision that was made in the 1970s. The development of ideas discussed at Woudschoten was interrupted by the Second World War. But in 1958, the distinguished linguist and key figure in ABS history, Eugene Nida, wrote a paper on "readers' helps" in which he showed how marginal notes in Bibles could provide helpful explanations and yet "avoid all doctrinal interpretation or emotionally charged accusations or innuendos".[17] More than thirty years later, in August 1989, Nida gave a lecture on Study Bibles to ABS translations staff and the CEV translations team.[18]

"ABS history", he said, "is one of not telling people what to believe, and of giving them even-handed options for understanding, and showing what, historically, have been those understandings. Among audiences, however, there are those who much prefer this, and those who prefer to be told what to believe".[19] But, historically, Bible societies have not seen

---

15. Kraemer, as quoted in Edwin H. Robertson, *Taking the Word*, pp. 9-10.

16. For mention of the report and the internal quote, see the essay by Paul Ellingworth, "How Far Have We Come? Reader's Helps and Study Bibles, 1939-1989," Unpublished keynote address at the Madrid Consultation on Study Bibles (UBS, September 1989).

17. Eugene Nida, "Marginal Helps for the Reader", *The Bible Translator*, vol. 9, no. 1 (January 1958).

18. [*Editor's Note*: CEV refers here to the edition then under preparation by the ABS, *Holy Bible, Contemporary English Version* (American Bible Society: New York, 1995).]

19. Quoted in David G. Burke, "Text and Context: The Relevance and Viability of the Bible Society Movement's Fundamental Principle — 'Without Doctrinal Note and Comment' — Past, Present and Future", UBS Background Paper, 21 March 2000, p. 29.

their task as engaging in detailed exposition of the Scriptures. This is the work of churches into whose hands Bible societies put those Scriptures.

In 1966, Laton Holmgren, who died in January 2004 at the age of 88 after a distinguished career in the ABS and the United Bible Societies, wrote a significant letter to General Secretary John Watson of the BFBS. He said that, without any policy change, the ABS Board had recently authorized the publication of a variety of helps for readers. These included historical introductions, explanatory footnotes, and glossaries that were understood as appropriate. The ABS Board had come to understand the "without note and comment" clause to restrict the use of doctrinal or sectarian notes, but not contextual and explanatory background materials that helped Bible readers better understand what texts from ancient times and cultures were saying. Holmgren concluded his letter by noting, "If I sense the current mood correctly, even further reader helps of a non-doctrinal character are likely to be approved in the near future".[20]

UBS/Vatican Guidelines and Bible Society Revisions

One of the happiest strands of Bible society history in the second half of the twentieth century has been the developing cooperation between the UBS and the Roman Catholic Church in Bible translation. In 1968, the UBS/Vatican *Guidelines for Interconfessional Cooperation in Translating the Bible* listed the following helps for readers that would not contravene the intention behind the "no note and comment" rule: alternative readings or renderings, explanations of proper names, plays on words (e.g., the ability of the Greek *pneuma* to mean spirit, wind, and breath), historical backgrounds, cultural differences, cross-references, and section headings. In addition, certain supplementary features, which Bible societies had previously avoided, were cleared for use: indices, concordances, maps, and illustrations.

In 1971, the ABS adjusted the wording of its constitution so that the phrase "without note or comment" became "without doctrinal note or comment". Although many other Bible societies later made the same change to their key documents, the BFBS never did so, perhaps because the Society decided that it was almost impossible to define what was and was not "doctrinal". The Bible Society did give itself more flexibility, however, in 1968 by altering the phrase to read: "without note or comment, other than such aids for readers as shall have previously been

---

20. L. E. Holmgren to J. T. Watson, 12 December 1966, internally quoted in Burke, "Text and Context," p. 10. The original letter is in BFBS Secretaries' Correspondence: Royal Charter and Bye-Laws, box 4 (BSA/D4/1/4).

approved by the General Committee".[21] These changes were based on the assumption that it wasn't notes and comments in themselves that were the problem but positioning or advocacy on issues where Christians were not in agreement. Readers' helps would enable Bible societies better to serve the needs of their audiences, but the aim would be to provide the helps in a way that avoided interpreting texts along lines that advocated divisive theological positions.

Writing on the issue of "without note or comment" in 1971, Archbishop of York and UBS Honorary President Donald Coggan remarked:

> As time goes by, the gap which yawns between the world in which the Bible was written and the world in which we live grows ever wider. It is not simply a matter of the passage of time. The difference is deeper and more subtle than can be measured in terms of centuries.[22]

He noted the difference between the pre-scientific world and the scientific world of today, the highly rural and pastoral context of the Bible and the high urbanization of today, and the technologically simpler world and the complexity of today. He argued that these changes justified the inclusion of non-doctrinally divisive notes in Scripture publications.

But there were limits to the relaxation. In 1977, the UBS Executive Committee (UBSEC) recommended to all societies that they should not disseminate the English *Living Bible* on the grounds that it was a paraphrase, straying too far in some places from the original Hebrew and Greek. With the establishment of BFBS's new publishing division in 1978, the Society embarked on a radical review of its publishing and distribution operations and rapidly expanded its range of products.

Meeting in Chiang Mai (Thailand) in 1980, the UBS Council suggested that Bible societies should examine afresh the fundamental "without doctrinal note and comment" principle to see what this meant if construed positively rather than negatively. Instead of asking "how far can a Bible Society go"? [without contravening the principle] the question should be "what do readers need to know to be better able to use and understand the Bible"?[23] On 13 July 1984, the BFBS took a related step. In a revision of its royal charter, the Society altered its main objectives by adding "use" of Scripture to its longstanding commitment to the "distribution" of Scripture. This fundamental change made it possible for the Society's product range to be dramatically broadened. The Society became for a period as much a wholesaler of "Bible helps" as it was a publisher of Bibles.

---

21. *Good News Is for Telling: One hundred and Sixty-fourth Report of the BFBS* (London: BFBS, 1969), p. 6.
22. Donald Coggan, *Word and World* (London: Hodder & Stoughton, 1971), p. 99.
23. Internally quoted in Burke, "Text and Context", p. 12. For the UBS Council meeting in Chiang Mai 1980, see the *Bulletin of the United Bible Societies*, no. 120/121.

Five years later Donald Coggan, no longer archbishop but still UBS president, wrote an article, "Without Note or Comment—Then and Now", comparing the idea of the appeal made by readers for help in understanding the Bible to the appeal in the book of Acts by the Ethiopian official to the apostle Philip for contextual help: "Do you understand what you are reading? How can I understand unless someone gives me the clues"? (Acts 8.30-31, NEB).[24]

Recent Guidelines for Bible Society Publishing

In 1989, the UBS Europe-Middle East Region put out guidelines entitled *What Should Bible Societies Publish?* These guidelines allowed "non-prescriptive" readers' helps that "assist readers in making up their own mind on how Bible texts should be interpreted".[25] In March 1990, the ABS followed with a vision statement for the 1990s that included the statement, "the Bible cause is more than production and distribution. It is the promulgation of effective Bible reading in terms of changed lives".[26] In all this, the fundamental assumption was that the BFBS founders intended to avoid comment that was *divisive,* thus hindering the fundamental objective of ensuring the widest possible collaboration of all Christians in the cause of distributing the Scriptures and making them heard.

When in May 1992, the UBS approved a new and comprehensive set of guidelines for Study Bible preparation, the document embodied an important and long-held Bible society conviction that the Bible is self-authenticating, and that in its words readers/hearers will encounter God speaking to them—that the Bible is always its own best evangelist. The 1992 guidelines continued:

> Study Bibles like other Bible Society publications exclude doctrinal note and comment. "Doctrinal" in this context is understood to refer to contentious theological and denominational issues. Study Bibles accordingly should not include material which imposes post-biblical doctrinal formulations, expresses the distinctive tenets of a particular denomination or theological tendency, or prescribes any specific contemporary application. [They] should be written so as to allow the readers to discover applications to their own situations.[27]

---

24. Coggan cited in Burke, "Text and Context", p. 11.

25. *What Should Bible Societies Publish? Editorial Guidelines of Bible Societies in Europe-Middle East* (UBS: Haarlem, 1989), cited in Burke, "Text and Context", p. 14 n. 70.

26. "The vision of the ABS for the 1990s" (ABS Board internal document, 9 March 1989), cited in Burke, "Text and Context", pp.12-13.

27. "UBS Guidelines for Study Bibles" (UBS: Reading, May 1992), cited in Burke, "Text and Context", p. 14.

As ABS translations staff began in the 1990s to prepare study editions for both the *Good News Bible/Today's English Version* and the *Contemporary English Version*, they also worked at updating their guidelines and principal documents to incorporate the reality of Study Bibles. When the ABS Board approved a set of "Guidelines for Study Bibles and Study Helps" in September 1996, the document addressed, in addition to the more usual kinds of helps that had become well accepted by this time, the possibility of such features as articles on the nature and canon of the Bible, thematic indices, questions for reflection, and even suggested readings and study methods. The introduction to the "Guidelines" states:

> All such helps are designed to provide important background information and should in no sense be *prescriptive* as to what doctrines people should believe [italics added]. These helps are, however, extremely important in providing historical and cultural information that would have been obvious to original audiences, as well as the best scholarly evidence as to what the writers of the various books of the Bible intended to communicate.[28]

In essence, the intention in the 1970s of the introduction of the word "doctrinal" into the classic formulation "without note or comment" was to avoid division. This corresponded with the objectives of the Society's founders. Any kind of positioning that would be divisive had to be avoided so as to prevent the Bible from being used as a means for promoting discord.

When the BFBS published a *Good News Study Bible* in 1997, it followed the same principles. Bible societies, when they act as publishers, continue to uphold the position that the interpretation of Scripture is the role of the churches, not of the societies. While it is possible for Study Bibles to be produced within this understanding of Bible Society policy, "Application Bibles" will probably never be acceptable within such a policy. The current thinking is that Application Bibles (which seek to help the reader apply the Biblical narrative to his or her everyday life) tend to close off options for readers to draw their own conclusions by imposing the commentator's or note writer's understanding or by prescribing a conclusion for the reader to adopt. Applications can "deafen" the reader to other possibilities in the text because of an implication that a comment or suggested response represents the only correct understanding.

In an important paper reflecting on the change of policy to "without doctrinal note and comment", published as a UBS Background Paper, David Burke of the American Bible Society put the new approach in context:

---

28. "Guidelines for Study Bibles and Study Helps" (ABS Translations Department internal document, September 1996), p. 1, cited in Burke, "Text and Context", p.15.

Coming toward the last quarter of the twentieth century, with the advent of wide and growing biblical illiteracy, modern communications technology, and increasing knowledge of the Bible, Bible times, Bible manuscripts and languages, the use of notes on cultural-historical realities, text issues, word meanings, and so on, become crucial for helping modern readers who have so little shared information with people of Bible times to bridge the gap and read with increased meaning.[29]

The Nottingham Campaign and the Future

The aim of the Bible Society's campaign in Nottingham in the autumn of 2003 was to get people talking about things that matter to them and, with an open mind, to start to see how the Bible might connect with these things — an attempt to move from how we live to the world in which we would like to live. As part of an assessment of the campaign in the spring of 2004, the Society's Board of Trustees began a detailed consideration of the opportunities presented by such a campaign to make the Bible heard and how they fit with the traditional no note or comment stance of Bible societies.

Clive Dilloway, current chairman of the BFBS trustees, believes that the mandate to work without note or comment in the Society's objective has earned it widespread respect for the conscientious way in which it has published unbiased versions of the Scriptures. In consequence he thinks that the Society is now well placed to serve as a unifying influence within the church by providing a neutral meeting point around a common belief in the importance of the Scriptures. Without compromising its doctrinal neutrality, the Society needs to use that influence to encourage greater use of the Bible throughout the church.

One reason for the remarkable success of the Bible Society in its first two hundred years certainly has been the unprecedented broadmindedness of its principles. From the start there was no doubt that the Society would not be confined to any one section of the Christian church, or to any party within the church. The first prospectus laid down that

> The *principles* upon which this undertaking will be conducted are as comprehensive as the nature of the object suggests that they should be. In the execution of the plan, it is proposed to embrace the common support of Christians at large; and to invite the concurrence of persons of every description, who profess to regard the Scriptures as the proper Standard of Faith.[30]

---

29. Burke, "Text and Context", p. 11.

30. Published as Appendix 1 of the *First Report of the BFBS* (London, 1805), and internally quoted in William Canton, *A History of the British and Foreign Bible Society*, 5 vols. (London: John Murray, 1904-1910), vol. 1, pp. 21-22.

On the whole the Society has kept well to this principle, but like every organization in the world it has had to make do with flawed individuals to run it, work for it, and support it. Some have had a better appreciation of what the Society was about than others. Generally though, the open-hearted principle has been well understood. "If we cannot reconcile all opinions, let us at least unite all hearts", the Society's second president said.[31]

Was the "without note or comment" principle too restrictive? Did it restrict the British and Foreign Bible Society and other Bible societies from pursuing new approaches to presenting Scripture to the world, or from publishing a wide range of Bible-related material, or from interpreting their mission to the world and to the church in imaginative ways? Historically (and surely when at its best) the Bible Society has thought of itself, and been seen by others, as a partner with and provider for churches of all traditions across the ecclesiastical spectrum — Protestant, Catholic, Orthodox, Pentecostal. The phrase "without doctrinal note or comment" was a sort of self-denying and self-limiting posture that encapsulated the genius of the vision of the BFBS founders in 1804, and has been a secret of the widespread acceptance and rapid growth of the Society and its offshoots all over the world. In this sense, the "without note and comment" principle captured the essence of Bible Society identity. It has been the means by which a breadth of interdenominational involvement has been assured. Since 1804, the success of the Bible Society and its followers around the world in restraining themselves from divisive positioning in favour of one side or another over contentious issues of biblical interpretation has been an unusual, if not unique, achievement. Maintenance of this historic principle has enabled hundreds of inter-confessional Bible translation projects to be agreed upon and implemented by teams of Protestant, Catholic, and Orthodox scholars in many countries.

Adherence to the principle has also accorded to churches their own historic role in the interpretation of Scripture, and the application of Scripture to church practice. That interpretive role has not been usurped by Bible societies. By retaining their founding principle, Bible societies have upheld a view of the Bible as an unpredictable vehicle by which God has disclosed himself, and which is bigger than we are. The principle represents an intelligent insight into both the nature of Scripture and the characteristics of our frail humanity. Scripture is, like the God who gave it, mysterious, surprising, always beyond us. Men and women are great but fallen – prone to compete, argue, and divide. The principle ensures that Scripture is not seen by any reader or group as a weapon with which to

---

31. Nicholas Vansittart [Lord Bexley], internally quoted in Canton, *History*, vol. 2, p. 167.

launch attacks on others who hold different views or as a tool for demonizing opponents. The Bible society way is the path of cooperation rather than condemnation. The Bible cause is a mission in support of which all Christians can unite, even if they are in other ways divided by disagreements on theology or interpretation.

This fundamental philosophy of the Bible society movement means not only that the societies will continue to adhere to the "no note or comment" principle in their publishing, but also that where they enter into partnerships with other organizations they will try to avoid giving the impression that they align themselves predominantly with any particular church grouping—evangelical, Catholic, Orthodox, or Pentecostal. Happily, in any case, there is evidence that the habit of rigidly professing undying allegiance to any one of these labels is declining in the church. Christians are often ready, perhaps more frequently than in the past, to have their faith enriched by the insights of traditions other than the one in which they were brought up or with whom they currently align themselves. More importantly, when they meet and work together as members of Bible societies, Christians from different traditions will see "agreeing to disagree" about doctrine as a more immediate priority even than being enriched by each other's insights.

LONDON BIBLE HOUSE IN THE 1950S:
AN ILLUSTRATED REMINISCENCE

John Dean

Describing its London Bible House in a popular 1932 sixpenny booklet, the British and Foreign Bible Society commented that "it is in accord with the fitness of things that the world's chief distributing centre for the Book of books should stand in the heart of the world's greatest city".[1] Something of that confidence, of that pride and consciousness of being at the centre of things, was very much in my mind as I joined the staff of the British and Foreign Bible Society on the last day of December 1956. How thrilled I was as a twenty-year-old, newly converted Christian, fresh from the provinces, to be working for such a Society in such a location, within a stone's throw of the office of *The Times,* close to St. Paul's Cathedral and the river Thames, and in the heart of *one* of the world's greatest cities!

The Bible House, described by architectural historian Nikolaus Pevsner as "a good quiet Italianate palazzo", was built between the years of 1866 and 1869.[2] It replaced the Bible Society's earlier building in Earl Street, which was pulled down when the great thoroughfare of Queen Victoria Street was built over the old site. Construction of the new building was funded entirely from voluntary contributions, which were additional to the regular income of the Society, and the property was purchased at a total cost of £61,000. Until well into the 1960s, it was valued on the balance sheet at just £87,000.

The elegant, regular exterior concealed an internal structure that was nothing less than labyrinthine. To enter from Queen Victoria Street was not to enter on the ground floor but rather to enter the basement.[3] This was because the building was erected on a site that sloped upwards from front to back, to such an extent that the back door was located one floor higher than the front entrance. On both the west side and on the front of

---

1. *The Bible House* (London: British and Foreign Bible Society, 1932).
2. Nikolaus Pevsner, *London I: The Cities of London and Westminster* (London: Harmondsworth, 1957), p. 239.
3. British terminology is used throughout this article for architectural features.

Picture 7. *Bible House, 146 Queen Victoria Street.* Reprinted from *The Bible House* (London: BFBS, 1932).

the building facing south onto Queen Victoria Street, the structure rose to six storeys. The warehouse area, however, in the rear northeast part of the building, was seven storeys above street level. That is why, if one climbed up the elegant staircase on the office side from the second floor to the next floor, one reached not the third but the fourth floor. Is all that perfectly clear? Well, let's take a tour.

The visitor who entered the front door—at the basement level—was immediately confronted by what looked like two large tombstones, which were in fact plaques erected in commemoration of the founding fathers of the Society: the president, the vice-president, and the first General Committee—in those first days, of course, they were exclusively founding *fathers*. To the left of the entrance, the imposing main staircase led to the upper floors, and behind the staircase in the southwest corner of the building was the bookshop, or "depot" as it was then called, which had its own street entrance. The depot was an imposing and somewhat daunting study in brown mahogany, and most of the Scriptures available for sale were kept in locked glass cases and wall cabinets. The friendly depot staff were, however, always willing to open up for the potential purchaser.

Picture 8. *Bible House Main Staircase*. Reprinted from *The Bible House* (London: BFBS, 1932).

Deeper into the basement was the room in which the outgoing post was sorted and franked, and in which the Braille press was also located. There, Ron Hagger spent his days laboriously punching out large sheets of zinc. It took him about a year to produce the plates for a complete Bible in Braille, which ran to some forty-five volumes. In addition to making the plates, he printed out the sheets on heavy brown paper. Near the post-room was the crypt, a cavernous, dark, dusty, many-pillared room with a beautiful fan-vaulted low yellow-tiled ceiling, in which many of the Society's archives, dating back to 1804, were located. Just beneath the basement was the boiler room, which was off limits to all staff except for the caretaker. The rest of the basement floor consisted of warehouse space (printed sheets were stored on this level awaiting shipment to the bindery) and the packers' tearoom, out-of-bounds to everyone else and usually full of cigarette smoke.

I nearly forgot to mention the dungeon. This was the name given to a large walk-in safe in the basement, in which finance department records were kept, including accounts going back to the earliest years of the Society. It was in the dungeon that I searched for and found records of the Bible Society of Ethiopia, going back to the 1930s, which provided documentary evidence of the sequestration of a building in Addis Ababa by the Italian occupying forces. As a result, the Society was successful in obtaining compensation from the Italian government some thirty years later.

Moving up to the ground floor, which also went by the name of "mezzanine floor", one reached the reception hall, an open space at the bottom of the main central staircase and the location of a few special items. Here could be found a table made of wood from Wycliffe's pulpit, a portrait of William Tyndale, and a magnificent globe bearing the names of languages into which the Bible had been translated at the time the globe was presented to the Society. The donor was His Imperial Highness Haile Selassie, the emperor of Ethiopia, who presented it to the BFBS during his exile in Britain at the time of the Italian occupation of Abyssinia.

Also on the ground floor were the offices of the finance department and the publishing department. The main office in the finance department was known as the "general office". This photo of the general office was taken in the 1930s, but the place had changed little some twenty-five years later, apart from the introduction of more modern desks. My first boss was Bernard Tattersall, a keen mountaineer, who had served previously as finance director of the Bible Society of India. In a separate compartment of the finance department was the cashier's office, presided over by William Mitchell, known to everyone as Mitch. Mitch's curmudgeonly manner failed to mask a kindly spirit, though he did thoroughly enjoy grumbling about what was wrong with the Bible Society of the day. He served faithfully and well for over fifty years, but it was not until a couple of years before his retirement that he switched from purchasing a daily railway ticket to a season ticket — he'd not been sure whether he was going to stay.

Picture 9. *Bible House Mezzanine Floor*. Reprinted from *The Royal Visit to Bible House* (London: BFBS, 1949).

Picture 10. *Bible House General Office*. Reprinted from *The Bible House* (London: BFBS, 1932).

In charge of the publishing department was the lively Norman Bratt. In addition to his technical skills, Norman had the gift of the gab and was much in demand as an interesting and amusing speaker at Bible Society meetings. Norman loved to quote the old verse, which he claimed was published in *Punch* some time in the nineteenth century:

> Holy Bible, Book Divine
> Leather bound at one and nine;
> Satan trembles when he sees
> Bibles sold as cheap as these.

The largest single area on the ground floor was the packing room, the most important room in the warehouse. Here men packed Scriptures into wooden crates, which had stencilled on them such exotic destinations as Cape Town, Port au Prince, Takoradi, and Yokohama. Those were the days when the lion's share of worldwide Bible production was carried out in Britain. It is said that when King George VI and Queen Elizabeth visited Bible House in 1949, the King asked one of the warehousemen how many people worked in the building. "About half, Your Majesty", was the reply.

Picture 11. *Bible House Packing Room*. Reprinted from *The Royal Visit to Bible House* (London: BFBS, 1949).

Moving up to the first floor was to move up to what was thought of as the most important floor in the building, though as will be explained later on, it could well be argued that the most important work of the Society was done on the floor above. Here on the first floor were the Committee room and the offices of the two general secretaries of the day and their immediate support staff.

Life in the Bible House in those days was a somewhat formal affair. It was *de rigueur* for gentlemen to wear suits and ties. Shirtsleeves might be permissible in one's office in the summertime, but certainly not while walking about the building. Ladies were not allowed to wear short dresses, or anything so unsuitable as a pair of sandals. First names were never used except between close friends. Committee and staff members were always addressed as Brigadier Swift, Dr. Platt, Miss Clapham, etc.[4] In this context it should be understood that the first floor, housing the general secretaries, was looked upon as some kind of inner sanctum. Any conversation in the corridors was quickly suppressed. The atmosphere was not unfriendly, but it *was* formal.

One important responsibility among many others exercised by the general secretaries was to supervise the work in the Society's overseas agencies and in a growing number of what were then called "daughter societies" around the world. One of the general secretaries of the day was always an Anglican clergyman and the other a Nonconformist minister, and they shared the world between them as "Secretary A" and "Secretary B". Secretary A primarily related to Europe and Latin America, and Secretary B to Africa, Asia, and Australasia.

In 1956, the Society's Secretary A was the Reverend Norman Cockburn, a Scottish Episcopal clergyman. Norman was a deeply spiritual, kindly, and saintly man, who was a fine priest, but who did not exactly shine as an administrator. As far as he was concerned, budgets and accounts were a matter for the finance department, which is why quite early on in my career I found myself sitting in his office discussing major questions relating to funding the Society's work around the world with Bernard Tattersall and Dennis True (my finance department bosses) and Laton Holmgren and Charley Baas, the two most senior officers of the American Bible Society (ABS).

At the end of the first floor was the office of Dr. William J. Platt. Bill, who lived to be one hundred, had a large office, which I was later to occupy for a few years. (The photograph, from the 1920s, shows a previous general secretary, Dr. John Ritson.) It was in that office around 1960 that Laton Holmgren of the American Bible Society tried to persuade Bill Platt that ABS should share in the administration of Bible Society work in Africa. This was in the days when the work around the world was still primarily supervised by ABS, BFBS, and a few other European Bible societies, before the United Bible Societies' regional structure was established.

---

4. The only exceptions were cases such as "Sir Roderick" or "Your Excellency".

Bill pointed to a large map of Africa on the wall of his office and said, "Laton, I want you never to forget—that is BFBS territory".

Picture 12. *Office of an BFBS General Secretary.* Photograph from the private collection of John Dean.

The committee room was the most imposing room in the Bible House, with a high, decorated ceiling and tall, elegant windows looking out over the bombed remains of the church of St. Andrew by the Wardrobe, which was later restored. The room was impressively furnished with substantial leather chairs, a splendid table around which the senior staff sat during meetings of the General Committee, and fine red carpeting in the Persian style. In one corner was a Blüthner grand piano, used on Tuesday mornings for prayers, at Christmas for an annual carol service, and also, for a time, by the short-lived Bible House music group. On the walls were a varied collection of pictures, including one that I already knew from my childhood reading of the Children's Encyclopædia: the Venerable Bede on his deathbed, dictating the last words of John's Gospel. There were other pictures, including some rather fine ones, such as those of the Reverend Thomas Charles and of Mildred Cable, and a rather less impressive, more modern attempt at a portrait of William Wilberforce.

And what of that august body, the General Committee? In my early years I was somewhat dispirited by the impression I received that the work of the Committee had become something of "a hobby for old gentlemen". This was a result of the practice whereby, after retiring from the Committee, members were usually immediately elected as vice presidents

Picture 13. *Bible House Committee Room.* Reprinted from *The Royal Visit to Bible House* (London: BFBS, 1949).

of the Society, which gave them the right to continue attending General Committee meetings. These retired senior bankers, diplomats, naval and military men, industrialists and businessmen, all of them in their seventies and eighties, were thus able to dominate the decisions of the Society for many years, until a revolutionary change was introduced in the early 1970s, which prohibited service on the General Committee beyond the age of seventy.

The committee room was not only used for meetings of the BFBS General Committee. It was also used by a number of specialized committees of the Society, dealing with finance, property, translation, the overseas work, and other topics. In addition, it was frequently the site of meetings of representatives of different church or mission groups that needed a neutral Christian location for their discussions.[5]

---

5. For a number of years I co-chaired with Michael Bordeaux of Keston Institute a quarterly meeting of Christian groups working inside the Soviet Union. Those operating through legal channels (which included the Bible Society) always spoke freely of their work, while those who represented smuggling organizations said nothing at all.

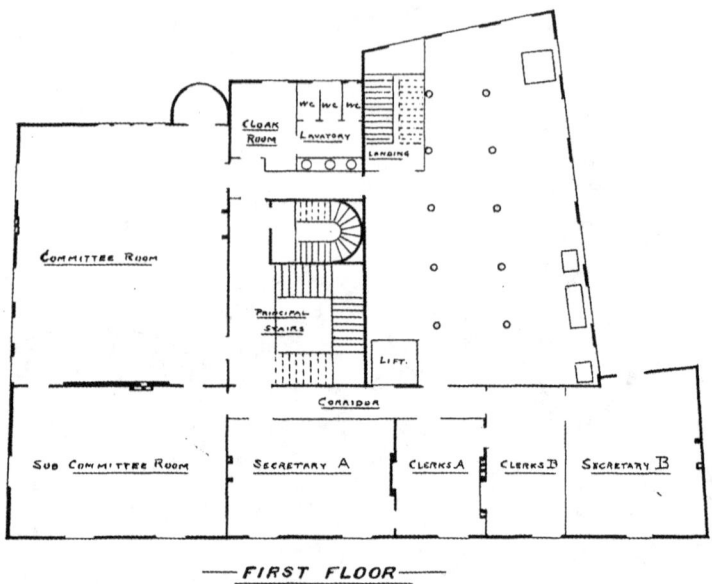

Picture 14. *Plan of Bible House First Floor, Early 1900s.* Drawing courtesy of BFBS collections, Cambridge University Library.

The committee room was also the place where every Tuesday morning the staff met for prayers. Until just prior to my joining the Society, these devotions had always been led by a member of the clergy, but lay members of staff were now invited to lead the devotions. As a result one senior member of the finance department decided to stay away, remarking as he did, "I like to get my religion from a clergyman". At prayers all the ladies sat on the left, and all the men on the right. After a few years some of us younger staff decided that on the next Tuesday morning we would swap over and sit on the "wrong" side. In the event, our courage failed us and we slunk into our usual places. So ashamed of ourselves were we, however, that the very next Tuesday we made the switch, and at a stroke the days of segregation were gone forever without a murmur of complaint.

A great event every year was the Christmas party, when the Committee room again became the focus of attention. There was always a wonderful buffet (sometimes in the Committee room, sometimes in the upstairs canteen), as well as games and other entertainments, often including a dramatic sketch, which for a few years I would write until the pressures of work became too heavy. Last, but not least, the General Committee room was also home once a month to the London Youth Group. It was the LYG, under the inspiring leadership of Bernard Tidball and Elizabeth Goodin, which kept me going in the Society during those early years. I began to realize that the Bible Society was a lot more than "a hobby for old gentlemen" and was indeed the focus of a worldwide Christian movement of great importance. Today, nearly fifty years later, I am still in touch with several former LYG members who continue to be staunch supporters of the Society as a result of their earlier involvement.

We go next to the second floor, which after all was perhaps the most important floor, because it was here that the translations department was located — at that time an unrivalled global centre of expertise in Bible translation theory and practice. Led by Wilfred Bradnock and Harold Moulton, and later by Gwen Anderson, this department and its team of manuscript examiners faithfully and rigorously served hundreds of translators around the world. Most of the translators in those days were missionaries, who did their work together with a team of what were then called "native informants". This was before the days of translation by mother-tongue speakers, assisted on the spot by a team of UBS translation consultants, as is now the case.

Perhaps the crowning glory of the Bible House was its library of some thirty thousand Bibles and other Scriptures, the rich collection of scriptural treasures that have now become a part of Cambridge University Library. I sometimes used to accompany visitors while the librarian of the day pointed out, in addition to the famed Codex Zacynthius and the fourth-century Coptic Gospel of John, such wonders as the "biscuit tin" Bible, the "Treacle" Bible, the "Bug" Bible, the "Breeches" Bible, and, of course, the "Wicked" Bible.[6] The library was also the place to which scholars from all over the world came to study the Society's archives.

The second floor also housed an office called "minutes and receipts" and, in a far corner, two very small offices, which at that time constituted the space given over to the United Bible Societies. These small offices were occupied by Olivier Béguin, a great UBS general secretary until his untimely death in 1972, and Edwin Robertson, the UBS study secretary, plus two support staff.[7] Few could have imagined then that the UBS would in a few short years, under the leadership of Olivier and later of Uli Fick, grow into a global organization, providing support services to Bible societies in all parts of the world.

In the 1950s, the Society's warehouse occupied much of the third floor in the north-eastern part of the building. Later (like the rest of the warehouse), the third floor was converted into office space, when the warehouse was moved down to New Cross in south London in the mid-1960s.

---

6. *The Bible House* brochure of 1932 coyly states that this Bible "omits the negative in one of the commandments".

7. A prolific writer and broadcaster, Edwin Robertson had previously been the assistant head of religious broadcasting at the BBC and went on to become executive director of the World Association of Christian Communication (WACC).

Picture 15. *Bible House Library*. Reprinted from *The Royal Visit to Bible House* (London: BFBS, 1949).

The main staircase came to an end on the fourth floor under a glass dome, from which point one went on to the editorial and home departments. The editorial department produced the quarterly magazines, *The Bible in the World* and *For Every Land*, the latter a publication for children, as well as an annual *Popular Report*, a short alternative to the impressive annual BFBS *Report*, which was a mine of information about Bible Society work all over the world. Here too was the office of Youth Secretary Bernard Tidball, who was such an influence for good on hundreds of young Christians in the 1950s and 1960s. I suppose the days of Bible Society youth house parties have gone forever; but how inspiring they were in their day, and how much fun! The home department had the heavy responsibility of raising funds in England and Wales, largely through the hundreds of auxiliaries (later called "action groups") that were served by some fifteen district and regional secretaries who lived in different parts of the country. In those days too the Society had a separate office for "women's work" on the fourth floor.

Also on the fourth floor was the office of the Good News Transport Fleet, a special campaign through which children saved up donations to pay the cost of shipping Scriptures from Bible House to all parts of the world.[8] Nearby was Stamp Corner, presided over by the redoubtable Miss Davis, known affectionately to all as Auntie Davis. A tiny figure, always dressed in black, Auntie Davis came into Bible House two or three times a week, supervising the sorting and sale of stamps sent in by supporters in Britain and around the world. Auntie's way of crossing busy Queen Victoria Street on her way to and from Bible House consisted of holding her rolled black umbrella high in the air and stepping boldly off the pavement. Unfortunately on one occasion this provided insufficient protection and she was knocked down. Within a few weeks, however, she was back at work, and continued faithfully to manage the Stamp Corner until her death in her late eighties.

The fourth floor also contained a room in which the mail was opened each day, and where a rigorous procedure for the handling of money and other valuables was practised. On this floor too one found the caretaker's comfortable flat, as well as a cinema. The cinema was used for both slide shows and for films. In those days the Society sponsored the production of a distinguished series of films by the noted English director Ray Kinsey, including *This is the Bible Society* (1960), which took as its topic the daily work done in Bible House, and an excellent film about Bible translation in Eritrea called *The Leaves of the Tree*, a reference to Rev. 22.2: "and the leaves of the tree were for the healing of the nations". This last reference was presumably unknown to the keen Bible Society supporter who wrote in and asked to borrow the film, *The Leaves in the Tea*.[9]

Up on the fifth floor, immediately below the roof, were the magazine department, a photographic darkroom, the small pageant office (a place where costumes of all shapes and sizes could be found, a treasure much exploited by the London Youth Group), and the office of Vera Pearson, the Society's calligrapher, who spent her days producing very beautiful illuminated bookplates for inclusion in presentation Bibles. Last, but not least, on the fifth floor was the canteen, where solid but not particularly appealing lunches were provided to the staff—free of charge, however, so one should not complain. The quality of meals was to be greatly improved a decade later when the warehouse moved out to New Cross and a modern cafeteria was opened in the basement.

Those who have followed my description to this point will by now have realized that in the mid-1950s, and for some time to come, the

---

8. Once a year these children were invited to a Bible Society birthday party in the City of London Guildhall, where they received a slice of an enormous cake shipped to England by the Bible Society in Australia.

9. Some of these films have survived, and have been preserved in BFBS collections at Cambridge University Library in the "BFBS Film Collection (BSFILM)". For these two films, see *This is the Bible Society* (BSFILM 10) and *The Leaves of the Tree* (BSFILM 30).

Society carried out within the walls of Bible House quite a large number of specific technical and other functions. This was before the days of outsourcing, and none the worse for that. The reader will also well understand how attractive and interesting the building was — simply as a place to visit. Parties came from far and wide to take a tour of Bible House, to see a film, or to hear a speaker with first-hand experience of Bible Society work, and to go away having a better understanding of — and one hopes enthusiasm for — the worldwide Bible cause.

There are two other features well worth describing. First there was the roof. Although later declared to be out-of-bounds (and wisely so, for safety reasons), the roof of Bible House on sunny summer days was where several of the staff would sit enjoying their lunch or afternoon tea. There was a fine view to the southwest, past the ruined St. Andrew's church,[10] the *Times* building, and Blackfriars station. Although the powers-that-be never found out about it, a few of us on one occasion played an impromptu cricket match, using a stick and a few pebbles that had somehow found their way on to the roof. After a couple of hits for six, people down in the street started looking up and gesticulating, and our match came to a sudden halt. We never played again.

Picture 16. *BFBS Staff on Bible House Roof.* Photograph from the private collection of John Dean.

10. During World War II a stick of incendiary bombs fell on the church and on the Bible House. While firemen hosed the building with water from the river Thames, Bible Society staff on nightly fire-watching duty managed to throw the bombs into the street, where they were extinguished. The water in the river was so low, however, that the supply then ran out, and the interior of St. Andrew's was completely gutted.

The other feature had to do with the methods used for getting about the building. In addition to the main staircase, there was also in the northeast corner of the building a dark and dingy "back staircase", as it was called, which linked the warehouse floors. Ancient, dusty bundles of archives were stored on every landing. There were also two lifts, one more unusual than the other. The back lift in the warehouse consisted of an open-fronted wooden box, which was propelled up and down from floor to floor by means of a rope. Office staff were not supposed to use it, but I did ride in it a couple of times, accompanied by a warehouseman. The front lift was a more elaborate affair with outer doors and inner concertina-like gates, which had to be opened and closed by hand. Its most memorable feature was that it had no memory. This meant that at the moment an occupant left it, a person on a different floor who was pressing the button took precedence over other people elsewhere who had pressed their buttons earlier. At busy times, such as the afternoon tea break, one could wait for a long time while the lift went up and down, and up and down again. This led to a lot of irate but useless tapping on the outside doors by those left waiting as the lift passed their floor.

I have very happy memories of my thirty years in London Bible House. In those early days the staff worked long hours for low pay, but this was later to improve.[11] Job satisfaction was very high. In that connection, I love J. B. Phillips's paraphrase of Ephesians 5.15: "Live life, then, with a due sense of responsibility, not as men who do not know the meaning and purpose of life but as *those who do*" [italics in Phillips].[12]

The BFBS finally sold the Bible House in 1985 and moved to Swindon. Before moving to my UBS office (not to Swindon but a few hundred yards to Carter Lane, just by St. Paul's Cathedral), I took a walk all by myself through the empty building. Memories came flooding back, although it was in fact the very first time that I had been into those parts of the Bible House that had always been off limits: down into the boiler room, along a long narrow passage full of lumber at the back of the top floor, into the caretaker's kitchen — all places I had never seen before and would never see again. And, as I thought about my thirty years in that lovely old building, I realized that I had at some time or another worked in an office on every floor except the basement.

---

11. For many years salaries were kept unreasonably low by virtue of the fact that the chairman of the salary review committee, an English colonel retired from the Indian army, would not agree that the general secretaries should earn more than his pension of £600 per annum.

12. J. B. Phillips, *Letters to Young Churches: A Translation of the New Testament Epistles*, 21st rev. ed. (London: Geoffrey Bles, 1957).

Today the property is the home of British Petroleum's exploration department, and thankfully it has been restored in such a way as to retain quite a few of the most important architectural features. But as I reflect on the fact that this building is now used to promote the exploitation of a precious and soon to be exhausted resource, I remember with gratitude the fact that for a hundred and twenty years, as London Bible House, it was the place where an infinitely more precious and inexhaustible resource was faithfully translated, produced, and distributed to the ends of the earth. That work still continues. Buildings come and go, and people come and go, but as one can still read over the entrance to 146 Queen Victoria Street, "The Word of the Lord endureth for ever".

Part Two

THE BFBS ABROAD

John Hill and the Early Attempt to Study a West African Language

Patricia Mirrlees

In May 1808, when the British and Foreign Bible Society (BFBS) was in its fifth year, John Hill wrote to Joseph Tarn, assistant secretary of the Society, stating that he had sailed to Gorée, the small island off the coast of Senegal, reaching there in November 1807.[1] "Being bred, born & Educated in Edinburgh" and a craftsman of edge tool making, Hill had missionary connections and West African experience.[2] In communications with the BFBS, Hill hinted at his wish to work for the Society in some capacity, especially in connection with his interest in the Wolof language, which he called Jaloff. But he was ahead of his time, for the BFBS was not then employing people as linguists.

---

1. Hill to Tarn, Goree, 31 May 1808, BFBS Home Correspondence Inwards (BSA/D1/1/3). See also the pocket book of John Hill (Hampshire Record Office: Mildmay Papers, 15M50/1574) containing *inter alia* accounts in dollars and pounds (November 1806–May 1808); vocabulary of the Jaloff language; diary, Africa (1808); and diary of a trader or missionary in Africa, with mention of Gorée and Senegal (November 1807–October 1808). Catalogued as anonymous, this pocket book was identified by Patricia Mirrlees in the 1970s as the work of John Hill. Hereafter it will be cited as the Pocket book of John Hill. For a detailed account of Hill's life and journal, see Patricia Wilson [Mirrlees], "Christian Linguists in the Senegambia Area, 1800-32," M.Th. Thesis, University of Aberdeen, 1978, chaps. 1–4 and appendix A. Zachary Macaulay writing to Governor Ludlam in Sierra Leone stated that his letter would be dispatched on a ship belonging to Bowers, "called the Lively bound to Rio Pongas." See Macaulay to T. Ludlam, London, 12 October 1807, Hull University Library (HUL), DTH/1/2. Hill therefore sailed on the *Lively* shortly after that date.
2. Hill to A. Clarke, George Town, Sierra Leone, 28 September 1809, Egerton MS. 933, British Library (BL). Since the knowledge of crafts was often passed down within a family, it is possible John Hill came from a family of smiths. Of the Hill families in Edinburgh that produced sons named John and recorded their births, there was one John Hill, a smith by profession, and his wife Ann. Under the registration of 9 March 1771 is the entry: "John Hill, Journeyman Smith in New North Kirk parish and Ann Smith his spouse a Son named John, Witnesses James Adam and Andrew Finlay both Journeymen Smiths in Edr. The Child was born 1st Curt." General Register Office, Edinburgh: Parochial Registers, Co. of Edinburgh, 1769–1771, 685/33, 9.

From the outset, John Hill's travels were associated with his missionary interests. As a result of evangelical zeal, missionary societies had been founded in the main cities of Britain, beginning with the influential London Missionary Society (LMS) in 1795, followed by societies in Edinburgh (1796) and Glasgow. In 1796, the LMS chartered the *Duff* to carry missionaries to the Pacific Islands. In a second voyage in 1798, the Edinburgh Missionary Society (EMS) "was invited to bear a part" and readily accepted.[3]

The Reverend Greville Ewing, secretary of the EMS, wrote to the LMS with the news that they had "three Missionaries, two of them possessing medical knowledge, and one an edge toolmaker, whom they had some thoughts of sending out in the Duff." In a subsequent October 1798 letter to the LMS Board, Ewing named the Edinburgh missionaries as "Mr. John Beattie, and Mr. John Hill, married persons, and Mr. Greig who is engaged and wishes to marry."[4] John Hill and his wife, Mary, would have undergone scrutiny and training before being regarded as suitable and ready for the field.[5] After his arrival in London, Hill was ordained by the LMS on 20 November 1798.[6] He seems to have been one of the more able missionaries. Writing about the second voyage of the *Duff*, William Gregory

---

3. Richard Lovett, *The History of the London Missionary Society, 1795-1895...* (London: Henry Frowde, 1899), vol. 1, pp. 2-41; William Ellis, *The History of the London Missionary Society...* (London: Snow, 1844), pp. 23-25, 37-38, 43-46; William Brown, *History of the Propagation of Christianity among the Heathen Since the Reformation*, 3rd ed. (Edinburgh: W. Blackwood, 1854), vol. 2, pp. 415, 454; Elizabeth Glendinning Kirkwood Hewat, *Vision and Achievement, 1796-1956: A History of the Foreign Missions of the Churches United in the Church of Scotland* (London: Thomas Nelson and Sons, 1960), p. 8; James Wilson, *A Missionary Voyage to the Southern Pacific Ocean...* (London: S. Gosnell for T. Chapman, 1799). *Report of the Directors of the Edinburgh Missionary Society, to the General Meeting of the Members of that Society, held at Edinburgh, the 30th day of July 1799* (Edinburgh), vol. 4, p. 49, hereafter *Report of the Directors of the EMS*.

4. *The Missionary Magazine for 1798*, vol. 3, no. 29 (15 October 1798), p. 475. CWM/LMS Home Board Minutes Box 1/2, Board Minutes 2, 1798-1801, 4 and 29 October 1798 (School of Oriental and African Studies).

5. *Abstract of Proceedings and State of the Funds of the Edinburgh Missionary Society, 20th July 1797*, pp. 2-3. John Hill and his fellow missionaries had been educated "for a considerable time" under the inspection of the directors of the Society. *Report of the Directors of the EMS*, p. 49.

6. *The Missionary Magazine for 1798*, vol. 3, no. 31 (17 December 1798), pp. 569-70. *The Missionary Magazine for 1799*, vol. 3, no. 34 (18 March 1799), pp. 112-13. CWM/LMS: Journals 1, South Seas, 1796–1803, Copy of a diary of J. L. Vardy, 19 December 1798-15 February 1799. Joshua Lambert Vardy was one of the missionaries who accompanied John Hill on the second voyage of the *Duff*. Like Hill, he was ordained before the commencement of the voyage and ceased his connection with the LMS on his return to England. His diary is the one source that mentions that John Hill's wife was named Mary. For the possible marriage entry for John and Mary Hill, see the General Register Office, Edinburgh: Register of Proclamations and Marriages, 1751–1800: "Hill/Lugton,

includes extracts from the journals of several of the missionaries including John Hill, fragments of whose journal (14 December 1798 to 8 January 1799) are to be found in his Pocket book.[7]

The *Duff* sailed from Portsmouth on 20 December, but on 20 February 1799 the ship was apprehended by a French vessel, *Le Grand Buonaparte*, and the missionaries were taken to Montevideo, Uruguay, where the *Duff* was sold and Captain Robson was offered another ship, the *Postillahio d'Amerique*. The missionaries decided at a meeting on April 21 to proceed to the Cape of Good Hope. Failing that they would go to Sierra Leone, where the LMS also had a mission. Embarking on May 8, they sailed the following day for the African coast.[8] This ship, too, was captured, by a Portuguese commodore commanding a large ship and a frigate, and the missionaries were divided among the three vessels, John and Mary Hill being on the commodore's ship, the *Meduza*, where the treatment was worse than on the other two. Reaching Lisbon on 21 September, Mary Hill, who had acted as a midwife on the journey, gave birth to a stillborn child.[9]

Many of the missionaries ceased their connection with the LMS when they finally got back to London, for as a result of all their misadventures some had come to believe that God's will was against such missions. The Reverend David Bogue, a director of the LMS and an advocate of well-trained missionaries, suggested however that some of the missionaries had left Britain from "impure and inferior motives," and that early in the voyage it was evident a ship was needed to return to Britain those who

---

Edinburgh, 4 January 1798. John Hill, Smith, and Mary Lugton, both in High Church Parish, Daughter of George Lugton, Gentleman's Servant, Edinburgh."

7. Pocket book of John Hill (Journal of a voyage from London to Monte Video, Rio de la Plata South America, in the Missionary Ship Duff of London Captn Robson Bound for Otaheite, Begun Decr 20 1798). See also William Gregory, *The Second Edition of a Visible Display of Divine Providence; or, The Journal of a Captured Missionary, Designated to the Southern Pacific Ocean, in the Second Voyage of the Ship Duff . . . With extracts compiled from the Journals of the Rev. Peter Levesque, Rev. John Hill, Dr Turner, James Jones, John Levesque and other Missionaries captured in the Duff* (London: J. Skirven, 1801).

8. Journal of William Soddy, November 1798-October 1799, "Account of an unsuccessful voyage by LMS missionaries to the South Seas, to found a mission," copied by T. E. Soddy, Baptist Missionary Archives (BMSA), Regent's Park College, Oxford University. Gregory, *Second Edition of a Visible Display*, pp. 14-199; William Howell, *Some Interesting Particulars of the Second Voyage made by the Missionary Ship, the "Duff"* (Knaresborough: Hargrove and Sons, 1809), pp. 9-139. T. Robson to Directors, at sea, the Rock of Lisbon, 21 September 1799, CWM/LMS Home Incoming Correspondence Box 1, 1795–1800. Lovett, *History of the LMS*, vol. 1, pp. 477-79, 481-97. Brown, *History of the Propagation*, vol. 2, pp. 415-20.

9. Journal of William Soddy. Gregory, *Second Edition of a Visible Display*, pp. 210-79. Howell, *Some Interesting Particulars*, pp. 139-260. Robson to Directors, 21 September 1799.

were not suitable.[10] In the event, when John Hill reached London on 12 November 1799, he too resigned from the LMS.[11] Although his formal connection had ended, his name appears in the minutes of a meeting of the LMS directors on 13 October 1800: "Mr. Hill one of the Missionaries that had returned home after the capture of the *Duff* was in very straitened Circumstances and had applied for some further assistance, it was Resolved that the sum of £10 be allowed him."[12]

From October 1800 to March 1806, there is seemingly no reference to the whereabouts of John Hill. Then, in a letter in the archives of the Church Missionary Society (CMS), dated March 1806, Hill wrote from Sierra Leone to the London bookseller Robert Ogle, saying he had little news except that his wife was beginning to recover from a serious illness, which he regarded as a "mirical," and that if she returned to Britain he might accompany her, although he claimed to be in good health. There was no indication how long he had been in Sierra Leone. This letter caused some concern to the CMS, since in it John Hill criticized the missionaries in Freetown.

Zachary Macaulay, secretary of the Sierra Leone Company, had transmitted Hill's letter, indicating it had been written by an employee of the company, to Mr. Ogle, the bookseller in Turnstile, "wherein he particularly notices the present want of efficiency in Missionary attempts." The CMS requested to see the letter, and it was duly handed over to the correspondence subcommittee for consideration.[13] Zachary Macaulay's remarks revealed that John Hill was in the service of the Sierra Leone Company, which had been founded by an act of Parliament in 1791. The position held by Hill is given in a list of company servants dated 13 July 1807, where he is described as a clerk with a salary of £120 per annum.[14]

---

10. Lovett, *History of the LMS,* vol. 1, pp. 61-62. Howell, *Some Interesting Particulars,* p. 134. John Owen Whitehouse, *London Missionary Society: A Register of Missionaries Deputations, etc., from 1796 to 1896* (London: LMS, 1896), pp. 6-11. James Bennett, *Memoirs of the Life of the Rev. David Bogue, D.D.* (London: F. Westley and A. H. Davis, 1827), pp. 217-18.

11. Lovett, *History of the LMS,* vol. 1, p. 62. Gregory, *Second Edition of a Visible Display,* p. 158. LMS: Committee Minutes, Book 1, 18 November 1799. CWM/LMS Home Candidates Examination Committee Box 1, Book 1, 27 May 1799–10 June 1816, 18 November 1799. Whitehouse, *London Missionary Society,* p. 9.

12. CWM/LMS: Home Board Minutes Box1/2, Board Minutes 2, 1798-1801, 13 October 1800.

13. Hill to R. Ogle, Freetown, Sierra Leone, 21 March 1806, CMS (CAI/E1/42); CMS Committee Minutes, vol. 1, 2 and 9 June 1806 (G/Cl); CMS Minutes of Subcommittee, 4 June 1806 (GSC/1).

14. Christopher Fyfe, *A History of Sierra Leone* (London: Oxford University Press, 1962), pp. 26-27. Macaulay to E. Cooke, Sierra Leone Office (London), 13 July 1807, "A

In the CMS archives, there is a letter instructing Peter Hartwig, a Lutheran pastor from Berlin and one of the first two CMS missionaries to Sierra Leone, to gather information about the spread of Islam and the use of Arabic in the Mandinka and Susu areas. The letter, dated Freetown, 9 April 1806, contains next to the signatures the notation, "Exd. J Hill," an example of Hill's clerical duties. Having access to this and other communications may have encouraged John Hill to collect information and manuscripts in a systematic fashion.[15]

An extract from a surgeon's report for the Sierra Leone Company for the year 1807 mentions that it was thought "necessary for Mr. Hill to return to Europe; he had suffered much from repeated Attacks of fever, affection of the Liver and Spleen; and at the time he left this place I was very apprehensive he would become dropsical." John Hill was invalided home after November 1806, according to that month's account written in his Pocket book. In August 1807, Macaulay wrote that "the Court of Directors have remitted to Mr. Hill, who is now pretty well, the balance of his account, and have advanced him a little money for his present support till he can obtain employment." It can be assumed that Hill was paid off between the company list dated July 13 and Macaulay's letter of August 28.[16]

Despite the ill health he had suffered in Sierra Leone, John Hill made the decision, perhaps for financial reasons, to return to West Africa, sailing on the *Lively* in October 1807 for Gorée. In his letters to the BFBS during 1808 and 1809, he attempted to solicit employment, meanwhile accepting whatever work he could obtain.

Hill most likely had visited the small island of Gorée on his way to and from Sierra Leone, as he records in his journal in 1808 meeting up with former Sierra Leone Company colleagues when their ships stopped briefly at the island. Hill wrote from Gorée that communications from London should be directed to him through George Fraser, a brother of Lt.-Colonel John Fraser, commandant of Gorée from 1800–1804. George Fraser, listed

---

List of the Servants of the Company at Sierra Leone with their Salaries," Public Record Office (PRO: WO/1/352).

15. T. Ludlam, A. Smith, A. Vanneck to P. Hartwig, Freetown, Sierra Leone, 9 April 1806 (CMS: CA1/E1/46).

16. Extracts from Surgeon's Report, 1807 (PRO: CO/267/24); Pocket book of John Hill (the next entry for his accounts is dated November 1807, a year later); Macaulay to Ludlam, London, 28 August 1807, Papers of Thomas Perronet Thompson, 1783-1869 (HUL: DTH/1/2); and Macaulay to Cooke, "A List" (PRO: WO/1/352). Hill's loss of employment may have been linked to his ill health, or the fact that the Company was due to be liquidated and its holdings transferred to the Crown on 1 January 1808. See Fyfe, *History of Sierra Leone*, p. 97.

as a merchant who had furnished the garrison at Gorée with supplies, may have been in a working partnership with Hill.[17]

Although Hill had given up his missionary life some years previously, he still retained connections with evangelical societies. He was, for example, in contact with the Religious Tract Society (RTS), which according to the RTS minutes of October 1807, resolved that "tracts to the Amount of £3.3.0. be placed at the disposal of Mr. John Hill for distribution at Gorée and Sierra Leone."[18]

Discovered by the Portuguese and under Dutch, French and British domination from 1617, the tiny island of Gorée was described in terms both flattering and uncomplimentary. Less than a mile in length and half a mile in width and having only about 45 acres of land mass, it was pictured by John Lindsay in 1758 as "resembling nothing so much as a ham of bacon," and by Edward Bickersteth of the CMS in 1816 as "not unlike a shoulder of mutton."

It included a high volcanic rock on which a fort was erected. Below lay the town and toward the northern point was a natural mole. The barren rock, "qui ne peut rien produire," had a severe water supply problem. Water, foodstuffs and fuel were brought from the mainland.[19]

This unprepossessing island not only provided safe anchorage for shipping, but also developed into a thriving depot for slaving and trade. Britain had at various times gained control of Gorée from the French, during almost the whole period from 1800–1817, for example. Of the many accounts

17. Hill to Tarn, Goree, 31 May 1808, BFBS Home Correspondence Inwards (BSA/D1/1/3); Pocket book of John Hill. *The Post-Office Annual Directory for the Year 1805* (London: Printed by T. Maiden for the proprietors, 1805), p. 96. Here Fraser is described as a merchant of 8 New City Chambers, Bishopsgate. See also Hill to Tarn, Goree, 9 August 1808, BFBS Home Correspondence Inwards (BSA/D1/1/3). In this, Hill said that George Fraser was the only person who could forward his letters.

18. Minutes of Religious Tract Society, vol. 3, 6 October 1807, Archives of the United Society for Christian Literature. Hill recorded distributing the tracts on Gorée. See Pocket book of John Hill, 25 March 1808. Also Hill to Tarn, 31 May 1808, BFBS Home Correspondence Inwards (BSA/D1/1/3).

19. On Gorée, see C. Toupet, "Gorée, Jadis et Aujourd'hui," *Notes Africaines* 75 (July 1957), pp. 85-86. W. F. Lord, "Goree: A Lost Possession of England," *The Nineteenth Century* (May 1897), pp. 759-68. John Lindsay, *A Voyage to the Coast of Africa, in 1758, Containing A Succinct Account of the Expedition to, and the taking of, the island of Goree* (London: S. Paterson, 1759), pp. 48-50. "Journal of a visit to Sierra Leone by Edward Bickersteth, Secretary of the CMS," 1815–1816, vol. 1 (CMS: Z.26). S. Meinrad Xavier Golberry, *Fragmens d'un Voyage en Afrique, fait pendant les années 1785, 1786 & 1787* (Paris: Chez Treuttel et Würtz, 1802), vol. 2, pp. 56-58, 66-67. M. Saugnier, *Rélations de Plusieurs Voyages à la Côte D'Afrique, à Maroc, au Senegal, à Gorée, à Galam* (Paris: Chez Gueffier jeune, 1791), pp. 252-53.

Picture 17. *The Island of Gorée*. Reprinted from Jean Baptiste Labat, *Voyage du chevalier Des Marchais en Guinée, isles voisines, et à Cayénne, fait en 1725, 1726 & 1727* vol. 1 (Paris: Pierre Prault, 1730), facing p. 47.

by Europeans who had lived on or visited Gorée, two were published during this period of British control. John Hill was familiar with the one by Joseph Corry, but he made no mention of the more detailed account of Francis Spilsbury.[20]

Hill's journal provides a unique and historically valuable account of daily life on Gorée from November 1807 to October 1808.[21] In it he mentions 16 people connected to the garrison, 34 residents of Gorée (or people he met on the mainland), and 12 individuals connected to Sierra Leone. The population consisted of a few Europeans, a large number of people of African-European descent, and Africans, both free and enslaved. By 1811, their number was estimated at just over 3,000, of whom only 10 were Europeans. The Europeans mentioned in Hill's journal were the officers of the Royal African Corps, who numbered about a dozen at any given time.[22]

---

20. Golberry, *Fragmens d'un Voyage*, vol. 2, pp. 68-70. Lord, "Goree," pp. 766-68. Joseph Corry, *Observations upon the Windward Coast of Africa, the Religion, Character, Customs etc. of the Natives*, reprint ed. (London: Frank Cass & Co., 1968), pp. 10-23. Francis B. Spilsbury, *Account of a Voyage to the Western Coast of Africa, Performed by His Majesty's Sloop Favourite, in the Year 1805* (London: Printed for Richard Phillips, 1807), pp. 12-18.

21. Pocket book of John Hill. See also Patricia Wilson [Mirrlees], "Christian Linguists in the Senegambia Area," appendix A.

22. "Answer to the Questions proposed to Lieut. Col. Maxwell, Lieut. Gov. of Senegal & Goree," by HM Commissions for Investigating the Forts & Settlements in Africa, St. Louis, 1 January 1811 (PRO: CO/267/29). Golberry, *Fragmens d'un Voyage*, vol. 2, pp. 60-61. Golberry thought the population was about 1,800. Le Citoyen Pélletan, *Mémoire*

Those of African-European ethnicity, the "Mulattos", or "Inhabitants," as they were called at that time, comprised an influential and powerful group, involved in trading and local administration. Prior to the abolition of the slave trade, they had been largely slave traders, and even after 1807 some continued in the trade illicitly. Their connections with France were strong. Many spoke and read French and were Roman Catholics, though Edward Bickersteth remarked that they seemed to know nothing about the subject. They also had family and trading links to the Senegalese mainland.[23]

On an island as small as Gorée, relationships were of the utmost importance, and much of Hill's journal mentions dining, dancing, and playing cards with the officers from the garrison and with "the Inhabitants ... who on all occasions treated me with respect & friendship!" Shipping was another preoccupation, since ships brought trade, news, visitors, and variety to the island. Hill kept a record of many of the ships that stopped at Gorée.[24]

Observing the Roman Catholics on Gorée, Hill notes on 3 January 1808:

> They appear to have no church or Priest and seldom meet above once a year to worship, when one of the Principal Inhabitants reads a few prayers in Latin, neither himself nor any of the rest understanding a single word! The time they meet is on Christmas Eve & part on the Xmass morning! The Room fitted up for worship is hung round with some pictures chiefly of departed saints, the place where (If they had a Priest) the Sacrement would be partook of, is ornament with a Crucifix, the virgin Mary above them on canvas the representation of the Saviour on the cross the whip that scorged him the spear that pierced him, the cock that crow'd on Peter's accot [account].

---

sur la Colonie Française du Sénégal, avec quelques considérations historiques et politiques sur la traite des Nègres (Paris: Ve Panckoucke, [1801?]), p. 25. Pélletan estimated 2,000, and Corry, *Observations* (p. 10), 3,000 to 4,000. J. A. Carnes, *Journal of a Voyage from Boston to the West Coast of Africa* (Boston: John P. Jewett & Co., 1852), p. 37, thought the population was not more than 2,000. Pocket book of John Hill. On 1 January 1806, there were 16 officers, 14 sergeants, 6 drummers, and 161 rank and file stationed at Gorée. John Joseph Crooks, *Historical Records of the Royal African Corps* (Dublin: Browne & Nolan, 1925), p. 47.

23. J. D. Hargreaves, "Assimilation in Eighteenth-Century Senegal," *Journal of African History* 6, no. 2 (1965), pp. 177-84. Hargreaves writes that the children of European fathers were usually educated, sometimes in France. See also H. O. Idowu, "Café au Lait: Senegal's Mulatto Community in the Nineteenth Century," *Journal of the Historical Society of Nigeria* 6, no. 3 (December 1972), pp. 272-84. Corry, *Observations*, p. 13. "Journal of... Edward Bickersteth", vol. 1 (CMS: Z.26). C. Becker and V. Martin, "Mémoire inédit de Doumet (1796): Le Kayor et les pays voisins au cours de la seconde moitié du XVIIIe siècle," *Bulletin de l'Institut français de l'Afrique noire* (BIFAN) 36, b. 1 (1974), pp. 32-33.

24. Hill to Clarke, 28 September 1809, Egerton MS. 933. Pocket book of John Hill.

According to Brooks, the church had been burnt "in one episode of unbridled license" on Christmas Eve 1799. On February 28, Hill noted that the young people of Gorée started to celebrate Mardi Gras.[25] He observed Good Friday and Easter Sunday, when the "inhabitants opened their church for worship in the forenoon," the afternoon being spent in "eating & drinking & visiting — they appear to take great pride in appearing fine & richly dressed."[26]

Perhaps to ease his financial problems, Hill began in 1807 to tutor the son of a leading family, the Pepins. He also began to teach a young man attached to the garrison. Writing to Joseph Tarn in May 1808, Hill stated that if the BFBS would send him some school books, paper, and pens, he felt sure he would be of use to the young people of the island, adding that "indeed the want of them has prevented me from being useful in a school department in which the Coll. offered to patronize me." This suggestion was not taken up by the BFBS.[27]

Hill's income was finally supplemented by a government appointment in May 1808 but there is no indication in his journal what the appointment was. He wrote that Lloyd, the commandant, had apologized, saying "he was sorry he could not at present give me a better." Major Charles Maxwell, who in September 1808 replaced Lloyd on Gorée, wrote in a letter to Governor Thomas Perronet Thompson of Sierra Leone on 4 April 1809 that he had found John Hill "in the situation of Provost Martial to which office he was appointed by Lieut. Colonel Lloyd."[28] The duties of the provost martial were to enforce military discipline and to secure

---

25. Pocket book of John Hill, 3 January 1808. George E. Brooks, Jr., *Yankee Traders, Old Coasters, and African Middlemen: A History of American Legitimate Trade with West Africa in the Nineteenth Century* (Boston: Boston University Press, 1970), p. 38. Lindsay, *Voyage to the Coast of Africa*, pp. 75-76. Lindsay had noted in 1758 that although there was no priest, there was a "gentleman (although a negroe) of extraordinary good sense, a good education, and withal polite... On Sundays, and other holidays, his house becomes a chapel, where a very decent and considerable community meet together, the gentleman himself officiating to them as pastor." Hill to Tarn, 31 May 1808, BFBS Home Correspondence Inwards (BSA/D1/1/3). Probably Bickersteth was referring to Mardi Gras on 25 February 1816 when he concluded that Lent was observed by the people "going to a dance in a kind of procession, some of them in masquerade grotesquely & absurdly dressed." See also the "Journal of... Bickersteth," 25 February 1816 (CMS: Z.26).

26. Pocket book of John Hill, 15 and 17 April 1808.

27. Pocket book of John Hill, 31 December 1807 and 18 March 1808. Hill to Tarn, 31 May 1808, BFBS Home Correspondence Inwards (BSA/D1/1/3). In May 1815, a school was established on Gorée by a British couple, Mr. and Mrs. Hughes. See R. Hughes to J. Pratt, Gorée, 8 December 1815 (CMS: CA1/E5); also Idowu, "Café au Lait," p. 273.

28. Pocket book of John Hill, 19 May 1808. Maxwell to Thompson, Goree, 4 April 1809 (HUL: DTH/1/67).

prisoners until brought to trial. Just before Lloyd handed Hill the appointment, in May 1808, he asked Hill to attend to a prisoner from the garrison, who was to be executed, and to read the death sentence to him. Maxwell asked Hill to read the prayers to the garrison, since he understood that Hill was "a fit person for that business." John Hill therefore began reading prayers to the soldiers on Sundays.[29]

In the journal there are a few pages of entries devoted to a mission undertaken by John Hill to visit the Damel of Kayor—the head of the Wolof state—Amari Ngone Della Kumba Fal, who ruled from 1790 to 1809. Although the journal entries precede Hill's description of his life on Gorée, the visit to the Damel occurred later, in December 1808. Hill appears to have been sent to procure a horse for Major Maxwell.[30]

In September 1809, Hill wrote to Dr. Adam Clarke, the Methodist preacher and scholar, stating that along with his letter he was sending the original copy of his journal, recorded during his visit to "King Damel," since he had been unable to make a copy.[31] This journal was sent with a vocabulary. Hill's letter and vocabulary are in the British Library, but unfortunately the journal has not been located. Although John Hill was evidently pleased by the information his journal contained about "the Jaloff Customs," his visit was not a success, for the Damel was "less Courteous than perhaps he otherwise would have been."[32] In keeping an account of this visit, Hill was possibly trying to emulate his famous fellow countryman, Mungo Park, and other travellers. From various references Hill made to Park, it is clear he had read Park's book about his travels in West Africa published in 1799. Park had set out on his second attempt to find the source of the Niger from Gorée in 1805, and rumours about his disappearance and fate were reaching Gorée, as Hill noted.[33]

---

29. Pocket book of John Hill, 15 and 16 May; 3, 12, 23, and 25 September 1808.

30. Pocket book of John Hill, 9 to 17 [December], 1808. Félix Brigaud, *Histoire du Sénégal, des origines aux traites de Protectorat* (Dakar: Editions Clairafrique, 1964), vol. 1, pp. 25, 63. See also T. L. Fall, "Recueil sur la Vie des Damel par Tanor Latsoukabé Fall," introduit et commenté par C. Becker et V. Martin, *BIFAN* 36, b. 1 (1974), pp. 123-25.

31. Hill to Clarke, 28 September 1809, Egerton MS. 933. Adam Clarke commanded several languages, including Arabic. See his entry in *Dictionary of National Biography*. The BFBS so appreciated his translation work that they appealed to the Methodist Conference to allow him to remain in London to continue it. See BFBS Minutes of the Committee, 15 June and 5 October 1807, vol. 3, pp. 40, 62 (BSA/B1/3).

32. A vocabulary of the Jaloff language, prepared by Hill at Goree and Senegal, with a letter from Hill to Clarke, 28 September 1809, Egerton MS. 933. Hill gave reasons for the Damel's treatment. The Damel was disappointed because Hill came dressed in "plain clothes," when Damel had expected a "Commissioned Officer in full & rich uniform!" Hill had offered no presents, and the Damel was prejudiced against those from Gorée as some of his soldiers had been sold there as slaves.

33. Mungo Park, *Travels in Africa*, ed. R. Miller for Everyman's Library (reprint,

Before leaving England in 1807, Hill had agreed to collect information for the BFBS "respecting the knowledge the natives of this part of the Coast had of the Arabic language." He was able to report that their knowledge of Arabic was good, and to give proof of this he sent the Society several Arabic manuscripts he had collected.[34] Books and manuscripts being highly valued among Muslims in West Africa, there was broad support at the end of the eighteenth century for disseminating Christianity through the translation of the Scriptures into Arabic. Mungo Park related that he had been shown an Arabic edition of one of the Gospels, and in *The Missionary Magazine* of May 1798, a query appeared whether any Bible societies had considered printing an Arabic Bible for distribution in Africa. In 1799, inspired by reports that Arabic was read extensively in parts of Africa, J. D. Carlyle, professor of Arabic at Cambridge, proposed publishing a new edition of the Scriptures in Arabic. Carlyle's unexpected death and a difficulty over the contract for types put a stop to the work for some time. The CMS, interested in the distribution of Arabic tracts, cooperated with the Edinburgh Missionary Society in 1805 to print an Arabic tract addressed to "Mahometans," written by the first Susu translator, Henry Brunton.[35]

The BFBS became involved in the project in 1806 at the suggestion of Bishop Porteus of London and Bishop Shute Barrington of Durham. Porteus wrote to Lord Teignmouth that the decision to print an Arabic version of the Scriptures for Africa would "redound no less to the credit of the Society than to the benefit of that numerous unenlightened race for whom it is designed, *the Moors of Africa*" [emphasis in the original]. He felt African Muslims were more ripe for conversion than non-Muslims.

London: Dent, 1969), p. 241. Pocket book of John Hill. Hill to Tarn, 9 August 1808, BFBS Home Correspondence Inwards (BSA/D1/1/3), in which Hill says that the view prevailed that Park had been murdered. Hill to Tarn, 28 September 1809, BFBS Home Correspondence Inwards (BSA/D1/1/4). In this subsequent letter Hill stated that reports had been received that Park had passed "Jenne" in his boat with Lieut. Martyn and a private, and that the "King of Jenne sent a party after them with orders to drown them in the Joliba!" Not until 1811 was the full story of Park's death reported.

34. Hill to Tarn, 31 May 1808, BFBS Home Correspondence Inwards (BSA/D1/1/3). Enclosed with this letter were four Arabic manuscripts. Two are single sheets, probably for amulets; the other two consist of 8 and 16 pages, respectively. They are now in the BFBS manuscripts collection (BSMS 492).

35. Park, *Travels in Africa*, p. 241. *Missionary Magazine for 1798*, no. 24, p. 231; *Missionary Magazine for 1799*, no. 35, pp. 217-18; no. 39, pp. 337-41. John Owen, *History of the Origins and First Ten Years of the British and Foreign Bible Society*, 2 vols. (London: Tilling and Hughes, 1816), vol. 1, pp. 299-304. It is clear that Park's information had influenced the attitudes of those engaged in Arabic translations. CMS Committee Minutes 1, 1, 15 April 1799-3 May 1813, 1 July 1799, 4 March and 1 July 1805 (G/Cl); Minutes of Subcommittee, 6 March 1805 (GCS/1).

Henry Ford, Reader in Arabic at Oxford, continued Carlyle's work, and the Arabic version of the Bible was eventually printed in 1811.[36]

It is not surprising therefore that John Hill was asked to collect information by the Society. In his journal, Hill recorded how he collected the specimens in Arabic. The first mention was on 14 January 1808, when two men from "fottah" (Futa) came to ask him for paper. In exchange for this, they wrote some Arabic for him. Later that month he similarly obtained another specimen from a "Mahomedan from Ducar." The following day another man from Dakar asked for paper, to which Hill agreed in return for a "full sheet of Arabic" and some sugar. Hill added that he had some difficulty in getting the writer to leave his room, "for perceiving that I was much pleased with his performance he multiplied and repeated his requests until I almost got out of temper." Another problem for Hill was his limited supply of paper, this being the most acceptable form of payment for the written Arabic. Demanet had observed that paper was in great demand because the Marabouts used it to write *grisgris* using parts of the Qur'an.[37]

Hill's other disadvantage was not having a copy of Richardson's standard Arabic grammar with him. Park had recorded showing it to a Marabout, who admired it, and to some "Slatees on the Gambia," who were "astonished to think that any European should understand and write the sacred language of their religion." Thomas Winterbottom, the Sierra Leone Company doctor in 1794, reported a similar experience. He had shown some Africans Richardson's Arabic dictionary, and they had pronounced the words "very nearly as they are there written, and in general explaining the meaning of them very exactly." Hill had read Park's book and perhaps was aware of Winterbottom's account.[38]

---

36. *al-Kitāb al-muqaddas wa hiya kutub al-`ahd al-`atīq wa'l-`ahd al-jadīd/The Holy Bible... in the Arabic Language* (Newcastle-upon-Tyne: Sarah Hodgson, 1811). The BFBS contributed £250 to this publication. See T. H. Darlow and H. F. Moule, comps., *Historical Catalogue of the Printed Editions of Holy Scripture in the Library of the British and Foreign Bible Society*, 2 vols. in 4 (London: BFBS, 1903–1911), no. 1663 (hereafter DM). See also Owen, *History*, vol. 1, pp. 281-29, 305-307; and Charles J. Shore, *Memoir of the Life and Correspondence of Lord Teignmouth*, 2 vols. (London: Hatchard and Son, 1843), vol. 2, pp. 104-107. William Canton, *A History of the British and Foreign Bible Society*, 5 vols. (London: John Murray, 1904–1910), vol. 1, pp. 133-34. BFBS Minutes of the Committee, 5 January, 2 February, 7 September 1807; 4 January, 7 March, 18 April, 6 June, 4 July 1808, vol. 3, pp. 2, 8, 55, 83, 96, 122, 133, 144 (BSA/B1/3).

37. Pocket book of John Hill, 14, 23, and 24 January 1808. Hill to Tarn, 31 May 1808, BFBS Home Correspondence Inwards (BSA/D1/1/3). M. l'Abbé Demanet, *Nouvelle Histoire de l'Afrique françoise* (Paris: Chez la veuve Duchesne, 1767), vol. 1, p. 248.

38. Hill to Tarn, 31 May 1808, BFBS Home Correspondence Inwards (BSA/D1/1/3). John Richardson, *A Grammar of the Arabick Language* (London: William Richardson for J. Murray, and D. Prince, 1776). Also John Richardson, *A Dictionary of Persian, Arabic*

In a letter of 31 May 1808, Hill stated that the *Lively*, which had brought him to Gorée, had recently arrived, and that he had borrowed a copy of Richardson's Arabic grammar from Captain Blakesley, who "will not part with it under one Guinea." When Hill had shown parts of the book to a Wolof on the island, the man had expressed his astonishment in Arabic and read sections with "facility." To verify if the man understood what he had read, he was asked to explain the meaning in Wolof and by signs, which satisfied Hill that the man had "perfectly understood what he had read; even the different verbs with their conjugations were intelligible to him." In October, while visiting Dakar, Hill showed a copy of Richardson's book to some Muslims,

> but could only find one or two who seemed to have any knowledge of it. The Arabic Characters being printed with a type so much finer & smaller than they are accustomed to, besides the different formation of the vowel points as well as the different placing of them, renders them more difficult to be understood.

While at the Damel's residence, Hill showed an "ambassador" the Arabic grammar, and the man was "astonished to find his favorite language so clean & beautifully written."[39]

If Christianity in Senegal and on Gorée showed traces of the African cultural heritage, Islam also was "cast in an African cultural mould." Captain George Howland, who travelled to Gorée and the mainland in 1811 and visited a Qur'anic school where the children were learning Arabic, spoke of the Wolof being Muslim "mixed in with their own native idolatry and paganism." Of the Muslim festivals, Hill wrote of only one, on 7 February:

> This day I am informed is a great day among the Mahomedans & tho' part of it is spent by them in acts of worship or Offering which They call *Tobasky*, yet the other part is spent in the same manner English spend an Holy-day.[40]

and *English*, 2 vols. (Oxford: Clarendon Press, 1777). Park, *Travels in Africa*, p. 242. Thomas Masterman Winterbottom, *An Account of the Native Africans in the Neighbourhood of Sierra Leone to which is added an Account of the Present State of Medicine among them*, 2nd ed. (reprint, London: Frank Cass & Co., 1969), vol. 1, p. 221.

39. Hill to Tarn, 31 May 1808, BFBS Home Correspondence Inwards (BSA/D1/1/3). Pocket book of John Hill, 4 October and 14 [December] 1808. Hill did not say to whom Richardson's *Grammar* belonged.

40. L. G. Colvin, "Islam and the State of Kajoor: A Case of Successful Resistance to Jihad," *Journal of African History* 15, no. 4 (1974), p. 593. For Captain Howland's account, see Norman R. Bennett and George E. Brooks, Jr., eds., *New England Merchants in Africa: A History Through Documents, 1802 to 1865* (Boston: Boston University Press, 1965), pp. 60-61. The latter includes an account of Capt. George Howland, who made another recorded visit in 1822–1823. Pocket book of John Hill. *Tobasky* is 'Id al-Adha and is celebrated in Senegambia.

Hill differentiated at times between Muslim Wolof and "Khefer Jaloffs" or "Pagans," saying that the Muslims learned to read and write Arabic, whereas the "Khefers" did not. He believed the majority of "Mahomedans in Kajor & the Jaloff Kingdom are originally Jaloff Khefers or Pagans. Many to my knowledge are connected by family ties to Pagan families."[41]

Writing to Tarn in May and June 1808, Hill asked the Society to send him a copy of Richardson's Arabic grammar, as well as any parts of the Scriptures that had been translated into Arabic, but he felt that it would be difficult to introduce an Arabic Bible "or prevail on the Mahometans to peruse it." However, as the Muslims in the area were "particularly fond of the Storry of Joseph & his brethren, & many other of Moses writings," he suggested introducing these first.[42]

The Arabic manuscripts that Hill sent to the BFBS at the end of May 1808, were reported by Adam Clarke to be "very fair, tho' not elegant specimens of the African Nisk." Clarke felt certain any printed Arabic Bible sent to the area would be easily read. He suggested sending John Hill copies of Richardson's Arabic grammar and his Persian and Arabic dictionary, as well as a supply of paper, all of which Hill received at Sierra Leone in 1809. Clarke also stated that John Hill was of the opinion that if the Scriptures "were printed in the *Jaloff* language, they would be recd [received], & read by a numerous class of Mahamedans who speak that Language." He added that, to show the Society what the language was like, Hill had "with considerable pains & industry formed a short vocabulary."[43]

John Hill compiled his Wolof vocabularies while at Gorée or when on the Senegal mainland. He had seen the work of at least three other Europeans — namely, Golberry, Park, and Corry — who had listed Wolof words in their books, and he criticized all of them for their pronunciation and

---

41. Hill to Clarke, 28 September 1809, Egerton MS. 933. While the minority of Western scholars in recent years have accepted the antithesis of Muslim Wolof and non-Muslim or semi-pagan Wolof, Colvin has refuted this as a misinterpretation caused by "our ethnocentric perspective." The true antithesis was between the clerical and secular parties. Instead of viewing the Wolof as only partly Islamised, "it would be more appropriate to see the idiosyncracies of Wolof Islam as revealing a depth of faith in a predominantly unlettered society very similar to medieval Europe." See Colvin, "Islam and the State of Kajoor," pp. 593, 602.

42. Hill to Tarn, 31 May and 10 June 1808, BFBS Home Correspondence Inwards (BSA/D1/1/3). Hill also wrote a letter on 10 June to "Mrs H" (see Pocket book of John Hill). After that there is no further mention of Mary Hill in his journal or letters.

43. Report of Adam Clarke, 2 January 1809, BFBS Correspondence Book no.3, p.121 (BSA/D1/5/3); BFBS Minutes of the Committee, 2 January and 6 February 1809, vol. 3, pp. 195-96, 202-203 (BSA/B1/3). At the latter meeting, the Committee were presented with a revised report by Clarke, and they agreed to encourage John Hill and send him Richardson's books and a supply of paper.

errors. Golberry had "most egregiously misapplied the greater part of his Jaloff Nouns! Neither has he divided the words in a sentence as they ought to be!" And Corry had "unblushingly" copied Golberry. Hill's work differed from those earlier lists in that he set out to make a study of Wolof so that his work might be useful in having Biblical texts translated into the language. If he remained in the area for any length of time, he expected "to be able to translate some of the most important parts of the sacred writings." He worked in the hope that his efforts would be recognized. Only his genuine intellectual interest and ambition could have sustained him, for he admitted that while at Gorée, his work "met with some little Jeerings from some in this place."[44]

What prompted Hill to take an interest in Wolof is not known. His contact with the BFBS certainly influenced him, and in his earlier years he would have known of the activities of Peter Greig and Henry Brunton, who had been sent to Sierra Leone by the Edinburgh Missionary Society in 1798. Indeed, Brunton had compiled the first books in Susu, published in 1802. Also, during Hill's employment with the Sierra Leone Company, he had seen missionary work and was familiar with the recommendation that missionaries acquire a knowledge of the area's indigenous languages.[45]

On 16 January 1808, Hill wrote in his journal that he had made "some application to the Jeoliff language, Completed in words and sentences about Three hundred and fifty — of such as are correct." This was the first indication of his interest in Wolof, just two months after his arrival at Gorée. Two days later, he again recorded spending time on the language. He made an attempt "to join a few Jeoliff words & sentences & to translate them into English." His exercise was: "My Excellent girl, come to my heart. I love you. You are beautiful in my eyes. You are very young but very good. Kiss me. My heart beats with pleasure." This was not the example he sent back to the Society. On January 25, he again "applied to the Geoliff." While not again specifically mentioning his work on Wolof, he wrote various journal entries in the language. This should not give the impression that he was able to speak Wolof, for he found it difficult to follow conversations and required an interpreter when he visited the Damel.[46]

44. Wolof Vocabulary of John Hill, Goree, 1 June 1808, BFBS manuscripts collection (BSMS 490). Hill to Clarke, 28 September 1809, Egerton MS. 933. Hill to Tarn, 31 May 1808, BFBS Home Correspondence Inwards (BSA/D1/1/3). Hill's vocabularies and Pocket book have been prepared for publication by Professor David Gamble and Patricia Mirrlees.

45. P. E. H. Hair, "The Sierra Leone Settlement — The Earliest Attempts to Study African Languages," *Sierra Leone Language Review* 2 (1963), p. 7. Brown, *History of the Propagation of Christianity*, vol. 2, pp. 415-20.

46. Pocket book of John Hill, 16 and 18 January 1808.

In his letters, Hill revealed more of how he compiled his vocabularies. He wrote to Adam Clarke that "it was by frequent excursions to several places on the mainland in the company with some of the principal Inhabitants ... as well as a pretty constant intercourse with the youth of both sexes, that I was enabled to collect my Vocabulary!" He found that the Wolof spoken on the mainland was much purer than that on Gorée, so that when he mentioned words for parts of the body, "some of the oldest and most intelligent Inhabitants of Goree could not understand," although they were "perfectly intelligible & familiar to people in the interior of the Jaloff Country." Edward Bickersteth wrote that the Wolof spoken on Gorée would "hardly be understood in some other parts" as it incorporated French, English and Portuguese.[47]

Hill repudiated Golberry's assertion that the language was poor and said that it was "both appropriate, copious and significant," thus echoing the words of Mungo Park. He said that he had an ardent desire to study the language but that it required someone with more general knowledge and abilities "whose circumstances might enable him to appropriate his time chiefly to its study." Hill stated that one of his own early vocabularies was so correct that he never read it to the Wolofs "without exciting in them the greatest surprise." Of his last vocabulary he wrote that it was more correct than the previous one, and as to its correctness all the principal Inhabitants of Gorée were "willing to certify the same by their signatures, if I thought it necessary, before I left that place!"[48]

In all, John Hill compiled four vocabularies in Wolof and English. One was a draft vocabulary that was a part of his journal. It was probably the earliest and consisted of about 454 words and 26 phrases, the days of the week, and numerals from 1-1200. The first vocabulary he sent to the BFBS, dated 1 June 1808, included an introduction on pronunciation, about 460 words and 227 phrases, the days of the week, numbers from 1-30, the qualities of palm wine, and an attempt at translating the Lord's Prayer into Wolof. His third vocabulary, finished on 10 August 1808, was an improved and revised version, which he also sent to the Society. It had an introduction on pronunciation, about 663 words and 168 phrases, the days of the week, numbers from 1-1100, and points of the compass. It was not until he had received some response from the Society, and Adam Clarke in

---

47. Pocket book of John Hill. Hill to Clarke, 28 September 1809, Egerton MS. 933. "Journal of... Edward Bickersteth," 28 February 1816 (CMS: Z.26). Hill to Tarn, 9 August 1808, BFBS Home Correspondence Inwards (BSA/D1/1/3).

48. Hill to Clarke, 28 September 1809, Egerton MS. 933. Hill to Tarn, 8 August 1808, BFBS Home Correspondence Inwards (BSA/D1/1/3). Park, *Travels in Africa*, p. 12. Here Park described Wolof as "copious and significant." Hill to Tarn, 31 May 1808, BFBS Home Correspondence Inwards (BSA/D1/1/3).

particular, that he sent his fourth and last vocabulary to Dr. Clarke. Finished in September 1809 while Hill was in Sierra Leone, it was "considerably enlarged." It consisted of about 826 words with a few phrases, numbers from 1-1000, months of the year, days of the week, the points of the compass, and a rudimentary grammar section on declension of nouns, pronouns, comparison of adjectives, and verbs of various tenses.

One of Hill's main problems had been the spelling of Wolof. In his introduction to the first vocabulary he sent to the BFBS, he wrote, "I am persuaded that no two persons will be found to spell it in the same way... I have seen Mr Park's & a Frenchman's manner of spelling the numerals, & when I compare them with my own, I see we all differ." Professor David Gamble was to write almost 150 years later that the spelling of Wolof is "in an extremely confused state." Hill experimented with various ways of spelling the guttural sounds in Wolof. In the first vocabulary he sent to the Society, he used a symbol to denote the guttural sound; in the second one, he used *kh*, as in Arabic, at the beginning of a word, and *gh* at the middle or end. Similarly, he also indicated the difficulties with sounds like *j* or *g*, which were nearer to *gy* or *dy*. Thus the word for hatred could be written *dyepa* or *jepa*.[49]

Hill felt that it was a "misfortune" that *gh* had lost all its sound in "fashionable English." As a Scot, he had an advantage in being able to easily pronounce the guttural Wolof sounds. He wrote that the sounds he wished to produce in Wolof, such as *gh*, were "exactly the same as they would produce in the following words if pronounced by an old fashioned Scotsman, viz., laugh, cough, sought, bought, caught, Daughter, slaughter, not lauff, couff, sout, baut, Dauter, slauter; a pronunciation like this where the spelling & original sound is so different appears to me highly incompatible."[50]

---

49. Pocket book of John Hill (Vocabulary of the Jaloff language). Wolof Vocabulary of John Hill, Goree, 1 June 1808, BFBS manuscripts collection (BSMS 490); Wolof Vocabulary of John Hill, Goree, 10 August 1808, BFBS manuscripts collection (BSMS 491); and Wolof Vocabulary of John Hill, 27 September 1809, Egerton MS. 933. David P. Gamble, *The Wolof of Senegambia Together with Notes on the Lebu and the Serer* (London: International African Institute, 1967), p. 22. Since the 1970s the script has been standardised by law.

50. Wolof Vocabulary of John Hill, Goree, 10 August 1808, BFBS manuscripts collection (BSMS 491). Hill said he was aware that the guttural sounds seemed "uncouth" to an Englishman. See Lindsay, *Voyage to the Coast of Africa*, p. 55. Lindsay found Wolof a "very uncouth dialect" and stated he could not distinguish pleasantries from threats. If Wolof reminded Hill of Scottish pronunciation, it reminded John Morgan, a Methodist missionary at the Gambia, of Welsh. See Rev. John Morgan, *Reminiscences of the Founding of a Christian Mission on the Gambia* (London: Wesleyan Mission House, 1864), p. 41.

Hill's vocabularies provide a window into Gorée society and the Wolof Senegalese environment at that time. Comparing his fourth vocabulary with that of Angrand in his *Manuel Français-Wolof*, there are many similarities of words. Regarding the weather, Hill included words such as *guelany* (tornado), which Angrand spelled *nguelane*, and *Tow* (rain), rendered by Angrand as *tao*. Geographical references are *degh*: a river (Angrand-*dekh*); *soof*: the ground, sand (Angrand *souf*). For the concept of time Hill had words such as *utt*: a year (Angrand *atte*); *ulluck*: tomorrow (Angrand *elek*). The parts of the body that he listed are numerous and detailed, such as *legaite*: a scar (Angrand *léguète*); *hom*: a knee (Angrand *om*). He also included illnesses and body functions such as *wotiow*: to vomit (Angrand *votchiou*); *logh*: palsy (Angrand *lokh*). There are words to describe occupations such as *sama*: shepherd (Angrand *samme*); *togacat*: cook (Angrand *toguekat*). Hill included many words for animals, birds, fish, insects, and reptiles, and words connected with them, such as *jergoine*: spider (Angrand *diargogne*); *khointan*: firefly (Angrand *khouyantane*). There are also words connected with hunting, fishing, eating, and agriculture.[51]

Some of the observations he made with his fourth vocabulary are of interest. *Ndupa* was a "narrow piece of plain or striped cotton, about two inches wide used by the Jaloff women in wraping round the head." *Ndowla* was also a piece of cloth for the head, broadest in the middle "consisting of a square of near twelve inches. This square is for covering the crown of the head & defending it from the sun." He added that the ladies of Gorée generally did not wear these to visit but would substitute instead "elegant coloured Handkerchiefs which they fasten round the head in a very decent & agreeable manner!" For the word *diangallee*, meaning to pillage or plunder an enemy, he added that "the Inhabitants of Senegal and Goree apply this word to Privateers and man of wars, stationed on the western coast of Africa! It was particularly often applied to the late Captain Parker of H.M.S. Darwent, & chiefly in consequence of his seizing their craft coming from the Gambia & other rivers with slaves!"[52]

---

51. Wolof Vocabulary of John Hill, Egerton MS. 933. Armand-Pierre Angrand, *Manuel Français-Ouolof* (Dakar: Librairie Maurice Viale, 1940.), pp. 29-54. Professor Gamble pointed out in a note to Patricia Mirrlees that Angrand was not a linguist and his spelling was derived from French, with a French readership in mind. While Hill had collected a great number of words, he had not understood the construction of Wolof grammar and would substitute word for word Wolof for English in sentences, often producing nonsensical Wolof.

52. Wolof Vocabulary of John Hill. Egerton MS. 933. Capt. Frederick Parker arrived at Gorée in February 1808 on his ship *HMS Derwent*, visiting the island again in May and June. He had been involved in the capture of two American ships carrying slaves, and this was brought before the court at Sierra Leone. He drowned during the capture of St. Louis in June 1809. It is possible that Hill had met him. See Pocket book of John

The majority of the phrases Hill included occurred in the first and second vocabularies that he sent to the Society. They were arranged in alphabetical order and were of a miscellaneous nature. With regard to numbers, Hill said that the Wolofs could easily calculate to one million. The "Kheffer Jaloffs," who had no knowledge of writing or numbers would use the forefinger or middlefinger of the right hand to "strike off so many marks in the sand, & then multiply these by such a number as may be required, such a number of Multiplicand being merely conceived of! It is only, however, in matters of importance that they have recourse to this method!" When Clarke studied the Wolof numbers that Hill sent, he concluded that because they counted by fives, the Wolof were an ancient and "unmixed people; as this was the mode in numberation which prevailed among the aboriginal inhabitants of the world, in their rude & barbarous State."[53]

Adam Clarke assessed the Wolof language as "irregular gibberish, adorned here & there with arabic words, which may be easily detected." He felt Hill's observations of the language were imperfect because of the little time Hill had to study it, but he stressed that it was curious and "of considerable importance even in a philological point of view." He then wrote to Hill in March 1809, and asked him to attempt to analyze the language to form a grammar, giving him a structural basis from which to work. It was in response to this that Hill attempted a grammatical analysis in his last vocabulary.[54]

In the spring of 1809, because of financial difficulties, John Hill decided to leave Gorée, despite his fondness for the island and its people and his increasing interest and work on the Wolof language. Hill wrote that his government appointment had been "but barely sufficient to support the necessary expences of a very economical and plain method of housekeeping: And as the Commandant (tho' very willing) could not better my income without advices from home, I resolved trying my fortune once more at Sierra Leone!" In his letter to Governor Thompson of Sierra Leone, Major Maxwell wrote in April 1809 that Hill was about to leave for Sierra Leone "to Solicit some employment" and that he had conducted himself to Maxwell's satisfaction. He had found Hill "forward in executing any

Hill. Hill to Tarn, 28 September 1809, BFBS Home Correspondence Inwards (BSA/D1/1/9). Fyfe, *A History of Sierra Leone*, pp. 106-107.

53. Wolof Vocabulary of John Hill, Goree, 1 June 1808 (BSMS 490); Wolof Vocabulary of John Hill, Goree, 10 August 1808 (BSMS 491); and Wolof Vocabulary of John Hill, Egerton MS. 933. Report of Dr. A. Clarke, 2 January 1809, BFBS Correspondence Books, no. 3, p. 121 (BFS/D1/5/3).

54. Report of Dr. A. Clarke (BFS/D1/5/3). Clarke to J. Hill, London, 1 March 1809, BFBS Correspondence Book no. 3, pp. 120-122 (BSA/D1/5/3).

Service" he required of him. Maxwell added that Hill had "met with some disappointments in his views, in life; and is anxious to be employed so as to be useful to the community and to benefit himself."[55]

Worried over money, and having received no intimation of employment from the BFBS for whom he had collected and dispatched Arabic manuscripts and compiled Wolof vocabularies, John Hill set sail for Sierra Leone on 6 April 1809. Unknown to him, the Society had a month earlier sent replies, along with copies of Richardson's books and a supply of paper. It was typical of his bad luck that these arrived after he left. He later wrote that, if he had received them while at Gorée, he would have remained there, whatever the financial problems. He reached Sierra Leone on 21April. Having shown his letter of recommendation from Commandant Maxwell to Governor Thompson, Hill was given a government appointment. On 6 May he was made superintendent of the Smiths Department at a salary of £150 per annum. In his letter to Adam Clarke of September 1809, Hill wrote that because he had been trained as an edge tool maker, the governor had thought him the "fittest person" for the Smiths Department, "where all kinds of work for gun carriages & in short iron work for every part of Public works is done." On 12 September he was appointed for the year ensuing as a "Commissioner of Requests."[56]

Hill did not envision his stay in Sierra Leone as permanent, stating his desire to return to "the dear little island, which I shall always love," and that Major Maxwell had told him "that if I did not meet with a situation at Sierra Leone to my liking, he would make me hearty welcome to resume my situation at Goree!" To continue his linguistic work and form a Wolof grammar, it was imperative that he return to Gorée or Senegal, and he suggested to Clarke that if the BFBS or any other "whose object may be, the Civilizing or christianizing of Africa, would allow me a small salary (say £200 stg.) or otherwise provide for annual necessaries," he would work for them in whatever capacity was required. He continued, "There are now a number of good houses built on Dakar by the Inhabitants of Goree, in any one of which a person employed by the Society might live with comfort and safety! I am certain the rent would be but trifling." While someone who was employed by the government would "ease the Society of the burthen of a Salary...it would be altogether uncertain, what

55. Hill to Tarn, 28 September 1809, BFBS Home Correspondence Inward (BSA/ D1/1/4). Hill to Clarke, 28 September 1809, Egerton MS. 933. Maxwell to Thompson, 4 April 1809 (HUL: DTH/1/67). In July 1808, Hill had spent a few days with Governor Thompson when he stopped at Gorée en route for Sierra Leone. See Pocket book of John Hill.

56. Hill to Tarn, 28 September 1809, BFBS Home Correspondence Inwards (BSA/ D1/1/4). Hill to Clarke, 28 September 1809, Egerton MS. 933. Copy of Minutes of Council Papers, Sierra Leone, 6 May 1809 (HUL: DTH/1/57).

time or opportunities, a person in such a case might have to the study of the great object of the Society." Hill added that if the BFBS, "which I am chearfully willing to serve should approve of the above hint," he hoped Dr. Clarke would let him know as soon as possible.[57]

In earlier letters, Hill had mentioned Gorée or Dakar as a suitable place for a Christian mission. He observed that they were as favourable as any other place "to attempt an introduction of the scriptures or any part of them, as any Mahomedan country in Africa," mainly because of the character of the "King of Dakar." Son of a Marabout, Dial Diop was regarded as a learned man who had successfully liberated his people, the Lebu, from the yoke of the Damel of Kayor. Hill admired him, writing in May 1808 that he was "a humane and rational man, much esteemed, not only by all his subjects, but by every person who has any knowledge of him, & a person who would be even proud to protect any well behaved European, who might reside in his town or any part belonging to him." In June 1808, Hill wrote further that although Dial Diop was a "strict Mahomedan, he is devested of all bigotry & has no doubt but Christians worship the same God as he does, and as sincerely too. He is very rational in his conversation, & appears well acquainted with human life!" Hill said he was "astonish'd that none of the Missionary Societies have ever thought of trying a Mission in this part of Africa... I think this part of the coast while Goree is in the hands of the English quite as promising to any leeward. I am certain a Mission might at least be tried with much less expense." Hill in his final letter of September 1809 suggested to Clarke that Gorée would be a good place for a "prudent, well behaved person, employed by the Society for Missions to Africa and the East."[58]

In letters to Adam Clarke and Joseph Tarn, John Hill stated his intention of leaving Sierra Leone as soon as possible, and he thought it might be toward the end of October, "in a vessel then expected to sail to Goree." With his return imminent, Hill asked the Society to send him up to three hundred copies of the Bible or New Testament in French, as these would be easily read by the men on Gorée, but less so by the women, who though more religiously inclined, were "suffered by their parents to grow up without the least knowledge of letters!" After these letters of September 1809, the BFBS received nothing more from John Hill. Similarly, after the Council minutes of October 1, there is no further mention of John Hill. Neither

---

57. Hill to Tarn, 28 September 1809, BFBS Home Correspondence Inwards (BSA/D1/1/4). Hill to Clarke, 28 September 1809, Egerton MS. 933.

58. Hill to Tarn, Goree, 31 May, 10 June, and 9 August 1808, BFBS Home Correspondence Inwards (BSA/D1/1/3). Hill to Clarke, 28 September 1809, Egerton MS. 933. For Dial Diop, see Armand-Pierre Angrand, *Les Lébous de la Presqu'île du Cap Vert* (Dakar: Distributeur E. Gensal, 1946).

The Sierra Leone Gazette nor *The African Herald* contains any reference to his death. There are, however, two brief references to Hill in the Public Record Office. One, dated 10 March 1810, is found under the heading of "Sundry Debts." It reads, "Due from the estate of the late John Hill and Bills drawn by Govr. Thompson on Cashier £71.9.0¾. Signed late cashier, F. Leedham." On 24 March 1810, in a "Book of Debts in the Civil Store," there is the entry, "John Hill, £6.11.6."[59]

In the minutes of the Bible Society for 30 April 1810, it was recorded that Hill's letter of 28 September 1809 had been received and read, but after that there is no further reference to him. John Hill's death occurred between 1 October 1809 and the date of the list of debts, March 1810. During his earlier period in Sierra Leone, illness had forced him back to England. The climate on Gorée had been healthier because of the sea breezes and cooler temperatures. Indeed one visitor heard it described as "the Hospital of Africa," since many came to recuperate on the island. In his last letter of September 1809, Hill had related that the rains were very severe and that many were ill, and that he had suffered from one "pretty smart attack of fever, which with God's goodness, I have got pretty well over."[60]

The first book to be published in Wolof and English as a linguistic work appeared in 1820. Its author was Hannah Kilham, a member of the Society of Friends, who was helped by her two Wolof-speaking African assistants, Mahmadee and Sandanee. Jean Dard, who had taught in Senegal from 1817 to 1820 and had studied Wolof there, published his Wolof-French dictionary in 1825 and a Wolof grammar in 1826. The first portion of the Bible printed in Wolof was the Gospel of Matthew, translated by A. Villéger of the Paris Missionary Society, and published by the Bible Society of France in 1873.[61]

---

59. Hill to Tarn, 28 September 1809, BFBS Home Correspondence Inwards (BSA/D1/1/4). Hill to Clarke, 28 September 1809, Egerton MS. 933. "Sundry specie on hand according to the Current prices amounting to Paper Money of the Sierra Leone Company... Sundry Debts, including 'Book Debts due to the Civil Store at Sierra Leone,' as it was left by Gov.Thompson," 24 March 1810 (PRO: CO/267/27).

60. BFBS Minutes of the Committee 30 April 1810, vol. 4 p. 173 (BSA/B1/4). "Journal of . . . Edward Bickersteth," 29 February 1816 (CMS: Z.26). Hill to Tarn, 28 September 1809, BFBS Home Correspondence Inwards (BSA/D1/1/4).

61. Hannah Kilham, *Ta-re Wa-loof, Ta-re boo Juk-a: First lessons in Jaloof* (London, 1820). The Kilham work was published anonymously. Jean Dard, *Dictionnaire Français-Wolof et Français-Bambara, Suivi d'un Dictionnaire Wolof-Français* (Paris: Imprimerie royale, 1825); *Grammaire Wolof, ou Méthode pour Etudier la Langue des Noirs qui Habitent les Royaumes de Bourba Yolof, de Walo, de Damel, de Bour Sine, de Saloume, de Baole en Sénégambie, Suivi d'un Appendice où Sont Etablies les Particularités les Plus Essentielles des Principales Langues de l'Afrique Septentrionale* (Paris: Imprimerie royale, 1826). For the 1873 Gospel of Matthew, see *Sounou Evañsil ou Borom Yésou-Krista naka Mato mou sèlã*

John Hill's four vocabularies and his attempt at a grammar differ from the travel accounts of his day and are the earliest study of Wolof so far discovered. Their value lies not only in their accuracy and the richness of their vocabularies, but also in the early material they provide for the historical study of the development and changes of the Wolof language. They predate Dard's work by about nine years, and Kilham's by twelve. They also include words found in neither of the earliest Wolof books. It was unfortunate for Hill that during his lifetime his work was not given more support, and that with his death his vocabularies and journals were scattered and disappeared for so long into obscurity. Hill's life was never free from financial insecurity, and it was his misfortune to lack influence, wealth, and luck; hence, his unsuccessful attempts to seek the patronage of Adam Clarke and the BFBS, and to win recognition for his Wolof work. Had he lived, might that patronage have been forthcoming?

---

mŭ (Paris: Société Biblique de France, 1873), noted also in G.E. Coldham, *A Bibliography of Scriptures in African Languages* (London: BFBS, 1966), no. 1165.

ANONYMOUS BIBLE TRANSLATORS: NATIVE LITERATI AND THE
TRANSLATION OF THE BIBLE INTO CHINESE, 1807–1907

Thor Strandenaes

In her novel *The Exile*, China-born Pearl S. Buck, winner of the Nobel Prize in literature, has given a beautiful portrait of her mother Carrie ("Carie").[1] Touching briefly also on the life-long Bible translation work of her father, the Rev. Absalom ["Andrew"] Sydenstricker,[2] she mentions another important person, his Chinese tutor and linguistic consultant: "One of the members of our household came to be the old, stooped Chinese scholar who came often at his request to consult with him about style and phrases".[3] Neither in Pearl Buck's biographical account of her mother nor of her father does the name of the scholar appear, only the names of other Chinese, such as the serving woman, Wang Amah, the adoptive daughter Precious Cloud, the evangelist Li, and the preachers, Mr. Ma and Mr. Rao.[4] In Pearl Buck's writings, the Chinese scholar remains anonymous, and nothing beyond the consultations on Chinese style and

1. Pearl S. Buck, *The Exile* (London: Methuen & Co., 1936). Pearl Sydenstricker Buck (1892-1973) received the Nobel Prize in 1938. In her Nobel lecture, she paid tribute to Chinese novelists and to literature in daily language. See Pearl S. Buck, *The Chinese Novel: Nobel Lecture Delivered before the Swedish Academy at Stockholm, Dec. 12, 1938.* (London: Macmillan & Co., 1939).

2. Carrie and Absalom Sydenstricker of the American Presbyterian Mission arrived in 1811 in China, where he prepared a version in Mandarin of the New Testament and also contributed to the Union Old Testament Mandarin Version. For editions, see Hubert W. Spillett, comp., *A Catalogue of Scriptures in the Languages of China and the Republic of China* (London: British and Foreign Bible Society, 1975), nos. 447, 490a, and 490b. On Sydenstricker's translation, see Jost Oliver Zetzsche, *The Bible in China: The History of the Union Version, or the Culmination of Protestant Missionary Bible Translation in China*, Monumenta Serica Monograph Series, no. 45 (Nettetal: Steyler Verlag, 1999), p. 311-14 and 330. The portrait Buck gives of her father reveals traits of a person who, though earnestly committed to his service among the Chinese, had only a superficial and non-committed relationship with his children. Pearl S. Buck, *Fighting Angel: Portrait of a Soul* (New York: P. F. Collier & Son, 1936).

3. See Buck, *The Exile*, p. 125.

4. See Buck, *The Exile*, pp. 89-91, 121, 147-49, and 140, respectively; also Buck, *Fighting Angel*, pp. 101, 179, 98, 130, and 179, respectively.

phrases is said of his work. It is known from other sources, however, that the scholar was Zhu Baohui, and that he later prepared his own version of the New Testament, translating from the Greek.[5] Here and elsewhere in the history of the first hundred years of Protestant Chinese Bible translation, it is rather typical that the names of the Chinese scholars are not mentioned, notwithstanding the obvious importance of their work.[6] When paintings or pictures of the missionary translators and their Chinese co-workers were publicized, the names of the latter were often only briefly identified. Whereas the names of the European and American translators can normally be found with full titles and academic degrees as well as the names of the missionary societies they represented, the information about their Chinese co-workers is either given in a block reference,[7] or in a reference using the Chinese surname only with, at most, the city, region, or province of his origin.[8]

---

5. Spillett, *Catalogue of Scriptures*, nos. 490a and 490b. According to Spillett, the Mandarin version is said to have been translated by A. Sydenstricker. Unfortunately no mention is made of the real translator, Zhu Baohui, and that this was his independent work. At first Zhu Baohui was A. Sydenstricker's co-worker and consultant on the Mandarin NT version Sydenstricker prepared, published in 1913 (Gospels) and 1929 (NT). See Zetzsche, *The Bible in China*, p. 311-14. When in 1929 Sydenstricker started to revise his Mandarin version, he was also assisted by Zhu Baohui. But at Sydenstricker's death in 1930, Zhu Baohui undertook on his own the preparation of an entirely new version of the NT (based on the Greek text), translating independently from Sydenstricker's version, albeit often making use of the text of the version prepared by the two of them. Zhu Baohui's version was published in Nanjing in 1936, with financial support from Pearl S. Buck, and republished in Hong Kong in 1993. For the information about Zhu Baohui's work, see Zetzsche, *The Bible in China* (pp. 339-43) and sources quoted there.

6. Thus, in Richard Lovett, *The History of the London Missionary Society 1795-1895*, 2 vols. (London: Henry Frowde, 1899), no mention is made of the Chinese linguistic consultants to Robert Morrison (see vol. 2, pp. 399-428). There is mention only of the first Chinese convert in 1814, "Tsae A-ko" (p. 414), and the following persons connected with the London Missionary Society in 1832, all of whom were converts: Leang-Afa, native teacher; Kew-Agang, assistant to Leang-Afa and lithographic printer; and Le-Asin, assistant to Leang-Afa (p. 426). Nothing is said of the contributions of native Chinese literati to the translation process. Only Morrison (pp. 408-28) and William Milne (pp. 421, 429-36) are credited for the work.

7. See, for example, the picture facing the frontispiece in William John Townsend, *Robert Morrison: The Pioneer of Chinese Missions* (London: S. W. Partridge & Co. [1911]): "The Rev. Robert Morrison, D.D., and his assistants in the translation of the Bible into Chinese. Engraved by W. Holl [f]rom the original painting by G. G. Chinnery, Esq".

8. See, for example, the picture of the Mandarin Union Version committee in the *Quarterly Record* (January 1918), p. 480 (a publication of the National Bible Society of Scotland [NBSS]). The picture has the following title and subtitle: "Revising the Bible in Mandarin, the spoken Language of 30,000 Chinese. 1. Mr. Lee (Peking), Chihli. 2. Rev. Chauncey Goodrich, D.D., Litt.D. (Chairman), American Congregational. 3. Mr. Yen,

Why is this so? First of all, the inferior role conceded to Chinese co-workers corresponds to the total dominance held by western missionaries in policymaking and administration during the first hundred years and more of Protestant missionary work in China. At the 1877 China conference of Protestant missionaries in Shanghai, there were 142 persons in attendance (72 from American societies and 49 from British/Scottish groups), but not a single Chinese.[9] At the Protestant missionary conference in Shanghai in 1890, there were only two Chinese among the 445 members.[10] Even at the Protestant centenary missionary conference in Shanghai in 1907, out of a total attendance of 1,170, only 6 or 7 Chinese were present.[11]

Second, the supposed superiority of western civilization and culture over against that of the Chinese influenced not only the minds of the politicians, but that of the missionaries as well. Their wish to see Christianity and western culture spread to China through the achievements of outstanding European or American individuals dominated both their thinking and their work.

Third, attention was on the accomplishments of the individual missionary rather than on the team of which he or she was a part, or the team's achievements. The nineteenth century, as well as a great part of the twentieth, was a time when the West focused on the individual achievements of great men and women.[12] The individual hero from the West received

---

Szûch'uan. 4. Rev. Spencer Lewis, D.D., American Methodist Episcopal. 5. Rev. C. W.Allen, British Methodist. 6. Mr. Wang (Peking). 7. Rev. C. E. Aiken, American Congregational. 8. Rev. F. Baller, British Baptist. 9. Mr. Liu, Shantung". Other examples can be found in *The Chinese Recorder and Missionary Journal* 37 (1906), facing p. 355, and 49 (1918), frontispiece to August number. An exception, however, is the frontispiece in W. H. Medhurst, *China: Its State and Prospects, with especial Reference to the Spread of the Gospel: Containing Allusions to the Antiquity, Extent, Population, Civilization, Literature, and Religion of the Chinese* (London: John Snow, 1842), which provides the following information: "Mr. Medhurst, in conversation with Choo-Tîh-Lang, attended by a Malay Boy".

9. *Records of the General Conference of the Protestant Missionaries of China, Held at Shanghai, May 10–24, 1877* (Shanghai: Presbyterian Mission Press, 1878), p. 1-9; see also Kenneth S[cott] Latourette, *A History of Christian Missions in China* (New York: The Macmillan Co., 1929), p. 413.

10. *Records of the General Conference of the Protestant Missionaries of China, Held at Shanghai, May 7–20, 1890* (Shanghai: Presbyterian Mission Press, 1890), p. 15-23; see also Latourette, *History of Christian Missions*, p. 414.

11. *Records: China Centenary Missionary Conference, Held at Shanghai, April 25 to May 8, 1907* (Shanghai: Centenary Conference Committee, 1907), p. 784-808; see also Latourette, *History of Christian Missions*, p. 665.

12. See Robert Morrison, ed., *Memoirs of Rev. William Milne, D.D., Late Missionary to China, and Principal of the Anglo-Chinese College; compiled from Documents Written by the Deceased, to which are Added Occasional Remarks by Robert Morrison, D.D.* (Malacca:

attention, but not his Chinese counterpart.[13] Biography was a popular literary genre, but biographies of Chinese in the West were extremely rare compared with those of American and European missionaries or scientists in China.[14] Even the Chinese, when and if presented to European and American readers, were generally portrayed in the same individualistic way.[15] Little attention was paid to collective achievements or joint cooperation between Chinese and foreigners.

The meagre attention paid to the identity and contributions of those Chinese persons who worked together with the foreign missionaries was in line with the general picture of the Chinese in the West and fitted well the normal way of presenting missionary work in Europe and America. In the case of Bible translation, a failure to understand the role of the Chinese co-workers in the process of translating may also have been one of the reasons that caused such indifference to them. The fact that, despite the missionaries' dependence on them, only very few of these Chinese had been converted to the Christian religion made it difficult to acknowledge their status as co-workers.[16] Even in the catalogues of Chinese Scriptures

---

Mission Press, 1824); [Eliza Morrison], *Memoirs of the Life and Labours of Robert Morrison, D.D....compiled by his Widow,* 2 vols. (London: Longman, 1839); Robert Philip, *The Life and Opinions of the Rev. William Milne, D.D., Missionary to China, Illustrated by Biographical Annals of Asiatic Missions, from Primitive to Protestant Times; intended as a Guide to Missionary Spirit* (London: John Snow, 1840).

13. See, for example, Howard and Geraldine Taylor, *Hudson Taylor in Early Years: The Growth of a Soul* (London: Religious Tract Society, 1911) and *Hudson Taylor and the China Inland Mission: The Growth of a Work of God* (London: Religious Tract Society, 1918).

14. For example, in the impressive bibliography of Latourette, *History of Christian Missions,* p. 845-99, only a few biographies of Chinese are listed, but those of western missionaries are plentiful.

15. Geraldine Taylor, *Pastor Hsi (of North China): One of China's Christians* (London: China Inland Mission, 1903).

16. There are a few known exceptions, such as Ju Dilang (Choo Tih-Lang), a native of Guangdong province who was the language teacher and Chinese secretary of W. H. Medhurst and who accompanied Medhurst on his return to England in 1836 as "amanuensis for the Sacred Scriptures", which the latter was engaged in translating into Chinese. Ju Dilang was baptized by Medhurst at St. Thomas Square Chapel, Hackney (near London), on 20 July 1838 and appointed Native Assistant in the service of the London Missionary Society in Canton. Alexander Wylie, *Memorials of Protestant Missionaries to the Chinese, Giving a List of Their Publications, and Obituary Notices of the Deceased, with Copious Indexes* (Shanghae: American Presbyterian Mission Press, 1867), p. 40. In 1840 Ju Dilang was excluded from the church at Macau for opium smoking. Carl T. Smith, *Chinese Christians: Élites, Middlemen, and the Church in Hong Kong* (Hong Kong: Oxford University Press, 1985), p. 215. Lian Yinghuang, one of Samuel Isaac Jacob Schereschewsky's co-workers was a Christian. Two other anonymous Christian co-workers were mentioned by his wife, Susan M. Schereschewsky (1937-1909), née

prepared by Darlow and Moule, and by Spillett, the names of the Chinese co-workers are rarely mentioned.[17]

Ever since I first ventured into research on the principles of Chinese Bible translation, the question has therefore continued to puzzle me: what was the role of the Chinese in translation work during the first century of Chinese Bible translation?[18] Historical records and books that have presented the work of translators in China are often silent on this subject or tend to deal with it rather superficially. But information conveyed through private and official correspondence, diaries, journals, and certain historical records, leaves one with the impression that the Chinese had a key role, and that their role has been neglected for too long. The occasion of the bicentennial of the British and Foreign Bible Society (BFBS) — the first Bible Society to support Protestant Bible translations in China — is a welcome opportunity to identify the Chinese role more clearly.

This essay therefore addresses a few of the more dominant Chinese versions of the Bible during the first century of Protestant missions in China, with a view to determining the role(s) that Chinese literati played in the translation work initiated by European and American missionaries.[19] Unless it was subsequently documented, the oral information that might have been secured from nineteenth-century European and American translators and their Chinese co-workers was lost with their deaths. The obstacles posed by the nature of the existing written sources, as well as the complexity and magnitude of the topic, do not make the task any easier. In spite of such source limitations, the available material is sufficient to give some qualified answers to the question of anonymous nineteenth-century Chinese Bible translators.

Fortunately, the recent works by Irene Eber and Jost Oliver Zetzsche have contributed greatly to the history of Chinese Bible translation and to

---

Waring; see Irene Eber, *The Jewish Bishop and the Chinese Bible: S. I .J. Schereschewsky (1831–1906)*, Studies in Christian Mission, vol. 22 (Leiden: Brill, 1999), p. 110 n. 71 and p. 161.

17. T. H. Darlow and H. F. Moule, comps., *The Historical Catalogue of the Printed Editions of Holy Scriptures in the Library of The British and Foreign Bible Society*. 2 vols. in 4 (London: BFBS, 1903–1911); Spillett, *Catalogue of Scriptures*. Exceptions are, of course, versions translated independently by Chinese during the late nineteenth century. Even in such cases, however, the identification of some co-workers is lacking.

18. See Thor Strandenaes, *Principles of Chinese Bible Translation as Expressed in Five Selected Versions of the New Testament and Exemplified by Mt 5:1-12 and Col 1*, Conjectanea Biblica: New Testament Series 19 (Uppsala: Almqvist & Wiksell International, 1987), p. 77.

19. The focus here is not upon Bible translations done directly by Chinese, for which they have been duly credited. See, for example, Spillett, *Catalogue of Scriptures*, pp. 251-55, and Zetzsche, *The Bible in China*, appendixes, pp. 405-422.

the identification of the names of many of the Chinese co-workers of Protestant missionary translators, as well as listing some of the achievements of these co-workers.[20] In particular, Zetzsche, in his doctoral dissertation, has paid special attention to the role of what he calls the "Chinese assistants".[21] But much remains undone. In fact, detailed studies of the contributions of the individual Chinese literati and their lives are worthy subjects of future dissertations. Through individual enterprise and knowledge of research done by Chinese scholars, as well as joint international efforts to uncover information from the rich archival materials available especially in China, Japan, Europe, and America, one may be able to discover, systematize, and publish much more factual knowledge than has hitherto been done.[22]

The So-called One-Man Missionary Versions

In the case of the pioneering translation for which Robert Morrison was responsible, it is possible to define the two main roles of Morrison's Chinese co-workers: that of the secretary or scribe on the one hand, and that of the language teacher and linguistic consultant on the other.[23] The Chinese businessman Rong Sande (Yong Sam Tak)[24] had helped Robert

---

20. Eber, *The Jewish Bishop and the Chinese Bible*; Zetzsche, *The Bible in China*. Zetzsche's book has been translated into Chinese, giving Chinese readers access to valuable and detailed information on the history of Chinese Protestant Bible translation. See, You Side (Jost Oliver Zetzsche), *Heheben Yu Zhongwen Shengjing Fanyi*, tr. Cai Jintu (Daniel K. T. Choi), IBSHK Monograph Series on Bible Translation (Hong Kong: International Bible Society of Hong Kong, 2002). The article soon to be published by Jost Oliver Zetzsche, "The Missionary and the Chinese 'Helper': A Re-Appraisal of the Chinese Role in the Case of Bible Translation in China", *Journal of the History of Christianity in Modern China* (forthcoming), may shed more light on this area of research. See also You Side's note 2, p. v, in the introduction to *Heheben Yu Zhongwen Shengjing Fanyi*.

21. Zetzsche, *The Bible in China*, pp. 39-41, 91-93, 109, 142 n. 20, 158, 251, 260-64, 319, and 366; see also the corresponding pages in the Chinese version of his book (You Side, *Heheben Yu Zhongwen Shengjing Fanyi*).

22. Zetzsche lists much valuable research work already accomplished by the Chinese. See the preface (pp. 13-17) and bibliography (pp. 370-99) in his *Bible in China*. He also includes a list of NT and OT versions, in whole or in part, prepared or under preparation by Chinese scholars, pp. 405-22.

23. An analysis of principles of translation followed in Morrison's version of the NT, together with a brief historical introduction, may be found in Strandenaes, *Principles of Chinese Bible Translation*, pp. 22-46. For details on Robert Morrison's life and work, see William Milne, *A Retrospect of the First Ten Years of the Protestant Mission to China* (Malacca: The Anglo-Chinese Press, 1820); E. Morrison, *Memoirs*; and Townsend, *Robert Morrison*.

24. E. Morrison, *Memoirs*, vol. 1, p. 217. For other suggestions as to the characters of his Chinese name, see Zetzsche, *The Bible in China*, p. 32 n. 42. The transliterations used

Morrison before he left England for China to transcribe a manuscript translation in Chinese of major parts of the New Testament.[25] This manuscript, which is in the British Library, contains a Roman Catholic Chinese translation of a Gospel harmony, the Acts of the Apostles, and Paul's letters, as far as Hebrews 1. It is known as the Sloane MS. 3599.[26] Although Rong Sande also helped Morrison later in China, his attitude to the English missionary was rather complex and caused Morrison much worry.[27]

In Macao, Morrison was introduced to two important persons, Mr. Abel Yun (Yun Kwan-ming) and Mr. Li, both members of the Roman Catholic church.[28] Mr. Li was a native of Canton who had spent twelve years in Portugal where he had studied at the college of the Jesuits to become a priest. When he came to China, he married and therefore had to find another profession (he ended up as a security merchant). However, owing to oppression by Chinese government officers, he had failed in his business and had become a poor man. Mr. Li and later his son Li Shigong — also a Roman Catholic — were hired by Morrison to teach him Cantonese, Chinese writing, and literary Chinese.[29] According to Morrison,

---

by Morrison for the names of his Chinese co-workers were inconsistent, and it is not always possible to tell whether he was giving a Mandarin or a Cantonese pronunciation of the Chinese names. Hence it is difficult to know which Chinese characters he used. For this problem, see also Zetzsche, *The Bible in China*, pp. 39-41, especially notes 71 and 76.

25. Morrison (1782-1834) arrived in China on 4 September 1807.

26. Morrison was always frank about the use he made of this manuscript version (translated by the priest Jean Basset). See Morrison to the BFBS, Canton, 11 January 1814, BFBS Correspondence Books, no. 6, p. 286 (BSA/D1/5/6), quoted in *Eleventh Report of the BFBS* (London, 1815), p. 27. See also Morrison to the LMS, Canton, 25 November 1819, South China and Ultra Ganges, incoming correspondence, box 1, folder 3, CWM/LMS Archives, School of Oriental and African Studies (SOAS), London. For a full account of the contents of this manuscript, see Thor Strandenaes, "The Sloane MS 3599 — An Early Manuscript of an Incomplete Version of the New Testament", *Theology and Life* (Lutheran Theological Seminary, Hong Kong), no. 6 (1983), pp. 61-76; see also Zetzsche, *The Bible in China*, pp. 28-36.

27. "He has behaved very well and very friendly, assists me all he can in getting books & teachers & domestics.... On comparing him with others I find that he is not himself qualified to teach. He is not master of his own language; and his temper unfits him for communicating what he does know." R. Morrison to LMS, Canton, 10 December 1809, South China and Ultra Ganges, incoming correspondence, box 1, folder 1, CWM/LMS Archives.

28. Townsend, *Robert Morrison*, p. 43. For the characters of Yun's Chinese name, see Zetzsche, *The Bible in China*, p. 40 n. 76.

29. Morrison to LMS, Canton, 1 November 1808, South China and Ultra Ganges, incoming correspondence, box 1, folder 1, CWM/LMS Archives. See also E. Morrison, *Memoirs*, vol. 1, p. 168; and John Chalmers, "Sketch of the Canton Protestant Mission", *Chinese Recorder* 7 (1876), p. 174.

Mr. Li "possesses considerable knowledge of Chinese, writes an excellent hand, and having obtained one degree as a man of letters, is not so afraid as some of the trades-people are".[30]

In the painting of Robert Morrison by George G. Chinnery, Li Shigong is the person seated at the table writing, with Chen Laoyi standing behind.[31] Chen Laoyi came into Morrison's employment as language teacher and linguistic consultant in the later part of Morrison's Bible translation project, after Mr. Gao had to leave. Abel Yun, a native of Shanxi and aged 30 (in 1807), had spent a great deal of his life with the Roman Catholic missionaries in Beijing, where he had learned Latin, which he spoke fluently. He taught Morrison spoken Mandarin (1807-1809), but was unable to teach him the written Chinese as his "knowledge of his own language is very imperfect, and much more his knowledge of ours".[32]

Two other persons also helped Morrison during this period. From 1808 until 1814, Mr. Gao (Kŏ-mow-ho)[33] taught him Mandarin, and Chinese writing, and together they studied the works of Confucius and other Chinese classics. Morrison found Mr. Gao both able and very willing to serve him. Yet another helper was Lo-Xien (Low-Hëen), who was Morrison's companion, Chinese tutor, and secretary.[34] Morrison characterizes Lo-Xien briefly as "mild, but insincere. He writes a good hand, and is very useful in writing for the press".[35] About Mr Gao he says, "His grandfather

30. Quoted in E. Morrison, *Memoirs*, vol. 1, p. 168.
31. In her *Memoirs* (vol. 2, p. 483), Eliza Morrison identified Mr. Li in the painting by Chinnery (1774-1852), but not Chen Laoyi, the person standing next to him. This painting—in an engraving by Jenkins—faces the frontispiece of vol. 2. The original, dated about 1828 and in the possession of Eliza Morrison at the time the biography of her husband Robert Morrison was published, was destroyed in a fire in 1874. Today only printed copies and engravings survive, for example, the work by Jenkins used as the aforementioned frontispiece and the work by W. Holl used as the frontispiece in Townsend's *Robert Morrison*. Chalmers identified both the Chinese co-workers by name in his "Sketch" (p. 174).
32. Robert Morrison to LMS, Canton, 22 December 1812, South China and Ultra Ganges, incoming correspondence, box 1, folder 2, CWM/LMS Archives. Elsewhere Morrison says that "he has not had time to learn the characters of his native language" (quoted in E. Morrison, *Memoirs*, vol. 1, p. 163).
33. Transliteration given by William Milne in a letter from Mr. Gao to LMS, Canton, 11 January 1815, South China and Ultra Ganges, incoming correspondence, box 1, folder 4, CWM/LMS Archives.
34. Toward the end of 1812, Mr. Gao was 45 years old and Lo-Xien about 30. E. Morrison, *Memoirs*, vol. 1, pp. 238, 274, and 293. This is probably a romanization either of Lo-Xien, Lou Qian, or even "the Elder/Senior Xien"; see Zetzsche, *The Bible in China*, p. 40 n. 79, and You Side, *Heheben Yu Zhongwen Shengjing Fanyi*, p. 29 n. 79.
35. Morrison in his journal of 12 October 1812, quoted in E. Morrison, *Memorials*, vol. 1, p. 343.

Picture 18. *Robert Morrison (seated right), with Chinese Co-workers Chen Laoyi (standing) and Li Shigong (seated).* From a painting by G. G. Chinnery, reprinted from the frontispiece of W. J. Townsend, *Robert Morrison: The Pioneer of Chinese Missions* (London: S. W. Partridge & Co., [1911]).

was a Mandarin of some rank. He is of a mild and amiable disposition, of good natural parts, and has been accustomed all his life to teach". Morrison also notes that he "revises what is translated. They both do their parts without scruple".[36] He further reports that Mr. Gao "cheerfully corrects the idioms of my translations; helps to examine the pages that are written for the type-cutter; and joins in family prayer".[37] Not only did Morrison make use of his services as a language teacher, secretary, and scribe, but whenever the opportunity came, he also let him read portions from the New Testament, which Morrison in turn expounded to him.

One gathers from this that it is possible to distinguish between the functions of a Chinese language advisor/consultant and language teacher, on the one hand, and that of a Chinese secretary giving assistance in direct Bible translation, copying, and proofreading for printing, on the other. Whereas Rong Sande and Lo-Xien assisted Morrison as Chinese secretaries and consultants, Abel Yun functioned more as his informant, advisor, and dialogue partner on matters of Chinese language and cultural customs, with regard to the Roman Catholic church and Chinese society in general. Mr. Li, both father and son, were Chinese secretaries, as well as language teachers and consultants. Their assistance included introducing and explaining the use of Chinese words, expressions, and phrases, suggesting sentence structure, and giving advice on grammatical rules, structure, and style of Chinese, literary and spoken, as well as guidance on the cultural pitch of the Chinese translation.

Mr. Gao was Morrison's language teacher, advisor, scribe, and aide in translation work for almost six years. He also saw the completed New Testament version through its printing. This meant that he did both proof-writing of the manuscripts and proof-reading at different stages in the translation process. When political conditions forced Mr. Gao to leave Morrison in February 1814 after the completion of the New Testament version in High Wenli, he did so only very reluctantly. Not long before Mr. Gao's departure, Morrison had written in his journal:

> Jan 11. Kō Sëen-sãng and his son are obliged to flee from my house, and think it prudent to retire from their own. They are informed by a person on whom they depend, that the police-officers are endeavouring to apprehend them... Kō Sëen-sãng says that he is very sorry to leave me, and the

---

36. Morrison in his journal of 12 October 1812, quoted in E. Morrison, *Memorials*, vol. 1, p. 343.

37. Morrison to LMS, Canton, 22 December 1812, South China and Ultra Ganges, incoming correspondence, box 1, folder 2, CWM/LMS Archives. His letter shows that he was uncertain about whether to refer to Mr. Gao as his assistant or as his Chinese teacher. Writing in 1809, he referred to him as "a regular schoolmaster". Morrison to LMS, Canton, 14 December 1809, South China and Ultra Ganges, incoming correspondence, box 1, folder 1, CWM/LMS Archives.

duties in which he has daily engaged. He has been thinking what he shall do to remunerate me; and he determined to endeavour to promulgate the doctrines which I have taught him, as the best thing he could do to recompense me.[38]

It is known that Morrison undertook his language studies and Bible translation under extremely severe political conditions.[39] An edict against Christianity was issued in 1812 in the name of the emperor Ren Zong (1796–1821; reign name: Jia Qing).[40] And on 12 December of that same year, Mr. Yun told Morrison that the Roman Catholic bishop of Macao "issued an anathema against those who have intercourse with me or give Chinese books to me [i.e., Morrison]".[41] Under these strict conditions it was extremely difficult for Morrison to socialize freely with the Chinese, to learn the language, or to employ Chinese personnel with higher academic degrees. He was fortunate to get services at all from any persons who had literary training, such as Mr. Li or Mr. Gao.

When Morrison had completed and printed the entire Bible in Chinese in 1819, he did give some credit to the help that Chinese "teachers of the language" had rendered to his translation work, but not to the extent that his addressees could fully comprehend the extensive and true nature of their contribution. The contribution of Morrison's co-worker William Milne to this version was his translation of Deuteronomy, Joshua, Judges, and 1 Samuel – Job.[42] In the following letter, Morrison also expressed his own attitude to translation:

> The duty of a translator of any book is two-fold; first, to comprehend accurately the sense, and to feel the spirit of the original work; and secondly, to express in his version faithfully, perspicuously, and idiomatically (and, if he can attain it, elegantly), the sense and spirit of the original. For the first part of this duty, a Christian student will be much more competent than a heathen translator generally is; for the second part of the work, of course, a man who translates into his mother tongue (other things being

---

38. Morrison in his journal of 10 January 1814, quoted in E. Morrison, *Memoirs*, vol. 1, p. 377. In spite of his favourable attitude to Morrison's teaching, Mr. Gao did not convert to Christianity.

39. See, for example, Morrison's letter from Canton, 9 December 1809, quoted in E. Morrison, *Memoirs*, vol. 1, p. 285.

40. A translation of the edict was given by Morrison in his letter to LMS, Canton, 2 April 1812, South China and Ultra Ganges, incoming correspondence, box 1, folder 2, CWM/LMS Archives.

41. Morrison in his journal of 12 December 1812, quoted in E. Morrison, *Memoirs*, vol. 1, p. 347.

42. Morrison in a letter accompanying the Bible in Chinese High Wenli sent to the LMS, Canton, 25 November 1819, quoted in E. Morrison, *Memoirs*, vol. 2, p. 10; see also p. 2. Morrison and Milne revised each other's work, and the rest of the Bible was translated by Morrison and his Chinese co-workers.

equal) will much excel. Till those who are now heathen literati, cease to be heathens, these qualifications will not easily be found, in tolerable perfection, in the same individual.[43]

In his first duty as a translator, Morrison was alone. But in accomplishing the second part of his work, the Chinese in his employment had been useful for him. They had been engaged in teaching him Chinese and in consultant and tutoring functions, on the one hand, and had been serving in the role of Chinese secretary, scribe, and copyist, on the other. When political conditions prevented Morrison from associating with the Chinese at large, and with the scholarly, trained literati in particular, his Chinese co-workers loyally performed their duties as best they could, while in danger of harsh punishment or loss of their lives.[44]

When the names of Robert Morrison or William Milne (1785–1822) are remembered in connection with this particular Chinese translation of the Bible, so also should be the achievements of the Chinese persons who contributed in so many ways to the successful completion of the work.[45] Thus, the "one-man missionary version" was not the achievement of the one missionary alone. It was the result of a team process, and although no one can deny Morrison's chief responsibility for the project, he (and Milne) arrived at the result together with language teachers and linguistic consultants, Chinese secretaries, and scribes. The Chinese text reveals that Morrison relied less on the assistance from Chinese advisors than he might have done.[46] However, to the extent that this Chinese version was able to express perspicuously, idiomatically, and elegantly the sense and spirit of the original, it was thanks to the contribution of the Chinese co-workers. And, whenever the Chinese version does not read idiomatically or offers a poor style or inaccurate renderings of words and expressions, it may be due to any, or all, of the following reasons: the failure of Morrison to convey the exact meaning of the original text to his co-workers, the lack

---

43. "In the second part of my duty, viz. rendering the sense of the Scriptures into Chinese, my helps were, British Museum MS; several Roman Catholic works in China, MS. Dictionaries of Chinese; and Native Teachers of the language" (quoted in E. Morrison, *Memoirs*, vol. 2, p. 2).

44. Characterising the conditions of the early days of the China mission, Alexander Wylie writes that "the printing and circulation of the Scripture, even on the borders of the empire, was a question of penalties, stripes and imprisonment; and it was found necessary to remove to Malacca, or some place outside the empire, in order to carry on the printing to any great extent". See Wylie, "The Bible in China", in *Chinese Researches*, part 1, *Literary* (Shanghai, 1897), p. 105.

45. On Milne's contribution to the translation work, see Morrison, *Memoirs of Rev. William Milne*, p. 72.

46. Strandenaes, *Principles of Chinese Bible Translation*, pp. 37-41; see also Zetzsche, *The Bible in China*, p. 56.

of proficiency Morrison exhibited in literary as well as spoken Chinese,[47] the limited liberty of the Chinese co-workers to propose and use idiomatic Chinese and to employ a style acceptable to the reader, and the rather limited formal education of some of Morrison's (and Milne's) Chinese co-workers.[48] Among these reasons, the limited liberty given to the Chinese co-workers to influence the translation actively must account for the version's lack of idiomatic Chinese.

One must also keep in mind that the practice of employing Chinese personnel as language teachers and consultants, or as secretaries and scribes, created a delicate patron-client relationship. On the one hand, the employee was vulnerable to the whims and wills of his or her employer, and could easily be fired. But on the other hand, the loyalty of the client to the patron might well have prevented the person from being frank or speaking up, unless encouraged to do so. It is obvious that Morrison tried his best to maintain an amiable and respectful relationship with his employees, but this did not relieve him of the patron role or of the attitude to services that easily enter a patron-client relationship, namely that the labour which is paid for by the patron belongs to the patron. Hence the person who has produced the services for payment normally gets far less credit than the one who has these services at his or her disposal.

After the political events that led to the Treaty of Nanjing in 1842, five ports were opened for foreign settlement, trade, and mission work, namely, Canton, Amoy, Foo-Chow, Ningpo, and Shanghai; and Hong Kong was ceded to England as a British settlement.[49] This greatly enhanced the chance of securing qualified Chinese co-workers in translation work, as they could be recruited without fear of government reprisals or penalties, but it also meant that Chinese co-workers would be allowed a greater influence in securing idiomatic Chinese in the versions described below.

---

47. On the Chinese proficiency of Milne and Morrison, see Zetzsche, *The Bible in China*, pp. 39-42.

48. For a discussion on the degree of Chinese co-workers' involvement, see Zetzsche, *The Bible in China*, p. 40.

49. An account of the terms of this treaty, and the preceding friction and open hostilities between Britain and China that led to it, can be found in Kenneth Scott Latourette, *The Development of China*, 4th rev. ed. (Boston: Houghton Mifflin Co., 1929), pp. 139-48; W. C. Costin, *Great Britain and China, 1833–1860* (Oxford: The Clarendon Press, 1937); Wolfram Eberhard, *A History of China*, tr. E. W. Dickens, 4th ed. (London: Routledge & Kegan Paul, 1977), pp. 297-301. For a more thorough presentation of cultural and political factors, see John K. Fairbank, ed., *The Chinese World Order: Traditional China's Foreign Relations* (Cambridge: Harvard University Press, 1968); Jerome Ch'en, *China and the West: Society and Culture, 1815–1937* (London: Hutchinson & Co., 1979); and Raymond Stanley Dawson, *Imperial China* (London: Hutchinson & Co., 1972).

The limited formal recognition of the Chinese co-workers, noted in what might be called the "Morrison team version", coincides with what is known about the anonymous or semi-anonymous status of Chinese co-workers associated with other so-called one-man versions. An example is the work of Bishop Samuel Isaac Joseph Schereschewsky (American Episcopalian, 1831-1906), who translated the Old Testament both into Peking Mandarin and Easy Wenli, and the New Testament into Easy Wenli.[50] Schereschewsky spent years of his life translating the Bible and was highly respected for the lasting value and influence of his literary achievements, but in spite of all his diligent efforts, he was not working alone. There were a number of Chinese who made his translation possible. Whereas the names of Schereschewsky's Chinese co-workers during his first period of translating the Bible into Chinese are unknown,[51] Irene Eber and Jost Oliver Zetzsche have successfully traced the names of several Chinese tutors, literati, and secretaries who assisted him during the last years of his life, which he spent in Shanghai (1895-1897) and Japan (1897-1906). In Shanghai, he employed two Chinese scholars to help him put his Romanized manuscript into Chinese characters. After a short time, these scholars were replaced by a Chinese woman, Wei Jianmin (1848?-1932), who had been educated in an Anglican school and was thus able to understand English and to read his manuscript.[52] And while in Japan, Schereschewsky had with him Mr. Jin Shihe, Mr. Ye Shanrong, Mr. Yu Baosheng, Mr. Zhang Jiezhi, Mr. Lian Yinghuang, and a Mr. Liao. Mr. Zhang worked with Schereschewsky for one year, Mr. Yu for two years, and Mr. Lian for almost five years — Schereschewsky's final years.[53]

50. Schereshewsky, a Jew born in Lithuania, emigrated first to Germany, where he became a Christian, and then to the United States, where he studied theology and became a missionary to China. A pioneering biography portraying S. I. J. Schereschewsky was prepared by James A. Muller, *Apostle to China: Samuel Isaac Jacob Schereschewsky, 1831-1906* (New York: Moorehouse Publishing Co., 1937). Eber's *Jewish Bishop and the Chinese Bible* is, however, the first work to deal comprehensively with the life and achievements of the Lithuanian-born American missionary to China. The work demonstrates his immense contributions to scholarly translation of the Old Testament into Chinese and the lasting influence of his translation of both the OT and NT into Mandarin (OT 1874, NT 1886). See Spillett, *Catalogue of Scriptures* (nos. 319 and 347) and in literary Chinese (Easy Wenli NT, 1898; OT, 1902; complete Bible, 1910), see nos. 163, 274, and 285. For Schereschewsky's translation work, see also Zetzsche, *The Bible in China*, pp. 151-60.

51. Based on information found in Muller, *Apostle to China* (p. 139), Zetzsche (*The Bible in China*, p. 152 n. 82) thinks a Mr. Liu was Schereschewsky's Chinese co-worker in the late 1870s and early 1880s.

52. Zetzsche, *The Bible in China*, p. 158; see also Muller, *Apostle to China*, p. 223.

53. Lian Yinghuang was a Christian from north China who had studied at the Presbyterian College in Dengzhou. He can be seen in a photograph from 1902 together

Both before and after the sunstroke that left him lame (1881), Schereschewsky was highly dependent on the assistance that various Chinese scholars offered him. Irene Eber has aptly assessed the role and contribution of the Chinese literati who assisted Schereschewsky in his Bible translation work:

> The Chinese scholars whom Schereschewsky employed throughout the years were indispensable to his endeavours. Without them, even prior to his infirmity, the translations would have been less perfect stylistically. How much more so thereafter when he could not write and when his speech was difficult to understand. Despite their crucial role in the translation process, little is known about these men. They were not given credit for their share in the work and they are not always mentioned by name in the correspondence. Yet, they were the ones who were really responsible for the initial steps in the Sinofication of Christianity. Like the first Buddhist Sutra translators two thousand years earlier, it was they who began the process of imbuing the foreign teaching with Chinese forms. Their knowledge of written Chinese was required for selecting the right characters, proper idiomatic expressions and correct grammatical forms. Even Schereschewsky, who was completely dependent on these co-workers for the last eleven years of his life, failed to praise their accomplishments in the correspondence.[54]

The above examples show that it is necessary to reconsider how to refer to the Chinese "one-man missionary versions". The missionary may have been in charge of the version, and indeed have been its chief entrepreneur, but the successful completion of any missionary translation project in China during the first century of Protestant missionary activity would not have been possible without the active participation of Chinese co-workers. This is even more true when dealing with versions in literary Chinese, since it was not a spoken mode of the language and required years of hard study and training to master, even for the Chinese themselves.

---

with Schereschewsky and the latter's Japanese copyist/scribe, Mr. Bun. See Eber, *The Jewish Bishop and the Chinese Bible*, appendix with illustrations, p. 2. Ye Shanrong (Eber refers to him as Ye Shandang) came from Shutao (and was still alive in 1936); Mr. Jin Shihe came from Nanjing (d. 1934) and spent only a short time in Japan in 1897 before returning to China, as was the case with Mr. Liao who also left for China. For further information about these individuals, see Eber, p. 161; and also Zetzsche, *The Bible in China*, p. 158.

54. Eber, *The Jewish Bishop and the Chinese Bible*, p. 161.

The So-called Missionary Committee Versions

In spite of the great efforts of Robert Morrison, William Milne, and their Chinese co-workers, it was soon concluded that their version needed a thorough revision. At first John Robert Morrison (1814-1844), the translator's son, was expected to carry out a revision alone, but his duties as official translator of the East India Company did not allow him the time required. Then, Walter Henry Medhurst (1796-1857) took up the task. Nominally, the version was the work of a committee consisting of Medhurst, Karl Friedrich August Gützlaff (1803-1851), Elijah Coleman Bridgman (1801-1861), and John Robert Morrison, but the New Testament has been understood to be chiefly the work of Medhurst, and the Old Testament that of Gützlaff.[55] The New Testament version was published in 1836, and the Old Testament version in 1838, both privately.[56]

Zetzsche has characterized as "immense" the influence of these Old Testament and New Testament translations on later Protestant versions, especially with regard to terminology and transliteration of proper names.[57] But in these translations, no name of any Chinese co-worker is revealed. At the time, Mr. Ju Dilang was in the employment of Medhurst as Chinese teacher and secretary and must — for one — have been engaged also in the translation project. He went to England with Medhurst in 1836-1838, after the version was finished.[58] Seeing Medhurst's positive attitude to his Chinese co-workers, on the one hand, and yet his failure to mention their active involvement in the translation work, on the other, leads one to conclude that Medhurst's silence about their participation was prompted by fear of negative reactions from the BFBS or the London Missionary Society (LMS) for letting non-Christian or newly converted Chinese appear too dominant in the Bible translation work.

---

55. Wylie, *Memorials,* pp. 31 and 61; see also Spillett, *Catalogue of Scriptures,* nos. 376 and 377.

56. Spillett, *Catalogue of Scriptures,* nos. 37 and 38. They were revised several times in the period 1838-1855; see nos. 41-44, 48, and 69, among others. For a full acount, see Zetzsche, *The Bible in China,* pp. 59-71. The BFBS did not support the publishing of this version for two main reasons: 1) disagreement with the principles of translation followed in the version, and 2) lack of respect for Morrison's (and Milne's) work, which the inititative to undertake a new version — not only a revision — seemed to reflect. As Zetzsche (*The Bible in China,* p. 64) has pointed out, "Medhurst portrayed for the first time a concept of Bible translation which was not bound to the letter of the base text but to its meaning in a non-Christian culture". For the work on this version, see Zetzsche, *The Bible in China,* pp. 59-75.

57. Zetzsche, *The Bible in China,* p. 66.

58. Wylie, *Memorials,* pp. 26, 40. Mr. Ju is one of a few Chinese listed by Wylie (p. 40), who also gives the Chinese characters for his name. If these are correct, the transliteration should be Ju Délàng. See also note 16, above.

Picture 19. *Walter Medhurst (seated left), a Malay Boy (standing), and Chinese Co-worker Ju Dilang (seated).* From the frontispiece of W. H. Medhurst, *China: Its State and Prospects* (London: John Snow, 1842)

It was mainly because of the reactions of trustworthy native Chinese readers that Medhurst was convinced that a thorough revision of the Morrison team version was needed. Medhurst communicated to England the opinions of three of these Chinese readers, which had been conveyed to him (and the LMS and BFBS) in letters.[59] The evangelist Mr. Liang was of the opinion that "the style adopted in the present version of the scriptures is far from being idiomatic, the translation having sometimes used too many characters, and employed inverted and unusual phrases, by which the sense is obscured".[60] Mr. Lew Tse-chuen, a Chinese literary graduate, writes of the version that it "exhibits a great number of redundancies and tautologies, which render the meaning obscure". Also Mr. Ju Dilang, Medhurst's secretary, comments in the same direction, "It ought to be known, that in the Chinese, phrases have a certain order, and characters a definite application, which cannot be departed from with propriety".[61] And, he continues, "In a translation the sense ought certainly to be given according to the original; but the style should be conformable to native models: thus every one will take up the book with pleasure and read it with profit".[62] But Medhurst's initiative was met with great scepticism in the BFBS, and the Society refused to support it. In an article in the *Chinese Repository* in 1836, Gützlaff had also made suggestions regarding the manner in which improvement of the version in literary Chinese ought to be made, showing that Medhurst was not alone in seeing the need for improving the translation. In Gützlaff's opinion the following matters were important to secure: the idiomatic use of particles and the employment of them only when needed, the use of euphony and good rhythm in the translation, the employment of reduplication and pleonasm, and the conscious use of antithesis and climax. He concluded:

> In speaking of these peculiarities, we would by no means admit that the meaning of the text should in any case be altered or obscured by their use;

---

59. See the three following letters by Walter Henry Medhurst, "Memorial Addressed to the British & Foreign Bible Society on a New Version of the Chinese Scriptures", Hackney, 28 October 1836; "Remarks of Mr. Medhurst on the Letters of Messrs. Evans and Dyer, contained in a Letter to the Rev. J. Jowett", Hackney, 19 November 1836; and "Memorial Addressed to the Directors of The Missionary Society on the Projected Revision of the Chinese Scriptures", Hackney, 23 December 1836. The Memorial to the BFBS was printed separately; the other two are in *Documents Relating to the Proposed New Chinese Translation of the Holy Scriptures* [London: BFBS, 1836]. See BFBS Pamphlet Collection, vol. 36, nos. 9 and 11. The original letter of 19 November 1836 is in BFBS Foreign Correspondence Inwards, 1836, no. 3, p. 75 (BSA/D1/2/55). See also Strandenaes, *Principles of Chinese Bible Translation*, pp. 68-73.

60. Quoted in Medhurst, *China: Its State and Prospects*, p. 558.
61. Quoted in Medhurst, *China: Its State and Prospects*, p. 559.
62. Quoted in Medhurst, *China: Its State and Prospects*, p. 560.

yet so far as the sense of the original will allow, and especially where the introduction of these figures will render the language perspicuous, the translator though a foreigner ought to yield to the genius of the Chinese language.[63]

So the missionaries embarked on a new version in literary Chinese. A committee of delegates consisting of members from the different Chinese ports came together.[64] The committee consisted of William Jones Boone (d. 1891),[65] Walter M. Lowrie (1819-1847), and Medhurst (all representing the Shanghai and Ningpo stations), John Stronach (1810-1888, representing Amoy), Elijah Coleman Bridgman (representing Canton and Hong Kong), and William Charles Milne (1815-1863, the son of William Milne), who joined the delegates on Lowrie's death. The delegates met at the house of Medhurst from June 1847 until 24 July 1850, bringing the translation of the New Testament to a completion. For three full years, the committee met daily from 10 a.m. to 2:30 p.m., without pause except for a few months in 1847.[66] Unfortunately, there is no known photograph of this translation group, and only western missionaries were official delegates and considered to be members of the committee of translators. But all of them prepared the sessions and met in the committee together with their Chinese co-workers. Among the rules of order for the committee of delegates, decided upon in 1847, there are some that at least indirectly point to what might be recognition of the presence and the functions of the delegates' Chinese co-workers:

4) The Chinese secretary shall then produce a correct copy of the portion of the Scripture revised at the previous meeting; which after being read and approved, shall be kept on file upon the table for reference; and it shall be considered as the standard copy from which the work shall be printed.

5) The Chinese secretary shall note in a book kept for that purpose (the Englishman's Greek-English Concordance), the rendering into Chinese of each Greek word; which book is to be kept for the use of the several delegates...

---

63. *The Chinese Repository*, no. 4 (1835/1836), p. 398.
64. Zetzsche has given a thorough account of the work on this version. See Zetzsche, *The Bible in China*, pp. 77-110. For the principles of translation that it followed, see also Strandenaes, *Principles of Chinese Bible Translation*, pp. 48-75.
65. Bishop Boone was, however, unable to attend because of ill health.
66. William Charles Milne, *Life in China* (London: G. Routledge & Co., 1857), p. 504; see also Wylie, "The Bible in China", p. 103. See E. C. Bridgman's letter (Shanghai, 7 July 1849) to *The Chinese Repository*, no. 18 (1849), pp. 384-91, about the first meeting of the delegates in 1847; and also the announcement in *The Chinese Repository*, no. 17 (1848), p. 53.

8) The method of proceeding in Committee shall be to consider verse by verse, word by word, allowing each individual opportunity to propose any alteration that may be deemed desirable.
9) Any portion of the work that has been revised and approved may be reconsidered, if a motion to that effect be offered in writing.[67]

Although the function of Chinese secretary for the committee was formally held by one of the delegates, it is obvious that the Chinese co-workers—in spite of not being formal members of the committee—in reality had much influence on the committee work and on the final result. Milne, himself a member of the committee of delegates, tells of their work:

> The method of proceeding in committee was to consider verse by verse, word by word, allowing each individual opportunity to propose any alteration that he might deem desirable. The several members of the delegation had their native tutors with them, three of whom continued with us for six years in our daily sittings, rendering most valuable assistance.[68]

It would not be right to underestimate the extent of this "valuable assistance". The fact that the delegates' version of the entire Bible achieved such a good literary standard and as a result was printed repeatedly (even as recently as 1982 by the Bible Society in Taiwan) was due not least to the active participation of the committee's Chinese co-workers.[69] Unfortunately, only two of them have been identified: Mr. Wang Changgui (d. 1849) and his son Wang Lanqing (1828–1897), both of whom were co-workers of Medhurst. In a letter, Medhurst writes that Wang Lanqing (better known by his literary name, Wang Tao, or Wang Dao)[70] had been "engaged for the last six years in the Translation of the Scriptures", and that his father (Wang Changgui) "commenced the work, and assisted in the preparation of the Delegates version of the New Testament as far as the Epistle to the Romans".[71] The influence of Wang Lanqing on the delegates'

---

67. Bridgman's letter, p. 390.
68. Milne in *Life in China* (p. 505) relates that two of these Chinese had since converted to Christianity.
69. See Strandenaes, *Principles of Chinese Bible Translation*, p. 66.
70. Wang Dao moved to Hong Kong in 1863 and lived there until his return to Shanghai in 1884. He became closely associated with the Rev. James Legge on the translation of the Chinese classics that Legge was then preparing. Legge recognized him as having more knowledge of Chinese classics than any one he had ever known. When the *Tsun Wan Yat Po (Universal Circulating Herald)* started publication in February 1874, it was registered under Wang Dao's name (see Smith, *Chinese Christians*, p. 133), but Legge followed the attitude of westerners by publishing in his own name the translation of the Chinese classics without crediting Wang Dao.
71. Medhurst to the LMS, 11 October 1854, Central China, incoming correspondence, box 1, folder 4, CWM/LMS Archives. In his letter he tells of the baptism of his "Chinese teacher named Wang Lan-King" on 22 August 1854, aged 26. Medhurst

version was recognized in 1890 by the LMS missionary William Muirhead (1822–1900), who said that "the style of the Delegates' version is really the style of this younger Chinese scholar",[72] but as was typical of the westerners, Muirhead did not mention Wang Lanqing's name.

Following the completion of the New Testament version, a disagreement on guidelines for translation made it impossible for the delegates to complete the translation of the Old Testament together. The committee split, and the remaining members, Medhurst, Milne, and Stronach, formed the Old Testament committee, whose work was completed in the spring of 1853. This committee also met together with their Chinese secretaries during the committee sessions. This means that all five Chinese co-workers partook daily in the three-year process of translating the New Testament, and that three of them met for another three years during the Old Testament translation, that is, for the entire six-year period. The names of these Chinese co-workers were unfortunately not submitted by W. C. Milne in his report (see note 68), but Milne did recognize their contribution. A. J. Garnier in his *Chinese Versions of the Bible* mentions that, "The help of a Chinese named Wang, a man of considerable attainments as a scholar, was enlisted, with the result that the translation, at any rate from the point of view of style, is far in advance of any previous work".[73] Here, Garnier refers to Wang Lanqing *alias* Wang Dao. Another person who has been made anonymous is the individual who translated the delegates' version of the New Testament into Mandarin, the so-called Nanking version, printed in 1856.[74] The reason for preparing such a version in Mandarin was given by Medhurst in a letter to the LMS in 1854, in which he said:

relates that his father [i.e., Wang Changgui] "had an extraordinary amount of knowledge, so as to acquire the name of the walking literary". About Wang Lan-King, he says "his style of writing was said to be elegant, and his judgment mature. He was engaged accordingly [in 1849], and answered our expectations in every respect. Not only did he maintain a respectable position among other teachers much his seniors in point of age, but being of industrious habits, he took upon himself most of the labour connected with the preparation of the work, which was generally adopted after some corrections by his confreres".

72. William Muirhead, "Historical Summary of the Different Versions, with their Terminology, and the Feasibility of Securing a single Standard Version in Wen-li, with a Corresponding Version in Mandarin Colloquial", *Records 1890,* p. 35. See also John Hykes, "Dr. John R. Hykes Tells the Wonderful Story of the American Bible in China", *The China Press*, 12 November 1911, p. 3.

73. A. J. Garnier, *Chinese Versions of the Bible* (Shanghai: Christian Literature Society, 1934), p. 29.

74. Medhurst tells of the printing of 50,000 copies "in Mandarin colloquial" in a letter to LMS, Shanghai, 6 September 1855, Central China and Ultra Ganges, incoming correspondence, box 2, folder 1, CWM/LMS Archives. In 1856 William Muirhead reported

[Mandarin] is understood in every part of the empire, *and will* [emphasis in the original], if well translated, command the respect of the learned and the reader wherever it travels. Messrs. Medhurst and Stronach though separated, being well acquainted with each others views, and having been the chief agents now residing in China in the preparation of the Delegates' version, thought that they could do no better than undertake the Colloquial Mandarin also, the one taking the Gospels and Acts, and the other the Epistles; Remitting to each other their several productions and mutually availing themselves of each others corrections. This has accordingly been done, and the entire New Testament is now ready for the press in that dialect... The Mandarin Colloquial version has met with great favour among the Missionaries, and has been equally acceptable to the Chinese.[75]

The preceding passage is included in the same letter in which Medhurst tells of the baptism of Wang Lanqing. One wonders what holds Medhurst back from admitting Mr. Wang's contribution to this version, for it seems likely that Wang, at least as Medhurst's co-worker at the time, would have been involved. Was it because Wang was just a recent convert, or was Medhurst's way of thinking, in Zetzsche words, "[characteristic of] the attitude of the missionaries?"[76] One reason may have been the fear of negative reactions from the BFBS or LMS in England to such recognition. But also the patron-client relation, mentioned above, probably created a pattern among western missionaries that made them consider the work for which they paid Chinese co-workers as their own property. Also, since the missionaries were officially and administratively responsible for the project, and for approving the final version, they felt they should receive the honour as well. Very likely, therefore, it was Wang Lanqing who made the draft translation from the classical Chinese into Mandarin, whereupon it was submitted to Stronach and Medhurst for scrutiny. At least the involvement of a Chinese scholar is known to posterity. The scholar's young age and his position (after being involved with the delegates' version), as well as his being Medhurst's co-worker, all point to Wang Lanqing.[77]

---

that in a fire "a great part of the Mandarin Colloquial Version has been destroyed but we shall endeavour to replace it in as short a time as possible". See Muirhead to LMS, Shanghai, 30 June 1856, Central China and Ultra Ganges, incoming correspondence, box 2, folder 1, CWM/LMS Archives.

75. Medhurst letter to LMS, Shanghai, 11 October 1854, Central China and Ultra Ganges, incoming correspondence, box 1, folder 4, CWM/LMS Archives.

76. Zetzsche, *The Bible in China*, p. 142 n. 20.

77. William Muirhead ("Historical Summary of the different Versions", *Records 1877*, p. 36) stated: "The first Mandarin version was under the hands of Dr. Medhurst, who simply aimed at a faithful rendering of the Delegates' version of the New Testament. It was done by a native and is expressed in a free and racy style, which has been objected to as lacking in fidelity to the Greek". Garnier (*Chinese Versions of the Bible*, p. 46)

Looking into the work of other committee versions, mainly that of the committees preparing the Union versions in High Wenli, Easy Wenli, and Mandarin, the impression of active Chinese co-worker participation is confirmed, but one also sees the tendency to leave the contribution of the co-workers somewhat in darkness, even though their identity is increasingly becoming known. This is particularly true for the latter part of the work, that on the Old Testament, but can also be traced in the work on the New Testament.[78] In connection with the Mandarin translation, Zetzsche aptly concludes,

> the increasing role that they were given in the process of translation nevertheless shows that their contributions were highly valued. The Chinese translators were rarely mentioned in the reports of the first seven years, but as the work progressed, their importance was increasingly valued, so much so that eventually — under the new chairman Goodrich during the OT translation — they were given an equal vote with the foreigners.[79]

At the China Centenary Conference in Shanghai in 1907, during the presentation of the progress report on the Union Mandarin Version, the following could be read in the translators' report: "About the middle of the session [which lasted from 18 June to 2 September 1904], Dr. Goodrich was called away by severe illness in his family. He was represented to the end, however, by his experienced Chinese teacher, Mr Choong Hsi-hsin" (Zhang Xixin).[80] This, then, gave Zhang Xixin not only the status of a Chinese co-worker, but also of a committee member, and it serves as an

---

indicated: "The first draft of this work was done by a young Chinese scholar who had no access to the original language". Spillett (*Catalogue of Scriptures*, no. 580) stated that it was translated "by a Chinese scholar supervised by W. H. Medhurst and J. Stronach".

78. Zetzsche, *The Bible in China*, has gathered and publicized pictures of several of the Union Version translation committees (pp. 251, 264, 266, 303, 320, and 321), and he has managed to find most of the names of the Chinese co-workers, at least the transliteration of their surnames. For a thorough history of the work on these versions, see pp. 193-330.

79. Zetzsche, *The Bible in China*, p. 260.

80. *Records 1907*, p. 280. In the same volume the participation of Chinese assistants is also mentioned by D. Z. Sheffield on behalf of the High Wenli committee (p. 274). In the printed English preface to the first edition of the 1907 Union Mandarin New Testament Version, written by the chairman of the translation committee, C. W. Mateer, the following recognition is expressed: "The translation owes a great deal of whatever excellence it has to the faithful help of our Chinese assistants. One teacher continued without interruption throughout the whole course of the book. Another died after serving twelve full years. Others served shorter terms." In the Chinese printed text the two persons' names are given with titles; the longest serving is referred to as "Elder Zhang Xixin", the other as "Evangelist Zhou Liwen". See also note 83 below.

example of how the presence and role of the Chinese co-workers became gradually recognized.

In December 1917, the chairman of the Union Mandarin Version committee, Chauncey Goodrich (1835-1925, American Congregational), gave a written report after the revisers had completed their task. In the report, he makes the following statement, which explicitly underlines the importance of the Chinese co-workers in the results achieved by the committee. Although the co-workers were not regular members of the committee, their being "associated" with the committee members is also a recognition of their overall contribution, and not only to "matters of style":

> It should be added to the above, that in almost every instance terms in universal or almost universal use have been discovered; also that for the past four years we have had three exceptional Chinese scholars associated with us, who have given as earnest toil and patient search as their foreign brethren of the Committee. To them in matters of style we have gladly deferred.[81]

Goodrich's letter, when published in Scotland, was also accompanied by a picture of the committee, identifying the individuals.[82] It is again worth noticing that, whereas the western missionaries in the picture have been acknowledged with full names (or surnames with initials), and some even with academic degrees, country of origin, and church denomination or mission affiliation, the four Chinese co-workers in the picture are only identified by surname and place of origin. Knowing that the surnames Li, Yen, Huang, and Liu are extremely common in China, and that their place of origin tells next to nothing, it is extremely difficult or even impossible for an ordinary reader to trace their identity further.

This practice also signifies an attitude in the western Bible and missionary societies of the time. The missionaries were regarded as the persons of importance, the Chinese only as personal assistants and therefore of much less importance. It was, of course, the responsibility of the publishers of the *Quarterly Record* of the National Bible Society of Scotland to furnish detailed information to their readers by identifying clearly the persons in the pictures they published. But when such information is

---

81. Chauncey Goodrich in the *Quarterly Record* (January 1918), p. 481. See note 8 above for names of the persons pictured. The picture, probably taken in 1913, is identical with the one in Zetzsche (*The Bible in China*), p. 320), and was later publicized also in *The Chinese Recorder* (1918), frontispiece to the August number. The Chinese co-workers and the missionaries they assisted are: Mr. Li (C. Goodrich), Mr. Yan (S. Lewis), Mr. Wang (C. W. Allan), and Mr. Liu Dacheng (F. W. Baller).

82. *Quarterly Record* (January 1918), pp. 479-81. The committee had then worked since 1890. In the undated picture of the Union Version OT committee published by Zetzsche (*The Bible in China*), ill. 10, p. 303, the names of the Chinese Bible translators are unknown, only the names of the western translators are given.

missing, it illustrates again the difference of status between westerners and Chinese that was part of the mindset of many of the missionaries in the field and their corresponding bodies abroad.[83]

Conclusion

The above analysis leads to certain conclusions about the role of the native literati in the Chinese Bible translation projects headed by western missionaries. The Chinese co-workers who acted as secretaries transcribed manuscripts, both the manuscripts of the translator(s) and the manuscripts of others (see, for example, the Sloane MS. 3599). Additionally, these secretaries took notes or wrote down the translation, as dictated to them, and then revised what had been translated, corrected proofs, prepared manuscripts for publication, and saw the versions through the press.

Those literati who had more education and writing/teaching/translation experience took a more active part in the translation process itself, if and when permitted. They had a scholarly knowledge of the language and made suggestions to their colleagues about ways of translating the originals into the receptor language. This they did by offering synonyms or alternative words and expressions, by correcting idioms and grammatical structure, and by improving style and aspects of style in the final versions. And, in so doing, they greatly influenced the result and created versions that were more long lasting.

When it was difficult to employ well-educated Chinese literati, and as long as the foreign missionaries were hesitant to let their Chinese co-workers influence the translation work, the assistance the missionaries received was insufficient. This, in turn, led to wooden, too literal renderings and less idiomatic translations than was possible later. After 1842, when the five ports and Hong Kong had been opened for foreign settlement, and the legislation against translating and publishing foreign works into Chinese had become less strict, the missionaries had the freedom to hire better-trained co-workers who were able to render a more independent service to the translation projects. The improvement of idiomatic Chinese, including the style of both the literary versions and the versions in spoken Chinese, came about as a result of this new freedom to cooperate with native speakers and writers. One must keep in mind, however, that during the nineteenth century the Chinese literati were always paid co-workers in the service of foreign missionaries. Their freedom to express

---

83. Zetzsche, *The Bible in China*, p. 260, says that whereas both C. Goodrich and C. W. Mateer valued their Chinese scholarly co-workers highly, A. Sydenstricker criticized the respected position given to the Chinese "assistants". C. W. Mateer's high regard for the Chinese co-workers is described in note 80 above.

opinions was limited, and they did not enjoy a status equal to that of the missionaries in the translation project, even though they had better mastery of the Chinese language. Very much depended therefore on the atmosphere of cooperation created by each translator and by the western missionary members of the translation teams as a body. This means that in the three basic phases in the translation processes — analysis, transfer, and restructuring — the Chinese contribution was made in the latter two phases.[84] One has the definite impression, from the dominant translation projects looked at in this period, that the Chinese literati were respected for their opinions and had a favourable influence on the translations that came out of the projects, although in the case of the Morrison team version, Morrison did not allow them sufficient influence to make the translation fully idiomatic. In spite of employer-employee dependency, the Chinese literati became an integral part of the translation and revision teams, albeit without formal status, except in the latter part of the Union version projects. Their ignorance of the original languages of the Scriptures was balanced by the relevant knowledge of their own language. And, as the missionaries lacked the proficiency in Chinese that only native speakers have, the missionaries were dependent on their Chinese co-workers for achieving their goals.

It may be anachronistic to try to fit the work of the Chinese literati into the late twentieth-century *Procedures in Publishing Bible Translations* that guide modern translation practice. Nevertheless Jan de Waard and Eugene Nida have listed eight general procedures in translating that may be used in an assessment. They include:

> (1) background study, (2) amount of time and circumstances for the drafting process, (3) the phases of analysis, transfer, and restructuring, (4) translation units, (5) the mechanics of formulation of the text, (6) successive drafts, (7) order in which various books are to be translated or revised, and (8) the preparation of supplementary material.[85]

When reviewing the work of the Chinese co-workers in the projects dealt with in this paper, it is obvious that these co-workers were influential in all procedures except 1 and 3a (the phase of analysis). They contributed in the phases of transfer and restructuring, in the different translation units (in committee sessions as well as in the one-to-one basic unit), in the

---

84. This process is adequately described by Jan de Waard and Eugene A. Nida, *From One Language to Another: Functional Equivalence in Bible Translating* (Nashville: Thomas Nelson, 1986), appendix B, pp. 188-209. For a detailed description of the process, see Eugene A. Nida and Charles Taber, *The Theory and Practice of Translation*, UBS Helps for Translators, vol. 8 (Leiden: E. J. Brill, 1969).

85. For these "Procedures", see de Waard and Nida, *From One Language to Another*, appendix B, pp. 188-209.

process of formulating the text, and in developing successive drafts together with their missionary co-workers. In the committee versions, the Chinese literati individually assisted those persons to whom portions of the Scripture had been allotted for translation, seeing the assignment through not only up to the time when the committee met. Also, during the time when the translation committee was in session, they contributed constructively to the constant improvement of the Chinese texts. Interestingly, de Waard and Nida have observed, "It is almost impossible to take a stylistically wooden and awkward text and introduce proper stylistic features. On the other hand one can take a stylistically good translation and 'tighten it up' in terms of accuracy of content".[86] Thus, when the versions by the delegates, Schereschewsky, and the Union Mandarin version received the acclaim they did and were able throughout the text to influence the Chinese style so well, it was obviously because the Chinese literati had been active co-workers in the translation process from the beginning. They took seriously their role both as translators and as linguistic consultants. When the version published by Morrison's team needed an early revision, it was exactly because Robert Morrison and William Milne had failed to — or had not been able to — let the literati have sufficient influence on what was to be considered idiomatic and stylistically good Chinese.

In the first hundred years of Chinese Protestant Bible translation, western missionaries and corresponding societies failed to give sufficient recognition to the important work that was rendered by their Chinese co-workers. Many of these Chinese also remained anonymous, not because they desired anonymity, but because their names were not shared or publicized. Although further studies are needed to identify the names, academic training, professional skills, and specific contributions of all Chinese literati who contributed to Bible translation projects in China in the nineteenth and twentieth centuries, the present study has nevertheless shown that we know not a little about the role the Chinese literati played in the projects we have looked into. They were part of translation teams, and they assisted individual translators as well as groups of translators in preparing readable — sometimes even elegant — Chinese translations into literary and spoken Chinese. Their knowledge of the receptor language was needed, and so was the classical Chinese education and apprenticeship that many of them brought to the translation effort. Except for the fact that they were not theologically trained and had not studied the original languages of the Bible, and therefore could not translate *from* the originals, they were indeed translators who ably rendered the biblical texts *into* the receptor language, with which they were familiar. As such,

---

86. de Waard and Nida, *From One Language to Another*, appendix B, p. 200.

these Chinese literati deserve to be called Bible translators and consultants. Thus, their status has now been rectified. As for their anonymity, we have discovered that they are not all unknown. The western co-workers and their corresponding societies in Europe and America reduced them to anonymity. Since many have now been identified, more joint international efforts must be made to find information about them and the names and identities of others yet unknown to us.

In the new on-line edition of Darlow and Moule's catalogue of Scriptures (presently in preparation), care must be taken with the Chinese Scripture entries to ensure that, just as the names of the western co-workers are registered, the names of the participating Chinese co-workers are also added, including the full Chinese rendering of their names in characters with transliteration, since initials are insufficient. Furnishing such information should not be limited to those versions that are known to have been translated solely by Chinese, but should also include all the projects wherein Chinese literati have worked together with western co-workers as Bible translators and linguistic consultants. Whenever possible, additional information such as dates of birth and death, place of birth, and so on, should be listed as well. In this way, one after the other of these anonymous Chinese will eventually appear with the name by which they were known in their families and in contemporary society. In the same way, they should be remembered and honoured in churches and Bible societies, in history and research, just as is the case with their overseas missionary colleagues. They and their families deserve it; so do the Chinese people and the rest of us.[87]

---

87. In order not to reduce another person to anonymity, I hereby express my thanks to the Reverend David Lewis for editing the English text of my manuscript.

PROBLEMS IN TRANSLATING THE BIBLE INTO MANCHU:
OBSERVATIONS ON LOUIS POIROT'S OLD TESTAMENT

Erling von Mende

In the Vienna Kunsthistorisches Museum, I recently came across a Maria van Osterwijck (1630–1693) vanitas still-life on which there was a quote from the fourteenth chapter of the Book of Job. In the Revised Standard Version, the passage reads: "Man that is born of a woman is of few days, and full of trouble." So, I thought it might be interesting to see what the Jesuits had made out of this in Manchu and what the reaction of a possible Manchu reader might have been to their rendition. The sentence quoted above in English has been rendered in Manchu translation as *"hehe ci banjiha niyalma goidarakô jalan de bifi. beye jalu mangga gosihon ojoro teile."*

My interest in the Manchu translation of the Book of Job has a precedent, however, in a much earlier first-person account. In September 1835, following his return from St. Petersburg to London, George Borrow included in his report to the members of the Committee of the British and Foreign Bible Society (BFBS) an evaluation of Poirot's Manchu translation, pointing out that some passages really were of unsurpassable elegance, and that "this soaring tendency is particularly observable in the version of the Book of Job."[1] This essay reopens the evaluation of Poirot's Manchu translation.

The Manchus

In 1644 when they officially took over the Chinese Empire, the Manchus introduced their language into China, where it became occasionally, at least in the domain of state affairs, more significant than Chinese. For a long time its usage was as important as Chinese. In its final stage, when its relevance and circulation declined, it was kept artificially alive until the end of the dynasty.

Who exactly, one might ask, were the Manchu-speaking people? Scholars concerned with the history of biblical translation may well know more

---

1. T. H. Darlow, *Letters of George Borrow to the British and Foreign Bible Society* (London: Hodder and Stoughton, 1911), p. 89.

about these people than the average sinological scholar, despite the fact that Manchu culture and language have been rediscovered by Chinese and American scholarship in the last two decades. Twenty years ago, readers looking for information written on the Manchus in the English language were best advised to look at the sensible remarks authored, for example, by T. H. Darlow or at the reports and letters composed by individuals involved in BFBS and London Missionary Society (LMS) activities in Russia and its eastern territories.[2] The writers of such reports and letters were often familiar with Jesuit and Russian publications on China and the Qing dynasty. Additionally, they were acquainted with the French and, to a lesser extent, German research done on the Manchus in the early nineteenth century. Moreover, for chronological reasons these authors were untainted by Chinese historiography of the twentieth century, according to which the Chinese people had been victims of disgrace and humiliation visited upon them by the Manchu oppressors.

The Manchus were a more or less voluntary federation of Tungusic tribes, whose native language was for a long time based on an oral, not written, tradition. It was only in 1599, by the decree of a future emperor, that the Manchu language was given a script derived from Mongolian. This script was further improved and tuned to Manchu between 1632 and 1641, becoming the new script called *tongki fuka hergen-i bithe* — that is, the script with the diacritical marks. The new script provided a clear distinction between vowels on the one hand and consonantal stops and fricatives on the other hand, thus avoiding seemingly identical writings of different words.

Since they were conquerors and not scholars, most Manchus supposedly never really understood the importance of learning the new written language. Still, the use of this written language is fairly well recorded in documents, inscriptions, seals, and coins dating from the beginning of the seventeenth century. It is known that those who wrote the language were Manchus, Mongols, Chinese, and Koreans, working as scribes and interpreters in the early days of the Manchu administration. In that early phase, these scribes were the so-called *baksi* (from Chinese, *boshi*, or the widely learned). Later on, different bureaucratic departments employed lower-level *bithesi* (scribes). In addition, before the introduction of this new script, the Manchus used for some centuries, at least on official occasions, the rather unmanageable Jurchen script. Sometimes, they even employed the Mongolian script and language in their written communications.

It was only with the new script that the Manchus turned from a mostly oral society into an "alphabetized" civilization. This development coincided with Manchu settlement in predominantly Chinese surroundings.

---

2. Darlow, *Letters of George Borrow*, pp. 3-6.

In other words, the Manchus were competing both with the Chinese, who were by comparison much more refined, and with the Mongolians, who were also culturally more advanced. The new script, however, was used only in an official context. It never really became the medium in which the Manchus expressed themselves in their art and their beliefs. The development of Manchu as a more comprehensive medium happened only gradually, largely thanks to those from the West, who at the beginning of the twentieth century started to collect Manchu literature, rendering it in the Manchu script.[3]

In an overwhelmingly script-oriented society like China, Manchu writing was for the most part a means to learn about China. In addition, as the Tuoba, the Qidan, the Jurchen, and the Mongol precedents show, having a script of one's own gave additional credibility to legitimate and effective rule.

A Short Remark on Jesuits and their Manchu Language Activities

Allegedly the Manchu translation of the Old Testament, which was never published, was done prior to 1790 by Louis Antoine de Poirot (He Qingtai), who lived from 1735 to 1813. The dating has been made possible because of a note written about the translation in 1790 in a letter by Joseph Panzi (1733–before 1812) and recorded by Louis Pfister.[4] Poirot also translated the New Testament into Chinese, and it seems that he was renowned for his skills in both the Chinese and Manchu languages. Among those to whom he taught Chinese and Manchu were Jean-Joseph de Grammont (1736–before 1812) and the superior of the French Lazaristes, M. Raux. More importantly, Poirot was charged to translate from Latin to Manchu and vice versa the correspondence between Peking and St. Petersburg. As late as 1803, he was still busy working as a Manchu interpreter. He even

---

3. Most prominent is A. V. Grebenshchikov's recording of the tales of the Nishan shamaness. Those tales have also been translated into English, with transcription and analysis, in Margaret Nowak and Stephen Durrant, *The Tale of the Nišan Shamaness: A Manchu Folk Epic*, Publications on Asia of the Institute for Comparative and Foreign Area Studies, no. 31 (Seattle and London: University of Washington Press, 1977). Another example is Fedor Muromskii's recording of tales, which for Manchuists rather disappointingly proved to be mostly adaptations of Pu Songling's *Liaozhai zhi yi*. A final example is the Manchu epic, *Teptalin*, which was supposedly written down by S. M. Shirokogoroff in 1915, but has been lost since 1937. It seems that some traces of this text have been recovered in the meantime (Martin Gimm, verbal communication with author).

4. Louis Pfister, *Notices biographiques et bibliographiques sur les Jésuites de l'ancienne mission de Chine. 1552–1773*, 2 vols. (Chang-hai: Imprimérie de la mission catholique, 1932–1934; reprint, *Variétés sinologiques*, no. 59, 60 [San Francisco: Chinese Materials Center, 1976]), p. 969.

translated the *shengxun* (the sublime instructions) of the Kangxi emperor from Manchu into Italian.[5] Poirot's regular involvement in Chinese-Russian affairs helps to explain how the Russians acquired his Bible translation.[6]

There were other Jesuits who were perhaps even better versed in Manchu. These included Jean-François Gerbillon (1654–1707), Jean Domenge (1666–1735), Joseph Marie Anne de Moyriac de Mailla (1669–1748), Dominique Parrenin (1665-1741), Joseph de Prémare (1666–1736), Antoine Gaubil (1689–1759), Alexandre de la Charme (1695–1767), Pierre Foureau (1700–1749), Michel Benoist (1715–1774), and J.-F.-Marie-Dieudonné d'Ollières (1722–1780).[7] Clearly, this list is not exhaustive, for there were many others, including the famous Ferdinand Verbiest (1623–1688), author of the first western grammar of the Manchu language, and Jean-Joseph-Marie Amiot (1718-1793), compiler of the widely used Tatar-Manchu French Dictionary.[8] Amiot's dictionary was frequently mentioned by Protestant missionaries and was used also by George Borrow.[9]

---

5. Pfister, *Notices biographiques*, pp. 965-70. Joseph Dehergne, *Répertoire des Jesuites de Chine de 1552 à 1800*, Bibliotheca Instituti Historici S. I., no.37 (Rome: Institutum Historicum S.I.; Paris: Letouzey & Ané, 1973), p. 207.

6. Darlow, *Letters of George Borrow*, p. 5, even states that S. V. Lipovtsev of the Russian ecclesiastical mission to Peking met Poirot after 1800. According to Louis Wei Tsing-sing, *La politique missionaire de la France en Chine, 1842–1856. L'ouverture des cinq ports chinois au commerce étranger et la liberté religieuse* (Paris: Nouvelles Éditions Latines, 1960), p. 82, Poirot was admitted to the Jesuits' residence in Russia in 1802. The Jesuits continued to be very interested in the fate of their fellow brethren in China and even tried around 1800 to enter China by way of Siberia with the help of the Russian ecclesiastical mission.

7. Biographical accounts of these Jesuits may be found in Pfister, *Notices biographiques*, pp. 449, 505-506, 597-98, 670, 721, 734, 817, and 904-905. Regarding Parrenin, it was said: "P. Parrenin in negotiis tractandis dexteritatem miram, in loquendo sinice et tartarice facilitatem habet incredibilem." See Dehergne, *Répertoire*, pp. 195-96. Pfister, *Notices biographiques*, pp. 505-506, quotes a letter by P. Valentin Chalier (1697-1747): "Il fut constamment l'interprète de tous les Européens qui sont venu ici, des missionnaires, des légats du St.-Siège, des ambassadeurs de Portugal et de Moscovie. Il a fait près de 40 ans cet emploi dangereux, à la double satisfaction du prince devant qui il parlait et de ceux pour qui il parlait. On était surpris de lui parler également bien le tartare, le chinois, le latin, le français, l'italien, le portugais... Il a toujours été, en quelque manière, le mediateur dans toutes les contestations qu'il y a eu entre ces deux Cours de Pékin et de Moscou. C'est lui qui a dressé les articles de paix qui ont arrêtés entre ces deux nations (en 1726), qui les a mis en latin et en tartare." On Joseph de Prémare, see Knud Lundbæk, *Joseph de Prémare (1666–1736), S. J.: Chinese Philology and Figurism*, Acta Jutlandica 66, no.2, Humanities Series 65 (Aarhus: Aarhus University Press, 1991).

8. *Dictionnaire tartare-mantchou françois* (Paris: F. A. Didot l'ainé, 1789-1790). See also Pfister, *Notices biographiques*, pp. 338-62, 837-60.

9. "How Lavengro Learned Languages," the first 173 pages of which consist of an

The BFBS, the LMS, and their Interest in the Manchu Language

The Manchu translation of the New Testament by Stepan Vasil'evich Lipovtsev (1773–1841),[10] is better known than Poirot's rendition of the Old Testament, because it was published under the auspices of the BFBS. The translation was done for the first time between 1804 and 1808 for the Manchu Christians living in Beijing, but it was not approved by the Holy Synod.[11] It was retranslated by Lipovtsev for the BFBS between 1821 and 1826.

The Old Testament, on the other hand, was obviously never translated in its entirety into Manchu, and the parts that were actually translated were never printed, for various reasons, one of which was the Protestant distrust of any Catholic translation.[12] Already in 1820, William Swan had aired his doubts about the trustworthiness of Jesuit translation work:

> Our chief errand to Kiachta was to have an interview with the Russian Archimandrite Kamenskoe who is here on his way to Pekin. We wished him to procure for us at Pekin a Mongolian and Mandshur lexicon and other books connected with our missionary object... The Archimandrite himself spent ten or twelve years in Pekin in the capacity of a student and is well acquainted both with the Manjshur and Chinese language.
>
> According to appointment we called next day and spent several hours with the dignitaries of the Grk. Church... During his [Kamenskii's] residence in China, he had made the acquaintance of the Roman Catholic missionaries

English-Manchu vocabulary based on Amiot, among others (Norwich Public Record Office, MS. 11337).

10. Hartmut Walravens, "S. V. Lipovcov, A Little Known Russian Manchurist," *Manchu Studies Newsletter*, no. 1/2 (1977/1978), pp. 65-74. On Lipovtsev and two other Russians, Kamenskii and Voitsekhovskii, see also B. K. Paškov, *Der Beitrag russischer Gelehrter zum Studium der mandjurischen Sprache und Literatur*, tr. Hartmut Walravens (Hamburg: C. Bell, 1983), Han-pao tung Ya shu-chi mu-lu 13, pp. 5-7.

11. Hartmut Walravens, "Zur Publikationstätigkeit der Russischen Geistlichen Mission in Peking," in *Monumenta Serica* 34 (1979–1980), p. 529. See also Robert Pinkerton to E. H. Rönneberg, 16 November 1822, BFBS Foreign Correspondence Inwards, 1822, p. 180 (BSA/D1/2/9). The BFBS asked Abel Remusat to check the Manchu translation, at least parts of the NT, which he seems to have judged to be quite acceptable. George Borrow, too, seems to have felt qualified quite early in his Manchu studies to pass judgment on Lipovtsev's translation (see Darlow, *Letters of George Borrow*, p. 7).

12. LMS Directors to Stallybrass, Swan, and Yuille, London, 9 July 1823, LMS Archive, Russia, Box 2 (1825–1834), folder 4A (School of Oriental and African Studies, hereinafter LMS Archive): "We are not surprised to hear of the errors of the Jesuits' Manjur version. It is among the proofs of the essential importance of a mind spiritually enlightened & of that integrity of character which should always be its concommitant, to a translator of the Sacred Scriptures, whatever may be the extent or depth or accuracy of his erudition."

(the Jesuits), of them he spoke in terms of high commendation as great and learned men. He seemed rather dissatisfied that Dr. Morrison had not followed or rather adopted the translation which the Jesuits had made of various parts of the Scriptures. He had a thin volume of their work on the table before him—on enquiry we found that their version contained notes and explanations, and these in the most exceptionable form—not placed at the foot of the page, but printed along with the text. Such interpolations render their work unworthy of the name of a translation of the Word of God... I hinted that as the archimandrite was acquainted with the Manshur language it would be a good work for him to make a translation of the Scriptures into it. This was not the object of his mission he replied, neither would it be practicable to circulate the work among the people... He is however entrusted with a supply of Dr. Morrison's version of the New Testament—and will doubtless find means to disseminate them. He considers Dr. Morrison's dictionary a very great undertaking.[13]

In the same vein, William Swan wrote again two years later:

You will rejoice to hear that we have made a beginning of another important branch of our work, that of the translation of the Scripture; although it has been merely a beginning. During the weeks of harvest Mr. S[tallybrass] and I sat down to the translation of Genesis. I may call it a translation, although we had before us a Mongolian version of the first eighteen chapters made from the Manshur translation of the Jesuit missionaries in China, for as you may easily suppose there were so many departures from the original that the revision of it proved actually a re-translation.[14]

Allegedly, Poirot's Manchu translation of the Old Testament was copied by Archimandrite Petr Kamenskii in 1825–1826 and deposited first in the Aleksandr Nevskii Monastery in St. Petersburg and later in the Asiatic Museum, subsequently known as the Institute of Oriental Studies (Institut vostokovedeniia), under the signature Brosset XIV, N. 1.[15] Apparently another copy, either from the original or from Kamenskii's transcript,

---

13. Swan to William Alers Hankey, Selenginsk, 22 October/1 November 1820, LMS Archive, Russia, Box 1 (1804–1824), folder 4B.

14. Swan to Hankey, Selenginsk, 14 November 1822, LMS Archive, Russia, Box 1, folder 5D.

15. On this question, see Hartmut Walravens, "Zu zwei katholischen Katechismen in mandjurischer Sprache," in *Monumenta Serica* 31 (1974–1975), p. 522 n. 5. Another probable copy (or the original translation?) is in the Tôyô bunko, Sign. 100657. See Nicholas Poppe, Leon Hurvitz, and Okada Hidehiro, *Catalogue of the Manchu-Mongol Section of the Toyo Bunko* (Tokyo: Toyo Bunko and Seattle: University of Washington Press, 1964), no. 510. The Union Catalogue of Manchu holdings in 51 libraries of the People's Republic of China, *Quanguo Manwen tushu ziliao lianhe mulu* (Beijing: Shumu wenxian chubanshe, 1991), does not include any copy of the OT, but this is no proof, since manuscripts are only included sporadically in this catalogue. The original, kept in the Pe-t'ang library, was lost long ago (H. Verhaeren, "La Bibliothèque Chinois du Pet'ang," in *Monumenta Serica* 4 (1939–1940), p. 623).

was made by the medical doctor of the Russian mission, Iosif Voitsekhovskii. This is the one that Swan first heard of, but since Voitsekhovskii had given an asking price of 50,000 rubles if the BFBS wanted to buy it, Swan was rather permitted by Kamenskii to make a copy at no charge with the help of George Borrow.[16] In a letter dating from 1832, Swan quotes the front page of Voitsekhovskii's copy in Latin:

16. Erling v. Mende, "Einige Bemerkungen zu den Druckausgaben des mandjurischen neuen Testaments," in *Oriens Extremus* 19 (1972), pp. 215-16. See also Swan to William Ellis, St. Petersburg, 9 May 1833, LMS Archive, Russia, Box 2, folder 5A, regarding the time-consuming labour of copying the Manchu Bible. See also Swan to John Paterson, St. Petersburg, 7 June 1833, BFBS Paterson Papers, vol. 2, item 172 (BSA/F3/Paterson/2/2), wherein Swan indicates he is occupied with copying the Manchu manuscript and finds it a hard task. See also Swan to Ellis, St. Petersburg, 17 July 1833, LMS Archive, Russia, Box 2, folder 5A, wherein Swan writes about the Manchu Bible, indicating that Mongolian Bibles are found even in Peking. Similarly, in Swan to Thomas Wilson, St. Petersburg, 24 September 1833, LMS Archive, Russia, Box 2, folder 5A, Swan comments on copying the Manchu Bible, indicating at the same time that Borrow, who had come out to assist him, "has made some progress in the study of Manchoo." See also Swan to Joseph Jowett, St. Petersburg, 22 October 1833, BFBS Foreign Correspondence Inwards, 1833, no. 4, p. 59 (BSA/D1/2/44), wherein Swan adds a postscript that Borrow was then transcribing Daniel, and "only a very few books remain of the Manjur Testament." See also Swan to Jowett, St. Petersburg, 2 November 1833, BFBS Foreign Correspondence Inwards, 1833, no. 4, p. 69 (BSA/D1/2/44), wherein Swan writes, "I have been engaged during the present year, on account of the Bible Society [with copying] the Mandjur version of the SS. I have now to report the state of it as follows: 1. I have written out and compared the Pentateuch, 1 (and) 2 Chronicles, Esther, and Ezra; 2. The rest of the Historical Books were forwarded nearly three months ago through the Rev. R. Knill—but the receipt of them remain yet unacknowledged; 3. The Books of Job, Daniel, and Jonah with 14 chaps. of Matthew's Gospel—Mr. Borrow has copied; and 4. The only remaining books are Nehemiah and the Acts of the Apostles which Mr. B[orrow] will copy, and the whole will be compared and ready in the course of a few weeks—the above are all the books contained in the Mss. of Puerot's version (Could the Mss. be brought to England by Mr. Borrow?)." Finally, see also Swan to Jowett, St Petersburg, 5/17 December 1833, BFBS Foreign Correspondence Inwards, 1834, no. 1 p. 10 (BSA/D1/2/45), wherein Swan reports that the whole (Manjur) manuscript is ready for commission to London, as follows:

> The Pentateuch in slips Nos. 1-43; 1st Chronicles in slips Nos. 83-88; 2nd Chronicles in slips Nos. 89-97; Ezra in slips Nos. 98-99; Nehemiah+ in slips Nos. 100-102; Esther in slips Nos. 103-104; Job+ in 6 slips; Daniel+ in 4 slips, yielding a total of 75 slips.

Swan noted that those books marked with the "+" sign were copied by Borrow. Swan adds that "Mr. B[orrow] has also copied the Acts of the Apostles and the first fourteen chapters of Matthew's, but these have not been sent as he may find them useful if he obtain permission to print the N. Testament here. I willingly bear testimony to his

> Partes sacrae Scripturae veteris ac novi Testamenti in Chinense et Manzurica linguis proxime at textum sensum ac verbum S. Scriptura medio, aequali ideoque ad intelligendum uniuscuiusque Chinensium lectorum faciliori stylo, in capitali Chinensium urbe Bey-dzin (vulgo Pekin) versae, cum vasto in unumquodque caput quam sensus tam verborum explicatione, immediate unumquodque caput concomitante, ac in utraque linguarum in meliori Chinensi charta, accurato penicillo, linealiter conjugatim transcriptae, ita ut textus Chinensis eidem textui Mandzurico ubique correspondit.
> ... Partes S. Scripturae sunt sequentes: 1. Geneseos libri 4; 2. Exodi 2; 3. Levitici 2; 4. Numeri 2; 5. Deuteronomii 2; 6. Josue 1; 7. 8. Judicum et Ruth 2; 9. Regum 1 2; 10. Regum 2 2; 11. Regum 3 2; 12. Regum 2; 13. Paralipomenon 1 2; 14. Paralipomenon 2 2; 15. Tobias 1; 16. Judith 1; 17. Esther 1; 18. Job 2; 19. Daniel 2; 20. Machabeorum 4; 21. Evangelium Mathei 4; 22. Acta Apostolorum 2. (Subscrip. Missionis Russico-Chinensis Medicus Josephus Woycechofsky.)[17]

In 1849, the BFBS wanted to obtain another copy of the Manchu Old Testament. This was in response to a request from the Chinese Institution in Kassel, Germany, on behalf of the pioneer China missionary Karl Gützlaff, who hoped to revise and publish the Manchu Old Testament. Gützlaff's death in 1851 put an end to these hopes. Thereafter the BFBS exchanged letters with Walter Medhurst, an LMS missionary in Shanghai, asking him about possible publication of the Manchu Old Testament in China. Even though the Manchu font used for printing the New Testament did find its way to China, nothing came from the plans to print the Old Testament, and the manuscript remained with the BFBS in London. In fact, the manuscript suffered the same fate anticipated for the New Testament publication by many of those involved in the project, including George Borrow[18] and John Paterson.[19]

---

diligence in transscription. I have collated with him all he has done and hope he will succeed in the objects of his visit. A petition has been sent to the Minister of the Interior on the subject of permitting an Edition of the Mandjur N.T. to be printed, and I have even learned by private communication with an official person connected with that department, that the business is in train." All these letters were reported to the editorial subcommittee, including a letter from W. C. Gellibrand, St Petersburg, 15 June 1834, which accompanied the actual manuscript. See BFBS Minutes of Editorial Subcommittee, 26 September 1834, vol. 2 p. 43 (BSA/C17/1/2).

17. Swan described Voitsekhovskii's manuscript in a letter to Andrew Brandram, 10 November 1832, BFBS Foreign Correspondence Inwards, 1832, no. 4, p. 86 (BSA/D1/2/40).

18. Darlow, *Letters of George Borrow*, p. 23.

19. Paterson to Hankey, St. Petersburg, 21 July 1822 [old style], LMS Archive, Russia. Box 1, folder 5C. Paterson writes, "You will no doubt have heard that a translation of part of the Testament is preparing in the Manjure language; but from this we expect nothing at present as not a copy of it can be circulated among the people who speak that tongue, and it can only serve as a literary curiosity among the learned in

Because Swan had neither the time or health to make another copy, his former colleague Edward Stallybrass did the work between 1849 and 1851.[20] Stallybrass himself reports in two letters to T. W. Meller on the early progress of the copying and gives some additional information on the copying in St. Petersburg. In the first letter he states:

> An attack of sickness prevented me from beginning the transcription of the Manjoo O.T. as I intended. Now, however, I am considerably better, & commenced my work on Monday the 1st inst.; I hope, if health be granted, to give a full three months to it in this year.
>
> My friend, Mr. Swan, informs me that the transcription occupied him "about a twelvemonth, at the rate of ten to twelve hours a day for six days

---

Europe. This is the unanimous opinion of our Committee here and in a letter I had from Mr. Swan a few days ago he thus writes on the same subject. The Manjures as you know live within the Chinese territory, and without the sanction of His Imperial Majesty we conceive it would not be consistent with the duty we owe him to go beyond the purpose for which we were permitted to come hither. It is to be considered that our [Tracts] are a direct attack upon Dalai-Lamaism — a superstition sanctioned and supported in China, if they should get [into that] empire and excite the suspicions of that suspicious government, a representation would doubtless be [sent] to the Court of Russia, and our immediate removal from this place the probable consequence. His Excellency Mr. Speransky as well as Prince Galitzin and indeed our whole Committee were unanimous of the opinion that the Russian government could give no such sanction as Mr. Swan refers to and therefore would not allow the Manjures to be printed under the sanction of the Russian Bible Society but only gave permission to its being printed in St. Petersburg for the British and Foreign Bible Society. They only however permitted 500 copies to be printed, as this number will be sufficient to satisfy the curiosity of the learned in Europe."

The number of copies printed compares unfavourably, however, with other projects around the same time. Pinkerton reports the printing of 5,000 copies of a new edition of the Bible in Lithuanian, 2,000 copies in Tatar, and the same number of the Gospels of Luke and Mark in Mongolian and Kalmyk. See "Rev. Dr. Pinkerton's Letters," in *Eighteenth Report of the BFBS* (London, 1822), pp. 42, 44, and 45.

20. Stallybrass to Andrew Brandram, Dorchester, 2 June 1849, BFBS Foreign Correspondence Inwards, 1849, no. 1, p. 281 (BSA/D1/2/101). Stallybrass, noting his own very bad health, writes that it was Swan who copied the Manchu OT. See also Swan to Brandram, Edinburgh, 6 June 1849, BFBS Foreign Correspondence Inwards, 1849, no. 1, p. 285 (BSA/D1/2/101). Also, see Stallybrass to the Committee of the BFBS (with a separate note to Rev. George Browne), Clapton, 27 September 1851, BFBS Foreign Correspondence Inwards, 1851, no. 2, p. 103 (BSA/D1/2/110), in which Stallybrass indicates he has completed the transcription of the Manchu Old Testament and has tried to correct errors in the text. BFBS Archives today possess two manuscripts of the Manchu Old Testament, the one copied by Swan and Borrow (BFBS MS. 349), and the one copied subsequently in 1849-1851 by Stallybrass (BFBS MS. 351). Preparation of the second copy was owing to BFBS reluctance to send off the Swan/Borrow transcription.

of the week—often from twelve to fourteen hours. This (he says) was too much, but you know how time pressed."

Neither my health nor engagements will allow of my devoting so much time to the work. At present six hours close writing per diem is all that I could undertake...

The copy which I have to transcribe was made from a copy. It is not much to be wondered at, therefore, that many of the orthographical errors occur. As my friend, Mr. Swan, made the copy in St. Petersburg, separated from his books etc., he was unable to rectify many errors which he found. I am differently situated, having one Lexicon Manjoo & French, & another Manjoo & Mongolian. To correct the version I regard as no part of my business. But where I find the orthography manifestly wrong—sometimes conveying another sense—I do not like to perpetuate an error. Still, the corrections cost time, for reference to books etc., and impede progress.

Were it Mongolian it would be almost natural to write it correctly. With the Manjoo, however, it is different, as that language has not formed a part of our study.

Will you, dear Sir, favour me with your opinion as to the course I should adopt. In some cases the word is evidently left, as it was found, equivocal, uncertain. Should I imitate this, or take the time necessary to put it right?—If the Commee. wish to send the Ms., they need not, I presume, wait till the whole is finished, as a part might be sent when any favourable opportunity occurs.[21]

In another letter to Meller (12 November 1849), Stallybrass provides further information on the process of copying:

I was glad to receive your note on Saturday evening, as it gave me some idea of what the feeling of the Committee is, respecting the work which I have commenced. I have already said, and I wish to stand by, and act upon what I have said, that remuneration is not my chief object in undertaking the work. If, therefore, the Committee think that £250 is a full and equitable sum for the whole work, I am content to perform it—if life & health be spared—for that sum...

Mr. Swan is of all men best qualified to calculate the amount of time and labour involved in the work. And, I may add, to those who know him, beyond suspicion of cherishing any selfish motives. I thought you, perhaps, would wish to lay Mr. S.'s letter before the Commee—He would lay out for me more work than mere transcription. But the latter, I presume, is all that the Commee wish to have done here. And I can easily imagine that they would prefer having the work of revising and correcting the version executed by those who are more conversant with the language idiomatically than I profess to be. It is evidently made from the Vulgate; and will require many corrections to make it conformable to our present Hebrew textual reading, or to our own authorized version.[22]

21. Stallybrass to T. W. Meller, 5 October 1849, BFBS Foreign Correspondence Inwards, 1849, no. 2, p. 133 (BSA/D1/2/102).

22. Stallybrass to Meller, 12 November 1849, BFBS Foreign Correspondence Inwards, 1849, no. 2, p. 164 (BSA/D1/2/102).

Reasons for the BFBS to Consider a Manchu Version of the Bible

Certainly, BFBS interest in the Manchu language was not unique, judging by the well-informed, if misguided, article published in the *Chinese Repository*. There the anonymous author proposed the idea of turning Manchu into the *lingua franca* of the whole of East Asia.[23]

The LMS seems to have become actively interested in things Manchu in 1814, when John Paterson and Robert Pinkerton advocated the establishment of a missionary station in the neighbourhood of Irkutsk. From there one could also, in their view, try to target the Manchus and Chinese, as well as the Buryats and Kalmyks, because Irkutsk, or rather Selenginsk, was on the main route between Russia and China. Thus, in 1814, Paterson and Pinkerton wrote back to the London LMS offices with the following message:

> Since returning to Russia our thoughts have been much employed with the object about which we conversed so fully with you while in London: namely your sending missionaries to that part of Siberia which borders on China, for the purpose of spreading the glorious Gospel of the Blessed God among the numerous tribes of heathens in those extensive regions, and particularly with the view of translating the word of life into the Mongol and Manjur languages. Irkutsk or its neighbourhood was the place, which Mr. Pinkerton, after having with much labour examined into the present state of the nations of Siberia, considered as the most eligible for the establishment of such a mission. We are more than ever convinced that, as far as we are able to judge before hand, this is one of the most important missionary stations of the world, being so central, and surrounded by so many different tribes, and having been the chief place of communication between China and Russia...
>
> But we are of opinion that the mission established in this quarter should make it also a chief object to spread the Gospel among the Manjurs which are a still more numerous people than the Mongols, and the conquerors of China — the present Emperor of which is a Manjur, and their language is spoken at the court of China. Were the Gospel to gain access among this interesting people, a highway for its entrance would be opened, from this quarter, even into China itself. Their language has been much more cultivated than the Mongolian, with which it has some connection. Many of the Chinese books have been translated into it, the language is said to be easily learned, the grammar regular; and what is a great advantage, there exists a dictionary, Manjur and French, published in Paris. The Manjurs are not like the Buryats inhabitants of Russia; they inhabit that extensive tract of country called Chinese Tartary, which borders on Russia, and their language can easily be learned in Irkutsk.[24]

---

23. "Considerations on the Language of Communication between the Chinese and European Governments," *Chinese Repository*, vol. 13 (1844), pp. 281-300.

24. Paterson and Pinkerton to George Burder, St. Petersburg, 7 November 1814, LMS Archive, Russia, Box 1, folder 1.

Though the hope to penetrate China and the Manchu empire through Siberia proved as futile as a somewhat earlier attempt to do so by the Moravian brethren through Tibet—and not only because the Chinese/Manchus resisted, but also because of Russian policies—this hope was slow to die.[25] Therefore, even when they were still in St. Petersburg the LMS missionaries started learning Manchu alongside their Russian and Mongol.[26]

In a letter exchange dating from the end of 1818, Edward Stallybrass reported to William Alers Hankey about his busy linguistic schedule:

> I wish I could add that my attainements [in Mongolian] have kept good pace with my time and application; these however appear very small, compared with all other languages that I have learned… I never before knew the want of a grammar and lexicon in learning a language. Our teacher although he is reported to know the Mongolian tongue well, does not know it scientifically, and knows that a thing is so, rather than why it is so. I receive my instruction from him in Russ, and this you will easily perceive is an additional difficulty; for though on common subjects I can speak and understand with ease, but to enter into all the peculiarities of a language requires much more knowledge. I have however found this very useful in improving me in the Russian language. We have however 11 chapters of the Book of Genesis translated by our teacher, which we have read over and over…and also 100 dialogues with a Russ translation, some of which I have committed to memory. We have also the journal of a Chinese ambassador through Russia and Siberia [in the Mongolian language] of which a translation in Russ, French or German is to be obtained in St. P[etersburg]? and a little of the Manjur language, in each of which I could improve myself if necessary. The Mongolian books which we have, or which we can obtain, are all written, and we have employed persons here to copy the above for us at a moderate charge.
>
> With respect to your important question, I scarcely know how to answer. Perhaps you will have heard ere this that we have received a supply of Chinese Testaments and Tracts from our friends in Malacca, by Captain [Peter] Gordon, who has made a voyage to Ochotsk; but we are at a

---

25. How much Manchu was overrated as a medium for missionary work in China becomes evident also in a letter by Robert Pinkerton from St. Petersburg dated 1 December 1821 (see *Eighteenth Report of the BFBS* [London, 1822], p. 43), wherein he writes, "I enclose my agreement with the Manjur translator. The sum agreed on is lower than I expected; for the labour of translating into a language, in which Christian ideas are unknown, will be very great. Of its importance it will be sufficient to say, that it is one of the two languages spoken and cultivated in the vast Empire of China. It therefore is next in importance to the Chinese version for that Empire."

26. Stallybrass to Hankey, St. Petersburg, 14/26 August 1817, LMS Archive, Russia, Box 1, folder 1; Stallybrass to Hankey, Moscow, 3 January 1818, LMS Archive, Russia, Box 1, folder 1.

loss to know what to do with them. The governor has heard of our reception of them, and says it is impossible for us to distribute them, but if we let him have some, he will do it. This for many reasons we are unwilling to do without some further directions... In our late journeys we took Kiachta in our way, which is just on the frontiers of the Russian Empire, and close by those of China. We wished to see the Chinese town, about 4 versts from Kiachta, but the Director at Kiachta, to whom we had a letter of introduction, and who behaved very politely, told us that he thought it best for us not to go, because a report of hostility between China and England was current, and he said, he feared, not on our account, but for himself, thinking the Chinese (regarding us as spies) would suspect the Russians. In this and many other instances I have seen that the Russian people here fear doing any thing which would be likely to displease the Chinese, and unless some order were given of an Imperial kind, I fear it would not be practicable to distribute the Scriptures among them. So it appears to us at present, but when we remove beyond the Sea we may be able to learn something of which we are now ignorant. Our contemplated residence, Selenginsk, is only 100 versts from Kiachta, and from this we may be able to know more.[27]

---

27. Stallybrass to Hankey, Irkutsk, 21 October/2 November 1818, LMS Archive, Russia, Box 1, folder 2D. Several references in the Stallybrass letter can be clarified by reference to Charles R. Bawden, *Shamans, Lamas and Evangelicals: The English Missionaries in Siberia* (London: Routledge & Kegan Paul, 1985), pp. 54-56, 135, 220. Stallybrass's comment about his attainments reflects the fact he was not fluent in Buriat after a year's language study in Irkutsk.

The reference to use of the text of Genesis and the Russian dialogues reflects, as Bawden notes, that the missionaries had no grammar and no dictionary, and very little to read. Their reading matter consisted of eleven chapters of Genesis translated by their teacher, a book of dialogues — from Stallybrass's description probably a Mongolian version of the well-known Manchu-Chinese primer of conversation known as *Tanggô meyen*, or the *Hundred Chapters*, and a Mongolian version of what was undoubtedly the travel journal of Tulishen.

On the matter of instructional materials and the Manchu books, there is considerable correspondence from Russia, including the following: Paterson to Hankey, St. Petersburg, 13/25 December 1818, LMS Archive, Russia, Box 1, folder 2D; Stallybrass to Hankey, Selenginsk, 4/16 May 1820, LMS Archive, Russia, Box, folder 4B; Swan to Hankey, Selenginsk, 22 October/1 November 1820, LMS Archive, Russia, Box 1, folder 4B; Swan to Hankey, Selenginsk, 23 December 1821, LMS Archive, Russia, Box 1, folder 5B; and Robert Yuille to Hankey, Selenginsk, 1/13 October 1831, LMS Archive, Russia, Box 2, folder 4A. In fact, William Swan had already written to John Paterson on 13/25 June 1820, indicating that more missionaries were necessary if the Manchus were to be added to the task of the Selenginsk missionaries. Swan noted that "the Manjoor language can be acquired at Irkutsk under a well qualified teacher. If they [the directors of the LMS] have any thoughts of attempting the introduction of the Gospel among the Mandschurs [manjoors], the Lords of China, they must send other missionaries hither. Our hands are filled and I trust our hearts also with the work among the Mongolians." Swan was implying it was best for there to be a restriction to

162   Sowing the Word

From outside the missionary fold, the London Missionary Society's strategy to get a foothold in China via Siberia might indeed have looked like a clever strategy, as may be indicated by the exchange of letters dating from 1818 between Peter Gordon and George Burder on missions to Malacca, China, Japan, and Korea:

> The establishment of missionaries at Irkutsk leads me to suppose that your attention is occupied with the Mandshurs. Should that be the case I cannot but hope it may lead to the establishment of a mission about the isthmus of Sagalien which appears to be a very commanding and centrical station. It would most probably prove to be the key of the northern parts of Japan, of Sagalien, the coast of Tartary, and of Corea.[28]

A Sample of the Manchu Old Testament Translation with Interpretive Comments

In light of these missionary efforts to link Manchu translation with wider entry into China via Siberia and the Russian ecclesiastical mission to Peking, it is interesting to review a sample text from Poirot's Old Testament translation (*Yob sere nomun-i bithe, juwan duici fiyelen* [The book called Job, chap. 14], as follows:

---

one people and one language. See Swan to Paterson, 13/25 June 1820, BFBS Paterson Papers, vol. 2, item 68 (BSA/F3/Paterson 2/2).

In London, the BFBS later provided Borrow with the books available at that time in Europe to study the Manchu language. They also urged John Hattersley to study Manchu in case Borrow should fail (Darlow, *Letters of George Borrow*, p. 12). No mention is made of another apparently competent Manchuist available in London, William Huttmann, who as secretary to the Royal Asiatic Society in 1828 provided the BFBS with publications relevant to Manchu language studies and later was employed by the BFBS in translating the NT into Chinese. In the early thirties Huttmann supposedly was a member of the Congregational Dissenters (see his obituary in *Asiatic Journal*, vol. 4 [1845], pp. 104-105).

On Peter Gordon, see Bawden, *Shamans*, pp. 54-56. On the Chinese and Russian border near Kiakhta referenced in the Stallybrass letter, see William Coxe, *Account of the Russian Discoveries between Asia and America, to Which Are Added, the Conquest of Siberia, and the History of the Transactions and Commerce between Russia and China*, 4th ed. (London: Printed by J. Nichols for T. Cadell, 1804), p. 215, wherein Coxe writes, "Midway between, two posts about ten feet high are planted in order to mark the frontier of the two empires: one is inscribed with Russian, the other with Manshur characters."

28. Gorden to Burder, Ochotsk, 3/15 November 1818, LMS Archive, Russia, Box 1, folder 2D.

Mende *Problems in Translating the Bible into Manchu* 163

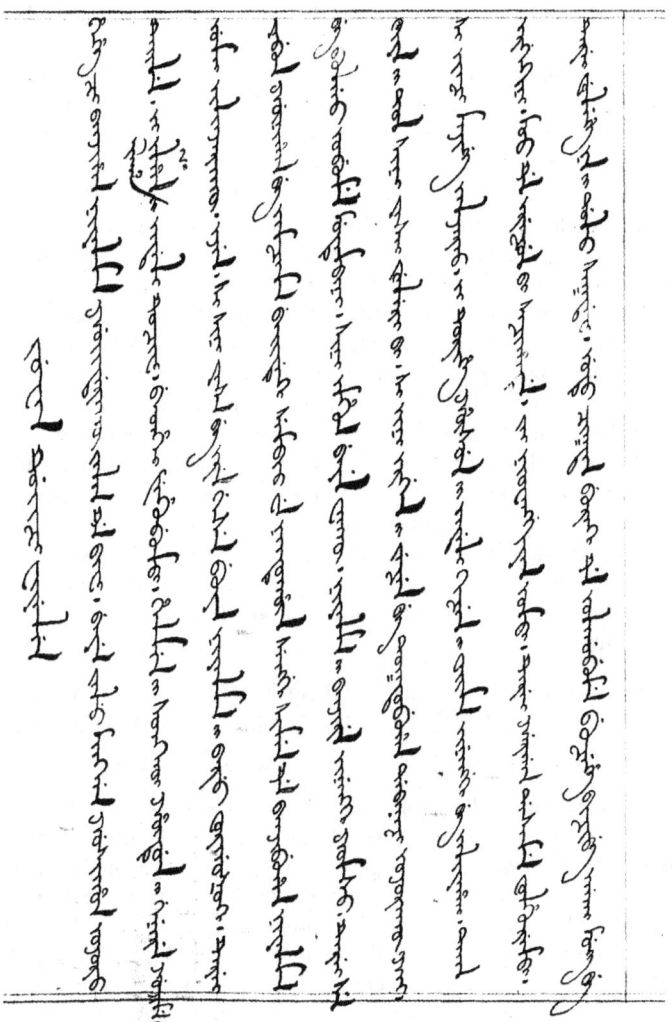

Picture 20. *Job, beginning of Chap. 14, in Manchu.* Specimen of BFBS MS. 349 courtesy of BFBS collections, Cambridge University Library

[1],Hehe ci banjiha niyalma goidarakô jalan de bifi. beye jalu mangga gosihon ojoro teile. [2] ilha [corrected by an obviously trained hand from *i ilha-i*] adali tucifi. bethei fehubumbi. helmen-i songkoi hôdun-i genere gojime. umai ilinjarakô. [3] ejen. si sini yasa be ere gese buya niyalma-i baru forgošoki. terei yabun gôniha be amcame beideki sembio [4] we nantuhôn senggi simen de banjibuha niyalma be bolgo obume mutembini. sini emhun beye wakao. [5] niyalma-i banjire inenggi komso. terei se biya-i ton sini yasai juleri bi. si ini ergen-i jecen be toktobuha dabanaci ojorakô kai. [6] si inci majige aljarao. i turihe hôsun-i adali kicen-i wajima inenggi be aliyahai. taka ergekini. [7] moo de erecun bi sacihade. jai niowanggiyan ombi. terei gargan

dasame fulhurembi. [8] terei fulehe na-i dolo sakdafi. udu ciktan buraki de olgobume bucehe bicibe ganji (?) [9] muke be (38) baha manggi arsun arsumbime geli tuktan tebuhe adali subehe abdaha be duin ergi ici banjimbi. [10] niyalma oci. akô oho. niohušun beye eifu de dosimbuha mukiyehe amala fonjime. aibide bi. [11] mederi. bira-i muke da ulan ci tucime gôwabsi genehede. mederi bira-i fere uthai fara adali. [12] niyalma inu emgeri bucefi. abka mohotolo. jai banjirakô. bucen-i emu ci geterakô. ilirakô. [13] we sini ere kesi be minde bahabuki ejen bairengge. si sini horonggo jili toroko de isitala. mimbe na-i fejile karmame dalireo. geli mimbe gosime ejere erin be minde toktoruo. [14] bucehe niyalma dahôn-i banjimbi semeo. na-i afara geren inenggi de mini beyei icemlere be aliyame bi. [15] si mimbe hôlaki. bi inu jabumbi. si hono sini banjibuha niyalma- baru gala be saniyaki. [16] si mini yabuhala baita be toloho ofi. yala geleci acambihe. ne mini waka babe guwebureo. [17] mini weile be fulhô de tebufi fempilaha gese. damu si mini ehe be dasihabi. [18] alin farsi farsi ome genehei teni (39) ulejembi. wehe da baci guribumbi. [19] aga sabdan sabdan-i wehe be šungkutu obumbi bilteme bisarara muke be na be ulhiyen ulhiyen-i efulembi. ejen si emu adali durun-i niyalma be mohobumbi. [20] majige hôsun be inde salgabuha sehe seme. i naranggi dulefi enteheme marinjirakô si terei cira be halhai. teni ere jalan ci tucibumbi. [21] ini juse omosi wesihun bicibe. fusihôn ocibe. i oron sarkô [22] ini yali beye emu jalan hôsime nimere ini sure fayangga aliha gosihon-i turgunališara teile.²⁹

If one then seeks to re-translate into English this commonly recognized selection of the Book of Job from Poirot's Manchu text, as copied in the BFBS manuscript, the result is something like the following:

[1]Man born by woman does not belong to a long-lasting species. His body experiences in full strong bitterness. [2] Like a flower he appears, downtrodden he disappears without lingering. [3] Lord, would you direct your eyes on such a wretched man? Would you discriminately judge his deeds and thoughts? [4] Can one say that? Man is born from impure blood and humours, who can purify him? Is that not you alone? [5] Man's lifespan is short. The number of his years and months is before your eyes, and you do not let him surpass the border destined for his life. [6] Would you just remove yourself a little from him, so that he could like a conscientious hired labourer abide the time until the last day. Would you in the meantime grant him respite. [7] There is hope for a tree. When it has been cut down, it can sprout again, and twigs will spring up again. [8] Even if its roots age below ground and its branches dry up to become dust and die, [9] as soon as it gets water, it sprouts again. As if planted for the first time, twigs and leaves grow in all directions. [10] Of man nothing is left. The naked corpse is buried, and when he has grown cold, one asks, where he is.

[11] If the waters of the seas and rivers leave their original bed and flow somewhere else and the bottom of the seas and rivers dries up, [12] then this is like man, who when he has died will not be reborn until the end of

---

29. BFBS MS. 349. This is the BFBS copy of the Manchu text transcribed by George Borrow.

Heaven. He will never wake from death nor get up again. [13] Who will for me obtain your grace? I am one who prays to the Lord: "Until You have softened Your terrible wrath, can you hide me beneath the earth for protection? Would it be that you fixed my time, when you might look mercifully upon me. [14] And tell: Can the dead live again?" All day long, when I fight on earth, I wait that I may be renewed. [15] Would You call me! I would answer. Would You give Your hand to man born by You. [16] I must fear that you count my deeds. Would my sins be forgiven! [17] Would my guilt be put into a bag, as if it was locked away! In this way you will have covered up my misdeeds. [18] A mountain piece by piece disappears, and in the end it crumbles completely. Stones are moved from their original place, [19] and rain hollows them drop by drop. Water that inundates all, slowly destroys all earth. Lord, in exactly the same way You cause hardship for man. [20] Let him have little strength, You said, so that at last he will never return. You change his face and let him leave this world. [21] Whether his sons and grandsons are honoured or humble, he would not know their position. [22] His body experiences pain the whole lifetime. His soul is depressed because of all pain encountered.[30]

To a great extent, this short extract seems to confirm the secondary remarks on Poirot's translation and the Swan/Borrow copy held in the BFBS archive. In fact, the translation is very close to the Vulgate,[31] with one possible exception — the last part of Job 14.17:

Vulgate: "sed curasti iniquitatem meam"
Manchu: "damu si mini ehe be dasihabi"

This passage seems to follow the rendering in the Revised Standard Version: "and thou wouldest cover over my iniquity," rather than the German translation of the Vulgate, which reads, "aber hast deine Aufmerksamkeit meiner Schuld zugewendet."

The Borrow/Swan copy (BSMS. 349) used by me in the BFBS Archives shows a somewhat clumsy handwriting and several spelling mistakes,[32] while the very few corrections in Job seem to derive from an individual with superior, if not native, training. The text is legible, with the exception of the word *ganji* (?), while the spelling mistakes mostly concern the writing of diphthongs. Diacritical marks are used at random. The translation itself seems to be basically admissable and understandable, at least from a grammatical viewpoint.[33]

---

30. A literal translation from the Manchu by the author.
31. *Biblia Sacra Vulgatae Editionis Sixti V. Pontifici Maximi Jussu Recognita et Clementis VIII*, 2nd ed., vol. 1. (Ratisbonae: Fridericus Pustet, 1903), pp. 1273-75 (with a German translation).
32. Walravens, "Zu zwei katholischen Katechismen," p. 525.
33. Surely, more serious research would have to include the other known copies of Poirot's translation.

There is one stylistic peculiarity, not only in this short piece, but throughout the translation, namely the constant use of the personal pronoun *si* (you), when God is directly addressed. Instead, one would have expected the rather formal and respectful *ejen* (Lord), or *abkai ejen* (The Lord of Heaven). As it happens, Borrow in one of his letters referred to a discussion he had had with Lipovtsev about what would better convey the relationship between God and man as expressed in the Bible. Borrow's preference was for the more familiar "you," while Lipovtsev argued for the impersonal third person:

> He replied that he had the best of reasons; for that amongst the Chinese and Tartars none but the dregs of society were ever addressed in the second person; and that it would be most uncouth and indecent to speak to the Almighty as if He were a servant or a slave.[34]

Borrow's own argumentation, on the other hand, focused on the kind of attitude men should have toward God — that is, one addresses Him "rather as children their father," which means that the man-God relationship is "a mixture of reverence and love." In this Borrow seemed to follow Poirot, who uses *si* and *sini* (your) throughout his translation. In fact, Borrow's pronominal preference is in perfect agreement with previous Jesuit translation work, as is clearly shown by the renditions of the *Pater noster* and *Ave Maria*.[35] Nevertheless, Lipovtsev surely had the better argument, not only because it was important to take into account social habits, but also because of the way the language was actually used. Similar to classical Chinese (*wenyan*) and even colloquial (*baihua*) Chinese, Manchu tended to drop the sentence's subject whenever possible. Manchu shamanist prayers or incantations, to take but one generic example, normally list at the beginning the names of the spirits or gods specifically addressed in the liturgy. In the remaining text no pronominal substitution takes place, thus making it impossible to distinguish the third from the second person.[36]

As to the expressions *abkai ejen* (Lord of Heaven) and *ejen* (Lord), which were chosen both by the Jesuits and Lipovtsev to translate the concept of "God," they are not found outside Christian texts. Still they convey the

---

34. Darlow, *Letters of George Borrow*, pp. 74-75.

35. Walravens, "Zu zwei katholischen Katechismen," pp. 527-33; 537.

36. This is found, for example, throughout the shamanist ritual of the Šušu Gioro Clan, written down in 1771. See Alessandra Pozzi, *Manchu-Shamanica Illustrata*, Shamanica Manchurica Collecta 3 (Wiesbaden: Harrassowitz, 1992). In the *Nišan saman-i bithe* (see, Nowak and Durrant, *The Tale of the Nišan Shamaness*), in the incantations to the spirits, personal pronouns are avoided, while the shamaness addresses the father of the son to be redeemed by her from Ilmun han, the ruler of the underworld, using the second person. The same is used when the shamaness and spirits of the netherworld argue with each other, obviously on equal standing.

original meaning very well, distinguishing themselves from the impersonal *dergi abka* and *amba abka* (High or Great Heaven) or the rather personal *abkai enduri* and *abkai han* (Spirit or Lord of Heaven). Semantically, *abkai ejen* is in fact analogous with Chinese *tianzhu*, coined by the Jesuits to name "God."

Elegantly rendered are also verses 16 and 17. *Waka ba* (sins; in the Vulgate, *peccati*) uses the rather concrete *waka* (having done something that is wrong), transforming it through *ba* which conveys the meaning of innate wrong-doing. *Weile* (transgression; in the Vulgate, *delicta*) originally means something like a misdeed that must be punished. Finally, *ehe* (iniquity; in the Vulgate, *iniquitas*) signifies in its basic meaning, "what is evil."[37]

The term "soul," as it occurs in verse 22, even though it was skipped by the Revised Standard Version, was translated by Martin Luther as "Seele" and as "anima" in the Vulgate. This concept might have been rather difficult to grasp, not only for the Manchus. The Manchus were familiar with the notion of forces implanted in man, both positive (*enduri*) and negative (*hutu*). This notion was semantically overlaid by Chinese influences to become *fayangga* (the yang-soul; Chinese, *hun*) and *oron* (the yin-soul; Chinese, *po*). Though one finds *sure fayangga* used in Manchu translation by Hauer (sub *sure*), he gives as his only source von der Gabelentz.[38] A random look at traditional Manchu dictionaries did not reveal such an entry. Apparently, this term is an ingenious, and yet at the same time for Manchus an easily understandable, neologism coined by the Jesuits, which can be retranslated as "the soul able of cognition" (*sure*; wise). By contrast, in shamanist usage the soul was the place of life, and the soul had to be summoned back (*fayangga hôlambi*) to save man from death.[39]

---

37. Durrant, in Nowak and Durrant, *The Tale of the Nišan Shamaness*, p. 89 (Manchu text, p. 164), translates *miosihôn ehe* as "sins and evils," but then, *miosihôn*, which has more the notion of "the wrong creed," or heterodoxy, would not have fit in this context.

38. Erich Hauer, *Handwörterbuch der Mandschusprache* (Wiesbaden: Harrassowitz, 1952-1955), p. 833.

39. The act of reviving the boy brought back from the underworld by the Nišan shamaness is described as *fayangga be oron beyede...singgebume sindahabi*, translated by Durrant in *The Tale of the Nišan Shamaness* (p. 85) as "(I) have infused a soul...into his empty body," while it rather should be — under Chinese influence — "I have infused his *hun*-soul into his *po*-soul." Durrant (p. 75 n. 21) quotes Sergei M. Shirokogoroff, *Psychomental Complex of the Chinese* (London: Kegan Paul, Trench, Trübner & Co, 1935), pp. 52, 135, wherein he says that the Manchus conceive of the soul as being composed of three elements, the "true soul," which may be compared with "consciousness" and which cannot leave the body without causing death; the "soul that precedes," which may temporarily leave the body during dreams or the loss of the soul, and which after death may be given to another child; and the "external soul," which returns to the underworld after death, at which time it may be reincarnated into another person or animal.

The plot of the Book of Job itself cannot have been too difficult to understand. God or the spirits testing the faith of men was not for the Manchus an extraordinary experience. The rich Baldu, one of the main characters in the *Nišan saman-i bithe*, a pious and charitable man, is twice tempted to lose his faith after the death of his two sons. To no avail, however, for Baldu remains a staunch believer. The similes of toppling mountains, dried-up seas and rivers, and raindrops hollowing out stones are as Chinese, or East Asian for that matter, as they are western. The first two mentioned have been *topoi* of Chinese culture at least since Han times, when they served as rhetorical devices to describe disorder or any major deviation from the natural order of things. As to the simile of the tree that contrary to man sprouts again, it seems to be western in nature. By contrast, the horror and grief experienced by man's not knowing what will happen to his children and grandchildren is not only a western obsession, but in fact very much Chinese.

To sum up this rather impressionistic treatment of one chapter of the Book of Job, the text does reflect both Chinese and Manchu experience, and can be appreciated as a reminder of how fragile a seemingly blissful life could be. The vanitas notion is not strange to the people of East Asia. Indeed, it was the one notion, detected by Matteo Ricci, that would enable Buddhists—and Chinese for that matter—to accept Christian ideas. This vanitas idea is represented in Chinese by the "Confucian" *xu* (emptiness), the Daoist *wu* (the non-existent), and the Buddhist *kong* (the void; *śūnyatā*). In Manchu the idea is expressed by *untuhun* (emptiness).[40]

---

40. Iso Kern, "Matteo Riccis Verhältnis zum Buddhismus," in *Monumenta Serica* 36 (1984–1985), p. 75.

THE BFBS PETERSBURG AGENCY AND RUSSIAN BIBLICAL TRANSLATION, 1856-1875

Stephen K. Batalden

Introduction

During the first fifty years of the life of the British and Foreign Bible Society, the Russian Empire was the scene for the Society's greatest international success and its most conspicuous failure. Initially, BFBS representatives John Paterson, Ebenezer Henderson, and Robert Pinkerton helped launch the most ambitious Bible publishing and translation center outside Britain—namely, in St. Petersburg. In a single decade, more than two million copies of Scripture were published in more than a dozen languages at a modern stereotype printing office that housed operations of the Russian Bible Society (*Rossiiskoe bibleiskoe obshchestvo*, 1812-1826).[1] The success of the Russian Bible Society owed in great measure to the entrepreneurial leadership of the great Scottish Congregationalist, John Paterson. Vivid accounts of the Society's activities often dominated the pages of the annual BFBS published reports. The Russian Bible Society produced the landmark *textus primus*, or first edition, of a Russian-language New Testament (all previous published editions had been in the

---

1. For a chronology of the founding of the Russian Bible Society from the arrival of John Paterson in Russia in August 1812 to the first session of the Russian Bible Society in January 1813, see Paterson's published memoir, *The Book for Every Land: Reminiscences of Labour and Adventure in the Work of Bible Circulation in the North of Europe and in Russia* (London: John Snow, 1858), pp. 164-93. On the Russian Bible Society, more generally, see the standard work of A. N. Pypin, "Rossiiskoe bibleiskoe obshchestvo," in his *Religioznyia dvizheniia pri Aleksandre I*, vol. 1 of 3: *Izsledovaniia i stat'i po epokhe Aleksandra I*, with introduction and notes by N. K. Piksanov (Petrograd: Izdatel'stvo "OGNI," 1916). The Pypin work was first published in *Vestnik Evropy* in 1868. The finest one-volume study on the Russian Bible Society in English is the unpublished dissertation of Judith Cohen Zacek, "The Russian Bible Society, 1812-1826," Columbia University, 1964. See also S. K. Batalden, "Printing the Bible in the Reign of Alexander I: Toward a Reinterpretation of the Russian Bible Society," in Geoffrey A. Hosking, ed., *Church, Nation and State in Russia and Ukraine* (London: Macmillan and University of London School of Slavonic and East European Studies, 1991), pp. 65-78.

Old Church Slavonic language), as well as printed editions of a Russian-language Psalter and an uncirculated printing in sheets of the first eight books of the Old Testament, the Russian Octateuch.

Nevertheless, responding to the concerns of Orthodox hierarchs and court officials who saw the unchecked energy of the Bible Society as a threat to mainstream Orthodox and Slavonic tradition, Tsar Nicholas I decreed in 1826 the closure of the Russian Bible Society, effectively proscribing all modern Russian biblical translation and publication. For the next thirty years, attempts at modern Russian biblical translation were relegated to the underground. The low point in this period of repression occurred when clandestinely circulated lithographed copies of a Russian Old Testament prepared in the 1830s by former Russian Bible Society activist and Hebraic scholar, Gerasim Petrovich Pavskii, were seized by the authorities. Throughout the empire, owners of all copies were interrogated, and the seized copies were burned. This so-called Pavskii affair (*delo Pavskogo*) yielded the greatest Bible conflagration of the modern era, representing a complete reversal in the fate of the Russian Bible in the second quarter of the nineteenth century.[2]

How is one to interpret the unprecedented success and, immediately thereafter, the unparalleled repression of modern Russian biblical translation in the first half of the nineteenth-century? And, how were the lessons of that early engagement of the BFBS in Russia reflected in the activities of the Petersburg BFBS agency when modern Russian biblical translation was once again allowed in 1856? To answer these questions it is necessary to contextualize what ultimately came to be called the *sinodal'nyi perevod*, or the Synodal translation of the Russian Bible completed in the 1870s.

In exploring the reasons for the quite remarkable success and subsequent failure of modern biblical translation in Alexander I's Russia, it is helpful to reflect upon the nature of the British and Foreign Bible Society itself, and its transforming impact on religious culture in the west. For, the remarkable thing about the BFBS was that it became both in Britain and in its far-flung overseas agencies a significant force for "modernity," or a distinctively modern religious culture. The use of the word "modernity" here draws upon a set of very specific meanings attached to the term by the German critical theorist Jürgen Habermas, who ironically, until recently, has largely failed to address religious culture. In his landmark work, *The Structural Transformation of the Public Sphere,* Habermas provides a clear focus for the often-muddled discussion of modernity. He writes that modernity is a distinct phase in history when, led by commercial,

---

2. S. K. Batalden, "Gerasim Pavskii's Clandestine Old Testament: The Politics of Nineteenth-Century Russian Biblical Translation," *Church History*, vol. 57, no. 4 (1988), pp. 486-98.

bourgeois agents, a powerful new discursive "public sphere" emerged, a sphere that was both distinct from the direct authority of the state—indeed was frequently at odds with the authority of the state—yet at the same time was separate from the vested interests of powerful families or a given social estate, such as the aristocracy or church hierarchy.[3] Both in its universalism and in its political, democratizing character, the public sphere ultimately came to be associated with the development of civil society in nineteenth-century Britain, a civil society determined not by privilege of birth, but by law and the rational appeal to public interest.

Although Habermas has written very little on religious culture, he argues that the same kind of discursive power that came to operate within the secular public sphere inevitably also came to function in the adaptation of religious culture to modernity. Thus, the quite extraordinary, unprecedented success of the British and Foreign Bible Society in the nineteenth century owed in good measure to the remarkable capacity of the Society to capitalize upon and manipulate this emergent public sphere in Britain. As Leslie Howsam has demonstrated in her work *Cheap Bibles* and in her essay on the BFBS as publisher within this collection, the BFBS Committee in the nineteenth century was invariably dominated by entrepreneurs who were prepared to link the latest technological developments in stereotype printing with modern management techniques both in the organization of their domestic biblical enterprise and in the development of their far-flung international chapters and auxiliaries.[4] The Society's universalizing, evangelical mission (what Habermas would call its ideology) could even be interpreted as fundamentally democratic in character, targeted to a public sphere that placed greater importance upon literacy, the marketplace, and Bible reading in prisons than upon the authority of bishops and church hierarchs. In short, the evangelizing, universalizing, democratizing, and commercializing goals of the British and Foreign Bible Society reflected a unique and powerful accommodation of religious culture to modernity and the emergent public sphere in nineteenth-century Britain.

Interpreting the Fate of the Russian Bible Society, 1812–1826

It is this remarkably "modern" religious culture, reflected in the leadership and operations of the BFBS, that helps to explain both the unprecedented initial success of the BFBS in Russia and, at the same time, the precipitous collapse of the Russian Bible Society in 1826. In interpreting

---

3. Jürgen Habermas, *The Structural Transformation of the Public Sphere: An Inquiry into a Category of Bourgeois Society*, tr. Thomas Burger (Cambridge: Polity Press, 1989).

4. Leslie Howsam, *Cheap Bibles: Nineteenth-Century Publishing and the British and Foreign Bible Society* (Cambridge: Cambridge University Press, 1991).

the fate of Russian biblical translation in the initial decades of the nineteenth century, the role of BFBS representatives, such as John Paterson, Ebenezer Henderson, and Robert Pinkerton, became part of the wider, politically charged engagement between Russia and the west—specifically in the case of the Russian Bible Society its linkage with British evangelicals in Alexander I's Russia.[5]

In the second decade of the nineteenth century, British evangelicals were welcomed into Petersburg, where their concern for religious awakening found resonance with the religious piety of Tsar Alexander I and his close aide, Alexander Golitsyn, whose multiple posts included that of the chief administrator, or ober-procurator, of the Holy Synod. Still traumatized by the invasion of Napoleonic French forces into the Russian heartland, the pious, Bible-reading Russian tsar no doubt welcomed BFBS representatives in Petersburg as much for their anti-Napoleonic British allegiance as for their religious piety. Once established in late 1812, the Russian Bible Society and its modern press, under the leadership of John Paterson, became the vehicle for a printing and management revolution that sought to replicate in the Russian Empire what the BFBS was already doing in Britain. Indeed, the Russian Bible Society proceeded to set up its own efficient stereotype printing establishment and modern book-binding operation, with annual contributions generously led by the tsar's own patronage and the eventual support of more than 250 local Bible society chapters and affiliates throughout the empire. With its president Alexander Golitsyn also capable of muting potential disaffection from the ranks of the Russian Orthodox Church by virtue of his position as lay head of the Holy Synod, the Russian Bible Society was able to launch modern Russian translation without concern for what normally would have been a controlling system of pre-publication spiritual censorship.

But there was always a crucial difference between the successes of the parent BFBS in London and those of the Russian Bible Society in Petersburg. In Britain, the BFBS functioned as a nongovernmental agency in a relatively open marketplace that Habermas would consider part of the public sphere. In Petersburg, by contrast, the existence of the Russian Bible Society rested entirely upon the authority of tsarist decree and official state patronage. Even though the multiplication of Russian Bible Society chapters and affiliates gave the veneer of a broad Russian public audience independent of state authority, the reality was that the Russian Bible

---

5. For a somewhat different approach to this engagement through the eyes of Ebenezer Henderson, see S. K. Batalden, "Musul'manskii i evreiskii voprosy v Rossii epokhi Aleksandra I glazami shotlandskogo bibleista i puteshestvennika" [The Muslim and Jewish Questions in Russia in the era of Alexander I through the Eyes of a Scottish Biblical Scholar and Traveler], *Voprosy istorii*, no. 5 (2004), pp. 46-63.

Society's freedom to publish without censorship and to organize local chapters and affiliates owed almost entirely to state patronage. Indeed, the Society's auspicious building adjacent to the Imperial Summer Gardens was nothing more than a generous tsarist gift. The Russian Bible Society was functioning like its efficient bourgeois publishing counterpart in Britain, but in an environment far removed from the emergent civil society of England. Indeed, it is ironic that by the time of the tsar's closure of the Russian Bible Society in 1826, its efficient production of Russian Scripture had begun to outstrip the demands of the relatively small Russian reading public. John Paterson's support for literacy projects in Petersburg, reflected in his call for the introduction of Lancastrian schools and his advocacy of prison reform, effectively sought to stoke the demand for Bibles in a public arena that was still only beginning to be fashioned. Faced with the lack of a viable public sphere in Russia capable of generating spontaneous market demand for Holy Scripture, the instinctive BFBS reaction was to try to forge such demand.

In the more reactionary post-Napoleonic setting, the Russian Bible Society, facing challenges to its existence from powerful privileged interests such as the church hierarchy and leading court officials, found no effective public arena to which it could appeal for support. In Britain, apart from the privileged authority resting with Oxford and Cambridge University presses for publication rights to the authorized King James Version of the Bible, the marketplace, not state or privileged authority, determined the success of BFBS funding appeals and scriptural editions. What the fate of the Russian Bible Society in Petersburg proved, despite its fleeting and remarkable successes, was that all the vital issues of authority for translation, publication, and distribution of Holy Scripture in Russia ultimately continued to be vested in privileged state and ecclesiastical institutions. Without a modern civil society and a marketplace responsive to the public sphere, it was impossible (even if it had been desirable) to replicate the work of the BFBS in Russia.

The Reopening of Officially Sanctioned Russian Biblical Translation

The important lesson of the Russian Bible Society's vulnerability was not lost upon the BFBS, which continued to operate in St. Petersburg after the 1826 closure of the Russian Bible Society, albeit much more quietly, with a small depot and one part-time agent (initially, the Congregationalist pastor, Richard Knill).[6] Indeed, it was this lesson — the need to be responsive

---

6. For a full listing of BFBS agents in Russia from 1812 to 1918, see S. K. Batalden, "Revolution and Emigration: The Russian Files of the British and Foreign Bible Society,

to and in creative tension with state and ecclesiastical authority — that the BFBS brought to the reopening of modern Russian biblical translation and publication in the post-Crimean War era.

The official resumption of work on the modern Russian Bible followed Russia's defeat in the Crimean War and the accession to the Russian throne of the "tsar transformer," Alexander II. Over the course of the following twenty years, 1856-1875, translation and publication of multiple editions of Russian Old and New Testaments culminated in the publication of a complete Russian Bible authorized by the Russian Orthodox Church — the *sinodal'nyi perevod*, or Russian Synodal translation of 1875. The Synodal translation, although it never replaced the Old Slavonic text in Orthodox liturgical worship, remained, as it does to this day, the most commonly circulated edition of modern Russian Scripture.

To understand what prompted the mid-century turnabout in the fortunes of modern Russian biblical translation, how the renewed translation and publication effort proceeded, and how the BFBS Petersburg agency contributed to the new opening, one must understand the broader transformation of Russian religious culture itself. For it was in the engagement with modern biblical translation, biblical text criticism, and the open circulation of such sacred texts that nineteenth-century Russian religious culture entered, however tentatively, into Habermas's public sphere — that print-mediated public realm that began to function with a measure of independence from narrow state, autocratic authority in the last decades of the Russian Empire. BFBS involvement in Russian biblical translation not only accelerated the translation process itself, but also effectively eased the Russian church toward modern religious consciousness — the distinctively reflexive religious consciousness that recognizes competing communities of faith, and other claims to truth. In short, the issues of authority reopened by modern biblical translation — the authority of texts, the authority to publish and disseminate Scripture, and the authority of the modern linguistic medium itself — became central in Russian religious culture's fledgling early engagement with modernity. In that engagement, the BFBS

1917-1970," in *The Study of Russian History from British Archival Sources*, ed. Janet M. Hartley (London: University of London School of Slavonic and East European Studies/Mansell Publishing, 1986), p. 162. Until 1865, the BFBS functioned in St. Petersburg with part-time agents who were either pastors working for the London Missionary Society's Petersburg parish or prominent British merchants serving on the local Petersburg agency committee. In the ninety years from the closure of the Russian Bible Society to the Russian Bolshevik Revolution, there was continuous representation of BFBS agents in Petersburg, as follows: Richard Knill (1826–1833); John Brown (1833–1840); Thomas Ellerby (1840–1853); Archibald Mirrielees (1853–1857, and continuing informally thereafter); William Mirrielees (1857–1865); Andrew Muir (1860–1869); Adalbert Eck (1865–1869); William Nicolson (1869–1897); and William Kean (1896–1918).

and its Petersburg agency became a critical catalyst in the awakening of a modern Russian religious culture.

The Opening Debate: A Conflict Between Two Prominent Russian Prelates

The reopening of modern Russian biblical translation in the 1850s was attended by a significant internal Russian church dispute that prefigured the engagement of the Russian church with issues of modernity and the public sphere. The dispute involved two of the most powerful Russian prelates of the mid-nineteenth century, the two Filarets—Metropolitan Filaret (Drozdov) of Moscow and Metropolitan Filaret (Amfiteatrov) of Kiev.[7] Moscow Metropolitan Filaret (1782-1867) was the most significant Russian churchman of the nineteenth century. A close observer and defender of Orthodox churches in the Near East and an apologist for tsarist autocracy and the institution of Russian serfdom at home, the Moscow metropolitan had served forty years prior as a member of the Russian Bible Society's governing committee. He had also been an active member of its crucial translations and publications subcommittee. Anxious to preserve the authority of the church and its institutions, particularly the institution of monasticism that he sought to reinvigorate, Filaret Drozdov openly advocated the reopening of Russian Bible translation and publication in order to address the growing public disaffection of a Russian laity and parish clergy, many of whom could no longer comprehend the Slavonic biblical text. The Moscow prelate had no interest in undermining the longstanding diglossia operating in Russia wherein there was both a churchly Slavonic language and a separate modern Russian literary language operating in tandem. Rather, Filaret Drozdov sought to provide a modern Russian text to accompany the Slavonic, especially for the private use of believers as they sought to understand and interpret the more difficult to read Slavonic Scripture used in liturgical worship.

Metropolitan Filaret (Amfiteatrov) of Kiev, in contrast, took the fundamentalist or essentialist position, arguing for the infallibility of the Slavonic text and the rejection of modern Russian translation. In his challenge to Filaret Drozdov of Moscow, the Kievan prelate posed three interesting arguments. First, in his response of 1857, Filaret of Kiev argued that translation and dissemination of the Bible in modern Russian undermined the authority of the Slavonic text.[8] What was needed in his view was not

---

7. For a full discussion of this debate, see the standard nineteenth-century history of Russian Bible translation, I. A. Chistovich, *Istoriia perevoda Biblii na russkii iazyk*, 2nd ed. (Spb.: Tip. M. M. Stasiulevich, 1899), pp. 261-323.

8. "Otvetnaia zapiska," *fond* S.-Peterburgskaia dukhovnaia akademiia, *delo* A.I.80,

renewed Russian translation, but more diligent training of the laity in the Slavonic tongue. Filaret Amfiteatrov argued that the Russian church schism of the seventeenth century and the controversy spawned by biblical translation during the era of the Russian Bible Society developed out of disregard for the holy Slavonic text. Metropolitan Filaret of Kiev had earlier been among those in the 1840s who had sought, over the opposition of Filaret Drozdov, to canonize the Slavonic text, declaring it to be infallible. In response to this, in a telling reflection of the nascent public sphere already beginning to be felt on the margins of Russian religious culture, the Moscow metropolitan believed it was no longer reasonable to expect everyone to gain access to Holy Scripture through the medium of the Slavonic text. In short, both Filarets were conditioning their arguments upon the assumption that, with or without intensified instruction in the churchly Slavonic language, "public accessibility" to Scripture was a defining issue.

The second argument deployed by Filaret Amfiteatrov asserted that if one gave support for scriptural translation into Russian, then the same would be necessary for Belorussian, Ukrainian, and other languages as well. While that point might readily be conceded by a sympathetic BFBS audience, what made the argument so fascinating in a Russian context was that it posed the question of whether the Slavonic Bible was not, in effect, being used as a political instrument to hold together the multi-ethnic, diverse Russian Imperium. Equally interesting, in this regard, was the response of Metropolitan Filaret of Moscow, who conceded the imperial argument, while rejecting translation into other Slavic languages on the following grounds:

> Because the Ukrainian and Belarusian languages are of a small minority and are little developed; because many (but not all) Ukrainians and Belarusians understand Russian and are able to read Holy Scripture in it; and, finally, for church and *civil unity* [italics added] it is more useful that a single Russian language rule in Ukraine.[9]

Predictably, Metropolitan Filaret of Kiev responded that Slavonic, just as much as Russian, could provide the civil unity sought by his Moscow counterpart. But, the point is that both the advocate of modern Russian biblical translation and its opponent recognized in the 1850s that scripture could be politically legitimizing — in short, that sacred texts were also instruments of symbolic power functioning in the public sphere.

ll. 95-104, ROGPB (Manuscript Division, State Public Library, St. Petersburg). See also Chistovich, pp. 269-83.

9. "*Konfidentsial'naia zametka o raznoglasii vzgliadov dvukh mitropolitov Filaretov... o perevode Sv. Pisaniia,*" *fond* S.-Peterburgskaia dukhovnaia akademiia, *delo* A. I. 80, *ll.* 111-111ob, ROGPB. See also Chistovich, p. 290.

A third and final argument posed by the Kievan metropolitan against modern translation was specifically focused upon the issue of Old Testament translation. The Kievan prelate, seeking to discredit earlier Russian Old Testament translations that had used a Hebrew Massoretic textual base, argued that Russian translation based upon the Hebrew Bible parted with the Orthodox textological tradition of the Slavonic Bible, grounded as it was upon the Greek Septuagint. His argument further noted that the Ecumenical Patriarch had earlier anathematized attempts to render the Holy Scriptures into Modern Greek. By engaging in modern Russian biblical translation, the Russian church in the eyes of the Kievan prelate would be condoning activity that was elsewhere spurned within the Orthodox family.

On this matter, Filaret of Kiev was not only challenging prior Russian translation efforts, but also the basic textological principles set forth by Moscow Metropolitan Filaret Drozdov.[10] The Moscow prelate was as much opposed to the canonization of the Greek Septuagint as he was to the earlier attempt to canonize the Slavonic Bible. For him, the Septuagint was an important textual base for the Old Testament, but it did not stand alone in that respect. His position on the issue of Old Testament textology was well known from his earlier treatise on the dogmatic value of the Greek Septuagint in which he argued that, while the Greek Septuagint had a special place in the Eastern church, it was nevertheless a translation — the oldest extant translation — from a Hebrew textual tradition that also needed to be embraced.[11] For good or for ill, Filaret Drozdov's effort to combine support for the Hebrew textual tradition with the accommodation of Russian clerical concern for the Septuagint text ultimately yielded a compromise

---

10. The position of Kievan Metropolitan Filaret (Amfiteatrov) is identified in Chistovich, pp. 270-71. The conflict between the two prelates, Filaret of Kiev and Filaret of Moscow, is amply documented in the secondary literature. In addition to the standard Chistovich history, see also *Serdechnyi privet. Sbornik statei, izdannykh S.-Peterburgskoi dukhovnoi akademiei v pamiat' piatidesiatiletiia sviatitel'skogo sluzheniia vysokopreosviashchenneishago Isidora Mitropolita Novgorodskago, S.-Peterburgskago i Finliandskago* (Spb., 1884). For the manuscript record of the exchange between the two prelates, see "Sbornik statei o raznykh predmetakh," *fond* S.-Peterburgskaia dukhovnaia akademiia, *delo* A.I.80, *ll.* 1-381, ROGPB.

11. Filaret (Drozdov), *O dogmaticheskom dostoinstve i okhranitel'nom upotreblenii grecheskago sedmidesiati tolkovnikov i slavenskago perevodov sviashchennago pisaniia* [On the dogmatic value and preservative use of the Greek Septuagint and Slavonic translations of Holy Scripture], published in *Pribavleniia k Tvoreniiam sviatykh ottsov v russkom perevode*, 1858, vol. 32, 2nd pagination, pp. 452-84. Metropolitan Filaret wrote the treatise in connection with the debate over canonization of the Slavonic Bible and Greek Septuagint in 1845, a debate in which he opposed such canonization.

that affected all subsequent editions of the Synodal translation of the Russian Old Testament. Synodally authorized editions then and now have sought to accommodate both textual traditions by the characteristic deployment of variant Septuagint readings footnoted throughout the pages of the Russian Old Testament. The bracketed footnotes, however, brought the Holy Synod and its modern Russian translation of the Old Testament into irreconcilable conflict with the BFBS's dogmatic commitment to editions that were exclusively "without note or comment."

By raising the issue of the Russian church's relation to the Ecumenical Patriarchate, the Kievan prelate had also posed issues of a more transparently political character. To this Filaret Drozdov responded with straightforward clarity and candor. The distinguished Moscow metropolitan was known for his principled independence on matters involving Russian ties with the Orthodox East, supporting the Ecumenical Patriarch's opposition to Bulgarian church autocephaly, despite strong domestic pan-Slavic sentiment in Russia that favored Bulgarian and other autocephalous movements. Yet, on the issue of modern Russian biblical translation, Filaret Drozdov saw no need to secure the approval of the Ecumenical Patriarch, whose opposition to demotic translation was well known. He noted that, even as the Ecumenical Patriarch was not consulted on Russian translations of the Greek patristic writers then being printed in Russian theological journals, so also no prior consultation was called for in the case of biblical translation. Aware of the weakened condition of the Ecumenical Patriarchate, Filaret argued that its Greek hierarchy did not have the necessary information on which to base a judgment regarding Russian biblical translation. Filaret noted that the Ecumenical Patriarchate was, after all, dependent upon an unbelieving government (the Ottoman Empire) that could depose it at will, and that therefore the patriarchate lacked the freedom necessary to pass judgment on Russian biblical translation.[12] Metropolitan Filaret of Moscow concluded that the reopening of modern Russian biblical translation was a matter for the Synod and the tsar to decide, not the Ecumenical Patriarch.

The BFBS Petersburg Agency and the Russian Synodal Text

Having carried the argument and secured the tsar's blessing, Moscow Metropolitan Filaret oversaw until his death in 1867 a translation process that divided responsibilities among scholars at each of the four major

---

12. Moscow Metropolitan Filaret's response on the Greek patriarchate is missing from the Chistovich history, but can be found in "*Konfidentsial'naia zametka...*," *fond* S.-Peterburgskaia dukhovnaia akademiia, *delo* A.I.80, *ll.* 111-111ob, ROGPB.

Russian theological academies — Moscow, St. Petersburg, Kiev, and Kazan. That collective process yielded publication of a complete Synodally authorized Russian New Testament by 1862. At the time of Filaret Drozdov's death, there had yet to be any Synodally authorized publication of a Russian Old Testament text, although underground translations dating from the second quarter of the nineteenth century had begun to be published in the more open, reformist atmosphere of the tsarist reign of Alexander II.[13]

How did the British and Foreign Bible Society respond to this reopening of modern biblical translation in the post-Crimean War era, particularly the thorny issue of Russian Old Testament translation? First, on the question of the 1862 authorized edition of the New Testament (*sinodal'nyi perevod*), the BFBS Petersburg agency quickly adopted the Synod's translation as its own. Already in 1860, upon initial publication of the Synodal Gospels, the agency had secured approval from London to market this edition in its Petersburg shop.[14]

Archibald Mirrielees, a British merchant in Petersburg who sat on the committee, wrote back to London heralding the significance of the first Synodal edition of the four Gospels:

---

13. Several of these early Russian publications are represented in the BFBS library, bearing the identifying numbers from the historical catalogue of the Bible compiled by Darlow and Moule. See T. H. Darlow and H. F. Moule, comps., *Historical Catalogue of the Printed Editions of Holy Scripture in the Library of the British and Foreign Bible Society*, 2 vols. in 4 (London: BFBS, 1903–1911), hereafter cited as DM. See, for example, Mikhail Guliaev's translation of Job (DM 7802: Viatka, 1860); Archimandrite Makarii Glukharev's translation of the Bible serialized in *Pravoslavnoe obozrenie*, 1860-1863 (including DM 7804 [Jeremiah and Lamentations]; DM 7808 [Ezekiel]; DM 7809 [Daniel]; DM 7826 [Daniel]; DM 7807 [Job]; and DM 7810 [Hosea-Malachi]); Leon Mandel'shtam's Pentateuch (DM 7812: Berlin, 1862); and Archpriest Gerasim Pavskii's Old Testament serialized in the journal *Dukh Khristianina*, 1862–1863 (DM 7813, DM 7814, DM 7818, and DM 7815, copies of separate offprint editions of Old Testament books).

14. The BFBS Editorial Subcommittee undertook only the most perfunctory review, sending a copy of the 1860 Gospels to former Siberian missionary for the London Missionary Society, Edward Stallybrass, who approved of the text (see BFBS Minutes of the Editorial Subcommittee, vol. 6, 5 June 1860, pp. 105-106; and the note of Stallybrass's support, p. 114 [BSA/C17/1/6]). A member of the Petersburg agency committee, W. Lee, also forwarded a positive evaluation of the text, but there is no indication that the BFBS submitted the Synodal New Testament to a careful editorial evaluation by a native speaker of Russian (W. Lee to W. H. Ropes, 31 May 1860, St. Petersburg, in BFBS Editorial Correspondence Inwards, no. 1, p. 322 [BSA/E3/1/4/1]).

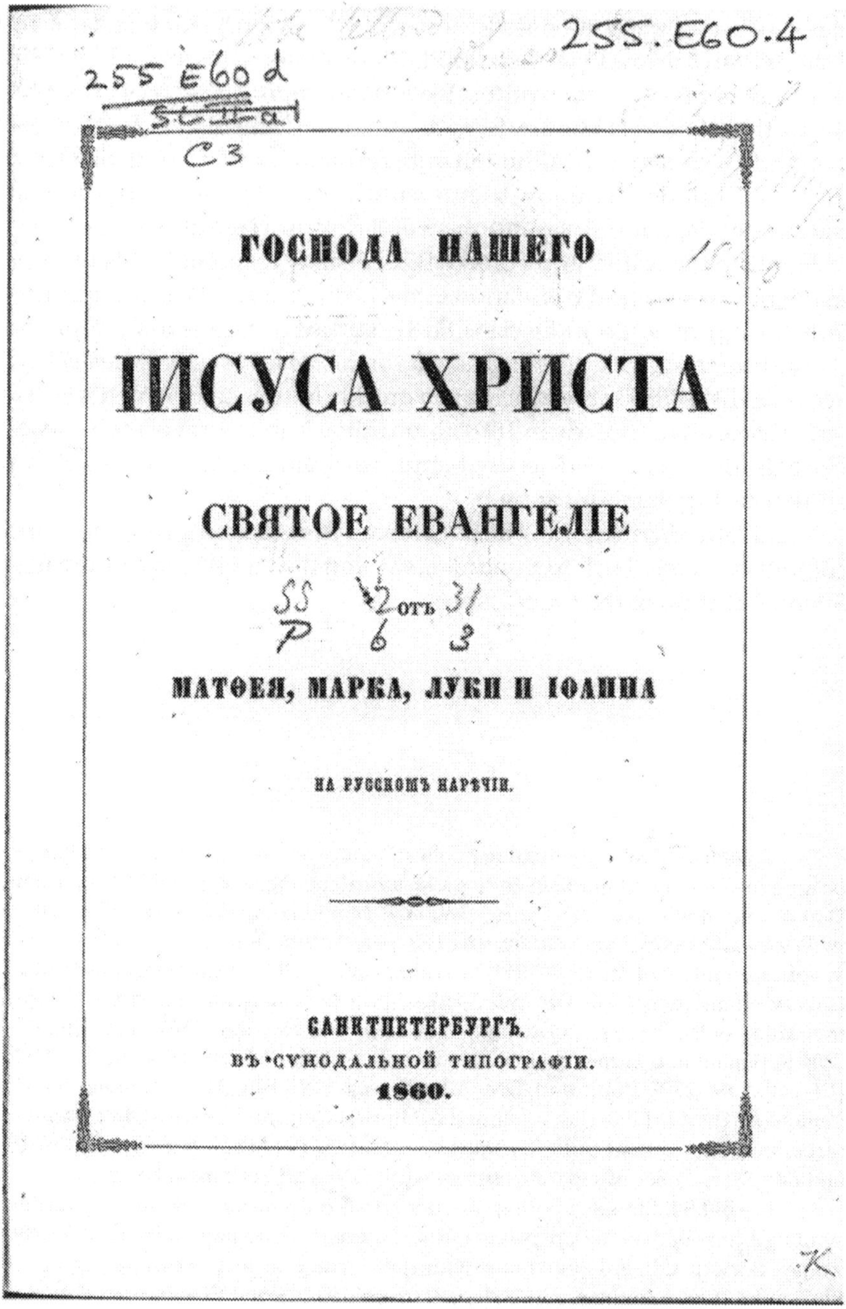

ГОСПОДА НАШЕГО

ІИСУСА ХРИСТА

СВЯТОЕ ЕВАНГЕЛІЕ

МАТѲЕЯ, МАРКА, ЛУКИ И ІОАННА

НА РУССКОМЪ НАРѢЧІИ.

САНКТПЕТЕРБУРГЪ.
ВЪ СУНОДАЛЬНОЙ ТИПОГРАФІИ.
1860.

Picture 21. *First Edition (1860) of the Synodal Russian Text of the Gospels.* Specimen courtesy of BFBS Library collection, Cambridge University Library

The demand has been very great, the shop being literally crowded and the number of copies sold to one applicant limited to 50 as the edition was likely to be soon exhausted. It is expected that the Acts will appear very soon and the Testament be completed shortly, also that the whole Bible is being proceeded with. This is partly attributed to a desire to prevent the necessity for Foreign Versions, and partly to there having arisen among the younger clergy a strong desire for reform in some matters. It is also thought that the wants of the schools which have been springing up everywhere of late has had some influence.[15]

Particularly notable was Mirrielees's reference to the Synod's contemplated work on the whole Bible, including the Old Testament, for Mirrielees recognized Russian concern that, unless they addressed the market themselves, they could not prevent the distribution of foreign, specifically BFBS, competing editions. Mirrielees knew very well what those competing editions were, because he and his father were working with the London BFBS editorial subcommittee in overseeing reprintings of the earlier Russian Bible Society New Testament and Psalter. Representing one of the most successful British merchant families in Russia — the patriarch behind the Muir and Mirrielees Department Store opposite the Bolshoi Theater in Moscow — Mirrielees understood that, in Alexander II's Russia, market competition could be a powerful stimulant to advance modern Russian biblical translation.

In the end, the BFBS accepted the Russian Synodal New Testament text without critical examination either of its textology or its Russian linguistic medium. Lacking a native speaker of Russian, the BFBS London editorial offices were not in a position to render independent judgment on these matters. The Synodal translation drew upon Slavonic and early nineteenth-century Russian translations, while grounding its Greek textology upon the sixteenth-century Erasmian *textus receptus*. Both of these issues, the textology and the language of the *sinodal'nyi perevod*, became the subject of renewed interest in post-World War II Russian biblical studies, but the politics of biblical translation in the Soviet period tended to mute challenges to the hegemony of the nineteenth-century Synodal text. Indeed, as regards the language question, the bureaucratic Russian of Soviet journalism and state publication lent, at least for much of the Soviet period, a kind of artificial nostalgic validation to the stylized churchly language used in the nineteenth-century Synodal text.[16]

---

15. A. Mirrielees to H. Knolleke, 13 June 1860, BFBS Editorial Correspondence Inwards, no. 1, p. 323 (BSA/E3/1/4/1).

16. Viktor M. Zhivov, the contemporary Moscow linguist, has published widely on hybrid churchly languages of the eighteenth and nineteenth centuries, including the modern Russian and Slavonic languages employed in churchly translations. See, for example, his volume, *Kul'turnye konflikty v istorii russkogo literaturnogo iazyka XVIII-*

Regularization of the BFBS Petersburg Agency and Depots

With the reopening of officially sanctioned Synodal translation and the potential for widespread distribution of the Synodal New Testament, the activities of the Petersburg BFBS offices began to outstrip the capacities of the part-time agents who were serving voluntarily for the BFBS while also pursuing their daily commercial activities. Andrew Muir, partner in the import-export firm of Muir and Mirrielees, co-chaired from 1860 the Petersburg BFBS agency committee with William Mirrielees. The demand noted above by the elder Mirrielees for the new Synodal Gospels and subsequently for the full Synodal New Testament ultimately forced the St. Petersburg agency to reorganize its operations in the decade of the 1860s, adding a full-time BFBS agent and launching an ambitious program of colportage that yielded annual agency sales by the turn of the century of more than a million copies of Scripture in whole or in part.[17] The BFBS became the largest wholesale purchaser of Russian New Testament texts from the publishing house of the Holy Synod in Petersburg.

In the spring of 1865, Andrew Muir added to his annual report to London an appeal for the appointment of a full-time paid BFBS agent for Petersburg, an appeal that was coupled with a petition to the Petersburg governor-general for state approval to operate the BFBS store as a retail agency with depots for biblical distribution throughout the Empire. Muir specifically recommended the Committee appoint Adalbert Eck, an assistant who had "taken an active and prominent part" in BFBS Petersburg operations for the previous nineteen years.[18]

The London BFBS Committee readily agreed to this Petersburg proposal, thus creating the first full-time BFBS staffing in Petersburg since the era of the Russian Bible Society. By the fall of 1865, the governor-general of St. Petersburg had sanctioned BFBS purchase of its own depot in Petersburg and had granted BFBS offices there the full authority to operate as an "agency" for retail sales under the direction of its new fulltime

---

nachala XIX veka (Moscow: Institut russkogo iazyka, AN SSSR, 1990); and his article, "Iazyk Feofana Prokopovicha i rol' gibridnykh variantov tserkovnoslavianskogo v istorii slavianskikh literaturnykh iazykov," *Sovetskoe slavianovedenie*, 1985, no. 3. Less charitably, the prerevolutionary Russian textologist Ivan E. Evseev described the language of the Synodal translation simply as "pre-Pushkin." See Evseev's *Stoletniaia godovshchina russkogo perevoda Biblii* (Petrograd, 1916).

17. See S. K. Batalden, "Colportage and the Distribution of Holy Scripture in Late Imperial Russia," in *Christianity and the Eastern Slavs*, vol. 2: *Russian Culture in Modern Times*, ed. Robert P. Hughes and Irina Paperno, *California Slavic Studies*, 17 (1994), pp. 83-92.

18. BFBS Minutes of the Committee, vol. 54, 17 April 1865, pp. 271-72 (BSA/B1/54).

Petersburg agent, Adalbert Eck.[19] Andrew Muir continued throughout the remainder of the 1860s to oversee issues of Russian biblical translation, but BFBS agent Eck took command of the expanded sales operations. Upon Eck's sudden death in 1869, his successor William Nicolson completed the efficient transformation of the Petersburg agency into a modern Eurasian center for multi-lingual biblical translation and dissemination.

Picture 22. *William Nicolson, BFBS Agent in St. Petersburg, 1869–1897.* Photo courtesy of BFBS 1879 photograph album, BFBS collections, Cambridge University Library.

From 1865 until the October Bolshevik Revolution of 1917, the BFBS agency in Petersburg, utilizing editions published largely from the printing press of the Holy Synod, became the largest distributor and retail sales office for Holy Scripture in the Russian Empire, with sub-agencies in Odessa and Ekaterinburg and satellite depots scattered throughout the Empire, notably in Moscow and Tiflis (Tbilisi, Georgia).

---

19. Confirmed in the letter of S. B. Bergne to A. Eck, 21 November 1865, BFBS Foreign Correspondence Outwards, 1865, no. 2, p. 151 (BSA/D1/4/1/73).

The Problem of the Russian Old Testament: The Source Text

The commercial success of the BFBS in its dissemination of Synodal Russian New Testaments tended to obscure the much more complicated and divisive issues facing translation and marketing of a modern Russian Old Testament. In the end, BFBS efforts in support of modern Russian Old Testament translation hastened the appearance of the Russian Holy Synod's own Old Testament text, an edition that was issued in four separate parts between 1868 and 1875. In the process, however, the BFBS confronted three intractable problems that ultimately thwarted its effort to circulate a modern Russian Old Testament — namely, the problems of the textual base of the Synodal translation, the identification of reliable BFBS translators, and the barriers to the marketing of BFBS Old Testament editions.

The first of these issues involved the conflict already noted between the BFBS and the Russian church over Old Testament textology and the placement of notations within biblical editions. On the matter of textology, BFBS editorial superintendents well into the nineteenth century considered the Greek Septuagint to be an inferior, "translated" text, upholding instead exclusive use of the Hebrew Massoretic text for Old Testament translation. Most odious to the Bible Society was the fact that the Greek Septuagint included deutero-canonical or apocryphal books that they had rejected, but that Russians sought to include in their Old Testament text. Russian inclusion of the deutero-canonical texts reflected the fact that these texts were traditional parts of the established liturgical text, the Slavonic Bible.

On the face of it, the appointment to the Synod's Old Testament translation commission of Daniil Avraamovich Khvol'son, a Jewish convert to Orthodox Christianity and a distinguished Semitic linguist at St. Petersburg University, might seem to have opened the door to some textological harmony between BFBS and Russian Synodal Old Testament translation efforts, inasmuch as Khvol'son, like the BFBS, was committed to the use of a Hebrew base text. But, as BFBS Petersburg agent William Nicolson later recounted from his conversations with Khvol'son, the Synodal Old Testament translation involved a very cumbersome process. Nicolson reported in 1870 to the BFBS editorial superintendent, Reverend R. B. Girdlestone, on his "very long conversation over the matter" with Khvol'son:

> He tells us that the Synod's translation is not altogether his work. There was a committee consisting of four persons appointed to examine the work after it passed through the hands of Dr. Chwolson and his coadjuters. He gave, I may remark by the way, no flattering account of the composition of that committee, there being scarcely a Russian ecclesiastic who knows anything

of Hebrew. The translation, so far as the Pentateuch is concerned, as he showed us, and Mr. Simpson and I had found out previously by collating the passages you mentioned besides a number of others, is a sort of hodge-podge between the Hebrew and Septuagint. In many passages, as for example, Gen. 4:7, the Hebrew text has been preferred, while the additions to be found in the Septuagint have been put within brackets. In other portions, however, the version of the Septuagint has been preferred (for example, in Gen. 47:3 and other instances).[20]

Commenting independently upon his joint meeting with Nicolson and Professor Khvol'son, the Reverend A. Simpson of the Petersburg agency committee noted that Khvol'son had "described the translation for the Synod as a 'conjectural translation.'" Simpson added, "It cannot be considered a faithful rendering of the Hebrew text, although in some instances in which it differs it is sustained by the New Testament."[21] (The reference to a text "that is sustained by the New Testament" may allude to passages in the Synodal Old Testament that, as in the Slavonic Bible, make explicit reference to Jesus Christ.) In noting for Nicolson the four scholars appointed by the St. Petersburg Theological Academy to work on Old Testament translation, Khvol'son had in mind, in addition to himself, M. A. Golubev, P. I. Savvaitov, and E. I. Loviagin. The death of Moisei Aleksandrovch Golubev in 1869 slowed the process of Synodal Old Testament translation, an additional concern that Khvol'son shared with BFBS agent Nicolson.[22]

While the Pentateuch, published in a Synodally authorized Russian edition in 1868, posed no problem over deutero-canonical books, all subsequent parts, including the second volume issued in 1869, contained deutero-canonical readings. Thus, by the 1860s, the BFBS London home office recognized — despite mild protestations from British merchants on the Petersburg BFBS agency committee, such as William Mirrielees, who could not quite understand the fuss over deutero-canonical texts — that a fundamental obstacle stood in the way of its Petersburg agency's sale of the Synodal Russian Old Testament text.[23]

20. Nicolson to R. B. Girdlestone, St. Petersburg, 3 December 1870, BFBS Agents Books, no. 125 (Russia), p. 230 (BSA/D1/7/125).
21. Simpson to BFBS, St. Petersburg, rec'd in London 8 December 1870, BFBS Agents Books, no. 125 (Russia), p. 234 (BSA/D1/7/125).
22. Nicolson to Girdlestone, St. Petersburg, 3 December 1870, BFBS Agents Books, no. 125 (Russia), p. 231 (BSA/D1/7/125).
23. The four parts of the Synodal Old Testament were issued under the general title *Sviashchennyia Knigi Vetkhago Zavieta v russkom perevode* and are identified in DM. They can all be found in the BFBS Bible collection at Cambridge University Library and carry the following numbers, beginning with 1868, DM 7840 (1. *Piatiknizhie Moiseeva*); 1869, DM 7846 (2. *Knigi Iisusa Navina – Kniga Esthir'*); 1872, DM 7854 (3. *Kniga Iova*,

The Problem of the Russian Old Testament: Securing Reliable Translators

Unable to overcome this insurmountable obstacle over the apocrypha, the Petersburg BFBS agency sought to confront a second major problem, namely, that of identifying a reliable translation team that might undertake for the BFBS its own Russian Old Testament translation. Drawing upon the early nineteenth-century Russian Bible Society edition of the Psalter and a printing of the first eight books of the Old Testament, the London home office had already issued reprintings and revisions of those texts, beginning with an 1852 edition of the Russian Psalter printed in Leipzig (DM 7798). Copies of the Russian Bible Society's original Octateuch printed in sheets had been bound and distributed by the BFBS agency in Petersburg until the supply was exhausted in the 1830s. With the reopening of biblical translation in the 1850s, the BFBS undertook the first formal publication of that Octateuch in a London 1861 edition (DM 7806) — curiously, an edition proofread for the Society by Russian émigré revolutionaries from the circle of Alexander Herzen in London.[24]

Yet, despite these editions of the Russian Octateuch and Psalter published for the BFBS in the west, the BFBS lacked its own reliable Russian text for the majority of the Old Testament at a time when both the Petersburg and Vienna BFBS agencies were experiencing growing demand for such a modern Russian text. Early in 1865, three years before the Synodal Old Testament editions began to be published, Andrew Muir responded to this demand by suggesting that the BFBS add its own competing Russian Old Testament text to those then surfacing in Russia:

> I annex a list of new translations of parts of the Old Testament into Modern Russ, which have lately appeared. As there seems no prospect of the Old Testament being published as a whole by the Synod here, and your

---

Psaltir', Kniga Pritchei Solomonovykh, Kniga Ekkleziasta ili Propoviednika, Kniga Piesni Piesnei Solomona, Kniga Premudrosti Solomona, Kniga Premudrosti Iisusa syna Sirakhova); and 1875, DM 7859 (4. *Kniga proroka Isaii, Kniga proroka Ieremii, Kniga plach' Ieremii, Poslanie Ieremii, Kniga proroka Varukha, Kniga proroka Iezekiilia, Kniga proroka Daniila, Kniga proroka Osii, Kniga proroka Ioilia, Kniga proroka Amosa, Kniga proroka Avdiia, Kniga proroka Iony, Kniga proroka Mikheia, Kniga proroka Nauma, Kniga proroka Avvakuma, Kniga proroka Sofonii, Kniga proroka Aggeia, Kniga proroka Zakharii, Kniga proroka Malakhii, Pervaia kniga Makkaveiskaia, Vtoraia kniga Makkaveiskaia, Tret'ia kniga Makkaveiskaia, Tret'ia kniga Ezdry*). Each title page includes the inscription that publication was at the Synodal Press in St. Petersburg.

24. For a background description of these earliest BFBS London Russian Old Testament editions, see S. K. Batalden, "Revolutionaries and Evangelicals in Concert: Alexander Herzen, Vasilii Kel'siev, and the British and Foreign Bible Society," unpublished paper delivered to the Russian Speaking Society, Cambridge, 10 February 2004.

ordinary edition of the Pentateuch [sic] might be revised if a competent person could be found, you could thus with little difficulty complete the work. Your doing this would perhaps hasten the movements of the Synod.[25]

Muir's note to London was revealing on several fronts. First, Muir, as in the case of his successor agents in Petersburg, understood how western involvement in biblical translation and publication could stimulate competitive Synodal action. Second, on the translation process itself, Muir reasoned somewhat simplistically that all the BFBS needed to do was contract with a local Russian scholar to provide a complete Old Testament text by combining revision of the existing BFBS edition of the Octateuch and Psalter with revisions of one or another of the formerly clandestine Russian Old Testament texts then being published in Alexander II's Russia. Toward that end, Muir recommended that the BFBS contact Leon Mandel'shtam, a distinguished polyglot scholar, who despite the restrictive atmosphere of Nicholas I's Russia, had been the first Jew to graduate from St. Petersburg University in 1843. Mandel'shtam was then in Berlin, but had earlier been employed by the Russian government to compose a Hebrew/Russian lexicon. According to Muir, Mandel'shtam might even be willing to relocate to London to undertake such an assignment.[26]

In the end, after Vienna BFBS agent Edward Millard raised questions about the appropriateness of employing a Jew for BFBS translations, the decision was rather made to employ a Jewish convert to Christianity, Vasilii Levison, for preparation of an independent and potentially competitive BFBS edition of the modern Russian Old Testament.[27] Indeed, with

25. A. Muir to H. Knolleke, St. Petersburg, 3 January 1865, BFBS Editorial Correspondence Inwards, no. 3, p. 309 (E3/1/4/3). The reference should be to the Octateuch.

26. Muir to Knolleke, St. Petersburg, 3 January 1865, BFBS Editorial Correspondence Inwards, no. 3, pp. 309-311 (BSA/E3/1/4/3). What Muir did not mention was that Mandel'shtam, whose remarkable personal library ultimately became the basis for the outstanding New York Public Library Judaica collection, had already completed sections of his Russian translation of the Hebrew Bible, which would later be widely disseminated throughout the Pale of Settlement in a Hebrew-Russian diglot edition. See DM 7812, *Thora, t.e. Zakon, ili Piatiknizhie Moiseevo: Bukval'nyi perevod v pol'zu russkikh evreev* (Berlin: K. Schultz Press, 1862). The title and the DM citation indicate that the entire Pentateuch is included. The British Library copy (3061.e.2), however, contains only the book of Genesis. Mandel'shtam's preface is addressed to Jewish schoolteachers and exhorts these teachers to train their children to read the Bible and also to teach them to be good citizens of the Russian Empire. The BFBS library contains a complete 1872 printing of the Mandel'shtam Pentateuch issued in Berlin in a Hebrew-Russian diglot (DM 7852). See also Mandel'shtam's separate, diglot edition of the Psalter, which was already in its third printing in 1872 (DM 7853a).

27. Millard to Knolleke, Vienna, 17 February 1865, BFBS Editorial Correspondence Inwards, no. 4 (BSA/E3/1/4/4). Millard urged caution on the matter of Mandel'shtam, saying in rather coded language that referenced Mandel'shtam's Jewish identity, "my

the hire of Vasilii Levison the BFBS committed itself to the preparation of its own rival Russian Old Testament text. Following his conversion to Orthodox Christianity at the age of twenty-five, Levison had moved from his German homeland to Russia, where he taught Hebrew from 1840 to 1860 in Catholic and Orthodox seminaries in Petersburg. Then he accompanied the Russian mission to Jerusalem, where he also came to the attention of missionaries from the London Society for Promoting Christianity among the Jews. Having translated several works of theology into German for the private reading of Nicholas I's wife, the Russian empress, Levison ingratiated himself into the tsarist family. Despite his knowledge of Hebrew, however, Levison had an insecure command of modern Russian. Thus, he hired a Russian native speaker, his former seminary student Petr Ivanovich Bogoliubov (d. 1880), to assist him throughout the translation process.[28] Bogoliubov had taught church history and Greek at the St. Petersburg Theological Seminary (not to be confused with the postgraduate Petersburg Theological Academy) before becoming director in 1854 of the St. Petersburg Home for the Upbringing of Poor Children (Dom vospitaniia bednykh detei). In addition, the BFBS Petersburg agency arranged for a two-person team of Russian correctors, professors Hoffman and Nikolai Astaf'ev, to review the translation and proofread the resulting publications that were printed in London.

Although BFBS agent William Nicolson later lamented the terms of the agreement whereby Levison was paid a lavish monthly salary, rather than specific remuneration for completed work, the BFBS Petersburg agency oversaw the translation and publication of the Old Testament books of 1 and 2 Samuel, Proverbs, and all the major and minor prophetic books.[29]

---

experience of birds of this feather is such as to advise great caution." After correspondence with BFBS agents in Vienna, Petersburg, and Odessa in winter and spring 1865, the BFBS Editorial Subcommittee in London authorized the hiring of Vasilii Levison in April 1865 at a salary of 200 rubles per month. See BFBS Minutes of the Editorial Subcommittee, vol. 8, 19 April 1865, pp. 56-58 (BSA/C17/1/8).

28. On Levison, see the attestation of Gottlieb Abramsohn to BFBS agent Millard, Berlin, 31 December 1864, BFBS Editorial Correspondence Inwards, no. 3, pp. 312-313 (BSA/E3/1/4/3). See also "Levison, Vasilii Andreevich, *Russkii biograficheskii slovar'*, vol. Labzina - Liashenko (Spb., 1914), p. 144.

29. The DM entries for these London publications, published at the press of W. M. Watts, are as follows: Proverbs (DM 7833: London, 1866); Isaiah (DM 7834: London, 1866); Jeremiah and Lamentations (DM 7837: London, 1867); Ezekiel (DM 7838: London, 1867); Daniel (DM 7842: London, 1868); and 1 and 2 Samuel (DM 7850: London, 1870). The volumes were issued in print runs of 2,500 copies each. See, for example, BFBS Minutes of the Depository and Printing Subcommittee, vol. 8, 29 November 1867, p. 50 (BSA/C10/1/8). On Nicolson's subsequent review of the history of this BFBS Russian Old Testament translation, see W. Nicolson to BFBS, 4 November 1881, BFBS

Upon the sudden death of Vasilii Levison in 1869, the BFBS Petersburg agency was again faced with having to locate a reliable translator for its Old Testament edition. By 1869, however, the Holy Synod had commenced publication of its own authorized Russian Old Testament edition, thus adding new questions for BFBS offices in Petersburg and London about the feasibility of proceeding with a separate BFBS Russian Old Testament. The unwillingness of the BFBS to circulate a Synodal Old Testament that included deutero-canonical books meant that they were required to hire a new translation team to complete the BFBS Russian Old Testament.

Within weeks of Levison's passing, BFBS Petersburg agency committee representative William Mirrielees wrote to BFBS Editorial Superintendent Girdlestone in London. He noted the recent progress of the Holy Synod in translating its own Russian Old Testament, which included apocryphal readings. Then, in an ingenious move, he urged the BFBS to hire the Synod's own translator, Daniil Khvol'son, to complete the BFBS translation of the Russian Old Testament from the Hebrew.[30] Girdlestone and the BFBS Editorial Subcommittee readily agreed that the Petersburg agency should engage the services of Khvol'son, a process that after protracted negotiation, led to the hiring of Khvol'son and his Russian colleague Pavel Savvaitov for the completion of the BFBS Russian Old Testament. Daniil Khvol'son was one of the finest European scholars of Semitic languages, who in addition to his command of Hebrew had mastered Old Syriac and several other key Near Eastern languages. As in the case of Levison, Khvol'son was a Jewish convert to Orthodoxy. Along with fellow Hebraic scholars, Gerasim Petrovich Pavskii and Vasilii Levison, Khvol'son had also participated in a landmark tsarist commission investigating the notorious "Saratov affair," one of the most serious cases involving blood libel in nineteenth-century Russia. For this, Khvol'son continued to be deeply respected within Russian Jewish circles. Savvaitov was also a distinguished biblical scholar, who taught at both St. Petersburg University and the St. Petersburg Theological Academy. The team of Khvol'son and Savvaitov, combined with proofreader-correctors Hoffman and Astaf'ev, gave the BFBS an able set of translators for Russian Old Testament

---

Editorial Correspondence Inwards, no. 16, pp. 133-141 (BSA/E3/1/4/16). Nicolson's rather negative assessment of the Levison translation was owing to the critical evaluation of the BFBS text written by Moscow Theological Academy Professor Nikol'skii in the Russian journal *Pravoslavnoe obozrenie* (M. Nikol'skii, "Russkii perevod Biblii i znachenie evreiskoi filologii," *Pravoslavnoe obozrenie*, 1876, t. 1 [April], 645-72). Nicolson subsequently urged BFBS revision of the Levison translations to make them conform to the BFBS Khvol'son translations noted below.

30. W. S. Mirrielees to R. B. Girdlestone, St. Petersburg, 15 July 1869, BFBS Editorial Correspondence Inwards, no. 7 (BSA/E3/1/4/7).

translation from the Hebrew.[31] There followed in fairly prompt succession the translations by Khvol'son/Savvaitov of those portions of the Old Testament that had not previously been translated by either the Russian Bible Society or the team of Levison and Bogoliubov.[32] Although Khvol'son urged the BFBS Petersburg agency to revise also the books translated by Levison and Bogoliubov to bring them into conformity with the language and translation practices of Khvol'son and Savvaitov, the BFBS postponed such an action, opting rather to appeal to the Synod for publication of a separate edition of the Synod's own Old Testament without the deutero-canonical books.[33]

---

31. After considerable haggling over what rate should be paid for the translation and whether the existing BFBS Russian Pentateuch needed to be revised, the terms of Khvol'son's engagement were confirmed in early 1871. See Nicolson to Girdlestone, St. Petersburg, 4 January 1871, BFBS Agents Books, no. 125 (Russia), pp. 253-54 (BSA/D1/7/125); and BFBS Minutes of the Editorial Subcommittee, vol. 10, 1 February 1871, p. 71 (BSA/C17/1/10). On Khvol'son and his relationship with Hebraic studies in Russia, see S. K. Batalden, "Nineteenth-Century Russian Biblical Translation and the Jewish Question," in *Kirchen im Kontext unterschiedlicher Kulturen: Auf dem Weg ins dritte Jahrtausend*, ed. K. C. Felmy, F. von Lilienfeld, et al. (Gottingen: Vandenhoeck & Ruprecht, 1991), pp. 577-87.

32. The remaining books were published in the following order: I and II Chronicles, Ezra, Nehemiah, and Esther (DM 7855: London, 1873); Job (DM 7856: London, 1873); a revised Psalter (DM 7857: London, 1873); and Ecclesiastes and the Song of Songs (DM 7858: London, 1873). In order to issue the complete Old Testament, the BFBS also needed to reissue its existing Octateuch in a compatible 12mo format. In doing so (DM 7861: London, 1875), the BFBS secured the services of the Khvol'son team in Petersburg to prepare the Society's new Octateuch, which Khvol'son and Savvaitov did by revising/Hebraicizing the Synod's newly published edition, rather than using the earlier Russian Bible Society and BFBS Octateuch.

33. For the extensive correspondence between William Nicolson and the BFBS regarding this negotiated Synodal edition without the apocryphal books, see BFBS Editorial Correspondence Inwards, nos. 14, 15, and 16 (BSA/E3/1/4/14, 15, 16), including letters from Nicolson to BFBS Editorial Superintendent Wright, 1880-1882. The counterpart correspondence from BFBS London offices to the BFBS Petersburg agency, including the draft of a letter prepared for submission directly to Alexander II that was never actually sent, is located in BFBS Foreign Correspondence Outwards, especially 1880, no. 2 (BSA/D1/4/1/103). After prolonged negotiations, BFBS Petersburg agent Nicolson procured Synodal publication of this edition (DM 7866: St. Petersburg, 1882) in 20,000 copies. Nikolai Astaf'ev, one of the BFBS correctors, was engaged in Petersburg to bring the Synodal Old Testament into conformity with BFBS concerns and to see the proofreading through the Synodal press. Each of the four Old Testament divisions as originally published by the Synod were dated 1882 and carried the inscription in Russian, "With the permission of the Most Holy Ruling Synod, for the English Bible Society." Until the twentieth century, this was the only such complete Old Testament edition published by the Holy Synod without the deutero-canonical books.

The Problem of the Russian Old Testament: The Right to Circulate

While the BFBS had managed to identify and engage competent, internationally recognized Petersburg translators to complete a BFBS edition of the Russian Old Testament in a uniform format by 1875, there remained the third hurdle of securing rights to the circulation and sale of its own or an appropriately modified Synodal translation. William Nicolson had managed to secure a contract for publication by the Synodal press of an edition of the BFBS Russian Old Testament without the apocryphal readings, but this one-time edition (1882) created lasting animus at the Holy Synod where Ober-Procurator Konstantin Pobedonostsev argued, with reason, that the Synod ought not to be publishing editions of Scripture in competition with its own. Indeed, that same argument doomed the possibility of Russian circulation of the BFBS Russian Old Testament. The one exception to this policy involved circulation of Old Testament diglot editions in Hebrew and Russian. Having been given the authority to circulate these diglot editions for the Jewish population in the Pale of Settlement, the Vienna BFBS agency issued several printings throughout the nineteenth and early twentieth centuries.[34] Thus, the conflict over circulation of variant Russian Old Testament texts meant that the BFBS Petersburg agency confined its circulation of Russian Scripture almost exclusively to the New Testament and Psalter published for the agency by the press of the Holy Synod. Bolstered by an army of colporteurs and hawkers, the Petersburg BFBS agency, despite its competition with the Holy Synod over Russian Old Testament translation, became the Holy Synod's largest purchaser of Holy Scripture during the course of the last half-century of the Russian Empire.

---

34. In November 1878, Edward Millard wrote to the London BFBS offices noting his sale of Old Testaments with parallel Hebrew text. See Millard to BFBS, Vienna, 26 November 1878, BFBS Editorial Correspondence Inwards, no. 14, p. 183 (BSA/E3/1/4/14). The Hebrew/Russian diglot employing the BFBS Russian Old Testament continued to circulate. See, for example, DM 7876 (Vienna: A. Holzhausen, for the BFBS, 1888), and subsequent reprintings. The Vienna BFBS agency also published numerous reprintings of the complete Bible in a Russian-only edition, composed of the BFBS Old Testament and the Synodal New Testament. For the first printing of that edition, see DM 7862 (Vienna: A. Holzhausen, for the BFBS, 1877). Although copies of that edition came to circulate in Ukrainian regions adjacent to Austro-Hungarian territory, such an edition was unable to be circulated in Russian territory with the blessing of the Holy Synod.

Conclusion

What conclusion can be drawn from this picture of competing translations and the dramatic growth of the BFBS Petersburg agency in the years following the Crimean War, when modern biblical translation was again possible in the Russian Empire? At the time of the closure of the Russian Bible Society in 1826, all the major questions of authority surrounding biblical translation and dissemination essentially remained unresolved: Who had the authority to translate modern Russian scripture? Who had the authority to disseminate modern Russian scripture? And, what linguistic medium was to be authoritative for Russian biblical translation? By proscribing modern biblical translation, Nicholas I had artificially closed off all official translation, leaving these issues of authority unanswered.

The reopening of modern biblical translation was accompanied by a flurry of publication, particularly of Old Testament texts that had been circulating underground during the thirty-year hiatus in modern Russian translation. Indeed, for a while it appeared as though there might be a more open religious marketplace, a "public sphere" in which multiple translations published in religious journals would be evaluated within an increasingly "modern" Russian Orthodox religious culture. The debates within the religious journals about the merits of one or another translation seemed to anticipate such a gradual transformation of Russian religious culture. Even Russian state authorities seemed to encourage the new religious marketplace, granting rail concessions to the BFBS as it transported its stock of Scripture to depots and colporteurs dotted along the Eurasian frontier.

Yet, in the years following the death of Moscow Metropolitan Filaret, reactionary circles within the Russian church hierarchy sought to restore the authority of the black (monastic) clergy, and with it the authority of the church to control translation and circulation of Holy Scripture. In contrast to a nascent "clerical liberalism" represented within the Russian white (parish) clergy, the renewed clericalism of the 1870s and 1880s demanded Synodal control of the translation process (except in the matter of non-Russian languages of the empire) and Synodal monopoly on biblical circulation. By the time of Alexander II's assassination in 1881, even though the Russian church had completed its landmark authorized Russian Bible (*sinodal'nyi perevod*), ecclesiastical leadership personified in the reactionary ober-procurator of the Holy Synod, Konstantin Pobedonostsev, had come to fear modernist forces and retreated into a period of conservative, hierarchical control. Although the debate over texts and the sophistication of biblical studies in the Russian theological academies advanced at the end of the nineteenth century, the wider picture of clerical reaction did not change in its essentials until the 1905 Russian Revolution and the renewed effort to secure church independence from state authority.

Within this shifting fate of Russian Orthodoxy in the last half of the nineteenth century, how should one evaluate the role of the British and Foreign Bible Society and its active Petersburg agency? First, the BFBS commitment to proceed with its own edition of the Russian Old Testament had the effect, at least initially, of stimulating more rapid completion of the Synod's own Russian text. Not only did the competition over the Old Testament speed the completion of the *sinodal'nyi perevod*, but the outpouring of rival Russian Old Testament editions in the 1860s and 1870s reflected an early, but ultimately abortive, engagement of Russian religious culture with the "public sphere" and the religious marketplace. It was natural upon the completion of the Synodal translation for the Holy Synod to assert its hegemonial interests in controlling the translation and circulation of Scripture, but the 1860s had left the important legacy of an open market for competing Russian biblical texts.

Meanwhile, as the BFBS Petersburg agency struggled through the death of its own initial translator in 1869, it faced the liability of the parent Bible Society's injunction against publication of "note or comment" in its scriptural editions. Amidst such setbacks, as well as fleeting moments of satisfaction when the BFBS Russian editions came off the press in London, the Petersburg agency had in reality also become a generous patron for its collaborating Hebraic scholars in Petersburg. While the Petersburg agency may at times have overpaid its translators and correctors, its positive and significant legacy in this respect was to be seen in its indirect support for those who built the solid tradition of Hebraic scholarship in Petersburg — a remarkably rich tradition that lasted well past the October Bolshevik Revolution of 1917. Moreover, the consistency of the translation principles underlying the BFBS Russian Old Testament remained the most important legacy of the BFBS and was deeply appreciated by those who had access to variant Russian Old Testament readings. Writing to BFBS Editorial Superintendent William Wright near the end of his career in Petersburg, BFBS agent William Nicolson noted the following curious testimony from Professor Ivan Troitskii, Khvol'son's successor as professor of Hebrew at St. Petersburg University and the Petersburg Theological Academy:

> I have to report an interview with Prof. Troitsky, Dr. Chwolson's successor as Professor of Hebrew in the St. Petersburg University, and an able Hebraist, as becomes a pupil of Chwolson's, in which he, a native Russian and Orthodox believer, testified, I confess somewhat to my surprise, that our translation is decidedly *better* [Nicolson's italics] than the Synod's — less wordy, simple and more idiomatic. He tells me in his own words that the Synod's is more paraphrastic.[35]

35. Nicolson to Wright, St. Petersburg, 7 June 1894, BFBS Editorial Correspondence

At the same time, the Bible Society's fixation on the Hebrew text, its opposition to publication of deutero-canonical texts, and its narrowly Protestant fear of any lectionary or other note or comment in its editions significantly weakened its capacity to be an even-handed broker in Orthodox Russia. While the Holy Synod welcomed the large wholesale purchases of Russian Scripture that kept their Synodal presses busy, there existed beneath the surface the fear that the Bible Society was a kept preserve for Protestant sectarians, indeed for colporteurs, who would hawk by day and proselytize by night.

Within this picture of renewed commercial success tempered by elements of latent distrust, the role of the BFBS Petersburg agent became critical in the last fifty years of the Russian Empire. No one played that role better than William Nicolson. He developed close personal ties with superintendents at the Synodal press. In his earliest years he cajoled Daniil Khvol'son and the BFBS translation team to maintain deadlines for timely submission of newly translated books, he secured free rail passage for transmittal of scripture to BFBS depots in outlying parts of the Empire, and he pioneered collaboration with Russian Turcologists in Kazan and elsewhere to address the languages of non-Russian speaking peoples of the empire.[36] He railed against sectarian BFBS colporteurs, who left the Petersburg agency vulnerable when they exploited their position to engage in illegal proselytizing alongside the sale of Scripture. Curiously, Nicolson even came to be respected by his nemesis at the head of the Holy Synod, lay ober-procurator Konstantin Pobedonostsev.

On more than one occasion, Nicolson was frustrated by the inability of the London home office to understand his situation, thrust as he was into a difficult position between the desires of the London Committee and the restrictions imposed upon the Petersburg agency by the ober-procurator. Once, in 1890, Nicolson was seeking to negotiate with the Synod the right for the BFBS to combine in a Hebrew/Russian diglot the earlier 1882 Russian text that had excised the deutero-canonical readings. The London BFBS Editorial Subcommittee, insensitive to the delicacy of such requests

---

Inwards, no. 32, p. 77 (BSA/E3/1/4/32). Troitskii later wrote his own moving tribute to Daniil Khvol'son upon Khvol'son's death in 1911. See Ivan Troitskii, "Professor D. A. Khvol'son," *Zhurnal ministerstva narodnago prosveshcheniia*, novaia seriia, vol. 34 (1911), no. 8, otd. 4, pp. 90-99.

36. The substantial work of William Nicolson with Turkic translations awaits scholarly examination in the BFBS archive. On the confirmation of free rail passage, see the BFBS Minutes of the Committee, vol. 91, 3 July 1893 (BSA/B1/91), wherein the BFBS Committee noted receipt of the notice from Nicolson that he had received a reply from the Minister of Ways indicating "that Scriptures of this Society would be conveyed free of charge on all Government Railways in Russia until further notice."

to the Synod, wrote back to Petersburg asking why Nicolson had not added, as per their request, an appeal to the Synod for the separate reissuance of the 1882 Synodal Old Testament without apocrypha. Responding to this insensitivity on London's part, Nicolson wrote back firmly:

> I regret to find that the Committee should feel it necessary to express their surprise that I am neglecting part of their resolution of November 6, 1889. I trust, however, that they give me the credit that I know the difference between the practicable and the impracticable in the circumstances in which I am placed.[37]

It was not always easy serving as the intermediary between London BFBS home offices and a Russian Holy Synod headed by Konstantin Pobedonostsev. Indeed, there must have been times when the seasoned BFBS Petersburg agent wondered which side was more understanding of his position.

Finally, there was one structural limitation in the BFBS Petersburg operations that came to be shared with the agency's twentieth-century successors involved in BFBS and UBS Russian translation — namely, the lack of an internal capacity to judge the quality of the Russian translations it was producing. In short, despite the Russian skills that agents such as John Paterson, William Mirrielees, and William Nicolson developed, none of them were native speakers of Russian capable of evaluating the texts they were publishing and circulating. In a prime example of the lack of independent native-speaker expertise, the Petersburg agency in the 1860s fell prey to a team of Russian correctors (Hoffman and Astaf'ev) too closely tied to translator Vasilii Levison, whose limited Russian slowed preparation of the BFBS Russian Old Testament text. The close ties between translators and correctors and the consequent lack of internal criticism meant, by extension, that the BFBS Russian Old Testament posed less of a challenge to the landmark *sinodal'nyi perevod* than it otherwise would have.

Again in the twentieth century the BFBS was limited by its inability to conduct an independent internal language evaluation of the Russian émigré New Testament of Bishop Cassian (Bezobrazov). Bishop Cassian, rector of the St. Sergius Institute in Paris, produced an extremely interesting New Testament Russian text using up-to-date Greek New Testament textology, but the work turned out to be functionally unusable owing to Cassian's belief that he could somehow replicate the original word order of the Greek New Testament in his Russian translation.[38] It is a

---

37. W. Nicolson to Wm. D. Wright [serving for his father, Wm. Wright], St. Petersburg, 1 April 1890, BFBS Editorial Correspondence Inwards, no. 25, p. 309 (BSA/E3/1/4/25).

38. On the Bezobrazov translation, see the essay by Father Sergei Ovsiannikov in this volume; also Batalden, "Revolution and Emigration," pp. 147-81.

commentary on the manifest lack of institutional memory that again, in 2004, amidst signs of the reengagement of Russian religious culture with a more open "public sphere," the United Bible Societies recently issued a note of redundancy to the only native speaker of Russian among its translation consultants for Eastern Europe and Eurasia. Given this disregard for the indigenization of its staff of translation consultants, the UBS would do well to consider the failures, as well as the remarkable successes, that distinguished the work of the British and Foreign Bible Society in nineteenth-century Russia.

BISHOP CASSIAN'S BFBS-SPONSORED
RUSSIAN TRANSLATION OF THE NEW TESTAMENT

Sergei Ovsiannikov

Introduction

After the fall of the Berlin Wall and the collapse of the Soviet Union, the opportunity arose for the United Bible Societies (UBS) to start interconfessional translation projects. The task of creating a partnership with the Russian Orthodox Church, the biggest Orthodox church in Europe, was a particular challenge for the UBS. In this respect a history of the so-called Cassian translation, despite its preparation forty years ago under the auspices of the British and Foreign Bible Society, is of special interest because of the insight and parallels it offers for the present situation facing modern Russian biblical translation. In fact, the Cassian translation project began as an interconfessional one. In retrospect, one can say that the final goal of the project was not achieved. But why did that happen? This paper is an attempt to analyze both the history of the translation and its unique characteristics with an eye toward uncovering the reasons that have so significantly limited the dissemination of Cassian's translation in Russia.

A brief historical overview of the Cassian translation has already been provided by Stephen Batalden in his article, "Revolution and Emigration: The Russian Files of the British and Foreign Bible Society, 1917–1970".[1] Therefore this paper will focus more directly on the inner motives of the project and its participants.

Plans

The first request for a revised Russian translation came from groups associated with the Russian Student Christian Movement outside Russia

1. Stephen K. Batalden, "Revolution and Emigration: The Russian Files of the British and Foreign Bible Society, 1917–1970", in Janet Hartley, ed., *The Use of British Archives in the Study of Russian History* (London: University of London School of Slavonic and East European Studies/Mansell Publishing, 1986), pp. 147-61.

(Russkoe khristianskoe studencheskoe dvizhenie, RKSD) who were concerned with youth work. They were aware that for the youth of the more recent Russian emigration during World War II, the existing Russian text of the Bible (the so-called Synodal translation) needed to be retranslated into the spoken idiom. They asked for an adjusted and simplified text. A similar request came from priests who were visiting the camps for "displaced persons" in postwar Germany. They reported that the language of the Synodal translation was rather difficult for those who had grown up in Soviet Russia. An opportunity for a revision (or new translation) was opened up because of the ecumenical atmosphere prevailing in the postwar period among Russian Orthodox circles in Europe. Within these circles, ecumenical organizations such as the Fellowship of St. Alban and St. Sergius, although not directly involved in the Cassian translation, played a significant role in preparing the scene for interconfessional collaboration between Russian Orthodox and western churches. Bishop Cassian (1892–1965),[2] the key figure in the future translation project, had been an active member of the fellowship, having made a presentation at the opening of the first conference organized by the group in 1927.[3] The Russian delegation, which numbered about twelve, consisted chiefly of professors and students from the newly founded St. Sergius Russian Orthodox Theological Institute in Paris.[4] Fortunately, it is possible to get a flavour of the time and the fellowship from the recollections of Nicolas Zernov, who was the Orthodox chairman of this first Anglo-Russian conference and served, at the same time, as the general secretary of the Russian Student Christian Movement. Zernov writes of one of the subsequent fellowship conferences:

> In 1936 the Fellowship held its conference in Paris. The sense of unity between Anglicans and Orthodox reached a notable climax during this gathering. Bishop Frere was invited by Metropolitan Evlogy to sing an

---

2. Bishop Cassian (Sergei Sergeevich Bezobrazov) was professor of New Testament studies in the St. Sergius Theological Institute, Paris, and was an active member of the Fellowship of St. Alban and St. Sergius and the Russian Student Christian Movement outside Russia.

3. The first conference is described in the memoir of Nicolas and Militza Zernov, *The Fellowship of St. Alban and St. Sergius: A Historical Memoir* (Oxford: [The Fellowship], 1979), pp. 4-5, wherein they write: "On the 11th January 1927, an unusual group descended from the train at St. Alban's station. It included bearded clerics in flowing robes, an Indian, a Copt, several Anglican monks from Mirfield and Kelham. The average British student was in the minority. For five days (11th–15th January), this incongruous community lived in St. Alban's Retreat House, praying together, debating theology, and trying to understand each other's point of view".

4. The St. Sergius Russian Orthodox Theological Institute, founded in Paris in 1925, gathered together many of the outstanding émigré theologians of the Russian church.

English Office in the St. Alexander Nevsky Cathedral. In full episcopal attire and in a building packed with Russians he conducted a service from a stand in the middle of the church reserved for the Orthodox bishops. This was the first occasion on which Anglican worship had taken place for a Russian congregation in an Orthodox church. It signified the liturgical recognition by a Russian diocesan bishop of the Anglican bishop as being his brother.[5]

Not surprisingly, among the various early proposals for a new Russian translation of the Scriptures were those made in 1946-1947 by the same Nicolas Zernov and his émigré acquaintance Yury Bezsonov. Although Zernov met with the General Committee of the British and Foreign Bible Society (BFBS), the proposals for new translation failed to secure support from the BFBS.[6]

At the same time in Paris, Russian émigré followers of the RKSD frequented the local offices of the Paris YMCA directed by Paul B. Anderson, a prominent American Russianist.[7] Anderson would provide an important linkage between the Bible Society and the Paris Russian religious intelligentsia. Anderson inquired of Father Georges Florovsky and other representatives of the St. Sergius Institute, reporting back to the American Bible Society General Secretary Eric North in the spring of 1950, that "they all quite agree that a new translation is desirable".[8]

On 4 May 1950, representatives of the Moscow Patriarchate, the Ecumenical Patriarchate (Russian Archdiocese), and the Russian Orthodox Church Abroad held a meeting in Paris at the YMCA office. The main topic of the meeting was a revision of the Russian translation of the Bible. Among the participants were G. Bobrovsky; Archimandrite Nicholas Yeremin, a representative of the Diocesan Council of the Exarch of the Moscow Patriarchate; Archpriest Victor Yuriev, chair of the committee on education for the Diocesan Council of the Ecumenical Patriarchate; Archimandrite Silvester (Ivan Haruns); Archimandrite Methodius (Vladimir Kul'man); and Peter Kovalevsky of the Ecumenical Patriarchate. Bishop Nathaniel, diocesan bishop of the Russian Orthodox Church Abroad (Munich Jurisdiction), sent his apologies for not coming, but at the same time gave his approval "to the idea of the need for modernizing the

---

5. Nicolas and Militza Zernov, *Fellowship of St. Alban and St. Sergius*, p. 9.
6. Batalden, "Revolution and Emigration", p. 157.
7. Paul Anderson (1894–1985) was one of the founders of St. Sergius Institute, and in 1948 was awarded the doctorate *honoris causa* from the Institute. Russians affectionately referred to him as *Pavel Frantsevich*. As late as the 1970s, Anderson served as a consultant for the Anglican-Orthodox Joint Doctrinal Commission.
8. Copy of letter from P. Anderson to E. North, 4 April 1950, BFBS Translations Department Language Files: Russian, file 3, June 1946–April 1952 (BSA/E3/3/501/3). See also Batalden, "Revolution and Emigration", p. 157.

scripture text".[9] Although the beginning looked very promising, disagreements over the approach to the translation were indicated from the very start. Kovalevsky reported that the Diocesan Council of the Ecumenical Patriarchate had made a decision to establish a committee on revision of the Russian text of the New Testament. According to him, the work should take a few years and it would not be just a "russification" of the text, but a critical edition based on the original texts. At the same time Bishop Nathaniel noted that he agreed with the idea of a new edition, but not an entirely new critical edition.[10]

The BFBS translations subcommittee decided to send its translations secretary, Wilfred J. Bradnock, to Paris to meet all the interested parties. Thus, in the spring of 1951 the question of forming a commission on Russian revision was discussed. It was decided that the commission should include the following parties: a) a permanent chairman or commission secretary (Donald Lowrie of the Paris YMCA);[11] b) a chief translator (Bishop Cassian); c) an executive committee of seven persons; d) a literary panel of three; and e) a group of critical assessors or consultants (eight to twelve in number).

In May 1951, the first session of the commission took place in Paris. For two days the members discussed the principles of the revision. At the opening session, Bishop Cassian made the following points:

1. The work should be regarded as a revision and not a new version, the Synodal version being used as the basis.
2. It should be made with full regard to New Testament scholarship of the last fifty years and to the profoundly significant changes that had occurred in both the Russian language and the political background.

---

9. Quote taken from the "Minutes of a conference concerning publication of the New Testament in the modern Russian language", Paris, 4 May 1950. A copy of the minutes appears to be attached to the letter of Olivier Béguin to W. J. Bradnock, BFBS Translations Department Language Files: Russian, file 4, July 1948–March 1957 (BSA/E3/3/501/4).

10. See the "Minutes" noted above, Paris, 4 May 1950, BFBS Translations Department Language Files: Russian, file 4, July 1948–March 1957 (BSA/E3/3/501/4).

11. Donald A. Lowrie (1899–1974), the replacement for Paul Anderson at the Paris YMCA, attended and minuted the sessions of the revision committee as local representative for the BFBS. It is interesting that Lowrie took part in the first meeting of the Russian Student Christian Movement in Přerov in Czechoslovakia. He later became one of those who initiated the St. Sergius Institute in Paris and, following the departure of Paul Anderson, he served as director of YMCA Press in Paris. Russians called him *Donal'd Ivanovich*. For a useful guide to the St. Sergius Theological Institute in Paris, see Donald Lowrie's work, *Saint Sergius in Paris: The Orthodox Theological Institute* (London: SPCK, 1954). Lowrie's French spelling of Russian émigré names has been followed for many of those identified below.

3. A very careful study of the relation of the Old Slavonic to the new version should be made.
4. The needs of a vast new generation brought up outside the Church should be constantly kept in view.[12]

Bishop Cassian gave a detailed analysis of the Synodal version, indicating the various types of correction and modification that he considered necessary. These were fully discussed in two sessions of one hour each. Summarizing the proceedings, Donald Lowrie wrote in a report to the BFBS:

> I was impressed by the ready comprehension of the nature of these problems by all members there and also by their acquaintance with recent NT studies. Bishop Cassian himself spent a further hour on a critical analysis and appraisal of the main NT commentaries and concordances etc. as an outline to his proposed method of procedure. He has access to such work in Russian, French, German and English.[13]

On the second day it was agreed that special regard should be paid to the following characteristics and problems of the existing Russian Synodal translation:

1. Removal of mistranslations
2. Archaisms
3. Ambiguities (in the Greek and in the version)
4. Infelicities
5. Lack of concordance
6. Tendentiousness of interpretation
7. Punctuation
8. Non-Greek words in the Greek NT (e.g., Corban, Amen, etc.)

It was also agreed that Bishop Cassian would start the translation with the Gospel of Matthew.[14]

A follow-up meeting of the Russian New Testament Commission took place at Melun near Paris, 12-14 December 1951. Donald Lowrie chaired the session, with G. A. Bobrovsky acting as secretary. Others in attendance besides Bishop Cassian (who would be chief translator) and Wilfred Bradnock (as representative of the sponsoring BFBS) included Boris Bobrinskoy, Father Anatolii Dreving, N. T. Gontcharoff, Vladimir Lossky,

---

12. Cited in the memorandum of W. J. Bradnock to the BFBS Translations and Library Subcommittee, 21 May 1951, BFBS Translations Department Language Files: Russian, file 4, July 1948–March 1957 (BSA/E3/3/501/4).

13. Lowrie to Bradnock, Paris, 21 May 1951, BFBS Translations Department Language Files: Russian, file 4, July 1948–March 1957 (BSA/E3/3/501/4).

14. See the memorandum of W. J. Bradnock to the BFBS Translations and Library Subcommittee, 21 May 1951, BFBS Translations Department Language Files: Russian, file 4, July 1948–March 1957 (BSA/E3/3/501/4).

Father Methodius, Prince Dimitri Obolensky, Bishop Sylvester, Robbins Strong (secretary-designate of the YMCA), and Boris Zaitseff. Father Dreving of the Anastasii Jurisdiction (Russian Orthodox Church Abroad) in Germany announced that he could only attend in a private capacity inasmuch as his bishop had formally withdrawn from association with the commission.

Picture 23. *Bishop Cassian and Russian Translation Committee*. Reprinted from the Bible Society's *Popular Report for 1955* (London: BFBS, 1956), facing p. 86.

To give the project a genuinely interconfessional character the BFBS sought a qualified representative from the evangelical churches. In December 1951, they found Pastor A. P. Vasil'ev (Wassilieff) from the Belgian Gospel Mission, and he was added to the committee. There were also Russian-speaking Roman Catholics among the consultants.

Later in the 1950s, by the time the initial trial edition (*probnyi vypusk*) of the Gospel of Matthew was published, the complete list of the members of the Commission was as follows:[15]

Bishop Cassian (France)
Wilfred Bradnock (UK)
Boris Bobrinskoy (France)
G. Bobrovsky (USA)
Georges Florovsky (USA)
N. T. Gontcharoff (USA)

---

15. Members of the commission and their consultants can be identified from the commission minutes in BFBS Translations Department Language Files: Russian, file 5, March 1952–August 1953 (BSA/E3/3/501/5).

Vladimir Lossky (France)
Donald Lowrie (France)
Bishop Methodius (France)
John Meyendorff (France)
Dimitri Obolensky (UK)
Vladimir Rayevsky (France)
Boris Sove (Finland)
Bishop Sylvester (France)
A. Wassilieff (Belgium)
Wladimir Weidlé (France)
Boris Zaitseff (France)

The consultants included the following:

Nicholas Afanasieff (France)
Nicholas Arseniev (USA)
Archimandrite Christophe Dumont (France)
Elizabeth Hill (UK)
Bishop John of San Francisco (USA)
Anton Kartashev (France)
Michael Koriakov (USA)
Grigoriy Lomako (France)
Paul Lutoff (USA)
Pierre Pascal (France)
Gleb Struve (USA/France)
Jean Train (France)
George Urban (USA)
Alexander de Weymann (Switzerland)
Valentina Zander (France)

As Batalden has noted, the commission membership read like a "who's who" of first-wave Russian émigré religious leaders.[16] Indeed, many of the commission members were professors at the St. Sergius Russian Orthodox Theological Institute in Paris.[17] Bishop Cassian, for example,

---

16. Batalden, "Revolution and Emigration," p. 158.

17. In addition to Bishop Cassian, the list includes the following scholars and professors at the St. Sergius Institute: Archpriest Boris Bobrinskoy (more recently, since 1993, dean of the Institute); Archpriest Georges Florovsky (1893–1979), Institute professor, and active member of the Fellowship of St. Alban and St. Sergius and of the Russian Student Christian Movement outside Russia, who later served as professor and dean of St. Vladimir Theological Seminary, New York; Vladimir Lossky (1903–1958), professor and dean of the Institute, and one of the leaders of the Fellowship of St. Alban and St. Sergius; Archpriest John Meyendorff (1926–1992), Ph. D., University of Paris [Sorbonne], professor at the Institute and at St. Vladimir Theological Seminary, New York; Boris Sove (1899/1900–1962), professor at the Institute; Wladimir Weidlé (1895–1979); Anton

was professor of New Testament there. It was no wonder that Constantinople Ecumenical Patriarch Athenagoras, within whose jurisdiction the institute operated, gave his blessing to the project.[18] The question that hovers over this project, however, is why, despite such an impressive list of commission members and consultants, the result of the work—the Cassian translation—was not only rejected by the Russian Orthodox Church (Moscow Patriarchate), but also failed to secure any significant readership. In fact, the translation clearly did not meet readers' expectations. To discover why the translation project met with such little interest on the part of readers requires a closer look at the history of the translation effort.

Ambitions

In January 1952, a "Statement on the New Translation of the Russian New Testament" was issued and signed by the translations secretary of the BFBS, Wilfred Bradnock, who in turn took responsibility for funding the translation project. The statement pointed out that two main principles would condition the work: 1) faithfulness to the original texts; and 2) intelligibility to the modern reader.[19] The critical edition of the Greek New Testament text (17th edition) would be used as a base text.[20] Reinforcing the provisions of the 1952 statement, Robbins Strong, who succeeded Lowrie on the commission, wrote to the members and the consultants of the commission in 1953:

> May I remind you that our work should be based on the following principles: Fidelity to the Greek original (Nestle, 17th edition, is used as a basis), and a clear and dignified text in modern Russian, comprehensible by everyone and still not unacceptable for those who know and love the old Synodal Russian translation.[21]

Kartashev (1875-1960); and Dimitri Obolensky (1918-2001), professor at Trinity College, Cambridge, later professor of Russian and Balkan History, Oxford University; and vice-president of the British Academy.

18. Copy of letter from Patriarch Athenagoras to Bishop Cassian, Constantinople, 24 April 1951, BFBS Translations Department Language Files: Russian, file 3, June 1946–April 1952 (BSA/E3/3/501/3)

19. For Bradnock's January 1952 "Statement", see BFBS Translations Department Language Files: Russian, file 4, July 1948–March 1957 (BSA/E3/3/501/4).

20. The critical Greek New Testament of Eberhard Nestle went through numerous editions in the twentieth century. See Eberhard Nestle and Erwin Nestle, comps., *Novum Testamentum graece, cum apparatu critico curavit,* 17th ed. (Stuttgart: Privilegierte Württembergische Bibelanstalt, 1949).

21. Strong to the Commission, 25 June 1953, BFBS Translations Department Language Files: Russian, file 4, July 1948–March 1957 (BSA/E3/3/501/4).

By August 1953, the trial edition *(probnyi vypusk)* of the Gospel of Matthew was sent to representatives of various Orthodox and other confessional groups. As a supplement to the translation, an "Introduction to the Tentative Edition of Matthew" (in English) was enclosed. Concerning the principles of translation the "Introduction" reiterated:

> ... In essence the old translation remains inviolate. Those changes that are being brought into it by the development of biblical science, do not affect the content of our faith, the ethical teaching of Christianity, nor our understanding of its historical course. Neither can we be indifferent to the letter of the Scriptures. We have no right to look upon the *'textus receptus'*, i.e., the generally accepted text since the 17th century, as being the best expression of the will of God.[22]

Publication of the trial edition of the Gospel of Matthew spawned an immediate and significant reaction, including a number of articles appearing in the pages of the *Journal of the Moscow Patriarchate* (*Zhurnal moskovskoi patriarkhii, ZMP*).[23] It is interesting to note how the author of one of these articles, A. Ivanov, approached the new translation:

> In 1951 ecclesiastical schismatic Russian circles in Paris started work on a new Russian translation... According to the statement of the Committee, His Holiness Patriarch Athenagoras and the Synod of the Ecumenical Patriarchate gave their blessing to this work. Nevertheless the Committee carries on its work without the blessing and consent of His Holiness the Patriarch of Moscow and all Russia Alexis and without representatives of the Russian Patriarchal Exarchate of Western Europe.[24]

Ivanov's statement was not quite correct. At least two persons on the committee, Vladimir Lossky and Vladimir Rayevsky, were under the jurisdiction of the Moscow Patriarchate. But the main point as noted below pertained to the principles of the translation. Bishop Cassian left a note in which he spoke about the principles of the translation, and this

---

22. BFBS Translations Department Language Files: Russian, file 4, July 1948–March 1957 (BSA/E3/3/501/4).

23. See, for example, A. Alekseev, "K voprosu o novom perevode na russkii iazyk Evangeliia ot Matfeia", *ZMP* (1954), no. 2, pp. 76-77; A. Osipov, "K izdaniiu russkoi Biblii", *ZMP* (1955), no. 8, pp. 58-66, and "Ob odnom novom zagranichnom izdanii russkoi Biblii", *ZMP* (1955), no. 10, pp. 48-53; A. Ivanov, "K voprosu o vosstanovlenii pervonachal'nogo grecheskogo teksta Novogo Zaveta", *ZMP* (1954), no. 3, pp. 38-50, and "Novyi perevod na russkii iazyk Evangeliia ot Matfeia", *ZMP* (1954), no. 4, pp. 45-55, and no. 5, pp. 38-47, and "'Novoe izdanie grecheskogo Novogo Zaveta [a review of the 1952 Nestle edition]", *ZMP* (1954), no. 12, p. 69, and "Novoe kriticheskoe izdanie grecheskogo teksta Novogo Zaveta", *ZMP* (1956), no. 3, pp. 49-58, no. 4, pp. 49-58, and no. 5, pp. 43-52.

24. A. Ivanov, "Novyi perevod na russkii iazyk Evangeliia ot Matfeia", *ZMP* (1954), no. 4, p. 49.

note can be found among the other notes to the translation of chapters 1–11 of the Gospel of Matthew. Bishop Cassian indicated that the project had to strive for 1) literal translation, 2) reconstruction of the word order of the original, 3) avoidance of archaisms, and 4) simple expressions.[25]

By way of comparison, Ivanov in his article in the *Zhurnal moskovskoi patriarkhii* identified the following set of translation principles that ought to have been followed in rendering Holy Scripture:

- A translation must be based on the best original, from the point of view of its clarity and uncorrupted character;
- A translation must express and translate the meaning of the original with absolute precision; the words and expressions must be clear and generally accepted but not vulgar;
- A translation intended for Russian Orthodox readers must be done with the blessing of the Russian Orthodox Church (ROC) and under her direct control.[26]

Obviously, these demands included rather idealistic requirements. For instance, what was meant by, "must be based on the best original from the point of view of its clarity and uncorrupted character", or by the demand to translate the meaning of the original "with absolute precision"? In fact, these statements were far removed from any linguistic principles or modern theory of translation. Ivanov's principles could be reformulated as three basic conditions: a) the issue of textology; b) the issue of language (the principle of exactness); and c) the issue of authority—that is, the blessing and control of the Russian Orthodox Church (for Ivanov, this meant the Moscow Patriarchate). Needless to say, the last condition undermined all possible attempts from outside Russia even to start a Russian translation of Holy Scripture. However, for the time being, setting aside the political considerations and considering the scholarly conditions—specifically the first two demands formulated by Ivanov, what would they have meant in practice in the case of the Cassian translation?

Textology of the Translation

The first point made by Ivanov was that "wrong" textology had been used in the new translation. He points out thirty-one cases in the Gospel of Matthew where the Cassian translation introduced textological brackets,

---

25. Bishop Cassian's Translation Notes on the New Testament, in Russian, the Gospel according to St. Matthew, leaf 15, BFBS Microfilm Collection, no. 37 (BSMF 37). Hereafter cited as Bishop Cassian's Notes (BSMF 37).

26. Ivanov, "Novyi perevod", p. 50.

twenty-five readings that were omitted by the translator, and ten cases in which the translator changed words. Two examples are illustrative of Ivanov's criticism and what Bishop Cassian says by way of response in the notes to his own translation. Ivanov suggested that it would not be correct to put in brackets the passage from Matthew 1.11 – "Josiah begot [Jakim and Jakim begot] Jeconiah and his brothers at the time of the exile to Babylon" (*Iosia rodil [Ioakima; Ioakim rodil] Iekhoniu i brat'ev ego, pered pereseleniem v Vavilon.*). Bishop Cassian comments as follows on this verse:

> The words of the Synodal translation 'Jakim and Jakim begot' must be omitted because they have no good support. St. John Chrysostom (Homily 4.1) already knew that Matthew's tabulation of fourteen names (verse 17) does not in fact take place.[27]

It is true that the insertion of Jakim as the father of Jechoniah brings the list into harmony with 1 Chronicles 3.15-16, but it produces fifteen names against Matthew's tabulation of fourteen. More than that, editors of the Slavonic Bible at the time of Peter I and Catherine II had already highlighted these words as unreliable. They put them between brackets or even in a footnote. The brackets were also kept in the New Testament published by the Russian Bible Society in the 1820s. Therefore, Bishop Cassian was acting in this case in full accordance with tradition and one can conclude the textological brackets were inserted correctly.

The second example of Ivanov's challenge to Bishop Cassian is in the translation of the Lord's Prayer (Matthew 6.12) where the words "as we also forgive (αφιεμεν) our debtors" were substituted by "as we also have forgiven (αφηκαμεν) our debtors". Bishop Cassian writes in the notes:

> The best form of the text is (αφηκαμεν) – "we have forgiven" (*prostili*)... Russian translation of the Lord's Prayer cannot pretend to have the same expressiveness as Slavonic. The latter is sanctified by its liturgical use and the use in other prayer services. Inevitably in the translation we have to put the Russian forms in place of the Slavonic. The translation must be based on contemporary biblical scholarship.[28]

It is interesting to observe that in spite of the liturgical significance of the traditional reading – "as we also forgive" – Bishop Cassian in this case gives preference to the critical edition.[29] It is typical for Bishop Cassian to give a reference to "the best text" or "the best form of the text". For example, in the note to Matthew 1.25 one reads:

---

27. Bishop Cassian's Notes (BSMF 37), leaf 1.
28. Bishop Cassian's Notes (BSMF 37), leaf 14.
29. In fact this reading is not unquestionable. See Bruce M. Metzger, *A Textual Commentary on the Greek New Testament* (London/New York: United Bible Societies [Biblia-Druck GmbH Stuttgart], 1975), p. 16.

The best manuscripts testify to the short form of the text—Υιον (Son/ *Syna*)—without the adjective: αυτης τον πρωτοτοκον—"Her firstborn" (*Svoego perventsa*).[30]

At the same time, Bishop Cassian was not uncritical in his use of the Nestle text. As he indicated, "In no way do I consider Nestle as a pattern to be followed in every case. In his rich apparatus Nestle himself gives sufficient material to criticise his own conclusions."[31]

Thus, one confronts here two very different positions of what should be understood as "the best text". The Paris committee and Bishop Cassian, in claiming to publish a landmark Russian translation based on the critical Nestle edition of the Greek text, follow the best text principle cautiously, but steadily. Ivanov, criticising the changes of text used in the translation, assumes that the textological principles start from wrong assumptions. According to his view, the best text is "the text commonly accepted by the Orthodox Church," by which he means the *textus receptus*. Yet, in upholding the Erasmian *textus receptus*, Ivanov failed to note the genuine and irreconcilable differences that exist between the *textus receptus*, on the one hand, and the varying Slavonic and Greek liturgical texts, on the other. He mistakenly thought all of those texts were based upon just one textological base, or one reading.[32] That is far from being the case.

Language of the Translation

The second point of Ivanov's critique—that a translation must express and translate the meaning of the original with absolute precision—coincided, practically speaking, with one of the principles of Cassian himself, who strove for "literal translation" and "reconstruction of the original word order". Nevertheless, Ivanov was not satisfied with the results. He demanded "an absolute" exactness of the translation:

> The new translation of the Gospel of Matthew does not satisfy the second requirement that we mentioned above, that is translating the meaning of the original with absolute precision [exactness]. Rather, undue liberties with regard to the original, deviations from it, and even distortions of the original in the new translation are numerous. They can be found from the very first words of the Gospel. From Mt. 1.1, in the Greek original the first words of the blessed message are read: Βιβλος γενεσεως; the Slavonic text translates this as "*kniga rodstva*" (a book of kinship); the Russian translation is close to the Slavonic: '*rodoslovie*' (genealogy) of Jesus Christ. The

---

30. Bishop Cassian's Notes (BSMF 37), leaf 2.
31. Bishop Cassian, "The Revision of the Russian Translation of the New Testament", *The Bible Translator* 5, no. 1 (1954), p. 29. See, for example, his notes on Mt. 6.13 and 15, and 8.10, in Bishop Cassian's Notes (BSMF 37).
32. Ivanov, "Novyi perevod", p. 48.

new translation suggests a new rendering — *Kniga o rozhdenii Iisusa Khrista* (The book about the birth of Jesus Christ), which is far from the original and does not correspond with the context. Since further in the text an account is given of the kinship/genealogy of Christ.[33]

Compare this statement with the note provided by Bishop Cassian:

> *Kniga o rozhdenii Iisusa Khrista, syna Davidova, syna Avraamova* (The book about the birth of Jesus Christ, son of David, son of Abraham); γενεσις (γενεσεως) — the birth — compare with Mt. 1.18; Lk. 1.14, where the parallel form γεννησις has fewer witnesses. In the best manuscripts the form γενεσις in 1.18 serves as an introduction to the story about the birth itself and at the same time gives us a reference to verse 1. In verse 2 and following, the verb εγεννησεν (*rodil*) explains the meaning of γενεσις in verse 1. (Compare also γεννηθεν in verse 20, γεννηθεντος in 2.1, and γενναται in 2.4). The Russian translation "genealogy" (*rodoslovie*) places under the heading of verse 1 a passage containing all of verses 2-17. The Slavonic translation — "*kniga rodstva*" (a book of kinship) — is simply incomprehensible. The suggested translation is close to St. John Chrysostom's understanding (Homily 2.1-3)[34]

The rendering suggested here by Bishop Cassian — *The book about the birth of Jesus Christ* — is probably not the best possible one. At the same time, taken as a whole, his translation corrected some of the mistakes of the previous Russian Synodal translation (see, for example, Matthew 3.16 and 9.18; and also John 10.9 where the passive form σωθησεται is used), and in some cases the old translation was improved (Matthew 3.15). Unfortunately, Bishop Cassian's desire for literal translation (and even replication of the Greek word order) made the translation rather unintelligible. Reading through all the notes, one is struck with the number of times he decided to keep the word order of the Greek original or to keep a passive voice (Matthew 3.3; 3.8; 3.10; 3.11; 3.14; 3.16 — and these examples are taken only from one chapter, Matthew 3).

While on the one hand, Cassian wanted to avoid using archaisms,[35] on the other hand, he often ended up introducing new archaisms into his translation. Thus, in his note regarding Matthew 3.16, he wrote:

> To keep the relationship between ανεβη and καταβαινον it is desirable to translate the first word as *vosshel* (archaic - went out). If this translation is acknowledged as being too archaic, it is possible to keep the old rendering *vyshel* (went out), in spite of all its insufficiency.[36]

---

33. Ivanov, "Novyi perevod", p. 38.
34. Bishop Cassian's Notes (BSMF 37), leaf 1.
35. See for example his notes to Mt. 3.10: *topor* in place of *sekira*; *derev'ev* in place of *derev* — in Bishop Cassian's Notes (BSMF 37).
36. Bishop Cassian's Notes (BSMF 37), leaf 5.

This remark can be compared with Bishop Cassian's general note on the Gospel of John:

> The Gospel of John has the seal of special solemnity that does not allow us to escape from archaisms in vocabulary and in the structure of translation. A suggested translation is just a compromise that the members of the Committee came to.[37]

Such an approach, involving the adoption of some archaisms and relatively rigid fidelity to the Greek word order, was opposed by certain members of the committee (notably Dimitri Obolensky and Anton Kartashev),[38] and Robbins Strong called it "a somewhat mechanistic reproduction of the Aramaic flavour in the Greek language and the Greek word order".[39] The Russian writer Boris Zaitseff particularly opposed this "mechanistic reproduction" and made numerous suggestions for improving the translation.[40] Nevertheless, many verses remained far from the literary standards of modern Russian (for example, John 13.1-2), and others were even incomprehensible (Romans 1.5).

Outcome

One can trace a fundamental disagreement in the definition of the translation project from the very beginning. It was not clear what the precise goal of the project was. Should it be a new translation or just a revision of the old Synodal translation? The BFBS considered the project to be a new Russian translation that could in the future replace the Synodal translation. Bishop Cassian, although he constantly insisted that what he was doing was only a revision, quite often contradicted himself. In 1954, giving an account of his work, he wrote an article for the UBS journal, *The Bible Translator*, in which he said:

> The work we are doing is conceived not as a new translation, but as a revision of the existing one by the Holy Synod of the Russian Church, dating from 1862 and being itself only a revision of the first translation published in the early twenties by the Russian Bible Society.[41]

---

37. Introduction, Gospel according to St. John, Bishop Cassian's Notes (BSMF 37).

38. See the early discussions minuted in the commission meetings, BFBS Translations Department Language Files: Russian, file 5, March 1952-August 1953 (BSA/E3/3/501/5).

39. Strong to Bradnock, 14 April 1953, BFBS Translations Department Language Files: Russian, file 5, March 1952-August 1953 (BSA/E3/3/501/5).

40. First-person testimony to the author in an oral interview with Archpriest Boris Bobrinskoy.

41. Bishop Cassian, "The Revision", p. 28.

Just one page after this statement, however, he wrote something very different:

> As it was clear from the beginning that what is needed is practically a new translation, there could be no doubt that this revised translation should be up to date; it should be on the level of contemporary Bible scholarship and free of all the deficiencies of the existing Russian text.[42]

In the case of both such approaches — revision of the Synodal text and a new translation — what the translator and the translation commission needed to do first of all was to define their attitude toward the existing tradition of Bible translation. That had been the intention of both the commission and Bishop Cassian. Unfortunately, the relationship between the new translation and established church traditions with respect to Russian biblical translation remained, in the end, ill defined.

The other problem clearly had to do with the language of the translation. In responding to this issue, the translator and the commission ought, in fact, to have addressed the matter of the intended audience. For whom was the translation to serve as a source for the Word of God? On the one hand, Bishop Cassian defended a common language translation, but on the other, he included archaisms and implemented in many cases a Greek word order that impeded reader understanding. Bishop Cassian told a very revealing story in his *Bible Translator* article:

> The evolution of the Russian language in the Soviet Union cannot be regarded as a normal one. It is not even a triumph of some popular form of Russian over the literary language of our generation. It involves a tremendous impoverishment of what constituted its richness, and at the same time, the accretion of a lot of artificial words, technical terms, abbreviations, etc. About the end of the last war I met in Greece a young officer of the Red Army who spoke this form of Russian. It was really awful. Strictly speaking, it could not be described as a "living" language... It would be *essentially wrong* to accommodate the language of the Russian Bible to this post-war and post-revolution Russian... It is self-evident that the faithful must understand the Bible, but the language of the Bible *must lift his own language to a higher level* [italics added, S. O.].[43]

That was not the argument of one committed to a common language text. On a similar note, Bishop Cassian offered a particularly interesting testimony that shed light on the history of the translation. The story was about how he had "converted" one man to his own "archaic" understanding of the language — a position he considered necessary for the translation:

---

42. Bishop Cassian, "The Revision", p. 29.
43. Bishop Cassian, "The Revision", p. 28.

> ...a young Displaced Person, a very gifted and enthusiastic man, took part in the discussions of our Commission. He was happy to enrich his vocabulary and not afraid at all of the archaic forms, which our people abroad tried to exclude at any price from the vocabulary of the same Displaced Persons! *Owing to his attitude, some archaic particles, conjunctions, prepositions, adverbs, which seemed to be condemned to death, have made their triumphant reappearance in our translation.*[44] (Italics added—S.O.)

Cassian concluded that, "the Commission felt obliged to give up the extreme simplification which had been formerly regarded as the main aim of the revision".[45]

Such comments regarding archaisms suggest that the intended audience for the translation had also not been clearly defined. The translation was rather a compromise between the convictions of Bishop Cassian and those of the commission. The discord between Bishop Cassian and other members of the commission can be traced throughout the translation process. Such differences not only made the translation weaker, but more importantly, ended up depriving the intended audience of the initial well-defined goals set forth at the outset of the project.

As a result, the BFBS, which was well aware of all the problems, had many doubts regarding publication of the translation, and the New Testament was published in its entirety only in 1970, five years after Bishop Cassian's death. In fact, the project had become a fiasco. Moreover, it had been the intention of the BFBS, after finishing the New Testament translation, to begin the translation of the Old Testament. A key figure in this project was to have been Anton Kartashev, professor at the St. Sergius Institute.[46] The debacle over the New Testament, however, meant that the Old Testament project was never implemented.

It is probably unjust to stigmatize the Cassian translation as a failure. That was far from being true. Recently republished (in the mid-1990s) by the renewed Bible Society in Russia (BSR), Bishop Cassian's translation has gained some popularity, mainly among students of theological seminaries and people who have some knowledge of the Greek New Testament. That was the reason the BSR, having decided to publish a diglot Greek-Russian parallel edition, chose the Cassian translation as the one best suited to appear as a parallel text alongside the critical Greek New

---

44. Bishop Cassian, "The Revision", p. 28.
45. Bishop Cassian, "The Revision", p. 31.
46. The early plan for an Old Testament counterpart translation, documented in BFBS Translations Department Language Files: Russian, file 5, March 1952–August 1953 (BSA/E3/3/501/5), was never pursued in light of the problems confronted with the New Testament.

Testament text.[47] Although such a narrow scholarly outcome was far from the initial goal, the translation intended for a wide audience turned out to be quite suitable for seminary students.

Conclusion

There can be no doubt that the textological issues and those relating to the intended audience were important, as was the need to connect any such new translation with established church traditions of Bible translation. However, the most important question raised in the critique of the Cassian translation within the pages of the *Journal of the Moscow Patriarchate* was one that remains to this day largely unresolved — namely, who has the final authority to bless and approve new translations for publication? In theory, for the Orthodox church, unlike for many of its western confessional counterparts, the answer to Ivanov's question ought to have been simple and straightforward — namely, the church gives its blessing for dissemination of new translations. But, for the Russian Orthodox Church (Moscow Patriarchate), as well as for some other Orthodox churches, such approval has become problematic. After all, there still exist two different forms of biblical text in use in churches in Russia: one for liturgical purposes and another for "home reading". The former is the Slavonic translation of the Holy Scriptures and the latter is the Russian Synodal translation. While it seems that a translation intended to bring better understanding of the Word of God would easily be accepted by the church and the public, great difficulties stand in the way of the recognition of a new translation.

First of all, the Russian Synodal translation has been gradually elevated toward the sphere of a sacral, or pseudo-sacral, existence, with the result that any attempt to replace the old translation is considered a kind of revolt against established church authority. After all, the Russian Orthodox Church is greatly concerned about the unity of the church and cannot approve initiatives that might threaten that unity. Today, the integral unity of the church is endangered not so much by dogmatic questions or issues of theology, but more by very practical considerations such as the calendar question or questions of liturgical language. That is why the church, particularly its hierarchy, seeks to hide under the carpet the major question of a new liturgical Bible translation. It is well known to all that the Slavonic translation is largely unable to be understood by the Russian people. Nevertheless, the church is unprepared even to begin a discussion about biblical translation for liturgical worship.

---

47. *Novyi Zavet na grecheskom i russkom iazykakh*, ed. Anatolii A. Alekseev (Moscow: Bible Society in Russia, 2002).

To understand Orthodox practice in this regard, one needs to compare reverence for the Bible with the practice of venerating icons. An Orthodox believer venerates the icon by kissing it. The same act of veneration occurs in the liturgical service with respect to the gospel, for the believer recognizes in the reading of the gospel the meeting with Christ as the Word. Just as the icon is blessed by church authority as recognition of the real presence of the Kingdom of God within it — as a window to the Kingdom — so must the translation of the Gospels be blessed in recognition of the words of Christ. The translation in this sense is also an icon, a window to the Kingdom. The believer is kissing not the text itself, but Christ as the Word of God. In fact, translation is not just a matter of the text that is read, it is a translation of the reader/listener into another sphere, the sphere of the Spirit. That is why even the Synodal translation, not just the Slavonic version, is considered to be an icon, the sacral text of the Holy Scriptures.

What lesson should the Bible societies learn from the story of the Cassian translation? In this respect it worth reconsidering a comment that Stephen Batalden made many years ago:

> The British and Foreign Bible Society no longer has a role in the Soviet Union, and it is still too early to determine whether the United Bible Societies can be as resourceful as their British parent.[48]

This was written in 1986. I believe it was not just a rhetorical comment, and it may now be possible to respond. At that time, no one could have imagined that a renewed Russian Bible Society would soon appear in Russia, but now there is an unprecedented opportunity for Bible work in Russia. This paper is not the place for analyzing the activity of BSR/UBS since the day of their reestablishment in 1990, and one can find an impressive description of Russian Bible Society activity on the Internet.[49] I only want to point out a striking parallel between today's situation and the Russian Bible Society's activity in the early nineteenth century. The contemporary Bible Society in Russia started its publishing programme with republication of the Slavonic Bible.[50] The very same was done at the beginning of the nineteenth century, prior to the launch of modern Russian translation in 1816, by the Russian Bible Society (*Rossiiskoe bibleiskoe obshchestvo*). It is quite understandable that there should be such a remembrance of the past, and perhaps that is why the bulk of contemporary BSR publications now consist of reprints of nineteenth-century works.[51] As in

---

48. Batalden, "Revolution and Emigration", p. 161.
49. www.bsr.ru
50. *Biblia na tserkovnoslavianskom iazyke* (Moscow: BSR, 1993).
51. See, for example, such republications as the *Piatiknizhie Moiseia v perevode arkhimandrita Makaria* (Moscow: BSR, 2000); *Novyi Zavet v perevode K. P. Pobedonostseva*

the past, the Bible Society in Russia continues to work with the translation of the Bible into different languages of the Russian Federation.[52]

While it has been relatively easy to reissue editions of the Slavonic Bible, much more complicated has been the path of new biblical translations into Russian. For example, a recent translation of the New Testament published by the Bible Society in Russia met with hostility from the Russian Orthodox Church.[53] A new translation of the Old Testament is now also in preparation, but this translation has no chance of being accepted by the Orthodox church either because it is based on the Hebrew Masoretic text.[54] Interestingly enough, the Russian Orthodox Church has taken a position with regard to new translations that is remarkably similar to that taken by the church at the time of the reopening of biblical translation in the middle of the nineteenth century. As a result, publications of new translations are appearing openly in contemporary religious journals.[55]

One of the sad ironies in this regard is that the first new Russian translation of several books of the New Testament recognized at last by the Russian Orthodox Church was launched with support from the United Bible Societies, but then rejected by the Bible Society in Russia and the project terminated.[56] It is hard to escape the conclusion that the policy of the Bible Society in Russia with regard to the Russian Orthodox Church is one of keeping its distance from the church and its leadership. The need

---

(Moscow: BSR, 2000); and *Novyi Zavet v perevode Rossiiskogo Bibleiskogo obshchestva 1824* (Moscow: BSR, 2000).

52. Projects include those of the Chuvash Old Testament, the Ossetian Old Testament, the Yakut Old Testament, the Altai Old Testament, and others.

53. See the so-called "Kuznetsova translation", a *Good News*-type translation. *Radostnaia Vest': Novyi Zavet v perevode s drevnegrecheskogo.* (Moscow: BSR, 2001)

54. The liturgical text of the Old Testament in the tradition of the Russian Orthodox Church is based largely on the Septuagint.

55. See, for example, Sergei S. Averintsev, "Ot Luki Sviatoe Blagovestie", in *Tserkov' i vremia*, vol. 1, no. 10 (Moscow: DECR, 2000), pp. 9-72; [Anatolii A. Alekseev], "Deianiia Sviatykh Apostolov (novyi perevod)", in *Tserkov' i vremia*, vol. 4, no. 13 (Moscow: DECR, 2000), pp. 171-229; and Sergei S. Averintsev, "Ot Marka Sviatoe Blagovestie", in *Tserkov' i vremia*, vol. 1, no. 14 (Moscow: DECR, 2001), pp. 222-61.

56. *Evangelie ot Marka, Evangelie ot Ioanna, Poslanie k rimlianam, Apokalipsis* (Sankt-Petersburg: Slavianskii Bibleiskii Fond, United Bible Societies, 1997). Translators were Sergei Averintsev, Anatolii Alexeev, Archimandrite Iannuary, and Fr. Sergei Ovsiannikov. A foreword to the translation was written by Metropolitan Filaret, Patriarchal Exarch of Belarus', who is the head of the Synodal Theological Committee of the Russian Orthodox Church.

for new Russian biblical translation acceptable to the Russian Orthodox Church has been discussed neither by the Orthodox church nor by the Bible Society in Russia. Thus, the problem of modern Russian biblical translation remains today much as it existed at the end of World War II, when Bishop Cassian and his Russian translation commission met in Paris to address the question of the Russian New Testament.

MINORITY LANGUAGE BIBLICAL TRANSLATION WORK IN RUSSIA:
THEN AND NOW[1]

David J. Clark

From its earliest contacts with Russia, the British and Foreign Bible Society (BFBS) was interested in the translation of the Bible into minority languages. This article will focus on two important minority languages now referred to as Kalmyk and Yakut. Both groups had some Bible translation published in the 1890s, and in both groups there was further translation work during the 1990s. It was my privilege to be involved in the latter projects as a translation consultant of the United Bible Societies (UBS).

The Kalmyk People and Their Background

The Kalmyks are a Mongol people who emigrated westward in the seventeenth century and settled in the steppes between the Caspian Sea and the River Don, in the area now comprising part of the Republic of Kalmykiia (Russian Federation).[2] This area is fairly low-lying, though not particularly fertile, and the climate, cold in winter and hot in summer, does not suffer the extreme variations of temperature found in Siberia. The Kalmyk population totalled 174,000 in the 1989 census.[3] Russian-Kalmyk bilingualism is widespread, but in mixed marriage families the children often do not learn Kalmyk well. Kalmyk belongs to the Mongolian branch of the Altaic language family.[4]

The Kalmyk people have retained Tibetan Buddhism as their traditional religion, and a new Buddhist temple was built near the capital city

---

1. My warm thanks go to the following people who have patiently read over a draft of this article: Marianne Beerle-Moor, Kathleen Cann, Glenys Clark, John Dean, Barbro Lindström, and Beth Long. All have earned my gratitude by providing additions and/or corrections on matters of fact or typography.

2. Bernard Comrie, *The Languages of the Soviet Union* (Cambridge: Cambridge University Press, 1981), p. 56.

3. Cited in Marianne Beerle-Moor, ed., *Rozhdestvo Iisusa Khrista: Evangelie ot Luki 2:1-10 na 80 iazykakh SNG* [The Birth of Jesus Christ: Luke 2.1-20 in 80 Indigenous Languages of the CIS] (Moscow: Institute for Bible Translation, 2000), p. 167.

4. Comrie, *Languages*, pp. xxi, 54-56

Elista during the 1990s. The Kalmyks now claim to be the only Buddhist group indigenous to Europe. In 1943, the entire Kalmyk population was exiled to Siberia and Central Asia because Stalin suspected them of sympathy for the invading Germans. In 1957, under Khrushchev, they were allowed to return to Kalmykiia, and many did so. They have not been strongly influenced by Orthodox Christianity, but since 1991 several Protestant congregations of various persuasions have been established among them.

Even before the foundation of the Russian Bible Society in 1812, BFBS had sent funds to support the publication of Scripture in a language then variously spelt Calmuc, Calmuck, Kalmuk, and Kalmuck,[5] and the Gospel of Matthew was printed in St. Petersburg as early as 1815. This publication was followed by the Gospel of John in 1820, the remaining Gospels and Acts in 1820–1821, and the New Testament in 1827.[6] Interest in Kalmyk continued throughout the nineteenth century, and the Gospel of John was reprinted in 1878.[7] Further progress in translation is documented in issues of the annual BFBS *Report* between 1880 and 1896. The publication of a new translation of the four Gospels, the work of Aleksei Pozdneev, was reported in 1887,[8] together with editions of each Gospel separately.

Translation work continued, and in 1895 publication of the remaining books of the New Testament (Acts to Revelation) was reported, also in St. Petersburg.[9] At least some copies of this were bound in with the 1887 Gospels to form a complete one-volume New Testament, which was printed in the old vertical script, no longer usable today. The individual Gospels were reprinted in Shanghai in 1896,[10] but there seems to be no evidence of any further reprints after that.

---

5. James Moulton Roe, *A History of the British and Foreign Bible Society, 1905–1954*, (London: British and Foreign Bible Society, 1965) p. 8. "Kalmyk," the form used in this article, is the modern spelling of the language name in roman script, transcribed from the current Russian spelling.

6. T. H. Darlow and H. F. Moule, comps., *Historical Catalogue of the Printed Editions of Holy Scripture in the Library of the British and Foreign Bible Society*, 2 vols. in 4 (London: British and Foreign Bible Society, 1903–1911), hereafter cited as DM. See DM 6830 for the 1815 Gospel of Matthew. For the 1820 Gospel of John, see DM 6831; for the 1820-1821 Gospels and Acts and the 1827 New Testament, see DM 6832-6834a.

7. DM 6835.

8. DM 6836. DM romanizes his name "Pozdneyeff", whereas "Pozdnejeff" is used in the BFBS *Report*. "Pozdneev" is in accordance with the Library of Congress romanization system used in this volume.

9. According to DM 6837, the publication actually took place in the previous year, 1894. The sizes of the print runs are not stated in DM for any of the Kalmyk editions.

10. DM 6838.

Kalmuk.

ГОСПОДА НАШЕГО
IИСУСА ХРИСТА
mark
СВЯТОЕ ЕВАНГЕЛІЕ ОТЪ МАРКА.

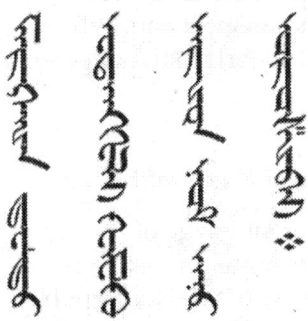

ИЗДАНІЕ ВЕЛИКОБРИТАНСКАГО И ИНОСТРАННАГО БИБЛЕЙСКАГО ОБЩЕСТВА.

САНКТПЕТЕРБУРГЪ.
ДЕПО ВЕЛИКОБРИТАНСКАГО И ИНОСТРАННАГО БИБЛЕЙСКАГО ОБЩЕСТВА.
НОВОИСААКІЕВСКАЯ № 4.
1887.

Picture 24. *Gospel of Mark in Kalmyk (1887)*. Specimen courtesy of BFBS Library collection, Cambridge University Library.

From the point of view of a translation consultant, the most interesting item in the BFBS *Report* from those years is the comment from 1887:

> The version was produced in the following manner. Professor Pozdnejeff first made a draft translation of the Gospels. These he sent to Archimandrite Smirnoff, in Astrakhan, for revision. When Professor Pozdnejeff had collated M. Smirnoff's criticisms, he proceeded to the steppes to test the translation by reading it to the Kalmuks. In this way he was able to conform his version to the style understood by the people, and to acquire information for further translation. Professor Pozdnejeff made three journeys to the steppes for the purpose of testing his work. On his return home he carefully revised the translation once more, and prepared copy for the press.[11]

It is good to see that the translation procedures in use today (including drafting, checking, comprehension testing, and revision) have such an honourable pedigree. The combination of modern linguistic and exegetical advances with modern transport and technology has made the process both more complex and faster, but the stages of the work remain broadly comparable.

The Yakut People and Their Background

Yakut is the easternmost language of the Turkic language family.[12] The Yakut people occupy a vast area of eastern Siberia known officially within the Russian Federation as the Sakha Republic (more popularly called Yakutiia), with its capital at Yakutsk on the River Lena. This is the coldest inhabited region on earth: most of the area is permafrost and agriculture is virtually impossible. The climate is very severe, with the temperature at minus forty degrees centigrade or below for weeks on end in winter, and as high as plus forty degrees centigrade during the short summer. The population was 382,000 in the 1989 census.[13] The Yakut language is flourishing in both oral and written traditions despite ever increasing bilingualism with Russian.

The traditional vigour of the Yakut language and culture is clearly reflected in BFBS records in a letter dated 9 October 1896 from William Nicolson, BFBS agent in St. Petersburg (1869–1897). Nicolson reports that according to Walter Davidson, the BFBS agent in Siberia (1889–1918), Russian merchants in Yakutiia, even in Yakutsk itself, learnt to speak Yakut

---

11. *Eighty-third Report of the BFBS* (London, 1887), p. 454.
12. Comrie, *Languages*, pp. xxi, 42. [Editor's note: According to the Library of Congress system followed in this volume, the Russian "я" is romanized as "ia". An exception has been made for Yakut and Yakutiia, for which the initial "Я" has been rendered with the more common "Ya".]
13. Cited in Beerle-Moor, *Rozhdestvo*, p. 133.

for trading purposes rather than the Yakuts learning Russian. Nicolson was well aware that this demonstrated "a remarkable tendency certainly not general in intercourse of civilized and savage peoples", as he quaintly expressed it.[14]

Orthodox Christianity reached Yakutiia as early as 1632 with the founding of Yakutsk, but although many of the Yakut people became nominally Orthodox, the traditional shamanism has continued to be practised down to the present day. Since 1991, Protestant Christianity (primarily Baptist) has also been significantly in evidence, and there are several Yakut-speaking congregations in Yakutsk and elsewhere.

The first two portions of the Bible in the Yakut language were printed in Moscow in 1858, one volume containing a translation of the Gospels, and the other the Acts, the Epistles, and Genesis; neither translator nor publisher is known.[15] In 1887, a translation of the Psalms was published in Kazan by the Orthodox Missionary Society.[16] BFBS became involved by supporting the publication of a new rendering of the Gospels. With the approval of the Orthodox Missionary Society, the translation was prepared by D. A. Kuchnev under the supervision of N. Bobrovnikov. The edition was published in 1898 at Kazan in a print run of 3,000 copies. At least one reprint was made in 1975, when with the consent of BFBS the Institute for Bible Translation (IBT) reprinted 2,000 copies at Örebro in Sweden.[17]

It is notable that in these two languages as in many others, BFBS cooperated both with the Orthodox church and with other Bible agencies. This open-minded attitude has continued to the present day through BFBS membership in the United Bible Societies (UBS). In the 1990s, it was IBT that initiated fresh translations of the New Testament in Kalmyk and Yakut (as well as in many other minority languages of Russia), and as a partner organization requested translation consultant help from UBS. The recently re-established Bible Society in Russia concurred, and this cooperation led to my own assignment to work with these projects.[18]

---

14. Nicolson to Charles Finch, 9 October 1896, BFBS Editorial Correspondence Inwards, no. 35, p. 75 (BSA/E3/1/4/35).

15. For the Gospels, see DM 9535; for the volume containing the Acts, the Epistles, and Genesis, see DM 9536.

16. DM 9537.

17. DM 9538 (the 1898 edition). The 1975 edition published in Stockholm (East Bible Institute) was reprinted by photography from the 1898 edition, including the original title, a new half-title, preface, and introduction (BSS 505.F75).

18. The cooperation between UBS and IBT has led to the migration of staff in both directions. The current UBS translation coordinator for the Europe-Middle East Region, Simon Crisp, was recruited from IBT. Following my own retirement from UBS, I have also served IBT as an honorary translation consultant.

Modern Translation Projects

IBT was founded in 1973 in Sweden with the aim of supplying scriptures in the non-Slavic languages of the USSR. It did initiate some new translations in major non-Slavic languages for expatriate communities in other parts of the world, but until the end of the Soviet period concentrated on reprinting older translations. Thereafter it was free to initiate new translation projects in various languages, among them Yakut in 1992, and Kalmyk, also about 1992. During the course of the translation, sample portions were published as follows: in Kalmyk, Luke appeared in 1996 (3,500 copies); and in Yakut, Mark was printed in 1995 (5,100 copies), Luke and Acts in 1998 (in one volume, 15,000 copies), and the Gospel of John and the Epistles of John and James in 2000 (all in one volume, 17,000 copies).

The new version of the Kalmyk New Testament was published in 2002, and the complete Yakut New Testament is due to appear in 2004.

The two projects are similarly structured. There is a team of translators, who are native speakers of the receptor language, together with an exegetical adviser and a linguistic adviser and/or stylist. In Yakut the (part-time) translators were Mariia Egorovna Alekseeva (a civil servant), Aita Shaposhnikova (a journalist), and Sargylana Afanas'evna Leont'eva, who also functioned as an exegetical adviser and worked full time on the project. Linguistic and stylistic advice has come from various people at different times. In Kalmyk, the translators were Vera Kirguevna Shugraeva, Nina Badmaevna Avashkieva, and Olga Borisovna Solomova, who all worked full time.[19] The exegetical adviser was Sergei Anatol'evich Sychov, and the linguistic adviser was Professor Petr Tsedenovich Bitkeev. Exegetical advisers are able to read Greek, and understand the receptor language, though they may or may not be native speakers. They work in close contact with the translators throughout the drafting process. The drafts are then shared with the linguistic advisers and/or stylists, who are also native speakers, and any necessary changes are made. The second draft is next given comprehension testing with people not involved in the project, and if further changes are needed, they are made. Finally, the draft is worked over again with the translation consultant, who may raise questions of various kinds, textual, linguistic, exegetical, literary, cultural, or even occasionally theological. The draft may receive further changes, usually of a minor nature at this stage, and then it is read over once more by at least one native speaker of the language before being published.

---

19. Vera Shugraeva at the age of four was among those exiled to Siberia, and Nina Avashkieva was born in Siberia. Olga Solomova and Vera Shugraeva are both published poets in Kalmyk, the latter being the author of the anthem of the Kalmyk republic.

Иоанн Үөрүүлээх Илдьит

Суруктар

Иаков суруга

Библияны тылбаастыыр институт
Москва
2000

Picture 25. *Gospel of John and Epistles of John and James in Yakut (2000)*. Specimen courtesy of BFBS Library collection, Cambridge University Library.

Translation consultants must have a good knowledge of linguistics and of the biblical languages, as well as being sensitive to cultural issues, but rarely will they know the receptor language. They must, however, have a common language with the translation team. In the case of the Kalmyk and Yakut projects, when I met with the team, they would provide me with an oral back-translation of their draft into Russian, and I would pose questions as far as possible in Russian. In both teams the exegetical advisers had an adequate knowledge of English and could help me out when my knowledge of Russian reached its limits. Checking sessions thus constantly involved the use of four languages: Greek, Russian, English, and the receptor language. Since nobody was completely at home in all four, there was always plenty of give and take, and checking sessions, though dealing with serious questions, also brought lots of fun.

The rest of this article will illustrate the types of problems encountered in the checking sessions. The examples are taken from notes made during the checking of the Pauline letters in Kalmyk and Yakut.[20] For present purposes these letters are defined as all those that claim to be written by the apostle Paul, namely Romans to Philemon. They provide an extensive and varied corpus of a size still manageable within the limits of this article.

For the historical record, the chart below shows exactly when and where the checking sessions were held:

BOOK	KALMYK		YAKUT	
	DATE	PLACE	DATE	PLACE
Romans (Rom.)	1/99	Moscow	4/01	Yakutsk
1 Corinthians (1 Cor.)	3/99	Moscow	6/02	Moscow
2 Corinthians (2 Cor.)	3/99	Moscow	6/02	Moscow
Galatians (Gal.)	3/98	Elista	6/99	Yakutsk
Ephesians (Eph.)	3/98	Elista	6/99	Yakutsk
Philippians (Phil.)	6/99	Moscow	6/96	Yakutsk
Colossians (Col.)	3/99	Moscow	4/01	Yakutsk
1 Thessalonians (1 Thess.)	11/96	Moscow	5/98	Moscow
2 Thessalonians (2 Thess.)	7/97	Elista	5/98	Moscow
1 Timothy (1 Tim.)	8/97	Elista	6/99	Yakutsk
2 Timothy (2 Tim.)	8/97	Elista	6/99	Yakutsk
Titus (Tit.)	8/97	Elista	5/98	Moscow
Philemon (Phlm.)	11/96	Moscow	5/98	Moscow

The checking of the Pauline epistles in Kalmyk was spread over two and a half years from November 1996 to June 1999, whereas their checking in Yakut was spread over six years from June 1996 to June 2002. This

---

20. If any similar notes were ever made during the nineteenth-century translation projects, they do not appear to have survived.

difference arose in some measure from the contrast between having parttime or full-time translators, but was also a reflection of the greater distances involved and the more difficult working conditions in Yakutiia.[21] For instance, in the winter of 1996-1997, there was a major computer crash, serious accommodation problems for one of the team, and a prolonged dispute involving electricity workers in Yakutsk, which greatly reduced the number of hours that translators had light and power and could be active in their work. In the absence of drafts ready for checking, I did not meet with the translation team between June 1996 and May 1998.

Typical Translation Problems

The average person who has never been involved in a Bible translation project probably thinks of translation as transferring the words of one language into the equivalent words in another language. While there is some truth in this, it is very far from being the whole truth. It is more appropriate to think of translation, especially Bible translation, as transplanting a message from one culture to another, with language as the primary tool. Thus, translation problems can be usefully considered in two general categories, linguistic and cultural. Since this volume is not oriented principally toward people who are specialists in New Testament Greek, linguistics, or translation, my article does not deal with technical questions of textual criticism or exegesis, but illustrates linguistic and cultural problems, and then examines an area where they intertwine, namely the translation of figurative language.

Linguistic Problems

A language is a highly structured combination of interlocking systems: a sound system, a morphological system, a syntactic system, and a lexical system, to mention only the most obvious. Linguistic problems in translation arise from the mismatch between the various systems of the source language and those of the receptor language. For example, English, like Greek, can accept several subordinate clauses within a single sentence. However, languages like Kalmyk, which belong to a very different language family, have strict limitations on subordinate clauses, and in particular typically insist on placing them before the main clause of a sentence. This makes unavoidable the radical restructuring of Paul's long sentences in his letter to the Ephesians. In a parallel manner, the head word in a phrase has to come last, with any descriptive matter preceding it. A clear

---

21. From Moscow it is only about 750 miles by air to Elista, but to Yakutsk over 3,100 miles.

example of the complications that can arise from this pattern is found in the first part of 2 Tim. 2.8. In the Revised Standard Version (henceforth RSV), it reads "Remember Jesus Christ, risen from the dead, descended from David…" In Kalmyk, the main verb "remember" has to come last, and the two other pieces of information must come in reverse order with the head noun "Jesus Christ" after the description of him, thus: "David-from descended the-dead-from risen Jesus Christ remember". If the two items describing Jesus Christ were kept in the same order as the Greek ("the-dead-from risen David-from descended Jesus Christ"), the phrase "the-dead-from risen" would then be taken as applying to David, and the sense would be completely mangled.

The need to put verbs at the end of a clause in Kalmyk means that certain literary structures cannot be preserved. In 1 Cor. 1.19, Paul quotes from the Septuagint rendering of Isaiah 29.14, preserving in Greek the verb phrase//noun phrase//noun phrase//verb phrase chiastic structure of the Hebrew. In the RSV (with // to indicate phrase boundaries) this is represented as

> I will destroy // the wisdom of the wise, //
> and the cleverness of the clever // I will thwart.

In Kalmyk, the clauses must both keep the verb at the end, so that they become parallel in structure rather than the second being a mirror image of the first. The Good News Bible (henceforth GNB) has done something similar in English, but with the verbs at the beginning of each clause, as befits English sentence patterns. In Kalmyk, however, there is a compensating literary effect in the presence of line-initial rhyme according to the conventions of Kalmyk poetry.

The mismatch of vocabulary structure between languages can be illustrated from Rom. 13.7, in which the Greek has two words for two different kinds of tax, rendered in GNB as "personal and property taxes". Kalmyk has only one term to cover all kinds of tax. In the same verse, the Greek has two words, rendered as "respect and honour" in GNB. Again Kalmyk has a single term to express both concepts. Thus, the verse in Kalmyk is significantly shorter than it is in Greek or English, but nothing is missing (except the Greek alliteration, which is also lost in English versions). In translating 1 Cor. 7.34 into Yakut, there is only a single term available to cover the words rendered as "unmarried" and "virgin" in the New Revised Standard Version (henceforth NRSV), something like "without a man". A slightly different problem occurs in Kalmyk in 2 Thess. 1.9, in which RSV uses the phrase "eternal destruction". Kalmyk has no term for "destruction" that can be used to refer to people, only a word that means physical decomposition. So the phrase has to be rendered as "eternal death".

A common feature of non-Indo-European languages is an obligatory lexical distinction between older and younger brothers and sisters. Thus, in Yakut there are four separate terms for older brother, younger brother, older sister, and younger sister. So in 1 Thess. 5.1 when Paul addresses church members with the Greek vocative — rendered "brethren" in RSV, and "brothers and sisters" in GNB and NRSV — four words are required in Yakut to represent the same degree of comprehensiveness. This is not mindless political correctness imposed from without, but natural style in the receptor language. The vocative "brother" in Phlm. 7 becomes in Kalmyk "younger brother", as best fits what is known of the context of the letter.

Another area in which languages differ in their lexical structure is double negatives. In Rom. 1.13, Paul says literally, "I do not want you to be ignorant", and this can be retained in English, as in the King James Version, "I would not have you ignorant". However, it does not sound very natural, and more recent versions say, "I want you to know" (RSV) or "You must remember" (GNB). A similar adjustment is required in Yakut in order to avoid sounding unnatural. However, in 2 Tim. 1.6, the boot is on the other foot: the Greek word translated "rekindle" in RSV is expressed in Yakut as a double negative, "do not extinguish".

Sometimes there is a fixed order of words in a phrase, and to violate it would sound as strange as saying "chips and fish" in English. Thus, in Yakut in Eph. 6.2, the order has to be "mother and father" rather than the Greek "father and mother", and in 1 Thess. 2.9 and 3.20, the Greek "night and day" has to become "day and night" in both Yakut and Kalmyk. In 2 Tim. 2.20 in Kalmyk, "gold and silver" must become "silver and gold".

Cultural Problems

In this article, "cultural" is used in a very broad sense, to include the ecological as well as the social environment of the translation, and the worldview of the speech community. In terms of the ecology, Yakutiia is very different from the Mediterranean area where the New Testament writings took shape. The absence of agriculture, and particularly of fruit trees, means that the common biblical picture of "fruit" as representing the result of something is impossible. In some contexts, such as Rom. 1.13, it is expressed in plain language as "a good result". In Eph. 5.9, "the fruit of the light" (NRSV) becomes "light encourages goodness to grow", which is still pictorial language, but less specific. In Gal. 5.22, "the fruit of the Spirit" is rendered with a parallel expression, "the harvest of the Spirit". The concept of harvest is known even in a non-agricultural society, but the impact of the picture is probably not high.

A different kind of problem arises in 2 Cor. 5.4, in which the human body is spoken of rather disparagingly as "this tent". Since the Yakut attitude toward tents is positive and associated with warmer summer weather, the connotations arising from a literal translation would be misleading, so the phrase was rendered as "this poor temporary home".

In 2 Tim. 4.21, Paul asks Timothy to come to him "before winter", and the question arises as to when winter begins. In the Mediterranean world, this would be reckoned as late September or early October, around the time of the Day of Atonement (Acts 27.9), after which travel by sea was considered dangerous. In my experience of Yakutiia, the Yakut winter begins about the end of August, at least in terms of the temperature. If so, then "before winter" would have a different meaning. However, the translation consultant is not always right, and the hardy Yakuts assert that they reckon winter as beginning about the end of October, when the rivers freeze over! It is not clear what St. Paul would have thought about this, but at least the phrase "before winter" is not seriously misleading in terms of the time of year.

In many cultures, the most common member in a class of related items may be used to represent the whole class. Thus "bread" in the prayer "Give us this day our daily bread" stands for food of all kinds, and not just for literal bread. In both Yakut and Kalmyk cultures, the common alcoholic drink is vodka, and it has come to stand for all alcoholic drinks. This term fits appropriately in Kalmyk in Rom. 13.13, where the topic is drunkenness in general. However, in 1 Tim. 5.23, when Paul tells Timothy to "take a little wine for the sake of your stomach" (NRSV), the translation would naturally come out as "take a little vodka". Since such a command would be open to misinterpretation(!), the Yakut translation in this case is more specific, "take a little vodka made from grapes".

It sometimes happens that the social values of a culture will influence its members to understand biblical statements in a manner that is different from that of the original readers, but not erroneous or misleading. For instance, among the Kalmyk the traditional and culturally valued sports are wrestling and horse racing, so when Paul refers to an athlete in 1 Cor. 9.25 and 2 Tim. 2.5, that athlete will be understood to be a wrestler unless otherwise stated. Because the point of the reference is to emphasize the importance of training and self-discipline, it would distort Paul's focus to complicate the translation by describing in detail the particular sport he had in mind. In similar manner, when Paul writes in 2 Tim. 4.7, "I have finished the race" (NRSV), the Kalmyk reader would naturally think first of a horse race. This in no way skews the apostle's focus on the importance of finishing the course, and so does not need to be cancelled out.

When varying interpretations of a passage are possible, the cultural background may sometimes push translators toward one option rather than another. In the Greek of Gal. 5.12, Paul writes literally about his wish that false teachers who insist on circumcision would "cut themselves off".

This may mean simply "separate themselves" from the Galatian Christians. On the other hand, it may mean "castrate themselves", as GNB and NRSV understand it. The Kalmyk version chose the latter option, as they have a folk memory of the existence of eunuchs in the time of the Mongol khans. The Yakuts on the other hand preferred the first option, "separate themselves", because they have no tradition of the practice of castration.

Cultural factors may also have some influence on section headings, where these are included. At Eph. 4.17, both GNB and NRSV use a section heading referring to new life. Because the Kalmyk religious worldview is drawn from Tibetan Buddhism, the heading at this point had to be worded very carefully to avoid any impression that the reference is to reincarnation. In Yakut, it was decided to have a section heading before 1 Cor. 7.10, because divorce is a serious contemporary social problem, and it would be useful to indicate clearly in the translation where the Bible speaks about it.

Another example of a worldview clash occurred in Yakut at 2 Cor. 12.2, where Paul speaks of being "caught up to the third heaven" (RSV), a phrase which in terms of a Jewish worldview was "the highest heaven" (GNB). The Yakuts, however, traditionally think of nine heavens, so the third one would be perceived as not very far up the ladder. They therefore followed the GNB rendering of "the highest heaven" to avoid wrong connotations.

Figurative Language

Figurative language is much more common than people usually realize, and indeed some figures of speech are so common that they are no longer regarded as figurative. Naturally, pictorial language is drawn from the cultural experience of the speakers, which varies widely in different parts of the world, so translation problems inevitably arise.

The most common figures of speech are similes, with the form "x is like y" (for instance, "the day of the Lord will come like a thief in the night" in 1 Thess. 5.2 RSV), and metaphors, with the form "x is y" (for instance, "you are God's field" in 1 Cor. 3.9 RSV). In similes, it is at least explicit that a comparison is being made, and that the language used is not literal, so in general similes cause fewer translation problems. In metaphors, however, the presence of a comparison is covert, and the potential for cross-cultural misunderstanding is therefore increased. There are of course other types of figurative language, but the focus here will be primarily on metaphors.

In linguistic terms, there are several ways in which a metaphor in the source language may be handled in translation. The first, and ideal, situation is when the metaphor will be readily understood in the receptor language and will carry the same meaning as in the source language. If this happens, then the metaphor can be retained. The less culture-specific a metaphor is, the more likely it is to be understood correctly in a receptor language. Fire, for example, is known in all cultures, so the statement in Hebrews 12.29, "our God is a consuming fire", can often be translated literally with no loss of understanding.

It is, however, the less than ideal situations that are the most interesting. If metaphors are unfamiliar rather than incomprehensible in the receptor culture, a second approach is to modify them in such a way as to turn them into similes. This keeps the picture, but makes it explicit that it is a picture. Thus, in Hebrews 12.29, one might say, "our God is like a consuming fire".

A third approach, if a metaphor carries the wrong meaning or is considered to be unintelligible, offensive, or grotesque, is to substitute a picture that is familiar in the receptor language and carries the same meaning. In John 2.17, a literal translation of the Greek is "Zeal for your house will consume me" (NRSV), the word "consume" meaning "eat up". While not impossible, this is not a very natural metaphor in English. GNB in its rendering has exploited the double meaning of "consume" in English to change to a related figure and thus says, "My devotion to your house, O God, burns in me like a fire". In doing this, GNB has also changed the metaphor into a simile. A frequent metaphor in the Old Testament is the term, "cut off", in the sense of "destroy". This is unnatural in English, and is often rendered in modern versions by "wipe out", a different but much more natural metaphor.

If all else fails, it may be necessary to resort to a fourth course, dropping the metaphor completely and expressing its meaning in plain language. This course is sometimes unavoidable, but if used too often, will make a translation seem flat and lifeless (note the metaphors creeping in spontaneously!) in comparison with the original. So it is helpful if translators look out for places where they can redress the balance by introducing new metaphors in the translation where there are none in the Greek. If they do this, the new metaphor must be natural in the receptor language, and carry the right meaning, and must not introduce anything historically or culturally incompatible with the first-century Mediterranean world. Such new metaphors bring the translation to life in a culturally relevant way and are likely to have a high impact on the reader.

All of these approaches can be illustrated from the Kalmyk and Yakut translations. Yakut is able to keep the Greek metaphors in such places as 1 Cor. 15.6 (sleep standing for death), 1 Tim. 6.1 (slavery as a yoke), and 2 Tim. 4.17 (the lion's mouth, probably representing a death sentence). Both Kalmyk and Yakut translations retain the metaphor of quenching the Spirit in 1 Thess. 5.19. The Kalmyk expands it to say, "Do not extinguish the flame of the Holy Spirit".

Of greater interest are the places where changes have to be made. In Kalmyk, metaphors are adjusted in such places as Rom. 3.23, where "fall short" is rendered as "distance themselves from (the glory of God)", in Gal. 3.1, where "who has bewitched you?" (RSV) is expressed as "who has twisted your brains?" and in 1 Thess. 2.19, where the "crown of boasting" (RSV) becomes the "height of victory". The metaphors are both expanded and turned into similes in Eph. 3.17, so that "rooted and grounded in love" becomes "like a tree putting down deep roots and like a house built on a rock". In similar fashion in Phil. 3.2, the enigmatic characterisation of false teachers as "dogs" is explained as "those who behave like wild dogs".

In Yakut, "the depth of the riches and wisdom and knowledge of God" in Rom. 11.33 (RSV) becomes "the frontierless riches and wisdom of God". In 1 Cor. 13.8, the Greek says literally, "love never falls", a metaphor that is not reflected in major English versions. It comes out much more vividly in Yakut as "love never collapses", where the verb "collapse" is associated with whipped cream that subsides as the air escapes from it. In 1 Cor. 14.9, "speaking into the air" (RSV) is transmuted to "speaking into the wind", which surely carries the notion of futility in a more forceful way. In 2 Cor., other adjustments to metaphors are found at 3.14 and 4.8. In the former, "their minds were hardened" becomes "their intelligence was blinded", and in the latter the Yakut has "we are...not driven into a corner". This is arguably closer to the Greek figure of being forced into a narrow place than is the English rendering "we are...not crushed" found in RSV and GNB.

In Col. 4.6, a situation arises in which the retention of the Greek metaphor, "seasoned with salt" (RSV), is culturally possible, but would carry a strong overtone of rebuke that hardly fits with "Let your speech always be gracious" (RSV) in the earlier part of the verse. The Yakut translation therefore renders it with a different metaphor drawn from horse riding, "having bridles and reins". This conveys the idea of discipline and self-control that fits the context better.

The Greek metaphor in 1 Thess. 2.17 is literally one of being orphaned, and English versions offer a variety of ways of handling it. NRSV retains it but adds an explanation of the meaning with "we were made orphans by being separated from you". RSV uses a modified form of the metaphor that sounds somewhat archaic, "we were bereft of you". GNB drops the metaphor altogether and translates the text in plain language as "we were separated from you". The Yakut substitutes a different but very effective metaphor with "we were robbed of you". In 2 Tim. 2.17, there is an example of a modified simile: "godless chatter" (RSV) is described in Greek as "like gangrene" but in Yakut as "like cancer".

There are a number of places where Kalmyk and Yakut have no alternative but to drop a metaphor and express its meaning in plain language.

In Rom. 6.23, the Kalmyk has "the result of sin is death" rather than "the wages of sin". In this case it is because the word for "wages" is a Russian loan word, and the aim was to keep such words to a minimum. In Rom. 10.15, quoting Isaiah 52.7 and Nahum 1.15, "How beautiful are the feet of those who preach good news", there is a figure called a synecdoche, in which "feet" stand for the whole person in the act of walking. This figure remains natural in some modern languages, but not in Kalmyk, which follows the example of GNB in saying something like "How wonderful is the coming of messengers who bring good news". In Phil. 2.11, another synecdoche, "every tongue", is replaced in both Kalmyk and Yakut by its plain meaning, "every person". In Yakut in Col. 3.17, however, there is some compensation in the form of a new synecdoche: "whatever you do, in word or deed" (RSV) becomes "whatever you do with tongue or hand".

In 1 Cor. 12.13, NRSV keeps the Greek metaphor in saying, "we were all made to drink of one Spirit". This sounds so strange in Kalmyk that the metaphor is dropped in favour of saying "we all received". Likewise in Eph. 4.24, "clothe yourselves with the new self" is sufficiently unnatural that it is rendered simply, "become new people". In 1 Tim. 6.10, both Kalmyk and Yakut had problems with the mixed metaphor, "pierced their hearts with many pangs" (RSV). In Kalmyk the problem was the metaphorical use of birth pangs, and in Yakut, the metaphorical use of the verb "pierced". Thus, in Kalmyk the translation says, "they have caused themselves to suffer very severely", and in Yakut, "they have found many troubles".

The number of places where figures of speech are lost is significant, so it is appropriate to make up for this reduction in literary impact by the introduction of new figures wherever possible and appropriate. In Kalmyk, for instance, in Gal. 1.14, "so extremely zealous was I" (RSV) becomes "I ardently fulfilled". The spontaneous selection of new metaphors was something that the Yakut translators were particularly adept at. In Rom. 1.18, the plain statement, "men who ... suppress the truth", becomes "men who ... strangle the truth". In Rom. 15.4, "in order that we might have hope" (GNB) is expressed as "that we might scoop out hope". The same figure recurs in 2 Cor. 10.8, where "if I boast a little too much of our authority" (RSV) is rendered "if I scoop out too much about our authority". In 1 Cor. 15.17, "you are still in your sins" (RSV) is more vividly stated as "you are still under the burden of your sins". "Tamper with God's word" (RSV) in 2 Cor. 4.2 becomes "bend God's word". A few verses later "perplexed, but not driven to despair" (RSV) in 2 Cor. 4.8 is rephrased as "our hope is like a thread, but it does not break". In Eph. 5.11, "expose them [the unfruitful works of darkness]" becomes "unmask them". As a final example, "unkind" (RSV) in 2 Tim. 3.3 is rendered with a climatically appropriate metaphor, "icy hearted".

Idioms
A further translation category is that of idioms, expressions in which the meaning of the whole cannot be derived from the sum of the meanings of the parts. This is often illustrated by the English idiom "a pretty kettle of fish", which in its totality says nothing about fish, kettles, or prettiness. Occasionally a translation can be enlivened by the use of an idiom from the receptor language. This is the case in Kalmyk in Rom. 12.17, which reads in NRSV, "Do not repay anyone evil for evil, but take thought for what is noble in the sight of all". The Kalmyk says, "If someone throws a stone at you, throw fat at him". The fat of meat is regarded as a luxury, so to throw fat at someone is to show kindness to the person publicly.

Yakut offers other examples of idioms, as for instance in 1 Cor. 1.18, where "the message about the cross is a sheep's head [that is, foolishness] to those who are perishing". In 1 Cor. 4.12, "we grow weary from the work of our own hands" (NRSV) becomes "we work with red hands", that is to say, very hard. In 2 Cor. 8.20, "no one should blame us" (RSV) comes out as "no one should put their fingers in our eyes". In 2 Cor. 11.6, "I am unskilled in speaking" is conveyed by the idiom, "I cannot hold water in my hands". From the same chapter in v. 29, "indignant" is expressed as "falling into fire and water". In Phil. 2.16, "I did not run in vain" (RSV) becomes "I did not run on dew or on snow". In Tit. 1.7, the word "violent" comes out as "having the law in his fist".

Conclusion
Enough has been said to demonstrate that translating the Bible is very much more than transferring the words of one language into the words of another. Language and culture are intimately connected, and a culture is deeply influenced by the ecological environment and philosophical worldview of its members. The result is that far from being a mechanical task that could be taken over by a machine, the translation of the Bible requires a deep understanding of and empathy with both the source language and culture and the receptor language and culture. It will continue to demand the highest level of skill, creativity, discipline, and commitment on the part of its practitioners. Happily, such qualities are readily available.

Enlightening "A Poor, Oppressed, and Darkened Nation":
Some Early Activities of the BFBS in the Levant

Richard Clogg

Within a few years of its foundation in 1804, the British and Foreign Bible Society (BFBS) turned its attention to securing Bible translations that would be readily intelligible to the Greek populations of the Levant, populations that were, with the exception of those in the Ionian Islands, still under Ottoman rule. This paper considers some of the activities of the Bible Society in the region between the founding of the BFBS and the early 1820s, when the outbreak of the Greek War of Independence brought a temporary halt to the Society's work in the Greek Orthodox world. As early as 1808, the attention of the Society's Oriental Subcommittee was drawn to the need for a Greek version of the Scriptures that would be accessible to the Orthodox *plērōma*, or flock, for most of whom the Greek of the Septuagint and the Koine New Testament would have been in large measure unintelligible. The subcommittee's minutes of 8 February of that year record that the "Rev. Mr. Usko" had reported that the Scriptures were so scarce among the fifty to sixty thousand Greeks in Smyrna (İzmir) as to be almost non-existent. He went on to suggest that "Mr. Corai", whom he described as "an admirable scholar in the Modern as well as the Ancient Greek", and who was resident in Paris, be approached for advice as to "the best mode of furnishing the Modern Greeks with such a version of the Scriptures as would be likely to be accepted and understood by them".[1]

Johann Friedrich Usko, a Prussian, had been appointed by the town of Danzig to be the Lutheran pastor to the German community in Smyrna, and in 1789 he was additionally appointed chaplain to the British Levant Company's factory in the city. By his own account he was a prodigious linguist, having learnt "grammatically" German, Polish, Latin, Ancient and Modern Greek, Arabic, Hebrew, Syriac, Chaldaic, Turkish, Persian, English, Italian, French, Spanish, and Dutch. He was married to a Greek native of Smyrna, "whom", he wrote somewhat patronizingly, "I had

---

1. BFBS Minutes of the Oriental Subcommittee, 8 February 1808, p. 21 (BSA/C19).

educated myself".² It was presumably from his Greek relatives and acquaintances in Smyrna that he heard of the reputation of "Mr. Corai". This was Adamantios Korais, perhaps the foremost scholar in the Greek world during the decades before independence. Born in Smyrna in 1748, Korais lived in Paris from 1788 until his death in 1833. He was in the highest rank of European classical scholars, respected even by the great Cambridge don Richard Porson, who had nothing but contempt for most of his contemporaries.³ Although his livelihood came in the main from collating manuscripts, Korais's overriding passion was the emancipation of his compatriots from the tyranny of the Ottomans. Indeed, in his autobiography he wrote that the mere word Turk was enough to induce in him strange spasms.

Usko duly wrote to Korais, who replied in November 1808. As far as the New Testament went, Korais said that all that was required was to reprint the version published in London in 1703, with revisions and corrections.⁴ He suggested that the Society's translation of the Old Testament be made from the Hebrew rather than the Septuagint. In this connection he urged the Society to oversee the training of two young Greeks "in the Hebrew, & other Oriental languages which facilitate the understanding of the Hebrew". He said that he had recommended "students of humble circumstances, because young men of fortune, or even those above want, would not be very easily induced to go & study Hebrew among you". Rather than following up Korais's suggestion, however, the Society preferred to test the waters by reprinting in London in 1810 the diglot translation of the New Testament that had been printed in Halle in Saxony in 1710. This was a version apparently unknown to Korais. It had been and was to be criticized. With his letter of 19 November 1808, Korais's connection with the Bible Society ended.⁵

2. See the autobiography of Usko, *A Brief Narrative of the Travels and Literary Life of the Reverend John F. Usko, Chaplain to the Factory at Smyrna* (London, 1808), p. 30.

3. On Korais as a classical scholar, see, *inter alia*, my article, "The Correspondence of Adhamantios Korais with Thomas Burgess, 1789–1792", *Anzeiger der phil.-hist. Klasse der Österreichischen Akademie der Wissenschaften*, 106 Jahrgang (1969), pp. 40-72.

4. It was this edition that had been burned in the courtyard of the Ecumenical Patriarchate. See Alexander Helladius, *Status praesens Ecclesiae Graecae* (Altdorf/ Nürnberg, 1714), pp. 238, 247.

5. Korais's brief connection with the Society is recorded in my article, "The Correspondence of Adhamantios Korais with the British and Foreign Bible Society (1808)", *Greek Orthodox Theological Review*, vol. 14 (1969), pp. 65-84. Korais's letter (Paris, 19 November 1808) is translated from the French and transcribed in the Minute book of the BFBS Oriental Subcommittee, numbered from the back, pp. *114-*120 (asterisks in the original), and is republished in "The Correspondence of Adhamantios Korais", pp. 74-76. More generally, on the question of the translation of the Holy Scriptures into modern Greek during the nineteenth century, see the thorough study by Geōrgios

The Society's activities in the Levant increased significantly with the improved communications that followed upon the ending of the Napoleonic wars. After the example of the Russian Bible Society, which was the first one established in the Orthodox world (in 1812), a Bible society was founded in 1817 in Malta, subsequently to emerge as a principal centre of Protestant missionary endeavour in the Mediterranean region. This was followed by the foundation of the Ionian Bible Society in Corfu in 1819, with auxiliary societies being established in Cephalonia and Zante, the Ionian Islands at the time being a British protectorate. In the same year, a Bible society was established in Athens. The previous year, 1818, a Bible society had also been founded in Smyrna (İzmir) on the initiative of the Reverend Charles Williamson, chaplain to the Levant Company's factory in that city, and a committed supporter of the work of the Bible Society.

Willliamson was able to enlist the support of a number of prominent members of the city's Greek community, including the Orthodox metropolitan, for the newly established society. British merchants and foreign traders also offered support, and representatives of such well-known Levantine families as Hochepied, Vanlennep, La Fontaine, Missir, Barker, Whittal, and Wilkinson subscribed to the Society. In the *Fourteenth Report of the British and Foreign Bible Society* (1818), it was recorded that 20 Hebrew Old Testaments, 100 Hebrew New Testaments, and 300 Italian Testaments, together with "other Scriptures in various languages", had been despatched to Williamson, presumably for the newly established Bible society.[6] The Smyrna Bible Society proved, however, to be short-lived, for Williamson died in late 1820, and a few months later the city was caught up in the turmoil of the outbreak of the Greek War of Independence.[7] The year before his death, during the course of a visit to Ayvalık (Kydonies), a small coastal town near Pergamum and the seat of perhaps the most advanced academic institution in the Greek world at the time, Williamson had hoped to establish a branch of the Bible society in the flourishing commercial centre there. He reported that the masters

---

Metallinos, which makes extensive use of the archives of the British and Foreign Bible Society, the Church Missionary Society and the London Missionary Society, *To zētēma tēs metaphraseōs tēs Agias Graphēs eis tēn neoellēnikēn kata ton 19 aiōna (epi tē vasei tōn arkheiōn tēs B.F.B.S., C.M.S., L.M.S., tou K. Typaldou-Iakovatou kai tou Th. Pharmakidou)* (Athens, 1977). See also Nomikos Michael Vaporis, "The Controversy on the Translation of the Scriptures into Modern Greek and its Effects, 1818–1843," unpublished Ph.D. dissertation, Columbia University, 1970; and his *Translating the Scriptures into Modern Greek* (Brookline, Mass. 1994).

    6.   *Fourteenth Report of the BFBS* (London, 1818), p. 295.

    7.   See my "Foundation of the Smyrna Bible Society (1818)", *Mikrasiatika Chronika*, vol. 14 (1970), pp. 31-49.

at the Ellēnomouseion, or College, were "extremely pleased" to learn of the existence of the British and Foreign Bible Society and had expressed

> ... an ardent wish for a similar institution in their own country. Had it not been for the mutual jealousies and mistrust of each [other], one of the greatest misfortunes of the Greeks, I am persuaded I should [have] succeeded in establishing a Bible Society in Kydonia; unhappily I [could] find none having courage enough to take the lead.[8]

Sir Adolphus Slade, who for seventeen years served as an admiral in the Ottoman fleet, took a somewhat cynical view of the Society's activities in the Levant, especially in Smyrna. If those who supported the Society's activities but knew of the local reaction then, he maintained, they would prefer to give money to their poor compatriots:

> God knows it would be a more praiseworthy action. But then the patronage of appointing missionaries, Bible distributors etc. would cease... Bibles are given to the Turks, printed very rationally in the Turkish character – (one hundred and ninety-nine of two hundred cannot read). A Turk...either keeps it as a curiosity, or tears it as waste paper... The Hebrews...carefully destroy the New Testaments and place the Old Testaments in their synagogues, sneering at the donors. The Albanian klepthes make wadding for their guns of the leaves of the Society's Bibles, if they have no other... Vast numbers of Bibles are annually distributed, or sold cheap, to the Greeks: these tell their priests, and their priests, as in duty bound, relieve them of the charge of keeping such forbidden books... If I do not mistake, it was said in one of the Bible Society reports, "that the Smyrniote Greeks were to be seen sitting at their shop-boards diligently reading the Bibles distributed by the Society, every moment they could spare from their work"... I cannot help remarking on so astounding a misrepresentation, made for an interested motive. I have often been at Smyrna, a great deal in the bazaars, and among the Greeks; but I have never seen one of them read a Bible... When a Greek has done his work he goes to dance, and to sing, and to drink; attending mass satisfies his conscience.[9]

In 1818, Williamson visited Constantinople on behalf of the Bible Society, with a view toward securing a new Modern Greek version of the Bible to replace the Society's much-criticized 1810 edition. In 1814, the Reverend Henry Lindsay, chaplain to the British Embassy to the Ottoman Porte, had secured the written approbation of Ecumenical Patriarch Kyrillos VI of the Bible Society's 1810 diglot version, although the patriarch had declined to sanction the publication of the Modern Greek translation without the

---

8. See Richard Clogg, "Two accounts of the Academy of Ayvalık (Kydonies) in 1818–1819", *Revue des Etudes sud-est européennes*, vol. 10 (1972), p. 659.

9. Adolphus Slade, *Records of Travels in Turkey, Greece, etc., and of a cruise in the Black Sea, with the Capitan Pasha, in the years 1829, 1830, and 1831* (London: Saunders and Otley, 1833), vol. 2, pp. 462-63, 476-77.

original. The text of Kyrillos VI's *imprimatur* gave permission to use, read, and sell the edition, published *"ellēnisti kai romaisti"* (in New Testament Greek and "Romaic", i.e., Modern Greek), to all pious Orthodox Christian *omogeneis*.[10]

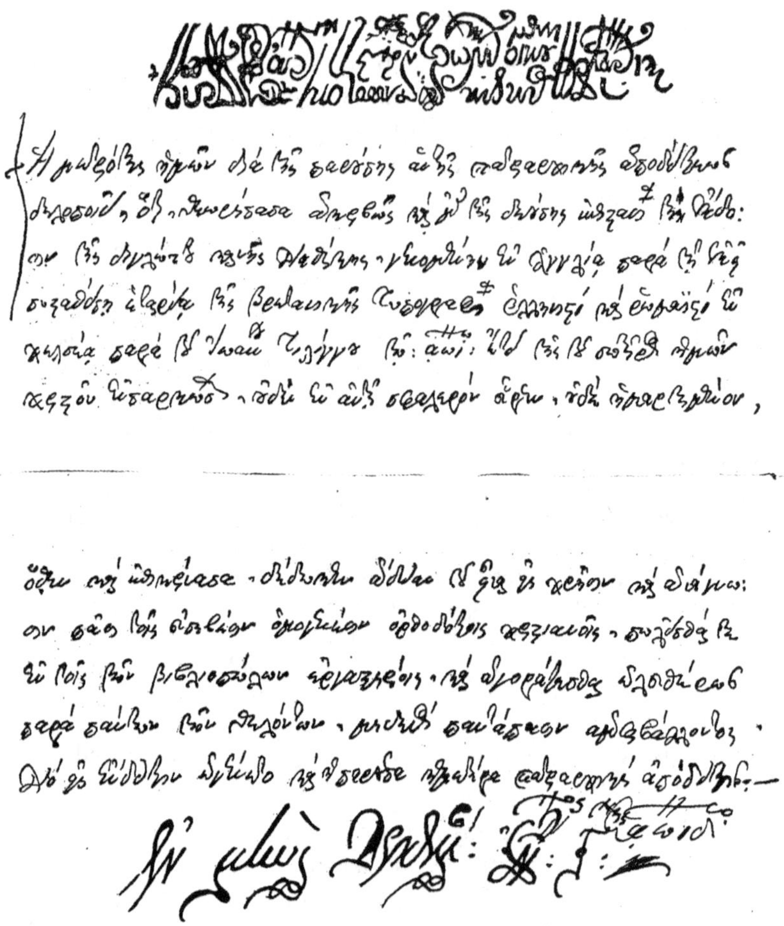

Picture 26.

10. For the text of Kyrillos' *imprimatur*, together with the lithographic reproduction, see the *Eleventh Report of the British and Foreign Bible Society* (1815), p. 164 (shown here). This is also published in Metallinos, *To zētēma tēs metaphraseōs tēs Agias Graphēs*, parartēma engraphōn, pp. 3-4.

164   ELEVENTH REPORT.   [1815.

(Translation.)
CYRIL, ARCHBISHOP OF CONSTANTINOPLE, NEW ROME, AND ŒCUMENICAL PATRIARCH.

Our Lowliness notifies by this present Patriarchal Declaration, that having examined accurately, and with the necessary attention, the Edition of the New Testament in two languages, Hellenic and Romaic, published in England by the Society there established, of British Typography, by John Tilling, at Chelsea, in the year one thousand eight hundred and ten of the incarnation of Christ our Saviour, we have found in it nothing false, or erroneous; wherefore we have judged right to give permission for it to be used, and read by all pious, united, and orthodox Christians; to be sold in the Booksellers' shops; and to be bought freely by all who wish it, without any one making the least hesitation: for the manifestation of which, this our present Patriarchal Declaration has been issued,

In the thirteenth day of the month of December, 1814.

Pictures 26 and 27. *Imprimatur of Patriarch Kyrillos VI for the BFBS New Testament in Modern and Ancient Greek, with English translation.* Reprinted from the *Eleventh Report of the BFBS* (London: BFBS, 1815)

It was suggested that this patriarchal *imprimatur* be recorded in the Society's Modern Greek Testaments, but this was not done, presumably because it infringed the Society's cardinal rule that its translations be published "without note or comment". Nonetheless, Benjamin Barker, who in April/May 1823 embarked on an extended tour of Thrace in order to survey at first hand the possibilities of Bible distribution by the BFBS, believed that the best way to provide villages in the region with Bibles would be "thro' the channel or with letters of recommendation from the Patriarch of Const[antino]ple".[11]

In 1811, soon after the 1810 edition had been printed, "two Greek gentlemen... Messrs. Johannes and Plato," the latter probably being Platon Petridis, a Constantinopolitan Greek sent to study in England by Lord Elgin, had voiced their criticisms in person to the Committee of the Society. Platon stated that in his opinion the 1810 edition reflected a dialect in use during the previous century and that it contained "many foreign words, particularly Turkish, which would be considered barbarous, and particularly in a religious book, it being in many instances a

11. For the Barker journal, see BFBS Foreign Correspondence Inwards 1824, p.14 (BSA/D1/2/12), published in Richard Clogg, "Benjamin Barker's journal of a tour in Thrace (1823)", *University of Birmingham Historical Journal*, vol. 12 (1972), p. 249.

literal translation, without attention to the idiom of the modern tongue."[12] Kōnstantinos Oikonomos o ex Oikonomōn, "a learned and well disposed Greek, a respectable priest, Principal of the College at Smyrna" (the Philologiko Gymnasio in Smyrna), was to characterise the 1810 version both as "imperfect and very inelegant" and the "performance of an Englishman or Foreigner".[13] "Mr. Plato" had urged the Society to take the publications of Korais as its linguistic model, they being "in the pure modern dialect, most approaching to the Ionic and Doric".[14] Usko was to argue, however, that Korais's language was "so exalted, so much approaching to the hellenistical idiom, at least in words, if not in phrases, and so difficult to readers who have not learned the Ancient Greek, that it cannot be supposed to be generally understood by all the Greeks." Korais's language, in Usko's view, was "fit for learned treatises and investigations, rather than for the common understanding of the Greek Nation in general, and better adapted for men versed in the ancient Greek, than for those who have no idea of it, as is the case of the greatest number of the Greeks who live in the Ottoman Empire".[15]

In an effort to remedy these deficiencies, Williamson secured the services of Archimandrite Ilarion of Mount Sinai to translate both the Old and New Testaments into Modern Greek. Ilarion, born on the island of Crete, was at this time *ēgoumenos*, or abbot, of the *metochion* of the monastery of St. Catharine on Mount Sinai in Balat, close to the Ecumenical Patriarchate. He was subsequently to become the metropolitan of Tyrnovo (1821–1827; 1830–1838).[16] In his dealings with Ilarion, Williamson was assisted by his friend, Dionysios Kalliarkhis, the metropolitan of Ephesus, whom he regarded as "the person of the greatest weight in the Synod of Constantinople".[17] Ilarion was described by another of the Bible Society's agents, the extraordinarily energetic Robert Pinkerton, as "the man whom

12. See BFBS Minutes of the Committee 7 October 1811, no. 5, p. 128 (BSA/B1/5). The full text of Platon's opinion is provided in BFBS Foreign Correspondence Books, no. 4, pp. 161-62 (BSA/D1/5/4). The text is published in Clogg, "The Correspondence of Adhamantios Korais", p. 70.

13. Kōnstantinos Oikonomos o ex Oikonomōn quoted in Clogg, "Foundation of the Smyrna Bible Society", p. 42.

14. See footnote 12 above.

15. Usko's letter is dated Orsett, Essex, 6 November 1818, BFBS Home Correspondence Inwards (BSA/D1/1/8). The letter has been published in Clogg, "Correspondence of Adhamantios Korais", pp. 80-81.

16. On Ilarion, see V. Sphyroeras, "Ilarion Sinaitēs o Kris (?1765–1838)", *Epistēmonikē Epetēris Philosophikēs Scholēs Panepistēmiou Athēnōn*, vol. 10 (1969/1970), pp. 225-310.

17. See the BFBS manuscript of T. Pell Platt, "[An Account of All the Translations Circulated by the Society]", 12 vols., compiled 1827–1829, vol. 7, "Modern Greek", pp. 15-20 (BSA/E3/8/1/7).

the general suffrage of the learned in Greece, at least all with whom I have spoken on the subject, consider as best qualified for translating the Holy Scriptures from the ancient into the modern Greek language".[18] Ilarion was likewise well regarded by Charles MacFarlane, who lived for some time in Constantinople in the late 1820s. MacFarlane described him as follows:

> ...perhaps the most learned and most indefatigable of the Greek hierarchy. From personal acquaintance, I should consider him entitled to occupy a distinguished place even among the literati of Europe, and as a man whose mind and energies, if afforded the opportunity of action, could not fail of producing the most beneficial effects on his long-degraded, but still talented and susceptible countrymen.[19]

Although Williamson, Pinkerton, and MacFarlane may have had a high regard for Ilarion, the abbot was something of a bugbear to progressive Greeks, one of whom, Stephanos Kanelos, accused him of seeking to set up a kind of index of prohibited books originating in Europe.[20] Korais, who had earlier expressed himself favourably about Ilarion, in 1820 described him as "blind".[21] It would appear, however, that these criticisms of Ilarion had more to do with his politics than with his aptitude as a translator.

Williamson contracted to pay Ilarion for his translation work 6,000 piastres, which he estimated to be the equivalent of about £220 to £240, a substantial sum in its day, and he urged the BFBS Committee to consider having some two thousand or more copies of Ilarion's translation printed at the press of the Ecumenical Patriarchate. He stressed

> the great recommendation of the patriarchal press, the only one at Constantinople, and the advantage of native Modern Greek printers and correctors! The Greeks also having very little idea of true religion, would find great fault, as they always do, however good the intention of the work, with errors in the orthography and accentuation, which must unavoidably happen in a

---

18. Pinkerton letter of 19 October 1819, recorded in T. Pell Platt's manuscript, "[An Account]", pp. 15-21 (BSA/E3/8/1/7).

19. Charles MacFarlane, *Constantinople in 1828. A Residence of sixteen months in the Turkish Capital and Provinces, with an account of the present State of the Naval and Military Power, and of the Resources of the Ottoman Empire* (London: Saunders and Otley, 1829), p. 400.

20. In publishing Kanelos's letter, Andronikos Dimitrakopoulos termed Ilarion half-educated, an egomaniac, and highly impertinent. See the letter in *Epanorthōseis sphalmatōn en tē Neoellēnikē Philologia K. Satha, meta kai tinōn prosthēkōn* (Trieste, 1872), p. 51.

21. D. Gkinēs, "Krētonos Stokhasmoi", in *Epitropē Anegerseōs Andriantos Adamantiou Koraē en Chio, Eranos eis Adamantion Koraēn*, (Athens, 1965), p. 145.

country totally ignorant of the language they print [i.e., Britain, where the Society's 1810 edition had been printed].[22]

Williamson also reported to the Committee that he had discussed his plans for a new Modern Greek translation with the "Patriarch's chief printer", Alexandros Argyrammos.

During his 1818 visit to Constantinople, Williamson negotiated with Ilarion on behalf of the Bible Society. Acting also for the Religious Tract Society, Williamson arranged for the printing of translations of a number of tracts of a markedly Protestant character, at a cost of £60, with the work again to be done at the press of the Ecumenical Patriarchate. These translations included the Reverend Legh Richmond's *Negro Servant* and Charles Leslie's *Short and Easie Method with the Deists,* as well as his *Happy Man, or The Life of William Kelly*. Only one of the tracts could be described as being of Orthodox provenance, namely, "Extracts from St. Chrysostom on the reading of the Old and New Testament". In a letter of 21 September 1818 to BFBS Foreign Secretary K. F. A. Steinkopf, Williamson explained that he had used the term Old and New Testament in the title of this tract in preference to the Holy Scriptures, for otherwise "the greater part of the Greeks through ignorance, and some thro' bigotry would have understood it to mean the writings of some of the numerous saints of their own making. They do not know the word Bible in the sense that we understand it". Williamson told Steinkopf that "those priests that are hostile to the protestant doctrines dare not open their mouths in disapprobation seeing the Tracts stamped with the Patriarchal authority", a reference to the double-headed eagle device of the press of the Ecumenical Patriarchate that appeared on the title-page of the tracts.[23]

The Chrysostom tract was reprinted on the island of Chios in 1820 at the behest of two American Congregational ministers, Pliny Fisk and Levi Parsons, who had been despatched by the American Board of Commissioners for Foreign Missions to work on behalf of the Western Asia Mission. A press had recently been established on Chios, an island that was one of the principal educational centres in the Greek world at the time,

---

22. Recorded in T. Pell Platt, "[An Account]", p. 18 (BSA/E3/8/1/7).

23. Williamson to Steinkopf, Smyrna, 21 September 1818, BFBS Foreign Correspondence Inwards, 1818, p. 54 (BSA/D1/2/5). While stationed in Smyrna, Williamson sent to Steinkopf on 1 May 1819 a graphic account of the martyrdom of Athanasios, an Orthodox neo-martyr. See Richard Clogg, "A Little-known Orthodox Neo-martyr, Athanasios of Smyrna", *Eastern Churches Review* 5 (1973), pp. 28-36. Nomikos Vaporis follows Williamson's account of Athanasios's martyrdom in his *Witnesses for Christ: Orthodox Christian Neomartyrs of the Ottoman Period, 1437–1860* (New York: Saunders and Otley, 2000), pp. 322-23. See, by the same author, "The Religious Encounter between Orthodox Christianity and Islam as Represented by the Neomartyrs and their Judges", *Journal of Modern Hellenism*, vols. 12-13 (1995–1996), pp. 257-325.

and the Chrysostom tract was one of the few productions of this press before it was destroyed on the outbreak of the Greek War of Independence. The tirage of three thousand copies was very considerable for that day. The efforts of the two Americans to establish a Bible society on Chios on the model of those already established at Corfu, Athens, and Smyrna, met with a somewhat equivocal response, however, from the Orthodox metropolitan. Fisk and Parsons, who had studied Greek with Neophytos Vamvas (the principal of the prestigious academy on the island and one of the two Greeks whom Korais had recommended to the Bible Society), were able to submit, in Greek, their proposal for the establishment of such a society. But on reading the proposal, the metropolitan would only reply "this is very good", before remarking on "the utility of Bible Societies in different parts of the world".[24] In the event, no Bible society was established on the island.

Williamson died in November 1820. Soon afterwards (in January 1821), Henry D. Leeves, recently appointed as the British and Foreign Bible Society's first full-time agent in the Levant, arrived in Constantinople. In addition to overseeing the Modern Greek translation already contracted for with Archimandrite Ilarion, Leeves was to be involved in promoting other versions. A Turkish translation (with the printing in Arabic, Armenian, and Greek characters), as well as Albanian, Bulgarian, Serbian, Kurdish, and Judaeo-Spanish or Ladino (Spanish printed in Hebrew characters) versions were all to be undertaken. Leeves arrived in the Ottoman capital at an inauspicious juncture, however, for the city was about to be caught up in the turmoil occasioned by the outbreak of the Greek War of Independence. So threatening did the situation become that, sometime between August 1821 and May 1822, Leeves had to move to Odessa, entrusting Ilarion's draft translation of the New Testament into Modern Greek to the safe-keeping of Lord Strangford, British ambassador to the Ottoman Porte. There was now no question of printing the Modern Greek New Testament at the press of the Ecumenical Patriarchate, as had been intended, for the Ecumenical Patriarch Gregorios V was hanged at the gate of the Patriarchate in reprisal for the Greek insurgency, and his printing press was broken up. When the chaplain to the British Embassy, the Reverend Robert Walsh, inspected the damage, he found sheets of the second volume of a massive lexicon of the Greek language, in press at the time of the attack, floating in a tank of water. This was the *Kivōtis tēs Ellēnikēs Glōssēs* or *Ark of the Greek Language*. Walsh recorded that "notwithstanding the dismal solemnity of all the circumstances", the Greek

---

24. Daniel O. Morton, *Memoir of Rev. Levi Parsons, first missionary to Palestine from the United States, containing sketches of his early life and education, his missionary labours in this country, in Asia Minor and Judea...* (Burlington, VT, 1830), pp. 288-89.

"who attended to show us the state of things could not help smiling at the idea of the Turks floating the Ark in the water".[25]

Once the situation in the Ottoman capital had calmed sufficiently for Leeves to return, efforts to revive the Ilarion translation were made. But Ilarion was not pleased when the manuscript of his version of the New Testament was eventually returned by the Bible Society in London with fifty-four pages of suggested amendments. In response, Ilarion apparently threatened to see that this revised text would be denied permission by the Holy Synod to circulate among the Orthodox faithful.[26] The main thrust of the criticism against Ilarion was that his manuscript was more of a paraphrase than a translation. T. Pell Platt of the BFBS expressed the Society's objections in the following terms: "the sense of each passage was indeed generally given, but the words of the original were not strictly followed...most frequently of all, additions of one or more words were observed, intended, apparently to render the sense plainer, but, as it appeared to me, not at all necessarily required".[27] Despite Ilarion's negative response, however, the Gospels were published by the Society in London in 1827 in their revised form as *Ta Tessara... Agia Evangelia, diglōtta...meta pasēs epimeleias neosti metaphrasthenta*.[28]

Also suspended as a result of the outbreak of the Greek War of Independence were the Society's efforts to publish in Constantinople a translation of the New Testament in Turkish, but printed in Greek characters, for the Turkish-speaking Orthodox Christians of the Ottoman Empire, who were particularly numerous in Asia Minor. These Orthodox Christians are known as the *karamanlides* in Greek and the *karamanlılar* in Turkish. Many of the Armenians of Asia Minor were likewise Turcophone, employing the Armenian alphabet to write Turkish. The need for Bible translation into Turkish written in Greek characters (*karamanlidika* in Greek[29] and *karamanlıca* in Turkish) for these Turcophone Christians had first been

---

25. Robert Walsh, *A Residence at Constantinople during a Period including the Commencement, Progress, and Termination of the Greek and Turkish Revolutions* (London, 1836), vol. 1, p. 324.

26. Vaporis, "The Controversy on the Translation of the Scriptures," p. 87.

27. Metallinos, *To zētēma tēs metaphraseōs tēs Agias Graphēs*, p. 173.

28. T. H. Darlow and H. F. Moule, comps., *Historical Catalogue of the Printed Editions of Holy Scripture in the Library of the British and Foreign Bible Society*, 2 vols. in 4 (London: BFBS, 1903–1911), no. 4970 (hereafter DM).

29. On literature in *karamanlidika*, see, *inter alia*, Janos Eckmann, "Die karamanische Literatur", in Jean Deny et al., *Philologiae Turcicae Fundamenta*, vol. 11 (Wiesbaden, 1964), pp. 819-35; Robert Anhegger, "Hurufumuz Yunanca: ein Beitrag zur Kenntnis der karamanisch-türkischen Literatur", *Anatolica*, vol. 7 (1979/1980), pp. 157-202; and "Nachträge zu Hurufumuz Yunanca: ein Beitrag zur Kenntnis der karamanisch-türkischen Literatur", *Anatolica*, vol. 10 (1983), pp. 149-64.

brought to the notice of the Bible Society by a correspondent in Mardin in Asia Minor. In a letter dated 20 February 1816, the correspondent wrote that among what he termed "the Angora Christians", the only language that was understood was "the Turkish, which they are unable to read in its proper character. Some Bibles in the Turkish language, but in Armenian or Greek letters, would be very acceptable there". A Greek priest had shown him what he said was the Testament printed in Turkish with Greek characters. It had been published in 1811 in Venice, as were so many books destined for a Greek readership during the years of the *Tourkokratia*, the period of Turkish rule. On inspection, however, this had turned out to be not a translation of the New Testament but "some lessons of Scripture with reflections and exhortations".[30] It was probably the *Aziz Apostolosların ameleri ve mektupleri* published in Venice in 1811.[31]

Soon afterwards the Society received much more detailed information on the need for Bible translations in *karamanlidika* from the indefatigable Robert Pinkerton. Pinkerton, who had been active in the foundation of the Russian Bible Society, wrote to the Committee on 8 June 1816, saying that few of the Greeks of Mariupol on the Sea of Azov and its hinterland knew Greek: they were "in a most lamentable state of ignorance; very few of them, comparatively, understand the Modern Greek. The Tartar, which they brought with them from the Crimea, is the only language which is generally spoken among them".[32] In fact, it appears that the Turkish-speaking Orthodox Greeks of Mariupol spoke a form of Ottoman Turkish rather than Tatar Turkish. Some three weeks later, on 26 June 1816, Pinkerton wrote to the Committee from Odessa with a full account of the need for Bible translations in *karamanlidika*. In travelling from Taganrog through the Crimea to Odessa he had "to the utmost of my power" sought to secure "authentic information respecting the state of the Holy Scriptures among the Christian inhabitants of Anatolia". With this object in view he had "sought out, and conversed with, intelligent men from almost every quarter of Asia Minor". His inquiries had demonstrated that much remained to be done "by Bible Societies for the poor, ignorant, and oppressed Christians of Lesser Asia, the majority of whom, in the present day, have almost entirely lost the knowledge of their native language, and speak and understand nothing but Turkish".[33]

30. *Thirteenth Report of the BFBS* (London, 1817), p. 23.
31. See Sévérien Salaville and Eugène Dalleggio, *Karamanlidika: Bibliographie analytique d'ouvrages en langue turque imprimés en caractères grecs*, vol. 1, *1584–1850* (Athens, 1958), pp. 148-51.This consisted of readings from the Acts and Epistles to be read each day in church (kilisede her gün okunur).
32. Robert Pinkerton, Kaffa (or Theodosia), 8 June 1816, in *Thirteenth Report of the BFBS* (London, 1817), p. 70.
33. Robert Pinkerton, Odessa, 26 June 1816, in *Thirteenth Report of the BFBS*, pp. 76-77.

Pinkerton had been assured by a number of "worthy" Greeks that "the cruel persecutions of their Mahomedan masters have been the cause of their present state of ignorance, even in regard to their native tongue". Pinkerton's interlocutors claimed that there had been a time "when their Turkish masters strictly prohibited the Greeks in Asia Minor even from speaking the Greek language among themselves". Those who disobeyed "this their barbarous command" had had their tongues cut out or had been punished with death. The cutting out of tongues was a commonly held, popular explanation for the abandonment of Greek in favour of Turkish, although there is no evidence that such a practice had ever occurred. "It is", Pinkerton wrote, "an indisputable fact, that the language of their oppressors has long since almost universally prevailed, and that in a great part of Anatolia even the public worship of the Greeks is now performed in the Turkish tongue". He appended a list of publications in *karamanlidika*, five of which he had been able to purchase. He concluded that, in his "humble opinion,"

> in order to effect more thoroughly the benevolent object of the Bible Society, among the Christians of Anatolia, we ought to print an edition of the Turkish Testament in the Greek, and another in the Armenian character, and strive to distribute these, with our Greek and Armenian Scriptures, among our poor Christian brethren in Asia Minor.[34]

From Odessa, Pinkerton proceeded to Vienna, where he inquired about the possibility of having the entire *karamanlidika* New Testament printed on behalf of the Society. He decided, however, that Venice, with its long tradition of publishing for the Greek world, would be a more appropriate place in which to issue the Society's proposed edition. He was told by Armenian Mekhitarist monks from the island of San Lazzaro degli Armeni that "the common people" among the Armenians and Greeks of Asia Minor understood "nothing but the common Turkish dialect spoken in Anatolia, and that all their business is transacted in that language, written with Greek or Armenian characters — that thereby their affairs are kept secret from the Turks whose Arabic alphabet not one in a thousand of the Greeks and Armenians knows how to read, or ever attempts to learn".[35]

Nothing came of Pinkerton's initial proposal that the *karamanlidika* New Testament be printed by the House of Glykys in Venice. Constantinople was now seen as the appropriate city in which to publish the proposed Turkish-language translation for the Greeks and Armenians of Asia Minor. In a letter of 12 October 1817 to the Reverend William Jowett of the Church Missionary Society, Pinkerton wrote that he had been in touch with the

---

34. Robert Pinkerton, Odessa, 26 June 1816, in *Thirteenth Report of the BFBS* (London, 1817), p. 76-77.
35. Letter from Vienna, 1 September 1816, in *Thirteenth Report of the BFBS*, pp. 98-99.

Armenian patriarch in Constantinople for advice in connection with the proposed Armeno-Turkish version.[36] It was planned that the *karamanlidika* and Armeno-Turkish editions be based on the Society's Arabic-character Turkish New Testament, then in the process of being printed in Paris. In Constantinople, Pinkerton had been assured by M. Ruffin, a leading French orientalist, that the proposed Arabic-character translation "was not in the pompous style of the Divan, a mixture of Arabic and Persian, but chaste and elegant, which would be read with pleasure by the man of letters and be understood by the lowest in Society".[37]

The Society's Arabic-character editions of the New Testament (1819) and the Old Testament (1827) were published in Paris. They were based on a largely unpublished translation compiled in the mid-seventeenth century by Albert Bobowski (Bobovius). Of Polish birth, Bobowski had been sold as a slave in Constantinople, given the name Ali Bey, and employed as dragoman to Sultan Mehmet IV. With the encouragement, and possibly also the assistance, of Levinus Warner, the resident of the States General of the Netherlands in Constantinople, Bobowski completed his translation of the Bible into Turkish. Warner sent the manuscript to the University of Leiden with the intention of its being published, but in fact, only chapters 1 through 4 of Genesis were printed (in Leipzig) in 1739.[38] Not until 1814 was the first effort made to publish the Bobowski translation in full. At that time, the British and Foreign Bible Society borrowed the manuscript from Leiden, after Pinkerton had examined it for suitability. Initially, the task of revising the manuscript for publication was entrusted to Baron Heinrich von Diez, a former Prussian ambassador to Constantinople. After the death of von Diez in 1817, the work was continued by John Daniel Kieffer, a Lutheran and the first secretary and interpreter of oriental languages to Louis XVIII of France.

Once satisfied as to its suitability, Pinkerton commissioned "Alexander Petropolis", whom he described as "the chief Turkish Secretary of the Patriarch", Gregorios V, to transcribe the text into Greek characters. Pinkerton reported that he had received the "unqualified approbation" of the patriarch for the proposed publication in *karamanlidika*. He also received the backing of the metropolitan of Caesarea, "next in dignity to the Patriarch", as well as the support of the archbishop of Sinai and the patriarch of Jerusalem. He was gratified that the Orthodox clergy "seemed to enter warmly into the cause of the universal dissemination of the

---

36. *Missionary Register for 1818*, p. 299.

37. Letter from Constantinople, 7 October 1819, *Sixteenth Report of the BFBS*, (London, 1820), p. 17.

38. N. W. Schroeder, *Quatuor prima capita Geneseos Turcice et Latine* (Leipzig, 1739).

Holy Scriptures" and believed that the proposed edition would be "most extensively useful not merely in Asia Minor, and different parts of Syria and Palestine, but also here in Constantinople, where the Turkish is so well understood by the lower classes of the Greek population".[39] He was certainly correct in this last assertion. Manouēl Gedeōn, *Megas Chartophylax* and *Chronographos* of the Ecumenical Patriarchate, the historian *par excellence* of *ē kath'imas Anatolē* (our Greek East), wrote that in the eighteenth century there were few among the Orthodox Christians of any part of the Ottoman capital who could understand the Holy Scriptures or ecclesiastical encyclicals written in Greek.[40]

Despite Ruffin's assurances to Pinkerton as to the accessibility of the Bobowski/Kieffer translation, the 1819 Paris edition had attracted criticism for being too literary and containing too many words of Arabic or Persian derivation. Its circulation was temporarily suspended while the opinion of leading European orientalists and those working on the *karamanlidika* edition, including Petropolis and Leeves, was canvassed. Ebenezer Henderson, who had strenuously criticised the 1819 edition, engaged in a vigorous polemic on the issue with Samuel Lee, professor of Arabic at Cambridge University.[41] Lee, in response to Henderson's strictures, invoked "a Turkish translation of the Psalms, made by Seraphim the Metropolitan of Angouri (Ankara), which was printed at Venice in Greek characters, in 1810, with a preface…addressed…to all the orthodox Christians in Anatolia",[42] a text that had been brought to his attention by G. C. Renouard, Arabic reader at Cambridge University and formerly chaplain to the Levant Company's factory in Smyrna. Lee argued that publications such as this, written or translated expressly for the *karamanlides*, should be used as a linguistic standard by the Bible Society in its own publications. If it could be "shewn that they [the Orthodox Christians in Anatolia] have adopted the same renderings with Ali Bey [Bobowski], that

---

39. Pinkerton letters of 25 and 27 October 1819, in *Sixteenth Report of the BFBS* (London, 1820), pp. 23, 25.

40. M. Gedeōn, "To kērygma tou Theiou Logou en tē Ekklēsia tōn katō chronōn", *Ekklēsiastikē Alētheia*, vol. 8, pt. 2 (1888), p. 200.

41. Henderson's criticisms were formulated in his work, *An Appeal to the Members of the British and Foreign Bible Society on the Subject of the Turkish New Testament Printed at Paris in 1819; Containing a View of its History, an Exposure of its Errors, and Palpable Proofs of the Necessity of its Suppression* (London: B. J. Holdsworth, 1824).

42. This is the *Psaltirion David Padişah ve Peygamberin tesbihatlarılan beraber… Yunanı lisanindan, Türk diline tercüme olundu*, translated by Serapheim of Antalya, published in Venice in 1810. Two copies of this work, one of them seemingly in its original binding, are in the BFBS Library (DM 9450).

circumstance may, perhaps, be considered as decisive..."[43] Henderson, however, was not persuaded and retorted that

> it was well he [Lee] inserted the doubtful particle "perhaps" in this place; for assuredly, whatever may be his individual opinion on the subject, such of our readers as are at all acquainted with the state of Christian knowledge among the Greeks of the present day, will be disposed to consider the practice of "Turkish Christians" as entitled to very little weight in deciding this, or any other question connected with Biblical science.[44]

It is clear that the Society's 1819 Paris edition of the Turkish New Testament was written in too "pure" a form of Turkish. Leeves accordingly engaged Theoctistus, a priest, schoolmaster, and later bishop of Aleppo, a man whom he found to have "the eye and look of a scholar" and who had been recommended to him by the metropolitan of Bursa, to prepare the text of the *karamanlidika* New Testament, based on the Bobowski/Kieffer version. In 1826, at De Castro's press in Galata in Constantinople, this version was published in three thousand copies as *Rabbi İsa el Mesihin Ahdı Cedidin yunanı lisanindan türk lisanina tercümesi*.[45] It was but the first of the numerous translations in Turkish with Greek characters that the BFBS published in the nineteenth and early twentieth centuries, making the Bible Society by far the largest publisher, in terms of the size of its editions, of works in *karamanlidika*.

This brief overview of the British and Foreign Bible Society's activities in the Levant, during the first twenty years of so of its existence, demonstrates that the Society was extraordinarily energetic in publishing and preparing translations in Modern Greek and *karamanlidika*, in arranging for their distribution, and in establishing local Bible societies among the numerous Greek- and Turkish-speaking Orthodox communities of the Ottoman Empire. Despite the difficulties occasioned by the Napoleonic wars and the outbreak of the Greek War of Independence in 1821, the Society's agents were able to lay the groundwork for the Society's later activities in the Orthodox world. Particularly manifest is the great care the Society took to ensure the accuracy of its translations of Holy Scripture into Modern Greek and Turkish with Greek characters. The extent to

---

43. S. Lee, *Remarks on Dr. Henderson's Appeal to the Bible Society on the Subject of the Turkish Version of the New Testament printed at Paris in 1819...* (Cambridge: J. Smith, 1824), p. 30.

44. E. Henderson, *The Turkish New Testament Incapable of Defence, and the True Principles of Biblical Translation Vindicated: In Answer to Professor Lee's "Remarks on Dr. Henderson's Appeal to the Bible Society..."* (London: C. and J. Rivington, 1825), pp. 80-81. Lee made a final rejoinder, entitled *Some Additional Remarks on Dr. Henderson's Appeal to the Bible Society...* (Cambridge: J. Smith, 1826).

45. DM 9455.

which the various editions of the Scriptures circulated by the Society among the Orthodox populations of the Ottoman Empire were actually read is not easy to assess, in part because of the difficulty of determining levels of literacy.

In the course of the visit to the Ellēnomouseion of Ayvalık in 1818 by William Jowett, agent of the Church Missionary Society and a committed Bible Society supporter, Gregorios Saraphis, the "principal master" and teacher of Greek and theology at the academy, referred to the Society's forthcoming Turkish New Testament:

> We know that there is a time foretold in prophecy, when the Wolf shall dwell with the Lamb, and the Leopard shall lie down with the Kid; when nation shall not rise up against nation, neither shall they learn war any more... We know that the Gospel is in its nature made to be universal. May we hope that the Turkish New Testament will have the effect of softening our present masters![46]

Any expectations, however, on the part of the Bible Society and its agents in the Levant that they might be able to work among the Muslim populations of the Ottoman Empire were doomed to failure.[47] The Society's activities in the Levant were to be strictly limited to work among the non-Muslim populations.

---

46. Quoted in Clogg, "Two accounts of the Academy of Ayvalık", p. 653.

47. Charles Williamson had experienced what he termed "the extraordinary fear" that the "highest Greeks" had of offending Muslim sentiment. When he had secured his coup of printing Charles Leslie's *Short and Easie Method with the Deists, Wherein the truth of the Christian religion is demonstrated...as...incompatible with the fabulous histories of the heathen deities, the delusions of Mahomet, or any other imposture whatsoever*, at the press of the Ecumenical Patriarchate, the head printer Alexandros Argyrammos, as Williamson reported, "would not upon any consideration insert the name of Mahomet as in the original, asserting that he would endanger his life, should he dare to print anything in derogation of Mahomet or his religion". The Ecumenical Patriarch himself, Gregorios V, had backed up Argyrammos on this point. See Clogg, "Two accounts of the Academy of Ayvalık", pp. 653, 662.

THE BIBLE SOCIETY'S SOUTH SLAVIC BIBLE IN THE BALKAN MAELSTROM

Peter Kuzmič

Until recently, the most widely distributed book of any kind in the South Slavic languages was the Serbian Bible translation of Vuk Karadžić (New Testament) and Đuro Daničić (Old Testament). Scholars consider this work historically influential because of its impact in popularizing and standardizing the linguistic reforms introduced by Vuk Karadžić and supported by Đuro Daničić. Vuk is generally considered to be the father of the modern Serbian literary language, and the role of his Bible translation into the Serbian vernacular has been compared to the impact of Martin Luther's translation on the German language. The journey toward the first complete Serbian Bible, however, was not an easy one. It was a half-century-long struggle, full of complex historical twists and painful setbacks, but ultimate victories. At the center of this struggle were the translators and their sponsor, the British and Foreign Bible Society (BFBS), whose work became an important vehicle for the cultural renewal of the South Slav peoples.

Kopitar's Comprehensive Vision

The story begins with the influential Slovene linguist Jernej Kopitar and his comprehensive vision for the cultural enlightenment of the South Slavs. As early as 1809, Kopitar, resident in the Austrian Empire, showed interest in the Serbian language and culture, and attempted to engage others in the movement for wider South Slavic intellectual and cultural renewal, a renewal stimulated by the European enlightenment. In Vienna, at the end of 1813, Kopitar encountered the recently arrived Vuk Stefanović Karadžić (1787-1864), described by a contemporary as "one who writes in wonderful Serbian."[1]

---

1. Kopitar as quoted in Jovan Skerlić, *Istorija nove srpske književnosti* (Beograd: Prosveta, 1967), pp. 243-44. Compare with *Slovenski biografski leksikon* (Ljubljana: Jugoslovanska tiskarna, 1932), vol. 1, p. 511.

Picture 28. *Vuk Karadžić about 1816*. Reprinted with permission from Duncan Wilson, *The Life and Times of Vuk Stefanović Karadzić* (Oxford: Oxford University Press, 1970).

The twenty-six-year-old Vuk had just arrived in Vienna for the first time, as a refugee, following the failure of the First Serbian Uprising against Turkish domination. Kopitar provided fundamental philological education for the young autodidact and widened his general literary and cultural horizons. Although unusually gifted, Vuk had never dreamed of a vocation in literary studies. Yet through the encouragement and mentorship of Jernej Kopitar, Vuk emerged as a leading reformer of the literary language, an historian, and an ethnologist. Kopitar recognized Vuk's literary gifts and brought him into the world of European scholarship by gradually introducing him to the western cultural milieu of the times. He first assigned Vuk a role in the gathering of Serbian folk treasures that circulated by oral tradition. He also encouraged Vuk to work toward the formation of a Serbian literary language that would correspond more closely to the spoken language of the largely uneducated Serbian population. Kopitar enabled Vuk to see the possibilities and the justification for codifying the vernacular language and for laying the foundations of a new type of literary language based on a phonological orthography in which the written word precisely reflected the spoken word. This concept was popularized by the slogan "one letter for every sound." The consistent application of the phonological principle produced a reformed Cyrillic alphabet and orthography superior to the Old Church Slavonic (OCS) and the hybrid Slavo-Serbian. The new alphabet and orthography were standardized in the first grammar of the Serbian language (1814) and the first Serbian dictionary (1818). Literary reforms were further clarified during lengthy controversies that arose over the new standards for the Serbian language. The twentieth-century Serbian literary historian Jovan Deretić summarized the immensity of Vuk's undertakings: "During his fifty years of tireless activity, he accomplished as much as an entire academy of sciences."[2]

These literary reforms took place during the time when a new Serbian culture and literature were also developing. The earlier and persistent attempts to impose Old Church Slavonic as the literary language of the Serbian people had not been successful, for OCS could neither be read nor understood by the majority of the Serbian-speaking people. Zaharija Orfelin's 1768 effort to modernize OCS by incorporating Russian elements did not make the language any more intelligible, but rather resulted in chaos. Dositej Obradović (1742-1811), the central figure in Serbian culture and literature in the eighteenth century and a man influenced by the

---

2. Jovan Deretić, "Literature in the Eighteenth and Nineteenth Centuries," in *The History of Serbian Culture*, ed. Pavle Ivić and tr. Randall A. Mayor (Edgware: Forthill Publishers, 1995), p. 3, located at the following website: http://www.serbianunity.net/culture/history/Hist_Serb_Culture/chl/Old_Literature.html.

ideas of the European Enlightenment, proposed a reformation of the literary language by introducing the "despised" vernacular. Though the idea was supported by some of his followers, the struggle for the affirmation of the vernacular as the literary language was a long and painful one, eventually won by its most persistent and systematic leader, Vuk Karadžić.

Cultural activity among the Serbian people, paralleled by their movement for political liberation, was immensely accelerated in the first decades of the nineteenth century. Schools were established and foundations laid for cultural and scientific advancement. A greater openness to European influences was felt throughout South Slav regions under Austrian rule. As the pressure for some kind of Russian-Serb church alliance decreased so did the suspicion of non-Orthodox cultures and progressive western European ideas and influences, thus facilitating the introduction of new literary genres. The spirit of liberation of the national ethos was enhanced by the two Serbian uprisings against Turkish domination (1804 and 1815) and by the gradual transformation of traditional patriarchal culture through links with Europe.

In March 1815, Kopitar began to encourage the talented but poor Vuk to think of one day taking on the task of translating the Bible, "for the English Bible Society and for good payment."[3] That September, Kopitar wrote to the "dean" of philological studies in Europe and proponent of Bible translation into numerous languages, the influential Baron Silvestre de Sacy, asking him to intercede on his behalf with the British and Foreign Bible Society (BFBS), for whom he would propose Bible translations into the languages of southern Austria, especially the Serbian, Romanian, Bulgarian, and Albanian languages. Kopitar knew of de Sacy's influence on the leadership of the Bible Society and counted on his recommendation for the support of translations "for the peoples who are certainly just as deserving of the Bible as the wild tribes of America."[4] Kopitar's letter was significant not only for its pioneering influence on behalf of the first translation of the Bible into the Serbian language, but also because it was the first written commendation of Vuk's extraordinary giftedness. Kopitar

3. Ljubomir Stojanović, ed., *Vukova prepiska* (Beograd, 1907), vol. 1, p. 490.

4. de Sacy to Steinkopf, Paris, 10 September 1815, with an extract of a letter from Kopitar, Vienna 10 August 1815, BFBS Home Correspondence Inwards (BSA/D1/1/16). This and other correspondence I have located in the rich archives of BFBS during the research for my book *Vuk-Daničićevo Sveto Pismo i biblijska društva na južnoslavenskom tlu u XIX stoljeću* (Zagreb: Kršćanska Sadašnjost, 1983). I have published most of the important correspondence, relevant excerpts from the minutes of BFBS committees, and other documents related to Bible translation in the appendix. Some of these documents have been published earlier and others for the first time in my own study. For the sake of easier accessibility, in addition to the original source, I also provide reference to my own work (Kuzmič, *Vuk-Daničićevo Sveto Pismo*, p. 48).

praised him as "an excellent young man," who has collected Serbian folk songs, written the first Serbian grammar, and who will produce a Serbian dictionary and "as far as the purity of the Serbian language goes, produce a translation without a match or comparison among other peoples."[5] From the same letter, it is evident that Kopitar had already met the BFBS secretary for Europe, K. F. A. Steinkopf, and that he understood the important role the Bible Society could play. Kopitar saw the translation of the Bible as a significant part of his overall vision for the cultural renaissance of South Slav peoples and as a vehicle for the promotion of Vuk's far-reaching language reform.

S. de Sacy wrote to London several times, both to Steinkopf and to BFBS Secretary John Owen, urging them to pay serious attention to the proposal of Kopitar, "a man worthy of all confidence." In London, the decision was made to send Kopitar's proposal to St. Petersburg, where the BFBS had helped establish the Russian Bible Society (RBS) at the end of 1812. A representative of the BFBS in St. Petersburg, Robert Pinkerton, prepared a reply on behalf of the Russian Bible Society—a reply that displayed considerable knowledge of the evolution and difficulties of the Serbian language:

> A translation of the Scriptures into…modern Servian is a desirable object …but the difficulties attending the reform of this kind are so great that… nothing has yet been attempted…you need to know how these [difficulties].are to be removed, and whether the abilities of the young Servian are commensurate to such an undertaking. Such a work, in my opinion, should be carried on in Servia itself, with the assistance of the most learned of the Bishops, in order that it may be properly done, and permission granted to circulate it.[6]

Pinkerton further anticipated the need for his own travel to Serbia and wondered whether the potential translator "intends translating from the original languages (for the Slavonian Old Testament is translated from the Septuagint)" and "whether he translates for the Servians belonging to the Catholic Church (who I understand are pretty numerous, and who use only the Latin Scriptures), or for the members of the Greek Church."[7] Pinkerton was obviously under the influence of the Russian opinion that the Croatian Catholics were actually ethnic Serbs of a different faith, which was also the controversial opinion held by Vuk Karadžić.

These initial contacts and the sharing of basic information led to an intensive and substantial exchange between Kopitar and the leading

---

5. de Sacy to Steinkopf, 10 August 1815 (BSA/D1/1/16). Kuzmič, *Vuk-Daničićevo Sveto Pismo*, pp. 254-55.

6. Robert Pinkerton, St Petersburg, 24 October 1815, in *Twelfth Report of the BFBS* (London 1816), pp. 79-80. Kuzmič, *Vuk-Daničićevo Sveto Pismo*, pp. 255-56.

7. *Twelfth Report of the BFBS*, pp. 79-80.

representatives of the BFBS. Kopitar had extensive conversations with Steinkopf in Vienna, and on 26 November 1815, he submitted to Steinkopf a comprehensive proposal, known as Kopitar's "Pro-memoria," for Bible translations into several South Slavic languages, as well as translations into the languages of other ethnic groups dwelling in the region. Kopitar saw himself, and was recognized by Steinkopf, as "in many respects so advantageously situated that he could best promote the following translations of the whole Bible or at least of the New Testament." These Kopitar programmatically listed under the heading, "in the living Slavonian dialects":

a) A Serbian version with Cyrillian types for the benefit of 4 millions of people professing the Greek religion
b) A Serbian with Latin Types for 1½ millions of Roman Catholics
c) A Croatian for about 800,000 Catholics
d) One or perhaps two for the Windes in Styria and Uppercarinthia. They read the Carniolan yet with difficulty
e) The inhabitants of Carniola are already provided by the excellent Clergy of that province
f) A Bulgarian in which language nothing exists in print with the exception of that which is mentioned by Mr. Martin Leake in his researches in Greece. This dialect is of peculiar importance with regard to the Slavonian dialect used for Ecclesiastical purposes. There are 800,000 people who use this dialect
g) A Rusniak for the people in the eastern parts of Austrian Galicia and in southern Russia.[8]

In addition to the above translations, Kopitar also proposed translations for the Wallachians and the Albanians. Obviously encouraged by Steinkopf, he requested that BFBS supply financial support "to enable him to proceed to these versions in the most effectual manner and the utmost possible expedition." An annual salary of between £200 and £300, he claimed, would enable him to devote all of his free time to this work and would cover the expenses of correspondence as well as "a suitable Room for Bible meetings and collation of procuring literary resources, and perhaps even a tour in the summer to inspect all these countries." Kopitar further assured the Society that he would personally work with the translators and that he "would know to render moderate" their honoraria.[9]

---

8. Kopitar, "Pro-memoria," Vienna, 26 November 1816, transcript in BFBS Foreign Correspondence Books, no. 4, pp. 108-110 (BSA/D1/6/4). Kuzmič, *Vuk-Daničićevo Sveto Pismo*, pp. 59-60, 256.
9. "Pro-memoria," (BSA/D1/6/4).

Kopitar's "Pro-memoria" displays the erudition, organizing capacity, and comprehensive vision of its author. He was by far the person best informed about the cultural situation among the South Slav peoples of his time, for he participated at the highest level of scientific discourse and comparative linguistics in the political decision making related to questions of the culture, language, and literature of the region. At the same time, his document provides evidence of the esteem the young Bible Society already enjoyed within the circles of cultural visionaries in the heart of the Austrian Empire.

Kopitar's proposals were taken seriously by the BFBS Committee in London, which recommended that Pinkerton follow up with his own research, as well as a personal meeting with Kopitar. The first meeting between Pinkerton and Kopitar took place in Vienna in the summer of 1816 and was prepared through the combined efforts of de Sacy, Steinkopf, and Owen. Pinkerton officially traveled to Vienna to meet with Metternich and negotiate the establishment of a Bible society in Austria.[10] During the same visit, Pinkerton and Kopitar had extensive conversations about translations into South Slavic languages, in general, and about the proposal to engage Vuk Karadžić to translate the New Testament into Serbian, in particular. Pinkerton provided additional information about the scope and importance of the work of the Bible Society at a time when its work was being vehemently opposed by Catholics in Austria and elsewhere in Central Europe. Encouraged by Pinkerton and concerned about safeguarding the freedom of Bible societies to do their work among the South Slavs and other Balkan peoples, Kopitar became a strategic ally and public apologist for the Society. In this context, it is important to mention his article "Über die Bibelgesellschaften" ("On Bible Societies"), published in the influential *Wiener allgemeine Literaturzeitung*. The article describes the founding and the work of the Bible societies and their importance not only for the Christian faith, but for the development of linguistic sciences and literature as well.[11]

The BFBS's Search through the Slavic Maze

Pinkerton learned a great deal from Kopitar about the ethnographics, the spiritual climate, and the state of the languages of the region. It is obvious that much of Kopitar's information was based on the extensive knowledge brought to Vienna by Vuk Karadžić. On 28 September 1816, Pinkerton

---

10. Robert Pinkerton, Vienna, 1 September 1816, in *Thirteenth Report of the BFBS* (London, 1817), p. 94. Kuzmič, *Vuk-Daničićevo Sveto Pismo*, p. 61.

11. Kopitar, "Über die Bibelgesellschaften," in "Intelligenzblatt," *Wiener allgemeine Literaturzeitung*, 1816, pp. 310-15.

sent a fascinating report from Vienna, full of significant data and observations. His studious survey deserves to be quoted here at length (without orthographic corrections or modernization of expression). After referring to the most "deplorable condition" among the Bulgarians, Pinkerton went on to provide a well-informed and contextually situated description of the condition of the Serbian people and language:

> Next to the Russians, Poles and Bohemians, the Servians are the most numerous tribe of Slavonian origin. They inhabit a large tract of country, south of the rivers Danube, Save and Culpa; and together with their colonies in Hungary and Slavonia, amount to nearly five millions of souls. To the Servian stock must be referred all the Slavonians who live in Istria, Dalmatia, Montenegro, Herzegowina, Bosnia, Turkish Croatia, and Servia Proper; because they all speak the Servian dialect of the Slavonian language. About two millions of this tribe are subjects to Austria, of whom one half are Catholics, and the other half belong to the Greek communion. The other three millions are still under the Turkish yoke, and of the Greek Church. The million of Servians, who are of the Roman Catholic confession, make use of the Latin characters only, and have, as yet, but a small part of the Holy Scriptures in their own language. The four millions belonging to the eastern church still continue to use the Slavonian character and churchbooks, and possess only the ancient Cyrilian version of the Bible, which is very rare among them. Among the Servians, under the dominion of the Turks, there are no public schools, or places of instruction, except in some of the monasteries where their clergy are educated. The small proportion of the people who understand to read, are either self-taught, or have been instructed by their neighbours: for many of them are said to teach one another to read: but among the Servians of both confessions, belonging to Austria, regular schools have been established by Government, for the common people, and also seminaries, in which young men are prepared for becoming teachers. The Cyrilian version of the Scriptures, which was made in the ninth century, and is still the only translation used among all the Slavonian tribes belonging to the eastern church, is not easy to be understood by the modern Servians; for, although the language which they now speak and write, is nearer the Biblical Slavonian than the modern Russian, yet the difference remains so great, that a translation into the modern Servian, for the use of about four millions of people, becomes a most desirable object.[12]

In this comprehensive and reliable written report to the BFBS Committee, Pinkerton progressed to an outright recommendation for both the Serbian translation and the potential translator. While the translator was described as an unknown "young Servian" in the earlier correspondence, he was now perceived as "a learned Servian," whom the authoritative

---

12. Robert Pinkerton, Vienna, 28 August 1816, in *Thirteenth Report of the BFBS* (London, 1817), pp. 89-93. Kuzmič, *Vuk-Daničićevo Sveto Pismo*, pp. 257-58.

Kopitar considered to be "very competent to the undertaking." Unfortunately, Pinkerton did not meet Vuk during this visit, since Vuk was away from Vienna working on his major project, the Serbian dictionary. Vuk was a guest of the archimandrite, later archbishop, Lukijan Mušicki (1777–1857), head of the monastery in Šišatovac. Mušicki at the time was a supporter of Vuk and had been approached by him about the translation of the New Testament. Along with other higher clergy of the Orthodox church, Mušicki later became an opponent of Vuk's translation on linguistic and religious grounds. Pinkerton writes:

> I observe, that, in the few literary productions which have, of late years, appeared among the Servians, they seem to strive at modifying their language, in many respects, after the modern Russian, whose civil character they have already adopted in printing; yet the difference between the modern Servian and the modern Russian is still such, that the modern Russian translation will never be thoroughly understood by the Servians. I have, therefore, conversed fully with Mr. Kopitar, of the Imperial Library, respecting the proposal which he made, last year, through Baron Silvestre de Sacy, to engage a learned Servian, named Wick Stephanovitch [Karadzic], to translate the Scriptures into the modern Servian: Mr. Kopitar considers him as very competent to the undertaking. He has already published the first Grammar of the modern Servian, and is now engaged in compiling a Dictionary of the same language, for which the excellence of his Grammar has already procured him a great number of subscribers among his countrymen. I am very sorry that I have not met with this Servian, here; as he is now living in a Monastery in the country, where he has the aid of a learned Archimandrite, in composing his Dictionary. Having duly considered the matter, I ventured to assure Mr. Kopitar, that, should a good translation of the New Testament be made into the modern Servian, by Mr. Wick Stephanovitch, and receive the approbation of some of the first Dignitaries of the Graeco-Servian Church, the Committee of the British and Foreign Bible Society would most willingly aid the printing of it.[13]

Pinkerton's report at this point becomes a survey of the somewhat more positive situation of the availability of the Scriptures in the Slovenian (Carniolan) language, in which both Protestant and Catholic translations already existed, and new ones were being undertaken. This is followed by a brief yet precise summary of the situation in Croatia:

> The Croatians speak another dialect of the Slavonian, which seems to be a medium between the Servian and the Carniolan, yet to have most affinity to the latter. The Croatian is considered to be one of the purest of the Slavonian dialects, because the tribe, by which it is spoken, is surrounded by Slavonians. The Croatians are reckoned at between 8 and 900,000, and are all of the Roman Catholic communion. They have no part of the Holy Scriptures in their language, except the Gospels for Sundays and Holy-days. However,

---

13. Pinkerton, in *Thirteenth Report of the BFBS*, pp. 89-93. Kuzmič, p. 258.

a certain Canonicus, in Agram, named Korolya, is said to be engaged in translating the New Testament into the Croatian.[14]

In a later paragraph, Pinkerton spells out his own vision of an alternate historical development, namely, a "Cyrillic alphabet for all Slavic nations," and shows that he understands the nuances of the differences and affinities of the languages in question. He also notes his appreciation of BFBS fieldwork for philological studies in Britain and his commitment to the universal mission of the Society. Here are his final fascinating observations and deliberations:

> While comparing the different dialects of the Slavonian language, and travelling among the nations and tribes where they are spoken, I have often regretted that the Cyrillian alphabet had not been universally adopted among them; for thereby, I am fully of opinion, these fifty millions of people would still have been able to understand the writings of each other. But the rupture between the eastern and western churches arrested the progress of the Slavonian character and Scriptures, and prevented their adoption by the Slavonian tribes of the west. This has also been a chief cause of the divisions and sub-divisions of this mighty nation: so that their common tongue, the strongest band by which nature could unite them together, has been confounded, and divided into different dialects. How unfit is the Roman alphabet to express the numerous complex, yet harmonious sounds of the Slavonian language! Hence we find, among the Slavonian tribes who use it, eight or ten systems of an imperfect and unnatural orthography, where one—that of Methodius and Cyril—would certainly have become universal. Even under the present distorted forms of a multitude of Slavonian words, when written with Latin characters, as in the Polish and Croatian, or with German, as among the Bohemians, Wends and Protestant Poles, I find myself capable of understanding tolerably well what is written in these dialects, by the knowledge I have of that Biblical Slavonian, and the modern Russian; yet I read with much more ease what is written in the Cyrillian character. This is a strong proof of the great affinity still existing among the nine dialects of the Slavonian language, which bear an affinity to each other, nearly in the following order: Russian, Servian, Croatian, Carniolan, Bohemian, Wendish, Second Wendish, Polish. The ninth dialect is the Bulgarian, which, being the most corrupt, I have not classed with the foregoing. But, as the Bulgarians still use the Slavonian characters and Bible; their dialect, ought, I think, to be placed in the first class, viz. Russian. Indeed so great is the affinity between some of the above mentioned dialects of the Slavonian, that I find a greater difference between dialects of the English, as spoken among the common people in different provinces of Great Britain, than between the Polish and the Bohemian, the Croatian and the Servian, the Carniolan and the Croatian. Excuse this philological deviation from my usual subject. The observations contained in it, may, perhaps, be of use to our British Linguists who have never had, and perhaps never

---

14. Pinkerton, in *Thirteenth Report of the BFBS*, pp. 89-93. Kuzmič, p. 259.

may have, the advantages and opportunities with which I have been favoured in studying this interesting subject; and, in a certain point of view, they are strictly connected with the object of the British and Foreign Bible Society, which is, to furnish every nation, and people, and tribe, with the word of God in a language, or dialect of a language, which they understand.[15]

Karadžić's Translation: Opposition and Impact

Of the many plans and proposals Jernej Kopitar made to the BFBS, the most problematic one, prolonged by lengthy struggles and delays, turned out to be the most successful. The credit for this achievement belongs not only to the vision and initiatives of Vuk Karadžić and to the dogged persistence of Vuk's disciple, Đuro Daničić, but also to the creative and pragmatic visionaries and administrators in the BFBS. They encouraged Vuk to undertake the translation and then employed their excellent diplomatic skills and unparalleled leadership to overcome what appeared to be unsurmountable political, ecclesiastical, and cultural obstacles on the way to the first Serbian Bible.

Following extensive communications between Kopitar, de Sacy, and Pinkerton, the BFBS and Kopitar convinced Vuk that he was the best-qualified person to translate the New Testament into the Serbian language. Though Vuk thought for a while that Mušicki, as a learned clergyman, should do the work, the two parted company, and Kopitar persuaded the impoverished Vuk to return to Vienna to do the work "against good payment."[16] Vuk decided to begin the translation as soon as he completed his major undertaking of the time, the publication of the Serbian dictionary, in November 1818. Vuk was now ready to undertake the long journey to St. Petersburg to sign a contract with the Russian Bible Society. Kopitar and Pinkerton again paved the way. The payment of £500 was agreed upon by the BFBS, and at the beginning of December 1818 Vuk was on his way to Russia. He was warmly welcomed by John Paterson, one of the founders of Russian Bible Society, and the formal contract was signed on 15 April 1819.[17] The work on the translation was soon begun with the help of Kopitar, because Vuk did not know Greek and relied mostly on the Old Church Slavonic translation as well as on Martin Luther's Bible.

Since the work of the Bible societies was forbidden in Austria, Vuk's translation could not be published there as agreed upon in the contract.

15. Pinkerton, in *Thirteenth Report of the BFBS*, pp. 89-93. Kuzmič, pp. 259-60.
16. Stojanović, *Vukova prepiska*, p. 490.
17. See "Vukov Novi zavjet i Rusko biblijsko društvo," in Kuzmič, *Vuk-Daničićevo Sveto Pismo*, pp. 67-81.

Also, the Russian Bible Society added new conditions, stipulating that the translation must be approved by the Serbian hierarchy before it could be printed. Because Vuk was not a priest and because his language reforms ran contrary to the traditional, conservative conceptions of the Serbian hierarchy, which insisted that Old Church Slavonic was the only proper language for religious expression, it was impossible for Vuk to receive such an approval. In fact, all of Vuk's literary work was vehemently opposed by the powerful head of the Serbian Orthodox Church, Metropolitan Stratimirović of Sremski Karlovci.

After lengthy and tedious negotiations, Vuk finally, though reluctantly, agreed to send the manuscript to St. Petersburg, where the Society tried to secure ecclesiastical approval of the translation. It asked for the approbation of two individuals: former metropolitan of Belgrade, Leontije, who was a Greek with limited knowledge of Serbian, and the writer and physicist, Athanasije Stojković, who was a Serb. Leontije and Stojković both disapproved of Vuk's language and rejected his translation. The Russian Bible Society then engaged Stojković himself as a new translator.[18] His dubious translation used a combination of Old Church Slavonic and Serbian orthography, a combination that was commonly used by the few Serbian writers working in the transitional era before Vuk's linguistic reforms were accepted. Stojković's translation was published in 1824, but it also failed to receive the needed church approbation. And, it was never distributed, because the Russian Bible Society's work was suddenly stopped by imperial decree in 1826.

Vuk was, of course, furious. He felt both betrayed by the Society and plagiarized by Stojković. In order to prove the priority he gave to Bible translation and to demonstrate the superiority of his work, he published a selection of New Testament passages under the title *Ogledi svetoga pisma na srpskom jeziku* (*Samples of the Holy Scriptures in the Serbian Language*) in 1824.[19] Thus began the long and complex history of Vuk's struggle to get his New Testament published. A number of his influential friends, including John Bowring, Leopold Ranke, Jacob Grimm and, of course, Jernej Kopitar, did their best to persuade the BFBS to publish Vuk's translation, but the BFBS instead published another two editions of Stojković's translation in 1830 and 1834. Vuk also made attempts to get his New Testament published with approval and support from the Serbian prince Miloš Obrenović and from the head of Montenegro's Orthodox church, the poet and prince Petar Petrović Njegoš, but without success. It was not until

---

18. For a detailed discussion of this translation and related controversies, see "Stojkovićev prijevod umjesto Vukova," in Kuzmič, *Vuk-Daničićevo Sveto Pismo*, pp. 82-92.

19. Published in Leipzig by Breitkopf and Hertl, 1824.

1847 that Vuk finally achieved sufficient fame and the material welfare accompanying it to enable him to publish a private edition of his embattled translation.[20] Its distribution in Serbia was forbidden, however, by the Belgrade Ministry of Education, under enormous pressure from the Orthodox hierarchy, conservative intellectuals, and Prince Miloš himself.

With the help of John Bowring and Pinkerton, who remembered the earlier promises made to Vuk, and with the literary recommendations of Jacob Grimm and Kopitar's successor, Professor Karol Kuzmany, the BFBS bought one thousand copies of Vuk's privately published translation in 1851 and secured the rights for future editions. A second edition was published by the BFBS in Berlin in 1857, followed by numerous other editions and reprints up to the present time.[21]

The First Serbian Bible and its Croatian Version

Vuk died in January 1864. The same year, a third Cyrillic edition of his New Testament translation was published along with the first edition in the Latin alphabet for the readers in Croatia. Vuk's most faithful disciple and friend, Đuro Daničić (1825-1882), who was working for the Bible Society at the time as the final editor of Vuk's Testament, oversaw these works as well the subsequent publications until 1871. It deserves to be noted that publication of the 1864 edition was urged by Alexander Thomson, agent of the BFBS for the lands under Turkish rule, after his visit to Bosnia and Hercegovina.[22] Thompson established a distribution center in Sarajevo in 1863 and asked London for a new publication of Vuk's New Testament to meet the great need for Serbian Bibles in Bosnia. It is symbolic that Vuk's Serbian New Testament officially entered his native Bosnia in the year of his death.

Of great significance for the history of the Serbian and Croatian Bible is Vuk Karadžić's programmatic letter sent on 10 September 1850 to Pinkerton. In it, along with a renewed offer of his New Testament, Vuk proposed to translate the Psalms as well, and he urged the Society to publish them along with the New Testament in both the Cyrillic and Latin

---

20. *Novi Zavjet Gospoda Nashega Isusa Hrista* (Vienna: Jermenski Monastery, 1847). For a complete listing of Serbian and Croatian Bible texts, in whole or in part, see T. H. Darlow and H. F. Moule, comps., *Historical Catalogue of the Printed Editions of Holy Scripture in the Library of the British and Foreign Bible Society*, 2 vols. in 4 (London, 1903–1911), hereafter DM. The entry for the 1847 New Testament is DM 8091.

21. Kuzmič, *Vuk-Daničićevo Sveto Pismo*, pp. 107-116. For the 1857 New Testament, see DM 8092.

22. BFBS Minutes of the Committee, 6 July 1863, vol. 52, pp. 135-36 (BSA/B1/52). Kuzmič, *Vuk-Daničićevo Sveto Pismo*, p. 115.

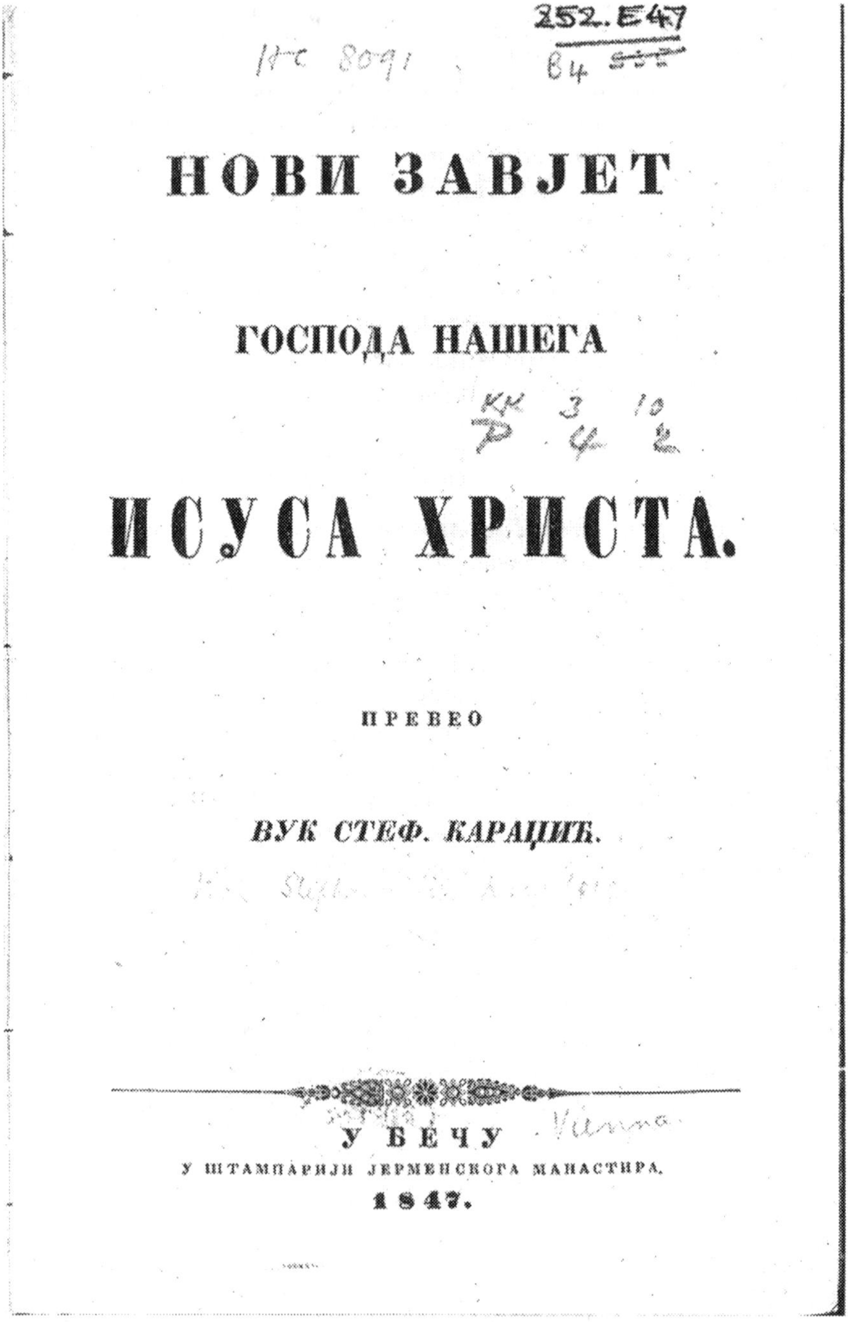

НОВИ ЗАВЈЕТ

ГОСПОДА НАШЕГА

ИСУСА ХРИСТА.

ПРЕВЕО

ВУК СТЕФ. КАРАЏИЋ.

У БЕЧУ
У ШТАМПАРИЈИ ЈЕРМЕНСКОГА МАНАСТИРА.
1847.

Picture 29. *Serbian New Testament (1847)*. Specimen courtesy of BFBS Library collection, Cambridge University Library

alphabets.²³ It is known from his correspondence with Grimm that for some time Vuk had thought of commencing the translation of the Old Testament. Since he did not know Hebrew, the Society rejected his first offers, and from 1851 to 1858 there was no further mention of translating the books of the Old Testament.

Edward Millard, who continued from Berlin to oversee Bible work in Serbia despite Austrian interventions that led to his temporary removal from the BFBS agency in Vienna, received in December 1858 an unexpected letter from Vuk, offering for publication a finished translation of the Psalms by Đuro Daničić. The editorial committee in London rejected the translation for the same reason it did not accept the offer Vuk had made seven years earlier, namely that the translation was not made from the original language. Such a decision surprised and angered Vuk, who accused the BFBS of unnecessary rigidity in the face of the excellence of the translation. Millard reports:

> Mr. Wuk thinks it would under these circumstances be not only unnecessary, but a sin to withhold so excellent a book as the Psalms from the Servian people until—God knows when—some one shall unite an accurate knowledge of Hebrew with the knowledge of Servian... Wuk hopes it may please God...for the publication of this work now declined by the Society.²⁴

Thus began another intensive struggle, this time for translation of the Old Testament into the Serbian language. The key role was played by the extraordinarily capable Edward Millard, who ultimately persuaded the Committee in London that there were no Serbian scholars with a reliable knowledge of both ancient Hebrew and the modern Serbian language, and that a more qualified translator than Đuro Daničić could not be found. The compromise stipulation of the Bible Society was that the translation be made from the literal Latin translation of the Scriptures by Tremelius and Junius. Thus, in 1864 Daničić's translation of the Psalms appeared in both Cyrillic and Latin scripts along with the third edition of Vuk's New Testament. In the next three years, Daničić translated the rest of the Old Testament, whose revision was provided by another successor of Kopitar, the Slovene scholar Franc Miklošič, and the whole project was carefully supervised by Edward Millard.²⁵ Four years after Vuk's death, in 1868, his

---

23. Vuk Karadžić to Pinkerton, Vienna, 10 August 1850, BFBS Foreign Correspondence Inwards, 1850, no. 2, p. 66 (BSA/D1/2/105).

24. Edward Millard to BFBS, Berlin, 15 September 1859, BFBS Editorial Correspondence Inwards, no. 1, pp. 171-72 (BSA/E3/1/4/1). Kuzmič, *Vuk-Daničićevo Sveto Pismo*, p. 272.

25. For a detailed and documented history of this process and gradual publications of translated parts before the whole appeared, see Kuzmič pp. 119-69. For the

translation of the New Testament was published together with Daničić's translation of the Old Testament as the first complete version of the Bible in the Serbian language. This was also the year of the final triumph in which Vuk's orthography was officially introduced and accepted in Serbia.

The appearance of the Vuk-Daničić translation of the Bible in the Latin alphabet did not go unnoticed in Croatia. At the opening of the national Academy of Arts and Sciences in Zagreb in 1867, its founder, the progressive and ecumenically minded Bishop Josip Juraj Strossmeyer, praised the Bible translation. The bishop, a supporter of Vuk and Daničić (who became at that time the first to serve as secretary of the academy), expressed the hope that a new Saint Jerome might arise among the people, dedicating his talents to "the precise and perfect translation into our language, such as other Slavic peoples are already priding themselves with."[26]

Ironically, from both an ecumenical and linguistic standpoint, the Vuk-Daničić Serbian Bible became the most widely distributed Croatian Bible for an entire century. Up to the time of Daničić's translation, the Bible societies had not, mainly under the influence of Vuk, sufficiently distinguished between the Serbian and Croatian languages. Their thinking was that the edition of the Vuk-Daničić Scriptures in the Latin alphabet would be sufficient for the Croats. By this time, the Croats already had two translations of the whole Bible (Katančić, 1831, and Škarić, 1858–1861). The appearance of the Vuk-Daničić Bible made especially evident, however, the need for a more contemporary Croatian translation. The limited space and scope of this article does not allow for an examination of parallel nineteenth-century developments in the evolution of the Serbian and Croatian modern languages and of the way in which Vuk influenced the standardization of the Croatian language.[27] The Vuk-Daničić Bible was at first received with enthusiasm by many Croats, including well-known clergy like Strossmayer and Franjo Iveković. Further development of the Croatian literary language and the differences in liturgical terminology and in proper names, however, demanded either a new translation or an adaptation that would make Vuk-Daničić acceptable to the Croats. Through the fieldwork and valiant efforts of Edward Millard, the Bible Society gradually came to the realization that the Croats had their own ethnic, religious, and linguistic

---

complete Bible, see *Sveto Pismo Staroga i Novoga Zavjeta* (Pešt/Beograd: BFBS, 1868). For the Serbian edition published in Beograd, see DM 8108; the Croatian edition published in Pešt is DM 8109.

26. Josip Juraj Strossmayer, "Besjeda preuzvišenoga gosp. pokrovitelja," *Rad* (Zagreb: Jugoslavenska akademija znanosti i umjetnosti, 1867), knj. 1, pp. 27-43.

27. For a history of these developments, see Zlatko Vince, *Putovima hrvatskoga knjizevnog jezika : lingvisticko-kulturnopovijesni prikaz filoloskih skola i njihovih izvora* (Zagreb: SNL, 1978).

identity. Thus, in accordance with BFBS editorial policy, Millard made great efforts to engage the best-qualified Croatian scholars for a Croatian revision of the Vuk-Daničić Bible. The first revision was prepared by the Zagreb linguist and writer Bogoslav Šulek.[28] A Slovak by birth and a Lutheran by confession, Šulek played a significant role in the evolution of the Croatian literary language. Šulek's revision of Vuk's New Testament and Daničić's Psalms was published in 1877 and reprinted many times. The second Croatian revision of the whole Serbian Bible took place in 1895, changing basically only the liturgical terms and proper names to make them agree with standard Croatian Catholic liturgical terminology. This was done by Milan Rešetar,[29] another outstanding Croatian linguist whose scientific work focused on the same concerns as did Kopitar's in the academic circle of Vienna at the beginning of the century.

The British and Foreign Bible Society, by assigning the task of Bible translation to the most able Serbian writers of the nineteenth century, Vuk Karadžić and Đuro Daničić, and by involving in the work such outstanding Slavic scholars as Jernej Kopitar, Franc Miklošič, Bogoslav Šulek, Milan Rešetar, and Vatroslav Jagić, and by making the Serbian Vuk-Daničić Bible and its "Croatianized" editions the most widely distributed book of any kind in the region, made a significant contribution to the religious and cultural progress of the South Slav peoples. The linguistic qualities of the translation are beyond dispute. It has contributed to the affirmation and popularization of Vuk's orthography and has also influenced, to some extent, the evolution of the Croatian literary language. It has become a kind of *textus receptus* that cannot be ignored by subsequent Serbian and Croatian translators.

There is general agreement among Slavic scholars that Vuk's language reforms were crowned by his excellent translation of the New Testament, and that Vuk's initiative led to the later accompanying edition of the Old Testament by his disciple and associate Đuro Daničić. Leading Slavic scholars consider this first Serbian Bible to be "the most beautiful monument of the Serbian literary language ever."[30] Its publication and wide distribution by the BFBS have played a groundbreaking role in the popular acceptance of the new standard Serbian language and, to a lesser extent, the Croatian language.

---

28. Edward Millard to BFBS, Prague, 21 June 1876, Editorial Correspondence Inwards, no. 12, pp. 147-48 (BSA/E3/1/4/12). Kuzmič, *Vuk-Daničićevo Sveto Pismo*, p. 286. For the Šulek 1877 revision of the New Testament and Psalms, see DM 8115.

29. Henry Millard to BFBS, Vienna, 6 February 1894, Editorial Correspondence Inwards, no. 31, pp. 275-77 (BSA/E3/1/4/31). Kuzmič, *Vuk-Daničićevo Sveto Pismo*, p. 287. For the Rešetar 1895 Croatian revision of the Bible, see DM 8120.

30. Deretić, *History of Serbian Culture*, p. 4.

ROBERT PINKERTON: PRINCIPAL AGENT OF THE BFBS IN THE KINGDOMS OF GERMANY

Wayne Detzler

According to Lord Teignmouth, who served as the first president of the British and Foreign Bible Society (BFBS), Robert Pinkerton (1780–1859) was the "most diligent of all the Society's agents."[1] Pinkerton's birth in Scotland in 1780 gave no hint of his future significance. His death in 1859 at Reigate in Surrey was almost as obscure as his birth.[2] Between those two dates Pinkerton compressed a life of valiant service for the cause of Scripture distribution. Nevertheless, his work has been largely ignored by the Germans and unknown to the British despite frequent mention of him in annual BFBS *Reports*. The significance of Robert Pinkerton was demonstrated recently when his book on Russia was offered at auction in London by the firm of Helen R. Kahn & Associates. Pinkerton wrote of his experience under the title *Russia: or, Miscellaneous Observations of the Past and Present State of that Country and its Inhabitants* and accompanied his work with valuable original illustrative prints from the region.[3] The auction house, early in 2004, offered Pinkerton's 1833 imprint at a starting price of £850. This paper seeks to build upon such interest in Pinkerton's work and observations, dividing his Bible Society career into four phases: The Russian Years; His Hopes for War-Torn Europe; Surviving the Apocrypha Crisis; and Pinkerton's New Path in Frankfurt.

---

1. Robert Steiner, "Robert Pinkerton," *Die Bibel in der Welt*, vol. 6 (1963), p. 151.
2. Wayne Detzler, "Robert Pinkerton," *Evangelisches Gemeindelexikon*, ed. Erich Geldbach, Helmut Burkhardt, and Kurt Heimbucher (Wuppertal: R. Brockhaus, 1978), p. 414. Much of this material is also drawn from the author's unpublished Ph.D. thesis, "British and American Contributions to the 'Erweckung' in Germany, 1815–1848" (University of Manchester, 1974).
3. Robert Pinkerton, *Russia: or, Miscellaneous Observations on the Past and Present State of that Country and Its Inhabitants, Compiled from Notes Made on the Spot, during Travels, at different Times…and a Residence of Many Years in that Country* (London: Seeley & Sons, 1833).

Picture 30. *Robert Pinkerton (1780–1859)*. Portrait courtesy of BFBS collection, Cambridge University Library

The Russian Years: From Frontier to the Front Rank of BFBS Agents

When he was twenty-five years old Robert Pinkerton left his native Scotland to settle near the Caucasus Mountains as a member of the Edinburgh Missionary Society. The objects of Scottish missionary interest were the Tatars who lived in and around Karass between the Caspian and Black Seas. The raw climate soon took its toll on the fragile health of the young Scot, however, and in 1809, Pinkerton left Karass for an appointment as private tutor to the family of Prince Meshcherskii in the relative comfort of Moscow.[4]

It was during Pinkerton's residence in Moscow that Karl Friedrich August Steinkopf contacted him on behalf of the British and Foreign Bible

---

4. Steiner, "Robert Pinkerton," p. 151.

Society. From 1795 to 1800, Steinkopf had been secretary of the evangelical Deutsche Christentumsgesellschaft (German Christian Association) based at Basel. In 1801, Steinkopf moved to London to take up the pastoral charge of the German Lutheran church in the Savoy. From this vantage point he became foreign secretary of the BFBS soon after its founding in 1804.[5] Later, in 1812, Steinkopf also founded the venerable Württembergische Bibelanstalt in Stuttgart.[6]

It was Steinkopf who encouraged Pinkerton to work toward the formation of a Bible society in Moscow, but these efforts were frustrated by Napoleon's invasion. Meanwhile, in Finland, another Scottish missionary, John Paterson, had helped to form a Bible society in 1811, and it gained the tsar's patronage. In 1812, Paterson went to St. Petersburg, partly to organize the printing of a Finnish Bible, and partly, at the encouragement of Steinkopf, to see what the possibilities were for a Bible society in Petersburg. Paterson and Pinkerton met in Moscow in early September, but had to leave hurriedly as the Napoleonic armies approached. Back in St. Petersburg, as the Napoleonic invasion of Russia raged on, Paterson set about seeking support among the aristocracy, notably gaining the patronage of Prince Alexander Golitsyn, a powerful Russian tsarist official friendly to evangelical causes. A plan for a Bible society was presented to Tsar Alexander I, and tsarist approval was granted in December 1812. Pinkerton hastened to St. Petersburg to join Paterson for the first formal meeting of the St. Petersburg Bible Society (later the Russian Bible Society) held in January 1813. The first auxiliary of the Petersburg committee was established in Moscow in July 1813 through the efforts of Pinkerton.[7]

The success of Pinkerton and Paterson did not escape the attention of BFBS headquarters, and a grant of £500 was dispatched by the Committee in London to its counterpart in St. Petersburg.[8] The propaganda value to

---

5. Adolf Risch, *Festschrift zur Jahrhundertfeier der Priviligierten Württembergischen Bibelanstalt* (Stuttgart: Priviligierten Württembergischen Bibelanstalt, 1912), p. 60. The Deutsche Christentumsgesellschaft sought to combat what it considered to be "rationalism" by the promotion of biblical doctrine and Christian ethics. It implemented this goal through auxiliary associations that sprang up throughout Germany and Switzerland. Johann Urlsperger, its founder, was inspired to found the Christentumsgesellschaft when he observed similar voluntary societies in England.

6. Paulus Scharpff, *Geschichte der Evangelisation* (Giessen: Brunnen-Verlag, 1964), p. 95. Charles I. Foster, *An Errand of Mercy: The Evangelical United Front, 1790–1837* (Chapel Hill: University of North Carolina Press, 1960), p. 102.

7. John Owen, *The History of the Origin and First Ten Years of the British and Foreign Bible Society*, 2 vols. (London: Tilling and Hughes, 1816), vol. 2, pp. 237-38; also George Browne, *A History of the British and Foreign Bible Society, From Its Institution in 1804, to the Close of Its Jubilee in 1854*, 2 vols. (London: BFBS, 1859), vol. 1, pp. 321-23.

8. Owen, *History*, vol. 2, p. 246.

the BFBS of such an exotic establishment as the Russian Bible Society was quickly realized, and Paterson and Pinkerton were invited back to England. There they addressed a captive audience at the tenth anniversary celebration of the BFBS in 1814.[9] In May of that year, BFBS supporters gathered from throughout England for the large anniversary meeting in London at the Freemasons' Hall. Financial contributors flocked to hear stirring stories of the Society's progress, and a flood of donations flowed into the Bible Society's coffers. Pinkerton's initial labors in the north of Europe had been crowned with success.

His Hopes for War-Torn Europe

Soon after the anniversary celebration Pinkerton and Paterson set off for the continent. Their ultimate destination was Russia. Whilst Paterson traveled through Scandinavia, his colleague Robert Pinkerton crossed through Holland, Germany, and Poland. As they traveled they left a string of local Bible societies newly formed in strategic centers, such as Amsterdam, Elberfeld, Hanover, Berlin, and Dresden.

Pinkerton started a Bible society in Amsterdam. It was there that he initially honed his method. First, influential men in the fields of politics, religion, and scholarship were won for the cause. Second, stimulated by a grant of funds from the BFBS offices in London, a local governing committee for the Bible society chapter was formed. Third, a well-defined area of activity was assigned to the committee.

A similar pattern of Bible society organization followed in Hanover. After the withdrawal of Napoleon's forces, Hanover had been proclaimed a kingdom at the Congress of Vienna, and was ruled in personal union with the crown of England. Adolphus Frederick (1774–1850), Duke of Cambridge and tenth child of King George III, served as viceroy of Hanover, 1816–1837. Of the Hanoverians, John Russell, a traveler, wrote: "The return to their native sovereign was to them the re-creation of their country, which Napoleon had blotted out from among the states of Germany."[10]

Through the good offices of Abbot Salfeld and Baron von Arnswaldt, a cabinet minister, Pinkerton was able to attract forty influential men to the founding meeting at Hanover on 25 July 1814. The ecumenical character of the meeting was pointed up by Pinkerton who wrote:

---

9. Owen, *History*, vol. 2, p. 246.

10. John Russell, *A Tour in Germany and some of the Southern Provinces of the Austrian Empire*, 3rd ed., 2 vols. (Edinburgh: A. Constable & Co., 1825), p. 398. The restoration of the national identity of Hanover represented triumph over France. In this view both the despotism and the rationalism of France were to be forgotten.

> In Hanover, as in Petersburg, I saw the Lutheran, Calvinistic, and Catholic Clergy join hands to promote the good cause: and some of these persons assured me, after the Meeting, that though they had been teachers of the same religion in this city for many years, yet they had never had an opportunity of speaking to each other. Oh! What a blessed plan, which is capable of bringing together the long divided parts of the Christian church.[11]

Alert to the political situation, Pinkerton emphasized that infidelity was at the root of the revolution in France and the consequent war across the continent. The most powerful antidote to anarchy was, in his estimation, the distribution of the Bible. The viceroy of Hanover concurred with the BFBS agent. So impressed was the duke of Cambridge with the potential of the Bible to preserve his position that he assumed the patronage of the Bible society. His minister von Arnswaldt became the committee's first president. To the Hanover committee Pinkerton also granted financial aid of £500.[12]

Departing from Hanover, Pinkerton directed his attention to the Prussian capital of Berlin. In many ways Berlin was more than the capital of Prussia. It was the center of that loosely knit association of German independent states sharing the German language. As Johannes Ball had welcomed Pinkerton to Elberfeld and Abbot Salfeld had introduced him at Hanover, so also in Berlin did Pinkerton have a patron. One of the leaders of the evangelical community then in Berlin was Baron Hans Ernst von Kottwitz (1757-1843). Not only was the baron an influential representative of the nineteenth-century *Erweckung*, he was also included in the small circle of royal confidants. To Pinkerton's delight von Kottwitz assented immediately to employ his prestige toward the founding of a local Bible society.[13]

The invitation to a founding meeting came from the pen of August Neander, who had been appointed professor in the university faculty of theology in Berlin one year earlier (1813). Neander's contribution to theological scholarship was the rejuvenation of ecclesiastical historiography. In a preface to the first edition of his *General History of the Christian Religion and Church,* Neander stated that his purpose in writing was devotional. Church history was, for him, "a living witness of the divine power of Christianity and a school of Christian experience." Professor Neander's

---

11. *Eleventh Report of the BFBS* (London, 1815), appendix, p. 3.

12. Victor Borde, "Die Hannoverische Bibelgesellschaft," *Die Bibel in der Welt* 7 (1964), pp. 54-55. Letter from Baron von Arnswaldt, 18 November 1814, BFBS Foreign Correspondence Inwards 1803-1814, p. 63d (BSA/D1/2/1).

13. Letter from Robert Pinkerton, 3 August 1814, BFBS Foreign Correspondence Books, no. 1, p. 39 (BSA/D1/6/1). Friedrich Hauss, *Väter der Christenheit* (Wuppertal: R. Brockhaus Verlag, 1959), vol. 3, p. 173.

immense influence in Berlin added to the acceptability of the Bible society.[14]

In recognition of what they perceived to be God's intervention in delivering Prussia from Napoleon, a veritable *Almanach de Gotha* (a *Who's Who*) met to form the Bible society.[15] The tutor to the crown prince, Lieutenant-General von Diericke, assumed the presidency and all the vice presidents were ministers of state. Among the directors were further luminaries of the court. So prominent were the king's men, that Friedrich Nippold considered the involvement of the royal ministers and advisors to be detrimental to the society because the common people might be mistrustful of such an organization.[16] King Friedrich Wilhelm III heaped both praise and money on the Bible society.

The Central Prussian Bible Society was not the first such organization in Berlin. As early as 1805, Johann Jänicke had added to his missionary training institute the function of distributing Bibles. This modest effort had been assisted also by British funds, and the Prussian king lent his support. Jänicke readily threw his weight behind the new society in 1814, and his small stock of Scriptures was absorbed into the larger operation.[17]

Noble patronage might have caused concern to some of the lower classes, but it also gave impetus to the expansion of the cause of Bible distributing. Auxiliary Bible societies sprang up throughout all of the provinces of the Kingdom. Bibles soon flowed from Prussian presses. According to Adolf Bruckner, even in the impoverished parts of East Prussia where 32,000 families had no Bibles, Scriptures were sent to the huts of the poor in 1814.[18]

---

14. *Thirteenth Report of the BFBS* (London, 1817), appendix, p. 167. Early in the nineteenth century Neander, originally a Jew by the name of Mendel, came under the influence of Friedich Schleiermacher. At his conversion to Christianity in 1806, Mendel assumed the name Neander (Greek for "a new man"). See August Neander, *Allgemeine Geschichte der christlichen Religion und Kirche* (Berlin: H. G. Bohn, 1850–1852), vol. 2, p. vi.

15. Heinrich Hermelink, *Das Christentum in der Menschheitsgeschichte*, vol. 3 (Stuttgart: J. B. Metzler and R. Wunderlich, 1955), p. 308. Adolf Bruckner, Max Geiger, Johann Heinrich Kurtz, Friedrich Nippold, and Friedrich Zange all attributed the *Erweckung* to a national sense of thanksgiving for deliverance from French domination.

16. Friedrich Nippold, *Geschichte der Kirche im deutschen Protestantismus des neunzehnten Jahrhunderts*, vol. 5, in *Handbuch der neuesten Kirchengeschichte*, 3rd ed. (Leipzig: T. O. Weigel, 1906), p. 125.

17. Letter from Johann Jänicke, 23 November 1814, BFBS Foreign Correspondence Books, no. 2, p. 118 (BSA/D1/6/2).

18. Adolf Bruckner, *Erweckungsbewegungen: Ihre Geschichte und Ihre Frucht für die christliche Kirche* (Hamburg, 1909), p. 132, as quoted in Wayne A. Detzler, "British and American Contributions to the 'Erweckung' in Germany, 1815–1848," p. 62.

Pinkerton's record of success in establishing Bible societies at Elberfeld, Hanover, Berlin, and Dresden clearly contributed to the genesis of the German Bible society movement. The evangelical theologian, August Tholuck, called Robert Pinkerton "a humble, pious man who glows with the fire of life." A latter-day commentator on his work in Dresden pronounced Pinkerton "a born organizer with glowing gifts."[19]

Leaving Dresden in 1814, Pinkerton returned to Russia, where three frigid winters passed before he again toured Germany. In 1818 he crossed the continent on his way to the BFBS anniversary in London. Along the way, Pinkerton visited hospitals and prisons, giving Scriptures to prisoners and patients, but lamented his own failure to do enough of this in these places of need. He had urged the societies he had formed to undertake such charitable actions, and he continued to engage in his own direct distribution of Bibles, including copies delivered directly to prisons, where in many parts of Prussia he developed the practice of reading the Scriptures aloud before the prisoners.[20]

On his journey southward through Germany, Pinkerton also visited universities. The University of Göttingen was called "the fairest pearl in her [Hanover's] crown" by the duke of Cambridge. Here Pinkerton found the professors of the university "with one accord" joining the "sacred band" of Bible distributors. University Vice Rector Pott served as secretary of the Bible society.[21]

Professors at Heidelberg joined their colleagues from Göttingen in supporting the Bible societies' distribution effort. At Tübingen, university professors formed an auxiliary of the Stuttgart Bible Society.[22] In Halle, Chancellor August Niemeyer signed his name to a letter requesting the "London Bible Society" to grant two English printing presses to the old Canstein Bible Publishing House. The Canstein Bible House had been founded in 1710 by Baron von Canstein, but the Halle chancellor considered the English printing machines to be "much better and more durable than the German [ones]." Chancellor Niemeyer furthermore requested sample Bibles from the BFBS, since "the mere sight of such a Bible library could not fail of making a deep impression on a great number of our students at the University."[23]

Robert Pinkerton had indeed become a major initiator of local Bible societies throughout the Germanies. He originated Bible distribution in

---

19. August Tholuck, as quoted in Steiner, "Robert Pinkerton," p. 155.
20. *Fifteenth Report of the BFBS* (London, 1819), appendix, p. 56, 58.
21. Russell, *Tour of Germany*, vol. 1, p. 372. *Fifteenth Report*, appendix, p. 68. *Missionary Register*, London, May 1819, p. 227.
22. *Fifteenth Report*, appendix, p. 73.
23. *Sixteenth Report of the BFBS* (London, 1820), appendix, p. 120.

prisons and hospitals in post-Napoleonic Germany. As universities became drawn into the *Erweckung,* Pinkerton also found leadership for the Bible society movement from within the elite German universities of the day. All of this occurred during the first fifteen years of the Bible Society's existence. For the BFBS Committee in London, the success in its continental operations owed in good measure to the zeal and wisdom of Robert Pinkerton, whose reputation grew accordingly.

Surviving the Apocrypha Crisis

Peace persisted in the relationships between German Bible societies and the paternal BFBS for almost a decade after Pinkerton's triumphal tours of 1814 and 1818. That the German committees also felt an attachment to England could be accounted for by the £58,131 that poured into German Bible societies from the BFBS London offices.[24] Many of these grants of funds were recommended to the Committee in London by Robert Pinkerton, with the result that the continental committees came to see him as a direct channel of support from BFBS headquarters in Earl Street. Alongside the British generosity, the German societies increased their own scripture distribution, establishing in the process sound financial stability. From the vantage point of the twentieth century, BFBS historian William Canton considered the first decade of Bible society work in Germany to be an era of significant success and harmony. As he noted:

> From 1821 to 1825 these [German] Societies presented their fairest picture of prosperity. Their connection with the great mother organization was undisturbed in its affection and admiration by any breath of controversy.[25]

This "picture of prosperity" and harmony was about to be broken, although one must scrutinize the records very carefully to decipher the roots of the controversy that ultimately choked off relations between Germany and England. The seed of the strife was a dispute over whether to include the apocryphal (deutero-canonical) books of the Bible in editions printed by and for the Bible societies. Over this matter, disagreement between the BFBS and the German Bible societies escalated in four fairly clearly defined stages.

Phase One. Initial signs of tension appeared already in 1812. With financial assistance from the BFBS, the Moravians near Königsberg were printing five thousand Lithuanian Bibles. Bibles in the Lithuanian language

---

24. Cumulative figure abstracted from the tenth to the twentieth annual reports of the BFBS (London, 1814–1824).
25. William Canton, *A History of the British and Foreign Bible Society,* 5 vols. (London: John Murray, 1904–1910), vol. 1, p. 432.

were "extremely scarce and extravagantly dear," and the BFBS grant enabled the Moravians to rectify this.[26] When Steinkopf toured the Continent in 1812 as an official representative of the BFBS he was charged by the Committee in London with the assignment of insuring the exclusion of the apocryphal books from the Lithuanian Bibles.[27] As a Lutheran churchman, Steinkopf found it difficult to understand the British evangelicals' concern that the apocryphal books should be deleted. Nevertheless, he informed his continental friends of the London Committee's concern. A storm of protest was unleashed by societies in Germany, Sweden, and Russia. Lutherans had never, according to the European committees, seen a Bible without the deutero-canonical texts. The British pressure, according to this view, would only reduce the market for Bible Society Scriptures.

Phase Two. The London Committee agreed, albeit reluctantly, to allow societies abroad to print Bibles at their own discretion.[28] Applying the standard BFBS principle, however, these Bibles must contain "no note or comment," a phrase that for most British evangelicals would have been interpreted to mean the exclusion of apocryphal texts. For such churchmen the Apocrypha was a mere human invention in contrast to the divinely inspired canonical Scriptures.

There the matter rested for nine years before a second threat to the unity of the international Bible society movement arose. In 1822, the Committee in London resolved that all future grants that local or national societies received from the BFBS would be solely for printing the canonical books "as they were generally received in England." The Committee's resolution made it clear that evangelicals in Britain, the main contributors to Bible Society funds, had applied pressure toward that end. On the other hand, continental committees were free to print the Apocrypha, or deutero-canonical texts, with their own funds. A system of double bookkeeping was thus introduced by which the expenditures of British and continental funds were kept separate.[29]

Such a system of accounting for funds received from various sources made sense to the accountant, but not to some of the strong-willed evangelical lay people and theologians. The evangelicals desired from their

---

26. *Seventh Report of the BFBS* (London, 1811), appendix, p. 48.
27. BFBS Minutes of the Committee, 6 July 1812, vol. 5, p. 291 (BSA/B1/5).
28. BFBS Minutes of the Committee, 7 June 1813, vol. 6, p. 106 (BSA/B1/6).
29. BFBS Minutes of the Committee, 29 August 1822, vol. 13, p. 59 (BSA/B1/13). Although most British church people, including some evangelicals, found no fault with the inclusion of the Apocrypha, a vocal majority of the BFBS supporters insisted on its exclusion. Since the lifeblood of any voluntary society is the generosity of its members and friends, the BFBS Committee was particularly sensitive to its supporters' demands.

continental counterparts an unconditional surrender on the Apocrypha issue. The pace of deliberations and debate quickened after 1822, and the heat generated by the discussions gained in intensity.

Phase Three. The conflict erupted again in 1824. The principal Catholic agent of the BFBS in Germany, Professor Leander Van Ess, requested aid from the Committee in London for the printing of eight thousand copies of his Bible translation. Since Van Ess held the chair in Catholic theology at the University of Marburg, his prestige insured relative freedom for the distribution of Scriptures among his fellow Catholics. His translation of the New Testament enjoyed local diocesan support, and thus during his tenure with the BFBS Van Ess was able to disseminate a half million copies of his New Testament. In 1822, Van Ess had resigned his position at Marburg to devote his time more fully to the Bible cause. His action presupposed continued generosity from London, and the timing coincided with the completion of the entire Old Testament translation. The Catholic agent argued that only Bibles containing the Apocrypha could be sold to Catholics, and the Committee in London voted him £500. He would have the canonical books printed with these funds, and supply the apocryphal books from other funds.[30]

It was at this point that open conflict erupted. The fuse that ignited the explosion was the Scottish revivalist, Robert Haldane. Although Haldane's fame was greatest in Scotland and in French-speaking Europe, where he had preached with success, he had many influential followers among the evangelicals in England. Haldane had expressed his disdain for the Apocrypha to the Committee of the BFBS as early as 1822. The decision to grant Van Ess £500 prompted new attacks from the Scottish preacher.[31]

Under mounting pressure from the north, the London BFBS Committee withdrew its grant to Van Ess on 6 September 1824.[32] On the basis of this case and in response to continued opposition from Haldane, the BFBS formulated a new principle in December 1824. Henceforth no grants would be made for editions of the Bible in which the canonical and apocryphal books were to be mixed. BFBS funds were to be applied only to the printing of canonical books.[33]

Needless to say, the Scots contested this settlement as well. It was still possible, they argued, for foreign societies to send out Bibles with the Apocrypha. Although the BFBS funds were applied only to the canonical books, money received from continental sources could be spent on what

---

30. BFBS Minutes of the Committee, 2 August 1824, vol. 14, p. 314 (BSA/B1/14).
31. Alexander Haldane, *Memoirs of the Lives of Robert Haldane of Airthrey, and his Brother, James Haldane*, 7th ed. (Edinburgh, 1860), p. 486.
32. BFBS Minutes of the Committee, 6 September 1824, vol. 14, p. 344 (BSA/B1/14).
33. Canton, *History*, vol. 1, p. 337.

Haldane called "the mongrel book."³⁴ In Haldane's estimation, the admixture of canonical and apocryphal books was detestable. Only a complete separation from any society that circulated the Apocrypha would silence the Scottish criticism, and in London the Committee was unwilling to acquiesce.

Haldane's fervor placed his Scottish friend, Robert Pinkerton, in a desperate dilemma. After all, Pinkerton was the most prominent BFBS agent in German-speaking Europe. Should Pinkerton concur with Haldane's conviction, he would be at odds with the policy articulated by the BFBS. On the other hand, conformity with the committee's resolution would require an open severance of his ties with Haldane and his Scottish evangelical supporters.

Phase Four. The final phase of the dispute formalized the positions of all parties involved: the BFBS Committee, Haldane and his Scottish supporters, and the German Bible societies. In November 1825, a fourfold policy was enunciated by the London BFBS Committee. First, the Scriptures were recognized as excluding the apocryphal texts. Second, no funds granted by the BFBS could be used to distribute the Apocrypha. Third, all Bibles and Testaments printed and funded by the BFBS were to be bound and thus safe from later insertion of the Apocrypha. Fourth, societies that sold Bibles with the Apocrypha were to return the proceeds from copies received through the BFBS to that organization. This was designed to eliminate the possibility of paying for printings of the Apocrypha with profits from BFBS Bibles.³⁵

Pinkerton visited local societies in seven German kingdoms and arrived at a prematurely positive conclusion that "their connection with the great mother organization was undisturbed."³⁶ He cited the continued distribution of Scriptures among the poor. Of course, the poor did not share the concern of many ecclesiastical authorities for a "complete" Bible containing the Apocrypha.

Within a year, however, Pinkerton's optimism had been shattered by reality. The tide of cordial cooperation had frozen into a sea of resistance. Four influential members of the Central Prussian Bible Society in Berlin released a pamphlet in which they argued that the Lutheran Church considered a Bible to be incomplete if it did not contain the Apocrypha.

---

34. Robert Haldane, *Review of the Conduct of the Directors of the British and Foreign Bible Society* (Edinburgh: W. Whyte & Co., 1828), p. 13.

35. BFBS, *Monthly Extracts from the Correspondence of the BFBS* (London, December 1825), p. 66. All four regulations were printed in the *Twenty-third Report of the BFBS* (London, 1827), and every year thereafter, at the end of the "Laws of the Society."

36. Canton, *History*, vol. 1, p. 432.

Therefore, the Central Prussian Bible Society found it impossible to comply with the BFBS's stipulations.[37]

An unfortunate by-product of the conflict followed in December 1826. Under pressure from his friends in Germany to reverse the BFBS decision and yet at the same time forced to uphold the policy of the Society for which he served as foreign secretary, Dr. Steinkopf resigned from the BFBS. Although the Bible Society explained Steinkopf's withdrawal by reference to his declining health—he had been seriously ill in 1826—it was also attributable to his genuine disagreement with the categorical exclusion of the Apocrypha. The relatively robust state of his health can be deduced from the fact that he attended the Jubilee of the Bible Society twenty-eight years later, when he was eighty-one years old.[38]

Steinkopf's resignation left the representation of the BFBS in Germany squarely on the shoulders of Robert Pinkerton. In an effort to explain the BFBS pamphlet concerning the matter, the Committee in London dispatched Pinkerton and R. Waldo Sibthorp on a tour of the German Bible societies. Sibthorp was a fellow of Magdalen College, Oxford, and later took charge of the Percy Proprietary Chapel in St. Pancras. Sibthorp and Pinkerton made a large circle around Germany visiting local Bible society committees. Here and there they found support for the BFBS position, but most committees were closed to the BFBS approach. In summing up the results of their tour, Sibthorp praised Pinkerton for his zeal and ability. "It would be doing an injustice to him," Sibthorp wrote, "were I not to state my full belief that no other individual connected with our Society could have effected so much in removing prejudice, softening angry feelings, and opening the continent, in some degree, to the reception of the Holy Scriptures, as they are now circulated by us."[39]

In spite of his admiration for Pinkerton, Sibthorp concluded that the door was closed and in most cases barred against the operations of the BFBS. The positive effects of the tour were two: misapprehensions were cleared away and distribution by sympathetic individuals emerged as a new means of operation. To support such a diversified network of Scripture salesmen a central depot at Frankfurt was needed.[40]

Both German and English sources agree with Sibthorp in fixing 1827/1828 as the commencement of a new era of individual initiative. German societies were forced to apply themselves with more zeal and sacrifice to

---

37. George Browne, *History*, vol. 2, appendix 2, pp. 518-19.

38. *Twenty-third Report of the BFBS* (London, 1827), appendix, p. 165. Canton, *History*, vol. 2, pp. 441-44.

39. *Twenty-fourth Report of the BFBS* (London, 1828), p. xxvi. Incidentally, Sibthorp later shocked his evangelical friends by becoming a Catholic.

40. *Twenty-fourth Report*, pp. xxiii-xxiv.

the task.[41] As Charles Shore has noted, fifteen years later Pinkerton would list three salutary effects of the crisis concerning the Apocrypha: first, many had become convinced that the Apocrypha should be deleted from the Bible; second, continental Bible societies had grown to meet the challenge; and third, the circulation of the Scriptures was aided materially by being committed into the hands of individuals.[42]

Pinkerton's New Path in Frankfurt

It was R. Waldo Sibthorp who first proposed the establishment of a central BFBS agency for all of German-speaking Europe. He saw this as an imperative forced upon the Committee in London by the dissolution of relations with the German Bible societies during the Apocrypha crisis.

The re-assignment of Pinkerton to such an agency became a matter of urgency. Reasons for this were cited in the 1831 *Report* of the Bible Society. First, the sudden severance of ties with the BFBS's principal Catholic agent, Leander Van Ess, demanded the attention of an on-site Bible Society agent.[43] Second, an agent stationed in Frankfurt and equipped with a depot stocked with Scriptures could expedite the supplying of these volumes to individual correspondents or colporteurs. Third, an accredited agent could enter into effective negotiations with printers and thereby reduce the cost of printing Bibles. Fourth, by traveling throughout the German kingdoms the agent could discover new distributors, establish subsidiary depots and supply Catholics who had formerly received Testaments from Van Ess.[44] Perhaps also the BFBS hoped by stationing its own representative in central Europe to win the war against those who would include the Apocrypha in the dissemination of Scripture on the continent.

Whatever the primary motivation, the BFBS Subcommittee for General Purposes recommended the assignment of Pinkerton to Frankfurt on 21 May 1830.[45] Three days later these minutes were confirmed by the BFBS Committee. The Subcommittee for General Purposes was charged with implementation of the plan.[46] The publication of this decision established

---

41. Johannes Adler, "Es began im 'Englischen Haus'," *Die Bibel in der Welt*, 7 (1964), p. 65.

42. Pinkerton cited internally in Charles J. Shore, *Memoir of the Life and Correspondence of John Lord Teignmouth*, 2 vols. (London: Hatchard and Son, 1843), vol. 2, appendix 1, pp. 597-98.

43. Van Ess's forced withdrawal was connected to alleged indiscretions with his housekeeper.

44. *Twenty-seventh Report of the BFBS* (London, 1831), pp. xxiv-xxvii.

45. BFBS Minutes of the Committee, 21 May 1830, vol. 20, pp. 71-72 (BSA/B1/20).

46. *Twenty-seventh Report*, appendix, p. 94.

Pinkerton, at least in the eyes of BFBS supporters, as the sole agent of the Bible Society in German-speaking Europe. By the end of May 1830, Pinkerton had settled in to the task in Frankfurt. A residence permit was forthcoming from the governing mayors, and a room was rented to house the depot.

A confirmation of the decision to dismiss Van Ess was explained by Pinkerton in these words: "the cloud upon his [Van Ess's] faculties seems denser than ever." Van Ess's nephew did not contest this assessment, since his uncle was unable to work further. Hidden in his agreement was the understanding that the BFBS would provide a pension for Van Ess.[47]

In the work of establishing a Frankfurt agency, Pinkerton received invaluable assistance from J. D. Claus, who had represented the interests of the BFBS in the Rhine-Main area (the region of Frankfurt and Darmstadt) since the rift over the Apocrypha. In April 1828, he became a salaried representative of the Bible Society and took journeys to Bavaria as well as to France.[48] Claus also provided schools with Bibles. As Catholic pilgrims passed through Frankfurt on their way to Walldürn he supplied them with a copy of the Catholic version of the New Testament.[49] Best of all, Claus was in wholehearted agreement with London over the Apocrypha issue.[50]

Pinkerton relied heavily on personal friendship with supporters of the Bible Society. This became the best means of circumventing the alienated German Bible societies. For instance, in 1831 a general officer of the Prussian Army approached one Samuel Elsner, secretary of the disaffected Central Prussian Bible Society. The general sought Scriptures for the soldiers under his command.[51] The Central Prussian society was unable to meet the enormous demand of the soldiers. Thus, Samuel Elsner laid down his role as secretary and launched the Military Bible Society in 1833. Because he was willing to circulate New Testaments provided by the BFBS, the Apocrypha issue was circumvented. Cost of printing the Testaments was divided between the BFBS, the crown prince (later Friedrich Wilhelm IV), and the soldiers themselves. Between 1831 and 1854, Pinkerton's agency provided no less than £4,467 to this project.[52] After more than ten years of uninterrupted activity on behalf of the young men of the military, Elsner summed up the significance of his

47. *Twenty-seventh Report*, appendix, p. 94.
48. BFBS, *Monthly Extracts* (London, October 1828), pp. 186-87.
49. *Twenty-sixth Report of the BFBS* (London, 1830), p. xxxv.
50. *Twenty-fifth Report of the BFBS* (London, 1829), p. xxxii.
51. This was probably General von Thile, who also served as president of the Prussian Society. See William O. Shanahan, *German Protestants Face the Social Question* (Notre Dame, Ind.: University of Notre Dame Press, 1954), p. 80.
52. Canton, *History*, vol. 2, p. 202.

progress: "We look upon the distribution of the sacred volume among the military as a glorious epoch in the history of the Bible Society."[53]

In a sense, Elsner's distributions to the military constituted mass circulation of Scripture. From the first, however, the Frankfurt center cultivated individual correspondents in almost every corner of the German kingdoms. During the first year more than one hundred individuals approached the Frankfurt agency for aid.[54] Most of these ordered a small store of Testaments and Bibles from Pinkerton and replenished their stock as copies were sold or given away. This method had three major advantages. First, societies opposed to the distribution of Scriptures without the Apocrypha could not hinder the circulation of these Scriptures by individuals. Second, the correspondents were in closer contact with needy individuals than were the titled and wealthier members of Bible society committees. Third, by selling Scriptures directly, even if at reduced rates, capital for further printing could be raised.

A perusal of the annual *Report of the BFBS* for the years of Pinkerton's service at Frankfurt reveals a list of correspondents that included people of notable influence. Several professors maintained a supply of Scriptures for their students. Among these were August Tholuck of Halle, professors Kraft and von Raumer of Erlangen, Professor Werner at Ehingen, and an anonymous professor at Augsburg. Clergy also kept Bibles and Testaments for their parishioners, and several deans, both Protestant and Catholic, supplied their colleagues. Pinkerton often visited these correspondents, and they in turn frequently called at Frankfurt. In fact, in one sample year alone, 1831–1832, more than twelve hundred visitors came to the central depot in Frankfurt.[55]

Members of the nobility, such as the widowed Countess Friedrike von Reden, also turned to Pinkerton. She took up from her husband the patronage of the Buchwald Bible Society in Silesia. Under her supervision the so-called Hirschberg Bible was printed and sent out to every elementary school in Prussia. At one point, Countess von Reden personally underwrote more than 120 Bible depositories in her domain. When Pinkerton settled at Frankfurt, the countess marked his arrival with these words: "May the Lord grant that assistance may be abundantly offered from London, and that we may have the unspeakable delight to see, through the generosity of England, a light never to be extinguished made to shine among the multitudes of our poor fellow-creatures who are groping in the deepest darkness."[56]

---

53. *Thirty-ninth Report of the BFBS* (London, 1843), p. lxii.
54. *Twenty-sixth Report* (London, 1830), p, xix.
55. *Twenty-eighth Report of the BFBS* (London, 1832), p. xxiv.
56. *Twenty-sixth Report*, p. xlviii.

Another source of allies were those affiliated with the London Society for Promoting Christianity Amongst the Jews (LSPCAJ), later known as the Church's Mission to the Jews.[57] Pinkerton recruited J. G. Bergfeldt to serve in Königsberg on the eastern edge of Prussia. In requesting a further grant of Bibles in 1830 he assured the BFBS that the poverty of the Prussian peasants made them receptive to Bibles, even if the Apocrypha was not included.[58] Johann Christian Moritz, another agent of the Jewish mission, worked in the Frankfurt area. Moritz was able to effect large distributions. He undertook a tour to Württemberg in 1833 during which he distributed Hebrew and German Scriptures among both Gentiles and Jews.[59] A third agent of the London Society for Promoting Christianity Amongst the Jews was J. Stockfeld, who confined his efforts to the Rhine Valley. Not only did he personally put Scriptures into the hands of Jews and Gentiles, he also enlisted "several pious persons in the work of disseminating the Scriptures among Gentiles and Jews." At one time more than thirty individuals were assisting Stockfeld in this project.[60] The fourth member of the LSPCAJ with whom Pinkerton corresponded was the Reverend F. W. Becker of Warsaw. Like Stockfeld, Becker employed colporteurs to distribute Scriptures. By this means he could report circulating 865 copies in a three-month period. One blacksmith bought New Testaments for all his workmen. He hoped thereby to prevent them from spending their wages in the public houses on Sundays. Theoretically, they would become interested in Christianity and cease to frequent the public houses. Sobriety on Sunday would also aid productivity on Monday.[61]

Despite occasional government prohibitions Pinkerton also employed and deployed colporteurs, door-to-door Bible salesmen. While Baron von Bunsen was praising the use of colporteurs at the BFBS anniversary in London in 1839, the president of the Prussian Bible Society, General von Thile, spoke out against the practice. Prussian authorities feared that the home distribution of Scriptures would encourage the publication and sale of liberal political pamphlets in the same manner. Therefore all colportage was banned in Prussia until after the 1848 revolution.[62]

Although the Prussians persisted in their rejection of the use of colporteurs, the Saxon Bible Society sent a man into the field in 1845. The

---

57. W. T. Gidney, *The Jews and Their Evangelization* (London: Student Volunteer Missionary Union, 1899), p. 91. See also the more recent work of Christopher M. Clark, *The Politics of Conversion: Missionary Protestantism and the Jews in Prussia, 1728-1941* (Oxford: Clarendon Press, 1995).

58. *Twenty-sixth Report*, p. xlvi.

59. BFBS, *Monthly Extracts* (London, October 1833), p. 65.

60. *Thirty-fourth Report of the BFBS* (London, 1838), p. xlvii.

61. *Thirty-fifth Report of the BFBS* (London, 1839), p. xxviii.

62. *Thirty-sixth Report of the BFBS* (London, 1840), p. xxvii.

Saxon government approved the assignment of a person by the name of Schuppan to travel among the rural communities in 1845. Within two years Schuppan was joined by two colleagues. Pinkerton attributed the prosperity of the Saxon Bible Society to their willingness to employ this controversial means of Bible distribution.[63]

An external witness to the debate over colportage was the German reformer Theodor Fliedner who lived in Kaiserswerth, not far from Elberfeld. Fliedner wrote, "If the Central Bible Society in Berlin would make a serious attempt to use agents [colporteurs], it would soon realize the need for further such men, their blessed effectiveness and their absolute indispensability."[64]

Despite the relative success of Bible societies during the nineteenth century, they did suffer rejection from the Catholic hierarchy. The contentious issue for the Catholic church was distribution of vernacular Scriptures, whose approval for general use would not come until the twentieth century. In 1814, during his triumphal march across Europe, Pinkerton proposed the establishment of a Polish Bible Society at Warsaw. Immediately this was opposed by the archbishop of Gniezno, the primate of all Poland. The archbishop wrote to the Vatican for guidance. Two years passed before Pope Pius VII responded in 1816 with a papal rescript. Vernacular Scriptures would undermine the very foundations of religion, he asserted, with a reference to the fact that vernacular Scriptures had earlier been placed on the Index of prohibited writings as early as 15 June 1757.[65]

In an effort to smooth the way for a Bible society in the Austro-Hungarian realm, Pinkerton met on 20 August 1816 with Prince Metternich in Vienna. He petitioned the prince for permission to establish a Bible society in Vienna. The prince delayed his answer for two full months while he conferred with the emperor. On 23 December 1816, an imperial edict prohibited the formation of a Bible society and the distribution of BFBS Bibles in the Austrian Empire.[66]

Almost a quarter of a century passed before Pope Gregory XVI issued an encyclical condemning the Bible societies. He vilified them as "daring Heralds of Infidelity and Heresy." In a thinly veiled reference to the "central Society of these Heretics and Infidels." he accused the BFBS of using

---

63. Wilhelm Thilo, *Geschichte der Preussischen Haupt-Bibelgesellschaft in ihrem ersten Halbjahrhundert 1814-1864* (Berlin: Preussische Haupt-Bibelgesellschaft, 1864), pp. 161-62. *Forty-third Report of the BFBS* (London, 1847), pp. xliv-xlv.

64. Theodor Fliedner, *Kollektenreise nach Holland und England*, vol. 1 (Essen), p. 300, as cited in *Evangelische Kirchenzeitung* (Berlin, July 1827), p. 39.

65. A handwritten copy of Pinkerton's English translation of the papal rescript appears in BFBS Foreign Correspondence Books, no. 5, pp. 319, 321, and 323 (BSA/D1/6/5).

66. Steiner, "Robert Pinkerton," pp. 161-62.

"falsified Bibles," "pestilent journals," bribes, and inflammatory addresses to snatch the faithful from the bosom of the church of Rome.[67]

In 1844, Pope Gregory XVI issued a bull in which he condemned the Bible societies. He spoke of the BFBS and its widespread influence. He condemned the circulation of Scriptures in the vernacular tongue with "no interpreter or guide." Then the Pope concluded: "we condemn anew, in virtue of our Apostolical authority, all the Bible Societies before alluded to and already disallowed by our predecessors."[68]

Pinkerton's Agency in Retrospect

The value of Pinkerton's work can be summarized in three ways. First, he channeled money and Scriptures to German-speaking Europe. During the period between its tenth anniversary in 1814 and the democratic revolution of 1848, the British and Foreign Bible Society sent £176,762 to the German kingdoms, and more than four million Scripture portions were distributed.[69]

Second, Pinkerton helped to link together the far-flung centers of the evangelical awakening, the *Erweckung*, in German-speaking Europe. Adolf Bruckner attributed the unification of the awakening to BFBS agents. In 1842, Pinkerton's report claimed partial credit for advancing the awakening.[70]

Third, Pinkerton founded Bible societies that were capable of survival on their own, despite the disruption of the Apocrypha crisis.[71] In his valuable essay on Pinkerton, Robert Steiner has asked: "Why, then, was Pinkerton largely forgotten in Germany?" Steiner answers, enigmatically, because he was not a German, but rather a Scot.[72] Pinkerton remains, nonetheless, among the most prominent nineteenth-century agents employed by the British and Foreign Bible Society.

---

67. Letter from Robert Pinkerton, BFBS Foreign Correspondence Inwards, 1840, no. 4, p. 61 (BSA/D1/2/71).

68. Quoted internally in *The Christian Observer*, August 1844 (London), p. 448.

69. Statistics here are drawn from annual reports, the eleventh to the forty-fourth, of the BFBS (London, 1815–1848). Adolf Risch, *Festschrift zur Jahrhundertfeier der Priviligierten Württembergischen Bibelanstalt* (Stuttgart: Württembergische Bibelanstalt, 1912), p. 71.

70. Bruckner, *Erweckungsbewegungen* (Hamburg, 1909), p. 132. *Thirty-eighth Report of the BFBS* (London, 1842), pp. xxii-xxiii.

71. *Thirty-eighth Report*, pp. xxii-xxiii.

72. Steiner, "Robert Pinkerton," p. 162.

OBEDIENCE AND DISOBEDIENCE: GEORGE BORROW'S IDIOSYNCRATIC
RELATIONSHIP WITH THE BIBLE SOCIETY[1]

Ann M. Ridler

George Borrow was introduced to the British and Foreign Bible Society in December 1832 by the Reverend Francis Cunningham of Lowestoft and had his first interview with the Society's governing Committee in January 1833. He was twenty-nine at the time and had spent the previous eight years trying to establish himself as a journalist and translator. During those years he lived in London, from 1824 to 1825 and again from 1829 to 1831. When not in London, he could be found either at home in Norwich or "wandering" the country. Whether he went abroad during this period is not conclusively known, for his habit of dramatizing his own experiences created the legend of Borrow as a mystery traveller.

This "veiled period" of Borrow's life, traditionally said to last from 1824 to 1832, is in reality a myth too long in the dying.[2] It is known, for instance, that although his journalistic efforts largely failed, those eight years were

---

1. This paper does not offer a comprehensive study of George Borrow's relationship with the Bible Society, but focuses instead on the kind of person he was, and how aspects of his personality affected his relationship with the Society. I have written elsewhere on Borrow's relationship as a linguist with the Society, and on his negotiations with them over his translation of the Gospel of Luke into Spanish Romani, or *caló*. See Ann M. Ridler, *George Borrow as a Linguist: Images and Contexts* (Warborough, printed for private circulation, 1996), particularly chap. 7, "The Linguist as Persuader: Borrow and the Bible Society", pp. 341-82. This is a revised version of my 1983 doctoral thesis bearing the same title. See also Ann M. Ridler, "Sidelights on George Borrow's Gypsy *Luke*", *The Bible Translator*, vol. 32, no. 3 (July 1981), pp. 329-37.

2. I have demonstrated in my own work of 1983, on Borrow's library subscriptions in Norwich and London, the many dates when he must have been in one or another city. Ann M. Ridler, "Norwich Libraries and George Borrow", *Library History*, vol. 6, no. 3 (1983), pp. 61-71; Ridler, "George Borrow as a Linguist", pp.173 n. 163; 185 n. 205; 289 n. 33; 353 n. 23. In 1987, Angus Fraser gave an important paper at the George Borrow Conference at Cambridge, on "The Unveiling of the Veiled Period", which included a detailed chronology of Borrow's activities in the years 1824 to 1832. See Gillian Fenwick, ed., *Proceedings of the 1987 George Borrow Conference* (Toronto, limited private edition, 1988), pp. 1-13.

Picture 31. *George Borrow (1803–1881)*. Detail from the 1843 portrait by Henry Wyndham Phillips, engraved by W. Holl, reprinted from George Borrow, *Lavengro* (London: John Murray, 1851)

ones of intense linguistic activity, mostly literary translations, from a remarkable range of languages. These included translations of poetry from German, Swedish, Danish, and Spanish, published during 1823 and 1824 in the *Monthly Magazine* and *New Monthly Magazine*; a full-length novel by the German writer Friedrich Maximilian von Klinger (1753–1831), published in 1825 as *Faustus: His Life, Death and Descent into Hell*; and an anthology of translations mainly from Danish, his *Romantic Ballads*, published in 1826. In addition, Borrow drafted *The Sleeping Bard* from the Welsh of Ellis Wynne, not published until 1860, and accomplished a huge amount of other poetic translations from a wide range of languages.³ And alongside all this, there arose his passion for Gypsies — their language and way of life — a passion that never left him. He had had no university education, yet the massive introduction he wrote from 1829 to 1830 for his abortive translation of "Songs of Scandinavia", which was to have been published in two volumes but failed to see the light, would stand comparison with many a graduate dissertation.⁴ He was not a biblical scholar nor even, as Cunningham admitted, of any "very exactly defined denomination of Christians" (though by mid-September 1833 Borrow describes himself as a "staunch Protestant").⁵ With all this behind him, one can imagine his reaction when, after those laborious years spent "digging holes in the sand", as he put it, he was sent home by the Committee to learn Manchu in six months.⁶ Even then, he had no idea that he would be offered the glamorous prospect of working in St. Petersburg, at the handsome salary of £200 a year, plus expenses. It was not until Borrow's thirtieth birthday, on 5 July 1833, that the Reverend Joseph Jowett, BFBS editorial superintendent, wrote to explain this possibility, and the letter confirming his appointment was sent only a week before Borrow's departure on 31 July.⁷

Borrow spent two years in St. Petersburg, from August 1833 to August 1835, initially engaged in transcription of portions of the Bible translated into Manchu and, for the greater part of his time, in editing and seeing through the press the New Testament in Manchu, which appeared in eight volumes in 1835. Toward the end of this period, Borrow published an anthology with the title *Targum*, meaning "interpretation," a collection of his translations from some thirty languages. In addition, he produced a modest booklet called *The Talisman*, which constitutes only the second appearance in English of any of Pushkin's poems.⁸ Each of these works appeared in an edition of one hundred copies in St. Petersburg in 1835.

3. Many of these were eventually published as part of the Norwich Edition of Borrow's *Works*, 16 vols. (London: Constable & Co., 1923–1924), though some still survive only in manuscript drafts.

4. The "Songs of Scandinavia" manuscript is in Rutgers University Library, Symington Collection, B737vii, New Brunswick, New Jersey.

5. Letter of Cunningham, Lowestoft Vicarage, 27 December 1832, cited internally in T. H. Darlow, ed., *Letters of George Borrow to the British and Foreign Bible Society* (London: Hodder & Stoughton, 1911), p. 1. For Borrow's self-description, see the same collection, p. 23.

6. W. I. Knapp, *Life, Writings and Correspondence of George Borrow*, 2 vols. (London: John Murray, 1899), vol. 1, p.138, from a letter Borrow wrote to his mother on 5/17 May 1835.

7. Darlow, *Letters of George Borrow*, pp. 16-17.

8. The first was by W. H. Leeds in an article published in 1832. Ridler, "George Borrow as a Linguist", p. 119 n. 209.

If Borrow had any private misgivings about his Russian assignment, he did not show them. In a characteristic letter to Jowett on 3 July 1833, written before his appointment was confirmed, he said: "I flatter myself that I am for one or two reasons tolerably well adapted for the contemplated expedition, for besides a competent knowledge of French and German, I possess some acquaintance with Russian, being able to read without much difficulty any printed Russian book, and I have little doubt that after a few months' intercourse with the natives I should be able to speak it fluently."[9] The term "natives" would raise eyebrows today, but it's unclear what resonance it would have had among the Russians of the 1830s! Borrow's social relations while he was in Russia were in any case cosmopolitan, and came from all classes of society. His letters reveal that he had dealings with Prince Alexander Golitsyn, with the Hon. J. D. Bligh, his Britannic Majesty's plenipotentiary to the court of the tsar, and with British Consul Dobell.[10] A key friend was that fine antiquary and orientalist with his own immense library, Baron Schilling von Canstadt, who in turn introduced Borrow to the Russian monk and pioneering orientalist, Iakinf (Bichurin), of the Alexander Nevsky Monastery. It was Ieromonakh Iakinf who gave Borrow lessons in Manchu in return for lessons in English.[11] There were also English and American merchants in St. Petersburg to whom Borrow had introductions, including John Venning and William Ropes, and other English people settled there, such as Sarah Biller, with whom he had left his translations into Russian of some of the homilies of the Church of England.[12] There were the professors of Arabic and Persian at the university;[13] and Borrow's scholarly colleagues working on the Manchu scriptures, including Stepan Vasil'evich Lipovtsev (1773-1841), the translator of the text Borrow was to edit, and the London Missionary Society missionaries William Swan and Edward Stallybrass.[14]

9. Darlow, *Letters of George Borrow*, p. 15. Although Jowett's letter was not sent until 5 July, he must have told Borrow of the prospect earlier, hence Borrow's letter of 3 July.

10. Most of these people are mentioned numerous times in his letters to John Hasfeld after his departure from Russia. See George Borrow's three letters to Hasfeld in *A Journey to Eastern Europe in 1844*, ed. Angus M. Fraser (Edinburgh: The Tragara Press, 1981); Borrow, *Letters to John Hasfeld, 1835-1839*, ed. Angus M. Fraser (Edinburgh: The Tragara Press, 1982); and his *Letters to John Hasfeld, 1841-1846*, ed. Angus M. Fraser (Edinburgh: The Tragara Press, 1984).

11. This is known from Alekseev's "Introduction" to the Russian translation of *Lavengro*. Ridler, "George Borrow as a Linguist", p. 359 n. 39.

12. C. K. Shorter, *George Borrow and His Circle* (London: Hodder & Stoughton, 1913), pp. 175-76. Unfortunately, according to Professor A. G. Cross, the manuscripts of his translations appear to have been lost.

13. Mirza Jafar and Mirza Achmed. Darlow, *Letters of George Borrow*, p. 78.

14. Darlow, *Letters of George Borrow*, pp. 21-27 and 78.

There were also Spaniards at the Spanish legation, whom he later remembered fondly, and of course his great friend the Dane, John Hasfeld, who worked at the Danish legation. In addition, Borrow had a manservant who spoke the Manchu Tatar of the steppes, and the printers he engaged were Estonians.

It is clear in his enthusiastic letters from Russia that Borrow was bowled over by the grandeur of the city, the cosmopolitanism of its inhabitants, and the sheer excitement of the vistas of unbounded knowledge opened up to him in Baron Schilling's library. Manchu he saw poetically as "a lake of learning overflowing with the tribute of a hundred rivers".[15] The traditional picture of Borrow as a man of the open road, consorting with Gypsies, not above practising pugilism, and somewhat rustic in his manners, has to be balanced by his "dream of study",[16] his passion for knowledge, however randomly acquired, his love of books, and his absorption in translation, which lasted some sixty years. As he once quoted from the Talmud: "Who is the wise man? He who learns from every body".[17]

When Borrow returned to England in 1835 to report to the Society, having completed his Manchu assignment, he was naturally eager to continue in their employment, and in the words of the Committee's resolution, it was agreed that he should "proceed forthwith to Lisbon and Oporto for the purpose of visiting the Society's correspondents there, and of making further inquiries respecting the means and channels which may offer for promoting the circulation of the Holy Scriptures in Portugal."[18] The resolution is quoted in full here, for it illustrates the kind of tension that arose between the Bible Society and their wayward agent. In every letter to them at this time, Borrow mentions Spain: "I should be most happy to explore Portugal and Spain"; "I wish it to be clearly understood that I am perfectly willing to undertake the expedition [i.e., to Portugal], nay, to extend it into Spain".[19] As is clear from the quotation, the resolution mentioned only Portugal, even though the Rev. Andrew Brandram, secretary to the Committee, in a letter to the Rev. E. Whiteley, chaplain at Oporto, admitted that "our correspondence about Spain is at this moment singularly interesting,

---

15. Knapp, *Life*, vol. 1, p.214, letter from Borrow to the Rev. F. Cunningham, 17/29 November 1834.

16. George Borrow, "Preface", in *Lavengro: the Scholar, the Gypsy, the Priest*, 3 vols. (London: John Murray, 1851), p. vii: "In the following pages I have endeavoured to describe a dream, partly of study, partly of adventure..."

17. Borrow chose this as the epigraph to an essay on "Songs and Literature of the Jews", of which a manuscript fragment is in the Humanities Research Center of the University of Texas at Austin.

18. Darlow, *Letters of George Borrow*, p. 102.

19. Darlow, *Letters of George Borrow*, pp. 98, 100.

and if it continues so, and the way seems to open, Mr. Borrow will cross the frontier and go and enquire what can be done there".[20]

Picture 32. *Andrew Brandram, BFBS Secretary 1823–1850*. Reprinted from Herbert Jenkins, *Life of George Borrow*, 2nd ed. (London: John Murray, 1924), facing p. 450.

Borrow eagerly seized the opportunity to get to Spain. Arriving in Portugal on 12 November 1835, he crossed the frontier on 6 January and travelled via Badajóz and Mérida to Madrid. From then on, apart from trips back to London and Norwich, he lived in Spain. Based in Madrid until 1839, he moved to Seville for a year, and continued to travel throughout the whole of Spain – with the single exception of Catalonia and the eastern seaboard, which formed the territory of a rival, unsalaried agent of the Society, Lieutenant James Graydon. During this period Borrow managed to complete a great deal of research for *The Zincali: An Account of the Gypsies of Spain*, published in 1841. He also kept journals and wrote numerous letters to the Society – writings that formed the basis for *The Bible in Spain*, a runaway bestseller in 1843. In addition, he produced the first ever published work in a Gypsy dialect, namely, his translation of the Gospel of

20. Darlow, *Letters of George Borrow*, pp. 102-103.

St. Luke into Spanish Romani, or *caló*, and he edited a version of this Gospel in Basque, both being published in Madrid in 1837.

It has to be said that, for a variety of reasons, Borrow's relationship with the Bible Society gradually began to deteriorate, and he left Spain for good in April 1840. Upon his return to England, he discovered at a final interview that there was no prospect of further employment with the Society. A short time later he married the widow Mary Clarke, who with her daughter had been staying at the house he had rented in Seville. Thereafter, the couple returned to her estate in Suffolk, and with the exception of the period 1871–1872, when he revised his Gypsy translation of Luke for a second edition, this episode of his life was closed.

Although the terms "obedience and disobedience" are used in the title of this article, one could equally well think of other antitheses: for example, "submissiveness and self-assertion", "compulsion and wilfulness", or "constraint and liberation". There are differences, however, in these four expressions: "obedience and disobedience", or "submissiveness and self-assertion" are both, in each case, aspects of Borrow's own mental attitude, whereas "compulsion" and "constraint" are intrusions from a second party, belonging to the sometimes unwelcome contingent reality within which Borrow has to function as the Bible Society's agent. Notions of this kind were not simply a question of Borrow's relationship with the Bible Society, or just a fragment of his day-to-day biography, but were more deeply symptomatic of the person he was, in so far as that can be discovered from his writings.[21] There seems to be a running dispute at the very core of his being, between the impulse to perform his allotted tasks thoroughly and well, and the conflicting impulse to escape, to open his life to random adventure and experience, the wilder the better, and to elude respectability by consorting with Gypsies and a motley crew of ruffians.[22] Borrow says little or nothing to the Bible Society about this

---

21. There is a telling example of this in *Lavengro*, chap. 15, where the adolescent hero discusses with his tutor, d'Eterville, the relative merits of reading Boileau and Dante. He finds French more difficult than Italian, and despite the urgings of his tutor, cannot get on with Boileau, whose didactic *Art poétique* of 1674 represents thraldom to rigid rules of prosody. By contrast, the boy's "mind would dwell on the sonorous stanzas of Dante, rising and falling like the waves of the sea". While the tutor characterized Dante as "a vagabond, my dear", Dante represented for Borrow freedom from restraint. See *Lavengro*, pp. 91 and 94 in the "definitive edition" (London: John Murray, 1900).

22. Much later in his life, in *Wild Wales: Its People, Language, and Scenery*, 3 vols. (London: John Murray, 1862), Borrow illustrates the impulse to elude respectability in conflict with docility to his wife, with a delightful vignette of his failed encounter with some wild Irish tinkers: "I saw a wild-looking woman with two wild children looking at me... I was going to address her, but just then my wife called to me from

directly, but glimpses can be picked up here and there in *The Zincali*, and they are a major theme of *The Bible in Spain*.

Borrow's willing obedience is evident in his first letter from St Petersburg, received at Bible House on 26 September 1833, less than two months after his arrival in the Russian capital. He writes: "I am...exerting myself to the utmost to fulfil the views of the Society". Referring in the same letter to the fine Bible versions produced by Jesuit missionaries, he notes somewhat sanctimoniously: "the Lord smiled not upon their undertakings. They thought not of His glory but of the glory of their order".[23] The rather glib use of a pious comment was unfortunately picked up by Borrow as readily as a television entertainer in the twentieth century impersonates a politician, and Borrow may have been surprised to be rebuked for it by Brandram. Such piety does indeed strike a false note from time to time and has led some writers to brand Borrow as a hypocrite. The truth about his beliefs, however, is more complicated. Having been given a challenging role to perform, Borrow flung himself into it ardently, and strove to please—but his actions still tended to come off as a performance with some air of theatricality. Much later, for instance, writing to Brandram on 4 September 1839 from Tangiers, Borrow describes what happened at the customs house of Sanlucár near Cadiz, where a supply of Spanish Testaments had been embargoed:

> As it was necessary to open the boxes to inspect their contents, we all proceeded to the courtyard where, holding a Testament in my hand, I recommenced my discourse. I scarcely know what I said, for I was much agitated and hurried away by my feelings, when I bethought me of the

---

the shop, and I went to her, and when I returned to look for the woman she and her children had disappeared, and though I searched about for her I could not see her, for which I was sorry, as I wished very much to have some conversation with her about the ways of the Irish wanderers. I was thinking of going to look for her up 'Paddy's dingle', but my wife meeting me, begged me to go home with her, as it was getting late. So I went home with my better half". Quotation is from the later "definitive edition," *Wild Wales* (London: John Murray, 1901), pp. 393-94. His wife Mary was in many ways a gently constraining influence on his wild restlessness, urging him, as she did in one of the small number of her letters that have survived, to "pray for belief in Jesus, By & thro' whom alone we can be saved." Letter of 26 July 1866, quoted in Angus Fraser, "George Borrow's Tour of Galloway and the Borders, 1866", unpublished but printed for circulation within the George Borrow Society, 2000, p. 31. Earlier, in letters to Borrow's mother written from Llangollen in 1854, she had written, "Last Sunday morning we *all* went to an English service at the Church here. In the evening we *all* went to the same", and as if to underline that George was under control, and again, "He is very regular in his morning and evening devotions, so that we all have abundant cause for thankfulness." Knapp, *Life*, vol. 2, p.111.

23. Darlow, *Letters of George Borrow*, p. 23.

manner in which the Word of God was persecuted in the unhappy kingdom of Spain.[24]

This statement may have a ring of truth, but it also illustrates the ambiguity of Borrow's role: he was not a missionary, but an agent of the Bible Society, whose sole concern was to publish and distribute the Scriptures. Others, including Graydon and agents of similar societies such as the Wesleyan missionary W. H. Rule, were performing a similar role in Spain, though not necessarily with the same publishing function. Brandram, in his letters to Borrow, frequently reminded him of the distinction between mission and distribution: "as far as our Society is concerned, it is our duty to leave the Bible to speak for itself... We must never forget we are not preachers", and again, "[a]n Agent of the Bible Society is a Reformer, not by his preaching or denouncing, but by the distribution of the Bible".[25] If Borrow was frequently disobedient in this respect, it was probably in spite of himself: the distinction between mission and distribution was important for the Society,[26] but was blurred by the fact that many missionaries in Spain, working within their own denomination, also distributed the Scriptures.

Borrow's seven years with the Bible Society are almost the only period of his life when he was subject to any form of external constraint, if one excepts the five years he spent as a solicitor's articled clerk, from 1819 to 1824. The need to earn his bread was an ineluctable constraint in the early years, but depended entirely on how he set his own agenda, even when it meant digging holes in the sand and filling them up again. The Bible Society, on the other hand, set a clear agenda for him. "[Fulfilling] the views of the Society" meant following a particular method of operation, a method that applied equally both in Spain and in Russia and involved production as well as distribution. For Borrow, production of the text consisted of three main tasks: first, he had to secure permission to print — no easy matter in either country — a task taking up several weeks and requiring great gifts of diplomacy.[27] It is doubtful if he had ever previously moved in such exalted circles, communicating with ambassadors and government ministers, yet despite having no models to guide him, such as contact with agents engaged in similar tasks, he seems to have impressed those he met.[28]

---

24. Darlow, *Letters of George Borrow*, p. 431.

25. Darlow, *Letters of George Borrow*, pp. 271 and 317.

26. This did not prevent the subcommittee from referring to Borrow's *Mission in Spain* in a formal resolution. Darlow, *Letters of George Borrow*, p. 450.

27. Herbert Jenkins, *Life of George Borrow*, 2nd ed. (London: John Murray, 1924), p.180.

28. In general there is only Borrow's word for it, but others did comment on their

Second, he had to be sure of his text, and this was always a matter for delicate negotiation between the Bible Society and Bible translators or advisers. In the case of the Manchu New Testament, although the tsar's imprimatur was essential, the choice of text for the Manchu scriptures did not have political implications. Much time however was spent, initially by William Swan, with Borrow's assistance, in transcribing Poirot's incomplete version of the Old Testament and the only two books available of the New Testament—the Gospel of St. Matthew and Acts. In the light of Borrow's comments on this version, the Bible Society asked him to "make a fresh report of the merits of Lipoftsoff's Manchou version of the New Testament",[29] but meanwhile Borrow had already secured permission to print from the Russian minister of the interior.

In Spain, on the other hand, the question of the text to be used was complicated by the Catholic authorities' adamant refusal to print the Scriptures without the Apocrypha, and without note or comment. At the same time, the political situation there was far more volatile and dangerous, so that any success achieved was always in danger of being reversed. Thus, no sooner had Borrow secured permission to print from Prime Minister Mendizábal than the latter resigned, and negotiations—this time with the new government—had to begin all over again. Fortunately, Borrow was able to enlist the support of George Villiers, the ambassador to Spain, and eventually permission was granted. All was not plain sailing, however, for in August 1836 the revolution of La Granja broke out, and it was not until early April 1837 that printing of five thousand copies of the New Testament in Spanish was finally completed.[30]

Borrow's third task was to commission printers and bookbinders to produce his Bible texts. He had had no direct experience of printing and publishing before he went to Russia, and the advice and information he had been led to expect from Isaac Jacob Schmidt, one of the Society's contacts in St Petersburg, was not forthcoming.[31] What is noteworthy about Borrow's approach to this task is his energy and zeal in sizing up what needed to be done and then putting appropriate measures into practice. He gave particular attention to paper quality and value for money, travelling three times to the paper mill at Peterhof some thirty kilometres

---

favorable impression. These included GeorgeVilliers and John Brackenbury, the British consul at Cadiz, who wrote to Brandram about Borrow in very cordial terms. On these issues, see Knapp, *Life*, vol. 1, pp. 254-55, 283, and 325-27.

29. Darlow, *Letters of George Borrow*, p. 28, 41. Unfortunately, Borrow's report does not seem to have survived.

30. Jenkins, *Life*, pp. 191-95.

31. Darlow, *Letters of George Borrow*, p. 29.

distant to discuss what was available,[32] and when not satisfied, having himself driven to "all the places in the vicinity of Petersburg where paper is made."[33] Ultimately, he appears to have secured paper at 25 rubles a ream, instead of the 75 or 100 originally quoted. He was equally thorough in his concern for typography in Manchu, and showed himself sensitive to the cultural impact of the finished work on its target readership, in terms of overall design and appearance. The Committee at one stage grew restive at the apparent delays, and asked what Borrow was doing. Borrow responded in a letter to Jowett of 8 [old style] October 1834,[34] firing off a passionately argued defence of his activities and progress. He had even learned to set up type in Manchu and prided himself on the accuracy of his proofreading.

Borrow was to show similar high standards in his editing of the New Testament in Spain. Although the text chosen was that of Scio, based on the Vulgate, Borrow was unsparing in his criticism of the editions he had had to use, which were printed in London:

> ...the work abounds in errors of every kind and reflects little credit on the person who edited it; no systematic order is observed either in the orthography or the use of accents or capitals, and whole sentences frequently appear in a mangled and mutilated state which renders them unintelligible.[35]

As for his own editorial work — he wrote that the edition had been "printed on the best paper, and no pains have been spared, at least on my part, to render it as correct as possible, having read every proof-sheet three times".[36]

This, then, is the submissive Borrow, faithfully performing the editorial tasks his employers required. But now comes the question of distribution. In Russia, Borrow had longed to take his Manchu Testaments to China, but the tsar refused him a visa to Siberia, and the idea had to be dropped — a bitter disappointment that only faded away after many years.[37] In Spain,

32. Darlow, *Letters of George Borrow*, p. 44.
33. Darlow, *Letters of George Borrow*, p. 47.
34. Darlow, *Letters of George Borrow*, pp. 55-63.
35. Darlow, *Letters of George Borrow*, p. 206.
36. Darlow, *Letters of George Borrow*, p. 206.
37. With some justification, Borrow resented a comment by Brandram in his 14 July 1838 letter internally quoted by Darlow: "I trust that we shall not easily forget your services in St. Petersburgh; but suffer me to remind you that when you came to the point of *distribution*, your success ended". See Darlow, *Letters of George Borrow*, p. 332. He must also have resented the figures suggesting that Graydon had been far more successful in the number of Bibles and Testaments distributed than he himself had been. Statistics are difficult to be sure of, given the number of times that Borrow's stocks of Testaments were impounded, but detailed figures are given in Jenkins, *Life*, p. 327. Jenkins makes the fair point that Graydon had kept to the towns and cities on

on the other hand, although the Bible Society agreed to Borrow's plans for distribution, the country was torn by ferocious civil strife (the Carlist wars), travel was extremely dangerous, and the Scriptures were being distributed in the teeth of furious opposition from the church authorities. As Kent Eaton has mentioned in his study of Brethren missions to Spain, even seminary students were forbidden to possess their own Bible. And the missionary George Lawrence noted:

> I was brought before the magistrates for giving a bible to a young priest nearly 5 years ago. The Lord delivered me out of their hands, but I never knew what became of the young man. I found him, and he was glad to see me. His mother said I had been his ruin. It appears that when he went back to college it was soon known that he had a Bible. He was brought before the bishop. It was proved that he had received and had been reading a Bible, and he was at once struck off the rolls from being a priest. He is now a chocolate maker...[38]

Such testimonies provide a valuable context for the study of Borrow's experiences thirty years earlier. Small wonder that in Spain, Borrow and his helpers were more than once thrown into jail.

As one might expect, it is in the matter of distribution that the *un*submissive Borrow comes to the fore, where he has the greatest freedom to work out the details of his personal agenda, within the broader framework agreed to by the Society. Toward the end of his St. Petersburg period, for example, in August 1835, he takes time off to visit Moscow in order to meet with Gypsies. He does not mention this journey in his letter to Jowett of 12 August 1835, or ask permission to incur the extra expense, but his experience takes up four printed pages in one of the remarkable reports he wrote for the Bible Society, dated September 1835.[39] It is typical of Borrow that he dwells on the theme of Russian Gypsies with apparently no perception of its relevance or otherwise to the Society's concerns! He comments on the wonderful Gypsy choirs of Moscow, and the fact that Gypsy women married into the highest levels of society. But what were the reverend gentlemen at Earl Street to make of the "great number of low, vulgar, and profligate females who sing in taverns...and whose husbands and male

---

the south [and east] coast, whereas Borrow had "circulated his books largely among villages and hamlets... He had gone out into the highways, risking his life at every turn, penetrating into bandit-infested provinces in the throes of civil war".

38. George Lawrence, *The Gospel in Spain, Some Accounts of Labours in that Country from Letters of Various Servants of the Lord* (London: Yapp and Hawkins, 1872), p.3, quoted from Kent Eaton, "The Awakening of Protestant Interest in Spain as a Mission Field", pt. 2, in *George Borrow Bulletin*, no. 27 (Fall 2003 [2004]), pp. 56-57. Lawrence was apparently describing events of the 1860s.

39. Darlow, *Letters of George Borrow*, pp. 92-95.

connections subsist by horse-jobbing and such kinds of low traffic"? Borrow justifies his fascination with low life by his reaction: "I...spoke to them upon their sinful manner of living, upon the advent and suffering of Christ Jesus". The Committee at Earl Street must have let it pass, but without forgetting that "we are not preachers".

This was the first of his unscheduled absences from duty, though it would be unreasonable to deny him a holiday after a strenuous two years. The second egregious example is his departure for "Barbary", or Morocco, described in the closing chapters of *The Bible in Spain*. Again, he does not seem to have asked permission from the Bible Society to leave Spain for six weeks, but simply told Brandram what he intended to do, shortly before his departure. His next letter of 4 September, addressed from Tangiers, which had no postal service to any part of the world, did not reach Brandram until 7 October! Borrow dresses up his escapade with an account of his plan to take spare copies of the Spanish Scriptures "to the Christian families established on the sea-coast of Barbary...the Spanish language being in general use among them", yet it is clear that he was pursuing a private agenda, a dream of discovery about Gypsies, Jews, and Moors.[40] This is only really known about from chapters 51 to 57 of *The Bible in Spain*, which also include an account of his unscheduled visit to Gibraltar.

If these were unscheduled and unapproved absences, there also seemed to be unscheduled delays in getting from A to B. One thinks especially of the ten days Borrow spent in the frontier town of Badajóz, in January 1836, consorting with Gypsies, as he describes in chapter 9 of *The Bible in Spain*. It was not until July 1836 that he sent Brandram an account that he thought might serve for the Society's *Monthly Extracts*.[41] As with his trip to Moscow, Borrow expands on the Romany way of life, and seems oblivious to the manner in which he is demonstrating his own infatuation with the Gypsies. Again, there is a veneer of sacred purpose: "I wished to become better acquainted with their condition and manners, and above all to speak to them about Christ and His Word". The real lure, however, is in the rabble he meets: "so much squalidness, dirt and misery I had never before seen...the Gypsy of Spain is a cheat in the market-place, a brigand and murderer on the high-road, and a drunkard in the wine-shop, and his wife is a harlot and thief on all times and occasions".[42] These passages may never have been published in the *Monthly Extracts*, but what an odd mixture they present of unspoken self-aggrandisement on the one hand and utter fascination with these wild people on the other. The unspoken

---

40. Darlow, *Letters of George Borrow*, p. 430.
41. Darlow, *Letters of George Borrow*, pp. 143-44, 167-71.
42. Darlow, *Letters of George Borrow*, pp. 168-69.

comment here alerts the reader that Borrow is capable of standing up to these rogues and villains without coming to harm or being robbed, that he has a special authority over them. Not until the publication of *The Zincali* in 1841, does one discover more.[43]

A similar unscheduled delay occurred when Borrow visited Córdoba for eleven days in December 1836. In his letters to the Bible Society he skates over his stay there: "I reached Cordova in three days, attended by the old Italian whom I mentioned... From Cordova I have ridden to Madrid in the company of a *contrabandista*, or smuggler".[44] In *The Bible in Spain*, however, this stay occupies two whole chapters, 16 and 17, and in *The Zincali*, there are various references to Córdoba, including some curious paragraphs on the frequent visits he had from an aged ecclesiastic, who had been an inquisitor.[45] One particular scene brings the opposite poles of his personality together: amidst a group of more than twenty Gypsies, "assembled in a long low room on the ground floor, in a dark alley or court in the old gloomy town of Cordova", "gathered round a huge brasero of flaming charcoal", Borrow proposes that they "endeavour to turn into the Calo language some pieces of devotion", and they "forthwith proceeded to the translation of the Apostles' creed".[46] Borrow makes no secret of the Gypsies' lawlessness and deceitful ways, and has no illusions as to their lack of response: "I cannot say that I experienced much success in my endeavours...being fully acquainted with the stony nature of the ground on which I was employed".[47] Yet he offers them the Apostle's Creed, that extraordinary controlling statement of Christian faith, demanding obedience. And he echoes Quaker beliefs in his assertion that "no individual, however wicked and hardened, is utterly *godless*".[48]

The third form of disobedience has already been touched on—his propensity to preach rather than to limit himself to distribution, and his desire to reveal his passionate anti-Catholicism. Much as Borrow deplored Graydon's activities, he resembled his rival far more closely than he knew! And like Graydon, he indulged in publicity of a kind hardly known at the time—posters and handbills in bright colours, a sandwich man

43. See George Borrow, *The Zincali; or, An Account of the Gypsies of Spain, with an original collection of their Songs and Poetry, and a copious Dictionary of their Language*, 2 vols. (London: John Murray, 1841). See also the 1901 "definitive edition" of *The Zincali* (London: John Murray, 1901), pt. 2, ch. 1, pp. 177-93.

44. Darlow, *Letters of George Borrow*, p. 194.

45. Borrow, *The Zincali*, pp. 133-34.

46. Borrow, *The Zincali*, pp. 201-202. The version of the Creed is reproduced in *caló* with a parallel English translation on pp. 418-19.

47. Borrow, *The Zincali*, p. 274.

48. Borrow, *The Zincali*, p. 275. Compare the traditional Quaker belief that "there is that of God in every man".

bearing a placard, and violent letters to the press inveighing against the Catholic church and the church authorities.[49] These activities naturally stirred up trouble, and the Committee, in the beginning moved to merriment, soon had misgivings: Borrow had been "swooped upon" by the priests and ordered to sell no more New Testaments. Mr. Brandram wrote: "we all deeply feel that we cannot be good judges here of what it is best to do in Madrid; but at the same time some did think your tricoloured placards and your placard-bearer were somewhat calculated to provoke what has occurred". [50] Thereafter, it seems clear that Borrow relied less on the printed word to relay his messages, and much more on a team of helpers, often people in humble circumstances, to engage in the task of distribution.

Another important aspect of Borrow's "disobedience" concerns the intrusion of personal desires in the map of his travels, particularly in his wish to go to the furthest reaches of the wilds of Spain, and to leave a Testament at Finisterre in the far northwest of Galicia. Borrow had written to Brandram setting out his plans on 14 January 1837: "I will ride forth from Madrid into the wildest parts of Spain, where the Word is most wanted, and where it seems next to an impossibility to introduce it". To this, Brandram had felt bound to convey the Committee's reaction: "You will see we do not quite enter into your plans. On hearing them a general and simultaneous question was asked. Can the people in these wilds read"? [51] As a result of his proposal, Borrow received qualified approval to make contact with the principal booksellers in the different towns of the northern and middle provinces of Spain, but no specific approval to go to Finisterre. He was able to strike up good relations with booksellers, most notably with Rey Romero in Santiago, and to establish local depots, but much of his travel was through sparsely populated areas, where any significant amount of distribution was out of the question, and indeed where travellers faced real danger from the local inhabitants. One only has to read accounts of shipwrecks on the Costa da Muerte, the Coast of Death, to understand how primitive these remote communities were.

Finally, there were Borrow's delaying tactics in the face of the Society's increasingly urgent requests for him to finish his work and come home immediately. Borrow was in beautiful Seville, basking in the sunshine, collecting materials for *The Zincali*, and spending "the greater part of each

---

49. Darlow, *Letters of George Borrow*, pp. 265-70, 274, and 315. "Resolved that Mr. Borrow be requested not to repeat the advertisement contained in the *Correo Nacional*... and that he be cautioned how he commits this Society by advertisements of a similar character".

50. Darlow, *Letters of George Borrow*, pp. 277-78, 281.

51. Darlow, *Letters of George Borrow*, pp. 198-201.

day in study, or in that half dreamy state of inactivity which is the natural effect of the influence of a warm climate".[52] One often marvels at how quickly letters were exchanged at a time before the penny post had come to Britain and before modern mailing systems were introduced elsewhere. Borrow, however, was a master at delaying his response. A letter would often be promptly dispatched but not followed by one from Borrow in return. He had already departed for Barbary when the Committee requested him "to return without loss of time to this Country". A letter sent in August 1839 he of course did not see until his return to Cadiz on 21 September.

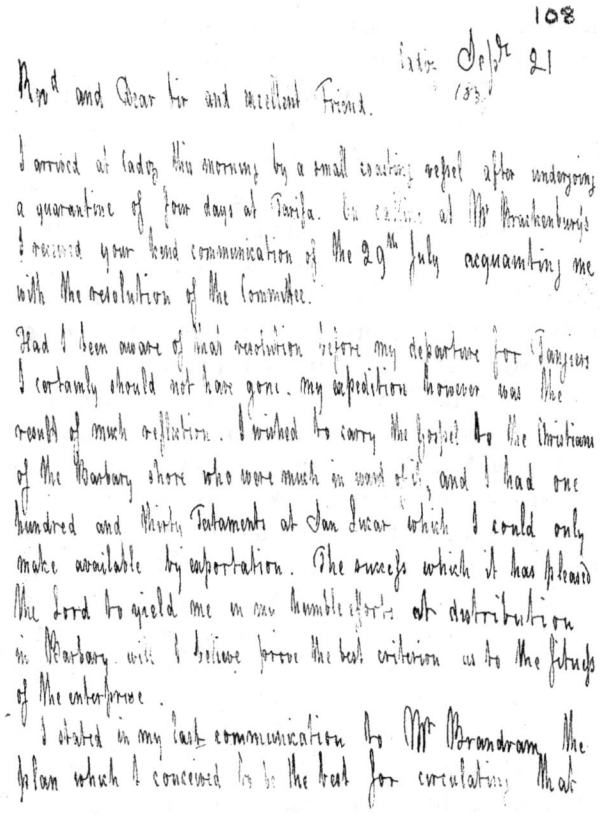

Picture 33. *Letter from George Borrow, Cadiz, 21 September 1839.* Specimen courtesy of BFBS Archives, Cambridge University Library

52. George Borrow, *The Bible in Spain; or, the Journeys, Adventures, and Imprisonments of an Englishman, in an Attempt to Circulate the Scriptures in the Peninsula*, 3 vols. (London: John Murray, 1843). The quotation here is taken from the later one-volume "definitive edition" of *The Bible in Spain* (London: John Murray, 1899), pp. 666-67. What would the Committee have thought of their energetic agent?

His response of the same date is a masterpiece of prevarication. He assures the Committee that he wishes to return to England as soon as possible, but then lists a number of obstacles. He adds disarmingly: "What should induce me to stay in Spain, as you appear to suppose I intend"?[53] He then reverts to his own agenda: "It is my intention in a few days to depart from hence on my expedition". He in fact returned to Seville, from where he wrote privately to Brandram that he planned to depart for La Mancha, "where I shall take up my abode for a few weeks" with a view to distributing Testaments to be sent him from Madrid. "I shall then move upon Madrid… I then purpose to make for France, passing through Saragossa…in which place I hope to accomplish some good in the Lord's cause. This is the outline of my plan, which I shall attempt to put into execution without delay".[54]

On 7 October, BFBS Secretary George Browne wrote: "The books you speak of as at Seville may be sent to Gibraltar, rather than to England, as well as any books you may deem it expedient or find it necessary to bring out of the country. As soon as your arrangements are completed, we shall look for the pleasure of seeing you in this country".[55] Nothing happened, however, for Borrow remained in Seville and even, briefly, from 24 to 25 November, spent time in jail there, following a dispute over his passport. And although Borrow had marked his letter of 29 September "private", it appears that it was read out to the subcommittee at its meeting on 1 November. By this time they had had enough: "resolved that this Sub-Committee cannot recommend to the General Committee to engage the further services of Mr. Borrow until he shall have returned to this Country from his Mission in Spain".[56] Borrow was released from prison by 26 November, and only then departed for Madrid, his object being to "demand redress" for his imprisonment, and "to make preparations for leaving Spain as soon as possible. There is nothing more to be done here for the present in the cause of the Gospel".[57] He does not acknowledge that the Bible Society had asked him to desist four months earlier, but at least he says no more of his proposed "expedition".

Borrow's original plans for leaving Spain via Zaragoza and France were not put into effect either. Instead, after three weeks in Madrid making representations about his imprisonment through the Hon. George S. S. Jerningham, first secretary of the legation, Borrow informed Brandram, in an extraordinary letter written on Christmas Eve 1839, that he had told

53. Darlow, *Letters of George Borrow*, p. 442.
54. Darlow, *Letters of George Borrow*, pp. 443-47.
55. Darlow, *Letters of George Borrow*, p. 450.
56. Darlow, *Letters of George Borrow*, p. 450.
57. Darlow, *Letters of George Borrow*, pp. 454-55.

Jerningham "that for some time past I have relinquished distributing the Scriptures in Spain—which is the truth... I shall return to England as soon as I can obtain some redress for this affair. It is then my intention to attempt to obtain an interview with some of the members of the House of Lords".[58] One is left open-mouthed at his effrontery! What exactly was the Society paying him for, at this stage? He returned to Seville on 2 January 1840, apparently impervious to the danger signals emanating from Earl Street. On 10 January 1840 came yet another resolution: "this Sub-Committee having referred to their Resolution of July 29th last year, respecting the recall of Mr. Borrow from Spain—which was confirmed at a Meeting of the Committee, held Aug. 5th—do again recommend to the General Committee to request him to return to this country without further delay". Unfortunately, Brandram, having noted that Borrow's letter of 2 January showed that he intended to return, informed Borrow of the resolution but did not formally transmit it to him, so that it did not have the impact intended.[59]

More than two months later, on 18 March 1840, Borrow, still in Seville, wrote a detailed explanation, which reads like a litany of excuses, describing why he did not return to England immediately after his departure from Madrid.[60] It appears that letters to and from the Society had genuinely gone astray, and Borrow says that "[for] upwards of five months" he has not heard a word from England in reply to the seven he had addressed to Earl Street. It appears, too, that between January and March he had been in correspondence with Brackenbury, the consul, about the possibility of getting married in Spain. In fact it was not possible for a Protestant marriage to be solemnized in Spain—but Borrow said nothing of his private affairs to the Bible Society. He at last promised to embark "on the third of next month", which indeed he did, with his future wife Mary Clarke, her daughter Henrietta, Henrietta's dog Craffs, his Moroccan Jewish manservant Hayim ben Attar, and—apparently by a later boat—his Arab horse Sidi Habismilk.[61] He had written to Brandram, "I wish much to spend the remaining years of my life in the northern parts of China... I hope yet to die in the cause of my Redeemer".[62] Alas, it was

---

58. Darlow, *Letters of George Borrow*, pp. 455-59. See also Ann M. Ridler, "George Borrow in Seville, Granada and Córdoba", *George Borrow Bulletin* 24 (2002), pp. 54-69. There is a delectable account of Borrow's imprisonment in a Spanish-language article by Professor Antonio Giménez Cruz: "La prisión de George Borrow en Sevilla", *Historia* 16, año XI, n° 120 (abril 1986), which provides a revealing insight into the official Spanish view of Borrow's behaviour and situation.

59. Darlow, *Letters of George Borrow*, p. 462.
60. Darlow, *Letters of George Borrow*, p. 463.
61. *George Borrow Bulletin* 24 (2002), p. 69 n. 28.
62. Darlow, *Letters of George Borrow*, p. 463.

not to be, and Borrow was to live the rest of his life subject only to the constraints of his marriage, and the exigencies of his writing, his publisher, and his public.

As Darlow notes, members of the Committee were in many ways unfair to Borrow in their partiality for Graydon, and can have had little practical awareness of the physical dangers and privations to which Borrow was exposed on his travels. Even his horses could not cope with conditions in Galicia. The minutes of the various Committees are terse and give no indication of the detail of discussions, so that one cannot know how far Borrow had been briefed on his duties, or what might be expected, whether in St. Petersburg or in Spain, though the Committee did make available introductions to persons of consequence. The hardships of travel by sea or land and the vast distances to be covered in Russia or Spain perhaps meant little to them. Yet as late as 1854, Borrow could still speak of the Society with affection:

> he went to Spain with the colours of that society on his hat — oh! The blood glows in his veins! Oh! The marrow awakes in his old bones [he was only 51] when he thinks of what he accomplished in Spain in the cause of religion and civilisation with the colours of that society in his hat, and its weapon in his hand, even the sword of the word of God! ...he bade it adieu with feelings of love and admiration.[63]

As for the Bible Society, whatever Borrow's wayward characteristics, they can only have been delighted at the publicity they gained through the success of *The Bible in Spain*. Borrow's letters to the Society are still the most remarkable sequence of communications ever sent to any public body, and the work that sprang from them remains enthralling for the depth and excitement of its creative energy. And Borrow's journeys fascinate the reader as every departure resembles the throw of a dice, and every page opens up new and unexpected discoveries and perceptions.

---

63. George Borrow, *The Romany Rye: A Sequel to "Lavengro"*, 2 vols. (London: John Murray, 1857). The quotation here is from the later "definitive edition" (London: John Murray, 1900), pp. 312-13.

The Bible in Spain and Gibraltar

Sue Jackson

In 1807, the British and Foreign Bible Society first established links with Gibraltar when it sent out a supply of English and Spanish Scriptures to two Methodists, Michael Caulfield and Thomas Davis. Caulfield and Davis were leaders in the Methodist church there, which had suffered severe persecution from the authorities, as well as the loss of their long-awaited first minister, who had died of yellow fever just a few weeks after arriving. Despite these difficulties and the fact that they both held full-time jobs, Davis and Caulfield continued the work of evangelism and tried to expand their efforts with the help of the Bible Society. The English Scriptures were for the British soldiers and sailors; the Spanish for the Spanish-speaking population of the Rock and also for distribution, whenever possible, in Spain.

Picture 34. *Gibraltar from the North-West, 1845*. Print from the private collection of John Dean.

Eventually other Methodist ministers were sent to Gibraltar, and they helped in the work of distribution. After the Methodist mission house was built in 1810, a depository was maintained there. James Gill, the Methodist minister in 1812, wrote to inform the Bible Society that "the distribution of the scriptures has been a principal cause in this place of the success of my Mission".[1] He reported that many soldiers, after receiving copies of the Bible, had become regular in their attendance at the church. Spanish, Portuguese, and Italian Bibles had also been distributed and received with much joy and gratitude. As it became known that Bibles were available, local people went to the mission house to ask for copies. Later, visitors from Spain and elsewhere also called upon the mission for Bibles. Supplies were given to anyone willing to help in the work of distribution. One such was Carolina Nicklin, a shopkeeper. Another was Captain John Gourly of the Royal Navy who wrote that "this unsettled way of life has given me many, very many opportunities of scattering the Scriptures far and wide".[2] Gourly was not a Methodist, but reported that "we are fellow servants and have one master and his glory is our chief desire".[3] Despite this ecumenical spirit from individuals, the relationship between Methodism and the Church of England in Gibraltar was poor at this time. Garrison chaplains did their best to hinder Methodist work in any way they could.

In 1821, Lieutenant John Bailey of the Royal Navy, who was the agent of transports at Gibraltar, began to take a leading role in the work of Bible distribution. Like Gourly, he was not a member of the Methodist church, but worshipped there frequently and worked tirelessly to distribute the Scriptures, even maintaining a depository in his own home. Through his efforts a corresponding committee was formed. It was not possible to start an auxiliary society without the governor's patronage, and the governor had given his support to the garrison chaplain's work for the Society for Promoting Christian Knowledge. Nevertheless, the formation of the corresponding committee led to "a more systematic and regular constitution", which greatly pleased the Bible Society, for it had referred to previous efforts in Gibraltar as "desultory and occasional".[4] Soon the Methodists also formed a Bethel Society, which organized preaching on board ships in the bay of Gibraltar. This activity presented good opportunities for distributing Scriptures.

---

1. James Gill to the BFBS, 16 September 1812, BFBS Correspondence Books, no. 5, pp. 28-32 (BSA/D1/5/5).
2. John Gourly to J. Tarn, 30 September 1809, BFBS Home Correspondence Inwards (BSA/D1/1/4).
3. John Gourly to [Mary Grey], 7 July 1809, BFBS Home Correspondence Inwards (BSA/D1/1/4).
4. *Eighteenth Report of the BFBS* (London, 1822), p. lviii.

After Bailey left Gibraltar in 1825, the work of the corresponding committee continued. New members came forward including Carolina Nicklin, the only woman on the committee, and Dr. John Hennen, the principal medical officer in Gibraltar. Although he too was not a Methodist, Hennen actively supported the Methodists' work and gave his professional services free to the ministers and their families. In 1828, when a yellow fever epidemic caused his death and that of several other members of the committee, including the Methodist minister William Barber, the work of distribution was temporarily suspended. The following year it was revived by Joseph Stinson, the new minister, and a colporteur was appointed to visit people in their homes and to distribute books to ships in the bay.

Throughout these early years, every opportunity had been taken to get Bibles into Spain itself, but the political and religious situation there made such activity virtually impossible, with the exception of small numbers of copies taken in by individuals travelling into Spain. By the 1830s, however, there were hopes for change. Spain was in a state of civil war over the succession to the throne. More liberal factions were emerging and the power and authority of the Roman Catholic church had been eroded. It was in this context that three men began to work in Spain: George Borrow, Lieutenant James Newenham Graydon, and William Harris Rule.

The first to enter the country was Graydon, who spoke Spanish and had offered his services to the Bible Society. Graydon had some private means and was willing to work without a salary as long as his expenses were paid and Bibles were supplied for distribution. At first he was rather discouraged by the difficulties he encountered, including the complete ban on the importation of books printed outside Spain. This ban of course included Bibles. However, a change of Spanish government and the hope that its policies might be different, led Graydon to believe he could solve the problem of the ban by printing Bibles himself. In 1836 he began to do this in Barcelona, claiming that the authorities in Madrid had given him informal, verbal permission to do so. By this time the Bible Society had appointed George Borrow as their paid agent in Spain. Borrow travelled to Madrid where he too gained permission to print Bibles, and began to do so in the same year 1836. All this Bible Society printing was undertaken despite the fact that Spanish law still prohibited the publication of Bibles without notes. As the printing runs were completed, the Bibles were put into circulation, with both Borrow and Graydon travelling around the country to distribute them.

Meanwhile, William Rule, Methodist minister in Gibraltar at the time, had been considering the possibility of founding a Protestant mission in Spain. Such a mission most certainly would have been against Spanish law, but Rule, like Borrow and Graydon, was hopeful that the laws would change. After exploratory excursions into Spain, Rule chose Cádiz for his base of operations because it was a busy port frequently visited by British and American ships. Rule was aware of the difficulties he might encounter, for he had already been expelled from San Roque, not far from Gibraltar, after holding meetings and distributing Bibles there. However, the Methodist authorities gave permission for an attempt to be made, and Rule travelled to Cádiz with James Lyon, a lay assistant, who was to undertake the actual work. Lyon preached in the bay to sailors, made contact with Spaniards, distributed Bibles, and eventually opened a mission school. Later Rule himself took over the work.

It is beyond the scope of this article to describe the work of these three men in detail, but perhaps the fact that all three were working in Spain at the same time proved too much for the Spanish authorities. Despite the changes in Spain because of the more liberal factions and the interest in reforming the Catholic church, the practice of Catholicism itself was not threatened from within, and Spain remained united enough to deal with any outside threats. Perhaps it is not surprising then that all three men were forced to leave the country. Borrow, who was briefly imprisoned, tended to blame his difficulties on Rule and Graydon, a view that many of his biographers share. Some of Borrow's biographers have also claimed that Graydon worked from Gibraltar, which was never the case.[5] All three men had acted rather incautiously at times, and each had broken Spanish law. Nevertheless, a good number of Scriptures were distributed during the time they spent in Spain. In 1838, however, a royal order was passed stating that all such Scriptures were to be seized, packed, and sealed for exportation. A small number of converts in Cádiz continued to meet after Rule was expelled from Spain, and he wrote them a weekly pastoral letter from Gibraltar.

The British authorities knew about the events in Spain, and the Foreign Office informed the Bible Society that it was aware the agents could "scarcely take a step without infringing some existing Law of Spain". At the same time, the Foreign Office warned the Society that if its representatives did act unlawfully it would be "impossible for the British Minister at Madrid successfully to defend them with the Spanish Government, or to afford them...protection".[6] It was clear that for the time being the

---

5. See William Canton, *A History of the British and Foreign Bible Society*, 5 vols. (London: John Murray, 1904–1910), vol. 2. p. 236; David Williams, *A World of His Own: The Double Life of George Borrow* (Oxford: Oxford University Press, 1982), p. 98; Herbert Jenkins, *The Life of George Borrow* (London: John Murray, 1924), p. 212; and William I. Knapp, *Life, Writings and Correspondence of George Borrow* (London: John Murray, 1899), vol. 1. p. 277.

6. This Foreign Office warning is quoted internally in T. H. Darlow, ed., *Letters of George Borrow to the British and Foreign Bible Society* (London: Hodder and Stoughton, 1911), p. 358.

work in Spain had to end, and even the work of distribution in Gibraltar ceased.

In 1845, the corresponding committee was revived by a new Methodist minister, Thomas Hull. By then a Presbyterian church had also been formed in Gibraltar and its minister, William Strauchan, joined the committee. The ministers of both churches continued to work together in this way for many years. A new depository was opened, and an advertisement was placed in the *Gibraltar Chronicle* to say that Bibles were for sale there.[7] In 1846, committee members formed themselves into small groups to visit ships in the bay on a regular basis.

In its correspondence with Thomas Hull, the Bible Society sought his opinion about renewed Bible work in Spain. Visitors from Gibraltar were taking Scriptures into Spain whenever they could do so and invariably found them to be well received. Hull thought it might be possible to work in Spain again and to print Bibles there. So the Bible Society appointed the Rev. Dr. James Thomson for two years, but the results were disappointing, as the Bible Society reported in its annual *Report*:

> In the first two years he travelled extensively, and endeavoured to get the Scriptures printed in the different towns in Spain, but uniformly failed. Arrangements were several times all but completed, when some evil influence interposed, and deterred the printer from proceeding. The importation of copies has been found all but an impossibility.[8]

In 1854 a revolution took place in Spain, which again raised the hopes of the corresponding committee in Gibraltar. Its members went into frantic action as all border restrictions were removed for a time and it became easy to get scriptures into Spain. All available copies were gathered together and a colporteur, Martin Escalante, was appointed to distribute them. The Methodist minister, George Alton, suggested that someone should be appointed to investigate the situation in Spain. The Bible Society responded by asking him to take on the assignment. He was a fluent Spanish speaker and the local committee wrote a glowing report on his suitability for the work. Eventually an agreement was reached between the Methodist Missionary Society and the Bible Society so that Alton could be released for the work. He and Escalante travelled into Spain together on an exploratory mission. The mission was not easy as cholera was raging in many parts of the country, and cordons around some areas limited where they could travel. Eventually arrangements were made for Alton to print some ten thousand Scriptures in Madrid. There was, of course, opposition to this work from Catholic priests, and Alton was occasionally away from

---

7. *Gibraltar Chronicle*, 22 September 1845.
8. *Forty-fifth Report of the BFBS* (London, 1849), p. xc.

Madrid on journeys to Gibraltar, where he still had some duties. It was not an easy time for him. He was also separated from his family who remained in Gibraltar. Whilst in Madrid, Alton began working on a revision of the Bible Society's Spanish version of the Bible. In 1855 he travelled to England to discuss the work with the Bible Society. He was authorized to seek official permission to circulate the Bibles once printing was finished and, if all went well, to continue printing.

All did not go well. Alton found upon his return to Gibraltar that one of his children had died during his absence. The printing in Madrid had been completed, but he encountered opposition from the church on the grounds that the Bibles had been printed without notes, which was contrary to the law. There was support from the civil authorities, but delicate negotiations had to be undertaken. It was a very stressful time for Alton, who was well aware of the need for caution and prudence. In May 1856 he moved his family to Madrid, but in August another revolution occurred, martial law was declared, and Alton realized he must leave Spain. He made arrangements with the printer, José Alegría, to store the Scriptures. However, their departure was delayed by the illness of their son George, who had typhoid. Once he was well enough to travel, the family fled for Valencia where they had to wait eight days for a steamer. Once on board, Amy Alton went into premature labour, giving birth to twins in the absence of a doctor or nurse. One twin, the little girl, survived, but the boy died some weeks later. Altogether the Altons lost seven of the ten children born during these years in Gibraltar.

Once again the door seemed to have closed on Spain but not entirely because the committee in Gibraltar, now described as an auxiliary, carried on its work and even managed to get some Scriptures into Spain. Alton avoided publicizing this work, explaining:

> Had I however been writing details of these efforts to everyone it would long ago have been impossible to do anything… Almost anything will be permitted by Spaniards provided what they call a 'scandal' is avoided.[9]

Somehow he managed to get thousands of Scriptures into Spain. Martin Escalante helped by continuing with the work of distribution in Gibraltar town and on board ships in the bay, and he also attended fairs in Spain itself.

Opposition to Protestant work in Spain continued. One Spanish Protestant, Francisco de Paula Ruet, was exiled from Spain where he had been preaching. In 1857 he went to Gibraltar and began Spanish preaching in the Presbyterian church. Such preaching already took place in the Methodist

---

9. Alton, 14 August 1857, Wesleyan Methodist Missionary Society Correspondence, Box 71, microfiche 700, no. 47 (London, School of Oriental and African Studies).

church where there was also a thriving mission school. The Bible Society supported this work by making regular grants of scriptures for the children.

In May 1859, the colporteur Martin Escalante was arrested in Spain and charged with "circulating the Scriptures printed in England, without notes, with a view to subvert the religion of the country—and for a second time".[10] The Bible Society was informed and responded with sympathy for his plight but was concerned that he had been breaking the law, which they feared would damage the Society's reputation. Escalante's work had been supervised from Gibraltar, but the Bible Society had been aware of his activities and had been informed of his earlier brief imprisonment.

It was not an easy situation for anyone, particularly Escalante, who languished in prison until his case was finally heard in December 1859. He was found guilty and sentenced to nine years' penal servitude. By then his health had deteriorated to such an extent that he was released on bail under house arrest but was expected to pay the expenses of his two guards. It was a very expensive time, paying for Escalante's needs in prison whilst continuing to pay his salary to his family, who would have been destitute without it. An appeal was lodged, and finally, a year after his arrest, he was acquitted. He returned to Gibraltar, but the Bible Society made it clear that he was not to do any more work in Spain. Unfortunately, this curtailment of his duties meant it was difficult to justify his salary, which was halved. This then proved insufficient for his needs, and the economic climate in Gibraltar made it difficult for him to find other work. As a result, Escalante asked the auxiliary for six months' salary in advance to enable him to move his family to Lisbon. Although this was given, Escalante in the end returned to Spain, rejoined the Catholic church, and denounced many of his Protestant contacts there, even though he knew only too well what the consequences were likely to be.

By then attitudes were hardening throughout Spain, and several Spanish Protestants were arrested: Manuel Matamoros, José Alhama, and Manuel Trigo amongst them. They were imprisoned in Granada and, in due course, were sentenced to long years of penal servitude. There was an international outcry at the severity of the sentences, and eventually, after the men had spent two and a half years in prison, the sentences were commuted to exile. In May 1863, the men and members of their families were taken from Málaga by the warship *Alerta* to Gibraltar. A number of them stayed in Gibraltar for several years, where they were joined by

---

10. Copy of letter from Warden in Gibraltar to S. Bergne, 28 June 1859, Methodist Church Archives, Gibraltar.

another Spaniard, Juan Cabrera, who feared for his safety in Spain in case it was known that he had corresponded with some of those exiled.

In 1868 yet another revolution occurred in Spain. This time there was hope that religious toleration would be granted, although everyone responded to the news cautiously at first. Some of the Spanish exiles from Gibraltar met with General Prim, one of the leaders of the revolution, who assured them that they were at liberty to return to Spain and preach there, which is exactly what they did. Some of them proceeded to found Protestant churches. In 1894, Cabrera, who remained a leading Spanish Protestant until his death in 1916, was consecrated as the first bishop of the Reformed Spanish church.

In January 1869, the Bible Society appointed the Reverend J. G. Curie as its agent in Spain. He opened a central depot in Madrid and established others around the country, appointing colporteurs to help with the work of distribution. The law still prohibited the importation of books printed outside Spain, and the Bible Society was anxious not to break any laws. However, the books that George Alton had printed, at such cost to himself and his family, were still safe and were now put into circulation. Soon an extensive printing programme began to ensure that a steady supply of Scriptures was available.

These developments meant that Gibraltar was no longer of strategic importance in the task of getting Scriptures into Spain, but work in Gibraltar itself continued. In 1871, the Presbyterian minister John Coventry made various suggestions about improving the work there. So, in February 1872, Richard Corfield, who had succeeded Curie as the agent in Spain, visited Gibraltar to supervise developments. A shop was rented, and a colporteur Stephen Froumou was appointed to run it with the help of his wife. Some of this work in Gibraltar was later undertaken in partnership with the seamen's mission, whose boat was used to visit ships in the bay. The seamen's missioner preached and Froumou offered Scriptures for sale. Over six hundred ships a year were visited in this way. Even though the sale of Scriptures did not cover the cost of the work, it was generally felt to be too important to abandon. Sales occasionally numbered one thousand copies in a year. In 1880, these sales included editions in thirteen different languages.

The Spanish agent continued to pay an annual visit to Gibraltar, and in December 1883, Anglican, Methodist, and Presbyterian clergymen attended the first public meeting ever to be held there in connection with the Bible Society.[11] It was a good opportunity to publicize the work of the Society and to gain subscribers.

---

11. *The Monthly Reporter of the British and Foreign Bible Society*, 1884, no. 2 (February 1884), p. 30.

Froumou continued to operate the Bible Society's depot until the summer of 1889, when he left Gibraltar suddenly. A successor was found and the depot was relocated. A kiosk was also opened in 1889, which in its first few days attracted quite a crowd of visitors of different nationalities. The kiosk remained open for some years, but dwindling sales led to its closure, and the direct work of the Bible Society in Gibraltar virtually ceased. A local committee continued to exist and an annual meeting was held to maintain interest in the work of the Society.

In Spain, the work of the Bible Society faced continued opposition and difficulties. In 1876 the Spanish Constitution was rewritten, granting a degree of religious toleration but also stating that "no manifestations or public religious observances will be permitted other than those of the State religion".[12] This was of course so vague that it could be interpreted in many different ways. In Madrid, the Bible Society had to remove its sign at the shop and depot. Bibles on display had to be closed and placed so that the titles could not be read. The strength of the opposition to Bible Society operations varied around the country, depending upon where sympathies lay. Colportage could be opposed on the grounds that it was "public" selling. Sometimes colporteurs were prevented from selling, had their stock seized and destroyed, were arrested or fined, and even subjected to physical, as well as verbal, assaults. It was surprising that anyone was willing to do the work at all, yet colportage did continue. The numbers employed varied from year to year but averaged around fifteen to twenty. Biblewomen were also employed in Madrid, working under the supervision of the agent's wife. Later, Biblewomen were employed in other parts of Spain.

By 1878, some 830,500 copies of the Scriptures had been printed in Madrid. Annual circulation varied but averaged around 69,000 volumes per year. A succession of agents worked in Spain, and all aspects of the work continued, despite the opposition. Eventually an annual Bible Sunday was instituted, and conferences for colporteurs were organized, which helped them to feel less isolated in their work.

In November 1916, the Spanish agent, William Summers, died. In the midst of the war it was not possible to find a replacement. So his assistant, Adolfo Araujo, was appointed as acting agent. He continued in the work, though he was usually described as the superintendent rather than the agent, and he became a prominent and respected figure in the Spanish Protestant church. Bible Society officials from England regularly visited Araujo to discuss the work.

---

12. The phrase from the Spanish constitution is quoted internally in Jacques Delpech, *The Oppression of Protestants in Spain* (London: Lutterworth Press, 1956), p. 19.

In July 1935, as the centenary of George Borrow's work in Spain approached, a motor caravan was dedicated in his memory at a Methodist church near Barcelona. Araujo, who spoke at the ceremony, had been much involved in planning the campaign to use the caravan in the work of distribution. In January 1936, other meetings took place to celebrate the anniversary of Borrow's work, but soon events in Spain were to curtail activities severely. Not long after the Spanish Civil War broke out, the Bible Society reported that many of the buildings in which these meetings had taken place had been destroyed, and three pastors were dead.

In 1937, despite the war, the Bible Society reported:

> The Madrid depot has been closed only one day since the beginning of hostilities. The Union Jack floats over it and a document is pasted on the door stating that it is under the protection of the British Embassy. Sales on a small scale are still taking place... [Araujo stays at his post,] carrying on with great courage, although two of his sons have fallen in the defence of the city.[13]

Araujo and his wife actually lived at the depot, which also housed a number of homeless refugees. He had little help with the work there because his two colleagues had been called up. He himself probably escaped conscription only because of his age. At some time the building was hit, but the shell failed to explode. It seems amazing that any work continued in war-torn Spain but it did, though not surprisingly circulation dropped from 211,286 in 1936 to 36,259 the following year.

After the war ended there was a great deal of uncertainty about what would be permitted. Under the Franco regime, life for Protestants became even more difficult than it had been before. Many Protestant missions had had schools attached, which were now banned. Bible Society work was curtailed because the Madrid depot was virtually closed by the authorities and colportage forbidden. Araujo continued to visit churches when he could and reported that "a quiet work in the circulation of the Scriptures is being carried on".[14] In the same report, the Bible Society paid tribute to him saying, "Our sympathy and prayers go out to Señor Araujo who, in the most difficult circumstances, has kept the flag flying". In 1948, he retired after nearly fifty years of work for the Bible Society. José Flores was appointed to succeed him, and a small amount of work continued. In 1954, it was estimated that only 26,000 Protestants lived in Spain, out of a population of 28,626,830. Circulation for that year was 21,834 volumes. However, the rules kept changing, and it was hard to know what was permitted and what was not. Flores soon reported:

13. *Hundred and Thirty-third Report of the BFBS* (London, 1937), pp. 30-35.
14. *Hundred and Forty-second and Forty-third Reports of the BFBS* (London, 1947), p. 20.

> While we still have our depot in Madrid, and it is officially known that we are circulating the Scriptures no permission exists either for printing or circulation. During the past three months more drastic action has been taken, refusing to admit supplies of the Scriptures from external sources.[15]

In April 1956, the Madrid depot was completely closed by the authorities, and the entire stock was confiscated "on the grounds that the books had been printed in Spain without permission and were being illegally circulated".[16] In December 1963, a new depot was opened in Madrid but the Spanish authorities placed a limit on the number of Bibles to be circulated. This was below the level of demand, but the existence of the new depot meant that the work was again going forward.

Today, forty years later, Spain has its own Bible Society, which is a member of the United Bible Societies. Its headquarters are still in Madrid. Although less than one percent of Spain's population is Protestant, the work goes on in a variety of ways. Bibles are still being printed, and translation work for new editions continues. Bible exhibitions are sometimes held in Catholic churches, thus fostering a growing relationship between Protestants and Catholics. In recent years a record label has been launched in an attempt to attract younger people.

Spain had proved to be a very difficult field for Bible Society operations, but despite all the difficulties and the strength of the opposition, millions of copies of Scripture were circulated by dedicated people who carried on the work despite the very real cost to themselves. They sacrificed a great deal to circulate what for them was the Word of Life.

---

15. *The Hundred and Forty-fourth and Forty-fifth Reports of the BFBS* (London, 1950), p. 18.

16. *The Hundred and Fifty-first Report of the BFBS, for the year ending December 31, 1955* (London, n.d.), pp. 19-20.

The BFBS and Native Language Literature in Nineteenth-Century Canada

Joyce Banks

Both aboriginal and white linguists laboured to translate the Scriptures into the languages of the native peoples of Canada. By publishing the results of this effort—in thousands of copies—the British and Foreign Bible Society (BFBS) made a remarkable contribution to the literature, and to the literacy, of thousands of native people. During the nineteenth century some sixty Bible translations, including revisions, were published by the BFBS in an estimated 52,000 copies. Edition size is known for many of the titles noted in this article. An estimate of 500 copies per edition has been made for the rest, but this may well be far fewer than the number of copies actually printed. Twelve native languages are represented, including Mohawk, Labrador Inuktitut, Ojibwa, Cree, Maliseet, Mi'kmaq, Slavey, Chipewyan, Baffin Inuktitut, Kwakiutl, Haida, and Blackfoot. All of these languages were used in the translation work done by Anglicans, Moravians, Methodists, Baptists, the Wesleyan Missionary Society (WMS), and the Church Missionary Society (CMS).

Translators not only prepared word lists and dictionaries, they also had to master the grammar and syntax of old and complex languages that had not previously been expressed in written form. The task of translation invariably began with the Gospels, and sometimes only one or two were ever published. If the translating activity was continued over an extended period, the Gospels were usually followed by the rest of the New Testament and Isaiah. In only a few cases was the translation of the entire Bible completed and seen through the press.

With one outstanding exception, the editions published by the BFBS for use in Canada complied with the Society's policy regulations that translations be accurate and appear without note or comment. All were printed on good-quality paper using clear typefaces; indeed, the Society did not hesitate to make use of exotic types to suit usage in the territories of the Hudson Bay Company. The books were soundly bound in cloth or roan, and most were octavo in format, reflecting the need to make something precious easily portable. During this period many of the native peoples were still nomadic hunters and trappers.

Most of the titles noted here are identified by T. H. Darlow and H. F. Moule in their splendid reference work, *Historical Catalogue of the Printed Editions of Holy Scripture in the Library of the British and Foreign Bible Society*. The BFBS Archives, now housed in Cambridge University Library, provide an invaluable resource on the Society's publishing policy as well as access to its annual reports, correspondence, and committee reports, as well as information on printing, typefaces, paper, and binding.

The earliest title published for use in Canada — indeed the first book in any language published by the BFBS — was the Gospel of John in the Mohawk language.[1] It was printed in London for the BFBS by Phillips and Fardon with the Mohawk and English on facing pages. Because no imprint date appears on the title page, it is not known whether it was published in 1804, the year the Society was established, or in 1805.[2] Printed in an edition of 2,000 copies, it was meant for the use of Britain's Indian allies, who were displaced after the American Revolution and given lands in Upper Canada to compensate for their territorial losses in the United States.

The translation was accomplished by John Norton, a Métis of Cherokee and Scottish heritage, who also prepared an accompanying commentary, *Address to the Six Nations*. In the *Address*, he exhorted the Mohawk Christians, who were mainly Anglican and literate, "to strictly adhere to what our Lord has transmitted to us in the Holy Scriptures, that thereby the unbelievers, in viewing us, may become enamoured of the Gospel".[3] Norton had the *Address* printed with the Gospel, but when the BFBS saw the first copies, they ordered it to be removed because of its incompatibility with their fundamental principle of publishing only Scripture.[4]

The bilingual *Address*, also printed by Phillips and Fardon, bears on its title page the imprint date of 1805, and was evidently printed together

---

1. T. H. Darlow and H. F. Moule, comps. *Historical Catalogue of the Printed Editions of Holy Scripture in the Library of the British and Foreign Bible Society*, 2 vols. in 4 (London: British and Foreign Bible Society, 1903-1911), no. 6797 (hereafter DM). James Constantine Pilling, *Bibliography of the Iroquoian Languages*, Smithsonian Institution, Bureau of Ethnology Bulletin no. 6 (Washington, D.C., 1888), p. 130.

2. DM 6797. Although the BFBS ordered English and Welsh scriptures in 1804, they did not appear until the autumn of 1805 (in the case of the English), and 1806 (in the case of Welsh) due to the delays in stereotyping. Thus, DM is clear that this is the first scripture item published by the BFBS. Thanks are owed to Rosemary Mathew, BFBS Library, Cambridge University Library, for answering questions about the Norton translation and other books printed for the use of Canadian native peoples.

3. "Introduction" to the *Address to the Six Nations: Recommending the Gospel of Saint John* (London: Phillips and Fardon, 1805), p. iv. See the entry under DM 6797.

4. See John Owen, *The History of the Origin and First Ten Years of the British and Foreign Bible Society*, 2 vols. (London: Tilling and Hughes, 1816), vol. 1, pp. 126-32.

with the Gospel of St. John. Signature collation of the *Address* and the Gospel strongly suggests that neither Captain Norton nor Phillips and Fardon were aware of the Society's policy. This was, after all, the first of the Society's publications. The *Address* is clearly signed A, and the Gospel begins with signature B. Even though most extant copies of the Gospel begin with signature B, many show clear evidence that preliminary material has been excised; moreover, some copies with the *Address* and the Gospel bound as one book have survived. On this evidence, it seems probable that the Gospel of John in Mohawk was published in 1805, the imprint date on the title page of the *Address*.

In 1811, the American Bible Society, and other interested groups in the United States, began the publication of Bible translations into Mohawk, mainly with the support of Methodist missions on both sides of the border. The BFBS did not issue any more editions in Mohawk during the nineteenth century, but in 1880 the Montreal auxiliary of the BFBS published the four Gospels in a print run of 1,000 copies.[5]

Among the early publications of the BFBS were translations prepared by the Moravians, who had laboured among the Inuit of Labrador from 1771. All of the Moravian translations were credited solely to Moravian missionaries, and the assistance of Inuit converts was not acknowledged. In 1809 the BFBS was in discussion with Moravian representatives about publishing their translations. They had prepared a Gospel harmony, but this was not acceptable to the Society, as it was an adaptation of the text. So, one of the Moravian missionaries, B. G. Kohlmeister, extracted and edited the Gospel of John from the harmony, and this was published by the BFBS in 1810.[6] This was followed by the Gospels of Matthew, Mark, and Luke in 1813.[7] The Society also published an Inuktitut translation of both the Acts of the Apostles (1816) and the Epistles (1819).[8] Inuktitut Old Testament translations published by the BFBS included the Psalms in 1830, Genesis in 1834, and Isaiah in 1837.[9] A revision of the Gospels appeared in 1839, and in 1840 the entire New Testament was published by the BFBS.[10] Having earlier published the Inuktitut translation of Genesis, the BFBS published the four remaining books of Moses for the Moravians

---

5. DM 5568; Pilling, *Bibliography of Iroquoian*, p. 131-32. DM 5568 classifies the language as "Iroquois."

6. DM 3508; Pilling, *Bibliography of the Eskimo Language*, Smithsonian Institution, Bureau of American Ethnology Bulletin no. 1 (Washington, D.C., 1888), p. 66.

7. DM 3509; the title page also mentions the Gospel of John, but it is not included. See Pilling, *Bibliography of Eskimo*, p. 16.

8. DM 3510 and DM 3511.

9. DM 3512, DM 3513, and DM 3514.

10. DM 3515 and DM 3516.

in 1841.[11] As Darlow and Moule note, "About this date, in gratitude for the copies of the Scriptures supplied to them by the BFBS, the Eskimo [Inuit] of Labrador, out of their poverty, sent a thankoffering of three gallons of seal oil".[12] Inuktitut editions of the books of Solomon, Jeremiah, Ezekiel, Daniel, and the Twelve Minor Prophets followed in 1849.[13] All of these titles were published in London in print runs of 1,000 copies. Four subsequent Inuktitut titles published by the BFBS for use in Labrador — Joshua-Esther (1869), Job-Song of Solomon, which completed the Inuktitut Bible in 1871, a revised edition of the Gospels and Acts (1876), and a revised New Testament (1878) — were printed by Gustav Winter in Stolpen.[14]

The first of the translations into Ojibwa to be published by the BFBS was the Gospel of John, printed in an edition of 1,000 copies in 1831.[15] It is a bilingual work with Ojibwa and English on facing pages. Translated by Peter Jones, a Métis of Welsh and Ojibwa parentage, this work followed two earlier editions of his translation of the Gospel of Matthew published in Upper Canada in 1829 and 1831, respectively.[16] As with Mohawk translations, several scriptural translations into Ojibwa, mainly for Methodist use, were published in the United States on both sides of the border. For example, in 1856 the Upper Canada Bible Society published an edition of the Psalms by Frederick A. O'Meara, who was attached to the Society for the Propagation of the Gospel.[17] His translation of the Pentateuch, published in Toronto, appeared in 1861.[18] In 1874 the BFBS published a translation of the Twelve Minor Prophets translated by Robert McDonald of the Church Missionary Society (CMS).[19] McDonald was a Métis of Cree and Scottish parentage. In 1897, yet another edition of the Gospel of Matthew was published, in Toronto, by the York Auxiliary Bible Society.

The first of the Bible translations published by the BFBS for use among the Cree in the Hudson Bay Company territories, or Rupert's Land, were the Gospels of Mark and John, both in 1855.[20] The CMS had published the

---

11. DM 3517.
12. Darlow and Moule, *Historical Catalogue*, vol. 2, part 1, p. 343 (DM 3517).
13. DM 3518
14. DM 3519 (1869), DM 3520 (1871), DM 3521 (1876), and DM 3522 (1878).
15. DM 3024; Pilling, *Bibliography of the Algonquian Languages*, Smithsonian Institution, Bureau of American Ethnology Bulletin no. 13 (Washington, D.C., 1891), p. 265. At the time, Chippewa and Ojibwa were used interchangeably, but Ojibwa is now standard.
16. DM 3022 and DM 3023; Pilling, *Bibliography of Algonquian*, p. 267.
17. DM 3036; Pilling, *Bibliography of Algonquian*, p. 380.
18. DM 3037; Pilling, *Bibliography of Algonquian*, p. 381.
19. DM 3039; Pilling, *Bibliography of Algonquian*, p. 324.
20. DM 3113 and DM 3114.

Gospel of Matthew in 1853.[21] Although the translations are credited to James Hunter of the CMS, or his wife, Jean Ross Hunter, much was owed to the labours of Henry Budd of the CMS, the first full-blood Cree to be ordained an Anglican priest. Jean Ross Hunter's translation of the First Epistle of John was also published in 1855.[22] All of these books were printed using the Latin alphabet.

In publishing biblical translations into the three dialects of the Cree language, the BFBS made full use of the syllabic characters — commonly known as "Cree syllabics" — a system introduced in 1840 and used for printing at the Rossville Mission north of Lake Winnipeg by James Evans of the Wesleyan Missionary Society (WMS). A simple system consisting of nine symbols, each expressed in four attitudes with finals to close the syllables, it was easily and quickly learned, an essential attribute in a vast territory peopled by ever moving nomadic bands of subsistence hunters and trappers, who could not linger at missions long enough to learn the Latin alphabet. Later adopted and developed by the both the CMS and Roman Catholic missionaries, Cree syllabics were widely used in Rupert's Land, which extended from beyond the East Main of Hudson Bay to the Rockies, and from the Arctic to the American border. Thousands of books were printed for the aboriginal peoples there using this highly developed syllabic system, which is still in use today.

In 1853 the BFBS was petitioned for a grant of paper to be used to print 1,000 copies of the Gospel of John at the Rossville Mission Press.[23] The stock of paper arrived at the mission in 1854 under the condition that the paper be used only for the printing of the stipulated number of copies of that Gospel or other scriptural translations, and the third Rossville Mission Press edition of the Gospel of John duly appeared in 1857.[24]

The first of the syllabic character translations into Cree to be published by the BFBS in London was the New Testament in Plain Cree, printed in an edition of 5,000 copies in 1859, using Watt's Cree No. 1 (14 pt.) type.[25] Although this translation has been credited to William Mason, the work is generally held to be that of Henry Bird Steinhauer (WMS), an Ojibwa, and John Sinclair (WMS), a Métis. The work of revising and editing, however, was undertaken by Mason, and particularly by his wife, Sophia Thomas Mason, a Métis, who worked for years both on this translation and on

---

21. DM 3112.
22. DM 3115.
23. David Anderson (Bishop of Rupert's Land) to the BFBS, 3 August 1853, BFBS Foreign Correspondence Inwards, 1853 (BSA/D1/2/113).
24. Bruce Braden Peel, *Rossville Mission Press: The Invention of the Cree Syllabic Characters, and the First Printing in Rupert's Land* (Montreal: Osiris, 1974), p. 37.
25. DM 3129; Pilling, *Bibliography of Algonquian*, p. 339.

that of the Old Testament. Mason, an experienced printer, and Sophia Thomas Mason, well educated and fluent in the Cree language, both used the syllabic system with ease.

The couple traveled to London to see the book through the press. But all of their knowledge and experience had not prepared them for a serious problem regarding BFBS policy on the translation of the word "baptize", which was not to suggest either dipping or sprinkling, but to embrace both interpretations.[26] Although the Society published nothing without checking translational accuracy, work on the Gospel of Matthew was already about one month advanced before the BFBS Editorial Subcommittee was apprised of the problem. Completion of the printing of Matthew was delayed, and twelve leaves (24 pages) had to be reprinted. In spite of the unforeseen problems, the New Testament—entirely in the Cree syllabic characters and printed in two columns—was completed by shipping time in June of 1859, and a grant of 2,000 copies was sent to Rupert's Land aboard the vessel *Kitty*. Unfortunately, the *Kitty* sank. Despite this setback, the following year a replacement shipment of 1,500 copies was sent to the CMS, with a grant of 700 copies to the WMS, and a gift of 6 copies to a correspondent in Red River.[27]

Not long after the publication of this New Testament, the CMS asked the BFBS to publish the Cree Old Testament, requesting an edition of 5,000 copies.[28] William Mason and his wife were still in London and remained to see the work through the press, although Sophia Mason's health was delicate. Concerned about the size of the volume proposed, Mason suggested that it be printed in large octavo format using a smaller typeface.[29] Watts Cree No. 2 (10 pt.) type was used for the double-columned publication, and the work was completed in 1861. Sophia Thomas Mason died just after the completion of the printing of Malachi.

William Mason remained to see through the press the second edition of the New Testament in syllabic characters, which was to be a companion volume to the Old Testament. Printed using Cree No. 2 (10 pt.) type, this book also featured the use of a boldface font designed and cast by Watts. The first letter in each sentence and the first letter in proper names were

---

26. This requirement, still in force, was expressed in *Rules for the Guidance of Translators, Revisers, and Editors Working in Connection with the British and Foreign Bible Society* (London: BFBS, 1917), p. 14. Although an unwritten rule in the nineteenth century, it was nevertheless firm policy.
27. *Fifty-seventh Report of the BFBS* (London, 1861), p.72
28. DM 3130; Pilling, *Bibliography of Algonquian*, p. 339.
29. W. Mason to J. Mee, London, 16 June 1859, BFBS Editorial Correspondence Inwards, no.1, p. 120 (BSA/E3/1/4/1).

distinguished by boldface. The printing of 5,000 copies was probably completed in February of 1862.[30]

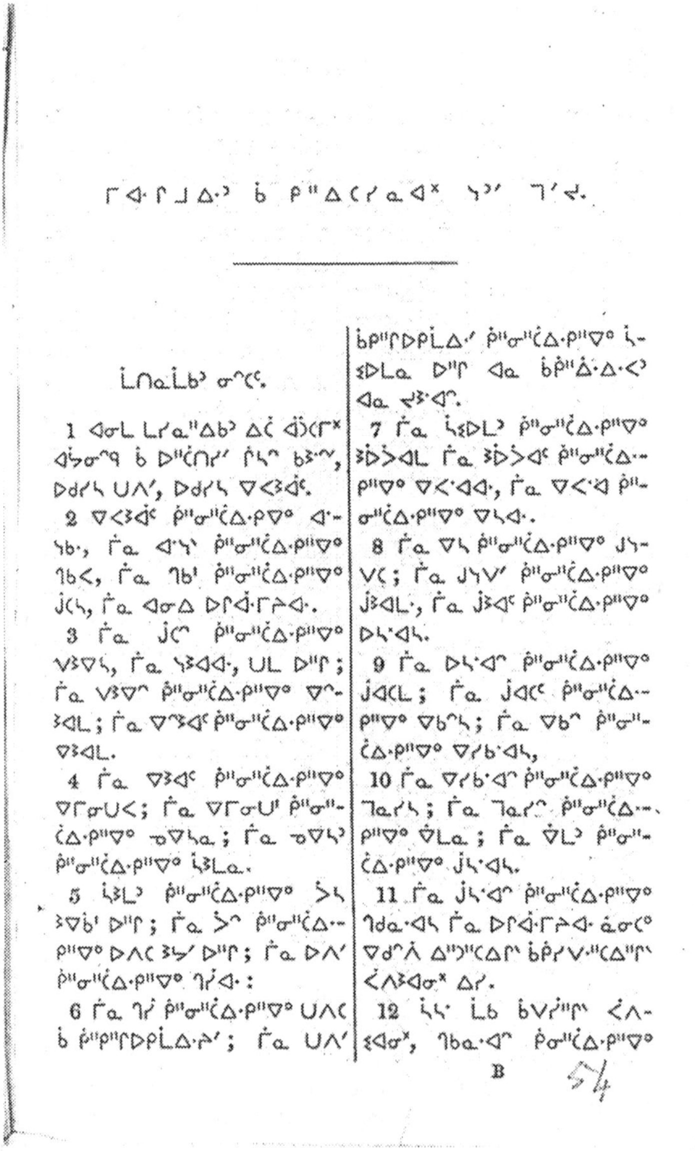

ᒥᐊᐧᒋᒧᐃᐧᐣ ᑳ ᑭᐦᐃᑕᓯᓇᐊᕽ ᓴᐣᐟ ᒣᐟᔫ.

ᒫᑎᓇᒫᑲᐣ ᓂᔥᑕᐟ.

1 ᐊᓂᒪ ᒪᓯᓇᐦᐃᑲᐣ ᐃᑖ ᐋᒍᑕᒥᕽ
ᐋᔮᓂᔅᑫ ᑳ ᐅᐦᒋᑎᓯᐟ ᒌᓴᔅ ᑲᐢᑐᐢ,
ᐅᑯᓯᓴ ᑌᐱᐟ, ᐅᑯᓯᓴ ᐁᐸᕒᐋᒼ.
2 ᐁᐸᕒᐋᒼ ᑮᐦᓂᐦᒑᐏᑭᐁᐤ ᐊᐧ-
ᓴᑳᐧ, ᒦᓇ ᐊᐧᓴᐠ ᑮᐦᓂᐦᒑᐏᑭᐦᐁᐤ
ᔦᑲᐸ, ᒦᓇ ᔦᑳᐠ ᑮᐦᓂᐦᒑᐏᑭᐦᐁᐤ
ᒨᑕᓴ, ᒦᓇ ᐊᓂᐃ ᐅᒋᒫᐏᒥᓯᐊᐧ.
3 ᒦᓇ ᒨᑕᐢ ᑮᐦᓂᐦᒑᐏᑭᐦᐁᐤ
ᐯᕒᐁᓴ, ᒦᓇ ᓭᕒᐊᐊᐧ, ᑌᒪ ᐅᐦᒋ;
ᒦᓇ ᐯᕒᐁᐢ ᑮᐦᓂᐦᒑᐏᑭᐦᐁᐤ ᐁᐢ-
ᕒᐊᒪ; ᒦᓇ ᐁᐢᕒᐋᒼ ᑮᐦᓂᐦᒑᐏᑭᐦᐁᐤ
ᐁᕒᐊᒪ.
4 ᒦᓇ ᐁᕒᐊᒼ ᑮᐦᓂᐦᒑᐏᑭᐦᐁᐤ
ᐁᒥᓂᑌᐸ; ᒦᓇ ᐁᒥᓂᑌᑊ ᑮᐦᓂᐦ-
ᒑᐏᑭᐦᐁᐤ ᓀᐁᓴᓇ; ᒦᓇ ᓀᐁᓴᐣ
ᑮᐦᓂᐦᒑᐏᑭᐦᐁᐤ ᓵᕒᒪᓇ.
5 ᓵᕒᒪᐣ ᑮᐦᓂᐦᒑᐏᑭᐦᐁᐤ ᐴᓴ
ᕒᐁᑳᑊ ᐅᐦᒋ; ᒦᓇ ᐴᐢ ᑮᐦᓂᐦᒑ-
ᑭᐦᐁᐤ ᐅᐱᑕ ᕒᐅᔾ ᐅᐦᒋ; ᒦᓇ ᐅᐱᐟ
ᑮᐦᓂᐦᒑᐏᑭᐦᐁᐤ ᔦᓯᐊᐧ:
6 ᒦᓇ ᔦᓰ ᑮᐦᓂᐦᒑᐏᑭᐦᐁᐤ ᑌᐱᑕ
ᑳ ᑮᐦᑭᐦᒋᐅᑭᒫᐏᔨᐟ; ᒦᓇ ᑌᐱᐟ
ᑳᑭᐦᒋᐅᑭᒫᐏᐟ ᑮᐦᓂᐦᒑᐏᑭᐦᐁᐤ ᓵ-
ᕒᐅᒪᓇ ᐅᐦᒋ ᐊᓇ ᑳᑮᐦᐄᐧᐃᐧᐸᐣ
ᐊᓇ ᔫᕒᐊᐧᐢ.
7 ᒦᓇ ᓵᕒᐅᒪᐣ ᑮᐦᓂᐦᒑᐏᑭᐦᐁᐤ
ᕒᐆᐴᐊᒪ ᒦᓇ ᕒᐆᐴᐊᒼ ᑮᐦᓂᐦᒑᐏ-
ᑭᐦᐁᐤ ᐁᐸᐊᐧᐊᐧ, ᒦᓇ ᐁᐸᐊᐧ ᑮᐦ-
ᓂᐦᒑᐏᑭᐦᐁᐤ ᐁᓴᐊᐧ.
8 ᒦᓇ ᐁᓴ ᑮᐦᓂᐦᒑᐏᑭᐦᐁᐤ ᒍᓴ-
ᐯᑕ; ᒦᓇ ᒍᓴᐯᐟ ᑮᐦᓂᐦᒑᐏᑭᐦᐁᐤ
ᒎᕒᐊᒪᐧ, ᒦᓇ ᒎᕒᐊᒼ ᑮᐦᓂᐦᒑᐏᑭᐦᐁᐤ
ᐅᓵᐊᓴ.
9 ᒦᓇ ᐅᓵᐊᐢ ᑮᐦᓂᐦᒑᐏᑭᐦᐁᐤ
ᒎᐊᑕᒪ; ᒦᓇ ᒎᐊᑦ ᑮᐦᓂᐦᒑᐏᑭ-
ᐦᐁᐤ ᐁᑲᐢᓴ; ᒦᓇ ᐁᑳᐢ ᑮᐦᓂᐦ-
ᒑᐏᑭᐦᐁᐤ ᐁᓯᑳᐊᓴ,
10 ᒦᓇ ᐁᓯᑳᐊᐢ ᑮᐦᓂᐦᒑᐏᑭᐦᐁᐤ
ᒪᓇᓯᓴ; ᒦᓇ ᒪᓇᓯᐢ ᑮᐦᓂᐦᒑᐏ-
ᑭᐦᐁᐤ ᐋᒪᓇ; ᒦᓇ ᐋᒪᐣ ᑮᐦᓂᐦ-
ᒑᐏᑭᐦᐁᐤ ᒎᓵᐊᓴ.
11 ᒦᓇ ᒎᓵᐊᐢ ᑮᐦᓂᐦᒑᐏᑭᐦᐁᐤ
ᔦᑯᓇᐊᓴ ᒦᓇ ᐅᒋᒫᐏᒥᓯᐊᐧ ᓈᓂᑕᐤ
ᐁᑯᐢᐄ ᐃᐦᑐᐦᑕᐃᒥᐢ ᑳᑮᓯᐯᐧᐦᑕᐃᐦᒥᐢ
ᐹᐱᕒᐊᓂᕽ ᐃᓯ.
12 ᓵᓵᐧ ᒫᑲ ᑳᐯᓯᔫᐦᒥᐢ ᐹᐱ-
ᕒᐊᓂᕽ, ᔦᑳᓇᐧᐊᐢ ᑮᓂᐦᒑᐏᑭᐦᐁᐤ

B 54

Picture 35. *Cree New Testament (1859), in Syllabic Script.* Specimen courtesy of BFBS Library collection, Cambridge University Library.

30. DM 3130; Pilling, *Bibliography of Algonquian*, p. 339.

When Mason returned to Rupert's Land in 1862, he took with him 125 cases of Bibles. The BFBS grant to the CMS comprised 1,000 Old Testaments and 3,000 New Testaments, plus a further grant of 12 Bibles to the WMS. Two separate books were printed, each with its own title page, signatures, and pagination, but they were usually bound together — a formidable tome! The Society had asked Mason for a report on distribution in Rupert's Land, for there was difficulty in shipping Bibles inland from their York factory on Hudson Bay. The season was dry that year, and the rivers were so low that for the first time in living memory the boats from Red River failed to reach the port. Indeed, many boats for the interior left with only half a cargo of supplies. Distribution was so slow that in the autumn of that year Mason had to pay more than £16 for a year's storage of cases of undistributed materials stored in the company's warehouse. He consequently decided to move the remaining cases to the quarters supplied to him as company chaplain, quarters not subject to storage costs. The BFBS *Report* for that year records Mason as writing, "And there you may see Bibles in my study, cases of Bibles in my kitchen, dining-room, and even in my bed-room".[31] The demand for Bibles continued, but the means of distribution became increasingly difficult. By 1869, Mason had been able to distribute only forty cases of the 125 shipped in 1862. He returned to England in 1870, leaving further distribution to his successors at the York factory.

Other Cree translations included in 1876 the Psalms, printed in the Latin script, the complete syllabic character edition of the New Testament in Moose Cree (1876), translated by John Horden of the CMS, and a new edition of the Gospel of Mark (1877) in the Latin script. The following year the BFBS published the Gospel of Matthew.[32]

All of the biblical translations into Mi'kmaq and Maliseet were done by Silas Tertius Rand, a man of remarkable tenacity and originality, who served among the native peoples of Nova Scotia, New Brunswick, and Prince Edward Island. Although he began his missionary career as a Baptist, he ultimately left the fold. The first Mi'kmaq translation by Rand to be published by the BFBS was the Gospel of Matthew, printed for the Society in Charlottetown, Prince Edward Island, by G. T. Haszard in 1853. The text was expressed entirely in the characters devised for Isaac Pitman's system of phonetic spelling. As Darlow and Moule record, "This

---

31. *Sixtieth Report of the BFBS* (London, 1864), pp. 262-63.
32. For the Psalter, see DM 3117; and Pilling, *Bibliography of Algonquian*, p. 246. For the New Testament in Moose Cree, see DM 3123; and Pilling, *Bibliography of Algonquian*, pp. 236-37. For the Gospel of Mark, see DM 3118; and Pilling, *Bibliography of Algonquian*, p. 245. For the Gospel of Matthew, see DM 3120; and Pilling, *Bibliography of Algonquian*, p. 243.

and the five following editions were printed in phonetic character, in order to enable even those who did not understand the language to read the books to the Indians".[33] Four translations in Mi'kmaq were all printed for the Society in Bath by Pitman—the *Gospel akordin tu Sent Luke* in 1856, the *Buk of Djenesis* in 1857, the *Buk ov Samz* in 1859, and Acts in 1863.[34] Translations printed in a Latin script in Halifax, Nova Scotia, at the expense of the BFBS were Exodus in 1870, a revised edition of the Gospel of Matthew in 1871, a revised edition of the Gospel of John in 1872, and a revised edition of the Gospel of Luke in 1874, plus the Gospel of Mark and an edition of Romans to Revelation in 1874, the latter two 1874 editions completing Rand's translation of the New Testament.[35]

Rand's translation into Maliseet of the Gospel of John was published by the Society in London in 1870. According to Darlow and Moule, the translation was made with "the assistance of an Indian named Gabriel Thomas".[36]

The Slavey language is used in the Mackenzie River region, and the first scriptural translations into that language were made by William West Kirkby of the CMS. Editions of the Gospels of Mark and John were published in syllabic characters by the BFBS in 1868 and 1870, respectively.[37] Both were printed in editions of 500 copies.

. Translations into Slavey were also accomplished by the colourful William Carpenter Bompas of the Church Missionary Society, and these were all rendered in the Latin script. Bompas was a man of strong convictions concerning CMS use of the syllabic system, which he eschewed. He saw the system as the instrument of the Oblates of Mary Immaculate, who were active in the same region, and therefore believed that its use by the CMS led to confusion. In fact, early in his tenure, he became so exercised about the use of syllabic characters in Rupert's Land that he offered to resign, saying, "I take the Alphabet to be a Divine gift to man and to be the foundation of all true knowledge".[38] He served as bishop in three dioceses in the far northwest, each more remote than the previous, and during his service in each of these sees he insisted that all translations be

33. DM 6781; and Pilling, *Bibliography of Algonquian*, p. 419.

34. DM 6783, DM 6784, DM 6785, and DM 6786. See also Pilling, *Bibliography of Algonquian*, p. 421.

35. DM 6787, DM 6788, DM 6789, DM 6791, DM 6790, and DM 6792. See also, Pilling, *Bibliography of Algonquian*, pp. 420-23.

36. DM 6609; and also Pilling, *Bibliography of Algonquian*, p. 422.

37. DM 8353 and DM 8354. See also Pilling, *Bibliography of the Athapascan Languages*, Smithsonian Institution Bureau of Ethnology Bulletin no. 14 (Washington, D.C., 1892), pp. 46-47.

38. Bompas to the Secretaries of the CMS, Fort Chipewyan, 6 July 1871, Church Missionary Society Archive, Birmingham University Library (C.1/M).

published in the Latin script. Bompas's translation of the New Testament into Slavey was published by the BFBS over a period years — the Gospel of Mark in 1874, all four Gospels in 1883, the book of Acts in 1890, and the completed translation of Acts to Revelation in 1891.[39] After Bompas left each diocese, much of his work was transliterated into syllabic characters by William Day Reeve of the CMS: separate editions of each Gospel (Matthew in 1886; Mark in 1886; Luke in 1890; and John in 1890), and Romans to Revelation in 1891.[40]

The New Testament was also translated into Chipewyan, by William West Kirkby (CMS), and published by the BFBS in syllabic characters in 1881, possibly in 500 copies. The New Testament edition was preceded by an edition of the four Gospels published in London by the BFBS in 1878.[41]

At this same time, in the eastern Arctic area, Edmund J. Peck (CMS) was preparing translations for the use of the Inuit of the Hudson Bay region. He had used Moravian translations prepared for the peoples of Labrador in his early efforts to master the Baffin dialect, and two of them were published by the BFBS in 500 copies each — the Gospel of Luke in 1881, and the four Gospels in 1897.[42] Both were expressed in syllabic characters, which had been introduced for use among the Inuit of Little Whale River on the East Main of Hudson Bay by Edwin A. Watkins (CMS) in 1855.

Books in Haida and Kwakiutl, published for use on the west coast, were all printed in Latin script. Charles Harrison (CMS) translated the first book in Haida to be published by the BFBS, the Gospel of Matthew, and it was printed in 1891 in an edition of 500 copies.[43] J. H. Keen (CMS) translated two more, the Acts of the Apostles published by the Society in 1898, and the Gospel of Luke, published in 1899.[44] Alfred James Hall (CMS) translated four titles into Kwakiutl, and all were published by the BFBS before 1900. They consisted of the Gospel of Matthew in 1882, the Gospel of John in 1884, the Gospel of Luke in 1894, and the Acts of the Apostles in 1897.[45]

The Gospel of Matthew was translated into the Blackfoot language by John William Tims (CMS) and published in the Latin script by the BFBS in 1890.[46]

---

39. DM 8355, DM 8356, DM 8361, and DM 8363. See also Pilling, *Bibliography of Athapascan*, pp. 113-14.
40. DM 8357, DM 8358, DM 8359, DM 8360, and DM 8362.
41. DM 3020 (1878) and DM 3021 (1881); Pilling, *Bibliography of Athapascan*, p. 47.
42. DM 3524 and DM 3525.
43. DM 5040.
44. DM 5041 and DM 5042.
45. DM 6046, DM 6047, DM 6048, and DM 6049.
46. DM 2173; see also Pilling, *Bibliography of Algonquian*, p. 487.

Conclusion

The value of the translations published for the use of native peoples of Canada during the nineteenth century goes beyond the traditional impact of missionary activity. Without the support of the British and Foreign Bible Society, much of this translation work would not have been published. In some cases the translations published by the Society were the first printed expression of a language, and in other cases they were the only expression. In both cases, the use of these written languages helped to rebuff twentieth-century efforts to assimilate the native peoples, efforts that included repression of the use of their languages. Without assessing the success or failure of missions to the aboriginal peoples of Canada during the nineteenth century, it is safe to say that the contribution made by the BFBS to the preservation of native languages and to the early spread of literacy have been of immeasurable and lasting value.

Sowing by Sea: Empowering Seafarers with the Gospel

Roald Kverndal

The Way of the Sea: How it All Began

"Sowing by Sea" — is not that at best a very mixed metaphor? By contrast, "Sowing the Word," the motto of the British and Foreign Bible Society, has solid biblical roots. It is found in the parable of sowing the seed of the Word, which talks about the four types of soil and the respective responses (Mt. 13.1-23). But there is also the biblical image of casting the bread of life "upon the waters" and finding it again "after many days" (Eccles. 11.1). Recognizing that the Christian community included many seafarers from its earliest origins, this paper addresses the formative role of the British and Foreign Bible Society in the modern rediscovery of seafarers and the seamen's mission movement.[1]

By the time of the Reformation, Protestant clergy of seafaring nations, profiting from recent developments in the art of printing, produced a whole series of homilies and other biblically based maritime devotional aids. These works were specifically produced to supply moral and spiritual self-help for sailors, so they could safely "navigate the oceans of life." Such mariners' manuals, as they came to be called, appeared already in the late sixteenth century and continued in a steady flow for centuries to come, some of them achieving quite extraordinary popularity.

Still, until the middle of the eighteenth century, there were no really convincing signs that mariners, as a group, would ever vindicate the early Christian vision of seafarers as carriers of the Bible to the world. The public image of seafarers as a group was still not any less negative than it had been for centuries. Many, not least those in evangelical ranks, continued to see seafarers as totally irredeemable. They had been, it was felt, beyond the pale of church and society for so long as to become almost impervious to spiritual or moral impressions. In fact, so entrenched had

---

[1] The subject of this study is addressed in greater detail in the author's published doctoral thesis. See Roald Kverndal, *Seamen's Missions: Their Origin and Early Growth* (Pasadena, CA: Wm. Carey Library, 1986). A parallel work in progress, *The Way of the Sea*, will constitute the author's companion volume on maritime missiology.

such prejudice become that it would be an important apologetic task for early advocates of seafarers' missions to overcome the "hopeless" image of the seafarer. According to his biographer, James Boswell, the renowned English lexicographer Samuel Johnson was asked in 1759 to define a sailor. His response was simple and to the point:

> No man will be a sailor, who has contrivance to get himself into a jail; for being in a ship is being in a jail, with the chance of being drowned.[2]

Why, therefore, did organized seafarers' missions finally emerge at the time they did and in the way they did? To explore these issues requires an examination of the role of the British and Foreign Bible Society in the development of seafarers' missions.

The Bible Society and the Rediscovery of the Seafarer

With the founding of the British and Foreign Bible Society in 1804, an institution was launched that would play a pivotal role in the global history of the Christian church. When activist pioneers of the BFBS fanned out to find those sectors of society most notoriously destitute of the Word, they quickly discovered the deprivation typical of seafarers. It is still largely unknown that the BFBS, from its earliest years, prioritized seafarers as a particularly important group.

Nevertheless, the BFBS was not, as is widely believed, the first Bible society in the United Kingdom. The first Bible Society had been launched twenty-five years earlier. It was on an autumn evening in 1779 that two Methodist laymen, so the story goes, were walking the streets of London through Soho Square, conversing after a meeting. These were troubled times, and they were discussing "the spiritual deprivation" of men in the armed forces. The outcome of their conversation was the founding, later that year, of a society whose express purpose was "for purchasing Bibles to be distributed among British Soldiers and Seamen of the Navy, in order (by the blessing of God) to spread abroad Christian knowledge and reformation of manners."[3]

At the time, the new organization was known simply as the Bible Society, for there existed no other agency devoted exclusively to the nationwide distribution of the Bible. Besides soldiers, the society originally focused on *naval* seafarers, not on seafarers in general. Even so, the Bible

---

2. James Boswell, *Boswell's Life of Johnson*, (London: Oxford University Press, 1953), pp. 46-47; Kverndal, *Seamen's Missions*, pp. 540-42.

3. Quotation from the anonymous tract, "The First Bible Society" (Religious Tract Society, 1874), as cited in Roald Kverndal, "The Two-Hundredth Anniversary of Organized Seamen's Missions, 1779-1979," *The Mariner's Mirror* 65, no. 3 (August 1979), pp. 255-63. See also, Kverndal, *Seamen's Missions*, pp. 71-90.

Society held the additional distinction of being the first seafarers' mission-related organization in the world.

Although Methodist-initiated, the Bible Society always remained essentially non-denominational. As such, it soon became the object of sustained Church of England support, especially by William Wilberforce and his evangelical Anglican colleagues (including the Reverend John Newton). However, it did not take the society long to discover that, despite such prominent patronage, demand for its publications was far outstripping the supply. Somehow the Bible Society managed to struggle on until 1803, when the outbreak of renewed international hostilities generated a sudden and even greater volume of requests for Bibles and New Testaments on British ships of war.

The following year, the founding of the more broadly based British and Foreign Bible Society presented the earlier society's leaders with a critical challenge that questioned their very reason for being. The outcome of the ensuing discussions was a resolve to stay the course as originally conceived, although with one significant concession. From 1804 onward the earlier Bible Society adopted a more narrowly defined organizational title, namely, the Naval and Military Bible Society (NMBS).

The Committee of the BFBS showed both sensitivity and restraint, choosing the role of supplementation rather than usurpation in relation to its somewhat less prestigious predecessor. Instead of targeting naval personnel in general, the BFBS elected to concentrate its early naval endeavors on particular categories. Foremost among these were the thousands of foreign prisoners of war jammed into old naval hulks anchored around the coast. By Christmas 1805, the first survivors from the shattered Franco-Spanish fleet at Trafalgar had barely been brought aboard their floating dungeons before the BFBS took up the challenge of providing for them.

The French and Spanish New Testaments that the BFBS Committee voted to supply to these survivors were only the first step in a rapidly expanding program for prisoners of war. In 1808, with exile to Australia becoming a favorite solution to Britain's overflowing jails, the BFBS began distributing Bibles to "convicts sailing for New South Wales." The BFBS also initiated Scripture distribution to the crews of revenue cutters and post office packets, as well as to the inmates of naval hospitals.[4]

---

4. *Reports of the British and Foreign Bible Society, with Extracts of Correspondence, &c. Volume the First, for the years 1805, to 1810, inclusive.* Reprinted from the original reports (London: BFBS, n.d.), pp. 158-59, 268, 396-97. John Owen, *The History of the Origin and First Ten Years of the British and Foreign Bible Society*, 2 vols. (London: Tilling and Hughes, 1816), vol. 2, pp. 56-57. William Canton, *A History of the British and Foreign Bible Society*, 5 vols. (London, John Murray, 1904–1910), vol. 1, pp. 17-55, 122-28. It is noteworthy

By 1810, with some 150,000 men under sail in the Royal Navy, there was growing demand for personal possession of copies of Scripture. Despite the efforts of the NMBS to cope with the situation, the need soon escalated to a point where the BFBS found it had no choice but to commit its far greater resources toward general naval distribution. As the NMBS repeatedly affirmed, there simply was no more effective means for sailors to overcome both moral laxity and the lack of preparedness for death than reading the Bible.

Other agencies involved in the distribution of Christian literature also took up the challenge.[5] However, for such a massive campaign to have any lasting effect, some system of shipboard "animators" was necessary. The Methodists found that their Nonconformist class-meeting traditions positioned them for crucial peer leadership in the burgeoning Bible-study cell group movement that began to take hold on the gun-decks of ships of war. The resulting revival came to be known as the "Naval Awakening."

The phenomenon was by no means limited to the lower deck. Noteworthy among the many evangelical officers involved in the movement was an unassuming lieutenant, Richard Marks (1778-1847). After serving with distinction at Trafalgar, Marks experienced a radical conversion, became the leader of an embattled but growing Christian community on board, and was later ordained. He became a pioneering advocate for Anglican seafarers' missions.[6]

It fell to the lot of a Baptist minister, once a sailor serving under Admiral Nelson, to play a unique role in the long-term impact of the Naval Awakening, as founder of the seafarers' mission movement. The Rev. George Charles Smith (1782-1863), while a pastor in the port of Penzance, launched an initiative that would become known as the "naval correspondence mission." Smith was astonished at the news of how his former fellow-sailors were struggling to withstand the ridicule and persecution of their peers in order to gather in groups for Bible-study and prayer on ships of the line. Seeing the need for a form of pastoral follow-up and fellowship, Smith, aided by teams of volunteers, corresponded with hundreds of his floating flock in the five-year period from 1809 to 1814.[7]

---

that in the United States the BFBS very early came to be recognized as owing its "parentage" to the NMBS. See Israel P. Warren, *The Seamen's Cause* (New York, 1858), p. 3.

5. Kverndal, *Seamen's Missions*, pp. 83-90, 99-103.

6. Kverndal, *Seamen's Missions*, pp. 91-111. See also the author's contribution, "Richard Marks," in the *Oxford Dictionary of National Biography* (Oxford: Oxford University Press, 2004).

7. Roald Kverndal, "George Charles Smith," *Oxford Dictionary of National Biography* (Oxford: Oxford University Press, 2004). See also, Kverndal, "George Charles Smith: Founder of the Seafarers' Mission Movement," *Maritime Mission Studies* 1 (1998),

Among Smith's many enthusiastic sponsors, Lady Mary Grey (1770-1858), wife of Sir George Grey, commissioner of the naval dockyard at Portsmouth, was conspicuous. Beginning in 1806 and continuing for two decades, she circulated "immense quantities" of Scriptures and Christian literature among active naval personnel through the BFBS and NMBS. For these and her many other means of ministering to the needs of seafarers, "the Commissioner's Lady" deserves to be remembered as the first female engaged in mission with seafarers.[8]

Besides playing an indispensable role in the Naval Awakening, the BFBS was destined to become the first organization anywhere to assume responsibility for Scripture distribution among seafarers in their *merchant* capacity. In so doing, the BFBS assumed an important position at the dawn of the seafarers' mission movement. During most of the Society's first decade, there was no question of outreach to merchant seafarers, but when such outreach began it was foreign merchant seafarers, not British seafarers, who became the Society's first beneficiaries. Many of these foreign merchant seafarers belonged to a category already noted, namely, prisoners of war. Large numbers of them were from the crews of foreign privateers and trading vessels seized as prizes. Over 27,000 were French, but thousands more were Scandinavian and Dutch, as well as American.

From 1805, merchant seafarers belonging to this category benefited from liberal annual grants given by the BFBS. Conspicuous in alerting the Society to the spiritual needs of their seafaring fellow-nationals were the pastors of the Scandinavian and Dutch resident communities in London. The Rev. Ulrick F. Rosing, for example, pastor of the Danish-Norwegian church in London, persuaded the BFBS to print and donate a special run of 5,000 Danish New Testaments for his incarcerated countrymen. With his assistance, the Society for the Promotion of Christian Knowledge provided 2,250 copies of the Danish hymnal. Apart from those interned, other seafarers also received wartime distribution of Scripture from the BFBS. Among the most prominent activists on behalf of seafarers were the Rev. K. F. A. Steinkopf of the German Lutheran church of the Savoy, Lady Mary Grey of Portsmouth, and Samuel Allen, who maintained a special depository for foreign seafarers in his St. Katherine's warehouse.[9]

pp. 9-21; Kverndal, *Seamen's Missions*, pp. 113-32; and the letter from G. C. Smith, 3 February 1812, which provided the BFBS Committee with a selection of letters from Smith's sailor correspondents, BFBS Home Correspondence Inwards (BSA/D1/1/10).

8. Kverndal, *Seamen's Missions*, pp. 125-26, 136; Kverndal, "Lady Mary Grey," *Oxford Dictionary of National Biography* (Oxford: Oxford University Press, 2004). The BFBS Home Correspondence Inwards (BSA/D1/1) from 1808 onward holds numerous letters from Lady Grey.

9. *Reports of the British and Foreign Bible Society...1805 to 1810*, pp. 138-39, 158-59;

There soon developed an alternative channel for Scripture distribution to merchant seafarers. Whereas during its early years, the BFBS had to rely solely on unpaid agents for general domestic distribution purposes, for its foreign distribution the Society found itself depending heavily on seafarers themselves. Thus, seafaring fellow-workers early on served to validate the inclusion of the words "and Foreign" in the self-designation of the new British and Foreign Bible Society. Referred to as "agents afloat," these seafaring distributors of Scripture formed a fascinating chapter in the Bible Society's early years. As masters of merchant vessels (and sometimes even as naval commanders), these highly motivated co-workers offered free transportation and use of their worldwide contacts to bring Bibles in different languages to every conceivable corner of the globe.[10]

Prominent in this unique category of collaborators was Captain Francis Reynalds of Hull. In a series of letters from the year 1810 onward, Reynalds reported on the distribution of Scripture in various languages to the inhabitants of ports of call as far apart as the Mediterranean and Baltic Seas, and the Caribbean basin. Grateful recipients included even the president of Haiti. Reynalds did not forget his fellow-seafarers, both British and foreign. Soliciting Scripture on their behalf before leaving for Malta, he wrote on 2 September 1811 to BFBS Assistant Secretary Joseph Tarn:

> ...and when the exhortation in Isa 42.10, with the promises recorded in Isa 24.24, and 60.5 is considered, I have no doubt but the Committee will continue to remember that class of men who seam to be neither numbered with the Living or the Dead. I expect to sail in a short time.

Two years later, in a letter of 24 June 1813, dated off the Mother Bank, Reynalds could write to tell Tarn of the formation among his crew of the first floating marine Bible association on record. After a meeting of all hands, convened by the captain, they had unanimously agreed to the following joint commitment:

Reports of the British and Foreign Bible Society, with Extracts of Correspondence, &c. Volume the Second, for 1811, 1812, and 1813, reprinted from the original reports (London: BFBS, 1813), pp.177-78. Samuel Allen to Joseph Reyner, 25 March 1815, BFBS Home Correspondence Inwards (BSA/D1/1/15). BFBS Minutes of the Committee, 29 April and 6 May 1816, vol. 7, pp. 374, 381 (BSA/B1/7). See also Owen, *History*, vol. 2, pp. 567-68; Canton, *History*, vol. 1, p. 9; Kverndal, *Seamen's Missions*, pp. 135-36, 592-95.

10. Canton, *History*, vol. 1, pp. 128-42; Kverndal, *Seamen's Missions*, pp. 136-38, 229, 242, 414, 552, 595, 620-21. Letters in the BFBS Home Correspondence Inwards (BSA/D1/1) indicate that many of the merchant and naval agents afloat were in touch with Lady Mary Grey.

That the crew of this vessel do form themselves into an Association for the purpose of contributing towards the circulation of the holy scriptures, both at home and abroad, and that this Association be denominated "The Ship Vigilant (of Hull) Bible Association."[11]

Like his fellow agents afloat, Captain Anthony Landers of Sunderland also seemed willing to "bear a hand" wherever needed in the "kingdom cause." In a letter to Tarn of 4 October 1816, he shares how, when visiting New York, he had left a large quantity of Sunday school books with "a Public Spirited Lady" (presumably Mrs. Divie Bethune). On his return, he was amazed to find that she had "fill'd the City with Sunday Schools." But Landers, too, looked with impatience to the dawn of organized mission for the benefit of seafarers. As he puts it, "so long as one of the greatest of all [missionary institutions] is wanting, I mourn and lament..." Meanwhile, with prophetic insight he warns that such mission must be particularized, because "the Means must be aim'd at them, & for them to do them good."[12]

Another entrepreneurial collaborator, Captain George Orton, wrote to the BFBS of his joy at having been the first to circulate the Society's Modern Greek Testament in the Mediterranean. Like his colleagues, Orton threw himself with enthusiasm into the nascent postwar organization of seafarers' mission activity — both ashore and afloat. In that process, the Bible Society's seagoing agents were positioned to provide a living link, and this they happily did.[13]

Marine Bible Societies

The Naval Awakening, by making Scriptures more widely available to seafarers, had created the precondition for the very first form of organization to emerge in the seafarers' mission movement of the early nineteenth century, namely, the marine Bible societies. These would draw much of their support from the thousands who were returning from ships of war

---

11. Francis Reynalds to Joseph Tarn, 2 September 1811 and 24 June 1813, BFBS Home Correspondence Inwards (BSA/D1/1/7 and BSA/D1/1/12); *Twelfth Report of the BFBS* (London, 1816), appendix pp. 91-92. Reynalds refers in his letter of 2 September to the legend of a philosopher of antiquity who, when asked about the ratio between the living and the dead, replied: "First you will have to tell me where I am to place seafarers — among the living or the dead?" See also Kverndal, *Seamen's Missions*, pp. 136-37, 140, 229.

12. Anthony Landers to Tarn, 4 October 1816, BFBS Home Correspondence Inwards (BSA/D1/1/18). Kverndal, *Seamen's Missions*, pp. 137-38, 243, 620-21.

13. Four letters from George Orton 1812, 1825, 1826, 1831, BFBS Home Correspondence Inwards (BSA/D1/1/9, 46, 50, 67). See also *Reports of the British and Foreign Bible Society...for 1811, 1812, and 1813*, pp. 416-17. Kverndal, *Seamen's Missions*, pp. 137, 203, 209, 220.

and French prison depots and seeking employment in the postwar merchant fleet.[14]

Captain Landers and his fellow agents afloat would still have to wait until 1818 for the formation of any seafarers' mission organized in a more comprehensive sense. But five years earlier, the first British society ever organized to promote the spiritual welfare of specifically merchant seafarers was formed, namely, the Thames Union Bible Committee (TUBC). This was the original name of the first marine Bible society — among many others — that emerged in Britain and abroad between 1813 and 1820.

The new organization was the brainchild of Charles S. Dudley of Camberwell, a man whose exceptional organizing ability later led to his appointment as the first full-time domestic agent of the BFBS. As an active member of the Society's Southwark auxiliary, Dudley toward the close of 1812 visited some merchant ships on the Thames. As Dudley later described the situation:

> ...the result of his casual inquiries induced a belief, that an unexpected and deplorable dearth of the holy scriptures existed among the British and Foreign sailors resorting to the port of London. In order to ascertain the fact, eleven ships were indiscriminately visited by him, and only *one* Bible found, and this aboard a *Swedish* vessel.[15]

Further investigation only served to confirm Dudley's initial impression. Accordingly, during the winter, Dudley devoted himself to a plan for meeting the Bible needs of those on board the merchant ships, and this he did with the assistance of a colleague, Benjamin Neale, who was a member of Parliament. The resulting proposal recognized the obligation of all BFBS auxiliaries bordering the waterfront of any seaport — in this case the banks of the Thames — to band together in so-called unions, in order to supply visiting seafarers with the Bible. For this purpose, they needed to form a committee — hence the proposed name of the organization, the Thames Union Bible Committee, eventually launched on 21 June 1813 at the Three Tuns Tavern in Southwark.[16]

Four BFBS auxiliary societies, Southwark and Blackheath on the south side and the City of London and East London on the north, agreed to form a joint committee. At the request of the TUBC, Dudley prepared a multi-language address to mariners. He sought to motivate seafarers to

---

14. Kverndal, *Seamen's Missions*, pp. 130-38.

15. Charles S. Dudley, *An Analysis of the System of the Bible Society throughout its Various Parts* (London: R. Watts, 1821), pp. 293-94.

16. Minutes of Southwark Auxiliary Bible Society (SABS), 12 May 1813 and 14 July 1813 (BSA/F1/London17/1). *Reports of the British and Foreign Bible Society, with Extracts of Correspondence, &c. Volume the Third, for the years 1814 and 1815*. Reprinted from the original reports (London: BFBS, 1815), pp. 201-2. Dudley, *Analysis*, 204, 294.

make use of the committee's listed depositories, posing the provocative question: "Will *you* [seafarers] be the last in supplying yourselves with this teacher of the way to heaven, and in sharing the happy privilege of conveying it to foreign lands?"[17] Whatever such arguments may (or may not) have contributed, the initial response was recorded as positive. Within a year, however, two major problems had surfaced, serious enough to jeopardize the fledgling organization's future. First, most foreign seafarers were unable to afford even the greatly reduced prices for Scripture asked for by the TUBC. Second, volunteer TUBC members were unable to commit to all the time-consuming person-to-person work entailed.[18]

Meanwhile, exciting news arrived of Captain Francis Reynalds' innovative ship-based Bible association, launched only three days after the Thames union committee was formed. Similar grassroots Bible associations (in affiliation with individual BFBS auxiliary societies) had already become popular ashore. With their minimal subscriptions and stimulus to self-help, they made Dudley wonder whether this was the way to go with seafarers. Again, he went to work with his colleagues, and came up with new published plans — and another address to mariners — for marine Bible associations throughout the merchant service. In July 1815, the Thames Union Bible Committee became the Thames Marine Bible Association Committee.[19]

Despite high hopes, it soon became apparent that even more radical change was inevitable. For the third time, Dudley was enlisted to come up with a plan as well as another address to mariners. By now it was clear that nothing short of a new national organization was called for. It would need to be directly affiliated with the BFBS itself, since its declared purpose rendered it "too important to continue merely as an appendage to other institutions." As a result, the Thames Marine Bible Association Committee transferred its resources to the Merchant Seamen's Auxiliary Bible Society (MSABS), established in January 1818, at a public meeting chaired by the Lord Mayor of London at his Mansion House residence.[20]

---

17. Dudley's "Address to Mariners" is appended to his *Analysis*, appendix no. 11, pp. 33-34.

18. Copy of TUBC resolution, May 11, 1815, enclosed with letter from Allen to Reyner, 25 March 1815, BFBS Home Correspondence Inwards (BSA/D1/1/15); Joseph Shewell to Tarn, 6 December 1815, BFBS Home Correspondence Inwards (BSA/D1/1/16). Minutes of the SABS, 12 July 1815 (BSA/F1/London17/1).

19. Minutes of the SABS, 12 July 1815 (BSA/F1/London17/1). Owen, *History*, vol. 2, pp. 586-87; For this "Address," see Dudley's *Analysis*, appendix no. 11, pp. 34-35.

20. Minutes of the SABS, 14 February 1816, 12 March 1817, 8 October 1817 (BSA/F1/London17/1). MSABS, *Address* (London, 1818), pp. 1-4; *Prospectus and Regulations*, 1818, pp. 20-21.

The new MSABS never became more than a metropolitan organization, and financial frustrations persisted. Nevertheless, in two key areas it registered such remarkable success that the justification for this third attempt was never in doubt. First, the MSABS introduced a proactive policy of ship visitation, rather than relying on seafarers themselves to search out Bible depositories ashore, and — equally important — the society secured as its first full-time agent the uniquely qualified Lieutenant John Cox of the Royal Navy.

Cox had already come to the attention of the BFBS as early as 1806, with his persistent concern for Scripture distribution on prison ships in the Thames off Woolwich (where he was then serving). Shortly afterward, he also single-handedly started — and for years continued to run — a kind of volunteer shipping agency that constantly sought opportunities to ship Scripture consignments from the BFBS overseas on outbound naval vessels. When sharing personal contacts in the course of frequent correspondence with the Bible Society's secretary, Joseph Tarn, the enterprising young lieutenant made no effort to conceal his Methodist partiality, as shown by the following postscript to an 1809 letter:

> P.S. I shall not fail to look out for those who savour of Methodism as bearers of your commands and you know the stronger they smell the better..."[21]

The Bible Society had no problem making their choice when, in the midst of postwar officer redundancy, they needed to fill the vital new MSABS agency position at Gravesend. Confronted with this novel call, Lieutenant Cox commenced without a day's delay, on 26 February 1818, to respond to their appeal. His weekly ministry reports were replete with dramatic details of his daily encounters on board, as he rowed his "Bible-boat" between ships in the roadstead awaiting departure. Typical in these reports was the candid confession of one "honest tar" who simply said: "We sailors have been swearing quite long enough. It is high time we begin to pray. Let me have a Bible." A Scottish seafarer told how he had gladly risked his life to rescue his New Testament during shipwreck on his previous voyage. Two New Testaments that were given to a Spanish crew induced them to follow the agent with thanks "a thousand times," even after he had left their ship far behind.[22]

---

21. Letters from John Cox to Reyner, 4 June 1806, and to Tarn, 30 June 1809, BFBS Home Correspondence Inwards (BSA/D1/1/2 and D1/1/4).

22. The Cox quotations are from the first report of the MSABS, published in the *Fifteenth Report of the BFBS* (London, 1819), p. 266.

Picture 36. *Distributing Scriptures to Sailors.* Reprinted with permission from Roald Kverndal, *Seamen's Missions* (Pasadena, CA. Wm. Carey Library, 1986)

The Bible Society was quick to capitalize on the public relations potential of their agent's exploits. Published extracts were regularly reproduced in the religious press and eagerly read, both nationwide and even across the Atlantic. In the long term, the appointment of the MSABS agent at Gravesend would prove to be a significant new development in at least three ways. First, in terms of maritime mission history, given the February 1818 date of his appointment, John Cox unwittingly became the world's first full-time seafarers' missionary on record. Second, in terms of maritime mission strategy, Cox confirmed the key motivational role of ship visitation as a means of reaching such a marginalized group both in their own element and in their own way. Third, in terms of maritime mission advocacy, inasmuch as the church could not adequately fulfill its obligation to bring the gospel to seafarers solely by means of its established ministry, the inauguration of a particularized maritime ministry became the only viable option.[23]

23. *Fifteenth Report of the BFBS*, pp.263-65; *Monthly Extracts* (London: BFBS, March 1819), pp. 77-78; MSABS, *Annual Report* (1826), pp.15, 30, 35. In the United States, see the Bible Society of Philadelphia, *Annual Report* (1819), pp. 50-52. See also, the American Bible Society, *Annual Report* (1820), pp. 171-74. Kverndal, *Seamen's Missions*, pp.143-46, 150.

In contrast to the sometimes painful process of experimentation in the metropolis, the organization of Scripture distribution among merchant seafarers in Britain's provincial ports met with far more success. Here, too, the ground had usually been prepared by an existing local auxiliary of the BFBS. Conspicuous among the provincial marine Bible societies that emerged as a result of those BFBS efforts were the ones located in the strongholds of Methodism in the northern counties. The first of these was the Tyne Union Bible Committee, founded in 1814 and modeled after the Thames version of 1813. Initially meeting with indifference, even outright sneers, the pioneers persevered and were soon "hailed with pleasure," as they carried on throughout the 1820s. Meanwhile, in 1817, Tyneside's neighbor to the south, Sunderland, followed suit with a special subcommittee fashioned out of the local auxiliary Bible society.[24]

Even more impressive were the results of the three seagoing marine Bible associations based in Whitby, Hull, and Aberdeen, founded in 1816, 1817, and 1818, respectively. In the Hull-based association alone, in which Francis Reynalds played a leading role, some seven hundred to eight hundred seafarers rapidly enlisted. By 1821, these three port-city parent associations could report that a total of twenty-five ship-based marine Bible associations had now been formed at sea. A major motivation was doubtless the fact that these seafarers were not treated primarily as objects of charity, but rather confronted with, and empowered by, cooperative responsibility. Such local responsibility had by then proved a key factor in the lay-led Bethel movement that originated precisely during this period (see below).[25]

In other provincial port cities, too, societies were founded for merchant marine Bible distribution. For example, from 1818 onward thriving societies emerged in Lerwick, Liverpool, and Bristol.[26] Nor were the nation's inland waterways ignored, with their workforce of thousands of impoverished people laboring on barges and boats. In 1816, the Grand Junction and General Canal Bible Association was founded in Paddington, making it the first organization in the world specifically formed for the spiritual welfare of inland waterway mariners and their families. For the benefit of

---

24. The quotation is from a report of the Newcastle auxiliary, in *Monthly Extracts* (June 1825). See also BFBS Minutes of the Committee, 15 July 1816, vol. 8, p. 31 (BSA/B1/8); *Monthly Extracts* (February 1829), p. 214. Dudley, *Analysis*, pp. 297, 305-306. Kverndal, *Seamen's Missions*, pp.146-48.

25. *Fifteenth Report of the BFBS*, p. 290. Dudley, *Analysis*, pp. 298-305, 321-22, 336-38.

26. *Fifteenth Report of the BFBS*, p. 255. Edinburgh Bible Society, *Report* (1819), pp. 14, 53-55. *The Sailor's Magazine* (1820), pp. 305-308, 344. Dudley, *Analysis*, pp. 306-307, 316-19.

the underprivileged children, a so-called Canal School was shortly afterward established.[27]

Just as the British and Foreign Bible Society's engagement on the metropolitan waterfront resulted in a ripple effect in Britain's provincial port cities, the same happened overseas, notably along the north Atlantic seaboard of the United States. For the church in the United States, the return of peace in 1815 meant a renewal of British example and inspiration, as voluntary societies for an ever-widening variety of benevolent causes proliferated on both sides of the Atlantic. A striking example of the tenacity of such transatlantic ties was the action of the Massachusetts Bible Society, which in the thick of hostilities, both in 1813 and 1814, had compensated the BFBS for Scripture consignments lost on ships captured by American privateers. For, if Americans were at war with England, they were "not at war with her pious and benevolent institutions."[28]

Largely as a result of the bond with the BFBS — both as parent and as example — marine Bible societies surfaced in Philadelphia (1816), in New York (1817), and in an impressive number of east coast seaports.[29] In some respects, America's version of the marine Bible society movement manifested a greater degree of vigor than its British antecedent. By contrast, marine Bible distribution elsewhere overseas began on a far more modest scale. Much of it was initially the fruit of seafaring collaborators of the BFBS, from agents afloat to members of ship-based marine Bible associations. But in a small number of continental port cities, indigenous marine Bible associations did emerge. Where it happened, it was normally thanks to the rapidly growing BFBS network for general Bible distribution abroad.[30]

The first continental agencies for marine Bible distribution had principally naval personnel in mind, together with their frequently impoverished dependents. The BFBS nevertheless classified these agencies as marine Bible societies, like the rest. Sweden seems to have been the site of the first continental marine Bible society with Skeppsholms Auxiliary Bible Society (Stockholm's Admiralty Parish), founded in 1815. In 1819, a

27. *The Sailor's Magazine* (1822), pp. 109-110. Dudley, *Analysis*, pp. 341-42.

28. Massachusetts Bible Society, *Report* (1814), pp. 5-6, 199-224; *The First Hundred Years* (Boston, 1909), pp. 14-17; *Reports of the British and Foreign Bible Society...1814 and 1815*, pp. 36-37, 120-23. Kverndal, *Seamen's Missions*, pp. 412-24.

29. *Reports of the British and Foreign Bible Society... for 1811, 1812, and 1813*, pp. 25-26. Robert Ralston to Josiah Roberts, 8 March 1816, BFBS Home Correspondence Inwards (BSA/D1/1/19). Bible Society of Philadelphia, *Report* (1816), pp. 17-23, 48, and (1817-1821), passim. New York Bible Society, *Annual Reports* (1810-1817), passim. *The Christian Herald* (1816-1818), passim. Marine Bible Society of New York, *Annual Reports* (1817), passim. American Bible Society, *Annual Report* (1822), pp. 212-13.

30. Kverndal, *Seamen's Missions*, pp. 148-49.

grant of £200 offered by the Rev. Ebenezer Henderson of the BFBS led to the founding of the Swedish Naval Bible Society, located at Carlscrona (known as the Portsmouth of Sweden).[31]

In 1816, another naval Bible society was founded at Kronstadt, Russia's key commercial and naval base. The Kronstadt society was initiated by Henderson's colleague, John Paterson, and Robert Pinkerton worked with the group later. Besides the BFBS outreach to visiting merchant seafarers, the domestic impact of the society prompted Russian Bible Society president Alexander Golitsyn to assert that Russian sailors had now "learned to value the Scriptures, and the use of them was becoming general."[32]

In 1820, agencies for Bible distribution among seafarers were established in Denmark (Copenhagen) and the Netherlands (Amsterdam and Rotterdam), later also in Germany (Hamburg-Altona). In all cases, BFBS sponsorship appears to have been a decisive factor.[33] And yet, half a century would elapse before more diversified seafarers' mission activities were developed on the European continent. Still, continental marine Bible societies did represent the first, and largely ignored, organized form of such mission in these parts. As to the British and American manifestations of the marine Bible society movement, their decisive impact on the emergence of more comprehensive seafarers' mission organization would shortly be discernable.

The Vision Restored

When Bible distribution and other mission initiatives among seafarers began gathering momentum as an authentic seafarers' mission movement, it was not because of bureaucratic action by the institutional church. It began rather with a movement of seafarers themselves, and eventually came to be known as the Thames Revival. The movement started in the summer of 1814, with groups of seafarers gathered for prayer and the sharing of Scriptures on board north-country collier-ships anchored in the lower pool of London's Thames. In 1817, as the numbers of these seafarers swelled, they adopted their own emblem, hoisted at the masthead as a signal for lay-led worship on board. While the emblem depicted the

---

31. Swedish Bible Society, *Reports* (1816), pp. 42-43; (1819), p. 23; (1820), pp. 20-21; (1821), pp. 35-36; (1822), pp. 29-30. *Twelfth Report of the BFBS*, p. 19; *Fifteenth Report of the BFBS*, p. 319. Canton, *History*, vol. 1, pp. 217, 448.

32. *Thirteenth Report of the BFBS* (London, 1817), pp.268-69; *Seventeenth Report of the BFBS* (London, 1821), pp.54-55). NMBS, *Report* (1818), pp. 11-12. Canton, *History*, vol. 1, pp. 407-408.

33. Danish Bible Society, *Monthly Reports*, no. 6, 1820, pp. 73-80; *Reports*, 1821, p. 35; 1822, pp. 33-34. *Seventeenth Report of the BFBS* (London, 1821), p. xxiii; *Eighteenth Report of the BFBS* (London 1822), pp. xxvi-xxvii.

Star of Bethlehem and Noah's Dove of Peace, its principal feature was the word "Bethel" (Hebrew for "House of God"). Together these images signified a profession of faith symbolized by the three major events in the Christian calendar — Christmas, Easter, and Pentecost.

The ensuing Bethel Movement was brilliantly promoted and coordinated by the Rev. George Charles Smith, who envisioned its global potential from the very start. Ashore, in the wake of initial shipboard Bethel meetings, port-based and national societies for seafarers' mission emerged from 1818 through the 1820s, both in Britain and America. Afloat, British and American Bethel captains and their crews carried the mission work to every corner of the globe. In these far-flung places, with the cooperation of local Christian merchants or missionaries, including BFBS emissaries, the ground was frequently laid for local shore-based maritime ministry at some later point. Thus, these Bethel captains carried on in the tradition of the early BFBS agents afloat.[34]

Tracing the continuing saga of seafarers' missions through the nineteenth and twentieth centuries has been undertaken elsewhere.[35] The Merchant Seamen's Auxiliary Bible Society (MSABS) continued to exist until 1855, although the BFBS eventually turned to supporting scriptural distribution through the various seafarers' missions instead. The Naval and Military Bible Society, which in 1825 decided to include merchant seafarers, has continued direct marine distribution up to the present — now as the Naval, Military and Air Force Bible Society (NMAFBS). Today, among the broad range of regular recipients of maritime-related NMAFBS Scripture portions are also the Catholic seafarers' mission agencies.

This paper has noted the crucial foundational role played by the British and Foreign Bible Society during the dawn of organized maritime mission. That role might in one way be compared to a spiritual transplant operation. Without the empowerment mediated by the Society's concerted campaign to make the Scriptures available to seafarers of the day, the story would have been very different. As it was, thousands of seasoned veterans, infused with the rugged spirituality of the Naval Awakening, sought employment in the post-Napoleonic merchant service. There, reinvigorated by the marine Bible society movement and the Thames Revival, they developed the dynamic momentum of the Bethel Movement.

In essence, the Bethel Movement represented the first fruits of a restoration of the missionary role of seafarers. Such a vision, although recaptured amidst the spontaneity of the initial Bethel era, was placed virtually

---

34. Kverndal, *Seamen's Missions*, pp. 151-68, 197-251.
35. See Paul G. Mooney, *Serving Seafarers under Sail and Steam*, IASMM Occasional Paper no. 2 (York, 2000); and his "Maritime Mission in the New Millennium," (Th.D. diss., Univ. of Brussels, 2002). Kverndal, *The Way of the Sea*, in progress.

on hold by the institutionalization of seafarers' missions that developed and continued during the ensuing 150 years. These missions entailed a more holistic approach. Nevertheless, the process all but eclipsed the original grassroots peer model of ministry with a welfare-based institutional model. Coupled with the increasing secularization of twentieth-century society, this inevitably resulted in a paternalistic view of seafarers as essentially beneficiaries or passive objects of mission, rather than, as originally envisioned, fellow-workers or active subjects of mission.

Globalization has had a radical contextual impact in the seafaring world as elsewhere. The so-called shipping revolution, which registered in real earnest from the mid-1970s, led to the hiring of crews from the low-cost labor markets of the world's developing nations, particularly from Asia, and no longer from the traditional seafaring nations of the western world. This has confronted contemporary seafarers' missions with awesome challenges, both in terms of relating to seafarers who come from a predominantly non-Christian background, and in advocacy for the victims of human rights abuse at sea.

In this situation, several seafarers' mission agencies have launched Bible-based pastoral programs for maritime follow-up ministry. Since the early 1980s, these have been accompanied by a remarkable proliferation of seagoing cell groups, or so-called maritime base communities, in many ways reminiscent of the heyday of the Bethel Movement. By providing Christian community on board ship, such groups have been able to offer a non-coercive gospel alternative to non-Christian fellow-seafarers. Empowered by a biblical understanding of human self-worth, they have also come into the forefront in resisting dehumanizing conditions at sea, and many of their members have been returning with a new-found faith to home communities in countries now closed to conventional Christian mission.[36]

In his doctoral dissertation, "Maritime Mission in the New Millennium," Anglican theologian Paul Mooney has delivered a powerful, well-argued challenge to the global maritime mission community. He has called for responding to the radically changed context in the maritime industry by embracing a corresponding paradigm shift in maritime ministry. This will mean moving from the agency-centered model of current shore-based welfare ministry to the seafarer-centered model of a ship-based peer ministry. Centers ashore will in the future need to give

---

36. Kverndal, "Maritime Christian Fellowship," *Maritime Mission Studies* (IASMM), no.1 (1994), pp. 1-15. During the late 1970s, the Rev. Ray Eckhoff, of Tacoma in the Pacific Northwest, developed a Bible study correspondence course called the *Ministering Seafarers' Program*, which reached thousands during the following two decades. In 2003, this led to the production of *Water Words*, an innovative series of scriptural "Sea passages" for Bible study, edited by the Rev. Dr. Robin Dale Mattison (Mall Maritime Library, Beach Park, Illinois).

priority to a supportive, yet no less essential, resource role.[37] Without doubt, the wave of the future points toward an emerging new Bethel movement, one where the centrality of the Scriptures will again be paramount. For the British and Foreign Bible Society, this may well mean that the maritime dimension of their global mission has yet to see its greatest glory.

---

37. Mooney, *Maritime Mission*.

APPENDIX: A SUMMARY CATALOGUE OF THE BFBS ARCHIVES (BSA)

Kathleen Cann

This is a summary of the British and Foreign Bible Society Archives catalogue compiled during the period 1999-2002 by Kathleen Cann, Gotthelf Wiedermann, and Robert Steiner, with funding assistance from the Research Support Libraries Programme (RSLP). The RSLP supported the compilation of the catalogue as part of the project, "Missionary Collections in the UK". The full online version of the catalogue of the BFBS Archives can be seen at http://janus.lib.cam.ac.uk. Other detailed finding aids, including card indexes of nineteenth-century correspondents and of pamphlets, can be consulted at Cambridge University Library. Please note that the Society operates a fifty-year closure period and that therefore not all the records described here are available for research.

The arrangement of the archives reflects the structure of the Society itself: at the top was the general meeting of members that appointed the governing Committee. The Committee appointed subcommittees to deal with specialized areas of the work, and also appointed the secretaries, who acted as chief executive officers. Beneath the secretaries were the departments, linked to the specialized subcommittees. The archives also contain records created outside London, but deposited at headquarters later, including records of local branches in the United Kingdom, records of overseas societies and agencies, and the papers of individuals connected with the Society. In creating a new classification for the archives, an alphanumeric scheme was adopted, giving a letter for the main categories, as follows:

- A Constitutional records
- B Records of the Committee
- C Records of subcommittees
- D Records of the secretaries
- E Records of departments
- F Deposited papers
- G Publications

Each section is then subdivided by using numbers: thus, A1 contains records of general meetings, A1/1 being the first minute book of those meetings. Not all of the subdivisions are recorded here. The archives as a whole have the designation BSA (Bible Society Archives) parallel with the Scripture library, whose classification begins BSS (Bible Society Scriptures). While the new codes serve as shelfmarks and for ordering items from the archives, the titles of the individual series and items should continue to be cited for purposes of clarity of documentation, alongside use of the new BSA codes.

BSA/A: Constitutional Records

Until the grant of a Royal Charter in 1948, the BFBS was a voluntary society, responsible to a general meeting of its subscribers. This section consists of the formal minutes of such meetings, an early document appointing trustees to hold the Society's funds, and the records of the Incorporated BFBS Association, set up as a limited company to own and manage property and related investments.

- A1 Minutes of General Meetings (1804–1951)
- A2 Declaration of Trust (1806)
- A3 Incorporated BFBS Association (1907–1966)
    - A3/1 Documents of incorporation (1907–1952)
    - A3/2 Minute books (1907–1964)
    - A3/3 Property account ledgers (1905–1939)
    - A3/4 Property account journals (1905–1925)
    - A3/5 Annual accounts (1919–1966)
    - A3/6 Register of members and directors (1930–1948)
    - A3/6a Signed membership forms (1910–1962)
    - A3/7 Letterbook (1907–1933)
    - A3/8 Draft powers of attorney (1933–1937)

BSA/B: Records of the Committee

The Committee, or "General Committee", was the body that controlled the Society's day-to-day business. Its minutes (B1) contain, typically, summaries of the letters presented to the Committee, and the resolutions passed. There are 127 volumes, each with a detailed index. Volumes 3-115 (1807–1914) have been microfilmed. Note that the first two volumes are missing, and also volumes 9, 12, 17, 21-25, 30, and 33.

- B1 Minutes of the Committee (1807–1984)
- B2 Rough minutes (1841–1851)
- B3 Foreign agenda (1830–1846)
- B4 Agenda, draft minutes, and supplementary papers (1938–1963)

B5 By-laws (1804–1928)

B6 Business at Committee meetings (1863–1870)

B7 Visitors' attendance book (1816–1868)

BSA/C: Records of the Subcommittees

For matters requiring detailed consideration the Committee appointed small subcommittees. A number of standing subcommittees soon emerged, which were reappointed each year. In addition, special subcommittees were set up from time to time to deal with specific issues. The whole committee system was reorganised in 1939 and further streamlined in 1966, 1969, and 1972, drastically reducing the number of subcommittees.

At first, minutes of all subcommittees were contained in one series of volumes (C1/1). As standing subcommittees became established they acquired their own series of minute books, except for the General Purposes Subcommittee, whose minutes were incorporated into the volumes of the minutes of the Committee (B1) from 1819 until the subcommittee ended in 1878. In 1882 another series of general volumes was begun (C1/2), which again contain the earliest minutes of subcommittees that later acquired their own minute books, for example C21 and C22. Nearly all the volumes have indexes. The subcommittees have been grouped by subject, as follows:

General volumes, policy, and administration

    C1 Miscellaneous subcommittees (1804–1952)
        C1/1 minutes (1804–1833)
        C1/2 minutes (1882–1905)
        C1/3 minutes (1912–1926)
        C1/4 minutes (1947–1952)

    C2 Staff Subcommittee (1904–1939)

    C3 General Purposes Subcommittee (1939–1966)

Finance and property

    C4 Finance Subcommittee (1816–1966)

    C5 Committee of Auditors (1810–1885)

    C6 Estimates/Property Subcommittee (1903–1969)

    C7 House Subcommittee (1) (1815–1817)

    C8 Building Subcommittee (1863–1870)

    C9 House Subcommittee (2) (1868–1937)

Publishing and warehouse

    C10 Printing and Depository Subcommittee (1817–1972)

Home work and publicity

    C11 Accommodation/Anniversary Subcommittee (1833–1937)

    C12 Local/Agency Subcommittee (1833–1854)

    C13 Home Organisation Subcommittee (1888–1972)

    C14 Publications/Publicity Subcommittee (1888–1968)

    C15 Women's Advisory Subcommittee (1942–1979)

    C16 Education Advisory Subcommittee (1955–1972)

Translations and library

    C17 Editorial/Translations Subcommittee (1830–1978) (with minutes of Library Subcommittee from 1816)

    C18 Library Subcommittee (1909–1936)

Work overseas

    C19 Oriental Subcommittee (1804–1809)

    C20 Foreign Depots Subcommittee (1852–1939)

    C21 China, Japan, and Korea Subcommittee (1905–1938)

    C22 India and Africa Subcommittee (1905–1939)

    C23 Colonial Subcommittee (1904–1907)

    C24 Australia and New Zealand/Overseas Dominions Subcommittee (1919–1939)

    C25 Overseas Administration Subcommittee A (1939–1965)

    C26 Overseas Administration Subcommittee B (1939–1964)

    C27 Europe and Latin America Subcommittee (1965–1969)

    C28 Asia Subcommittee (1965–1969)

    C29 Africa Subcommittee (1964–1969)

Short-term subcommittees

    C30 Special subcommittees:
        C30/1 Jubilee Committee (1852–1854)
        C30/2 River Colportage Subcommittee (1855)
        C30/3 Centenary Subcommittees (1901–1903)

C30/4 Authorized Version Tercentenary Subcommittee (1910-1911)
C30/5 Staff Subcommittee for Review (1919-1923)
C30/6 Motor Cars Subcommittee (1929-1935)
C30/7 Pensions Subcommittee (1933-1938)
C30/8 Investigation Subcommittee (1938-1939)
C30/9 Post-War (Overseas) Planning Subcommittee (1941-1945)
C30/10 Home Planning and Survey Subcommittee (1943-1945)
C30/11 Special Sealing Committee (1949-1962)
C30/12 Economy and Review Committees (1950-1952)
C30/13 Third Jubilee Executive Committee (1950-1954)
C30/14 Policy Advisory Committee (1956)
C30/15 Translators' Aids Subcommittee (1956-1964)

BSA/D: Records of the Secretaries

The BFBS secretaries were the Society's chief executive officers, responsible to the Committee. Three were appointed in 1804: one Anglican, one Dissenter, and one representative of foreign churches, all ordained men. The BFBS foreign secretary resigned in 1826, and his post was discontinued. It seems there was no distinction between the duties of the BFBS secretaries until about 1890, when the overseas work was divided between them on a geographical basis. During the nineteenth century, they were helped by an assistant secretary, an accountant, and an assistant foreign secretary, and the correspondence of these officials is included in the main series.

During the nineteenth century, correspondence was filed in long chronological series of incoming and outgoing letters, divided into "Home" and "Foreign" series. These are not complete, the most serious loss being that of the incoming correspondence from 1857 to 1900. Two series of copybooks partly fill this gap, the Agents' Books for the ten-year period, 1867 to 1877 (D1/7), and letters on translations from 1858 to 1897 (E3/1/4).

D1 Main Correspondence (1804-1931)

D1/1 Home Correspondence Inwards (1804-1856, 1902-1905), indexed to 1836
D1/2 Foreign Correspondence Inwards (1804-1856, 1901-1905), indexed to 1856
D1/3 Home Correspondence Outwards (1820-1906), indexed
D1/4 Foreign Correspondence Outwards (1819-1880, 1900-1931), indexed
D1/5 Correspondence Books (Home and Foreign) (1804-1839), indexed
D1/6 Foreign Correspondence Books (1814-1819), indexed

D1/7 Agents' Books (1867-1877), indexed and arranged by agency: France (7 vols.), Belgium and Holland (3 vols.), Germany (3 vols.), Austrian Empire (3 vols.), Italy and North Africa (4 vols.), Spain and Portugal (4 vols.), Russia (4 vols.), Turkish Empire (5 vols.), South America (2 vols.), China (1 vol.)

D2 Special correspondence (1804-1931): Correspondence and papers relating to specific individuals or events either kept out of or removed from the main series

    D2/1 Thomas Charles of Bala (1755-1814): letters and papers (1804-1814)
    D2/2 William Wilberforce (1759-1833), reformer: letters and speeches (1804-1837)
    D2/3 Apocrypha Controversy: copybook (1812-1825), letters on the controversy
    D2/4 Trinitarian Controversy: copybook (1831-1832), letters from supporters on the subject of the BFBS constitution
    D2/5 George Borrow (1803-1881), author and linguist: letters to the BFBS (1833-1843), published as *Letters of George Borrow to the British and Foreign Bible Society* (London: Hodder & Stoughton, 1911)
    D2/6 Earl of Shaftesbury (1801-1885), philanthropist and BFBS president: letters to the Society (1851-1878)
    D2/7 BFBS Jubilee 1854: miscellaneous papers (1853-1854)
    D2/8 Samuel Bergne (1805-1880), BFBS secretary: report of European tour (1872)
    D2/9 Secretaries' confidential letters outgoing (1886-1915)
    D2/10 Greece: correspondence on difficulties in distributing a Modern Greek Bible translation (1902-1914)
    D2/11 Colombo: correspondence about purchase of property (1879-1911)
    D2/12 Indian Million Testament Campaign: correspondence (1928)
    D2/13 Tercentenary of the Authorised Version: miscellaneous papers (1910-1911)
    D2/14 John Ritson (1868-1953), BFBS secretary: "Black Books" (travel notes) (1900-1930)

D3-D10 Twentieth-century subject filing
Files of incoming and outgoing letters, memoranda, and miscellaneous papers, arranged on a subject basis. Most of the material dates from the 1930s, but earlier material is included. The files have been grouped under the following subject headings:

D3 General filing series
    D3/1 Anglican secretary's filing (1931-1964)
    D3/2 Compilations (1936-1970)
    D3/3 Miscellaneous (1950-1965)

D4 Constitution and internal administration
    D4/1 Royal Charter and By-laws (1938-1975)

        D4/2   Administrative structure (1956–1973)
        D4/3   Internal meetings (1939–1986)

D5 Home work, publicity, campaigns
        D5/1   Annual Meetings (1927–1979)
        D5/2   Home work (1922–1960)
        D5/3   Publicity and fundraising: general (1961–1964)
        D5/4   Campaigns (1953–1970)

D6 Translation and publishing
        D6/1   English versions (1901–1966)
        D6/2   Selections (1940–1968)
        D6/3   Publishing for the blind (1950–1965)

D7 Overseas policy, inter-Bible Society relations
        D7/1   Post-war planning (1943–1945)
        D7/2   Colportage (1949–1953)
        D7/3   Overseas tours (1931–1971)
        D7/4   Inter-Bible Society conferences (1909–1970)
        D7/5   United Bible Societies conferences (1939–1961)

D8 Country files

Correspondence with and papers relating to individual countries where the BFBS maintained a presence. The files deal with administration, committees, staff, finance, meetings, colportage, translations, visits, and a wide range of other matters. The countries are grouped by region, as follows:

        D8/1   Europe (1892–1972)
        D8/2   Near and Middle East (1920–1972)
        D8/3   Africa (1918–1974)
        D8/4   Asia (1896–1981)
        D8/5   Oceania (1925–1979)
        D8/6   Northern and Central America (1901–1969)
        D8/7   Latin America (1925–1969)
        D8/8   Compilations by country

D9 Relations with churches and other organisations
        D9/1   Roman Catholic Church (1959–1973)
        D9/2   World Council of Churches (1946–1960)
        D9/3   British Council of Churches (1950–1966)
        D9/4   Conference of British missionary societies (1949–1972)
        D9/5   Anglican organisations (1918–1971)
        D9/6   Miscellaneous organisations (1944–1959)

D10 Personnel records
        D10/1   Patrons: election, obituaries (1942–1973)
        D10/2   Committee members: election, correspondence (1939–1973)
        D10/3   Staff (confidential records) (1888–1985)

BSA/E: Records of the Departments

E1   Finance Department
An accountant was appointed in 1804, and the post was combined with that of assistant secretary in 1810. During the nineteenth century the accountant's correspondence was mostly filed in the main correspondence series (D1/1-4). A major overhaul of the accounting system took place in 1938-1939, when modern practices were introduced. In 1861 the work of keeping the foreign accounts was entrusted to one clerk, and grew to considerable proportions, until it was transferred to the United Bible Societies in 1966. Records of properties owned by the Society, at home and overseas, were also kept by the Finance Department.

    E1/1   General and home accounts
            E1/1/1   Cash books (1804-1810, 1869-1901)
            E1/1/2   General ledger (1807-1963)
            E1/1/3   Audit books (1804-1939)
            E1/1/4   Auxiliary registers (1814-1941)
            E1/1/5   Grants (1804-1968)
            E1/1/6   Legacies (1809-1951)
            E1/1/7   Letterbooks (1897-1924)
            E1/1/8   Draft accounts (1929-1960)
            E1/1/9   Special funds records (1891-1918)
            E1/1/10 Miscellaneous records (1825-1975)
    E1/2   Foreign accounts
            E1/2/1   Foreign accounts letters (1816-1876)
            E1/2/2   Foreign accounts current (1817-1939)
            E1/2/3   Foreign accounts schedules (1881-1966)
    E1/3   Property records
            E1/3/1   Letters and papers (Bible House) (1865-1974)
            E1/3/2   Letters and papers (United Kingdom) (1944-1953)
            E1/3/3   Plans (home and foreign) (1816-1977)
            E1/3/4   Photographs/illustrations (home and foreign) (1819-1990)
            E1/3/5   Legal documents (home and foreign) (1840-1979)
            E1/3/6   Property fund (1914-1957)
            E1/3/7   Letters and papers (foreign) (1888-1977)

E2   Warehouse and Publishing Department:
The department was responsible for the warehousing of the Society's publications and the despatch of these printed works to customers. It also negotiated with printers, papermakers, and binders for the production of the Bibles. The records of the department are fragmentary, most series being incomplete.

    E2/1   Legal records
            E2/1/1   Agreements with L. B. Seeley, bookseller (1808-1818)

                E2/1/2 Agreements with R. Cockle, depositary, and executors (1839-1851)
                E2/1/3 Agreements with Watkins & Co., bookbinders (1869-1896)
        E2/2   Depositary's ledgers (1826-1869)
        E2/3   Registers
                E2/3/1 Grants and engagements (1820-1839)
                E2/3/2 Depot books (1870-1939)
                E2/3/3 British issues (1933-1939)
                E2/3/4 Foreign issues (1929-1939)
                E2/3/5 Foreign issues ('7') (1931-1938)
                E2/3/6 Import book (1937-1939)
                E2/3/7 Foreign shipments (1938-1974)
                E2/3/8 Versions books (1935-1969)
                E2/3/9 Binders' ledger (1934-1938)
                E2/3/10 Quire stock book (1933-1938)
                E2/3/11 Trade cash book (1938-1939)
                E2/3/12 Scriptures issued (1911-1939)
        E2/4   Correspondence
                E2/4/1 George Cowan's letterbooks (1918-1919)
                E2/4/2 Letterbooks 'S' (1924-1939)
                E2/4/3 George Cowan's correspondence (1930-1939)

E3 Editorial/Translations Department:
The supervision of the Society's versions was at first delegated to the General Purposes Subcommittee, special subcommittees, or individual editors. By 1830 the need for a more permanent arrangement was apparent, and a BFBS editorial superintendent was appointed, together with an Editorial Subcommittee (C17). The records of the department survive, with few breaks, from 1830 to the 1980s, and most are arranged or indexed by language, making it relatively easy to follow the progress of a specific version. In particular, a series of copybooks (E3/3/4) preserves the texts of letters no longer extant. Subject filing was introduced in 1909, the majority of "subjects" being individual languages (E3/3). The records of the library and archives are also included in this department.

        E3/1   Correspondence (incoming) (1832-1908), indexed by writer and language
                E3/1/1 Editorial Correspondence Books (1832-1834)
                E3/1/2 General Committee letters (1841-1856)
                E3/1/3 Editorial Department letters (1856-1857)
                E3/1/4 Editorial Correspondence, Incoming (1858-1897); this series (E3/1/4) has been microfilmed.
        E3/2   Correspondence (outgoing) (1832-1908)
        E3/3   Correspondence (language files) (1909-1984); files of incoming and outgoing letters, arranged alphabetically by language (625 individual languages, and some multi-language files, about 1,360 files in all). Note that the language names used are those in use when the files were created and may not be the current names.

E3/4 Correspondence (subject files) (1910-1981)
E3/5 Correspondence (miscellaneous) (1811-1936)
E3/6 Library and archives (1822-1987)
E3/7 Compilations and registers (1804-1965)
E3/8 Histories of translations (1827-1907); drafts and papers for four unpublished histories, of which the most useful is the first (E3/8/1), compiled by Thomas Pell Platt (1827-1829); it gives a detailed account of the Society's early versions.

E4 Home Organisation Department

The department began in 1888 with the appointment of a BFBS home superintendent and a Home Organisation Subcommittee (C13). It inherited some earlier records, notably a series of County registers (E4/1/1), which list annually all auxiliary Bible Societies by county and thus are useful in tracing the history of any local society. Further records of the department remain uncatalogued.

E4/1 Home Superintendent/Secretary's records (1825-1972)
    E4/1/1 County registers (1825-1941)
    E4/1/2 Letter books (outgoing letters, main series) (1898-1938)
    E4/1/3 Letter books (outgoing, confidential letters) (1904-1916)
    E4/1/4 Letter books (outgoing, routine letters) (1905-1915)
    E4/1/5 Minutes of district secretaries' conferences (1915-1962)
    E4/1/6 Minutes of regional secretaries' conferences (1942-1972)
E4/2 Women's Work: letter book, outgoing letters (1935-1936)
E4/3 Youth Work: minutes of Schools Visual Aids Panel (1955-1958)
E4/4 BFBS Helpers' Association: minutes and registers (1889-1949)

E5 Literary/Publicity Department

A BFBS literary superintendent was appointed in 1888, together with a Publications Subcommittee (C14), to take responsibility for preparation of the Society's annual *Report*, as well as its other publications and publicity material. In 1943 an assistant literary superintendent, John Stirling, was appointed, who developed educational material and made innovations in Bible layout and illustration. The records of the department are incomplete.

E5/1 Letterbooks (outgoing letters) (1888-1900)
E5/2 Press cuttings and releases (1888-1972)
E5/3 Histories of the Society (1933-1967)
E5/4 John Stirling's papers (1943-1954)
E5/5 Religious Tract Society minutes (transcripts) (1802-1804)

BSA/F: Deposited Papers

F1 Papers of Auxiliary Bible Societies in England and Wales:

From 1809 local Bible societies were set up throughout the United Kingdom to support the work of the BFBS, by raising money and distributing Bibles. They increased rapidly in the decade 1810 to 1820 — causing alarm to those who saw the Society as a threat to the Church of England — and they contributed enormously to the Society's funds. As a result of the Apocrypha controversy of 1825 the Scottish societies broke off their connection with the BFBS, and ultimately formed the National Bible Society of Scotland. There was at first a hierarchy of societies: Auxiliaries were based in large towns, dependent branches in small towns, and Bible associations at village or parish level. Ladies' Bible associations were particularly widespread and successful. From 1882 the BFBS established trade depots to relieve auxiliaries of the work of keeping stocks and accounts. In 1904 these were abolished and the Society's sales were thrown open to the book trade generally. The work of the auxiliaries was henceforth limited largely to fundraising and publicity. From 1972 they began to be known as Bible Society action groups.

The records, usually deposited when a Bible Society unit was closed, consist mainly of committee minutes, with accounts, registers of subscribers, and some published annual reports and publicity material. There are currently records of 126 societies in the archives, which are arranged by county (using the names current before the 1974 local government reorganization) and are listed on the website.

F2 Overseas Bible Societies and Agencies

    F2/1 Norway (Christiania Agency) (1828–1898): The Norwegian Bible Society (founded 1816) broke its links with the BFBS as a result of the Apocrypha controversy. In 1828 the BFBS formed a committee in Christiania [Oslo] to print and distribute its own editions. A rapprochement with the Norwegian Bible Society led the BFBS to close its agency in 1894. The records consist of committee minutes, accounts, and correspondence with the BFBS and within Norway.

    F2/2 Denmark (Copenhagen Agency) (1890–1895): A BFBS agency was set up in Denmark in the mid–1850s; the surviving records (minutes and correspondence) deal mainly with developing cooperation with the Danish Bible Society, and the withdrawal of the BFBS.

    F2/3 North East Europe Agency (1919–1946): The agency was set up in 1920 with the aim of maintaining links with Russia as far as possible and also to supervise work in Finland and the Baltic states. The agents were Walter Davidson to 1925 and Wilfred Wiseman to 1930; Wiseman also kept later material on the agency. The papers consist of correspondence with BFBS

London, BFBS Berlin, Estonia, Latvia, Russia, and elsewhere, together with accounts, annual reports, and files on special subjects.

F2/4 Central Europe Agency: Romania (1913-1931), Poland (1931-1934). Two files only, containing letters to the BFBS agent in Berlin from contacts in Bucharest and from the BFBS agent in Warsaw.

F2/5 Western Europe Agency (1921-1940): Files of correspondence of the BFBS Secretary for Western Europe (Edwin Smith to 1923, then William Rainey) with BFBS London, and with the various countries making up the agency, namely, Belgium, France, Italy, Malta, Portugal, Spain, and Switzerland. There is also a little correspondence with Albania (1940) and Ethiopia (1938-1940).

F2/6 Malta Bible Society (1820-1834): The society was formed in 1817 and continued until 1834. Although it achieved some local distribution, chiefly among seamen aboard ships calling at Malta, its principal function was to maintain a depot of scriptures and organise their despatch throughout the Mediterranean area. The records consist of committee minutes, with a little outgoing correspondence.

F2/7 Isaac Lowndes: letterbook (1845-1847). Lowndes (1790-1873) was a member of the London Missionary Society's Greek Mission (1816-1844), and then joined the BFBS as its agent, based in Malta, until his retirement in 1861. This volume contains copies of letters to the BFBS and to correspondents around the Mediterranean, most of which deal with Bible distribution and accounts of sales.

F2/8 Turkish Agency (1856-1936): Established in 1820, the agency covered countries that were or had been part of the Turkish Empire. The headquarters was transferred from Smyrna (Izmir) to Constantinople (Istanbul) in 1854. In 1883, Egypt, Syria, Palestine, and Arabia were detached to form a separate agency. In 1920, a South East Europe Agency was set up, under a secretary resident in Belgrade; thereafter the secretary in Istanbul was responsible solely for Turkey. The records are not complete, and deal mainly with Bible distribution in Turkey, Greece, Albania, Macedonia, and Bulgaria, together with translation work into Albanian and Bulgarian. There is also correspondence with BFBS London, accounts, and miscellaneous papers.

F2/9 Equatorial Africa Agency (1936-1940): The agency covered Angola, Belgian Congo, French Cameroun, French Equatorial Africa, Gold Coast, Ivory Coast, Kenya, Madagascar, Seychelles, Mauritius, Nigeria, Nyasaland, Northern Rhodesia, Sierra Leone, Tanganyika, Uganda, and Zanzibar. The papers consist principally of correspondence between these countries and the agency secretary in England.

F2/10 Calcutta Bible Societies (1809–1876): These volumes are fragile, and microfilms must be used instead.
    F2/10/1 Calcutta Corresponding Committee: minutes and letters (1809–1818)
    F2/10/2 Calcutta Auxiliary Bible Society: minutes and letters (1815–1876)
    F2/10/3 Calcutta Bible Association: minutes (1846–1867)
F2/11 West Indies Agency (1923–1937): Established in 1923, with W. J. Mowll as secretary, the agency covered the West Indies, Venezuela, part of Colombia, Bermuda, British Honduras, and the three Guianas. When Mowll returned to England in 1937 the work was continued on a part-time basis by J. H. Poole of Trinidad. The papers consist of correspondence with BFBS London, local correspondence, accounts, and reports.
F2/12 Gibraltar Auxiliary Bible Society (1821–1929): Papers deposited by the Methodist Church in Gibraltar in 1999, containing correspondence on the general work of the Society and on the imprisonment and defence of colporteur Martin Escalante, together with accounts, lists of scriptures sold, and minutes — for 1908–1929 only.

F3   Personal papers

F3/Bialloblotsky: commonplace book (1828–1830). Christoph H. F. Bialloblotsky (1799–1868) was born and educated in Germany, worked with the Continental Society and the Wesleyan Methodist Missionary Society, and taught in England and Germany. He corresponded with the BFBS (1827–1832). The commonplace book contains diary entries, copies of letters, and exercises in a variety of languages.

F3/Delitzsch: papers on his Hebrew New Testament (1863–1886). Franz Delitzsch (1813–1890) held professorships at a number of German universities, and wrote on Old Testament and Rabbinic subjects. The BFBS published successive editions of his Hebrew translation of the New Testament. The papers consist mainly of comments and criticisms by fellow-scholars.

F3/Lewis: sermon notes and talks (1859–1896). W. Dickens Lewis (d. 1895) was BFBS District Secretary for North Wales and Shropshire. The papers consist of notes for sermons and talks, and notes on his tours in Syria and Palestine, France, Italy and Switzerland, and the United States of America.

F3/Montgomery: poems (1819–1833). James Montgomery (1771–1854) was a journalist, poet and hymn writer. These items comprise autographs of six poems (one apparently unpublished), and two letters to the secretary of the Sheffield Auxiliary Bible Society, of which Montgomery was a member.

F3/Moule: letters (1899–1933). Horace Frederick Moule (1874–1967), schoolmaster and bibliographer, was the chief compiler of the Darlow and Moule catalogue of the BFBS library (1903–1911). These letters deal mainly with bibliographical details.

F3/Moulton: letters, reports, drafts, and notes (1939-1982). Harold Keeling Moulton (1903-1982) was a Methodist missionary in South India, before becoming BFBS Assistant Translations Secretary (1957-1971). His papers contain correspondence and papers on the Tamil Bible, tour reports, and drafts for books and articles on the Bible and its versions.

F3/Mynors: papers on the New English Bible (1948-1974). Sir Roger Aubrey Baskerville Mynors (1903-1989) held professorships of Latin in Cambridge and Oxford. In 1948 he joined the Literary Panel of the New English Bible Revision Company, and these papers contain drafts, notes, and correspondence on that project.

F3/Paterson: memoirs and papers (1805-1850). John Paterson (1776-1855) was one of the earliest BFBS agents, working in Scandinavia and Russia. The memoirs form the basis for *The Book for Every Land*, edited by W. L. Alexander (London: John Snow, 1857).

F3/Shore: letterbook (1792-1833). John Shore (1751-1834), the first Baron Teignmouth, made a career with the East India Company in Bengal (1768-1798). On his return to England he devoted himself to religious and literary pursuits, and was the first president of the BFBS (1804-1834). The letterbook contains letters to him relating to India, the BFBS, and other topics.

F3/Smith: linguistic papers (1935-1941). Edwin William Smith (1876-1957) was a Methodist missionary and Bible translator in Central Africa. He joined the BFBS in 1916 as agent for Italy, then secretary for Western Europe (1921), literary superintendent (1923), and editorial superintendent (1933-1939). The papers mainly deal with language issues, but include a diary of his tour of India, 1938-1939.

F3/Stirling: correspondence and papers (1919-1958). John Featherstone Stirling (1884-1958) was a Methodist minister, worked for a publisher, and joined the BFBS as assistant literary superintendent in 1943. The papers deal mainly with various religious and literary projects. See also his papers in section E5/4.

F3/Thomson: Tour in Yucatan (1844-1845). James Thomson (1788-1854) worked for the BFBS in South America, Mexico, the West Indies, Canada, and Spain. This manuscript is an incomplete draft for an intended book and contains a resume of his career (1818-1832), a journal of his tour, October-November 1843 only, and notes and memoranda.

F3/Wiseman: correspondence (1930-1966). Wilfred James Wiseman (1891-1970) worked for the BFBS in South East Europe, North East Europe, and in India. He was secretary for Equatorial Africa (based in England), as well as being a district secretary during the war years. These files contain letters to him from the several agencies where he worked, and two drafts of his autobiography. For his work in North East Europe, see F2/3.

F3/Wylie: miscellaneous papers (1840-1911). Alexander Wylie (1815-1887) worked in China for the London Missionary Society and then for the BFBS in the period 1858-1859 and again in 1863-1877. This small collection contains a Chinese/English vocabulary, a scrapbook, an autograph book, and a few letters. For his letters to the Society (1872–1876), see Agent's Book D1/7/146.

F4 Other organisations

- F4/1 London Secretaries' Association (1819–1945): The association was formed in 1819 to provide a forum for discussion and an exchange of information for the heads of missionary societies with headquarters in London. The BFBS joined in the 1860s. Members met several times a year and discussed topics agreed beforehand, ranging from aspects of the theology of mission to the practicalities of payment and allowances for missionaries and their families. The records consist of minutes, a little twentieth-century correspondence, and a centenary history published in 1920.

- F4/2 Association of Church of England Secretaries of Missionary Societies (1900–1915): The association was formed in 1900 and was made up of the secretaries of Anglican Missionary Societies and the Anglican secretaries of non-denominational societies like the BFBS. It met several times a year to hear and discuss a paper on aspects of missionary practice or policy. The records consist of one volume of minutes.

- F4/3 World Missionary Conference, letterbooks (1908–1927): Three volumes of outgoing letters of John Ritson, dealing with preparations for the conference, which was held in Edinburgh in 1910, and with various follow-up initiatives, notably the continuation committee and several literature committees.

- F4/4 National Council for the Celebration of the Fourth Centenary of the Reformation (1932–1939): A movement to celebrate the fourth centenary of the Reformation and the order (1538) to place a Bible in English Churches began in the early 1930s. In 1935 a Council was established, which prepared educational booklets and publicity leaflets and encouraged the organisation of local celebrations. The papers consist chiefly of committee minutes, correspondence, and publicity material.

BSA/G: Publications

The published annual *Report of the BFBS* (1805–date) and its monthly magazine (1817–1972) are an essential starting point for research into the Society's history. They are noted here for completeness, but should be cited as ordinary publications. There are also published histories of the Society by John Owen (1816, 1820), George Browne (1859), William Canton (1904–1910), and J. M. Roe (1965). For any study of the Society's translations it is necessary to consult T. H. Darlow and H. F. Moule, compilers, *Historical Catalogue of the Printed Editions of Holy Scripture in the Library of the British and Foreign Bible Society*, 2 vols. in 4 (London 1903–1911). There are also a large number of controversial pamphlets and publicity material, which are noted in the card index at Cambridge.

BSA/X: Index of Foreign Correspondents, 1804–1897

This is an alphabetical list of people writing to the Society from overseas during the nineteenth century whose letters are extant, either as originals or transcripts. The information is taken from the card index at Cambridge, which in turn is an amalgamation of the entries in the contemporary indexes to the Foreign Correspondence Inwards (D1/2), the early Correspondence Books (D1/5-6), the Agents' Books (D1/7), and the Editorial Correspondence Books (E3/1). The list gives name of writer, place of writing, number of letters, and a note of the subject matter where possible.

List of Contributors

Joyce Banks (Ph.D., University of London) is former curator of the rare book collection of the National Library of Canada. Her publications, including articles on Native Canadian printing and the use of syllabic characters, address early missionary publications in Native Canadian languages.

Stephen Batalden (Ph.D., University of Minnesota) is professor of history and director of the Russian and East European Studies Center at Arizona State University. His recent publications, including *Reexamining Tradition* (in Macedonian, 1997) and an edited anthology, *Seeking God* (1993), explore problems in modern Orthodox religious history.

Kathleen Cann was the first archivist of the British and Foreign Bible Society, 1966-1987, and subsequently was employed in the Manuscripts Department, Cambridge University Library. Appended to this volume, her systematic catalogue of the BFBS archive offers for the first time an on-line descriptive guide to the rich holdings of BFBS collections in the Cambridge University Library.

David Clark holds an M.A. from the University of Cambridge, and B.D., M.A. and Ph.D. degrees from the University of London. He spent thirty years as a United Bible Societies translation consultant, twenty in the Asia-Pacific Region and the rest in the Europe-Middle East Region. He has co-authored three UBS translator's handbooks.

Richard Clogg, graduate of the University of Edinburgh, is a senior research fellow of St. Antony's College, Oxford. He has taught at the universities of Edinburgh and London where, latterly, he was professor of modern Balkan history. His published work includes *A Concise History of Greece*, which has been translated into numerous languages, including Chinese and Turkish.

John Dean was a British and Foreign Bible Society general secretary and United Bible Societies world services officer. Following the dissolution of the Soviet Union, he worked in the 1990s with the UBS Europe-Middle

East Region in assisting in the establishment of Bible societies throughout the newly independent states of Eurasia.

Wayne Detzler (Ph.D., University of Manchester) has taught at Trinity International University, Yale Divinity School, and Southern Evangelical Seminary. His writings include *The Changing Church in Europe, New Testament Words in Today's Language,* and the *Lion Handbook to the History of Christianity.*

Leslie Howsam (Ph.D., York University, Toronto) is professor of history at the University of Windsor (Canada). Her publications include *Cheap Bibles* (1991) and *Kegan Paul – A Victorian Imprint* (1998). She is general editor of the University of Toronto Press "Studies in Book & Print Culture".

Sue Jackson (Ph.D., Durham University) spent her childhood in Gibraltar and has had an interest in the history of Methodism on the Rock ever since. This interest is reflected in the subject of her doctoral thesis and the article in this anthology. After a career in social work, she has now taken up other interests including research.

Peter Kuzmič (Th.D, University of Zagreb) is founding president of the Evangelical Theological Seminary in Zagreb/Osijek, Croatia, and the Eva B. and Paul E. Toms distinguished professor of world missions and European studies at Gordon-Conwell Theological Seminary. He is editor of the Croatian journal, *Izvori*, and author of *The Gospel of John and Biblical Hermeneutics*. His contribution to this anthology builds upon his monograph, *Vuk-Daničićevo Sveto Pismo i biblijska društva na južnoslavenskom tlu u XIX stoljeću* (Zagreb, 1983).

Roald Kverndal, an author, lecturer, and independent consultant, is president emeritus and co-founder of the International Association for the Study of Maritime Missions. He has served as a merchant seafarer, marine lawyer, and an ordained clergyman. His prior publications include *Seamen's Missions: Their Origin and Early Growth* (1986).

Sarah Lane read theology at Durham University and taught religious education in schools before joining the staff of the British and Foreign Bible Society in 1990. In 1994, she was awarded an M.A. in Church, Religion, and Society by the University of Gloucestershire and Trinity College, Bristol. She is now education officer for Churches Together in England.

Roger Martin is President of Randolph-Macon College in Virginia. He was previously President of Moravian College and a dean at Harvard

University's Divinity School. He received degrees from Drew and Yale universities before attending Oxford University from which he received his doctorate. He is the author of *Evangelicals United: Ecumenical Stirrings in Pre-Victorian England* (1983).

Erling von Mende (Ph.D. and habilitation, Chinese and Manchu studies, Universität zu Köln) is a professor of Chinese history at the Ostasiatisches Seminar, Freie Universität, Berlin. His work in Chinese and Manchu studies and in East Asian economic history is reflected in publications on foreign relations of imperial China, Manchu-Chinese relations, and the history of Chinese agriculture and water conservation.

Patricia Mirrlees works on Projects and Liaison with China and Korea at the East Asian Institute, Faculty of Oriental Studies, Cambridge University. Her article in this anthology is based on part of her University of Aberdeen thesis on Christian linguists in the Senegambia area, 1800–1832.

Sergei Ovsiannikov (Th.D., St. Petersburg Theological Academy), UBS translation consultant in Eurasia and priest of the Amsterdam Russian Orthodox Church (ordained by the late Metropolitan Anthony of Sourozh), is a frequent participant in biblical seminars in Russia. He is a contributor to the *Russkaia Pravoslavnaia Entsiklopediia* (Russian Orthodox Encyclopaedia) and author of the popular Russian *Detskaia Bibliia* (Children's Bible).

Ann Ridler has been editor of the *George Borrow Bulletin* since the founding of the George Borrow Society in 1991, and chairman of the society since 1997. Among her publications are seminal works on George Borrow as a linguist. This is also the subject of her doctoral thesis subsequently published as *George Borrow as a Linguist: Images and Contexts* (1996).

Roger Steer has been a trustee of the BFBS since 1985. He is the author of twelve books, including biographies of George Müller and Hudson Taylor, *Letter to an Influential Atheist*, and *Good News for the World: The Story of Bible Society*. With a degree in modern social and economic history, he now works as an online tutor for three colleges in southwest England.

Thor Strandenaes (Th.D., Uppsala University) is associate professor of missiology at the School of Mission and Theology, Stavanger, Norway. He taught New Testament at Lutheran Theological Seminary, Hong Kong, 1981-1991. His publications include *Principles of Chinese Bible Translation as Expressed in Five Selected Versions of the New Testament* (1987).

INDEXES

(References to illustrations are in **bold** type)

1. GENERAL INDEX

1848 revolution, 283
Aberdeen, Scotland, 353
action groups, BFBS. *See* auxiliaries, BFBS
Address to the Six Nations, 68, 317
African Herald, The, 119
agencies, BFBS, 4, 6, 8, 87, 170, 171, 330, 339, 342
    German-speaking Europe, 280
    joint agencies, 7
    marine, 340
        Denmark, 340
        Hamburg-Altona, 340
        Netherlands, 340
        Vienna, 186, 187, 191
agents, foreign, threat from, 42, 48
Albania, 237
Albanian. *See* languages
Aleppo, 249
Alexander Nevsky Monastery, St. Petersburg, 289
alphabets. *See* scripts
American Bible Society (ABS), 72, 73, 74, 77, 87
    and Bible use, 76
    and Mohawk Scriptures, 318
    and note or comment, 70, 74
    and Russian translation, 199
    foundation, 6, 69
    Good News Bible (GNB), 8
    Guidelines for Study Bibles and Study Helps, 77
    in China, 7
    relations with BFBS, 7
    suggests association of national Bible Societies, 7
American Board of Commissioners for Foreign Missions, 242
American War of Independence, 67
Amoy, China, 133

Amsterdam, 271, 340
Anatolia, 245, 246, 248
Anglicans, 19, 39, 51, 87, 134, 198, 312, 316, 317, 320, 329, 342, *See also* Church of England
    alarm at BFBS activities, 42, 44, 45, 46, 48
    and the evangelical awakening, 50
    fear BFBS as a threat to SPCK, 40
    membership on BFBS general committee, 2, 25
    seafarers' missions, 330
Angouri (Ankara), 248
anniversaries, BFBS
    1839: 283
    1854: 34, 279
    2004: 1, 11, 125
Apocrypha, 4, 280, 282, 283, 295
    distribution policy, 70
    Russian translations, 184, 185, 189, 191, 194
    the Apocrypha crisis, 1812–1828, 4, 275-80
Application Bibles, 77
Aramaic. *See* languages
archives, BFBS, 1, 9, 13 *See also* Appendix, 344-359
    catalogue, 13, 18-20
    history, 14-18
Armenian. *See* languages
Asia Minor, 244, 245, 246, 248
Astrakhan, Russia, 220
Athens, 236, 243
Augsburg, 282
Australia, 3, 329, 346
Austrian Empire, 4, 251, 257, 284
auxiliaries, BFBS, 2, 5, 8, 10, 25, 26, 29, 32, 33, 34, 40, 41, 53, 58, 69, 92, 236, 270, 274, 306, 311, 334, 335, 338

Bath, 50
Blackheath, 334
City of London, 334
East London, 334
Gibraltar, 305-15
Montreal, 318
role of, 39
Southwark, 41, 43, 44, 45, 48, 334
Staffordshire, 69
Wallingford, 46
Badajóz, Spain, 291, 298
Baffin Inuktitut. *See* languages *and* Scripture:versions
Baptists, 39, 50, 221, 316, 323, 330
baptize, translation of word, 321
Barbary, 298, 301
Barcelona, 307, 314
Basel, 270
Basque. *See* Scripture:versions
Bavaria, 281
Beijing. *See* Peking
Belgian Gospel Mission, 202
Belgrade
  Ministry of Education, 263
Belorussian. *See* languages
Berlin, 102, 187, 197, 263, 265, 271, 272, 273, 274, 278, 284
Bethel Movement, 338, 341, 343
Bethel Society, 306
Bible. *See* Scripture
Bible Associations, BFBS, 25, 26, 29, 32, 34, 38-52, 41, 43, 45, 53, 58, 61, 335
  Benson, 46
  Covent Garden, 44
  Hackney, Clapton and Homerton, 57, 60
  Henley, 45, 46, 47, 48, 49, 51, 52
  Hertford, 50
  Hitchin, 43
  Liverpool, 49
  marine, 332, 339
    Aberdeen, 338
    Bristol, 338
    Grand Junction and General Canal, 338
    Hull, 338
    Lerwick, 338
    Liverpool, 338
    Whitby, 338
  White Church and Goring, 46
Bible House
  Earl St London, **15**, 25, 81, 275, 293
  Queen Victoria St London, 8, 9, 19,
    in the 1950s, 81-96, **82-94**
    warehouse, 86, 90, 91
  Swindon, 19, 95
Bible Nurses, 59
Bible Societies in Germany, 268-85
Bible Societies, affiliated to BFBS, 5
Bible Societies, auxiliary, *See* auxiliaries
Bible Society in Athens, 236
Bible society in Chios
  attempt to found, 242
Bible Society in Gibraltar, 305-15
Bible Society in Malta, 236
Bible Society in Russia (1991-), 13, 212, 214, 215, 216, 221
Bible Society in Smyrna, 236
Bible Society in the Republic of China (Taiwan), 140
Bible society in Vienna
  attempt to found, 284
Bible Society of India, 84
Bible Society, Swedish, 6
Bible Sunday, 313
Bible Translator, The, 210, 211
Biblewomen, BFBS, 33, 35, 36, 53, 55, 59, 60, 61, 313
Blackfoot. *See* languages
Blackfriars, London, 94
board of trustees, BFBS. *See* committees, BFBS:general committee
Bohemia, 258
Bohemian. *See* languages
bookbinding. *See* Scripture:production
Bosnia, 258, 263
Brethren, Christian, 297
British and Foreign Bible Society (BFBS)
  and book production technology, 9, 30
  and modernity, 9, 170
  as evangelical organisation, 10, 38
  as non-denominational organisation, 39, 272
  book trade, relations with, 24-37
  colonial enterprise, accused of being, 7
  commercial and missionary aims, 9, 36
  competition and overlap, 7
  distribution policy, 33-36, 43, 70, 294
  expenditure, 5
  foundation of, 1, 66
  history of, 1-14
  home organisation, 40
  international role, 10, 11

Indexes

not a charity, 53
other Bible Societies, encouragement of, 5
prayer at meetings, 47
public image, 5, 11, 36, 80
publishing role, 2-3, 24
staff, 5
subscriptions, 2, 33, 36, 49, 51, 54, 58, 60, 61, 335
youth work, 8, 92
British Levant Company, 234, 236, 248
British Petroleum, 96
Buchwald Bible Society, Silesia, 282
Buddhism, 168, 217, 229
Bulgaria, 258
Bulgarian. *See* languages *and* Scripture:versions
Buryat. *See* languages

Cádiz, 293, 301, 307, 308
Caesarea, 247
Caesarea Philippi, 64
Calcutta, 3
Calo. *See* languages
Calvinists, 272
Camberwell, England, 334
Cambridge University, 248
Cambridge University Library, 1, 13, 14, 19, 20, 21, 91, 317
    Missionary Archives Project, 20-23
Cambridge University Press, 28, 173
Canada, 3
    BFBS work in Canadian languages, 316-26
Canstein Bible Publishing House, 274
Canton, China, 127, 133
Cape Town, 86
Carlist wars, 297
Carlscrona, Sweden, 340
Carniolan. *See* languages *and* Scripture:versions
Caspian Sea, 217
Central Prussian Bible Society, 273, 278, 279, 281, 284
Cephalonia, Greece, 236
Chaldaic. *See* languages
Charlottetown, Canada, 323
Cherokees, 67, 317
Chiang Mai (Thailand), 75
China, 5, 6, 7, 62, 123, 125, 135, 144, 121-48, 149-68, 159, 296, 303
    Bible House, 7
China Centenary Conference, 1907: 143

China Conference 1877: 123
China Inland Mission, 62
Chinese. *See* languages *and* Scripture:versions
Chinese Institution, Kassel, 156
Chinese Repository, 138, 159
Chipeywan. *See* languages
Church Missionary Society (CMS), 101, 102, 103, 108, 246, 250, 316, 319, 320, 321, 323, 324, 325
Church of England, 19, 42, 48, 69, 289, 306, 329, *See also* Anglicans
Church of Scotland, 66
Church's Mission to the Jews. *See* London Society for Promoting Christianity Amongst the Jews (LSPCAJ)
Codex Zacynthius, 91
collectors, BFBS, 53, 58, 59, 60, 61
Colportage, 36
    importance of, 5, 6, 12, 182
    in China, 7
    in Germany, 280, 283, 284
    in Gibraltar, 307, 312
    in India, 5
    in Russia, 191, 192, 194
    in Spain, 309, 311, 312, 313, 314
    methods of, 33, 34, 35
committees, BFBS, 189, 194
    editorial subcommittee, 21, 321
    general committee, 265
    after Battle of Trafalgar, 329
    and Apocrypha, 276, 277, 278
    and auxiliaries, 53
    and Bible Associations, 44, 58
    and colportage, 35
    and George Borrow, 149, 286, 288, 290, 296, 298, 300, 301, 302, 303, 304
    and German Bible Societies, 275, 279, 280
    and Greek translation, 241, 242, 245
    and labour relations, 32
    and new technology, 28, 29, 171
    and note or comment, 67, 68, 75
    and Robert Pinkerton, 275
    and Russian Bible Society, 182, 194, 270
    and Russian translation, 199
    and Serbian translation, 257, 258, 259, 265
    and the role of women, 38, 45

and William Nicolson, 195
composition, 2, 10, 24, 25, 29, 36, 88
general committee room, London Bible House, 88, **89**, 90
handling correspondence, 16
missing minutes, 16
protocol, 87
Scriptures for Roman Catholics, 277
general purposes subcommittee, 280
oriental subcommittee, 234
printing subcommittee, 47
Confucianists, 168
Congregationalists, 39, 144, 169, 173, 242
Congress of Vienna, 271
Constantinople, 204, 237, 240, 241, 242, 243, 244, 246, 247, 248, 249
Coptic. *See* languages
Córdoba, Spain, 299
Corfu, Greece, 236, 243
Costa da Muerte, Spain, 300
Council of Trent, 70, 71, 72
Cree. *See* languages *and* Scripture:versions
Cree people, Canada, 320
Crete, 240
Crimean War, 174, 179, 192
Croatia, 258, 263
    Academy of Arts and Sciences, Zagreb, 266
Croatian. *See* languages *and* Scripture:versions

Dakar, Senegal, 109, 110, 118
Dalmatia, 258
Danish. *See* languages
Danzig, 234
Daoists, 168
Darmstadt, 281
De Castro printing press, Constantinople, 249
deutero-canonical books. *See* Apocrypha
Dissenters, 25, 40, 48, 49, 51, 65
district secretaries, BFBS, 92
Dresden, 271, 274
Dublin, 44
Durham, England, 46, 69, 108
Dutch. *See* languages
Dutch East Indies, 6

East India Company, 136

ecumenical movement, 39, 72
Ecumenical Patriarch, 178, 204, 237, 243
    imprimatur, **239**
Ecumenical Patriarchate, 177, 178, 199, 200, 205, 240, 241, 242, 243, 248
Ecumenical Patriarchate (Russian Archdiocese), 199
Edinburgh, 12, 98, 99, 351
Edinburgh Missionary Society, 99, 108, 112, 269
Ehingen, Germany, 282
Ekaterinburg, Russia, 6, 183
Elberfeld, Germany, 271, 272, 274, 284
Elista, Kalmykiia, Russian Federation, 218
English. *See* languages *and* Scripture:versions
Ephesus, 240
Episcopalians, 87, 134
Eritrea, 93
Erlangen, Germany, 282
Erweckung movement, Germany, 272, 275, 285
Eskimo. *See* Inuit
Ethiopia, Bible Society of, 84
evangelical awakening, 1, 2, 10, 38, 50, 285
evangelicals, 4, 6, 36, 38, 48, 51, 59, 60, 172, 276, 277
Eyre and Strahan, printers, 27

Fellowship of St. Alban and St. Sergius, 198
Films
    The Leaves of the Tree, 93
    This is the Bible Society, 93
Finisterre, Spain, 300
Finnish. *See* Scripture:versions
Finnish Bible Society, 270
Foo-Chow, China, 133
Foreign Office, British, 308
France, 5, 34, 105, 202, 203, 247, 281, 302
Frankfurt, 279, 280, 281, 282, 283
Freemasons' Hall, London, 271
French. *See* languages *and* Scripture:versions
French Bible Society, 72, 119
French Revolution, 2, 272
fundraising, BFBS, 6, 34

Gaelic, Scottish. *See* languages
Galicia, 256, 300, 304
Gambia, 109, 115

Georgian. *See* languages
German. *See* languages *and*
    Scripture:versions
German Bible societies, 275, 278, 279, 280, 281
German Christian Association, 270
Germany, 3, 4, 156, 198, 202, 268, 271, 274, 275, 276, 277, 279, 285, 268-85, 340, 346, 350
Gibraltar, 10, 302, **305**, 305-15
Gibraltar Chronicle, 309
Glasgow Missionary Society, 99
Glykys publishing house, Venice, 246
Good News Transport Fleet, BFBS, 92
Goodenough College, London, 1, 13
Gorée, Senegal, 97-120, **104**
Göttingen, University of, 274
Greek. *See* languages *and*
    Scripture:versions
Greek Orthodox Church, 234-50, 255, 258
Greek War of Independence, 234, 236, 243, 244, 249
Gypsies, 288, 290, 291, 292, 297, 298, 299

Habismilk, Sidi (George Borrow's horse), 303
Haida. *See* languages
Haiti, 332
Halifax, Nova Scotia, 3, 324
Halle. Saxony, 235, 274, 282
Hampton Court Conference, 1604: 65, 66
Hanover, 271, 272, 274
Heidelberg, 274
Hercegovina, 258, 263
Hibernian Bible Society, 44
Hong Kong, 133, 139, 145
House of Lords, 303
Hudson Bay Company, 316, 319
Hull, England, 332, 333
Hungary, 258

India, 3, 5, 19, 67
Indonesia, 72
Institute for Bible Translation (IBT), 221, 222
Inuit people, Labrador, 318
Inuktitut. *See* Scripture:versions
Ionian Bible Society, 236
Ionian Islands, 234, 236
Ireland, 40, 44
Irish. *See* languages
Irkutsk, 159, 162

Islam, 102, 110
Istanbul. *See* Constantinople
Istria, 258
Italian. *See* languages *and*
    Scripture:versions
Italy, 5
İzmir. *See* Smyrna

Jaloff. *See* languages:Woloff
Japan, 126, 134, 162
Jerusalem, 188, 247
Jesuits, 127, 149, 151, 152, 154, 166, 167, 293
Journal of the Moscow Patriarchate (ZMP), 205, 213
Journeymen Bookbinders' Union, 31
Jubilees, BFBS. *See* anniversaries, BFBS
Judaeo-Spanish. *See* languages

Kaiserswerth, Germany, 284
Kalmyk. *See* languages
Kalmykiia, Republic of, (Russian Federation), 217
Karass, Russia, 269
Kazan, Russia, 179, 194, 221
Kiachta, Russia, 153, 161
Kiev, 179
Königsberg, Germany, 275, 283
Korea, 6, 162
Kronstadt, Russia, 340
Kurdish. *See* languages
Kwakiutl. *See* languages

La Granja, Spain, 295
La Mancha, Spain, 302
labour relations, BFBS, 25, 30-33
Labrador, 316, 318, 319, 325
Labrador Inuktitut. *See* languages
lady superintendents, BFBS, 35
Lambeth Palace, London, 18
Lancastrian schools, 173
languages. *See also* Scripture:versions
    Albanian, 243, 254, 256
    Arabic, 102, 108, 109, 110, 111, 114, 117, 234, 243, 246, 247, 248, 289
    Aramaic, xi
    Armenian, xii, 244
    Baffin Inuktitut, 316
    Belorussian, 176
    Blackfoot, 316, 325
    Bohemian, 260
    Bulgarian, 243, 254, 260
    Buryat, 159

Calo, 299
Carniolan, 260
Chaldaic, 234
Chinese, 11, 121-48
   Mandarin, 128, 141, 142, 143, 144, 147
   Peking Mandarin, 134
   Wenli, Easy, 134, 143
   Wenli, High, 143
Chipewyan, 316, 325
Coptic, 91
Cree, 316, 320, 321, **322**, 323
Croatian, 259
Danish, 287
Dutch, 234
English, 3, 113, 224, 225, 234, 260
French, 4, 105, 113, 119, 152, 158, 234, 277, 289
Gaelic, Scottish, 3
Georgian, xii
German, 165, 234, 272, 283, 287, 289
Greek (ancient), xi, 66, 75, 122, 139, 195, 204, 222, 225, 230, 234
Greek (modern), 177, 234
Haida, 316, 325
Hebrew (ancient), 66, 75, 158, 177, 184, 185, 187, 188, 189, 190, 191, 193, 194, 215, 226, 234, 235, 265
Hebrew (modern), 283
Irish, 3
Italian, 4, 152, 234
Jaloff. *See* Wolof
Judaeo-Spanish, 243
Kalmyk, 159, 217-33, **219**
Kurdish, 243
Kwakiutl, 316, 325
Labrador Inuktitut, 316
Latin, 105, 128, 151, 155, 234
Maliseet, 316, 323
Manchu, 12, **163**, 149-68, 288, 289, 295
Mandinka, 102
Manx, 3
Mi'kmaq, 316, 323, 324
Mohawk, 10, 11, 67, **68**, 316, 317, 318, 319
Mongolian, 150, 158, 160
Moose Cree, 323
Ojibwa, 316, 319
Persian, 111, 234, 248, 289
Polish, 234, 260
Portuguese, 4, 113

Romanian, 254
Russian, 13, 160, 169-96, **180**, 197-216, **202**, 224, 260, 289
Serbian, 243, 253, 251-67, **264**
Slavey, 316, 324, 325
Slavonic, Old Church, 170, 185, 207, 253, 258, 260, 261, 262
Slovenian, 259
South Slavic, 251-67
Spanish, 4, 72, 234, 287
Susu, 102, 108
Swedish, 287
Syriac, 189, 234
Tartar, 152, 245
Turkish, 234, 239, 243
Ukrainian, 176
Wallachian, 256
Welsh, xii, 2, 3
Wend, 260
Wolof, 11, 97-120
Yakut, 217-33, **223**
Lazaristes, 151
Leiden, University of, 247
Leipzig, 186, 247
Levant, BFBS Activities in, 234-50
library, BFBS, 1, 9, 13, 14, 91, **92**
Lisbon, 100, 290, 311
literacy, incidence of, 60
Lithuanian. *See* Scripture:versions
Liverpool, 49, 57
London Missionary Society (LMS), 2, 99, 100, 101, 136, 138, 141, 142, 150, 153, 156, 159, 160, 162, 289
London Society for Promoting Christianity Amongst the Jews (LSPCAJ), 283
London Youth Group, BFBS, 90
Lowestoft, England, 286
Lutherans, 2, 4, 102, 234, 247, 267, 270, 272, 276, 278, 331
Lyme Regis, England, 32

Macao, 127, 131
Mackenzie River, Canada, 324
Madrid, 70, 72, 291, 292, 299, 300, 302, 303, 307, 308, 309, 310, 312, 313, 314, 315
Magdalen College, Oxford, 279
Malacca, 160, 162
Málaga, Spain, 311
Malta, 332
Manchu. *See* languages
Mandarin. *See* languages:Chinese

Indexes 369

Mandinka. *See* languages
Manx. *See* languages
Marabouts, 109
Mardin, Asia Minor, 245
marine Bible societies, 333-40
Mariupol, Sea of Azov, 245
Massachusetts Bible Society, 339
Mekhitarists, Armenian, 246
Melun, France, 201
Merchant Seamen's Auxiliary Bible Society (MSABS), 335, 341
Mérida, Spain, 291
Methodist Missionary Society (MMS), 309
Methodists, 10, 107, 305, 306, 307, 309, 311, 312, 314, 316, 318, 319, 328, 329, 330, 336
Métis people, Canada, 317, 319, 320
Mexico, 6
Military Bible Society, Prussia, 281
Mi'qmak. *See* languages
Missionary Magazine, The, 108
Missions to Seafarers, 327-43, **337**
Mohawk. *See* languages
Mongolian. *See* languages
Montenegro, 258
Montevideo, Uruguay, 100
Moose Cree. *See* languages
Moravians, 160, 275, 276, 316, 318, 319, 325
Morocco, 298
Moscow, 179, 181, 183, 221, 269, 270, 297, 298
Muslims, 108, 110, 111, 118, 246, 250

Nanjing, Treaty of, 1842, 133
Napoleonic wars, 2, 172, 173, 236, 249, 270, 271, 275, 329, 341
National Bible Society of Scotland, 4, 6, 7, 72
   Quarterly Record, 144
Native literati
   contribution insufficiently recognised, 121-48, **129**, **137**
Naval and Military Bible Society (NMBS), 2, 328, 329, 341
Naval Awakening, 330, 341
Netherlands, 271
Netherlands Bible Society, 6, 72
New Brunswick, 323
New York Bible Society, 339
Ningpo, China, 133, 139
non-denominational Societies, 2

Norwegian Bible Society, 72
Norwich, England, 26, 28, 286, 291
note or comment, 4, 8, 74, 78, 63-80, 316
   20th century developments, 72-78
   a Roman Catholic view, 63
   and distribution with personal advocacy, 44, 49, 58
   and Russian Orthodox Church, 178, 193, 194
   avoiding controversy, 39, 80
   BFBS policy, 25
   effect in Spain, 295
   exclusion of Apocrypha, 276
   marginal references and alternate readings, 70
   only bound books distributed, 30
   patriarchal imprimatur, 239
   readers' helps, 73
   without *doctrinal* note or comment, 74
Nottingham Campaign, 2003, 78
Nova Scotia, 323
Nürnberg, Germany, 3

Oblates of Mary Immaculate, 324
Ochotsk, Russia, 160
Octateuch, Russian, 170, 186, 187
Odessa, 6, 183, 243, 245, 246
Ojibwa. *See* languages
Ojibwa people, Canada, 320
Oporto, 290
Örebro, Sweden, 221
Orthodox Churches, 4, 13, 247, 249
Orthodox Missionary Society, 221
orthography. *See* scripts
Ottoman Empire, 5, 6, 10, 178, 240, 244, 249, 250, 234-50, 346
Oxford, 109
Oxford University Press, 28, 173

Pale of Settlement, 191
Palestine, 248
papermaking. *See* Scripture:production
Paris, 159, 195, 198, 199, 200, 201, 216, 234, 235, 247
Paris Missionary Society, 119
Patristics, 178
Peking, 128, 134, 151, 153, 156, 162
Pentateuch, 64, 185, 187, 319
Penzance, England, 330
Percy Proprietary Chapel, St Pancras, London, 279
Pergamum, Greece, 236

periodicals, BFBS
  Annual Reports, 5, 92, 169, 218, 236, 268, 280, 282, 309, 323
  For Every Land, 92
  Monthly Extracts, 298
  Popular Reports, 92
  The Bible in the World, 92
Persia, 6
Persian. *See* languages
Philadelphia Bible Society, 3, 339
Philippines, 6
Phillips and Fardon, printers, London, 317
Poland, 271
Polish. *See* languages
Polish Bible Society, 284
poor law, 40
Port au Prince, Haiti, 86
Portsmouth, England, 100, 331, 340
Portugal, 63, 290
Portuguese. *See* languages *and* Scripture:versions
Presbyterians, 39, 309, 310, 312
Prince Edward Island, 323
printing. *See* Scripture:production
Privileged presses, 26
Prussia, 272, 283
Prussian Bible Society, 283
Puritan Committee, 42
Puritans, 42, 65

Quakers. *See* Society of Friends
Qur'an, Holy, 109

Reformation, Protestant, 327, 351
regional secretaries, BFBS, 92
Reigate, England, 268
Religious Tract Society (RTS), 2, 55, 67, 103, 242, 349
Roman Catholic Church, 34, 72, 74, 255
  condemnatory Papal encyclical, 284
  hostility towards BFBS, 284
Roman Catholic seafarers' mission agencies, 341
Roman Catholics, 4, 26, 64
  cooperation with BFBS, 39, 272, 280
  Croatian, 259
  in Canada, 320
  in Central Europe, 257
  in China, 127, 128, 130, 131, 153
  in Spain, 63, 66, 307
  in West Africa, 105
  Russian-speaking, 202

Serbian, 256, 258
Romanian. *See* languages
Rossville Mission, Canada, 320
  mission press, 320
Rotterdam, 340
Royal African Corps, 104
royal charter, BFBS, 8
Royal Navy, British, 306, 330, 336
Rupert's Land, Canada, 319, 320, 321, 323, 324
Rusniak. *See* Scripture:versions
Russia, 5, 13, 150, 159, 160, 187, 197, 213, 217-33, 256, 261, 268, 270, 271, 274, 276, 289, 290, 294, 295, 296, 304
  Bolshevik Revolution, 1917: 6, 7, 183, 193
  Revolution 1905: 193
Russian. *See* languages *and* Scripture:versions
Russian Bible Society, 1812-1826
  and Alexander Golitsyn, 172
  and John Paterson, 169
  and seafarers, 340
  and the Russian Orthodox Church, 170, 175, 194
  and the Serbian Bible, 255, 261, 262
  as example for Malta, 236
  closure, 170-171, 173, 262
  subsequent BFBS work, 173, 182
  compared with BSR 1991-, 214
  context of, 172, 173, 192
  evangelical links, 172
  foundation, 3, 270
  propaganda value to BFBS, 271
  publications, 3, 169, 170, 181, 186, 207, 218
  technological advances, 172
Russian Orthodox Church
  and BFBS Cassian NT, 197-216
  Holy Synod, 172, 178, 184, 187, 194
  in Yakutiia, 221
  mission to Peking, 162
  relations with Russian Bible Society, 169-96
Russian Orthodox Church Abroad, 199
Russian Student Christian Movement (RKSD), 197, 198

Sagalien, isthmus of, 162
St. Paul's Cathedral, London, 81, 95
St. Petersburg, 149, 151, 154, 157, 158, 160, 173, 185, 193, 218, 220, 255, 261, 262, 270, 288, 289, 297, 304

Indexes 371

BFBS agency, 169-96, 169-96
St. Petersburg Bible Society, 270
St. Petersburg Home for the Upbringing of Poor Children, 188
St. Petersburg Institute of Oriental Studies, 154
St. Petersburg Theological Academy, 189
St. Petersburg Theological Seminary, 188
St. Petersburg University, 189, 193
St. Sergius Russian Orthodox Theological Institute, Paris, 195, 198, 203
Sakha Republic. *See* Yakutiia
San Lazzaro degli Armeni, 246
San Roque, Spain, 308
Sanlucár, Spain, 293
Santiago de Compostela, Spain, 300
Sarajevo, Bosnia, 263
Saratov Affair, 189
Saxon Bible Society, 283, 284
Scotland, 4, 25, 72, 144, 268, 269, 277
scripts
    Cree, 320
    Cyrillic, 253, 258, 260, 263, 265
    Latin, 258, 260, 263, 266, 320, 323, 324, 325
    Manchu, 151
    Slavonian, 260
    Slavo-Serbian, 253
Scripture
    and contemporary culture, xii, 8
    authority of, 5
    Braille, 83
    canon, 4
    distribution, 2, 11
        quantities distributed, 5
    production
        bookbinding, 30
        papermaking, 28-29
        printing, 26-28
    selections, 8
    study aids, 8
    translation
        base texts, 3
        Christian investment in, xi
        influence of, 12
        interconfessional, 13, 79, 197, 198, 202
        UBS/Vatican guidelines, 74
        machine translation, 233
        number of languages translated, 3

        theology of, xi
        typical translation problems, 225-33
        work of a consultant, 217-33
    use, 75
    versions. *See also* languages
        Baffin Inuktitut, 325
        Basque, 292
        Bulgarian, 256
        Carniolan (Slovenian), 256
        Chinese, 121-48
        Mandarin, 141
        Chipeywan, 325
        Cree, 319, **322**
        Croatian, 256
        Croatian (Katančić), 266
        Croatian (Škarić), 266
        English, 8
        Authorized version. *See* King James version
        Bishops' Bible, 65
        Contemporary English Version (CEV), 73, 77
        Douai-Rheims Bible, 65
        Geneva Bible, 64, 65, 66
        Geneva Bible Bible, 64
        Good News Bible (GNB), 8, 77, 226
        Good News Study Bible, 77
        Gospels in magazine format, 8
        illustrated Bible, 8
        King James Version (KJV), 26, 65, 66, 70, 173, 227
        Living Bible, 75
        New Revised Standard Version (NRSV), 226
        Revised Standard Version (RSV), 149, 165, 167, 226
        Today's English Version. *See* Good News Bible
        Tyndale, 63
        Finnish, 270
        French, 28, 118, 329
        German
        Hirschberg Bible, 282
        Greek
        Septuagint, 177, 184
        Greek (ancient), 204, 208, 234
        Greek (ancient & modern), **238-9**
        Greek (modern), 237, 333
        Greek (Septuagint), 177, 178, 185, 226, 234, 235, 255
        Greek-Russian NT, 212

Hebrew/Russian, 194
Inuktitut, 318
Italian, 306
Kalmyk, 159, 217-33, **219**
Latin
   Tremelius and Junius, 265
   Vulgate, 158, 165, 167, 296
Lithuanian, 275
Maliseet, 324
Mi'kmaq, 323
Mohawk/English, 317
Moose Cree, 323
Ojibwa, 319
Portuguese, 306
Rusniak, 256
Russian
   BFBS editions, 184-96
   BSR editions (1991-), 169-73, 215
   Cassian NT, 195, 197-216, **202**
   Synodal, 170, 174, 178, 179, **180**, 181, 182, 184, 185, 186, 187, 189, 191, 192, 193, 194, 195, 198, 200, 201, 204, 207, 209, 210, 211, 213, 214
Serbian, 251-67
   Cyrillic script, 256, **264**
   Latin script, 256
Slavey, 324
Slavonian dialects, 256
Slavonian OT, 255
Slavonic, Old, 174, 201, 214
Spanish, 293, 295, 306, 310, 329
Spanish Romani, 292
Turkish, 234-50
Welsh, 33
Windes (Wend), 256
Yakut NT portions, **223**
seafarers and the Bible Society, 10, 327-43, **337**
Seamen's Mission, Gibraltar, 312
Senegal, 97-120, 104
Senftenberg, Bohemia, 19
Serbian. *See* languages *and* Scripture:versions
Seville, 291, 292, 300, 302, 303
Shanghai, 123, 133, 134, 139, 143, 156, 218
Siberia, 159, 160, 162, 217, 218, 220, 296
Sierra Leone, 120
Sierra Leone Company, 101, 102, 109, 112
Sierra Leone Gazette, The, 119
Silesia, 282

Sinai, Mount, 240, 247
Šišatovac, Serbia, 259
Skeppsholms Auxiliary Bible Society, Sweden, 339
Slavey. *See* languages *and* Scripture:versions
Slavonia, 258
Slavonian. *See* languages *and* Scripture:versions
Slavonic. *See* languages *and* Scripture:versions
Slovenian. *See* languages
Smyrna, 6, 234, 235, 236, 237, 240, 243, 248
Society for Promoting Christian Knowledge (SPCK), 2, 40, 306, 331
Society for Promoting Christianity among the Jews, 188
Society for Promoting Religious Knowledge among the Poor, 2
Society for the Propagation of the Gospel (SPG), 319
Society of Friends, 11, 24, 39, 40, 119, 299
South Slavic. *See* languages
Soviet Union, 197, 211, 214
Spain, 5, 10, 66, 70, 71, 290, 291, 292, 293, 294, 295, 298, 300, 302, 303, 304, 305-15, 346
Spanish. *See* languages *and* Scripture:versions
Spanish Civil War, 314
Spanish Reformed Church, 312
Spanish Romani. *See* Scripture:versions
Sremski Karlovci, Serbia, 262
Stamp Corner, London Bible House, 93
Stanhope printing press, 28
stereotype, 9, 25, 28, 29, 33, 169, 171, 172
Stolpen, Germany, 319
Study Bibles, 73, 76, 77
Stuttgart, 270
Stuttgart Bible Society, 274
Sunday School Society, 2
Sunday schools, 19, 60
Sunderland, England, 333, 338
Susu. *See* languages
Sweden, 221, 222, 276, 339, 340
Swedish. *See* languages
Swedish Naval Bible Society, 340
Switzerland, 3, 203, 350
Sydney, Australia, 3
Syria, 248
Syriac. *See* languages

Taganrog, Crimea, 245
Takoradi, Ghana, 86
Tangiers, 293, 298
Tartar. *See* languages
Tartars, 269
Tartary, 159, 162
temperance societies, 60
textus receptus, 181, 205, 208, 267
Thames Revival, 340, 341
Thames Union Bible Committee (TUBC), 334
Thrace, 239
Tibet, 160, 217, 229
Tiflis, Georgia, 183
Toronto, 319, 353
Trades unions, 31
Trafalgar, battle of, 329
translation. *See* Scripture translation
Tübingen, Germany, 274
Turkish. *See* Scripture:versions
Turkish Empire. *See* Ottoman Empire
Tyne Union Bible Committee, 338

Ukrainian. *See* languages
United Bible Societies (UBS), 1, 9, 74, 315
  and Bible Society in Russia, 215
  and interconfessional work, 197
  and the Orthodox world, 13, 214
  BFBS membership of, 221
  Council, 75
  early attempts to establish, 7
  executive committee (UBSEC), 75
  first offices, 91
  foundation, 7
  growth of, 7, 8
  regional structure, 87
  translations consultants, 8, 196, 217
  world service budget, 8
Upper Canada Bible Society, 319

Vatican, 74, 284
Venice, 245, 246, 248
Vienna, 149, 246, 251, 253, 256, 257, 258, 259, 261, 265, 267, 284

Wallachian. *See* languages

Walldürn, Germany, 281
Warsaw, 283, 284
Welsh. *See* languages *and* Scripture:versions
Welsh Union, 42
Wend. *See* languages
Wenli. *See* languages:Chinese
Wesleyan Missionary Society (WMS), 316, 320
Wesleyans, 38, 294, 320
Western Asia Mission, 242
Windes (Wend). *See* Scripture:versions
Wolof. *See* languages
women and the Bible Society, 3, 38-52, 53-62, 92
  and social control, 62
  as a religious role model, 54
  financial importance, 39, 51
  ladies' Bible Associations. *See* British and Foreign:Bible Society (BFBS):Bible Associations
  meetings, participation in, 38
  opposition and support, 56-58
  origins of women's work, 54-55
  spiritual and temporal relief, 61
  voting rights, 38
  "Women" and "Ladies", 61-62
women workers
  employment of, 30-33, **32**
World War I, 7
World War II, 7, 8, 181, 198, 216
Woudschoten Conference, 1939, 72, 73
Württemberg, 283
Württemberg Bible Society, 270

Yakut. *See* languages
Yakutiia, Russian Federation, 220, 221, 225, 227, 228
Yakutsk, 220, 221, 225
Yokohama, Japan, 86
York Auxiliary Bible Society, Canada, 319
Young Men's Christian Association (YMCA), 199, 200, 202

Zante, Greece, 236
Zaragoza, Spain, 302

2. Index of Persons

Afanasieff, Nicholas, 203
Alegría, José, 310
Alekseeva, Mariia, 222
Alexander I, Tsar, 170, 172, 270
Alexander II, Tsar, 174, 179, 181, 187, 192
Alexis, Patriarch of Moscow, 205
Alhama, José, 311
Allen, Samuel, 331
Alton, Amy, 310
Alton, George, 309, 310, 312
Amiot, Jean-Joseph-Marie, 152
Anderson, Gwen, 91
Anderson, Paul, 199
Angrand, Armand-Pierre, 115
Araujo, Adolfo, 313, 314
Argyrammos, Alexandros, 242
Arnswaldt, Baron von, 271, 272
Arseniev, Nicholas, 203
Astaf'ev, Nikolai, 188, 189, 195
Athenagoras, Ecumenical Patriarch, 204, 205
Augustine, Saint, xi
Avashkieva, Nina, 222

Baas, Charles, 87
Bacon, Richard, 28
Bailey, John, 306, 307
Ball, Johannes, 272
Bancroft, Richard, 65
Barber, William, 307
Barker, Benjamin, 6, 236, 239
Barrington, Shute, 108
Beattie, John, 99
Becker, F W, 283
Bede, Venerable, 88
Béguin, Olivier, 91
ben Attar, Hayim, 303
Benoist, Michel, 152
Bergfeldt, J G, 283
Bergne, Samuel, 10, 35
Bethune, Divie, 333
Bezsonov, Yury, 199
Bickersteth, Edward, 113
Bill, E G W, 18
Biller, Sarah, 289
Bitkeev, Petr, 222
Blakesley, Captain, 110
Bligh, J D, 289
Bobowski, Albert, 247, 248, 249

Bobrinskoy, Boris, 201, 202
Bobrovnikov, N, 221
Bobrovsky, G, 199, 201, 202
Bogoliubov, Petr Ivanovich, 188, 190
Bogue, David, 100
Bompas, William, 324, 325
Boone, William, 139
Borrow, George, 10, **287**, **301**
    and Manchu, 155, 156, 163, 165, 166, 286-90
    biography, 17
    centenary, 314
    in Portugal, 63
    in Russia and Spain, 286-304
    in Spain, 70-72, 300, 290-95, 307, 308
    relationship with BFBS, 286-304
    The Bible in Spain, 34, 70, 298, 299
    The Zincali, 291, 293, 299, 300
Boswell, James, 328
Bowring, John, 262, 263
Bradnock, Wilfred, 91, 200, 201, 202, 204
Brandram, Andrew, 290, **291**, 293, 294, 298, 300, 302, 303
Brant, Joseph, 67
Bratt, Norman, 86
Bridgman, Elijah, 136, 139
Brooks, Henry, 48
Browne, George, 302
Bruckner, Adolf, 273, 285
Brunton, Henry, 108, 112
Buck, Carrie, 121
Buck, Pearl S, 121
Budd, Henry, 320
Bunsen, Baron von, 283
Burn, Thomas, 30
Butterworth, Joseph, 36

Cable, Mildred, 62, 88
Cabrera, Juan, 312
Cambridge, Duke of, 271
Cann, Kathleen, 13
Canstadt, Baron Schilling von, 289, 290
Canstein, Baron von, 274
Carlyle, J D, 108, 109
Cartwright, George, 32
Cassian (Bezobrazov), Bishop, 13, 195, **202**, 207, 197-216
Catherine II, Tsarina, 207
Caulfield, Michael, 305
Charles, Thomas, 2, 88

Charme, Alexandre de la, 152
Chen Laoyi, 128, **129**
Chinnery, George, 128
Choong Hsi-hsin, 143
Chrysostom, St John, 207, 209, 242, 243
Clapham, Barbara, 87
Clarke, Adam, 107, 111, 113, 114, 116, 117, 118, 120
Clarke, Henrietta, 303
Clarke, Mary, 292, 303
Claus, J D, 281
Cockburn, Norman, 87
Coggan, Donald, 75, 76
Confucius, 128
Conybeare, William, 44
Corfield, Richard, 312
Corry, Joseph, 111
Coventry, John, 312
Cox, John, 336, 337
Cunningham, Francis, 286, 288
Cunningham, J W, 47, 48, 49
Curie, J G, 312

Daničić, Đuro, 251-67
Dard, Jean, 119
Davidson, Walter, 220
Davis, Mildred, 93
Davis, Thomas, 305
Deretić, Jovan, 253
Diericke, Lt Gen von, 273
Diez, Heinrich von, 247
Dilloway, Clive, 78
Diop, Dial, 118
Dobell, Consul, 289
Domenge, Jean, 152
Dreving, Anatolii, 201, 202
Dudley, Charles, 36, **41**
 and Bible Associations, 33, 35, 40-52, 53-54, 57-58
 and literacy, 61
 and marine Bible Societies, 334-335
 and printing technology, 29
 and the poor, 59
 attitude towards women, 40
 in charge of home organisation, 40
 travels and meetings, 40
Dudley, Mary, 40
Dumont, Christophe, 203
Dunning, T J, 31, 33

Eck, Adalbert, 182, 183
Elgin, Lord, 239
Elizabeth, Queen, 86

Elsner, Samuel, 281, 282
Erasmus, 181, 208
Escalante, Martin, 309, 310, 311
Ess, Leander van, 277, 280, 281
Evans, James, 320
Ewing, Greville, 99

Fick, Ulrich, 91
Filaret (Amfiteatrov), Metropolitan, 175
Filaret (Drozdov), Metropolitan, 175, 192
Fisher, R B, 46, 47, 48, 51
Fisk, Pliny, 242, 243
Fliedner, Theodor, 284
Flores, José, 310, 311, 314
Florovsky, Georges, 199, 202
Ford, Henry, 109
Foureau, Pierre, 152
Franco, Francisco, 314
Fraser, George, 102
Fraser, John, 102
Friedrich Wilhelm III, King, 273
Friedrich Wilhelm IV, King, 281
Froumou, Stephen, 312, 313

Gao (Kō-mow-ho), 128
Garnier, A J, 141
Gaubil, Antoine, 152
Gedeōn, Manouēl, 248
George III, King, 271
George VI, King, 86
Gerbillon, Jean-François, 152
Gill, James, 306
Girdlestone, R B, 184, 189
Gisborne, Thomas, 69
Gniezno, Archbishop of, 284
Golberry, Meinrad, 111, 113
Golitsyn, Alexander, 172, 270, 289, 340
Golubev, M A, 185
Gontcharoff, N T, 201, 202
Goodin, Elizabeth, 90
Goodrich, Chauncey, 143, 144
Gordon, Peter, 160, 162
Gourly, John, 306
Grammont, Jean-Joseph de, 151
Graydon, James, 291, 294, 299, 304, 307, 308
Gregorios V, Patriarch, 243, 247
Gregory XVI, Pope, 284
Gregory, Olinthus, 50, 285
Greig, Peter, 99, 112
Grey, Lady Mary, 331
Grey, Sir George, 331

Grimm, Jacob, 262, 263, 265
Gurney, Joseph, 26
Gützlaff, Karl, 136, 138, 156

Habermas, Jürgen, 9, 174
Hagger, Ron, 83
Haldane, Robert, 277, 278
Hall, Alfred, 69, 325
Hankey, William, 160
Harrison, Charles, 325
Hartwig, Peter, 102
Hasfeld, John, 290
Haszard, G T, 323
Haven, William, 7
Henderson, Ebenezer, 169, 172, 248, 249, 340
Hennen, John, 307
He Qingtai. *See* Poirot, Louis
Herzen, Alexander, 186
Hewlett, J P, 36
Hill, Elizabeth, 203
Hill, John, 11, 97-120
Hill, Mary, 99
Hoffman, professor, 188, 189, 195
Holmgren, Laton, 74, 87
Hope, Maria, 57
Howard, Luke, 11, 24, 26, 29, 36
Howland, George, 110
Howsam, Leslie, 171
Hughes, Joseph, 2, 46, 67
Hull, Thomas, 309
Hunter, James, 320
Hunter, Jean, 320

Iakinf, Ieromonakh, 289
Ilarion, Archimandrite, 240, 241, 242, 243, 244
Ivanov, A, 205, 206, 207, 208, 213
Iveković, Franjo, 266

Jagić, Vatroslav, 267
Jia Qing, Emperor, 131
James I, King, 65, 66
Jänicke, Johann, 273
Jay, John, 69
Jay, Peter, 69
Jerningham, George, 302, 303
Jerome, Saint, 266
Jin Shihe, 134
John, Bishop of San Francisco, 203
Johnson, Samuel, 328
Jones, Mary, xii
Jones, Peter, 319

Jones, William, 139
Jowett, Joseph, 288, 289, 296, 297
Jowett, William, 246, 250
Ju Dilang, 136, **137**,138

Kalliarkhis, Dionysios, 240
Kamenskii, Petr, 153, 154, 155
Kanelos, Stephanos, 241
Karadžić, Vuk, 251-67, **252**
Kartashev, Anton, 203, 210, 212
Kayor, Damel of, 107, 110, 118
Keen, J H, 325
Khrushchev, Nikita, 218
Khvol'son, Daniil Avraamovich, 184, 185, 189, 190, 193, 194
Kieffer, John, 247, 248, 249
Kilham, Hannah, 119
Kinsey, Ray, 93
Kirkby, William, 324, 325
Klinger, Friedrich von, 287
Knill, Richard, 173
Koenig, Friedrich, 28
Kohlmeister, B G, 318
Kō-mow-ho, 128
Kopitar, Jernej, 251-67
Korais, Adamantios, 235, 240, 241, 243
Koriakov, Michael, 203
Korolya, Canonicus, 260
Kottwitz, Baron von, 272
Kovalevsky, Peter, 199, 200
Kraemer, Hendrick, 72, 73
Kraft, Professor, 282
Kuchnev, D A, 221
Kuzmany, Karol, 263

Landers, Anthony, 333, 334
Langley, John, 44
Leake, Martin, 256
Lee, Samuel, 248, 249
Leeves, Henry, 243, 244, 248, 249
Leont'eva, Sargylana, 222
Leontije, Metropolitan, 262
Levison, Vasilii, 187, 188, 189, 190, 195
Lew Tse-chuen, 138
Li, Mr, 127, 128
Lian Yinghuang, 134
Liao, Mr, 134
Lindsay, Henry, 103, 237
Lipovtsev, Stepan Vasil'evich, 153, 166, 289, 295
Li Shigong, 127, 128, **129**
Lloyd, Richard, 45, 48, 51
Lomako, Grigoriy, 203

Lossky, Vladimir, 201, 203, 205
Louis XVIII, King, 247
Loviagin, E I, 185
Lowrie, Donald, 200, 201, 203, 204
Lowrie, Walter, 139
Lo-Xien (Low-Hëen), 128
Luther, Martin, 167, 251, 261
Lutoff, Paul, 203
Lyon, James, 308

Macaulay, Zachary, 101, 102
MacFarlane, Charles, 241
Mahmadee, 119
Mandel'shtam, Leon, 187
Marks, Richard, 330
Mason, Sophia, 321
Mason, William, 320, 321, 323
Matamoros, Manuel, 311
Maxwell, Charles, 106, 107, 116, 117
McDonald, Robert, 319
Medhurst, Walter, 136-41, **137**,156
Mehmet IV, Sultan, 247
Meller, T W, 157, 158
Mendizábal, Juan, 71, 72, 295
Meshcherskii, Prince, 269
Methodius (Vladimir Kul'man), Archimandrite, 199
Methodius, Bishop, 199, 202, 203, 260
Metternich, Prince, 257, 284
Meyendorff, John, 203
Miklošič, Franc, 265, 267
Millard, Edward, 4, 187, 265, 266, 267
Milne, William, 131, 132, 133, 136, 139, 140, 147
Milne, William Charles, 139, 141
Mirrielees, Archibald, 179, 181, 182, 185, 195
Mirrielees, William, 182, 189
Mitchell, William, 84
More, Hannah, 38
Morgan, William, xii
Moritz, Johann, 283
Morrison, John Robert, 136
Morrison, Robert, **129**, 126-38, 146, 154
Moulton, Harold, 91
Moyriac de Mailla, Joseph de, 152
Muir, Andrew, 181, 182, 183, 186, 187
Muirhead, William, 141
Mušicki, Lukijan, 259

Nathaniel, Bishop, 199, 200
Neale, Benjamin, 334
Neander, August, 272

Nelson, Horatio, 330
Newton, John, 329
Nicholas I, Tsar, 170, 187, 188, 192
Nicklin, Carolina, 306, 307
Nicolson, William, 5, 10, **183**, 220
    and BFBS agency in St. Petersburg, 194
    and BFBS London committees, 194, 195
    and BFBS Russian translation, 188, 191, 193, 195
    and Russian Bible Society, 183
    and Russian Synodal Bible, 184, 185
    and Yakut, 221
Niemeyer, August, 274
Njegoš, Petar, 262
Norris, Henry, 50
North, Eric, 7, 199
Norton, John. See Tyonenhokarawen

O'Meara, Frederick, 319
Obolensky, Prince Dimitri, 202, 203, 210
Obradović, Dositej, 253
Obrenović, Miloš, 262
Ogle, Robert, 101
Oikonomos, Kōnstantinos, 240
Oliban, Alejandro, 70, 71
Ollières, J.-F.-Marie-Dieudonné d', 152
Orfelin, Zaharija, 253
Orton, George, 333
Osterwijck, Maria van, 149
Owen, John, 19, 255, 257

Panzi, Joseph, 151
Parish, John, 19
Park, Mungo, 107, 108, 109, 111, 113, 114
Parker, Captain, 115
Parrenin, Dominique, 152
Parsons, Levi, 242, 243
Pascal, Pierre, 203
Paterson, John, 270, 271
    and Finnish Bible Society, 270
    and Manchu, 156, 159
    and marine Bible societies, 340
    and Russian Bible Society, 169, 172, 173, 261, 270, 271
    and Russian language, 195
    and Scandinavia, 271
Pavskii, Gerasim Petrovich, 170, 189
Pearson, Vera, 93
Peck, Edmund, 325
Peter I, Tsar, 207
Petridis, Platon, 239

Petropolis, Alexander, 247, 248
Pfister, Louis, 151
Phillips, Richard, 40
Pinkerton, Robert, **269**
   and Armenia, 246
   and Bulgaria, 258
   and Croatian, 255, 259
   and Cyrillic alphabet, 260
   and good business practice, 10
   and Greece, 240, 241, 246
   and Russian Bible Society, 169, 172, 245, 268-85
   and seafarers, 340
   and Serbian, 255, 257, 258, 259, 261, 263
   and Slovenian, 259
   and Turkish, 247, 248
   Bible work in Austria, 257
   helps to launch new Bible Societies, 3, 4
   in the Crimea, 245
   Irkutsk agency, 159
Pitman, Isaac, 323, 324
Pius VII, Pope, 284
Platt, T Pell, 244
Platt, William, 87
Pobedonostsev, Konstantin, 191, 192, 194, 195
Poirot, Louis, 149-68, 295
Porson, Richard, 235
Porteus, Beilby, 108
Pott, Vice Rector, 274
Pozdneev, Aleksei, 218
Precious Cloud, 121
Prémare, Joseph de, 152
Pressensé, Victor de, 5
Prim, General, 312
Prochaska, Frank, 55

Ralston, Robert, 3
Rand, Silas, 323
Ranke, Leopold, 262
Ranyard, Ellen, 35, 55, **56**, 59, 60, 61
Raumer, Professor von, 282
Rayevsky, Vladimir, 203, 205
Reden, Countess Friedricke von, 282
Reeve, William, 325
Renouard, G C, 248
Ren Zong, Emperor, 131
Rešetar, Milan, 267
Reynalds, Francis, 332, 335, 338
Reynolds, John, 65
Ricci, Matteo, 168

Richardson, John, 109, 110, 111, 117
Ritson, John, 7, 87
Rivas, Duke of, 70
Roberts, Josiah, 3
Robertson, Edwin, 91
Romero, Rey, 300
Rong Sande, 126, 130
Ropes, William, 289
Rosing, Ulrick, 331
Ruet, Francisco de Paula, 310
Ruffin, Monsieur, 247, 248
Rule, W H, 294, 307, 308

Sacy, Silvestre de, 254, 255, 257, 259, 261
Salfeld, Abbot, 271, 272
Sandanee, 119
Saraphis, Gregorios, 250
Savvaitov, P I, 185, 189, 190
Schereschewsky, Samuel, 134, 135, 147
Selassie, Haile, 84
Selina, Countess of Huntingdon, 38
Seraphim, Metropolitan, 248
Shaposhnikova, Aita, 222
Shugraeva, Vera, 222
Sibthorp, R Waldo, 279, 280
Silvester (Ivan Haruns), Archimandrite, 199
Simpson, A, 185
Sinclair, John, 320
Slade, Adolphus, 237
Smirnoff, Archimandrite, 220
Smith, George, 330, 341
Solomova, Olga, 222
Sove, Boris, 203
Stalin, Josef, 218
Stallybrass, Edward, 154, 157, 158, 160, 289
Steinhauer, Henry, 320
Steinkopf, Karl, 2, 3, 242, 269, 270
   and Bible work in Austria, 257
   and British evangelicals, 276
   and German Bible Societies, 270
   and Russian Bible Society, 270
   and seafarers, 331
   and Serbian, 255, 256
   continental tour, 1812, 276
   resignation, 279
Stockfeld, J, 283
Stojković, Athanasije, 262
Strangford, Lord, 243
Stratimirović, Metropolitan, 262
Strauchan, William, 309
Stronach, John, 139, 141, 142

Strong, Robbins, 202, 204, 210
Strossmeyer, Josip, 266
Struve, Gleb, 203
Šulek, Bogoslav, 267
Summers, William, 313
Swan, William, 153, 154, 155, 157, 158, 165, 289, 295
Swift, Charles, 87
Sychov, Sergei, 222
Sydenstricker, Absalom, 121
Sylvester, Bishop, 202, 203

Tarn, Joseph, 14, 16, 19, 98, 106, 111, 118, 332, 333, 336
Tattersall, Bernard, 84, 87
Teignmouth, Lord, 46, 67, 108, 268
Theoctistus, Bishop, 249
Thile, General von, 283
Tholuck, August, 274, 282
Thomas, Gabriel, 324
Thompson, Thomas, 106, 116, 117, 119
Thomson, Alexander, 5, 10, 263
Thomson, James, 309
Tidball, Bernard, 90, 92
Tims, John, 325
Train, Jean, 203
Trigo, Manuel, 311
Trimmer, Sarah, 38
Troitskii, Ivan, 193
True, Dennis, 87
Tyndale, William, xii, 63, 64, 84
Tyonenhokarawen, 67, 317

Urban, George, 203
Usko, Johann, 234, 235, 240

Vamvas, Neophytos, 243
Vasil'ev, A P. *See* Wassilieff, A P
Venning, John, 289
Verbiest, Ferdinand, 152
Villéger, A, 119
Villiers, George, 71, 72, 295

Voitsekhovskii, Iosif, 155
Walsh, Robert, 243
Wang Amah, 121
Wang Changgui, 140
Wang Dao *also known as* Wang Lanqing *and* Wang Tao, 140, 141, 142
Warner, Levinus, 247
Wassilieff, A P, 202, 203
Watkins, Edwin, 32, 325, 348
Watson, John, 74
Wei Jianmin, 134
Weidlé, Wladimir, 203
Wesley, John, 38, 41, 50
Wesley, Susanna, 38
Weymann, Alexande de, 203
Whiteley, E, 290
Wilberforce, William, xiii, 9, 54, 69, 88, 329
Wilkinson, Arthur, 7, 236
Williamson, Charles, 236, 237, 240, 241, 242, 243
Wilson, Andrew, 28
Winter, Gustav, 319
Winterbottom, Thomas, 109
Wright, William, 193
Wycliffe, John, 84
Wynne, Ellis, 287

Yeremin, Nicholas, 199
Ye Shanrong, 134
Yong Sam Tak, 126
Yu Baosheng, 134
Yun Kwan-ming *also known as* Yun, Abel, 127, 128, 130
Yuriev, Victor, 199

Zaitseff, Boris, 202, 203, 210
Zander, Valentina, 203
Zernov, Nicolas, 198, 199
Zhang Jiezhi, 134
Zhang Xixin, 143

3. INDEX OF AUTHORS

Angrand, Armand-Pierre, 115

Batalden, Stephen, 197, 203, 214
Bickersteth, Edward, 105
Borrow, George, 288
Brooks, George, 106
Buck, Pearl S, 121
Burke, David, 77

Canton, William, 57, 275
Comaroff, Jean and Comaroff, John, 11
Corry, Joseph, 104, 112

Dard, Jean, 119
Darlow, T H, 148, 304, 317
de Waard, Jan, 146
Demanet, Abbé, 109
Dudley, Charles
   and Bible Associations, 33

Eaton, Kent, 297
Eber, Irene, 125

Garnier, A J, 141
Gisborne, Thomas, 69
Golberry, Meinrad, 111
Gorham, Deborah, 50
Gregory, William, 100

Habermas, Jürgen, 170
Handover, P.M., 26
Hauer, Erich, 167
Hodacs, Hanna, 6

Howsam, Leslie, 9, 171

Kilham, Hannah, 120
Knapp, William, 17

Lawrence, George, 297
Leslie, Charles, 242

Mooney, Paul, 342
Moule, H.F, 148, 317

Neander, August, 272
Nida, Eugene, 73, 146
Nippold, Friedrich, 273

Park, Mungo, 107
Pevsner, Nikolaus, 81
Phillips, J B, 95
Pinkerton, Robert, 268
Prochaska, Frank, 51

Richardson, John, 109
Richmond, Legh, 242
Russell, John, 271

Sanneh, Lamin, xii, 12
Shore, Charles, 280
Spillett, Hubert, 125
Spilsbury, Francis, 104
Steiner, Robert, 285

Zetzsche, Jost, 125
Zhu Baohi, 122